DAIDALOS

AND THE ORIGINS OF GREEK ART

Bronze figurine of seated helmet-maker, Geometric, eighth century B.C. H. .052 m. New York 42.11.42.

DAIDALOS

AND THE ORIGINS OF

GREEK ART

Sarah P. Morris

PRINCETON UNIVERSITY PRESS • PRINCETON, NEW JERSEY

Library of Congress Cataloging-in-Publication Data

Morris, Sarah P., 1954–

Daidalos and the origins of Greek art / Sarah P. Morris.

p.   cm.

Includes bibliographical references and index.

ISBN 0-691-03599-7

1. Art, Greek. 2. Daedalus (Greek mythology)—Influence.

I. Title.

N5633.M67   1992   91-23831

700'.938—dc20

This book has been composed in Linotron Palatino

Princeton University Press books are printed on acid-free paper,

and meet the guidelines for permanence and durability of the

Committee on Production Guidelines for Book Longevity of the

Council on Library Resources

Printed in the United States of America

1 3 5 7 9 10 8 6 4 2

72841

The Greeks, surpassing all men in their natural genius,
first appropriated most of these tales, then dramatized
them colorfully with additional ornaments, intending
to beguile with the pleasures of myths, they embellished
them in all sorts of ways. Thence Hesiod and the famous
poets of the cyclic epics made their own versions and
excerpts of *Theogonies* and *Gigantomachies* and *Titanomachies*,
which they circulated and thus defeated the truth. Our ears
have over the centuries become accustomed to and
prejudiced by their fabrications; they defend the mythology
they receive as a sacred trust . . . which, having been
wrought over time, has made its hold inescapable,
so that the truth appears to be nonsense,
and an illegitimate tale, truth.
—Sanchuniathon, from the writings of Philo of Byblos:
Eusebius, *Praeparatio Evangelica*
1.10.40

CONTENTS

DAIDALOS AND ATHENS

PART III. The Reincarnation of Daidalos

PART IV. From Daidalos to Theseus

ILLUSTRATIONS

FRONTISPIECE

Bronze figurine of seated helmet-maker, eighth century B.C. H. .052 m. New York 42.11.42 (Fletcher Fund, 1942). Courtesy of the Metropolitan Museum of Art, New York.

MAPS (*Pages xvi and xvii*)

1. The western Mediterranean in the Bronze and Iron Ages (T. Seymour).

2. The eastern Mediterranean in the Bronze and Iron Ages (T. Seymour).

FIGURES (*Endplates*)

1. Hephaistos, Thetis, and the arms of Achilles, 480–470 B.C. Interior of red-figure cup by the Foundry Painter, from Vulci. D. .305 m. Berlin F 2294. (For exterior, see Figures 58a, b.) Antikenmuseum Berlin, Staatliche Museen Preussischer Kulturbesitz.

2. Young helmet-maker, ca. 480 B.C. Red-figure cup by the Antiphon Painter, from Orvieto. D. .243 m. Oxford G.267 (ex-Bourguignon). Courtesy of the Ashmolean Museum, Oxford.

3. Hephaistos, Thetis, and the arms of Achilles, ca. 470 B.C. Red-figure Nolan amphora by the Dutuit Painter. H. .342 m. Boston MFA 13.188. Courtesy of the Museum of Fine Arts, Boston, Francis Bartlett Fund.

4. Manufacture of the chest for Danae and Perseus, ca. 490 B.C. Red-figure hydria by the Gallatin Painter, from Gela. H. .417 m. Boston, MFA 13.200. Courtesy of the Museum of Fine Arts, Boston, Francis Bartlett Fund.

5. Lakonian bronze statuette, ca. 525 B.C. From Mazi (Elis). H. .191 m. Boston MFA 98.658. Courtesy of the Museum of Fine Arts, Boston, H. L. Pierce Fund.

6. Gold crown, Syrian or Phoenician, late second millennium B.C. H. .116 m. Baltimore 57.968. Courtesy of the Walters Art Gallery, Baltimore.

7. Death of Agamemnon (above), and death of Aigisthos (below), ca. 470 B.C. Red-figure calyx-krater by the Dokimasia Painter. H. .51 m. Boston MFA 63.1246. Courtesy of the Museum of Fine Arts, Boston, William Francis Warden Fund.

8a, b. Daidalos (TAITΛE) and Ikaros (VIKAPE) in flight, 475–450 B.C. Etruscan gold bulla. H. .04 m, D. .024 m. Baltimore 57.371. Courtesy of the Walters Art Gallery, Baltimore.

9. Birth of Athena, with Hephaistos; Ikaros, ca. 560 B.C. Fragments of black-figure vase by the Painter of Akropolis 601, from Athens. Akropolis 601. Courtesy of Deutsches Archäologisches Institut, Athen.

10. Theseus, Ariadne, and the Minotaur (a); Athenian youths and maidens (b); rider: Minos or Daidalos? (c); in flight: Daidalos or Ikaros? (d), ca. 540 B.C. Black-figure skyphos ("Rayet skyphos") from Tanagra, Boiotia. H. .115 m., D. (rim) .164, (foot) .087 m. Louvre MN 675. Cliché des Musées Nationaux, Paris. Photograph by M. Chuzeville.

11. Daidalos fights Ares before enthroned Hera, late fourth century B.C. Phlyax vase from Bari. H. .378 m. London F 269. Courtesy of the British Museum, London.

12. Daidalos fastening wings on Ikaros, 420–400 B.C. Apulian skyphos fragment. Oxford 1922.208. Courtesy of the Ashmolean Museum, Oxford.

13. Birth of Athena from the head of Zeus, with winged artist-attendants, seventh century B.C. Neck scene on relief pithos from Tenos. Tenos Museum. Drawing by Deborah Nourse Lattimore.

14a–e. Photographs of relief pithos from Tenos (Figure 13). Courtesy of Deutsches Archäologisches Institut, Athen.
    14a. View of neck of relief pithos with birth of Athena. Neg. 83/464.
    14b. Central figure on throne (Zeus?), giving birth to Athena. Neg. 83/463.
    14c. Female attendant to left of throne, with sickle or knife: Eileithyia? Neg. 83/466.
    14d. Winged figure to upper right of birth scene: Daidalos or Ikaros? Neg. 83/467.
    14e. Winged assistant seated at cauldron to right of birth scene: Hephaistos or Daidalos? Neg. 83/468.

15. Egyptianizing cylinder seal, second millennium B.C. From Byblos. H. .05 m. Drawing by Deborah Nourse Lattimore, after P. Montet, *Byblos et l'Egypte* (Paris, 1928–1929), 62.

16. Egyptianizing cylinder seal, fourteenth century B.C. From Beth Shean, Israel. Drawing by Deborah Nourse Lattimore.

17. Phoenician gilded silver bowl, eighth century B.C. From Idalion, Cyprus. D. .185 m.

Louvre Museum, Département des Antiquités Orientales, AO 20134. Cliché des Musées Nationaux, Paris.

18. Achilles and Penthesilea (restored drawing), seventh century B.C. Terracotta shield from votive deposit on akropolis of Tiryns. D. ca. .38 m. Courtesy of Deutsches Archäologisches Institut, Athen, neg. Tiryns 1424.

19. Animal sacrifice, worship before altars with horns of consecration (above), and libations of liquid, lyre music, and offerings to dead (statue, tomb) (below), thirteenth century B.C. (Late Minoan III). Hagia Triada sarcophagus, Crete. H. .895 m., L. 1.375–85 m., W. .45 m. Heraklion Museum. Photographs courtesy of Alison Frantz.

20. Limestone statue of man wearing bull's head, sixth century B.C. From Golgoi, Cyprus. H. .435 m. (mask .205 m.). Louvre Museum, Département des Antiquités Orientales, AM 2758. Cliché des Musées Nationaux, Paris.

21. Terracotta figurine putting on bull's-head mask, 650–600 B.C. From Amathus, Cyprus; Tomb 20, no. 1. H. .132 m. Limassol Museum 714/1. By permission of the Director of Antiquities and the Cyprus Museum.

22. Terracotta figurine of ram-headed god (Baal-Hammon?), 600–550 B.C. From archaic sanctuary at Meniko (Litharkes), Cyprus. H. .185 m. Nicosia M.L. 1952/S83. Photograph courtesy of the Cyprus Museum, Nicosia. By permission of the Director of Antiquities and the Cyprus Museum.

23a. Wheel-made terracotta statuette of "hermaphrodite," sixth century B.C. From Ayia Irini, Cyprus. H. .362 m. Stockholm A.I. 2316. Medelhavsmuseet, Stockholm.

23b. Wheel-made terracotta statuette of warrior, sixth century B.C. From Ayia Irini, Cyprus. H. .353 m. Stockholm A.I. 1276. Medelhavsmuseet, Stockholm.

24a, b. Terracotta votive statues in situ around altar at Ayia Irini, Cyprus, sixth century B.C. Photograph courtesy of Medelhavsmuseet, Stockholm.

25. Syrian bronze mold-made plaque (nose or chest piece) from horse harness made for King Haza'el of Damascus, ninth century B.C. From sanctuary of Hera on Samos in a late sixth-century context. L. .273 m., W. .175 m. Courtesy of Deutsches Archäologisches Institut, Athen, neg. 88/1102.

26. Ivory lion's head, eighth to seventh century B.C. From Thasos. H. .05 m. Courtesy of École Française d'Archéologie, Athènes, neg, 27.991a.

27. Marble leaf drum in Aeolic style, sixth century B.C. From Thasos. D. .313–.22 m. Thasos Museum, inv. 1385. Courtesy of École Française d'Archéologie, Athènes, neg. 31.096.

28. Unfinished marble statue of ram bearer, early sixth century B.C. From quarries on Thasos. H. 3.5 m. Thasos Museum. Courtesy of École Française d'Archéologie, Athènes, neg. 46.739.

29. Limestone capital, seventh century B.C. From Arkades, Crete. Lower D. .247 m. Heraklion Museum, Crete. Photograph courtesy of Alison Frantz.

30. Limestone frieze of horsemen, seventh century B.C. From temple at Prinias, Crete. H. .84 m. Heraklion Museum 232. Photograph courtesy of Alison Frantz.

31. Limestone stele with maiden holding wreath, bird, seventh century B.C. From Prinias, Crete. H. .485 m. Heraklion Museum 396. Courtesy of Deutsches Archäologisches Institut, Athen, neg. 75/1062.

32. Two winged demons confronting each other, below sun disk in crescent, ninth or eighth century B.C. Basalt stele found at Aleppo, Syria. H. .95 m, W. .131 m. Aleppo 9955. Courtesy of the Aleppo Museum. Photograph by Anwar Abdel Ghafour.

33. Bronze helmet with pair of winged young men, snakes, late seventh century B.C. From Crete, said to be from Arkades. H. of helmet .21 m. Norbert Schimmel collection. Now in the Metropolitan Museum of Art, New York L. 1979.49.2. Drawing by Deborah Nourse Lattimore, after Suzanne Chapman.

34. Black-glazed sherd with graffito scene of "goblins" in workshop, last quarter of fifth century B.C. From workshop of Pheidias, Olympia. Pres. W. .115 m. Courtesy of Deutsches Archäologisches Institut, Athens, neg. Olympia 4203.

35a, b. Archaic bronze kouros, "Daedalic" style, ca. 600 B.C. From Delphi. H. .197 m. Delphi Museum. Photograph by École Française d'Archéologie, Athènes.

36. King Arkesilaos of Cyrene on *diphros*, ca. 560 B.C. Lakonian cup by the Arkesilaos Painter, from Vulci. D. .293 m., H. .20 m. Cabinet des Médailles 189. Courtesy of Bibliothèque Nationale, Paris.

37. Kroisos on the pyre (left), and Theseus and Antiope, Peirithoos (right), after 490 B.C. Red-figured belly amphora by Myson. H. .585 m. Louvre Museum, Département des Antiquités, G 197. Cliché des Musées Nationaux, Paris. Photograph by M. Chuzeville.

38. Herakles and the Kerkynian deer, after 490 B.C. Metope 19, east frieze (Hoffelner), from the Athenian treasury. .67 × .63 m. Delphi Museum. Courtesy of École Française d'Archéologie, Athènes, neg. 22352.

39. Theseus and Antiope, after 490 B.C. Metope 8, north frieze (Hoffelner), from the Athenian treasury. .67 × .63 m. Delphi Museum. Courtesy of École Française d'Archéologie, Athènes, neg. 22357.

40. The serpent column of the Plataian tripod from Delphi, in Constantinople. Ottoman miniatures (Ṣur-name), sixteenth century A.D. Topkapi Museum, Istanbul.

41. Bronze statue of god (Zeus or Poseidon), 470–460 B.C. Found off Artemision, Euboia. H. 2.09 m. Athens, National Museum (inv. 15161). Courtesy of Deutsches Archäologisches Institut, Athen, neg. N.M. 4533.

42. Athena with ἄφλαστον, 480–460 B.C. Red-figure lekythos by the Brygos Painter, from Gela. H. .34 m. New York 25.189.1 (Purchase 1925). Courtesy of the Metropolitan Museum of Art, New York.

43. Marble statue of running Nike dedicated for Kallimachos (*IG* I³ 794), 490–480 B.C. From Akropolis, Athens. H. 1.4 m. Akropolis 690. Courtesy of Deutsches Archäologisches Institut, Athen, negs. 68/140, 72/2933.

44. Harmodios and Aristogeiton (the tyrannicides), (left), and Greek and Amazon (right), late fourth century B.C. The Elgin Throne. H. .815 m., W. (front) .70 m. Malibu 74 AA 12. Courtesy of the J. Paul Getty Museum, Malibu.

45. Harmodios and Aristogeiton, ca. 400 B.C. Red-figure oinochoe, from the Dexileos grave precinct, Kerameikos, Athens. Pres. H. .14 m. Boston MFA 98.936. Courtesy of the Museum of Fine Arts, Boston, Pierce Fund.

46. Clay plaque from Akropolis, Athens, with running hoplite, after 490 B.C. "(ΜΕΓΑ-ΚΛΕΣ) ΓΛΑΥΚΟΣ ΚΑΛΟΣ." By Euthymides. W. .52. m. Akropolis 1037. Courtesy of Deutsches Archäologisches Institut, Athen, neg. Akropolis-Vasen 72/3011.

47. Greek fighting Persian (above, exterior), and two Greek warriors climbing out of tomb or altar (left, interior), ca. 460 B.C. Red-figure cup, name vase of the Painter of the Oxford Brygos Cup. D. .33 m. Oxford 1911.615. Courtesy of the Ashmolean Museum, Oxford.

48. Hero rising from tomb, ca. 470 B.C. Top of red-figure askos, near the Tyszkiewicz Painter (*ARV*¹ 188.59). Boston MFA 13.169. Courtesy of the Museum of Fine Arts, Boston, gift of E. P. Warren.

49. Hephaistos and Athena at the birth of Erichthonios from Ge, ca. 460 B.C. Red-figure stamnos by the Painter of Munich 2413. H. .39 m. Munich 2413. Courtesy of Staatliche Antikensammlungen und Glyptothek, Munich.

50. Hermes, Hephaistos, Athena, and Ge at the Birth of Pandora, ca. 450 B.C. Red-figure volute krater, related to the group of Polygnotos. H. .482 m. Oxford 525 (G 275). Courtesy of the Ashmolean Museum, Oxford.

51. Theseus and giant (Prokroustes?), marble statue group from Akropolis, Athens, before 480 B.C.? Akropolis 145 (Theseus: Pres. H. .63 m) and 370 (fragment: hand,

beard). Courtesy of Deutsches Archäologisches Institut, Athen, negs. Akr. 1702 and 72/2972.

52. Theseus and Antiope, after 490 B.C.? Pediment of the temple of Apollo, Eretria. H. 1.12 m. Chalkis Museum. Courtesy of Deutsches Archäologisches Institut, Athen, neg. Hege 1442.

53. Poseidon receiving libation from Nike, ca. 470–460 B.C. Calyx-krater by the Aegisthus Painter. H. .405 m. Yale 1985.4.1. Courtesy of the Yale University Art Gallery, New Haven, James N. Fosburgh (BA 1933) and Mary C. Fosburgh collection fund, Stephen Carleton Clark (BA 1903) Fund.

54. Poseidon and Theseus, ca. 470–460 B.C. Red-figured oinochoe, name-vase of the Painter of the Yale Oinochoe. H. .403 m. Yale 1913.143. Yale University Art Gallery, New Haven, gift of Rebecca Darlington Stoddard.

55. Theseus and Antiope ca. 490 B.C. Exterior of red-figure cup by Euphronios. D. .324 m. London E 41. Courtesy of the British Museum, London.

56. Theseus, Athena, and Amphitrite, ca. 500–490 B.C. Interior of red-figure cup by Onesimos (painter) and Euphronios (potter). D. .40 m. Louvre Museum, Département des Antiquités, G 104. Cliché des Musées Nationaux, Paris. Photograph by M. Chuzeville.

57. Theseus and the Minotaur (above, tondo) and deeds of Theseus (center and below, exterior), ca. 460 B.C. Red-figure cup by the Codrus Painter. D. .325 m. London E 84. Courtesy of the British Museum, London.

58. Bronze sculptor's workshop: manufacture of hoplite statue (above), and manufacture of athlete statue (below), 480–470 B.C. Exterior of red-figure cup by the Foundry Painter from Vulci. D. .305 m. Berlin F 2294. (For interior, see Figure 1.) Antikenmuseum Berlin, Staatliche Museen Preussischer Kulturbesitz.

59. Athena modeling a horse in bronze or clay, 470–460 B.C. Red-figure olpe from Capua, name-vase of the Group of Berlin F 2415. H. .215 m. Berlin F 2415. Antikenmuseum Berlin, Staatliche Museen Preussischer Kulturbesitz.

60. Athena in workshop of potter, metalworker, 490–480 B.C. Red-figure cup by the Euergides Painter, from the Akropolis, Athens. Pres. H. .13 m., D. .24 m. Akropolis 166. Athens, National Museum. Courtesy of Deutsches Archäologisches Institut, Athen, neg. Akr. Vasen 805.

61. Athena in bronze-sculptor's workshop, 480–470 B.C. Red-figure cup by the Foundry Painter, from Vulci. Munich 2650. Courtesy of Staatliche Antikensammlungen und Glyptothek, Munich.

62. King Dareios on his throne with Persian nobles, hearing Greek "warner"? Upper register: personifications of Hellas, Asia, Athena, and Apate. Late fourth century B.C. Apulian krater by the Darius Painter, from Canosa. H. 1.30 m., D. 1.93 m. Naples Museum 3253. After A. Furtwängler and K. Reichhold, *Griechische Vasenmalerei* (Munich, 1904–1932).

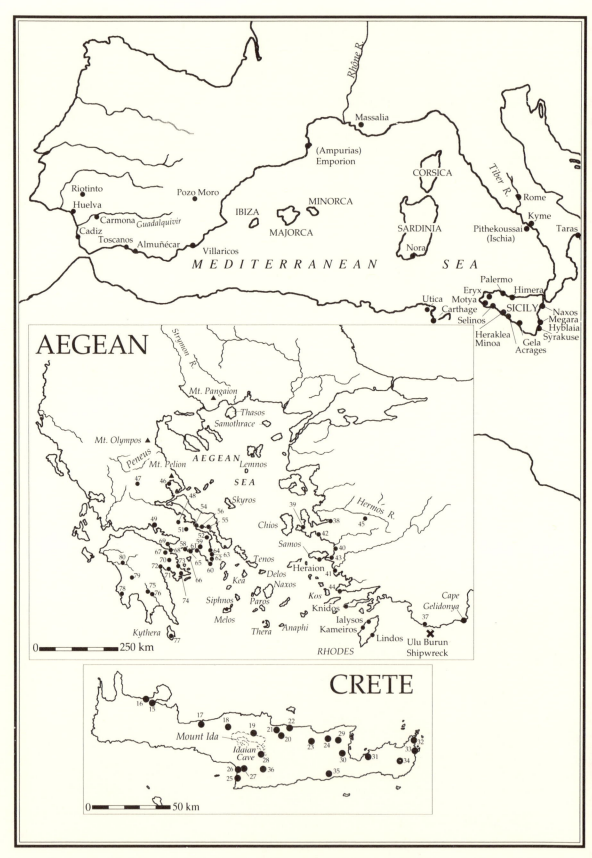

1. The western Mediterranean in the Bronze and Iron Ages with insets of the Aegean and Crete (T. Seymour).

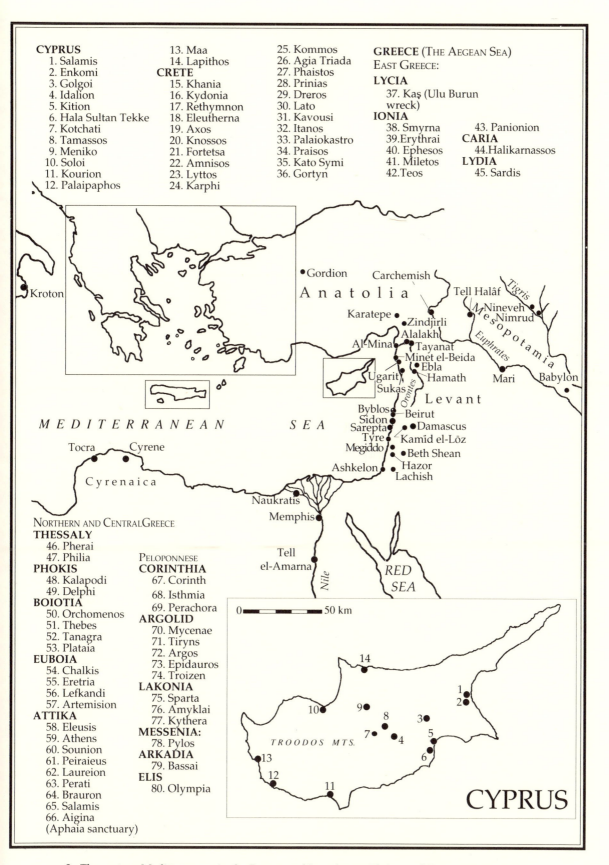

CYPRUS
1. Salamis
2. Enkomi
3. Golgoi
4. Idalion
5. Kition
6. Hala Sultan Tekke
7. Kotchati
8. Tamassos
9. Meniko
10. Soloi
11. Kourion
12. Palaipaphos
13. Maa
14. Lapithos

CRETE
15. Khania
16. Kydonia
17. Rethymnon
18. Eleutherna
19. Axos
20. Knossos
21. Fortetsa
22. Amnisos
23. Lyttos
24. Karphi
25. Kommos
26. Agia Triada
27. Phaistos
28. Prinias
29. Dreros
30. Lato
31. Kavousi
32. Itanos
33. Palaiokastro
34. Praisos
35. Kato Symi
36. Gortyn

GREECE (THE AEGEAN SEA)
EAST GREECE:
LYCIA
37. Kaş (Ulu Burun wreck)
IONIA
38. Smyrna
39. Erythrai
40. Ephesos
41. Miletos
42. Teos
43. Panionion
CARIA
44. Halikarnassos
LYDIA
45. Sardis

NORTHERN AND CENTRAL Greece
THESSALY
46. Pherai
47. Philia
PHOKIS
48. Kalapodi
49. Delphi
BOIOTIA
50. Orchomenos
51. Thebes
52. Tanagra
53. Plataia
EUBOIA
54. Chalkis
55. Eretria
56. Lefkandi
57. Artemision
ATTIKA
58. Eleusis
59. Athens
60. Sounion
61. Peiraieus
62. Laureion
63. Perati
64. Brauron
65. Salamis
66. Aigina (Aphaia sanctuary)

PELOPONNESE
CORINTHIA
67. Corinth
68. Isthmia
69. Perachora
ARGOLID
70. Mycenae
71. Tiryns
72. Argos
73. Epidauros
74. Troizen
LAKONIA
75. Sparta
76. Amyklai
77. Kythera
MESSENIA:
78. Pylos
ARKADIA
79. Bassai
ELIS
80. Olympia

CYPRUS

2. The eastern Mediterranean in the Bronze and Iron Ages with inset of Cyprus (T. Seymour).

PREFACE

A Reader's Guide and an Author's Apologia

A SCHOLAR, LIKE A GENTLEMAN, should never apologize or explain; this book excuses both gestures, as a courtesy to the general reader as well as the specialist. Before I emphasize some lessons of an already didactic text, my first apology is to Daidalos himself. The definitive work on his life and afterlife still remains to be written: he deserves, among other tributes, a lavishly illustrated assembly of his appearances in Western art (in the tradition of Nikolaos Yalouris's *Pegasus: The Art of the Legend*, published by Mobil Oil Hellas in 1975). Unlike such a book, this one purports to span multiple millennia and media, presents a curious mixture of close textual analysis with a selective survey of the archaeological evidence, speculates freely on mythology, etymology, and iconography, and recasts some dates and purposes of classical art. To combine the first chapters (in full ignorance of Semitic languages) with a detailed analysis of classical literature and art defies traditional divisions in professional specialties and competence.

I will defend some indulgences, in the Sokratic manner, from autobiography. I worked my way into Hellenism from the East, having excavated in Israel and Turkey before I ever saw Greece. When I finally did in 1978, I had just witnessed an unusual doctoral dissertation at Harvard University: "Greek Geometric Pottery in the East: The Chronological Implications," by Diane (Daniela) Saltz of the Department of Near Eastern Languages and Civilizations. Thanks to her obstinacy and her insights, I first saw early Iron Age Greece through Levantine eyes; she convinced me, in word, deed, and prose, that answers lay East. Her brilliant analysis of sites like Al Mina also introduced me to the perils of modern politics and persuasions, to the sad modern fate of the Phoenicians, and to the courage necessary to tackle these problems. I was fortunate to have an equivalent muse at the end of my odyssey in Patricia Bikai, an expert on the unhappy fate of the ancient and modern Phoenicians. I thank her not only for reading unmanageable drafts of Part II, but for her warmth, support, and insight.

On the professional side, my curiosity about the ancient Near East deepened during my doctoral venture into the Orientalizing period (published as *The Black and White Style*: see bibliography) but was hardly satisfied. Frustration as well as fascination led me to this investigation, neither a history of early Greek art, nor a biography of Daidalos, but a critical examination of a legend with roots in the East and of its fate in Greek hands. My aim was to explore first the Oriental component in those periods and genres it once fertilized and then its deliberate disarticulation in the classical period. The figure who gave his name to a century of Orientalizing art is more than just a convenient and poetic patron for such an investigation. The formation of his legend took place during early Greek contact and cohabitation with Levantines, which gave Greece an Oriental flavor, including an image of a craftsman with Near Eastern qualities. Later, his personality, like that of Kadmos, became progressively more Hellenized, eventually integrated into "native" dynasties of legendary kings. His repatriation demonstrates how classical Greek cities transformed traditions to suit an evolving historical consciousness, inaugurating a new phase of Greek myth and its uses. His fate recapitulates the progress of Greek art and thought in relation to the East, exemplifies an important pattern in Greek intellectual history, and lends insight for understanding similar configurations, especially in early Greek poetry and archaeology. In the last three chapters, the reader may lose track of Daidalos but should keep an eye on his fate: his transformation reflects such profound changes in Greek art and thought after the Persian wars in Athens in so many media that the scope of Part IV should explain itself. The nature of the break between pre-Persian and classical Greece, however artificial in historical periodization, cannot be overestimated at the intellectual, philosophical level. The accident of history that left Greece, and Athens, in a position of superiority determined much historical speculation thereafter, including the birth of the idea of Europe. In this classical restructuring of fragments of the past, Daidalos and his original world emerged in diffracted but informative illumination. Because these historical reorientations involve works of art occupying critical points in the chronology of Greek art, I have tried to suggest a number of threads of history to guide the scholarly community out of today's labyrinth, the stylistic chronology of late archaic and early classical Greek art. Hence my retracing of familiar ground in the late sixth and early fifth centuries, an attempt to elicit new arrangements of the evidence by other scholars, free of the acrimony now dominating the subject.

To admit that Daidalos is largely a literary creation, with a biography embroidered in classical and later periods (the subject of Part III), is hardly news. Most investigations have proceeded either "genetically" toward a diachronic synthesis of anecdotes and attributions that assumes a single, coherent tradition, or have synchronized his phases with contemporary art, to correlate "his" achievements with actual developments. Both methods have assumed two figures, a "mythical" and a "historical" Daidalos, and struggled to synthesize Panhellenic and local traditions in Athens and Crete, Greece and Italy, into a plausible stemma, as it were, of his testimonia. Instead, the very inconsistencies in the legends of Daidalos reward scrutiny, as they reveal the evolution of

Greek attitudes toward art and history. When the contradictions become the object of study rather than their obstacle, through a synoptic view of sources and art in a sequence of synchronic contexts, the results are fruitful and fascinating. Daidalos himself emerges as a movable beast, a creature most natural to the habitat of Greek myth. Born in an epic simile with enigmatic adjectives for parents, he was overshadowed by them for centuries. Dramatic changes in Greek art and life helped rediscover him and adapted him happily to far more numerous accomplishments than his poetic origins promised. Every feat claimed for him illuminates those occasions and attitudes that sponsored it, particular to a specific Greek city or tradition. It still remains to encourage the abandonment of the "historical sculptor" of the archaic period, enlisted to bolster ancient and modern theories of early Greek art. The fiction of a Cretan sculptor and teacher, if not father, of early Cretan artists conceals a convergence of prehistoric and Oriental elements beneath a classicizing perspective that arranges early Greek history into antecedents of classical art. The role of Athens in determining his classical persona is particularly vivid, and emerges in a close analysis of the intellectual atmosphere that succeeded victory over Persia (Part IV). Viewed under these conditions, each phase in the evolution of Daidalos reveals contemporary priorities in Greek art and its appreciation, and their collected sequence follows the prehistory of Greek art criticism and historiography.

The structure of this book has a point. In each of the two parts, the literature on Daidalos relevant to his archaic and classical personae (Parts I and III) is followed by a detailed exploration of the historical and archaeological background to each set of testimonia (Parts II and IV). This order documents my ἱστορίη and where it led me, but the results of my research could be read in different sequences, beginning with the insights I struggled to extract from years of analysis. This arrangement also demonstrates why each section goes unexplained without the other, a pedagogical, even polemical, strategy to integrate archaeology and philology, and advocate an interdisciplinary approach to the study of Greek history. In extant studies, the legend of Daidalos has already been deconstructed since the nineteenth century, and most recently and sensibly by Philipp, just as tragedy was newly analyzed for its barbarians by Hall, but such studies confine themselves to literature. This book asks that art inspire related disciplines to rethink Greece's relationship with the Orient, that philologists avail themselves more frequently of the rich banquet in the visual arts and share their own fare with historians and archaeologists, overcoming barriers of increasing specialization.

Another hope is to reunite prehistory and classical Greece as aspects of one culture. Greater minds have traced Greek art and culture to its Oriental roots, and pioneers like Frederik Poulsen and V. Gordon Childe are only absent from references because their influence is implicit. But more recent studies remain isolated within disciplines and confined to the Bronze *or* the Iron Age, with rare convergences. Those by Kantor and Smith concentrated on Bronze Age artistic motifs (now updated by Janice Crowley's *The Ae-*

gean and the East, Jonsered, 1989); however thorough, they omit more profound traditions in religion and literature, exchanged in the same "international age" and which lasted into the first millennium. Research on the Iron Age, including Burkert's remarkable integration of history, literature, and religion in his study of Near Eastern influence on Greece, confines itself to the parameters of Assyrian expansion, while archaeology now emphasizes much earlier contacts. A Levantine orientation in Greek culture transcended two or more phases and was a constant component of life in the Aegean. When united under one lens, prehistoric archaeology offers much in method to scholars of archaic and literary culture, while later phases of interaction made more vivid through the witness of texts can shed light on the silence of earlier years. The case of Daidalos becomes a welcome excuse for integrating periods as well as disciplines artificially and professionally separated.

The most important thing I learned from this book was how modern attitudes shape our view of the past, often blatantly in questions of cross-cultural contact, where they form a major impediment to understanding intimacy between East and West. Ancient and modern preoccupations with ethnicity, often specific to political and historical situations, easily turn innocent or convenient classifications of material and cultural evidence into racial properties. An attitude recognized as "Orientalism" has encouraged qualitative distinctions between cultural factors in a contest of rival claims. This approach involves not only "a style of thought based upon an ontological and epistemological distinction" between East and West but "a Western style for dominating, restructuring and having authority over the Orient," as defined by Said (*Orientalism*, 2–3). Bernal's analysis of the origins of classical scholarship (*Black Athena*, the first of four volumes on "The Afro-Asiatic Roots of Classical Civilization") blames modern European nationalism and anti-Semitism for the suppression of the Oriental contribution to Greek culture. Other factors contributed, some of them ancient; this book demonstrates how Bernal's "Aryan model" began in the fifth century, after the Persian wars, and not in modern Europe, such that the object of study—classical culture—already determined the mode of approach, long before the eighteenth century. A measure of prejudice remains traditional in modern studies of the Near East and in the field of classics itself: but an attitude toward classical antiquity somewhere between self-congratulation and self-flagellation can be found. As the pendulum swings in modern history from embracing to rejecting Oriental influence, it remains remarkable how different from its Eastern neighbors the Greek mind was—the forest that I hope does not disappear in the trees of this investigation.

ACKNOWLEDGMENTS

OF GREAT COMFORT, support and assistance to me during research and writing were colleagues in Greek and Near Eastern literature and art, at the institutions where I have taught (Yale University and the University of California at Los Angeles) and conducted research (the American School of Classical Studies at Athens). At Yale, I am particularly grateful to Professor Mark Smith of the Department of Near Eastern Languages and Civilizations and to Ulla Kasten of the Babylonian Collection. At UCLA, the Department of Classics invited me to join them after reading this as an unpublished manuscript, then helped me turn it into a book, in ways both scholarly and logistical. Emily Vermeule read more drafts than anyone, encouraged with premature praise, and offered a model difficult to follow. Irene Winter's example and advice were a frequent inspiration. Readers of the manuscript, solicited (including Henry Immerwahr and Eric Cline) and anonymous (for publication and academic reviews), provided generous criticism, helping shape and improve the book in ways they may not have suspected. The opportunity for informal presentations at the Johns Hopkins University, the University of North Carolina at Chapel Hill, and Yale exposed me to valuable counsel. Jane Carter has accompanied my progress and pitfalls through graduate school, teaching, research, and fieldwork; her discussions, criticisms, and contributions are too fundamental to this book to be specifically or adequately acknowledged.

I am grateful to all those who provided photographs and permission to publish them, often in record time: at the Antikenmuseum, Berlin, Wolf-Dieter Heilmeyer; at the Antikensammlung und Glyptothek, Munich, Friedrich Hamdorf; at the Ashmolean Museum, Oxford, Michael Vickers; at the Bibliothèque Nationale de Paris, Irène Aghion; at the British Museum, London, Dyfri Williams; at the Cyprus Museum, Nicosia, Athanasios Papageorghiou and Maria Hajinikolaou; at the Deutsches Archäologisches Institut, Athen, E. Lazarides and S. Rogge; at the J. Paul Getty Museum in Malibu, Karen Manchester; at the Medelhavsmuseet in Stockholm, Pontus Hellström; at the Metropolitan Museum of Art, Elizabeth Milleker; at the Musée du Louvre, Département des Antiquitiés Grecques et Romaines, Angelika Waiblinger and at the Département des Antiquités Orientales, Antoine Hermary; at the Museum of Fine Arts, Boston, Karen Otis; at the Walters Art Gallery, Baltimore, Ellen Reeder; at the Yale University Art Gallery, Susan Matheson. At UCLA, Deborah Nourse Lattimore and Timothy Seymour produced art under pressure, while Francis Deblauwe and Toni Pardi were welcome as careful editors.

The opportunity for a full year of salaried leave, on a Morse Junior Faculty Fellowship, was one privilege of teaching at Yale University; I am grateful to Susan Morse Hilles for her endowment and the Department of Classics at Yale University for my nomination. The manuscript could not have reached a press without the financial support of the Academic Senate of the University of California and the generosity of Dean Herbert Morris, or the assistance of the Department of Classics at UCLA. Joanna Hitchcock liked this book before I had written it, and assisted it into published form with patience and support. The opportunity to serve as classicist-consultant to MIT's human-powered flight team that launched the flight of "Daedalus" from Crete to Thera in April 1988 made me believe my research mattered, and often provided positive encouragement absent elsewhere. Finally, I am grateful to countless friends and family members who endured long years of excuses and absences, especially to the support of John Papado-poulos in the final struggle. I dedicate the result to the memory of my sister Margaret, who discovered the ancient Near East long before I did, and taught me the power of courage and love.

ABBREVIATIONS

AA	*Archäologischer Anzeiger*
AAA	Ἀρχαιολογικά Ἀναλεκτά ἐξ Ἀθηνῶν
AAAS	*Annales Archéologiques Arabes Syriennes*
AAP	*Atti dell'Accademia di Scienze, Lettere e Arte di Palermo*
AccLinc	*Rendiconti della Accademia Nazionale dei Lincei*
AE	Ἀρχαιολογική Ἐφημερίς
AESC	*Annales: Économies, Sociétés, Civilisations*
AfO	*Archiv für Orientforschung*
Agora III	R. E. Wycherley, *The Athenian Agora III: Literary and Epigraphical Testimonia*. Princeton, 1957
Agora XIV	R. E. Wycherley and H. Thompson, *The Athenian Agora XIV: The Agora of Athens*. Princeton, 1972
AJA	*American Journal of Archaeology*
AJAH	*American Journal of Ancient History*
AJP	*American Journal of Philology*
AK	*Antike Kunst*
AkkHw	W. V. Soden, *Akkadisches Handwörterbuch*. Wiesbaden, 1959–
AnatStud	*Anatolian Studies*
ANET	*Ancient Near Eastern Texts Relating to the Old Testament*, ed. J. Pritchard. 2d ed. Princeton, 1955
AntClass	*Antiquité Classique*
AOAT	*Alter Orient und Altes Testament*
APA	American Philological Association
ArchClass	*Archaeologia Classica*
ArchHom	*Archaeologia Homerica. Die Denkmäler des frühgriechischen Epos*, ed. A. Heubeck. Göttingen, 1974–
ARep	*Archaeological Reports*
ArtB	*Art Bulletin*
ARV	J. D. Beazley, *Athenian Red-Figure Vase-Painters*. 2d ed. Oxford, 1963
ARV¹	J. D. Beazley, *Athenian Red-Figure Vase Painters*. Oxford, 1942

ASAA	*Annuario della Scuola Archeologia di Atene*
ASNP	*Annali della Scuola Normale Superiore di Pisa*
ASOR	American Schools of Oriental Research
AthMitt	*Mittheilungen des Deutschen Archäologischen Instituts, Athen*
BA	*Biblical Archaeology*
BAR	*Biblical Archaeology Review*
BARep	*British Archaeological Reports*
BASOR	*Bulletin of the American Schools of Oriental Research*
BCH	*Bulletin de Correspondence Hellénique*
BClevMus	*Bulletin of the Cleveland Museum of Art*
BICS	*Bulletin of the Institute of Classical Studies* (London)
BIFG	*Bolletino dell'Istituto di Filologia Greca*
BonnJbb	*Bonner Jahrbücher des Rheinischen Landesmuseums. Bonn*
BSA	*Annual of the British School at Athens*
BSR	*Papers of the British School at Rome*
CA	*Classical Antiquity* (formerly CSCA)
CAH	*The Cambridge Ancient History.* Vols. 1–2, 3d ed.; vol. 3, 2d ed. Cambridge, 1970–
CBQ	*Catholic Biblical Quarterly*
CJ	*Classical Journal*
CMMS	*Corpus der minoischen und mykenischen Siegel*
CP	*Classical Philology*
CQ	*Classical Quarterly*
CR	*Classical Review*
CRAI	*Comptes Rendus de l'Académie des Inscriptions et Belles-lettres*
CronArch	*Cronache di archeologia e storia d'arte*
CSCA	*California Studies in Classical Antiquity*
CTA	*Corpus des tablettes en cunéiformes alphabétiques découvertes à Ras Shamra-Ugarit de 1929 à 1939.* Paris, 1963
CVA	*Corpus Vasorum Antiquorum.* Union Académique Internationale.
CW	*Classical World*
Deltion	Ἀρχαιολογικόν Δελτίον
DHA	*Dialogues d'Histoire Ancienne*
DMG	M. Ventris and J. Chadwick, *Documents in Mycenaean Greek.* 2d ed. Cambridge, 1973
EAA	*Enciclopedia dell'arte antica*
EADélos	*Exploration Archéologique de Délos*
EchCl	*Echos du Monde Classique* (*Classical Views*)

EPRO	Études Préliminaires des Religions Orientales dans l'Empire Romain
Ergon	Τὸ Ἔργον τῆς ἐν ᾿Αθήναις ᾿Αρχαιολογικῆς Ἑταιρεῖα
FdD	Fouilles de Delphes. École Française d'Athènes. Paris, 1902–
FGrH	F. Jacoby, Fragmente der griechischen Historiker. 14 vols. Berlin, 1923–1930; Leipzig, 1940–1957
Fifth Cretological Congress	Πεπραγμένα τοῦ Ε' Διέθνου Κρητολογικοῦ Συνεδρίου (῎Αγιος Νικόλαος, 25.8–1.10.1981). Herakleion, 1985
Fourth Cretological Congress	Πεπραγμένα τοῦ Δ' Διέθνου Κρητολογικοῦ Συνεδρίου (῾Ηράκλειον, 29.8.–3.9.1976). Athens, 1980.
FuF	Forschungen und Fortschritte
GGA	Göttingische Gelehrte Anzeigen
GHI	M. N. Tod, A Selection of Greek Historical Inscriptions. Oxford, 1948
GöttMisz	Göttinger Miszellen
GR	Greece and Rome
GRBS	Greek, Roman and Byzantine Studies
How and Wells	W. W. How and J. Wells, A Commentary on Herodotus. 2 vols. Oxford, 1928
HSCP	Harvard Studies in Classical Philology
HThR	Harvard Theological Review
ICr	Inscriptiones Creticae, ed. M. Guarducci. Rome, 1935–
IDélos	Inscriptions de Délos. Académie des Inscriptions et Belles Lettres, 1926–
IEJ	Israel Exploration Journal
IG	Inscriptiones Graecae. Berlin, 1873–
I.G.M.E.	᾿Ινστιτοῦτον Γεωλογικῶν καὶ Μεταλλευτικῶν ᾿Ερευνῶν
IrAnt	Iranica Antiqua
IstMitt	Mittheilungen des Deutschen Archäologisches Instituts, Istanbul
JANES	Journal of the Ancient Near Eastern Society of Columbia University
JAOS	Journal of the American Oriental Society
JARCE	Journal of the American Research Center in Egypt
JdI	Jahrbuch des Deutschen Archäologischen Instituts, Athen
JEA	Journal of Egyptian Archaeology
JESHO	Journal of the Economic and Social History of the Orient
JFA	Journal of Field Archaeology
JHS	The Journal of Hellenic Studies

JMA	*Journal of Mediterranean Archaeology*
JNES	*Journal of Near Eastern Studies*
JRAS	*Journal of the Royal Asiatic Society*
JRGZM	*Jahrbuch des Römisch-Germanischen Zentralmuseums, Mainz*
JSOT	*Journal for the Study of the Old Testament*
JSS	*Journal of Semitic Studies*
Kassel-Austin	R. Kassel and C. Austin, *Poetae Comici Graeci*. Berlin, 1983–
KrChr	Κρητικά Χρονικά
KTU	*Die Keilalphabetischen Texte aus Ugarit*, ed. M. Dietrich, O. Loretz, and J. Sanmartín. *AOAT* 24, vol. 1. Kevelaer, 1976
LIMC	*Lexicon Iconographicum Mythologiae Classicae*. Basel, 1975–
LSAG	L. H. Jeffery, *The Local Scripts of Archaic Greece*, rev. ed., ed. A. Johnston. Oxford, 1989
LSCG	F. Sokolowski, *Lois sacrées des cîtés grecques*. Paris, 1969
LSAM	F. Sokolowski, *Lois sacrées d'Asie Mineure*. Paris, 1955
MAAN	*Memorie dell r. Accademia di archaeologia, lettere e belle arti di Napoli*
MadrForsch	*Madrider Forschungen*
MadrMitt	*Mittheilungen des Deutschen Archäologischen Instituts, Madrid*
MarbW	*Marburger Winkelmannsprogramm*
MBaH	*Münsterische Beiträge zur antiken Handelgeschichte*
MDAIK	*Mittheilungen des Deutschen Archäologischen Instituts, Kairo*
MeditArch	*Mediterranean Archaeology*
MEFRA	*Mélanges de l'École Française de Rome, Antiquité*
MH	*Museum Helveticum*
MJb	*Münchener Jahrbuch der bildenden Kunst*
ML	R. Meiggs and D. Lewis, *A Selection of Greek Historical Inscriptions*. Rev. ed. Oxford, 1988
MonAnt	*Monumenti Antichi*, edti dell'Accademia di Lincei
MonPiot	*Monuments et Mémoires. Fondation Piot*
M-W	R. Merkelbach and M. L. West, *Fragmenta Hesiodea*. Oxford, 1967
Nauck	A. Nauck and B. Snell, *Tragicorum Graecorum Fragmenta*. Vols. 1–2. Göttingen, 1964
NC	*Numismatic Chronicle*
NJbb	*Neue Jahrbücher für das klassische Altertum*
NSc	*Notizie degli scavi di antichitá*
OJA	*Oxford Journal of Archaeology*
ÖJh	*Jahreshefte des Österreichischen archäologischen Institutes*

OLA	*Orientalia Lovaniensia Analecta*
OlFor	*Olympische Forschungen*. Berlin, 1944–
OLP	*Orientalia Lovaniensia Periodica*
OpAth	*Opuscula Atheniensia*
OpRom	*Opuscula Romana*
OrAnt	*Oriens Antiquus*
PAA	Πρακτικὰ τῆς ἐν ᾿Αθηνῶν ᾿Ακαδημίας
PAPhS	*Proceedings of the American Philosophical Society*
PapOxy	*Oxyrhynchus Papyri*. London, 1898–
PBA	*Proceedings of the British Academy*
PBF	*Prähistorische Bronzefunde*
PCPhS	*Proceedings of the Cambridge Philological Society*
PdP	*Parola del Passato*
PEQ	*Palestine Exploration Quarterly*
PGM	K. Preisendanz, *Papyri Graeci Magici*. Leipzig, 1928–1931
PMG	D. Page, *Poetae Melici Graeci*. Oxford, 1962
POM	A. Evans, *The Palace of Minos at Knossos*. 4 vols. London, 1921–1935
Praktika	Πρακτικὰ τῆς ἐν ᾿Αθήναις ᾿Αρχαιλογικῆς ῾Εταιρεία
ProcPS	*Proceedings of the Prehistoric Society*
PZ	*Prähistorische Zeitschrift*
QEDEM	Monographs of the Institute of Archaeology, Hebrew University, Jerusalem
QUCC	*Quaderni Urbinati di Cultura Classica*
RA	*Revue Archéologique*
Radt	S. Radt, *Tragicorum Graecorum Fragmenta: Aeschylus*. Vol. 3. Göttingen, 1985; *Sophocles*. Vol. 4. Göttingen, 1977
RAAN	*Rendiconti dell'Accademia di Archeologia, Lettere e Belle Arte di Napoli*
RAI	*Rendiconti dell'Accademia d'Italia*
RAss	*Revue Assyriologique*
RB	*Revue Biblique*
RDAC	*Report of the Department of Antiquities of Cyprus*
RE	A. Pauly, G. Wissowa, and W. Kroll, *Real-Encyclopädie der classischen Altertumswissenschaft*. 34 vols. Stuttgart, 1894–1962; Munich, 1973–1978
REA	*Revue des Études Anciennes*
REG	*Revue des Études Grecques*
RH	*Revue Historique*
RhM	*Rheinisches Museum für Philologie*

RHR	*Revue de l'Histoire des Religions*
RömMitt	*Mittheilungen des Deutschen Archäologischen Instituts, Rom*
RivStudAnt	*Rivista di Studi Antici*
RS	Ras Shamra
RSF	*Rivista di Studi Fenici*
RUB	*Revue de l'Université de Bruxelles*
SBL	Society for Biblical Literature
SCE	E. Gjerstad and others, *The Swedish Cyprus Expedition. Finds and Results of the Excavations in Cyprus*. Vols. 1–4. Stockholm and Lund 1934–1972
Second Cretological Congress	Πεπραγμένα τοῦ Β' Διέθνου Κρητολογικοῦ Συνεδρίου. 4 vols. Athens, 1968
SEG	*Supplementum Epigraphicum Graecum*
SIG	W. Dittenberger, *Sylloge Inscriptionum Graecarum*. 3d ed. Leipzig, 1915–1924
SIMA	*Studies in Mediterranean Archaeology*
SMEA	*Studi Micenei ed Egeo-Anatolici*
Snell	B. Snell, *Pindari Carmina*. Leipzig, 1971
SSA	*Studies in Sardinian Archaeology*
StEtr	*Studi Etruschi*
Studi Fenici e Punici	*Atti del Primo Congresso Internazionale di Studi Fenici e Punici (Roma 5–10 Novembre 1979)*. Rome, 1983
TAPA	*Transactions of the American Philological Association*
TAPS	*Transactions of the American Philosophical Society*
Third Cretological Congress	Πεπραγμένα τοῦ Γ' Διέθνου Κρητολογικοῦ Συνεδρίου (Ῥέθυμνον, 18–23.9.1971). Athens, 1963
Travlos	J. Travlos, *Pictorial Dictionary of Ancient Athens*. New York, 1971
UF	*Ugarit Forschungen*
WS	*Wiener Studien*
WZJena	*Wissenschaftliche Zeitschrift der Friedrich-Schiller Universität, Jena*
WZRostock	*Wissenschaftliche Zeitschrift der Universität, Rostock*
YUAG Bulletin	*Yale University Art Gallery, Bulletin*
ZaeS	*Zeitschrift für ägyptische Sprache und Altertumskunde*
ZAnt	*Ziva Antica*
ZAW	*Zeitschrift für alttestamentliche Wissenschaft*
ZDPV	*Zeitschrift des Deutschen Palästina-Vereins*
ZPE	*Zeitschrift für Papyrologie und Epigraphik*

DAIDALOS

AND THE LEVANT

· PART I ·

Daidalos and *Daidala*

in Greek Poetry

CHAPTER 1

Craft and Craftsmen in
Epic Poetry

[I]N *ILIAD* 18.592, Daidalos makes not only his first appearance in the Greek imagination, but also his only one in the corpus of Homeric poetry. Thus he is born as a *hapax legomenon* occasioned by a simile, the weakest of links for any epic phenomenon. Given the importance of this passage for his existence, a close examination of its context and epic associations is fundamental to explaining him in the context of poetic language.[1] His name requires reference to the epic corpus of "daidalic" words, since he obviously bears one of those *redende Namen* bestowed on other Homeric craftsmen and personifies specific qualities manifest elsewhere in cognates. Thus he keeps company with Τέκτων ("the builder"), Ἁρμονίδης ("the joiner"), and perhaps even Homer himself, all names for artists derived from their activity.[2]

An extensive family of words in the Homeric poems derives from a root of undetermined meaning, *δαλ reduplicated as δαιδαλ- to produce primarily adjectives (δαιδάλεος, δαιδαλόεις, πολυδαίδαλος); less frequently a neuter noun, used only in the plural (δαίδαλα), twice a verb in the present participle (δαιδάλλων), and, last but not least, Δαίδαλος himself.[3] The etymology of its root remains unknown: Indo-European sources (*del-*) and Semitic *dal-* (as in δέλτος, "writing tablet") have both been proposed, but neither demonstrates an independent connection with its epic manifestations.[4] No ancient usage that does not derive from its original epic context can be attested for any versions of the words. In poetry they describe, represent, or personify objects of intricate and expensive craftsmanship; expressions such as "well crafted,"

---

[1] According to principles and methods articulated by Leumann, *Homerische Wörter*, and Benveniste, *Problèmes de linguistique generale*, 289–90: "Le sens d'une forme linguistique se definit par la totalité de ses emplois, par leur distribution et par les types de liaisons qui en resultent." Cf. Householder and Nagy, *Greek: A Survey of Recent Work*, chap. 1; A. Dihle, "Leumann's Homerische Wörter und die Sprache der mündlichen Dichtung," *Glotta* 48 (1970) 1–7; A. Heubeck, "Zum Problem der homerischen Kunstsprache," *MH* 38 (1981) 65–80.

[2] Eckstein, *ArchHom II: L*, 1–22, on Homeric craftsmen; Lacroix, "Ikmalios"; Nagy, *Best of the Achaeans*, 299–300; Hoekstra, *Epic Verse before Homer*, 58–59, on *redende Namen* as individual invention.

[3] Frontisi-Ducroux, *Dédale*, 29–34, for forms and distribution.

[4] Chantraine, *Dictionnaire étymologique*, 246, s.v. δαιδάλλω etc., prefers the former. Cf. *Lexikon des Frühgriechischen Epos*, fasc. 10, ed. E.-M. Vogt (Göttingen, 1982), 195–96, s.v. δαιδάλεος.

"intricately worked," or "skillfully wrought" satisfy their meaning, encouraged by two instances as a verb for the activity of a craftsman at work. All ancient glosses and modern understanding of these words can be traced to their epic occurrences, which lend them meaning but also derive their narrative significance from them.

A survey of epic δαίδαλα in terms of metrical, syntactical, and thematic distribution reveals far greater powers of connotation than specific denotation. The most common form of these words in poetry is in adjectives; they account for twenty-eight of thirty-six appearances throughout the *Iliad* and *Odyssey*. Their morphology, identified by the -εος suffix, makes them material- or *Stoffadjective*, albeit of unfamiliar *Stoff*.[5] Neither position nor distribution of these adjectives shows them to be traditional epithets fixed in a metrical formula; they represent morphological units of greater flexibility within the technique of composition.[6] Since their greatest concentration is in the *Iliad*, and the artist himself is introduced in that poem, it forms an appropriate departure for this quest for Daidalos.

The most frequent manifestations of this word family involve armor, the man-made barrier between warrior and weapon, and often the outfit accompanying a hero into death and glory—hence their concentration in the narrative of the battlefield rather than in the *Odyssey*, an epic of return, where δαιδάλεος never describes armor. Nor is it surprising to find eight out of twenty-eight occurrences in the *Iliad* clustered in Book 18, devoted to the armor and arming of the best of the Achaeans, Achilles.

Most frequently qualified as δαιδάλεος (five times, of which four are πολυδαίδαλος) is the θώρηξ or cuirass, an outfit once rejected as a historical anachronism until archaeology confirmed its Bronze Age existence.[7] Paris (*Iliad* 3.358), Menelaos (4.136), Hektor (7.252), Diomedes (8.195) and Odysseus (11.436) are all endangered, at a moment in battle, by an arrow or spear that strikes them:

καὶ διὰ θώρηκος πολυδαιδάλου ἠρήρειστο.

and pierced through their much-decorated cuirass.

The practical assembly of armor in each of these passages has troubled scholars, who wonder how to wear θώρηξ, μίτρη, and ζώνη (cuirass, belly guard, and belt) together, but their combination is purely poetic.[8] The adjective is clearly fixed in an *iteratum* for-

---

[5] Leumann, *Homerische Wörter*, 131–33, considers δαιδάλεος but a variant of πολυδαίδαλος, itself a possessive denominative from δαίδαλον, "work of art"; *contra* Chantraine, *Dictionnaire étymologique*, 246: "Une telle hypothèse ne se laisse ni démontrer ni refuter," although he advocates a denominative morphology.

[6] M. Parry, *L'epithète traditionelle dans Homère* (Paris, 1928); and J. Hainsworth, *The Flexibility of the Homeric Formula* (Oxford, 1972), for these terms.

[7] On the Mycenaean cuirasse from Dendra, see "Neue Funde von Dendra," *AthMitt* 82 (1967) 1–35, pls. 2–17; H. Catling, "Panzer," and H. Brandenburg, "Mitra," both in *ArchHom. I: E Kriegswesen*, 1, 127–28; 1, 74–80, 96–100; and cf. Catling, "A Bronze Plate from a Scale Corslet Found at Mycenae," *AA* 85 (1970) 441–49. See subsequent discussion with nn. 15ff., on Kinyras and the cuirass of Agamemnon.

[8] H. Brandenburg, "Mitra–Zoma–Zoster," in *ArchHom I: E. Kriegswesen* 1, 119–25, 142–43, on the

mulaic for signaling a hero's proximity to death: "Despite the excellent workmanship of his armor, it failed to keep an arrow from his body, but prevented a fatal wound." For in all five passages, the hero is rescued from death. The Trojans save themselves: Paris avoids the spear of Menelaos through agility (ἐκλίνθη, "turned aside") and Hektor escapes a thrust by Ajax (7.252). The Greeks, in contrast, are saved by Athena: Menelaos is wounded, despite the protection of a ζωστῆρος δαιδαλέοιο, "elaborate belt") and a μίτρη (ἕρκος ἀκόντων, "barrier against spears") in addition to his θώρηξ πολυδαίδαλος, "much-decorated cuirass," but his skin is only grazed by the arrow, averted by the goddess to his most heavily protected part. As he assures his brother (4.184–87), various components of his armor saved him, and this time the ζωστήρ is praised as πανααίολος, "all-glittering," the μίτρη as the work of skilled craftsmen (χαλκῆες κάμον ἄνδρες: "bronze-workers made it"), without a repetition of δαιδάλεος. Likewise, Odysseus skins his ribs on the spear of Sokos (11.437), but Athena keeps the weapon away from his vulnerable internal organs, his ἔγκατα.

The fifth θώρηξ in the *Iliad* described as δαιδάλεος does not protect in battle: the armor of Diomedes is coveted by Hektor as a work of Hephaistos (8.195),

δαιδάλεον θώρηκα, τὸν Ἥφαιστος κάμε τεύχων,

the elaborate cuirass, which Hephaistos made, working it,

before the Trojan hero embarks on the rampage that recalls Patroklos into battle. Position and epithet for this θώρηξ also distinguish it from those described in battle, and the addition of the name of its maker, the god Hephaistos, gives it added prestige. As in the praise of other epic finery (for example, the throne of Penelope in *Odyssey* 19.57), the adjective δαιδάλεος participates in a hierarchy of praise expressions where it is subordinate to, but often linked with, the name of a craftsman.

These passages with cuirasses share special epic functions. They often follow or recall the hero's arming scene, the prelude to his moment in battle, his ἀριστεία, and his ritual preparation for κλέος, the glory his performance earns him in epic poetry.[9] The adjective itself, δαιδάλεος, can reverberate in action as in the description of armor, as if to reinforce those heroic qualities bestowed in arming scenes. Then, the *iterata* mark a close brush with death, a particular form of κλέος, and are linked to related passages, often with a twist of irony. In the case of Hektor, for example, an even more prestigious suit of armor than the one he covets is eventually captured—that of Achilles, worn by

---

difficulty of reconciling epic terms for armor with realia. Fenik, *Typical Battle Scenes in the Iliad*, 73–74, 78–79, 102–5, follows G. Murray, *The Rise of the Greek Epic* (Oxford, 1934), 155–58, in analyzing the θώρηξ as originally appropriate only to *Iliad* 11.436 (Odysseus), then attracted to similar moments involving other heroes whom it fits awkwardly. On the mechanics of

such *iterata* in the Homeric poems, see Strasser, *Iterata*.

[9] For example, the arming of Paris at 3.330–38 is succeeded by his evasion of a weapon at 3.358. On arming scenes, see n. 10. See Nagy, *Best of the Achaeans*, on the heroic values of κλέος and ἀριστεία.

Patroklos (*Iliad* 17.125). While Hektor's wish is fulfilled beyond expectation, that capture of armor costs him his life, and occasions the manufacture of a new outfit, the most "daidalic" in all of epic poetry. Indeed, Hektor's very boast, addressed to his horses, is returned in 17.448, where Zeus consoles the mourning horses of Achilles that their ἅρματα δαιδάλεα, "elaborate chariot-gear," will at least never carry Hektor. In this verbal network, the adjective that glorified the prize sought by Hektor in Book 8 and awarded him briefly with the slaying of Patroklos now describes the chariot that will drag his corpse around his own city (22.395–99) and the tomb of Patroklos (24.14–22). In examining the qualities bestowed by δαιδάλεος, this first category reveals the word's characteristic powers: it praises appearance but also signifies unexpected dangers. On a modest scale, these examples anticipate the fuller ambiguity of a complete set of armor, as explored in describing the armor of Achilles.

Other battle equipment praised as δαιδάλεα includes the ἔντεα (armor) of Aetion, the father of Andromakhe slain by Achilles long before the siege of Troy but buried with respect (6.418). The Cilician king received a proper hero's cremation burial "in all his elaborate armor," σὺν ἔντεσι δαιδαλέοισιν, crowned by a mound. This unusual treatment of Andromakhe's father, in a world where slain enemies are abandoned to dogs and birds on the battlefield (*Iliad* 1.4–5), contrasts gloomily with Achilles' initial mutilation of her husband's corpse. Eventually, in Book 24, Hektor's body is restored to his family and accorded proper burial, and the adjective at 6.418 helps qualify Achilles as the best of the Achaeans in social behavior as well as praising his armor and action in battle. Achilles' conduct of the funeral games in Book 23 at the end of the epic, for example, is characterized by respect for rank and social standing that represents a vivid departure from his μῆνις behavior, and his return of the body in Book 24 completes his reconciliation with contemporary social practices (see subsequent discussion with n. 37). Whether or not Andromakhe's narration of her father's funeral anticipates the end of the *Iliad* through a single word, Aetion's armor is distinguished as δαιδάλεος even after his death, or perhaps especially after winning κλέος from Achilles.

This heroic property of the adjective is manifest elsewhere in the *Iliad*, when elaborate armor, "δαιδάλεα ἔντεα," accompanies warriors at their moment of ἀριστεία. Idomeneus of Crete and his henchman or θεράπων also appear σὺν ἔντεσι δαιδαλέοισιν in 13.331, as do both the Aiantes and the Salaminians in the same book (13.719). While one could reduce this resemblance to the metrical fact that the phrase neatly fills a hexameter after the caesura, the adjective surely distinguishes the heroes of the moment. In the absence of Achilles, and with the wounding of Diomedes, Odysseus, and Agamemnon, it is Idomeneus, roused by Poseidon (13.210), and the two Aiantes (14.508–22) who ward off the Trojans from the Greek ships. Moreover, the first adjective recapitulates a recent and special arming process (254–305), when Meriones comes to fetch a spear to replace one broken in battle. The second use of δαιδάλεος for the Aiantes highlights armor all the more elaborate as their companions, the Lokrians, appear as bowmen alone (712–18).

Far more vivid is the praise lavished on the armor of Agamemnon as a prelude to his entry into battle.[10] As he assembles his gear for battle, every item of his bronze outfit (νῶροψ χαλκός) is described in loving detail as befits a hero embarking on his ἀριστεία (*Iliad* 11.15–46; cf. 3.331). While a simple hexameter line attaches his greaves,

κνημῖδας μὲν πρῶτα περὶ κνήμῃσιν ἔθηκε,

and first he placed his greaves around his shins,

it is augmented by an extra line of embellishment:[11]

καλάς, ἀργυρέοισιν ἐπισφυρίοις ἀραρνίας.

beautiful [greaves], fastened with silver ankle-points.

Next he dons his θώρηξ, again in one plain hexameter but followed by a praise line that reminds us that it is a ξεινήιος or guest gift from Kinyras, king of Cyprus. For the μέγα κλέος of the Trojan expedition had apparently reached Cyprus, whose king sent this military contribution, as it were, to the leader of the Greeks. The historicity of this figure is largely confirmed by the archaeological evidence for the θώρηξ, described in lavish detail. It features a series of bands called οἶμοι, a *hapax legomenon* in epic poetry. Ten are of dark blue κύανος (cobalt, lapis lazuli, or blue paste), twelve are of gold, and twenty of "cassiterite" or tin, that metal essential to bronze technology and Aegean prehistory.[12] Three snakes of κύανος crown the corslet around its neck and are compared to the rainbows of Zeus, "wonder of mortal men" (τέρας μερόπων ἀνθρώπων). Agamemnon then proceeds to don his next item, a sword worn from a shoulder strap (ἀμφὶ ὤμοισιν), studded with gold nails, as is its silver sheath. Next and most glamorous is his shield, whereupon the poet invokes πολυδαίδαλος to do justice to its qualities and θοῦρις ("breathing") to give it life. Three lines describe precisely what makes it beautiful (καλή). Ten bronze circles, twenty tin bosses surround a central one of κύανος, and the crowning touch is a Gorgon, whose ferocious visage (βλοσυρῶπις, an-

---

[10] On arming scenes, see Arend, *Typische Szenen*, 92–98, J. I. Armstrong, "The Arming Motif in the Iliad," *AJP* 79 (1958) 337–54; Nagler, *Spontaneity and Tradition*, 117–19, on the structural significance of such purely ornamental passages, including "brief arming scenes in which a traditional epithet is the only explicit allomorph of the all-important *charis* element."

[11] This technique was described by Parry as "unperiodic enjambement"; "the addition of an adjecti-

val idea . . . describing a noun found in the foregoing verse" (*Making of Homeric Verse*, 255).

[12] On κύανος and its Linear B counterpart, *ku-wa-no*, see R. Halleaux, "Lapis-lazuli, azurite ou pâte de verre? A propos de *kuwano* et *kuwanowoko* dans les tablettes mycéniennes," *SMEA* 9 (1969) 47–66; on lapis lazuli in the Bronze Age, including Cypriote industries (glyptic), see E. Porada, "The Cylinder Seals Found at Thebes in Boeotia," *AfO* 28 (1981) 6–8. Also see Chapter 5.

other *hapax* word), flanked by Fear and Terror, blaze from the center of the shield. Even the strap supporting this splendor is of silver with a cobalt snake with three heads. Finally, Agamemnon sets on his leather helmet, four-crested and horsetail-plumed, and grabs his two bronze spears. This spectacle inspires the applause of the gods in the form of thunder sent by Athena and Hera, as if visual splendor spilled over into sound and nature responded to human awe.[13]

This magnificent passage was long considered an interpolation, and its fabulous armor an anachronism, to excuse the singular appearance of Cyprus (never elsewhere in the *Iliad*) as well as its linguistic peculiarities (οἴμοι) and technical anticipations (the Gorgon).[14] Recent discoveries and scholarship have happily reconciled the passage with its immediate context and the rest of the poem. Kinyras plausibly represents the wealth and power of a Levantine king (his name has Semitic roots) in Late Bronze Age Cyprus, his gift an example of royal exchange of precious objects current in the ancient Mediterranean.[15] In commenting on this passage, Eustathius says that Kinyras promised fifty vessels to Agamemnon, but only sent one, the rest in clay (ὀστρακίνῳ στόλῳ), perhaps a reflection of Late Bronze Age ceramic trade with the Aegean carried by ships like those discovered at Cape Gelidonya and Kaş in Lykia (see Chapter 5). Plate fragments from genuine scale corslets, which the description in the *Iliad* implies, have turned up on Greek sites (see n. 7) and point to the occasional capture or bequest of a type of armor more familiar in the Near East. The gift of Kinyras recalls, in particular, the gold corslet and pectoral worn by Tutankhamon in his tomb, but the plate-corslet type represented in Greek finds has relatives in Cyprus and North Syria, where a workshop has been postulated.[16] The one worn by Agamemnon suggests that Near Eastern versions of such armor reached the Aegean, perhaps even through royal exchange, via the Levant and Cyprus.[17] Unlike the tin and lapis lazuli on his shield, the cuirass could have been a diplomatic gift or booty. What embellishes this passage is the role of the Near East as a

[13] Compare this climax to the arming of Achilles (*Iliad* 19.386—quoted subsequently in the text), where the hero's armor actually lifts him off the ground, in a moment of metaphor become reality.

[14] For traditional rejections, see Leaf and Bayfield's commentary on this line and Lorimer, *Homer and the Monuments*, 208; its authenticity is defended by Catling, in *ArchHom I: E. Kriegswesen*, 1, 78–79.

[15] C. Baurain, "Kinyras. La fin de l' Age du Bronze à Chypre et la tradition antique," *BCH* 104 (1980) 277–308; "Κινύρας et Κέραμος. Remarques à propos de Pline, *Hist. Nat.* VII, 195 et d'Homère, *Iliade* 5. 387," *AntClass* 50 (1981) 23–37. Pliny claims the same figure invented *tegulas*, which Baurain connects with copper mining in Cyprus rather than roof tiles.

[16] U. Öbrink, *Hala Sultan Teke 5*, SIMA 45: 5 (Göteborg, 1979), 44, N 6000, for scales from Cyprus.

W. Ventzke, "Der Schuppenpanzer von Kamīd el-Lōz," in *Kamīd el-Lōz 1977–81*, ed. R. Hachmann, Saarbrücker Beiträge zur Altertumswissenschaft 36 (Bonn, 1986), 161–82, cites (p. 182) V. Maag's article, "Syrien-Palästina," in *Kunstgeschichte des alten Orient*, ed. H. Schmökel, (Stuttgart, 1961), 447–604, esp. 500–501, for an armorer-workshop in Damascus which still supplied Neo-Assyrian royal kings. Cf. Figure 25, made in Damascus and found in Greece: Chapter 5, n. 192.

[17] Catling, *AA* 85 (1970) 441–49. Cf. an archaic bequest of Oriental armor: M.-Th. Picard, "Le 'thoraké' d'Amasis," in *Hommages à Deonna, Collection Latomus* 28 (Brussels, 1957), 363–70.; E. D. Francis and M. Vickers, "Amasis and Lindos," *BICS* 31 (1984) 125.

source for glamorous objects, an aspect of the Greek attitude that is the subject of this book.

An additional item of Agamemnon's battle outfit, neglected in this overture, is introduced later in the same book (11.236): a ζωστήρ παναίολος, "girdle all aglitter," belting the corslet around the body and, in fact, protecting the hero from the spear of Iphidamas in an encounter similar to those marked by the action of a δαιδάλεος θώρηξ. Such a belt not only reaffirms the Near Eastern connection but is conveniently illustrated by a corslet represented on a richly decorated ivory gaming box from Enkomi in Cyprus.[18] Thus elements of Agamemnon's entire outfit could allude to a Near Eastern ensemble, a royal gift from the Levant enshrined in the poetic tradition and embellished by a recent Greek innovation, the Gorgon.

This dazzling outfit, fit for a king and the leader of the Greeks, closes the repertoire of δαιδάλεος armor in the *Iliad* by introducing the most glamorous description of all, that of the "best of the Achaeans," Achilles himself. In his case, the request, manufacture, description, arming, and activity of the ensemble dazzle with the entire spectrum of forms of δαιδαλ- words, culminating in the introduction of Daidalos himself.

Thetis arrives at the house of Hephaistos, built of bronze by the craftsman-god, and finds him making twenty tripods with golden wheels attached to their feet (18.372–79):

> τὸν δ' εὗρ' ἱδρώοντα ἑλισσόμενον περὶ φύσας,
> σπεύδοντα· τρίποδας γὰρ ἐείκοσι πάντας ἔτευξεν
> ἑστάμεναι περὶ τοῖχον ἐυσταθέος μεγάροιο·
> χρύσεα δέ σφ' ὑπὸ κύκλα ἑκάστῳ πυθμένι θῆκεν,
> ὄφρα οἱ αὐτόματοι θεῖον δυσαίατ' ἀγῶνα
> ἠδ' αὖτις πρὸς δῶμα νεοίατο, θαῦμα ἰδέσθαι.
> οἱ δ' ἤτοι τόσσον μὲν ἔχον τέλος, οὔατα δ' οὔ πω
> δαιδάλεα προσέκειτο· τά δ' ἤρτυε, κόπτε δὲ δεσμούς.

She found him sweating, whirling around the bellows,
hard at work. For he was making twenty tripods, all
to stand around the broad megaron, against the wall.
And he placed gold wheels beneath each base,
for them to enter the divine assembly on their own,
and return back home, a wonder to behold.
But these were not yet finished, for he had not yet attached
their elaborate handles. He kept working at them, forging the links.

---

[18] F. Vanderabeele, "Some Aspects of Chariot-Representations in the Late Bronze Age in Cyprus," *RDAC* (1977) 103–4, pl. XXIV:2 (rejected by Catling, *AA* 85 [1970] 448, as "equivocal evidence" but accepted by Baurain, *BCH* 104 [1980]). Brandenburg, "Mitra–Zoma–Zoster," in *ArchHom. I: E. Kriegswesen 1,* 119–25, 142–43.

Form and technique of these marvelous creations have long been compared with Cypriote bronze wheeled stands, widely distributed in the Mediterranean and long-lived.[19] The continuity of their workshop traditions makes attempts to "date" their appearance in the epic tradition on the basis of archaeological evidence perilous, or at least disputed.[20] Their poetic description in Homer closely resembles the Biblical account of Hiram's Phoenician bronze stands for King Solomon (1 Kings 7.27). Like the cuirass from Kinyras, these tripods illustrate the convergence between Homeric and Levantine (in this case, Canaanite and Phoenician) culture to be explored in Part II. For the poet, the wheels lend magic to their burden by making the tripods αὐτόματοι, "self-moved," as if filled with invisible life, which enables them to come and go before the gods.[21] Thetis arrives before the final embellishment of these marvels: the attachment of their bronze handles, still in preparation at the forge while the rivets are being manufactured. Even in this unfinished state the handles are δαιδάλεα, as if the poet anticipates their final effect and praises them at the very moment of their manufacture.

Hephaistos gladly interrupts his work to welcome Thetis and invites her in for hospitality, ξεινία, beginning with a seat of honor on a throne studded with silver nails, καλοῦ δαιδαλέου, and places a footstool beneath her feet, ὑπὸ δὲ θρῆνυς ποσὶν ἦεν, as suits a goddess or woman of special rank (cf. *Homeric Hymn to Demeter* 190–96). The same special reception accompanies the seating of Penelope, Eurykleia, and Circe in the *Odyssey* (below, pp. 22f.) with lines identical to *Iliad* 18.389–90.

Implicit in this gracious reception of the goddess is the promise that Hephaistos will agree to make her son a new suit of armor, and hence save the Greeks. And indeed Hephaistos immediately responds to her plea for help by recalling the source of his obligation to her. Years earlier, Thetis rescued him after his rejection and injury at Hera's hands, and installed him as an apprentice to herself and her sister in a sea cave. For nine years, Hephaistos produced many δαίδαλα: pins, necklaces, spiral and floral designs. In gratitude for this refuge and training, the master craftsman is eager to reward her with ζωάγρια. He puts away his tools and approaches his guest, attended by marvelous ἀμφίπολοι or handmaidens,

χρύσειαι, ζωῇσι νεήνισιν εἰοικυῖαι.
της ἐν μὲν νόος ἐστὶ μετὰ φρεσίν, ἐν δὲ καὶ αὐδή
καὶ σθένος ἀθανάτων δὲ θεῶν ἄπο ἔργα ἴσασιν.

---

[19] U. Jantzen and R. Tölle, in *ArchHom II: P. Hausrat*, 76, fig. 14a; H. W. Catling, *Cypriote Bronzework and the Mycenaean World* (Oxford 1964), 207, n. 35, pl. 36a.

[20] Negbi, *Tel Aviv* (1974) 159–72; articles by Helzer and Lagarce, in *Studi Fenici e Punici*; Catling, *RDAC*

(1984), 69–91; *contra* H. Matthäus, in *Problems in Greek Prehistory*, 285–300; Muhly, in *Bronze-working Centres of Western Asia*, 333–37.

[21] Faraone, *GRBS* 28 (1987) 257–80; see Chapter 8, on magic and art.

golden, just like living creatures.

In them is mind and wits, in them too a voice

and strength, and they know the deeds of the immortal gods.

Surely these creatures are magic, like Hephaistos's tripods and his dogs in the palace of Alkinoos (*Odyssey* 7. 91–94; see n. 21 and also Chapter 8). Made of gold, yet able to move rapidly (ῥώοντο) like living maidens, they are further endowed with νόος, αὐδή, σθένος—mind, voice, and strength, the three senses vital to early Greeks and taught to them by the gods.[22] They are both attendants and creations of the smith-god, magic in a way only possible in an Olympic setting, but marvels in a way only visible to mortal eyes. Their specific services for Hephaistos are unclear: they almost carry him as they glide along effortlessly, as if his very presence, if not his craftsmanship, endows art with life. Their poetic descendants include Pandora (discussed at the end of this chapter) and their heritage encourages the characterization of the work of Daidalos.

In answer to her host's inquiry, Thetis launches into a long lament of her troubles, leading up to her request for a new suit of armor for her son, his last outfit in life. Hephaistos comforts her and returns at once to the fire to forge the armor. The entire passage recalls vividly the Ugaritic myth where Kothar-wa-Hasis, the Canaanite craftsman-god and metallurgist, works gold and silver for Lady Athirat of the Sea in the Epic of Baal. The convergences between these two passages and their historical context will be explored in Chapter 4, after the Greek tradition has been analyzed.

The materials are first to claim poetic attention—bronze, tin, gold, and silver—then the tools (anvil, hammer, forge), source of as much wonder in prehistoric society as precious metals. Then the poet concentrates on the fruits of this equipment. First and finest to be made is the shield itself, in a line ending in praise of its size and power, μέγα τε στιβαρόν τε. One might expect a second praise-line beginning with the familiar καλόν δαιδάλεον ("beautiful and elaborate") but no familiar adjective apparently sufficed to compliment this creation. Instead the poet makes rare recourse to the verb form by describing the smith-god as "crafting in all ways," πάντοσε δαιδάλλων. This form, the present participle, is the only form of the verb, *δαιδάλλω, presumably "to craft or make elaborate," in epic poetry and appears only once elsewhere, in an equally remarkable passage on the bed of Odysseus and Penelope (*Odyssey* 23.200). Morphologically, it is an artificial form inspired by analogy and not used in spoken language, meaningless outside poetry.[23] Like its counterpart in the *Odyssey*, it denotes technical activity involving the combination of precious materials (in the *Odyssey*, gold, silver, and

---

[22] J. Bremmer, *The Early Greek Concept of the Soul* (Princeton 1983), 53–63, on νόος and other components of the soul.

[23] Parry, *Making of Homeric Verse*, 339; cf. Leumann's definition of poetic words (*Homerische Wörter*, 15ff., 321ff., and 133, on the problematic δαιδάλλων).

ivory) without invoking a specific industry: inlaid woodwork is more appropriate for the bed in Ithaka, metal inlay in the *Iliad*. Its effect is busy, even fussy, but vague, and the primary impact of this verb is narrative, not technical.

This conspicuous use of the rare verb is followed closely (18. 482) by the noun, repeating the phrase used by Hephaistos himself in his autobiography (cf. 18.400): ποίει δαίδαλα πολλὰ ἰδυίῃσι πραπίδεσσιν ("he made many *daidala*, with his clever skills"). Even within a short passage, the same noun is equally appropriate to armor and jewelry, as if a measure of the same artist's skill rather than a reflection of common technical properties. Here, the noun serves as preamble to a detailed description of the subjects depicted on the shield, occupying the next 127 hexameter lines.

Few passages in the Homeric corpus have attracted as much modern speculation on art and civilization in early Greece. Archaeological reconstructions of the shield were common in scholarship and were once included in modern commentaries, with attempts to reconcile its description with Mycenaean realia.[24] In all likelihood, no such shield ever protected either a Mycenaean or Geometric warrior; its decoration is imagined by the poet, although it incorporates images from art and daily life into a poetic vision of the Greek world, a true microcosm. The δαίδαλα wrought by Hephaistos begin with Nature (18.483–89) and end with it (18.606–7): the great river Okeanos, "boundary of the world" (ἔσχατον γαίας), encircles the shield, and all the heavenly bodies and constellations blaze on it (483–88). Within these limits the poet stages a cultural panorama that still serves as the most important vision of early Greek civilization.

Two cities represent the Greek world, one at war, the other enjoying the fruits of peace—the cycle of harvest and festivals, harmony and dispute. The city at war is under siege by a divided enemy. An ambush is planned and executed, lead by Ares and Athena, a golden pair, καλὼ καὶ μεγάλω, "beautiful and big," but the narrative stops short of the battle's outcome, much as does the *Iliad*. Gentler scenes of civilized life succeed this carnage: a field under plough, another being harvested for its royal owner, a vineyard with its grape pickers, a herd of oxen, and a meadow with its sheepfolds. Only one violent scene disrupts the peace, when two lions attack an ox from the herd in a moment more inspired by art than life. The poet dwells with affection on these pastoral scenes, the rewards of war and ambush for the Greeks besieging Troy that anticipate the *Odyssey* and a welcome return to home.

It is the finale of this ode to the good life that invokes the persona of Daidalos before the poet closes his description with its circumference, Okeanos. The last scene on the shield to be described is a dance performed by young men and women in linen gar-

---

[24] Fittschen, *ArchHom II: N. Bildkunst, 1*, summarizes scholarship and archaeological evidence. du Bois, *History, Rhetorical Description and the Epic*, chap. 1, on the manufacture of the shield as an *ekphrasis*.   P. R. Hardie, "Imago Mundi: Cosmological and Ideological Aspects of the Shield of Achilles," *JHS* 105 (1985) 11–13.

ments, the girls in garlands and the youths sporting daggers. A crowd watches their skillful performance, led by two acrobats. In introducing this spectacle, the poet reaches for a simile and enters the legendary past:

ἐν δὲ χορὸν ποίκιλλε περικλυτὸς ἀμφιγυήεις
τῷ ἴκελον, οἷον ποτ᾽ ἐνὶ Κνωσῷ εὐρείῃ
Δαίδαλος ἤσκησε καλλιπλοκάμῳ Ἀριάδνῃ.

And on it the renowned, ambidextrous artist inlaid a dance,
like the one which once in broad Knossos
Daidalos crafted for Ariadne of the lovely hair.

The artist's appearance is sponsored by an unusual coincidence of poetic choices and eliminations. The verb ποίκιλλε is produced after exhausting the repertoire of verbs appropriate to the craftsmanship of Hephaistos: ἔτευξε, ποίησε, ἐτίθει ("he constructed, made, placed"}, even that last resort (albeit used first in the description), δαιδάλλων, for which a finite form (δαίδαλλε?) may have been too bold. Instead the poet here tries a *hapax* form, ποίκιλλε ("ornamented"), and follows the "plain" line with a praise line, this time a simile as a climax to his laudation. In turning to that versatile root, δαιδαλ-, the poet discovers that all its syntactical possibilities had been exhausted in the preceding episode, since Thetis arrived chez Hephaistos: adjectives first (lines 379, 390), then nouns (400, 482), and even the verb (478). All that was left was a personification, and the eponymous craftsman here found his poetic and professional entry into the Greek imagination.

Thus Daidalos enters the poem, and with it the Greek tradition, almost by accident, when simile relieves metaphor and a personification provides an alternative to other prolific cognates. Such a poetic occasion, if not this very one, accounts for his debut; his emergence is clearly a function of poetic variations on a root relevant to the praise of art. Had other epic descriptions of art survived in as long and elaborate a form as that in *Iliad* 18, Daidalos might have appeared on multiple occasions, if one can extrapolate from his *Iliad* debut to similar contexts in lost poems.[25]

In *Iliad* 18, this figure is made historical and plausible by two associations with Crete: the locale of his artistry, "wide Knossos," and his patroness, Ariadne. The artist's own nationality is not specified: one assumes that he is Cretan, but later readers took advantage of the imprecision in the allusion to repatriate him to locales like Athens (see Part III). Ancient commentators, familiar with the "historical" sculptor, expressed conster-

---

[25] Hoekstra, *Epic Verse before Homer*, 58–59, sees such "signifying names" for craftsmen as the invention of individual poets; Leumann, *Homerische Wörter*, 15–17 on Homeric "Neubildung und Nach-wirkungen"; W. Ingalls, "Linguistic and Formular Innovations in the Mythological Digressions in the Iliad," *Phoenix* 36 (1982) 201–2.

nation "that a god imitates a mortal" and even attempted various emendations to reverse the compliment, and have the mortal imitate the god.[26]

As to what precisely Daidalos made for Ariadne, context assures only that it must be a χορός comparable with that depicted by Hephaistos, if only in quality. Readers since antiquity have made him an architect, sculptor, or choreographer on the basis of this passage and its possible interpretations, beginning in the scholia. To begin with, the verb ἀσκέω is imprecise, if ornate. It usually supplements other verbs of manufacturing, such as τεύχω or ἀραρίσκω, as a participle emphasizing such careful craftsmanship as went into the bow of Pandaros (*Iliad* 4.110), or the famous bed made by Odysseus (*Odyssey* 23.198). It only appears twice as a finite verb, once in this passage and again in the *Iliad* (23.743) to describe the Sidonian manufacture of a golden mixing bowl. Most of these contexts involve metalwork or woodwork, but once it describes Athena's handiwork on the gown worn by Hera for seducing Zeus (*Iliad* 14.179). A similar distribution between metals and textiles, worked by men and women, respectively, marks the use of this word as an agent noun in Mycenaean Greek.[27]

Strictly within epic terms, χορός can be both an actual dancing floor, like the one prepared by the Phaiakians (*Odyssey* 8.260) or the dance itself, a few lines later (8.264) or, according to the meanings of ἀσκέω and the χορός it resembles on the shield, a representation of a dance. Pausanias accepted as the work of Daidalos a marble relief shown to him at Knossos (9.40.3), presumably a Neo-Attic work with dancing figures, while the epic description seems to have suggested a painting to Philostratos and Vergil.[28] For many, the architectural implications of this description have dominated interpretation and encouraged the view of Daidalos as architect. This interpretation began in antiquity, when scholiasts made χορός a place (τόπος), complete with columns and statues arranged in a circle.[29] Most recently, circular structures of the Late Minoan period newly discovered at Knossos have been identified as the χορός of Daidalos,[30] but there is no reason it need be round (the earliest round orchestra in Greece, in the theater at Epidauros, dates from around 300 B.C.), and Daidalos is not necessarily an architect until the late classical period. Whatever the precise form intended by the poet, unlike

[26] Thus Nicanor wonders πῶς ὁ θεὸς μιμεῖται τὸν ἄνθρωπον (in Venetus Graecus 822: Erbse, *Scholia Graeca in Homeri Iliadem*, 4:564–65) and decides that the works of Daidalos were more familiar to poet and audience than those of the god: Ἡφαίστου μὲν γὰρ ἔργον οὐδεὶς εἶδεν πώποτε, Δαιδάλου δὲ πολλοὺς πολλὰ εἰκὸς ἑωρακέναι.

[27] *A-ke-te* and *a-ke-ti-ri-ja* in Linear B are discussed by Canciani, *ArchHom II: N. 2*, 94; *Bildkunst*, cf. A. Morpurgo Davies, "Terminology of Power and Terminology of Work in Greek and Linear B," in *Colloquium Mycenaeum*, 91 n. 15, 99 n. 44.

[28] Frontisi-Ducroux, *Dédale*, 136 n. 8, for various ancient views.

[29] Scholia at 18.590 (from Venetus Graecus 822, and the Townley manuscript): Erbse, *Scholia Graeca in Homeri Iliadem*, 4:561. The adverb ἔνθα suggests a place, e.g., where people can dance. Cf. Becatti, *RömMitt* 60–61 (1953–1954) 25–28; G. Pugliese Caratelli, "Minos e Cocalos," *Kokalos* 2 (1956) 89–103, esp. 100–103.

[30] Warren, *BSA* 79 (1984) 307–24.

other works of art qualified as δαιδάλεος or δαίδαλα in epic poetry, the one work attributed to Daidalos himself is accompanied by almost no technical information or indication of materials. Yet these brief and ambiguous verses are the source of all Greek speculation about the nature and activity of Daidalos.

The poet has not finished with his encomium of the armor, or its δαιδαλ- qualities. The shield completed and encircled by Okeanos, Hephaistos continues with a shining θώρηξ and a helmet, καλήν δαιδαλέην (18.612) and with a golden crest; finally, greaves of tin (18.613). Thetis receives the gift with delight and carries it to her son in the Greek camp; when she dumps it before him on the ground (19.13), "all the *daidala* clanged aloud": τὰ δ' ἀνέβραχε δαίδαλα πάντα. Δαίδαλα is a fitting collective noun to enhance components praised individually as δαιδάλεος or δαίδαλα, and its aural reverberation resembles the rumble of thunder inspired by the arming of Agamemnon (*Iliad* 11.45–46). Moreover, Achilles appreciates his new outfit for the same qualities (19.19):

> αὐτὰρ ἐπεὶ φρεσὶν ἧσι τετάρπετο δαίδαλα λεύσσων,

> and he delighted in his heart, beholding the *daidala*,

a phrase that celebrates his grim joy and return to battle.[31]

The brilliant armor shines on in action as in its creation, and catches the poet's attention with a δαιδαλ- epithet twice more in the *Iliad*. The actual arming of Achilles (19.369–91) attracts the traditional vocabulary of praise preliminary to a hero's ἀριστεῖα. The shield itself, blazing light like a beacon fire for sailors, is καλὸς δαιδάλεος as if to recall the long and elaborate description of the previous book, liberally sprinkled with the adjective and its cognates. At the climax of this arming scene, after Achilles puts on his helmet, an extraordinary effect takes place (19.386):

> τῷ δ' εὖτε πτερὰ γίγνετ', ἄειρε δὲ ποιμένα λαῶν.

> And then [as if] wings grew on him, and lifted up the shepherd of the people.

Wearing all five pieces of his new and magic armor, the hero is literally levitated upward "as if on wings," in a moment of metaphor become reality. This imagined event, acceptable within poetry, bestows great powers on "daidalic" art and Daidalos, who is eventually credited with the invention of wings. In fact, this poetic vision could well have encouraged the legend that gave Daidalos man's first flight (see Chapter 6). If Hephaistos made a suit of armor that mobilized the hero, Achilles, with imaginary wings, it is not surprising that the manufacture of wings by Daidalos, who appears in

---

[31] Philipp, *Tektonon Daidala*, 11, claims this is the only passage where a character in the *Iliad* takes explicit delight in a work of art (as in *Odyssey* 5.73–74); Nagler, *Spontaneity and Tradition*, 178 n. 17, on the hero's return to battle.

the same epic context, borrows from the imagery of the *hoplopoiia*. Scenes of the manu-facture of the shield of Achilles, with the figures of Thetis and Hephaistos (Figures 1, 2), become a model for the figures of Daidalos and Ikaros, as Greek reliefs and their Roman copies. My reading of this line in the *Iliad* suggests that the miracle of winged works of art is transferred to the creation itself, as if this line contributed to the tradition that Daidalos, shadowy *Doppelgänger* to the epic craftsman-god, made wings himself. In the most fantastic scene of craftsmanship in early Greek art (Figures 13, 14), craftsmen, attendant figures, the god giving birth, and the work of art itself—the armed figure springing from the head of the god—are all wearing wings. The hexameter line where wings grow on the armor of Achilles and bear him aloft participates in this tradition, both poetic and visual, where wings characterize divine and magic qualities, and even-tually the means of flight itself becomes the object of a legend of manufacture (see Chapter 6).

After this metaphysical response to the armed hero, Achilles picks up a last weapon: his ashen spear, the legacy of Pelias and Cheiron. This is the only weapon not borne into battle by Patroklos in the guise of Achilles; it is also the weapon that delivers death to Hektor (22.317–19), as well as the most significant attribute of Achilles.[32] At a second critical occasion after Book 18, just before the final confrontation and death of Hektor, the power of the shield is summoned, as if in exhortation, with both simile and epithet (22.312–15):

> ὁρμήθη δ᾽ Ἀχιλεύς, μένεος δ᾽ ἐμπλήσατο θυμὸν
> ἀγρίον, πρόσθεν δὲ σάκος στέρνοιο κάλυψε
> καλὸν δαιδάλεον, κόρυθι δ᾽ ἐπένευε φαεινῇ
> τετραφαλῷ.
>
> And Achilleus rose up, and his spirit was filled with wild
> rage, and before him the shield hid his chest,
> beautiful and elaborate, and he nodded his shining helmet
> with its four crests.

Followed by the image of the spear of Achilles blazing like a star, in its final thrust against Hektor, this is the last time the adjective δαιδάλεος attends armor in the *Iliad*. It is retired from active duty, as it were, when Achilles retires from battle, and thereafter only attends civilized attributes of the hero.

In retrospect, the *Iliad*'s focus on Achilles is reflected in the poetic deployment of vocabulary, including δαιδάλεος and its cognates. The greatest of the heroes receives the greatest number of such praise words, but ultimately, outside the narrative frame-work of the *Iliad*, his armor proves as treacherous as in those passages where it fails to

[32] See R. S. Shannon, *The Arms of Achilles and Ho-meric Compositional Technique, Mnemosyne* suppl. 36   (Leiden, 1975).

protect other heroes from weapons. For Achilles is felled by a wound in the ankle, undefended by any armor, and all the δαίδαλα in the world cannot save him. In fact, his armor outlives him but goes on to claim another hero in the suicide of Ajax. Thus an ambiguous value is manifest for these "daidalic" words: glamorous but treacherous, qualities borne out in all their appearances.[33]

But not only the armor of Achilles and his action while wearing it are marked by significant uses of δαιδάλεος. In three other contexts outside of battle, his attributes are distinguished by the epithet in a way that contributes to his heroic image, and the occasions are auspicious. In his first appearance since the quarrel and his withdrawal in Book 1, the embassy of Greeks finds the hero in his tent, playing a lyre, καλὴ δαιδαλέη, with a silver bridge (9.187), a prize from the siege of Thebe, city of Andromakhe's father. Evidently, when Achilles buried Eetion σὺν ἔντεσι δαιδαλέοισιν, "in all his daedalic armor," he did not neglect to claim his share of Theban wealth, like this lyre. With this instrument, especially appropriate for a poet to praise, Achilles the hero has become a singer, perhaps even his own poet laureate. For his subject is κλέα ἀνδρῶν, the "fame of men" which makes epic poetry heroic and rewards warfare with the promise of immortality. Achilles' performance is a credit to his childhood tutor, Phoinix, who was instructed to teach Achilles "to be a speaker of words and a practitioner of deeds" (Iliad 9.443): μύθων τε ῥητῆρ᾽ ἔμεναι πρηκτῆρά τ᾽ ἔργων. The term invoked by Phoinix to describe the skills of the hero outside battle (ῥητήρ) appears only here in all of epic poetry, and only after the renunciation of his wrath does Achilles actually become a socially effective speaker (as in Book 23: see subsequent discussion). But only once does the hero perform as a poet. Having refused ἔργα, deeds of war, Achilles consoles himself with stories about them (μύθοι), and contemplates his own future as a hero.[34] His lyre, like his shield, is a window on the world where all this will be but poetry, as in the extraordinary passage at the opening of Book 12.[35]

A second possession of Achilles is distinguished as δαιδάλεος in a passage that formalizes, almost in ritual, the return of Patroklos into battle. In Iliad 16, Achilles reluctantly agrees to allow his beloved companion to enter the battle in his stead and in his armor. A powerful prayer to Zeus accompanies this decision, which sends Patroklos to his death (16.220–25):

αὐτὰρ Ἀχιλλεὺς
βῆ ῥ᾽ ἴμεν ἐς κλισίην, χηλοῦ δ᾽ ἀπὸ πῶμ᾽ ἀνέωγε

[33] Frontisi-Ducroux, Dédale, chap. 4, "Significations et valeurs," on their apotropaic and treacherous properties.

[34] M. Rocchi, "La lira di Achilleus," Studi Storico-Religiosi 4 (1980) 259–68; duBois, History, Rhetorical Description and the Epic, 18, includes "Achilles' harp" [sic] as "part of a system of daidala"; Thalmann, Form

and Thought in Early Greek Poetry, 176–77, notes the irony of consolation by singing with a lyre of past heroic ἔργα; Ford, "Early Greek Terms for Poetry," 74–82, distinguishes κλέα ἀνδρων from ἀοίδαι.

[35] R. Scodel, "The Achaean Wall and the Myth of Destruction," HSCP 86 (1982) 33–50; Thalmann, Form and Thought in Early Greek Poetry, 103–4.

καλῆς δαιδαλέης, τήν οἱ Θέτις ἀργυρόπεζα
θῆκ᾽ ἐπὶ νηὸς ἀγέσθαι, εὖ πλήσασα χιτώνων
χλαινάων τ᾽ ἀνεμοσκεπέων οὔλων τε ταπήτων.

But Achilles
went into his tent, and opened the lid of a chest,
beautiful and elaborate, which silver-footed Thetis gave
him on his ship, filling it well with woolen tunics
and cloaks and woven woolens to cover him from the wind.

From this chest Achilles takes a special cup that Thetis had placed inside, only to be used for libations to Zeus, cleanses it, and pours out to Zeus while praying for κῦδος for Patroklos. The chest is not described in detail beyond καλὴ δαιδαλέη, although one could imagine one of fragrant wood, perhaps inlaid with ivory or plated with gold and other precious materials.[36] But what attracted the adjective were its associations more than its appearance, beginning with its divine donor. For Thetis gave it to her son, Achilles, to much the same effect brought on by her gift of a new suit of armor: the death of a hero. Furthermore, it holds a ritual vessel, exclusive to the most solemn of ceremonies for the greatest of the gods. Yet prayer, cup, and chest save Patroklos no more than armor saves Achilles, and the adjective only helps distinguish the chest as a farewell gift from a mother who will not see her son return from war, and an instrument in the final scene between Achilles and Patroklos. For Zeus answers the prayer by awarding Patroklos his κῦδος, but in the form of death in battle, so the hopes pinned on the chest are disappointed.

Achilles' last appearance in the *Iliad* also coincides with the last use of δαιδάλεος in the poem. In Book 24, Achilles receives Priam in his tent and restores to him the body of Hektor in exchange for sumptuous ransom. After accepting the gifts and promising a share to the dead Patroklos, Achilles returns inside his shelter (24.597)

ἕζετο δ᾽ ἐν κλισμῷ πολυδαιδάλῳ, ἔνθεν ἀνέστη.

and he seated himself on the all-elaborate couch, from where he had stood up.

In this passage, the hero has reentered the social tradition that his μῆνις ("anger") rejected; he pronounces the reconciliation of the two enemies, prepares a meal, and provides his guest a bed for sleep. As in his arbitration of the games at the funeral of Patroklos, Achilles demonstrates civilized behavior at the end of the *Iliad*, here by agreeing to compensation for returning Hektor's body for burial.[37] Thus lyre and couch ac-

---

[36] S. Laser, *ArchHom II: P. Hausrat*, 68–69; cf. Simonides, frag. 543, and Chapter 2, for another chest described as δαιδάλεος; Carter, *AJA* 93 (1989) 355–78, on archaic decorated chests.

[37] Redfield, *Nature and Culture in the Iliad*, 203–18, on the purification of Achilles in the end of the Iliad.

quire their special significance, and δαιδάλεος adjectives, through association with the central hero of the poem, and in return help frame him as the best of the Achaeans through his attributes.

Outside of the armor of heroes and the attributes of Achilles, δαιδάλεος words are infrequent in the *Iliad* but complement their appearance in the *Odyssey*. Jewelry is one association, as in the apprenticeship of Hephaistos (18.400), where the line

τῇσι παρ᾽ εἰνάετες χάλκευον δαίδαλα πολλά

he worked many *daidala* in bronze, among them for nine years

introduces a list of items like pins and necklaces. The verb χάλκευον appears only here, a denominative form derived from the noun common in Mycenaean Greek, χαλκεύς (bronzesmith), and perhaps custom-designed for the smith-god.[38] The same noun, δαίδαλα πολλά, embraces the wondrous scenes on the shield some eighty lines later, where it is governed by the verb ποιεῖ, "he makes," to cover the variety of materials and techniques necessary to the manufacture of the shield. A third occasion in the *Iliad* allows δαίδαλα yet another artistic medium, in the domain of female ornament. In the famous Ἀπάτη or seduction of Zeus, Hera adorns herself with the assistance of the goddess of love and the handiwork of Athena (14.178):

ἀμφὶ δ᾽ ἄρ᾽ ἀμβρόσιον ἑανὸν ἕσαθ᾽, ὅν οἱ Ἀθήνη
ἔξυσ᾽ ἀσκήσασα, τίθει δ᾽ ἐνὶ δαίδαλα πολλά.

and around her she placed an ambrosial garment, which Athena
had made for her, and put on it many *daidala*.

The garment is the work of Athena, crafted as if in carpentry in a line that sounds lifted from a medium other than textiles. The verb τίθει, "[she] placed," hovers between two subjects: did Athena weave, embroider, or apply gold ornaments to Hera's dress, or did Hera herself add the ornaments as part of her strategic toilette? The former seems preferable, however ambiguous the syntax, for it credits Athena Ergane, goddess of manufacturing, with the total work of art, while still allowing Hera to put on her own jewelry in the next line (14.180). The technical background of the ancient textile industry supports the manufacture of garments with added ornaments of precious metal, most frequently gold foil.[39] Like the wardrobe of Pandora, Hera's strategic seduction outfit

---

S. Schein, *The Mortal Hero: An Introduction to Homer's Iliad* (Berkeley, 1984), 153–63, on the rehabilitation of the hero.

[38] Eckstein, *ArchHom II: L. Handwerk*, 1, 29: the verb anticipates the formation and function of δαιδάλλων later in the same episode or φαρμάσσων at *Odyssey* 9.293 (from φάρμακος).

[39] K. Brown, "Near Eastern Textile Decoration," 2 vols. (Ph.D. diss., University of Pennsylvania, 1980), 2:661–63, for woven and applied ornaments on Near Eastern garments, some removable; A. Oppenheim, "The Golden Garments of the Gods," *JNES* 8 (1949), 172–93; J. Canby, "Decorated Garments on Ashurnasirpal's Sculpture," *Iraq* 33 (1971) 47–49. Aegean

contributes to the poetic evolution of divine images. For in the archaic tradition, Greek statuary draws inspiration from poetry more than from ritual, whereby "Daidaleia" alone identifies a goddess (Figure 5), and the archetype of images, Pandora, is studded with *daidala* in literature (see Chapter 2).[40]

Hera's δαίδαλα partake of the same special qualities as related words in the *Iliad*. In this significant passage, which prepares for the withdrawal of Zeus from battle and a major turning point in the narrative, the description of Hera's toilette is not just an intimate genre scene. The goddess withdraws to a secret chamber made by Hephaistos (14.166–68); her wardrobe is sprinkled with exotic adjectives like ἀμβρόσιος (used four times in eight lines) as well as the more familiar καλὸς, χρυσέος, and the final effect is expressed in a favorite formula, χάρις δ' ἀπελάμπετο πολλή: "And much grace shone from it." She borrows divine trade secrets (Aphrodite's girdle) from the goddess of love and enlists the help of Hypnos with a bribe of a καλὸν θρόνον, "beautiful throne," in addition to receiving Athena's assistance in the form of an outfit.

In essence, this passage is an arming scene in drag: a goddess prepares to seduce, hence conquer, the king of the gods in order to save the Greeks. Hera's role is no less vital than that of Patroklos or another hero whose entry into battle turns the tide of destruction, and her preparation is no less painstakingly described. Her attire resembles the toilette of Pagat, daughter of Danel, in the Ugaritic epic of Aqhat. In preparing to avenge her brother's death, the Canaanite princess washes in the sea, applies purple from the sea and special cosmetics, then dons a hero's clothing and weapons beneath her female garments.[41]

In such a context, δαίδαλα πολλά are both jewelry and weapons, to dazzle and confound the enemy, and the word is chosen for its narrative impact as much as for its immediate semantic value.[42] As well as Hephaistos, Athena, and Daidalos, other legendary craftsmen in the *Iliad* are celebrated with δαιδαλ- words. A fitting example is Phereklos, son of Τέκτων ("the builder") and grandson of Ἁρμονίδης ("the joiner"), a

---

versions of these Oriental fashions include the wardrobes of the Shaft Grave Mycenaeans and their archaic counterparts (see Romano, n. 40).

[40] See the early archaic cult images from Delphi and Ephesus: Romano, "Early Greek Cult Images," 367–69.

[41] Coogan, *Stories from Ancient Canaan*, 46 (*KTU* 1.19, IV, 41–47). Cf. her sister Anat's veiled seduction of Aqhat: D. R. Hillers, "The Bow of Aqhat: The Meaning of a Mythological Theme," in *Orient and Occident*, 71–80. See also Chapter 4. Cf. the ceremonial dressing of Hittite queens and goddesses: J. Puhvel, *Homer and Hittite* (Innsbruck, 1991), 11–12.

[42] Frontisi-Ducroux, *Dédale*, 68, 72, calls such δαίδαλα "armes de combat" and "instruments de séduction"; H. Schwabl, "Traditionelle Gestaltung, Motivwiederholung und Mimesis im homerischen Epos," *WS* 16 (1982) 15–16, on the "Rüstung" of Hera and its typological relationship to arming scenes. Pucci, *Hesiod and the Language of Poetry*, 82–126, on Pandora, a related "arms and the woman" episode. I have profited from reading drafts of Ingrid Holmberg's Yale dissertation, "Gender and Deceit in Early Greek Hexameter Poetry" (in progress), and from her comments on this passage.

family of artists as distinguished as they are implausible (see n. 1, on such *redende Namen*):

ὅς χερσὶν ἐπίστατο δαίδαλα πάντα
τεύχειν· ἔξοχα γάρ μιν ἐφίλατο Παλλὰς Ἀθήνη.

whose hands understood how to make all forms of *daidala;*
for Pallas Athena loved him exceedingly.

This special patronage by Athena extended at least to carpentry in the form of ship-building, for it was Phereklos who made the "evil-bringing" (ἀρχεκάκους) ships that conveyed Paris and his stolen bride, Helen, from Sparta back to Troy. The nature of Phereklos's other works are unknown, but evidently they included not just intricate metalwork but large-scale projects in wood. The repertoire of epic δαίδαλα is considerably expanded by this passage, in terms of their potential size and medium. Context supplies symbolic meaning parallel to other δαίδαλα: the ships that carried Paris and Helen to Troy also brought destruction to that city and death to many Greeks, including Phereklos himself.[43] So the noun emphasizes a marvel with unhappy consequences, a combination characteristic for objects singled out by δαιδάλεος or δαίδαλον.

The most unusual *daidalon* in the *Iliad*, and the last to be considered here, involves a transferred epithet praising the skill of foreign craftsmen. At the funeral games of Patroklos, lavish prizes are assembled by Achilles, from his own property and booty aboard his ships, to be awarded to the victors in the individual events (23.257–61). In epic fashion, each event is introduced with a display of its rewards, as if to publicize the dimensions of κῦδος. After the controversial chariot race, the boxing and wrestling matches, Achilles sets out the gifts for the footrace, whose first prize is a magnificent vessel:

ἀργύρεον κρητῆρα τετυγμένον. ἔξ δ᾽ ἄρα μέτρα
χάνδανεν, αὐτὰρ κάλλει ἐνίκα πᾶσαν ἐπ᾽ αἶαν
πολλόν, ἐπεὶ Σιδόνες πολυδαίδαλοι εὖ ἤσκησαν,
Φοίνικες δ᾽ ἄγον ἄνδρες ἐπ᾽ ἠεροειδέα πόντον,
στῆσαν δ᾽ ἐν λιμένεσσι, Θόαντι δὲ δῶρον ἔδωκαν.

a krater made of silver. It held six measures
to pour, and in beauty it surpassed much for all time,
since Sidonians of many skills had made it well,

---

[43] Frontisi-Ducroux, *Dédale*, 68. Compare the Athenian ships sent to join the Ionian revolt in 499 B.C. and called ἀρχὴ κακῶν (Herodotus, 5.97) for their role in bringing Athens and Persia into conflict: see Chapter 11.

and Phoenician men had brought it across the wide sea,
and set it up in harbors, and gave it as a gift to Thoas.

This krater is valuable not just for its six-measure capacity but for its surpassing beauty, the work of Sidonians whose reputation earns them the epithet πολυδαίδαλοι and the rare finite verb form ἤσκησεν. The vessel's pedigree is no less distinguished: a Phoenician gift to Thoas, king of Lemnos, it passed to Thoas's grandson, Euneos (son of Jason), and was exchanged as ransom for Lykaon, son of Priam, to Patroklos. Thus Achilles commemorates Patroklos by bestowing as a prize at the fallen hero's funeral games the krater he won in war.[44]

In describing this impressive prize, the poet transfers his admiration from the object to its creators, to suggest an entire tradition of craftsmanship of which the krater is but an example. The compliment πολυδαίδαλος ranks the Sidonians with gods like Hephaistos, in its admiration for the work of Levantine workshops.[45] The historical dimensions of this reference are complicated: like another δαιδάλεος assembly, the armor of Agamemnon, it attributes to a foreign source an object of Greek admiration. The convergence of these qualities—the daidalic and the exotic—is no coincidence, for it dominates Greek taste in art in the prehistoric as well as the epic and archaic world. It is a fitting close to such configurations in the *Iliad*, and introduces a theme common to the Greek poetic tradition and its archaeological counterpoint.

In turning from the *Iliad* to the *Odyssey*, the shift from a military setting with martial themes and props to one dominated by seafaring and domestic scenes influences the frequency and function of δαίδαλα. There are simply far fewer occasions when an adjective associated primarily with armor is appropriate in the *Odyssey*—hence only eight appearances in contrast to the twenty-eight in the *Iliad*. Those eight uses embellish furniture and jewelry exclusively: the luxuries of a Homeric home, the pride of women's property and the elements of gift exchange—all themes essential to a story of return.[46]

Four times a special θρόνος, or seat for an important figure, as offered to Thetis by her host, Hephaistos (*Iliad* 18.390), invokes the epithet δαιδάλεος. The first is offered by Telemakhos to Athena, in disguise as Mentes but welcomed by the son of Odysseus (and perhaps by the poet) with the ceremony befitting an honored guest (*Odyssey* 1.130–31):

---

[44] Redfield, *Nature and Culture in the Iliad*, 205–6, on the history of this krater and its role at the funeral games.

[45] W. B. Stanford, "Homer's Use of Personal πολυ-Compounds," *CP* 45 (1950) 108–10; Leumann, *Homerische Wörter*, 131–33, classifies the adjective as a *Besitzkompositum*, on the analogy of πολύχρυσος ("with much gold"), which only evolved its metaphorical meaning later (cf. his views cited earlier in

n. 5, where he sees a *Stoffadjectif* in the morphology of δαιδάλεος). I prefer a transferred epithet to explain πολυδαίδαλος, also applied to gold as a raw material in the *Odyssey* (13.11), since all meanings prior to qualitative ones were probably lost well before extant epic tradition: see Chapter 4.

[46] C. Beye, "Male and Female in the Homeric Poems," *Ramus* 3, no. 2 (1974) 87–101; D. Frame, *The Myth of Return in Greek Epic* (New Haven, 1978).

αὐτήν δ᾽ ἐς θρόνον εἶσεν ἄγων, ὑπὸ λῖτα πετάσσας,
καλὸν δαιδάλεον. ὑπό δὲ θρῆνυς ποσὶν ἦεν.

And leading her, he placed her on a throne, spreading cloth beneath,
a beautiful, elaborate throne. And beneath her feet was a stool.

The entire arrangement—a throne spread with a soft linen cover, praised as καλὸς δαιδάλεος, and provided with a footstool—is traditional for a goddess, as for Circe (*Odyssey* 10.315, 367) or Thetis (*Iliad* 18.390), or for any guest whose status is thereby acknowledged by a host. In the opening of the *Odyssey*, Telemakhos's reception of the disguised Athena marks his manhood, for he is now capable of recognizing a distinguished guest and treating him or her with the reception expected from a mature host. So this θρόνος establishes a bond of patronage between goddess and young man of the nature of that enjoyed by his father, and represents one of the signs that Telemakhos is ready to assume the duties of an adult. With this seating of Athena, Telemakhos enters into that partnership essential to his personal odyssey, the *Telemakhia* of the first four books, and demonstrates his maturity. This coming of age in Book 1 culminates in his severe speech to his mother, when he assumes power in the household (1.346–59).

The next character to occupy a θρόνος, καλὸς and δαιδάλεος, is Odysseus at the house of Circe, the witch-queen and daughter of Helios who rules Aiaia. Unlike his less fortunate companions, who are collectively seated κατὰ κλισμούς τε θρόνους τε, "on couches and thrones," before transformation into swine (10.233), Odysseus is received more exclusively, as if to distinguish his fate from that of other guests. As he describes it himself (10.314–15):

εἶσε δέ μ᾽ εἰσαγαγοῦσα ἐπὶ θρόνου ἀργυροήλου
καλοῦ δαιδαλέου. ὑπὸ δὲ θρῆνυς ποσὶν ἦεν.

And leading me she sat me upon a throne with silver nails,
beautiful and elaborate. And beneath [my] feet was a footstool.

Offered the usual treatment of dire drugs (φάρμακα λύγρα) and a touch of the wand, Odysseus proves himself immune to both and is instantly recognized by his hostess as the one guest foretold as resistant to her magic. Having failed to bring her victim to the sty, Circe consoles herself with a visit to the bedchamber instead. Afterward, Odysseus is bathed, dressed, and offered the same seat in two lines identical to his reception (10.367 = 10.315), as if to reinforce his special status.[47]

The final appearance of a δαιδάλεος θρόνος in the Odyssey involves a roomful of such seats, in the great hall at Ithaka. When Telemakhos returns from his quest for his father, the nurse, Eurykleia, is the first to recognize him (17.31–33):

[47] G. Houston, "Θρόνος, Δίφρος, and Odysseus' Change from Beggar to Avenger," *CP* 70 (1975) 212–14; Strasser, *Iterata*, 63–66, on such "kontextbezogene Wiederholungen" which account for most epic *iterata*.

Τὸν δὲ πολὺ πρώτη εἶδε τροφὸς Εὐρύκλεια,
κώεα καστορνῦσα θρόνοις ἔνι δαιδαλέοισι,
δακρύσασα δ᾽ ἔπειτ᾽ ἰθὺς κίεν.

The first to see him by far was the nurse, Eurykleia,
spreading fleeces on the elaborate thrones,
and shedding tears she went straight to him.

The old woman is spreading fleeces on the δαιδαλέοισι θρόνοις, at the time empty and unconnected with any ceremony of reception as in most other passages. This collective expression suggests that many, if not all, of the chairs at Ithaka were as splendid as those offered to Athena, and is a reminder that Penelope treated her suitors, however reluctantly, with proper ξεινίη. Indeed, the adjective bestows on the great hall at Ithaka and its household those qualities tested in many foreign places by Odysseus. But the word is also linked, by suggestion, to a set of thematic and narrative conventions that dominate the latter half of the *Odyssey*: recognition and its variations.

The return and recognition of Telemakhos anticipate those of his father, just as his briefer travels are a junior version of his father's wanderings. Thus Eurykleia is the first to see the young man, just as she is the first member of the household to recognize the long-absent Odysseus (*Odyssey* 19.386–475). And the last two appearances of δαιδάλεος in the poem, as if anticipated in this set of θρόνοι, contribute to the narrative episode of recognition. In a subtle manner, several of the manifestations of these words participate in this theme of domestic reconciliation.

One conspicuous seat in the Odyssey where one might expect praise in the form of καλὸς δαιδάλεος receives an alternative compliment, and in fact a different name for furniture. In Book 19 (53–59), Penelope enters the great hall and is seated by the fire on κλισίη, seat or couch:

δινωτὴν ἐλέφαντι καὶ ἀργύρῳ ἥν ποτε τέκτων
ποίησ᾽ Ἰκμάλιος, καὶ ὑπὸ θρῆνυν ποσὶν ἧκε
προσφυέ᾽ ἐξ αὐτῆς, ὅθ᾽ ἐπὶ μέγα βάλλετο κῶας.

turned on the lathe, [inlaid] with ivory and silver. At one time
Ikmalios made it for her, and attached a footstool for her feet,
in one piece, and a great fleece was spread out.

Instead of a concatenation of epithets, a celebrated craftsman is invoked with a name that expresses his technical skills and possibly a foreign origin.[48] Several roots contend to explain his name: a verb attested in Cypriote, ἰκμάω, "to moisten," perhaps a reference to glue used for inlay of silver and ivory in furniture, or a Semitic root, *qamo'* "to

---

[48] On Ikmalios and its possible derivations, see Lacroix, "Ikmalios"; Canciani, *ArchHom II: N. Bild-* *kunst*, 2, 76, 98; S. Laser, in *ArchHom II: P. Hausrat*, 34–56, 102.

attach, bond, join." The Cypriote connection has been encouraged by the discovery of elaborate furniture, inlaid with ivory, in an eighth-century tomb at Salamis on Cyprus, as well as by other evidence for Levantine furniture popular in Iron Age Greece.[49] Whatever the etymology preferred, the name of Ikmalios adds itself to the half dozen *redende Namen* for craftsmen in epic poetry, including Daidalos if not Homer himself.[50] In this passage a hierarchy of conventions for praising art has substituted an actual artist, with a personifying name, for a formulaic compliment like καλὸς δαιδάλεος. This same principle inserted the name of a foreign king as gift giver in describing the armor of Agamemnon, leader of other Greeks whose armor is only καλὸς δαιδάλεος (*Iliad* 11.20), and added the personification of Daidalos to a description where every other form of praise had been exhausted (*Iliad* 18.590–92). Penelope, as queen of Ithaka and chief female figure in the *Odyssey*, is distinguished from other such figures by a seat whose description outranks theirs. In other words, this passage joins those cited here from the *Iliad* as demonstrations of the kinship between the naming of an artist and the praise of art that helped early Greek images of the artist grow out of the praise of art itself. This process is not exclusive to poetry: dedications name their maker in epic inscriptions, and Herodotus names artists like Theodoros and Rhoikos as if to increase the fame of certain artifacts. But in the pursuit of Daidalos it is important to recognize how difficult, if not impossible, it is to separate the conception of an artist from the praise of art; even in the fifth century the characterization of his art derives from epic conventions (see Chapter 8).

Another carpenter's triumph enters the daidalic domain and its narrative network through the significant epithet. In Book 6 (15–17), Nausikaa makes her first appearance in slumber, where she is visited by the disguised Athena and inspired to organize a laundry expedition. The goddess enters the house of Alkinoos,

> βῆ δ᾽ ἴμεν ἐς θάλαμον πολυδαίδαλον ᾧ ἐνὶ κούρη
> κοιμᾶτ᾽ ἀθανάτῃσι φυὴν καὶ εἶδος ὁμοίη.

> and went to go into her chamber, much elaborate, in which a girl
> slept, like the immortals in form and appearance.

The adjective inaugurates the lavish description of the palace of Alkinoos (7.81–132), whose interior decorators include Hephaistos, and of the Phaiakian gifts bestowed on Odysseus, including χρυσὸς πολυδαίδαλος (13.11). That the bedchamber of Alkinoos's unmarried daughter, Nausikaa, is called πολυδαίδαλος may call attention to her marriageable age and the subtle relationship, near courtship, between herself and Odysseus.[51] For in addition to being beautifully appointed, her bedroom is also a room un-

---

[49] V. Karageorghis, "Die Elfenbeinthrone von Salamis auf Zypern," in *ArchHom II: P. Hausrat*, 99–103; Canciani, *ArchHom II: N. Bildkunst*, 2, 98 n. 484.

[50] Nagy, *Best of the Achaeans*, 298–300.

[51] Murnaghan, *Disguise and Recognition in the Odyssey*, 93–94, 98 n. 11, 123 n. 7.

trodden by men, the room of a woman who first contemplates marriage with the arrival of Odysseus. Finally, the bedroom motif is an unconsummated rehearsal for the most famous bedroom scene in the *Odyssey*, the final recognition between Odysseus and Penelope. Their bedroom had been equally untrodden by men since the departure of Odysseus, and it is Odysseus's manufacture of that bed, narrated by himself with the rare verb, δαιδάλλων, that provides the final reconciliation. In *Odyssey* 6 a single word, πολυδαίδαλος, reactivates this chain of narrative and sexual motifs.

Three times in the *Odyssey*, precious metals are called δαιδάλεος as they are in the *Iliad* (the jewelry and vessels Hephaistos made, the ornaments worn by Hera); one occasion inspires the intensive version, πολυδαίδαλος. A quantity of gold, perhaps valuable for its raw material and future δαίδαλα, is presented to Odysseus as one of his farewell gifts from his host, Alkinoos (13.11):

> εἵματα μὲν δὴ ξείνῳ ἐϋξέστῃ ἐνὶ χηλῷ
> κεῖται καὶ χρυσὸς πολυδαίδαλος ἄλλα τε πάντα
> δῶρ', ὅσα Φαιήκων βουληφόροι ἐνθάδ' ἔνεικαν.

And clothes lie in the well-smoothed chest for the guest
and gold, well-wrought, and many other gifts,
as many as the elders of the Phaiakians brought there.

Raw materials rarely attract such daidalic compliments, and presumably the bullion's potential for δαίδαλα, or the workmanship of gold objects implied by the adjective but not specified, accounts for this praise.

A cluster of epic conventions for describing art attend the gifts of the suitors to Penelope in *Odyssey* 18, in an episode deliberately arranged by Athena in order to increase her τίμη—valor and value—in the eyes of her husband and son (291–301). The presents are inspired by her courageous and virtuous speech deploring their insolence, a delivery that delights Odysseus as proof of her virtue and fidelity (and, as he thinks, of her guile). The shower of gifts with which the suitors seek to stem her resistance and force her hand is enumerated in a list where each suitor and his offering challenges the poet to superlatives. Thus a peplos is beautiful (περικαλλέα) and decorated (ποικίλον); earrings of triple mulberry clusters, fit for the goddess Hera in the *Iliad*, radiate divine grace (χάρις) as they do in the same line in the *Iliad* (14.183); a necklace from Peisander is a περικαλλὲς ἄγαλμα. Without wearing them, Penelope assembles the elements of a wardrobe for a wedding or seduction. In the *Iliad*, Hera needs them to seduce her husband, any woman's most challenging suitor; in the *Odyssey*, such items are both gifts from suitors and proof to a husband that the queen of Ithaka is still attractive, yet chaste. Jewelry and compliments illustrate Penelope's unique position among Homeric women: she is seductive but still preserves her honor, dishonest but faithful, without giving herself or her kingdom to her suitors, and without revealing her recognition of her husband. Among these treasures is a necklace set with a rare material and compared to the sun itself (*Odyssey* 18.295–96):

> ὅρμον δ' Εὐρυμάχῳ πολυδαίδαλον αὐτίκ᾽ ἔνεικε,
> χρύσεον, ἠλέκτροισιν ἐερμένον, ἠέλιον ὥς.

> And Eurymakhos brought forth a necklace, much elaborate,
> of gold [beads], strung with amber [ones], [shining] like the sun.

Like the brooch by which Penelope recognizes her husband (*Odyssey* 19.225–31), archaeological realities correspond to these poetic descriptions in many details, without imposing an exclusive chronology on the composition of epic poetry.[52] These gifts replay the persuasive attempts of the suitors over the past twenty years, endured by Penelope in her husband's absence. The more lavish they can be made to appear now in his presence, the greater the demonstration of her loyalty in her resistance to the greed that ruined wives like Eriphyle.[53] Thus the poet deploys all the traditional artillery for praising art (περικαλλές, ἄγαλμα, χάρις, and πολυδαίδαλος) to attend the ἀριστεία of Penelope, much as armor described in equivalent terms, even praised with identical epithets, builds up the reputation of a hero. At the same time, this episode adds itself to the series of trials by which husband and wife test each other's faith and loyalty.[54]

The progressive revelation of ἀναγνώρισις in the last books of the *Odyssey* involves many such tests, of which two are marked by δαίδαλα. The first is the fabulous pin of Odysseus, described by its disguised owner to Penelope as proof of his "autopsy" of her missing husband (19.185–260). Penelope sets up this trial herself by inquiring what her husband wore; Odysseus cleverly describes the χλαῖνα, χίτων, and περόνη, that were gifts from his wife, even assuring her of the admiration they attracted from other women. Penelope's reaction is emotional, for she recognizes as σήματα ἔμπεδα what the stranger describes. In his account, he dwells on the golden pin in detail (19.225–31):

> χλαῖναν πορφυρέην οὔλην ἔχε δῖος Ὀδυσσεύς
> δίπλην· αὐτάρ οἱ περόνη χρυσοῖο τέτυκτο
> αὐλοῖσιν διδύμοισι· πάροιθε δὲ δαίδαλον ἦεν.

---

[52] On amber and ἤλεκτρον, see L. Deroy and R. Halleaux, "À propos du grec ἤλεκτρον: 'ambre' et 'or blanc'," *Glotta* 52 (1974) 36–52, on Homeric ἤλεκτρον. A necklace of gold and amber beads has recently been discovered in the Idaian Cave on Crete: I. Sakellarakis, "Some Geometric and Archaic Votives from the Idaian Cave," in *Early Greek Cult Practice*, 182–87, figs. 21–23. Like the "mulberry" earrings from Lefkandi (Coldstream, in *Phönizier im Westen*,

266, pl. 26d), these discoveries are probably as Levantine as they are Homeric.

[53] On the role of gifts in defining Penelope's status, see W. K. Lacey, "Homeric ἔδνα and Penelope's κύριος," *JHS* 86 (1966) 55–65. See *Odyssey* 11.326–27, for faithless wives like Eriphyle, who betrayed her husband for a necklace.

[54] Murnaghan, *Disguise and Recognition in the Odyssey*, chap. 4.

ἐν προτέροισι πόδεσσι κύων ἔχε ποικίλον ἐλλόν,
ἀσπαίροντα λάων. τὸ δὲ θαυμάζεσκον ἅπαντες,
ὥς οἱ χρύσεοι ἐόντες ὁ μὲν λάε νεβρὸν ἀπάγχων
αὐτὰρ ὁ ἐκφυγέειν μεμαὼς ἤσπαιρε πόδεσσι.

And godlike Odysseus wore a purple cloak of wool,
double thick; and for it a pin of gold was crafted
with double clasps, with a *daidalon* in front.
A dog was holding a dappled deer in its front paws,
gazing as it struggled. And everyone kept admiring it,
how—even though of gold—the one creature kept shaking the fawn,
but the other tried to escape in vain, thrashing with its legs.

The noun δαίδαλον makes its only appearance here in the singular in all of epic poetry, all other nominative forms being in the plural, collective for jewelry, armor, or other creations (in wood? *Iliad* 5.60). The object itself is such a marvel that no mere epithet will suffice, and this noun expresses a triumph of technique and design almost as an abstract quality. The specific properties of this pin defy modern classification: it has twin prongs, perhaps, and some ornament "in front" where an animal fight is depicted: a hound seizing a fawn in a struggle whose lifelike appearance amazes all. Even its philological properties are eccentric: the words for fawn and "thrashing," for example, appear here alone, with a coat dappled by nature or metallurgists. No extant pin demonstrates an archaeological prototype for this description, whose associations with Mycenaean and Orientalizing Greek art have been claimed with equal ferocity.[55] While fibulae are more appropriate to the Iron Age, animal fights are as popular on luxurious metal objects in the Mycenaean period, most vividly on the inlaid daggers from the Shaft Graves. Etruscan finery provides the closest visual parallel for form and decoration, but not the most helpful, historically. Like the shield of Achilles, this pin never existed in reality but may owe its properties to the poet's liberties with recognition signs of his own invention, encouraged by the urge to make plastic a poetic favorite, the animal fights beloved in Homeric similes.[56] In so doing, he deploys a favorite epithet, δαιδάλεος, and invokes the power of art-as-life: "even though made of gold," the one grasps, the other flails in vivid action. This poetic device is critical to the evolution of

[55] Canciani, *ArchHom II: N. Bildkunst*, 2, 41, 69, summarizes scholarly arguments since Helbig that favor an Iron Age parallel (the most popular example being the garish Orientalizing fibula from the Bernardini tomb in Praeneste, Italy: p. 69 n. 202). Philipp, *Tektonon Daidala*, 11–12, sees a significant difference between this passage, as a description of art, and equivalent lines in the *Iliad*.

[56] R. Hampe, *Die Gleichnisse Homers und die Bildkunst seiner Zeit* (Tübingen, 1952); W. Schadewaldt, "Die Homerische Gleichnisse und die kretisch-mykenische Kunst," in *Von Homer's Welt und Werk* (Stuttgart, 1959), 130–54; Vermeule, *Greece in the Bronze Age*, 41–42 n. 65, on animal similes and Mycenaean art.

theories of art, for eventually it develops into a philosophical concept and characterizes the work of Daidalos (see Chapter 8).

The *Odyssey*'s final δαίδαλον, and the last example in this survey of the Homeric poems, figures prominently in the climax of recognition between Odysseus and Penelope. For the final σῆμα, or proof of Odysseus's identity in the eyes of his wife, is his description of their bed, the ultimate bond of conjugal intimacy and fidelity.[57] In *Odyssey* 23, Penelope still holds back from full acknowledgment and welcome of her long-lost husband, even after their mock "wedding" (130–49). She devises the ultimate test by pretending to have his bed moved outside their bedroom, for separate sleeping arrangements until she should recognize him completely (177–80). She reminds him that he made the bed, himself, adding taunt to trial to provoke the truth from the master dissembler, and Odysseus falls for the bait. In an outburst of pride, love, and grief, he abandons his natural defense of cleverness and demands to know what man moved the bed from its original site, where he carved it out of a rooted olive tree. He describes his manufacture of the bed in bitter detail, including its decoration (199–201):

> ἐκ δὲ τοῦ ἀρχόμενος λέχος ἔξεον, ὄφρ᾽ ἐτέλεσσα,
> δαιδάλλων χρυσῷ τε καὶ ἀργύρῳ ἠδ᾽ ἐλέφαντι.

> Beginning from it [the tree] I carved the bed, until I had finished,
> crafting it with gold and silver and ivory.

The word δαιδάλλων is conspicuous, as the rare verbal reflexion of the root and the only example in the *Odyssey*, a verb exclusive to a craftsman-god in the *Iliad* (18.390) in the process of making the finery of the best of the Achaeans. Here it is delivered in the first person, by the hero of the *Odyssey*, to prove his own role in his manufacture of a marriage bed, and hence legitimize his claim to Penelope and Ithaka. His use of the words σῆμα, "sign," and ἔμπεδον, "sure, lasting" (in lines 188 and 202) are literal as well as literary, emphasizing the bed's immoveability and its role as physical evidence. The same words serve metaphorically for Penelope's recognition (206):

> σήματ᾽ ἀναγνούσῃ τά οἱ ἔμπεδα πέφραδ᾽ Ὀδυσσεύς.

> recognizing the clear signs which Odysseus spoke.

Penelope is triumphant, if in tears; her trick has succeeded, her husband is restored to her, and their reunion enjoys the benefit of a night whose duration is kindly prolonged by Athena.

---

[57] On the bed and its role in the return of Odysseus, see J.-P. Vernant, "Marriage," in *Myth and Society*, 62–66; J. N. O'Sullivan, "The Sign of the Bed," *GRBS* 25 (1984) 21–25; Warner, "The Bed of Odysseus," *Monuments and Maidens*, 99–100. Murnaghan, *Disguise and Recognition in the Odyssey*, 114–16, 140–41, 173 n. 46.

This climax of the epic and return of the hero, the reconciliation with his wife which is more challenging than slaying suitors and regaining power, depends on his creation of the bed, and δαιδάλλων marks the final σῆμα. In technical terms, the verb indicates the inlay of precious materials as decoration in wood, as implied for other wooden obejcts (chest, lyre, and couch of Achilles in the *Iliad*) and like the inlay work behind the verb's other appearance (*Iliad* 18.390). More important are the narrative affiliations of the verb in both of its contexts, where it is reserved for a single auspicious passage in both poems. The forging of the armor brings Achilles back into battle to deliver death to Hektor; it ultimately fails to save Achilles from his fate, and survives him to provoke a bitter quarrel and the suicide of Ajax. In the *Odyssey* the verb signifies the surrender of Odysseus to his wife, in an outburst releasing all the fears of betrayal that accompanied him on his long journey home. The weakest form, or that which is least plausible in spoken language, δαιδάλλειν, is used on a single occasion to express an act of supreme craftsmanship more essential to poetic narrative than to archaeology.

This consideration of the forms and uses of δαιδαλ- in Homeric poetry has focused deliberately on poetic context and function, excluding all later glosses, scholia, imitations, and explanations. Such strict analysis reveals a fascinating semantic field, rich with poetic potential; it also pares down the intrinsic meaning of δαιδαλ- to almost nothing. Scholars have tended to force the words into a consistent pattern of technical properties, exclusive to metal, for example.[58] Yet the epic instances embrace jewelry, armor, furniture, musical instruments, shipbuilding, and an enigmatic χορός, an unspecified work of art or architecture. Their only consistent feature is the cost, complexity, and reputation of their craftsmanship. Δαίδαλα claim no particular domain in the man-made world to the exclusion of any other, and the lack of clear etymology admitted at the onset is borne out by the absence of any firm denotative powers in context. Whatever technical associations these words may have once had—and they may always have been poetic—are buried beyond the reach of memory. No form of this word serves a technical description in Mycenaean Greek with its detailed repertoire of elaborately decorated furniture, vessels, and horse gear, where one would expect an appearance if any practical denotations had survived into this phase of Greek (see Chapter 4). In fact, the words may have already been moribund in the spoken idiom and active only in poetry, such that their very lack of vernacular life enriched their connotative powers as classic constituents of a *Kunstsprache*.[59] Thanks to their artificially sustained powers, the poet is free to apply them sparingly but emphatically, often as a powerful technique or narrative device. The qualities they mark include the exotic (Phoenician and Phaiakian arti-

---

[58] Frontisi-Ducroux, *Dédale*, chaps. 1 and 2, tries to establish "metallic" properties for the words; for a critique, see review by H. Philipp, *Gnomon* 51 (1979) 41–43.

[59] Canciani, *ArchHom II: N. Bildkunst*, 2, 84, complains of their "zu allgemeinen Sinn," a more prudent conclusion than Frontisi-Ducroux's semantic sweep (see the previous n.).

facts), magic (armor and costume assumed for strategic purposes), and ritual equipment—the chest with its vessel, a seat for special guests—along with objects that play a critical narrative role (the ship that carried off Helen, the bed Odysseus made for Penelope). The forms of δαιδάλεος, δαιδάλλω, and δαίδαλον can substitute for words of similar metrical and semantic nature: for example, ποίκιλος or ποικίλλω. But no other word complex describing art—χάρις, ἄγαλμα, περικαλλές—includes a personification like Daidalos, who bestows greater significance on his cognates than that enjoyed by words like ποίκιλλος.

Within the wider epic tradition, this word complex demonstrates signifying powers that are idiosyncratic to individual poems, much as the uses of δαίδαλα differ in the *Iliad* and *Odyssey*. Hesiod uses forms of these words equally rarely and emphatically, in fact exclusively as attributes for Pandora, the ultimate δαίδαλον and καλὸν κακόν, "beautiful evil," handiwork of all the gods and carrier of all ills.[60] In the *Theogony*, her κόσμος incorporates a panoply of epic embellishments, beginning with her δαιδαλέην καλύπτρην, "elaborate headdress," a gift of Athena. On her head, the same goddess places a crown of gold made by Hephaistos (581–84):

> τῇ δ᾽ ἐνὶ δαίδαλα πολλὰ τετεύχατο, θαῦμα ἰδέσθαι,
> κνώδαλ᾽, ὅσ᾽ ἤπειρος πολλὰ τρέφει ἠδὲ θάλασσα
> τῶν ὅ γε πόλλ᾽ ἐνέθηκε, χάρις δ᾽ ἀπελάμπετο πολλή.
> θαυμάσια, ζώοισιν ἐοικότα φωνήεσσιν.

And he worked on it many *daidala*, a wonder to see,
wild beasts, all that the earth nourishes and the sea,
of these he put many on it, and much grace shone from it,
wonderful creatures, like living creatures with voices.

Like the wardrobe of Hera in her seduction of Zeus in *Iliad* 14, the poetic embellishment of this mythical woman participates in early Greek craftsmanship applied to votive finery and the decoration of cult statues. Pandora's crown reflects actual objects in gold, in particular a type of headdress common in Cyprus and the Near East that is often decorated with human and animal figures (Figure 6).[61] Hesiod's marvelous crown bears many δαίδαλα, specified as creatures of land and sea, a source of wonder, grace, and as vivid as life. Greek artists honored Pandora's epic outfit even in the classical period, where she is represented wearing such a crown (Figure 50). Each of its qualities usually

---

[60] On Pandora as a symbol of the fundamental ambiguity of human existence, see Vernant, "The Myth of Prometheus in Hesiod," *Myth and Society*, 174–85; Warner, "The Making of Pandora," *Monuments and Maidens*, 213–40. On δαιδαλ- words in this passage, see Frontisi-Ducroux, *Dédale*, 73–77; Loraux, *Les enfants d'Athèna*, 7–97, 142 n. 98.

[61] Walters Art Gallery 57.968: V. Karageorghis, "Gold *Tiarae* from Cyprus," in *Insight through Images: Studies in Honor of Edith Porada*, ed. M. Kelly-Buccellati (Malibu, Calif., 1986), 129–32, for examples from the Cypro-Geometric I period (1050–950 B.C.).

appears alone in the Homeric corpus: in this concentration in Hesiod's poem, they challenge the magic and glamour of Hephaistos's handmaidens or Alkinoos's furniture, but also suggest the hidden evil that will bring misfortune to men.

Briefer and less vivid is Pandora's introduction in *Works and Days* (60–82), where only the loom she is taught to use by Athena is πολυδαίδαλος, not her wardrobe. As in the *Iliad* and *Odyssey*, this intensive adjective is transferred to sources of craftsmanship (in Homer, to Phoenician artists and unworked gold) from finished artifacts. The *Theogony* adds the skill of weaving and the medium of textiles to the domain of δαιδάλεος, increasing the verb's industrial range as it dilutes its technical focus. The association in Hesiod between textiles and Athena suggests that Hera's garment and its ornaments in *Iliad* 14 were both understood as the work of Athena, perhaps by Hesiod, and the later epic use helps clarify the Homeric syntax.[62]

The restriction of δαίδαλα in Hesiod's poems to the creation of Pandora, most splendid and most destructive artifice in all of epic poetry, designed to deceive and ruin mankind, seems deliberate and was not without influence. This artificial maiden inherits from Homer the "arming of Hera," the assistance of Athena, and the craftsmanship of Hephaistos. Pandora also receives instruction on the loom, πολυδαίδαλον ἴστον, Penelope's weapon against the suitors and often Helen's pastime, as when she first appears in the *Iliad*, weaving the substance of the *Iliad* itself (3.125–28). Despite ample opportunities, Hesiod nowhere applies δαιδάλεος to weaponry, except insofar as the assembly of Pandora is an arming scene in feminine garb and a prelude to the ἀπάτη of mankind by the gods. Her combination of qualities—the dazzling and the dangerous—attracted epic epithets that describe quality craftsmanship in Homer but also magic and unpredictable powers. Hesiod's highly specialized use of δαιδάλεος for the figure of Pandora, bringer of evils to men, suggests that he exploited, in a conscious and sophisticated manner, the connotative functions of such words in hexameter in order to frame her as dangerous.[63]

As well as confirming, or repeating, these symbolic functions of δαίδαλα in epic, the passages in Hesiod also initiate their poetic extensions in Greek literature. In particular, the creation of Pandora comes closest to the manufacture of a statue in all of archaic literature.[64] This description studded with δαίδαλα may have influenced speculation about Daidalos the sculptor, a classical reincarnation of the prehistoric craftsman, an artist of δαίδαλα, as artist of the monumental (see Chapter 9). Long before this devel-

[62] For the dependence of this passage on the Διὸς ἀπάτη in *Iliad* 14, see H. Neitzel, *Homer-Rezeption bei Hesiod. Interpretation ausgewählter Passagen* (Bonn, 1975), 20–34; Pucci, *Hesiod and the Language of Poetry*, 82–126.

[63] Vernant, *Myth and Society*, 175–76, 178, notes words expressing concealment (e.g., καλύπτρην) in

Hesiod's account; cf. Loraux, *Les enfants d'Athèna*, 85–86.

[64] As noted by Warner: "Pandora is made like a work of art" (*Monuments and Maidens*, 216). Cf. M. Erren, "Die Geschichte der Technik bei Hesiod," in *Gnomosyne. Festschrift für Walter Marg*, ed. G. Kurz, D. Müller, and W. Nicolai (Munich, 1981), 157–66.

opment, epic passages like Pandora's manufacture, with their poetic anthropomorphism of a mythological process, anticipate the creation of cult images. Such a pattern suggests itself for architecture, as well, where ἑκατόμπεδον appears as a poetic expression for the monumental (e.g., *Iliad* 23.164) that eventually became a technical concept in early Greek temple design. Under no circumstances do such passages testify to the existence of monumental sculpture and architecture, to complicate the chronology of early Greek temples and statues. Rather, they express a Greek impulse to personify and render colossal a religious concept, a drive that led, outside of poetry, to the invention of cult images.[65] Pheidias may have made a conscious allusion to the poetic manufacture of Pandora, as the ultimate epic source for a sculptor who would compare his handiwork with that of the gods. By portraying the myth on the base of his Athena Parthenos (see Chapter 9, 12), the Athenian sculptor may have suggested the divine character of his handiwork, or the "Panathenian" nature of the Akropolis project (Plutarch, *Perikles* 12–13) as a mortal equivalent of the manufacture of Pandora by all the gods.

In contrast to Hesiod's calculated use of these words, the *Shield of Herakles* (*Aspis*) displays a traditional, if not pedantic use of δαίδαλα that contributes to the argument for a separate poet.[66] Whoever its creator, its debt to the description of the shield of Achilles in *Iliad* 18 is manifest, particularly in its imitative application of δαίδαλα.

When Herakles arms for battle against Kyknos, his armor and arming occupy some two hundred lines of hexameter (122–320), much of it, especially lines 237–317, derivative from the *Iliad*'s shield.[67] Thus his greaves of bronze are praised as Ἡφαίστου κλυτὰ δῶρα (123), "illustrious gifts of Hephaistos," and his cuirass as a gift of Athena:

> δεύτερον αὖ θώρηκα περὶ στήθεσσιν ἔδυνε
> καλὸν χρύσειον πολυδαίδαλον, ὅν οἱ ἔδωκε
> Παλλάς Ἀθηναίη, κούρη Διός, ὁππότ' ἔμελλε
> τὸ πρῶτον στονόεντας ἐφορμήσεσθαι ἀέθλους.

> Second, he put on his cuirass around his shoulders
> beautiful, golden, much elaborate, which Pallas Athena
> gave him, daughter of Zeus, when he was first
> about to rush into grievous combat.

[65] B. C. Dietrich, "Divine Concept and Iconography in Greek Religion," *Grazer Beiträge* 12–13 (1985–1986) 171–92; Coldstream, *Deities in Aegean Art*.

[66] Thalmann, *Form and Thought in Early Greek Poetry*, xi–xxi, on the *Aspis* and the early epic corpus. Most scholars dispute the ancient attribution to Hesiod (e.g., Merkelbach and West, who exclude the poem from their *Fragmenta Hesiodea*) and date the poem to the sixth century: R. M. Cook, "The Date of the Hesiodic Shield," *CQ* 31 (1967) 208; R. Janko, *Homer, Hesiod and the Hymns: Diachronic Development in Epic Diction* (Cambridge, 1982), 200, fig. 41.

[67] Edwards, *The Language of Hesiod in Its Traditional Context*, 23–29, 196. Thalmann, *Form and Thought in Early Greek Poetry*, 62–64. H. A. Shapiro, "Herakles and Kyknos," *AJA* 88 (1984) 523–29.

Next come iron shoulder-guards, the quiver of death-dealing arrows, and his spear:

> κρατὶ δ᾽ ἐπ᾽ ἰφθίμῳ κυνέην εὔτυκτον ἔθηκε,
> δαιδαλέην ἀδάμαντος, ἐπὶ κροτάφοις ἀραρυῖαν,
> ἥτ᾽ εἴρυτο κάρη Ἡρακλῆος θείοιο.

And on his head he placed a well-made leather helmet,
well-wrought and unbreakable, fitting on the temples,
the helmet that guarded the head of dear Herakles.

The shield itself is next, "a wonder to behold": παναίολον, "all glittering," inlaid with τίτανος (?), ivory, amber, gold, and κύανος (blue stone). Its decoration is dominated by personifications like Fear and Discord, Pursuit and Flight, Din and Ker. Animals lend ferocity: δεινοί snakes, rows of boars and lions in struggle; then mythological themes mix men and beasts (Lapiths and Centaurs, Perseus and the Gorgons) before scenes from human civilization repeat motifs from the shield in the *Iliad*: cities of men at war and peace (237–313). Only at the close does the poet characterize its decoration, encircled by Okeanos, as πολυδαίδαλον (314), and nowhere does the personality of Daidalos suggest itself, although χοροί abound in the city at peace (277–85). Instead, the craftmanship of Hephaistos is praised repeatedly (219, 244, 297, 313) without the variation of a simile invoking a second, legendary artist. In addition, conventions abound praising art as close to life, "like living creatures," ὥς εἰ ζωοὶ ἐόντες, ὥς εἰ ζωοὺς ἐναρίζων, ζωῆσιν ἴκελοι or ἐοικώς as well as the more common θαῦμα ἰδέσθαι, "a wonder to behold." These expressions seem to mark a more popular view of art-as-life but cannot be taken as evidence for a more advanced or sophisticated attitude to art itself, as some have identified in this poem.[68] If anything, these phrases ring as repetitive and lack the variety demonstrated by the poet of the *Iliad* in his deployment of daidalic variants.

Shortly after the description of Herakles' shield closes, his opponent's shield is called δαιδάλεος by Athena in her advice to Herakles (334–35):

> ἔνθα κε γυμνωθέντα σάκευς ὕπο δαιδαλέοιο,
> ὀφθαλμοῖσιν ἴδης, ἔνθ᾽ οὐτάμεν ὀξέι χαλκῷ.

There where you see him naked under his elaborate shield
with your eyes, there you must wound with the sharp bronze.

---

[68] Philipp, *Tektonon Daidala*, 15–18, 35, 37, 42, 53–54, claims a major breakthrough in this poem—the distinction between art as a reality independent of life—as a result of archaic philosophical develop- ments. Cf. review by N. Himmelmann-Wildschutz, *Gnomon* 42 (1970) 292, and Kassel, *ZPE* 51 (1983) 1–12.

Its context matches closely those passages in the *Iliad* where this adjective distinguished a θώρηξ intended to protect a hero from a fatal wound (as previously noted), and indeed Herakles wounds Ares with the very method recommended by Athena, in a line that repeats her instructions complete with the significant adjective (460). In a triumphant finale that rewards his deeds, Herakles is swept off to Olympos in a chariot, a δίφρος πολυδαίδαλος, perhaps a variant on the ἅρματα δαιδάλεα of the *Iliad*.

In a poem as incomplete and as derivative of epic poetry as the *Aspis*, the narrative potential of a complex of words like δαιδάλεος enjoys far fewer opportunities. But these words complement a hero's armor in a traditional manner fully in agreement with their Homeric appearances, even indicating the hidden danger in glamour without strength, which marks epic equipment that fails to avert a wound. The glamour, power, and danger evoked by this word in Homeric poetry is sustained in the Hesiodic corpus, and its next poetic phase continues this tradition. The next phase also initiates the dialogue with religion suggested in the epiphany of Pandora, for these words claim new meanings in the realm of Greek cult.

CHAPTER 2

Daidala in Archaic Poetry
and Ritual

THE EPIC DIMENSIONS of Daidalos, as explored in the first chapter, spring from a complex network of words that mark a certain type of artifact for its role in epic narrative. These properties, independent of technical associations with the objects they describe, not only survive but flourish in subsequent Greek poetry, where they betray an unmistakable debt to the epic tradition and its "daidalic" occasions. Not surprisingly, it is the more prolific and poetically multivalent adjectival forms, plus an occasional plural noun (δαίδαλα), that are most popular in epic, lyric, and tragic poetry, where they are newly embellished by ambitious poets. Daidalos himself never reappears in Greek literature until his new role as a sculptor in the fifth century (see Part 3). Thus his brief role in *Iliad* 18 represents not only his first incarnation in the company of the words that inspired his name but his only literary role until the Attic stage.

The post-Homeric tradition technically begins with Hesiod, although his poems are better treated as components of the same epic tradition than purely as *Nachfolger* with imitative traits (see Chapter 1, nn. 61, 65). In the Hesiodic tradition, the analysis of δαιδάλεος and related words reveals how idiosyncratic to each composition can be such terms without technical limitations. Thus Pandora monopolizes this semantic field, as the dominant work of art in the *Theogony* and *Works and Days*, while in the *Aspis*, military equipment reasserts its claim to such descriptions. This deployment exclusive to a particular poem or poet manifests itself throughout archaic and classical Greek poetry.

In lyric and choral poetry, δαιδάλεος and its variations maintain their epic association with elaborate artifacts but show an increased emphasis on those descriptions that play a significant role in narrative. Not surprisingly, these adjectives appear only in mythological episodes in the poems of Pindar, Bacchylides, and Simonides, or in praise of art in epinician odes. Extended descriptions of art in the manner traditional to epic poetry, where length and detail often justify a ritual prelude to action while entertaining the visual imagination, have no place in brief poems of praise or selected mythological moments. Instead, two new categories attract expressions formed on δαιδάλεος: sacred objects in the religious domain, and the metaphorical extension of properties in art to the craft of poetry.

In Simonides' ode of uncertain meter about Danae and Perseus, his only preserved narrative poem, such an adjective qualifies the chest that carries mother and child to safety.[1] The preserved fragment, quoted in prose by Dionysios to illustrate the difficulties of restoring an unknown meter, begins:

> ὅτε λάρνακι
> ἐν δαιδαλέᾳ
> ἄνεμός τέ μιν πνέων
> κινηθεῖσά τε λίμνα δείματι
> ἔρειπεν,

> when in the elaborate
> chest
> the wind blowing
> and the sea heaving struck her
> with fear,

whereupon Danae throws her arms around her child and begins her lament. The magic chest is addressed by Danae a few lines later as ἀτερπής δορὺ χαλκεογόμφος "joyless wood, nailed with bronze," unusual epithets inspired by Homeric language.[2] The application of δαιδάλεος to a chest may well borrow its association from epic where it describes the chest of Achilles (*Iliad* 16.222), also a gift from mother to hero, just as it forms a bond between Danae and her son. Furthermore, the chest intended to carry them to an early and watery grave ends up saving their lives when it is discovered by fishermen on Seriphos (see nn. 3–5). Thus the adjective in the poem of Simonides designates an item with an important, still unfulfilled narrative role and with those ambiguous qualities that warrant the use of δαιδάλεος. For the chest is well made enough to keep them afloat from Argos to Seriphos but is designed as a coffin, before the quirk of myth makes it their cradle of rebirth through rescue; its strength and beauty are designed for death but foster life, unexpectedly. A word like δαιδάλεος may well have conveyed this mixture of qualities, to an ear tuned to epic conventions.

But the adjective also hints at a fuller description of this chest and its manufacture, either in the lost portions that preceded Dionysios's quotation of Simonides or in other poetic versions (e.g., Hesiod's *Catalogue of Women* or *Ehoiai*, frag. 135 M-W). For the chest itself, including its manufacture and maker, is regularly depicted in early classical red-figure vase illustrations of this myth as if it were an important traditional element.

---

[1] Dionysios of Halikarnassos, *De Compositione Verborum* 26.ii.140ff. = frag. 543. D. Page, "Simonidea," *JHS* 71 (1951) 133–40; Burnett, *Art of Bacchylides,* 11–14 nn. 20–25.

[2] A. E. Harvey, "Homeric Epithets in Greek Lyric Poetry," *CQ* 51 (1957) 206–23.

The popularity of this theme in classical vase painting probably derives from its publicity on the Attic stage.[3] For example, a hydria by the Gallatin Painter in Boston shows a bare-chested carpenter in the short chiton traditional to a workman, using a running drill on the lid of the chest (Figure 4).[4] Similar scenes cluster in the decades from 490 to 460 B.C. and demonstrate such consistency, including the role of the carpenter and the decoration of the chest, that inspiration by a single work of drama is highly attractive. The *Diktyoulkoi* from Aeschylus's tetralogy on the Perseus theme is a popular candidate in modern scholarship, for it narrated the chest's manufacture, sea voyage, and discovery on Seriphos.[5] Other possible sources include tragedies by Aeschylus and Sophokles, lyric or dithyrambic poems like the fragmentary one by Simonides, or even a monumental painting. Within this prolific classical tradition the poem of Simonides plays an uncertain chronological and literary role: it could have been inspired by other dramatic versions, or been influential enough if performed as a choral dithyramb to have contributed to the wave of vase paintings.

Whether in poetry or art, the episodes with the chest seem to have been among the most poignant and memorable, and its manufacture formed a crucial theme. And well it might: the chest is not only a universal motif in stories of abandonment or exposure and rescue, but its appearance must be glamorous enough to match its magic powers and attract the attention of fishermen. In narrative terms, its manufacture provided an occasion for dramatic irony in the form of a prolonged and tearful farewell, like that spoken by Euripides's *Alkestis* (280–368), unaware of the happy outcome ahead. In a classical context, in particular, the popularity of the "manufacture" theme in the early classical period inspired other scenes of craftsmen and workshops in vase painting (Figures 1–3, 58–61), and the celebrity of the ἔκφρασις of the shield of Achilles may have encouraged dramatic descriptions in the same vein.[6] The presence of the carpenter in the scenes with Perseus and Danae suggests such a craftsman could have appeared on stage, as a silent character. In terms of iconography, the association of craftsman and king represents a pattern of royal patronage and commission traditional to Homeric society and its Near Eastern counterparts. In the *Iliad* and the *Odyssey*, Hephaistos works at the request of Thetis (Figures 1, 3), just as Daidalos first made a work of art

[3] T. P. Howe, "Illustrations to Aeschylus' Tetralogy on the Perseus Theme," *AJA* 57 (1953) 269–75; Ch. Clairmont, "Danae and Perseus on Seriphos," *AJA* 57 (1953) 92–94; K. Schauenburg, *Perseus in der Kunst des Altertums* (Bonn, 1960), discusses thirteen Attic vases with this scene; J. Oakley, "Danae and Perseus on Siphnos," *AJA* 86 (1982) 111–15. J.-J. Maffre, "Akrisios," *LIMC* I.1, 449–52; "Danae," *LIMC* III.1, 336–37, nos. 41–70.

[4] Boston, Museum of Fine Arts 13.200; *ARV²* 247,

1.

[5] N. M. Holley, "The Floating Chest," *JHS* 69 (1949) 39–47; Howe and Oakley (cited in n. 3; M. Werre-deHaas, *Aeschylus' Dictyulci* (Leiden, 1961), 5–10; Sutton, *Greek Satyr Play*, 17–20. Simon, in *Eye of Greece*, 123–48.

[6] Philipp, *Tektonon Daidala*, 109–13, for an appendix of over fifty representations of workshops. Cf. discussion in Chapter 13.

for Ariadne, daughter of King Minos. Other craftsmen are associated with royal patrons in epic poetry: Phereklos made wooden ships for Alexandros (Paris), prince of Troy (*Iliad* 5.59–64); Ikmalios made an ivory throne for Queen Penelope (*Odyssey* 19.56–58); the goldworker Laerkes is summoned by Nestor, king of Pylos (*Odyssey* 3.425). The Levantine background to this tradition is suggested in the relationship of Kothar-wa-Hasis to divine patrons (Chapter 4) and in Phoenician craftsmen in the employ of Hiram of Tyre and King Solomon, according to the Hebrew Bible (1 Kings 5–7). In one of the earliest scenes of the act of creation (Figures 13, 14), the enthroned figure who gives birth to the work of art is assisted by assorted assistants, both female (midwife?) and male (craftsmen). In Greek art, patron and craftsman appear in a formulaic composition that lasts until the Roman period, including the manufacture of wings by Daidalos, who works in a seated position (on the Villa Albani relief, e.g.) while his son watches and waits, just as Thetis observes Hephaistos (Figures 1, 3).

In the story of the magic chest made for Danae at the orders of the Argive king, no artist is named, but the epithets lavished on the chest in poetry and the image of the carpenter in art reinforce his role. Simonides specifies artists in other poems (e.g., Hephaistos made the bronze giant, Talos: frag. 568). The word δαιδάλεος alone cannot guarantee a named craftsman or a second personification as in *Iliad* 18, but when combined with the evidence of vase paintings and other poetic fragments it abbreviates an entire tradition of the manufacture of marvelous and magic artifacts. In the *Iliad*, appearances of these words after the manufacture of the shield—for example, at 19.13, 19.19, 19.379—recapitulate the elaborate description in Book 18, and Simonides could have employed the word as a similar revival of an earlier description of the chest. In terms of the craftsman named Daidalos, this brief scrap assures that the epithets that sponsored him were not moribund in poetry and an archaic chest called δαιδάλεος must have contributed to his eventual reputation as a carpenter.

The poetry of Bacchylides, nephew of Simonides, reached modern readers late, in fragments, and amid high expectations, given Longinus's praise of him over Pindar. Adding to this unfair survival, his overlap in career and genre, often in patron and subject, with the formidable Pindar has reduced most scholarship to defensive and comparative work, until recently.[7] In the pursuit of a single root and its variants, as in this survey of *daidala*, the two poets demonstrate highly idiosyncratic innovations in their use of these words, epitomizing their poetic personalities as defined by other means. In short, Bacchylides indulges his taste for elaborate epithets as a narrative device, whereas Pindar explores the complex world of metaphor, both by means of the same family of words.

[7] M. Lefkowitz, "Bacchylides' Ode 5: Imitation and Originality," *HSCP* 73 (1969) 45–96, is typical of traditional scholarship, opening with "Bacchylides is a conventional poet, and no one begins to speak of him without apology" (p. 45). Burnett's *Art of Bacchylides* is a welcome tribute (on Pindar, pp. 1–3).

Bacchylides's fondness for epithets, including the coinage of new ones, some unique to his poems, did not neglect a word as rich in adjectival power as δαιδάλεος. His emulation of epic vocabulary inspired *hapax* forms like ὑψιδαιδάλτων τριπόδων (3.18), "high-wrought tripods," and χαλκοδαιδάλοισιν ἀσπίσιν, "shields elaborate in bronze," (frag. 2.2) as well as the more predictable εὐδαίδαλος (17.88, frag. 23.2) in company with the orthodox δαιδάλεος (5.140, frag. 4.2). Unlike Pindar, he never ventured to other parts of speech but remained faithful to his favorite poetic instrument, adjectives.[8] The contexts Bacchylides embellished with epithets include narrative passages where the word emphasizes significant thematic content, epinician occasions where δαιδαλ- praises a patron's dedications, and ritual settings where the adjective expresses respect and piety for the sacred, a poetic function new to the archaic period. The most traditional category, the first one of these three, is represented in a fragment quoted by the grammarian Didymos and by a scholiast to Pindar's tenth *Olympian Ode*, line 83 (Bergk 41, frag. 2):

> Ποσειδάνιος ὡς Μαντινέες τριοδόντα
> χαλκοδαιδάλοισιν ἐν ἀσπίσιν φορεῦντες . . .

> Like the Mantineans, bearing the trident of Poseidon
> on their elaborate bronze shields . . .

The "daidalo-brazen" shields are an obvious amplification of Homeric epithets applied to armor, in an era when the medium of bronze was already evocative of the age of heroes. This compound adjective, never repeated in extant Greek literature, typifies Bacchylidean language in general and his amplification of δαίδαλα in particular.

The most lavish of these variants was inspired by the quadriga victory of Hieron at Delphi in 470 B.C. In the third strophe of *Pythian* 3, the poet turns from a Syrakusan setting and pays tribute to the Deinomenid dedications at Delphi (17–22):

> λάμπει δ᾽ ὑπὸ μαρμαρυγαῖς ὁ χρυσός,
> ὑψιδαιδάλτων τριπόδων σταθέντων
> πάροιθε ναοῦ, τόθι μέγιστον ἄλσος
> Φοίβου παρὰ Κασταλίας ῥεέθροις
> Δελφοὶ διέπουσι.

> Gold shines forth with flashings
> from high-wrought tripods standing

[8] G. Kirkwood, "The Narrative Art of Bacchylides," in *The Classical Tradition: Literary and Historical Studies in Honor of Harry Caplan*, ed. L. Wallach (Ithaca, N.Y., 1966), 98–114, esp. p. 100 for epic epithets in Pindar and Bacchylides. G. Pieper, "Conflict of Character in Bacchylides' Ode 17," *TAPA* 103 (1972) 395, on epithets and characterization; C. Segal, "Bacchylides Reconsidered: Epithets and the Dynamics of Lyric Narrative," *QUCC* 22 (1976) 99–130.

before the temple, where lies the greatest grove
of Phoibos next to the Kastalian spring
and the Delphians serve him.

By means of a flattering maxim promising the dedicant happiness, the poet then introduces Kroisos as a fitting peer for such piety and happiness, much as did Pindar in his praise of the same Sicilian tyrant two years earlier (*Pythian* 1.93–95). The adjective ὑψιδαιδάλτος, "high-wrought," emphasizes both height and craftsmanship, qualities essential to any dedication that is to make a lasting impression at Delphi. The suffix -τος makes it a verbal adjective, artificial but more emphatic than the traditional but abstract Homeric epithet δαιδάλεος. With this compliment, Bacchylides flatters both the piety of the Deinomenids, their generosity to Apollo, and their success in battle, which inspired these lavish (gold, not bronze) tripods.

Miraculously, these tripods are among the rare δαίδαλα to have survived, at least in part, for comparison to their ancient esteem. Two inscribed bases found north of the temple pronaos at Delphi held tripods dedicated by the Sicilian tyrants.[9] The inscription adds a Nike and the sculptor's name to the information commemorated by Bacchylides; they are supplemented by other literary sources on these dedications. Theopompos (Athenaeus, 6.231f) and Diodorus (11.26.7) record that Hieron made the tripods of pure gold, delaying the dedication until such materials were available. This would allow the tripods, which share a single base, to represent simultaneous dedications by the two brothers for separate occasions, perhaps Gelon's Himera victory of 480 B.C. and Hieron's at Kyme in 474. Their placement next to the Plataian tripod juxtaposes Greek victories in the West with those in the East, a literal embodiment of the parallelism that obsessed historians (see Chapters 11 and 13). In poetry, Bacchylides compares Western prosperity with the legendary wealth of an Eastern ruler, Kroisos, just as early classical historiography envisioned the fortunes of Greece.

Whichever tripods Bacchylides had in mind, the most prominent must always have been those two near the temple. Proximity to the heart of the sanctuary and oracle conferred special status on dedications, as Pindar makes explicit in his praise of the Cyrenaean dedications suspended inside the temple (see my subsequent comments on *Pythian* 5). No less distinguished than their location was their craftsmanship, acclaimed by the sculptor's signature. No Homeric precedent associated δαιδάλεος with tripods, although Hephaistos's magic tripods have handles called δαίδαλα, and any object of gold would attract an epic epithet when pure gold alone can be praised as πολυδαίδα-

[9] Th. Homolle, "Les trépieds de Gélon," *BCH* 21 (1897) 588–90; F. Courby, *FdD* II: *Topographie et architecture. La terrasse du temple*, 1, 249–54, figs. 197–98; Th. Homolle, "Les offrandes Delphiques des fils de Deinoménes et l'epigramme de Simonides," in *Mélanges Weil* (Paris, 1898), 207–24; Tod, *GHI* 17, 22 = *ML* no. 28. B. Gentili, "I tripodi di Delfi e il Carme III de Bacchilide," *PdP* 8 (1953) 199–208; P. Amandry, "Les trépieds de Delphes et du Péloponnèse: Trépieds des Deinoménides," *BCH* 111 (1987) 81–89.

λος (*Odyssey* 13.11). As dedications and permanent property of the god, the Syrakusan tripods also participate in the realm of religious objects, which develop δαιδάλεος qualities in the archaic period.

Of the remaining δαίδαλα in the poems of Bacchylides, two compliment objects critical to mythological narrative, like the chest of Perseus in his uncle's poem. In fact, an identical noun-epithet pair—δαιδάλεος λάρναξ—plays a significant role in the fate of Meleager, narrated by the unlucky hero to Herakles in a victory ode for Hieron in 476 (the same occasion that sponsored Pindar's first Olympian ode). In a long passage laden with Homeric epithets (5.94–154), Meleager recalls how his ill-fated but ruthless mother, Althea (κακόποτμος, ἀτάρβακτος), removed the firebrand of her son's life "from its elaborate chest" (δαιδαλέας ἐκ λάρνακος) and burnt it (lines 140–41), thereby condemning her son to a swift and premature death.

Both language and motif—a chest that links mother and son—suggest deliberate allusions to the story told by Simonides. Conscious reference between the poems of uncle and nephew seems likely and carries thematic associations beyond archaic poetry as well. Like the χῆλος of Achilles in the *Iliad* (16.222), the chest that guards the source of Meleager's life is both a gift between parent and child and a precarious link between life and death. For Akrisios and Althea, parents of Meleager, the chest offers a means of eliminating their offspring. In both passages, the word δαιδάλεος carries dramatic qualities best translated as "fatal" and anticipates tragic diction, like the robe in the *Oresteia* made ominous by the same adjective (see Chapter 3). Assonance reinforces the qualities of this word: δαιδαλέας follows δαίμων (113) and δαΐφρων (122, 137), while the names Δαίπυλος (145) and Δαιάνειρα (172) echo sound.[10]

No less conspicuous is the ship of Minos in *Dithyramb* 17, probably a song for Apollo that celebrates the triumph of Theseus over Minos (Chapter 12). When the Cretan king delivers his challenge to Theseus, he commands a swift sailing course, downwind (86–89):

> τάφεν δὲ Διὸς υἱὸς ἔνδοθεν
> κέαρ, κέλευσέ τε κατ᾽ οὖ-
> ρον ἴσχεν εὐδαίδαλον
> νᾶα. μοῖρα δ᾽ ἑτέραν ἐπόρσυν᾽ ὁδόν.

And the son of Zeus was amazed within
his heart, and gave orders to hold
the well-built ship downwind.
But fate pursued another course.

[10] Burnett, *Art of Bacchylides*, 200 n. 18; cf. Hesiod, frag. 280. 10 (R. Merkelbach, *Die Hesiodfragmente auf Papyrus* [Leipzig, 1957], 26–81): διογενες [Μελ]έαγ[ρε δαΐ]φρονας Οἰνέος ὗιε and Phrynikhos's *Women of Pleuron* (Pausanias, 10.31).

The "well-built" ship no doubt draws from Homeric vessels with dangerous cargo praised as δαίδαλα, like the getaway fleet of Paris and Helen (*Iliad* 5.60–64). The ship of Minos in Bacchylides's poem could invoke the reputation of Cretan craftsmanship as well as narrative associations through its epithet. The Homeric connection between Daidalos and Minos's court at Crete, established in *Iliad* 18, may have been suggestive enough to influence Bacchylides's choice of epithet. If Daidalos made a χορός for Ariadne, why not a ship for Minos? The fleet of Minos acquired its new reputation in these decades of the fifth century, and its flagship deserved a "daidalic" epithet, if not a master craftsman. If these associations cannot be assumed as the poet's intention, that may have been the effect of an εὐδαίδαλος ναῦς belonging to Minos, just as δαίδαλα suspended near a Cretan statue (*Pythian* 5.63) helped nurture the legend of Daidalos as craftsman from Crete.

However "well-built," the ship of Minos fails its captain: it is Theseus who returns successfully from the sea to board the same vessel and amaze the Knossian commander. The chest commissioned by Akrisios for the dispatch of daughter and grandson (in Simonides, frag. 543) was praised in equivalent terms but, intended as a coffin, rescued mother and child instead of sinking them. The adjective common to both thus marks unexpected powers that turn against those who marshal them, producing a twist in the narrative.

Other Bacchylidean δαίδαλα distinguish religious settings by poetic properties. In a fragmentary paian (frag. 4, 26, quoted by Stobaeus) Bacchylides praises peace, source of πλοῦτος, song, and festival where sheep are sacrificed on δαιδαλέων . . . βωμῶν. In a hyperchorem quoted by Dionysios (*De Compositione Verborum* C 25 = frag. 11.3), Bacchylides praises the temple of Itonian Athena as εὐδαίδαλος, honoring the consecration of altars and temples in addition to their well-built proportions or decorations. This sacred property first attested here among the meanings of δαιδάλεος has no epic precedent and evolves in the archaic period to survive into the latest pagan expressions (see n. 45). It is accompanied by similar epithets in ritual contexts (festival and deity names) and testifies to the convergence between poetic and ritual language critical to archaic Greek culture.

In turning to the poems of Pindar, a richer selection of surviving works reveals the patterns demonstrated by Bacchylides in his deployment of δαίδαλα. Among the eleven examples preserved in the ampler Pindaric corpus, the three categories marked in the poems of Bacchylides by variants of the epithet—narrative, epinician, and ritual—repeat themselves. Of these, over half the occasions where Pindar elaborates on the Homeric root are devoted to his own craft, poetry, and five of them employ the rarest form of all—the verb δαιδάλλειν. Thus Pindar distinguishes himself, as in other criteria, from contemporary poets in bold departures from traditional phraseology and subtle incorporation of his innovations into a world of metaphor.

To begin with his more traditional expressions, three can be attributed to epinician concerns, where he praises the dedications and handiwork of his ode's audience. In *Pythian* 5, composed for Arkesilaos of Cyrene and no doubt performed in Libya, he lauds a quadriga victory that left the king's equipment unblemished by the effort: ἔντεα .... ἀκηράτοις ἁνίαις ("gear with undefiled reins"). Proof of this faultless victory is the display in the temple at Delphi of the winning equipment—χεριαρᾶν τεκτόνων δαίδαλα ("*daidala* of craftsmen with skilled hands")—in a location of unusual prestige (39–42):

> τό σφ᾽ ἔχει κυπαρίσσινον
> μέλαθρον ἀμφ᾽ ἀνδριάντι σχεδόν,
> Κρῆτες ὃν τοξοφόροι τέγει Παρνασσίῳ
> καθέσσαντο μονόδροπον φυτόν.

The cypress chamber now holds them,
close to the statue
which the bow-clad Cretans set up under the Parnassian roof,
carved from a single tree.

Roux has identified the κυπαρίσσινον μέλαθρον as the temple of Apollo, rebuilt after the sixth-century fire, and the ἀνδριάς as the cult image of Apollo, a wooden statue of Cretan manufacture. This topographic detail, unusual in an epinician ode, addresses an audience at Cyrene, according to Roux, whom Pindar sought to flatter with details of their city's prominence at Delphi.[11] The δαίδαλα themselves are the ἔντεα, harness and other chariot equipment traditionally praised as δαιδάλεα by Homer (*Iliad* 6.418; 13.331, 719). The most elaborate archaic versions could include bronze breast-plates, ivory cheekpieces, and other decoration; like other artifacts praised as δαιδάλεος, the most glamorous prototypes are Oriental (Figure 25).[12] In Pindar's vision, these traditional δαίδαλα are displayed adjacent to a cult image of Cretan manufacture, made of a single trunk (or block of stone).[13] This image combines Cretan sculpture, a branch of early Greek art that ultimately dominates the tradition of Daidalos, with the archaic and poetic δαίδαλα that sponsored his entry into Greek legend and art criticism. The ἀνδριάς itself claims only anonymous Cretan workmanship in this context, although this period already witnessed the elaboration of Daidalos as sculptor (see Part III). Moreover, the role of Cretans is attested among the professional personnel at Delphi, at least

[11] G. Roux, "Pindare, le prétendu trésor des Crétois et l'Ancienne Statue d'Apollon à Delphes," *REG* 75 (1962) 366–80.

[12] J. Wiesner, *ArchHom II: F. Fahren und Reiten*; H. Philipp, "Ein kyprischer Pferdebehang aus Olympia," *Bericht über die Ausgrabungen in Olympia 10*

(1981) 91–108; P. Brize, "Samos und Stesichoros," *AthMitt* 100 (1985) 53–90. On Figure 25, a North Syrian horse bridle found at Samos, see Chapter 5.

[13] Roux, "Pindare," 372–79, on the terminology and archaeology of this statue.

in poetry (*Homeric Hymn to Apollo* 388–544) and in other legends connecting Cretans to religious practices at Delphi (Chapter 6). In considering the sources that encouraged the classical legend of Daidalos as Cretan sculptor, one cannot underestimate the influence of such confrontations, literary if not archaeological, between "daidalic" words and early statues. In this Pindaric passage, the distance between poetic conventions and historical construct is maintained, but its chronological background is common to that which introduced the figure of Daidalos.

Praise for the property of patrons and audience must also have encouraged the language in a fragmentary Pythian ode for Hieron, quoted by Athenaeus in his surveys of regional specialties (1.28a = frag. 106). After extolling Lakonian hounds, Skyrian goats, Argive arms, and Theban chariots, Pindar culminates in:

> ἀλλ᾽ ἀπὸ τᾶς ἀγλαοκάρπου
> Σικελίας ὄχημα δαιδάλεον ματεύειν . . .

> but from fruit-bearing
> Sicily to seek a decorated cart . . .

The passage resembles Euripides's description of "multicolored chariots" (ποίκιλα ζυγά: cf. Bacchylides, frag. 1056), not to mention gaily painted modern donkey carts of Sicily and the Aegean, but in the context of Pindar's Sicilian patrons and their celebrated chariot victories, a mule cart of the type praised in *Pythian* 5 justifies the epithet. Mule races were a regular athletic event until the fifth century and often favored a Sicilian victor, like Hagesias of Syrakuse (*Olympian* 6.22–25) or Psaumis of Kamarina (*Olympian* 4.11, 5.1–3). The Sicilian vehicle for such victories attracted the praise of other poets, as Critias (frag. 1). Bacchylides and Pindar were so generous in their compliments to Sicilian tyrants that they attributed the invention of the first chariot to them (schol. Aristeides, 3.217). With such ample admiration, the attraction of an epithet like δαιδάλεος is almost predictable.

More generous but vague is Pindar's compliment to Athens, in a fragmentary dithyramb (frag. 75) apparently composed for performance at an Attic festival like the Dionysia. In this laudation, Pindar invites the Olympian gods to appear at the πολύβατον . . . ἄστεας ὀμφαλὸς θυόεντ᾽, ἐν ταῖς ἱεραῖς Ἀθάναις, "the fragrant, much-trodden navel of the city, in the sacred places of the Athenians," either the Akropolis or in the Athenian Agora.[14] The poet then invites them to an area, specific and separate from the "omphalos of the city," which he calls the πανδαίδαλον τ᾽ εὐκλέ᾽ ἀγοράν. If identical with the Athenian Agora, this would make the first area he describes, the "omphalos," more likely to be the Akropolis. Πανδαίδαλον is unique to Pindar and was probably his invention; it is assumed to refer to the multitude of private and public

---

[14] *Agora III*, 122; *Agora XIV*, 127; Camp, *The Athenian Agora*, 14–15.

dedications along the Panathenaic Way in the surrounding open public space of the Agora. Paired with εὐκλέα, a cult epithet that acquired historical significance after the Persian wars, the expression urges a date after 480–479 B.C., but during the period when the Agora and the Kolonos hillside were still in use as the principal theater of Athens.[15] Whichever monuments Pindar had in mind, the Athenians returned him the compliment with a bronze statue of the poet, visible somewhere in the northwestern Agora in the second century A.D. (Pausanias, 1.8.4; cf. Pseudo-Aeschines, *Epistle* 4.2–3). Pindar's epithet embraces an entire area rather than a single monument as in more common uses of δαίδαλος, and is intensified by πᾶν. This broad praise exceeds more conventional compliments and must reflect the exaggerated reputation that Athens had acquired for monuments after, and as a result of, the Persian wars. Eventually, this Athenian pride claimed Daidalos himself as a native Athenian, in a process explored in Parts III and IV. Thus Pindar's compliment agrees in timing as well as mood with the emergence of an Athenian monopoly in art and history.

Delphi and its temple attracted an equivalent compliment in a mutilated poem. Pindar's eighth paian survives in snatches of song on papyrus fragments, of which one (*PapOxy* 26.2442 = Snell, frag. 52) preserves the earliest *Baugeschichte* of a Greek temple.[16] In traditional Homeric manner, the πάντεχ[νοι] παλαμαί, "all-skilled hands," of Hephaistos and Athena are praised for their role in the bronze temple, the third in the legendary sequence of structures made of bay leaves, wax and feathers, and bronze, before the stone temple by two legendary architects (Pausanias, 10.5.5). According to Pindar, this magnificent building, with bronze walls, columns, and six golden acroteria, was destroyed by Zeus's thunderbolt. But what remained was endowed by Athena, an unusual agent of prophecy, with oracular powers, then praised by Pindar as a δαίδαλον or (Snell) δαίδαλμα. The crucial word is incomplete beyond the restored fourth letter and its syntactical and semantic function is unclear. It belongs to the description of the oracle, not the temple, and thus may express metaphorical qualities or ritual powers rather than visual properties of art or architecture. This use of δαιδαλ- may address two categories of archaic significance: the awesome effect of monumental arts, new since the culture that praised intricate minor arts as δαίδαλα, and the religious reputation of the Delphic oracle and its setting. The adjective's latter function survived, at least in a poetic context, until the last pronouncement of the oracle in the fourth century A.D. when the δαιδάλεα αὐλή (*Anthologia Graeca* 687) was stilled forever.

---

[15] *Agora XIV*, 126–29; C. M. Bowra, *Pindar* (Oxford, 1964), 408. On Artemis εὐκλε[ἴ]α see Sophocles, *Oidipous Tyrannos* 159–61; *Pausanias*, 1.14.5.; Harrison, *AJA* 81 (1977) 139 n. 14; and my discussion in Chapter 12. E. D. Francis and M. Vickers, "Leagros Kalos," *PCPhS* 27 (1981) 118–21 nn. 231–34, for an attempt to connect this passage with the position and date of the Leagros base; L. Gadbery, "Moving the Leagros Base," *AJA* 90 (1986) 194, for a new study of these Agora monuments.

[16] B. Snell, "Pindar's 8. Paian und die Tempel von Delphi," *Hermes* 90 (1962) 1–6; Philipp, *Tektonon Daidala*, 55–56.

Only one Pindaric myth involves an object both δαιδάλεος and critical to the narrative, in the manner popular with Simonides and Bacchylides. In *Nemean 4*, Pindar abbreviates Akastos's plot on Peleus's life in a cryptic manner (59–60):

> τᾷ [δαιδάλῳ] δὲ μαχαίρᾳ φύτευέ οἱ θάνατον
> ἐκ λόχου Πελίαο παῖς.

> With an elaborate knife he sowed his death
> by ambush, the son of Pelias.

All manuscripts transmit Δαιδάλου, "of Daidalos," as if the weapon belonged to the craftman or was his handiwork. Didymos's correction to δαιδάλῳ, assuming a lost *iota* after the "*o*," seems advisable.[17] Pindar's source is undoubtedly the epic version of the myth, which survives in a fragment of Hesiod quoted by an ancient commentator on Pindar's line (M-W, frag. 209):

> ἥδε δέ οἱ κατὰ θυμὸν ἀρίστη φαίνετο βούλη.
> αὐτὸν μὲν σχέσθαι, κρύψαι δ᾽ ἀδόκητα μάχαιραν,
> καλήν, —ἥν οἱ ἔτευξε περικλυτὸς ἀμφιγυήεις,
> ὡς τὴν μαστεύων. οἷος κατὰ Πήλιον αἰπύ
> αἶψ᾽ ὑπὸ Κενταύροισιν ὀρεσκώιοισι δαμείη.

> Now this seemed to him in his heart to be the best plan:
> to hold himself back, but to conceal an unexpected dagger,
> a beautiful one, which once the well-known clever one made for him
> when he was seeking one. In such a manner, under steep Pelion,
> he might be overcome by the mountain-dwelling Centaurs, at once.

Hesiod describes the knife as the work of Hephaistos, complete with a line lifted from Homer that describes its manufacture in formulas appropriate to the contexts of the adjective, δαιδάλεος. In other non-Homeric epics, Hephaistos is also responsible for the ashen spear given to Achilles by Cheiron (*Kypria* frag. 5: schol. *Iliad* 17.140), and the μαχαίρα makes sense as his handiwork. These references exclude the likelihood that the Pindaric word could be a genitive attributing the weapon to Daidalos, although one scholar has suggested that "Daidalos" is here used as an epithet of Hephaistos.[18] This agrees with the close resemblance between the two artists in poetry and art (Figure 11),

---

[17] Didymos's emendation in a scholion on this line: Drachmann, *Scholia Vetera in Pindari Carmina* (Leipzig, 1927), 3:80, 596; Farnell, *Critical Commentary to the Works of Pindar* (London, 1932), 270–71. Compare the emendation of Δαιδάλου to δαιδάλου at Euripides, *Herakles* 471: Chapter 3, n. 4. Martin, *Healing, Sacrifice and Battle*, 91–92, retains Δαιδάλου but translates "Daidalean," and admits the Hesiodic role of Hephaistos.

[18] H. Lloyd-Jones, *Aeschylus* (Cambridge, Mass., 1956), 2:547–48, citing Sophokles (A. Pearson, *Fragments of Sophocles* (Cambridge, 1917), 1:110.

if one can assume that Pindar employed a sophisticated trope on the names and functions of the two craftsmen, or that they were casual substitutes in the praise of art in poetry. However, the genitive of the craftsman's name would be unusual, nor would the dagger make sense as the property of Daidalos, never attested in myth. For syntactic rather than semantic reasons, poetic comparanda encourage ancient and modern corrections of Δαιδάλου to δαιδάλῳ. The text remains uncertain, and thus this passage is an ambiguous witness to the status of Daidalos as a named artist.

Whether adjective or possessive, this word expresses the treacherous nature of the object it describes, and its function in the legend. By hiding Peleus's weapon, Akastos hoped to expose him to certain death at the hands of the Pelian centaurs; as it turned out, Peleus was rescued by Cheiron (*Nemean* 4.60–61). The magic weapon, perhaps crafted by a divine craftsman, could kill its owner by its absence in the plot devised by the hero's enemy. The object described as the work of Daidalos or of equivalent quality also brings danger, in the epic domain invoked by the use of "daidalic" words.[19] In citing the dagger alone as the focus of the plot without further details, Pindar abbreviates the myth drastically but dramatically, thanks to the critical epithet. For in recalling a weapon attributed by Hesiod to Hephaistos as δαίδαλος / Δαιδάλου, Pindar is exercising the same poetic options that allowed an epic poet to choose between an attribution to a legendary craftsman (Athena, Hephaistos, Daidalos) or a traditional epithet like δαιδάλεος. In abbreviating the Hesiodic tradition by a single word, Pindar follows an epic technique popular in archaic poetry. Where Simonides condenses an earlier episode with detailed description into δαιδάλεα λάρναξ, vase paintings illustrated the lost portion he recalled. In the case of *Nemean* 4.59, the lines of Hesiod adduced by concerned scholiasts suggest the literary antecedent for Pindar's choice of epithet.

The δαίδαλ[ος] μάχαιρα of Peleus concludes the brief corpus of narrative props singled out with this epithet in archaic poetry. The weapon is instrumental to a dramatic event, a close brush with death: like the chest intended as a coffin for Perseus, or guarding the life-brand of Meleager, it becomes a threat (through its absence at a critical moment) to the life of a hero, but the dramatic outcome reverses in the hero's favor. In passages such as these, δαιδάλεος evolves into an instrument exploited on the Attic stage (see Chapter 3).

The greatest number of δαιδαλ- words employed by Pindar compliments his favorite art: poetry. The first instance involves a traditional adjective, δαιδάλεος, with which he describes a symposiast's lyre (*Pythian* 4.296) and seems conventional in context, at first glance. For it revives the noun-epithet pair from the *Iliad*, where the ambassadors find Achilles playing a lyre, a δαιδάλεαν φόρμιγγα (9.187, as noted in Chapter 1). In the

---

[19] As explored by R. Martin, *Healing, Sacrifice and Battle: Amechania and Related Concepts in Early Greek Poetry* (Innsbruck, 1983), 91–92. Cf. the divine μάχ-αιρα which took the life of Neoptolemos at Delphi: Pindar, *Nemean* 7.42.

Homeric passage, the phrase emphasized the hero's preoccupation with κλέα ἀνδρῶν while in voluntary but reluctant exile from the battlefield, as if to console himself for his loss of τιμή. The praise poet, Pindar, bestows this attribute on his friend, Damophilos, a Cyrenean in exile whom Pindar came to know in Thebes. In his eccentric plea on his friend's behalf for a return to Cyrene, the poet imagines him restored to his proper social setting. At a symposion, Damophilos will play the lyre, as distinguished as that held by Achilles, and, Pindar hopes, impress his friends with musical skills recently acquired in Thebes as the poet's guest.

This final passage in the ode is a digression unique to Pindar, a carefully phrased appeal aimed at community relations. With this invocation of a δαιδάλεα φόρμιγξ the poet lets his medium deliver the message: "If you will only welcome home Damophilos, you will enjoy the kind of poetry you now hear, and that I have taught him."

The epic associations of the expression, and the unusual social circumstances of its appearance in the epinician ode, justify this elaborate interpretation. The qualities attributed to the lyre in a single adjective are both heroic and prestigious, appreciated by wise citizens, σοφοί πολῖται. But ultimately the compliment derives from the poet's art, a genre embellished by Pindar through special applications of δαιδάλλειν.

On five occasions, Pindar employs a different form of this rare verb. Twice in *Olympian* 1 he turns to it, once as a participle (30):

> ἦ θαύματα πολλά, καί πού τι καὶ βροτῶν
> φάτις ὑπὲρ τὸν ἀλαθή λόγον
> δεδαιδαλμένοι ψεύδεσι ποικίλοις
> ἐξαπατῶντι μῦθοι.

> Truly there are many wonders, and especially where there is
> some report of mortals beyond the truthful account
> in colorfully elaborated lies
> with a deceiving story.

As in Bacchylides's ὑψιδαίδαλτος, the poet introduces the role of an agent through a deverbative form, here a perfect participle to express "tales crafted with colorful falsehoods," a poet's own description of mythological narrative. He redeems this pejorative image of art-as-deception by interjecting χάρις δέ, "but grace . . . ," in the next line, a traditional Homeric praise that rescues what is ἄπιστος, "untrustworthy," to make it πιστός, "trusted."

Later in the same ode, Pindar introduces the future infinitive of the same verb, promising to δαιδαλωσέμεν, to ornament the ἴδρις (wisdom) and δύναμις (strength) of Hieron in "folds of song." Once again, the metaphor derives from Homer, where the "folds" of Achilles's shield attracted multiple forms of δαιδάλλειν and inspired Pindar's juxtaposition.[20] But the -οω form of the verb is unique, and the epic future infinitive a Pindaric affectation. Together the two verb forms in a single ode demonstrate how Pindar adopted the language of art to the activity of the poet.[21]

He experiments with the participle again in *Nemean* 11, a brief ode celebrating not an athletic victory but the inauguration of a πρύτανις from Tenedos. Pindar predicts Aristagoras's reputation will be celebrated in two ways, on the lips of his fellow citizens and in song (17–18):

> ἐν λόγοις δ᾽ ἀστῶν ἀγαθοῖσιν ἐπαινεῖσθαι χρεών
> καὶ μελιγδούποισι δαιδαλθέντα μελίζεν ἀοιδαῖς.

> In the fine words of citizens he must be praised
> and he must be celebrated in song, in sweet-sounding verses.

Here, the passive participle makes the ode's honoree the object of poetic ornament: "he must be adorned with sweet songs." The expression reflects Pindar's own poem as well as an exhortation for Tenedos to carry on the tradition of craftsmanship.

In the final strophe of *Olympian* 5 (17–22), Pindar appeals directly to Zeus:

> Σωτὴρ ὑψινεφὲς Ζεῦ, Κρόνιόν τε ναίων λόφον
> τιμῶν τ᾽ Ἀλφεὸν εὐρὺ ῥέοντα Ἰδαῖόν τε σεμνὸν ἄντρον,
> ἱκέτας σέθεν ἔρχομαι Λυδίοις ἀπύων ἐν αὐλοῖς,
> αἰτήσων πόλιν εὐανορίαισι τάνδε κλυταῖς
> δαιδάλλειν, σέ τ᾽, Ὀλυμπιόνικε, Ποσειδανίοισιν ἵπποις,
> ἐπιτερπόμενον φέρειν γῆρας.

> Savior Zeus, with clouds on high, at home on the hill of Kronos,
> honoring the wide, flowing Alpheios and the sacred cave of Ida
> I come to you as a suppliant, speaking to Lydian flutes,
> begging you to celebrate this city of fine men;
> you, victor of Olympia, with the horses of Poseidon
> enjoy the reward of old age.

This time, the poet requests Zeus to grant the city fame, where δαιδάλλειν describes Zeus's favor and generosity to the city in the form of the ornament of fame, a divine complement to the poet's favor through song. The same kind of metaphor, where δαιδάλλειν indicates the acquisition of favorable properties, praises Theron of Akragas in *Olympian* 2.53:

> ὁ μὰν πλοῦτος ἀρεταῖς δεδαιδαλμένος
> φέρει τῶν τε καὶ τῶν

---

[20] D. Gerber, *Pindar's Olympian One: A Commentary* (Toronto, 1982), 158–60.

[21] Philipp, *Tektonon Daidala*, 37ff.; Nagy, *Best of the* Achaeans, 299–300. Cf. R. Harriott, *Poetry and Criticism before Plato* (London, 1969), chap. 5; J. Svenbro, *La parole et le marbre*, 186–212.

καιρὸν βαθεῖαν ὑπέχων μέριμναν ἀβροτέραν,
ἀστὴρ ἀρίζηλος, ἐτυμώτατον
ἀνδρὶ φέγγος.

For wealth amplified by virtues
also brings opportunity for other things;
it offers a deep cushion against cares,
bright as a star, the truest light
for a man.

Once again, the perfect participle is popular with Pindar: "wealth adorned with virtues" flatters prosperity with natural excellence that makes a man a star.

Throughout these appearances in verb form, δαιδάλλειν remains weak as a living verb describing physical activity, a weakness exploited for its metaphysical potential by Pindar. It is no surprise to discover how readily he applies the words to his own art, poetry, given both Pindar's self-conscious artistry and the Indo-European tradition where the language for poetry derives from the vocabulary of carpentry and craftsmanship.[22] Elsewhere, Pindar compares himself to a sculptor, as in the opening of *Nemean* 5:

Οὐκ ἀνδριαντοποιός εἰμ᾽, ὥστ᾽ ἐλινύσοντα ἐργά-
ζεσθαι ἀγάλματ᾽ ἐπ᾽ αὐτᾶς βαθμίδος
ἑσταότ᾽.

I am not a maker of statues, one to fashion
images that stand on the same base
unmoving.

Instead, the poet makes works that travel: poems that leave their isle of performance, departing from Aigina by boat, on the lips of singers and audience. His contrast of mobile and immobile images plays on the claim of statues that celebrate their size, base, and monolithism, as in the famous inscription on the base of the colossal "Apollo" of Delos, which boasts: τοῦ αὐτοῦ λίθου εἰμί, ἀνδρίας καὶ τὸ σφέλας: "I am of the same [piece of] stone, both the statue and the base."[23] In a related artistic vein, *Olympian* 6 begins with an elaborate architectural metaphor:

[22] Nagy, *Best of the Achaeans*, 298–300, on Greek and Vedic word patterns shared by poetry and carpentry, including the name of Homer himself; R. Schmitt, *Dichtung und Dichtersprache in indogermanischer Zeit* (Wiesbaden, 1967), 296–98; Vermeule, in *Troy and the Trojan War*, 86–87.

[23] P. Courbin, "L'inscription archaique du colosse naxien de Délos," in *Mélanges Helléniques offerts à Georges Daux* (Paris, 1974), 57–66, argues that the inscription makes a separate claim for its two monolithic parts, not that they belong to the same original block. More recently, see P. Bruneau, "Deliaca 55. Une idée de plus sur l'inscription archaïque de la base du Colosse," *BCH* 112 (1988) 577–82; F. Chamoux, "L'épigramme du Colosse des Naxiens à Delos," *BCH* 114 (1990) 185–86.

Χρυσέας ὑποστάσαντες εὐ-
τειχεῖ προθύρῳ θαλάμου
κίονας ὡς ὅτε θαητὸν μέγαρον
πάξομεν. ἀρχομένου δ᾽ ἔργου πρόσωπον
χρὴ θέμεν τηλαυγές.

As if placing golden columns below
the well-built porch of a chamber,
let us build, like a spectacular palace.
A masterpiece, once begun, needs a facade
to be placed, shining afar.

Pindar's metaphors of this nature borrow chiefly from the monumental arts, and this comparison confirms the function of columns in Greek architecture, where they enhance the visibility of a monument rather than serve practical or structural purposes. But subtler vocabulary, including words by then almost esoteric or exclusive to poetry, like δαιδάλλειν, held a natural attraction for a poet of subtle and self-conscious intricacy. The Homeric passages where that verb indicates the craftsmanship of a god or hero, alone, predestined its service for the noblest of the archaic arts, poetry.[24] Yet nowhere does Pindar conjure up Daidalos the artist (with the unlikely exception of *Nemean* 4.59), who owes his renaissance in the fifth century to sponsors outside poetry (Chapter 8). But through his fertile variations on this epic word-pattern, Pindar bears witness to the archaic function of these words in two critical domains: religion and poetry.

For parallel to their lives in poetry, δαιδαλ- words enter two fertile traditions—mythology and religion—for the first time in the archaic period. Legends about the craftsman became popular in the archaic period, according to a few eloquent documents (discussed in Chapter 8). More fascinating is the emergence of the adjectival forms of his name as ritual epithets for Greek deities and in votive formulas, a development closely linked to the evolution of poetic language into the terminology of Greek religion. This cult phenomenon is sustained, if not initiated, in poetry, where familiar epithets are applied to new priorities: the contents of Greek sanctuaries. Both innovations, religious and mythological, appear in widely dispersed areas of the Greek world and point to the role of poetry (and sanctuaries) as a medium in distributing new functions for the familiar in the archaic period. Its manifestations are not abundant but are linked in a diachronic tradition of *Kunstsprache* as *Kultsprache* that is maintained with affection, as an archaism, until the demise of pagan sanctuaries.

In poetry, adjectives derived from δαιδαλ- qualify temples, altars, and dedications in

---

[24] On Pindar's metaphors from art and architecture, see Philipp, *Tektonon Daidala*, 20, 37–38; Nagy, *Best of the Achaeans*, 298–300; Ford, "Early Greek Terms for Poetry," 326–28.

the odes of Pindar and Bacchylides. A votive inscription of the archaic period completes this liturgy by invoking a deity by this epithet, alone. This epigraphic contribution is provided on a bronze statuette of a peplos-clad kore from Mazi in Elis, now in Boston (Figure 5).[25] The figure represented, cast solid on a three-stepped base, seems to be the goddess Artemis, for she holds a bow in her left hand, but the Lakonian inscription running from right foot to right hip dedicates her from Chimaridas to ΔΑΙΔΑΛΕΙΑ.[26] The Lakonian letters match the Lakonian style of this bronze and seem to represent a Lakonian dedication to a goddess whose appearance resembles Artemis but whose epithet sufficed to identify her. The statuette's provenance and its inscription are both appropriate to archaic Spartan activity. Lakonian tiles and pottery were as widely distributed in the Peloponnese as was Spartan power, for they are common at Olympia and in remoter Arkadia.[27] In liturgical terms, the epithet as name for the goddess Artemis matches the Lakonian appellation "Ortheia" for a goddess ultimately identified with Artemis, but originally a distinct deity in the archaic period, not only in Sparta but on Mount Kotilion in Arkadia.[28] More elusive than Ortheia is the origin and meaning of the epithet δαιδαλεῖα, a personal possessive form derived from a proper name, like the Mycenaean da-da-re-jo- (explored in Chapter 4) , and not attested in Greek literature before a Euripidean fragment (Chapter 3 and Part III). The adjective would not seem to qualify a cult statue as the work of Daidalos or as endowed with aesthetic qualities conveyed by δαιδάλεος, δαίδαλον, or πολυδαίδαλος in poetry, although some have suggested that an aspect of such a statue (its clothing or lifelike qualities) is emphasized.[29] Instead, the epithet seems to have become formulaic for certain statues of goddesses, with an impact primarily ritual, beyond praise or other purely poetic functions. The process by which poetic language developed into religious formula emerges more clearly in the Boiotian counterpart to this Peloponnesian "Daidaleia," a counterpart that testifies to the reach of poetic tradition in distant areas of the archaic Greek world.

[25] Boston, Museum of Fine Arts B 2819; Richter, *Korai*, figs. 456–59; M. Comstock and C. C. Vermeule *Greek, Etruscan and Roman Bronzes in the Museum of Fine Arts, Boston* (Greenwich, Conn., 1971), 20–22, no. 19; F. Charbonneaux, *Les bronzes grecs* (Paris, 1958), 70; Frontisi-Ducroux, *Dédale*, fig. 6, 118–20. F. Brommer, "Gott oder Mensch," *JdI* 101 (1986) 39–40 n. 22.

[26] Jeffery, *LSAG*, 22, pl. 39; Richter cites Guarducci for a date in the last quarter of the sixth century B.C.: *Korai*, 187 n. 144.

[27] Lakonian roof on the temple of Hera at Olympia: A. Mallwitz, "Ein Scheibenakroter aus Olympia," *AthMitt* 83 (1968) 124–46; Lakonian tiles and pottery at the temples of Artemis and Apollo at Bassae and the Lykaion sanctuaries: F. A. Cooper, *The Temple of Apollo at Bassai* (Ph.D. diss., University of Pennsylvania, 1970; New York, 1978), 68–71, esp. 70 n. 10; N. K. Cooper, *The Development of Roof Revetment in the Peloponnese* (Göteborg, 1988), chap. 4.

[28] Ortheia is never called Artemis at Sparta until the Roman period and is addressed separately: e.g. Ἀρτέμι τᾷ Κοτιλεῷ καὶ τᾷ Ὀρθίᾳ in a fourth-century manumission inscription from Bassai (*IG* IV², 429): F. Cooper, "Two Inscriptions from Bassai," *Hesperia* 44 (1975) 224–33. For the Lakonian cult of (Artemis) Ortheia and its Near Eastern origins, see Carter, *AJA* 91 (1987) 375 n. 102; and my Chapter 5.

[29] Frontisi-Ducroux, *Dédale*, 118–20.

Sources of the Roman period provide detailed information about the Plataian festival for Hera involving multiple cult images called Δαίδαλα. These statues are cut from oak trees at festival occasions, to be burned in a holocaust of offerings on a pyre, along with sacrificial victims for Zeus and Hera.[30] The material for the statues comes from a special stand of oak trees at Alalkomene, presumably a sacred grove, a local cult element incorporated into this Boiotian festival.[31] The existence of two separate festivals—the Lesser and Greater Daidala—seems to correspond to Plataian and Panboiotian rituals, respectively, the latter the result of syncretism in the fourth century.[32] More recently, historical evidence for a date prior to the fourth century for the oldest elements of the festival has been adduced for a classical date.[33] The evidence of archaeology and comparative religion suggests much older origins for this ritual, probably in the Bronze Age and under the influence of Near Eastern practices. In particular, the manufacture of multiple images of women, with an emphasis on their nubile qualities, corresponds to the discoveries at Bronze Age Kea (Ayia Irini), where dozens of female statues in clay, many lifesized, formed part of some ritual now little understood.[34] Elsewhere in Bronze Age shrines, human figures are seen carrying what may be figurines in a procession, as in frescoes from the cult area at Mycenae.[35] Other examples of such practices may not have survived, especially if multiple images were made of perishable material such as wood or were regularly and ritually destroyed as in the Plataian rite. Burkert identifies such an image under conveyance in the "goddess on wheels" represented on an early Cretan pithos.[36] If this Cretan image is contemporary with the earliest festival in Boiotia, they

[30] The chief sources are Plutarch, *De Daedalis Plateensibus*, in Eusebius 3.1.3, 3.1.6, and Pausanias, 9.2.7, 9.3. L. Farnell, *Cults of the Greek States* (Oxford, 1896), 1:184ff.; Frontisi-Ducroux, *Dédale*, 193–216; Burkert, *Structure and History in Greek Mythology and Ritual*, 132–40; L. Prandi, "L'Heraion de Platea e la festa dei Δαίδαλα," in *Santuari e politica nel mondo antico*, ed. M. Sordi (Milan, 1983), 82–94. Donohue, *Xoana*, 134; 137–38, no. 108; 314–15.

[31] D. Birge, "Sacred Groves" (Ph.D diss., University of California at Berkeley, 1982); Prandi, in Sordi, *Santuari*, 87, calls this part of the ritual the oldest element, independent of the Hera cult.

[32] Schachter, *Cults of Boiotia*, 245–50; Frontisi-Ducroux, *Dédale*, 193–216. Donohue, *Xoana*, 145 n. 351, cautions against using antiquarian testimonia to reconstruct an authentic Plataian festival.

[33] Prandi, in Sordi, *Santuari*, 89–94, accepts only the entry of Thebes into the festival, after reconciliation with Plataia, as a fourth-century phenomenon. She argues that the ritual interval between celebra-

tions of the Greater Daidala (sixty years) which commemorates the estrangement of Plataia and Thebes corresponds to the interval between 447 and 386 in the fifth century, along with other "caratteri arcaici" (pp. 86–87, 91–92 n. 35).

[34] M. Caskey, "Ayia Irini, Kea: The Terracotta Statues and the Cult in the Temple," in *Sanctuaries and Cults in the Aegean Bronze Age*, 127–35; *Keos II.1: The Temple at Ayia Irini. The Statues* (Princeton, 1986).

[35] I. Kritseli-Providi, Οἱ Τοιχογραφίες τοῦ Θρησευτικοῦ Κέντρου τῶν Μυκήνων (Athens, 1982), 41–42, pl. 6a. Cf. N. Marinatos, "The Fresco from Room 31 at Mycenae: Problems of Method and Identification," in *Problems in Greek Prehistory*, 247–48, on other painted images sometimes identified as figurines.

[36] Burkert, *Greek Religion*, 23, 67; "Katagógia-Anagógia and the Goddess of Knossos," in *Early Greek Cult Practice*, 81–88, links the representation of a goddess on a ninth-century pithos from Knossos (J. N. Coldstream, "A Protogeometric Nature Goddess from Knossos," *BICS* 31 [1984] 93–104) not only with the

both appear in an area also connected with the Near East in legend, through the wanderings of Europa and Kadmos. Such activities—the dressing, bathing, and celebration of a cult image—represent a Greek religious practice probably derived from the Near East. Ritual texts specify that costly votive images were manufactured of materials like cedar and tamarisk wood, inlaid with gold and jewels, clothed, fed, and housed temporarily in a god's temple, only to be sacrificed (literally decapitated) and immolated on a pyre before the god.[37] The formation of Greek cult practices in the Late Bronze Age, under Near Eastern influence, is explored in greater detail in Chapters 5 and 6. A rite like the Plataian Daidala festival is likely to have its origins in the Bronze Age; in the archaic period, the terminology attending that festival reveals the emergence of Greek religious language in its poetic dimensions.

The name of the festival, in the various sources, introduces questions of terminology in art and ritual specific to the δαιδαλ- family of words. "Daidala" represents first of all the name of the festival, a term greatly expanded from an epithet for a specific deity as on the Mazi statuette. As a neuter plural (common) noun it also refers to the wooden images, according to the testimony of Pausanias (9.3.2):

Δαίδαλα ἑορτὴν ἄγουσιν, ὅτι οἱ πάλαι τὰ ξόανα ἐκάλουν δαίδαλα. ἐκάλουν δὲ ἐμοὶ δοκεῖν πρότερον ἔτι ἢ Δαίδαλος ὁ Παλαμάονος ἐγένετο Ἀθήνησι, τούτῳ δὲ ὕστερον ἀπὸ τῶν δαιδάλων ἐπίκλησιν γενέθαι δοκῶ καί οὐκ ἐκ γενετῆς τεθῆναι τὸ ὄνομα.

They conduct the festival called "Daidala," because long ago they used to call *xoana*, "daidala." And I think they called them so even before Daidalos, the son of Palamaon, was born in Athens, and I think that he later took the name from the statues, and was not born with this name.

Aside from the light his comments shed on the Athenian genealogy of Daidalos (Chapter 9), Pausanias proposes an important, if theoretical, connection between δαίδαλα and ξόανα, the latter a term he uses more frequently and consistently than any other ancient author. His own antiquarian fascination with wooden statues of gods, to which he consistently applies the term ξόανον, presumes its authority as an archaizing term, whereas neither statue nor his name for them represents a sculptural tradition attested in artifacts.[38] But however simplistic his equation of δαίδαλον, a traditional

Boiotian festival but with Homeric Daidalos and the Mycenaean place name *da-da-re-jo* attested in the tablets from Knossos.

[37] Such a rite is described in an Akkadian ritual text for a New Year's festival in Babylon: *ANET* 330–34; cf. I. Romano, "Early Greek Cult Images and Cult Practices," in *Early Greek Cult Practice*, 133.

[38] F. M. Bennett, "Primitive Wooden Statues which Pausanias Saw in Greece," *CW* 10 (1917) 82–86; "A Study of the Word ΞΟΑΝΟΝ," *AJA* 21 (1917) 8–21; Donohue, *Xoana*, 140–47; Burkert, *Structure and History in Greek Mythology and Ritual*, 132, accepts δαί-

term in this Boiotian ritual, with his own artificially ancient ξόανον, Pausanias derives an accurate conclusion by accident, in admitting that the proper name, "Daidalos," is more recent than the word attached to festival and statues. A similar process inspired the artist's name in Homer, as argued in Chapter 1. Pausanias recognizes the antiquity of the term relative to the "historical" Greek sculptor, although he testifies elsewhere to the family, pupils, and output of Daidalos (Part 3).

A few sentences later, Pausanias connects festival name and statues in contemporary usage. In a procedure that must derive from images of birds sitting on sacred trees, as on the pithos from Crete, the ritual selection of trees for statue wood begins by attracting crows with bait in a sacred wood:

ἐφ᾽ οὗ δ᾽ ἂν καθεστῇ, τεμόντες ποιοῦσιν ἀπὸ τούτου τὸ δαίδαλον. δαίδαλον γὰρ δὴ καὶ τὸ ξόανον αὐτὸ ὀνομάζουσι.

Wherever [the birds] may alight, cutting down that tree they make the *daidalon* from it and they call by "daidalon" the statue (*xoanon*) itself.

In this crucial statement, Pausanias equates his term, ξόανον, with the Boiotian one apparently in use at the time he investigates the ritual. This provides more useful information than his theoretical observation that "the ancients used to call *xoana*, 'daidala' "; here he testifies that the term was functional in rites of the second century A.D.

That the epithet expresses ritual concerns and not "ancient" technical terms for statues is supported by Plutarch, who records a familiar type of *aition*, an εὐηθέστερον μῦθον, to explain this festival (cf. Eusebius, *Praeparatio Evangelica* 3.1.6). According to his account, Zeus dressed up a wooden image, cut from the same oak grove where the Plataians obtain their festival images, as a false bride to provoke his alienated wife into a confrontation. The trick works: Hera descends from Kithairon, discovers that her jealousy was wasted on a wooden rival, and burns it in celebration of their happy marital reconciliation.

This legend justifies in local terms a marriage ritual, or *Hierogamia*, originally devoted to Plataian Hera before Panboiotian syncretism. Plutarch specifies which aspect of this colorful story attracted the term Δαίδαλα in his *aition*, which ignores the generic term δαίδαλον observed in use by Pausanias (*De Daedalis Plateensibus* 6 = Eusebius, 3.1.85 c–d). On the advice of Alalkomenes (an obvious personification of the sacred grove), Zeus learns

ὡς ἐξαπατητέον τὴν Ἥραν, σκηψάμενον γαμεῖν ἑτάραν. Συνεργοῦντος δὲ τοῦ Ἀλαλκομένους, κρύφα τεμόντας αὐτοὺς εὐκτέανον καὶ παγκάλην δρῦν μορφῶσαί τε αὐτὴν καὶ καταστεῖλαι νυμφικῶς, Δαιδάλην προσαγορεύσαντας· εἶτα οὕτω ἀνα-

---

δαλον as the "Greek word for roughly carved wooden image" but seems to derive this from Pau-   sanias.

μέλπεσθαι μέν τὸν ὑμέναιον, λουτρὰ δὲ κομίζειν τὰς Τριτωνίδας νύμφας, αὐλοὺς δὲ καὶ κώμους τὴν Βοιωτίαν παρασχεῖν.

Hera is to be deceived, by [Zeus] pretending to marry another woman. With the help of Alalkomenes, secretly cutting down a well-endowed and perfect tree, [they] shaped it into a woman and dressed it up like a bride, addressing it as "Daidale." Then [they] sang the wedding hymn, and the daughters of Triton brought bath water, and Boiotia provided flute-playing and dances.

The story told by Plutarch is sprinkled with eponymous figures, chief among whom is Δαιδάλη herself, a false bride adorned and celebrated with all the trappings of Greek marriage rites. She represents a mythological alternative to the bridal figure identified in Pausanias's account as the seated image of Νυμφευομένη, "Bride," a work of the sculptor Kallimachos (9.2.7) in the temple of Hera, the bride of Zeus he calls Πλάταια and the living γυναῖκα νυμφεύτρια who accompanies the wooden statues in the procession to Kithairon (9.3.4).[39] Δαιδάλη is also the feminine reflex of Δαίδαλος in Homer: an eponymous personification of a traditional epithet, here motivated by ritual rather than poetry.[40] Her manufacture and function suggest that the story recorded by Plutarch was enriched, perhaps with a touch of local pride, by the myth of Pandora as narrated in the poems of the Boiotian poet, Hesiod. For Pandora, too, is a false bride, designed by the gods to deceive, adorned by them, and given a name that derives from the motivation for her manufacture. And linking Pandora and Daidala is the host of δαιδαλ- words, applied by Hesiod to ornament his creation, serving as a ritual name for statues in Boiotia that beg and receive a myth with manifest influence from "native" poetry. In a phenomenon rare but by no means unique to Greek tradition, myth and cult derive from a common linguistic and thematic source older than epic itself, then cross-fertilize each other in an exchange between religious formula and personifying imagination.[41]

Whether the Plataian ritual itself derives from the story of Pandora is unlikely. Only the narrative justification familiar to Plutarch betrays a conscious debt to the Hesiodic tradition, and myth rarely precedes ritual in such a straightforward manner. But Pandora plays an important role in later theories about Greek sculpture and its origins, and her role as feminine trap is particularly close to the Boiotian marriage ritual, reinforced by the overlap in δαίδαλα nomenclature.

Beyond the *hieros gamos* rite, the application of the term to a statue reflects the same transformation of poetic categories into religious ones that explains the name of Δαι-

---

[39] As argued by A. Bergren, "Helen's Web: Time and Tableau in the *Iliad*," *Helios* 7 (1980) 27–28, the "Bride" also represents a marriage rite whose inversion is the Homeric Διὸς ἀπάτη.

[40] On the complex relationship between myth and ritual, see Burkert, *Structure and History in Greek Mythology and Ritual*, 1–58; see 132–34, on the Boiotian Daidala ritual.

[41] For a similar phenomenon in the realm of heroes, see Nagy, *Best of the Achaeans*, 67–210.

δαλεῖα from Mazi. The family of δαιδαλ- words experiences the same migration attested for the word ξόανον, which evolves from "intricate and luxurious work, with an Eastern cast of opulence," to a more restricted religious meaning in the context of divine imagery.[42] On the level of comparative religion and linguistics, this development is fundamental to Greek and Indo-European poetics, and appears in other semantic domains of the early Greek lexicon.[43] Within Greek culture, it demonstrates the incorporation of the exotic and Oriental into a cultural formula, even an intellectual concept. This is partly a function of history, as will be argued presently (Part IV). But this transformation of imported into native culture is seen by many as the most characteristic, if most perplexing, activity of the Greek mind: the process of "Orientalizing" involves an attempt to understand, to adopt the unknown to a familiar identity or active function within the home culture. The myth of the Plataian Daidala, for example, explains a practice borrowed from the Near East as a native story; the name of the ritual statue(s) and mythological "bride" has its own Eastern correspondences, as explored in Chapter 4, but lends the authority of tradition derived from epic literature. When Homeric epithets become cult titles of deities, they obey the same procedures; thus Artemis's title on the votive bronze statuette (Figure 5) may reflect a particular cult image in Lakonia that bore that title.

Within the historical background specific to this study, the evolution of δαίδαλον suggests a process that transforms the Mycenaean and epic heritage, a poetic and visual domain, to suit the archaic revision of the world in terms of religion. Ultimately this accounts for the religious functions absorbed by Daidalos and his linguistic cognates posterior to their epic generation. The imagery and terminology of prehistoric Greek religion emerged as late and obscure phenomena in a civilization whose monumental efforts were chiefly devoted to defense and death, palaces and luxuries, until the latest Bronze Age.[44] In the centuries that followed, palace yielded to *polis*, poetry as a performance art found a new home in sanctuaries and not just banquet halls, and poetic language found new functions in new contexts. In the archaic culture that evolved from prehistoric survivals, what was aesthetic and poetic fed the growing complexity of a religious imagination and its new creations —architecture and sculpture. Thus Daidalos, originally a poetic protagonist for visual wonders, enters the realm of religious art as does much epic stock, and his adjectives spread to altars, temples, votives, and statues, like these of a Peloponnesian Artemis and a Boiotian bride.

---

[42] According to the insightful analysis of Donohue, *Xoana*, 30–32.

[43] Leumann, *Homerische Wörter*, 131–33, on the Plataian δαίδαλα as a specialized meaning derived from poetic language; 326–29, on the afterlife of Homeric diction in Greek legal and cult expressions; Schmitt *Dichtung und Dichtersprache*, 195–284.

[44] Renfrew, *Archaeology of Cult*, 1–4, on the misidentification of cult in prehistoric Greece; cf. essays by Dietrich and Coldstream cited in Chapter 1, n. 65, on the late entry of divine image to the Greek imagination (see Chapter 5 on the archaeology of cult in the Late Bronze Age).

Thus modest archaic testimonia document this migration of poetic words to cult equipment, a transfer that ultimately makes of a prehistoric technician a sculptor of ancient or magic statues. Where historical events enriched an epic poetic tradition, activity in art survived on the level of cult far more complex than in prehistoric culture. And those archaic associations with cult lasted as an insignia of religious power, as in the archaizing expressions popular in epigrams of the Greek anthology, until the last oracular response of pagan antiquity:[45]

> εἴρατε τῷ βασιλεῖ· χαμαὶ πέσε δαίδαλος αὐλά
> οὐκέτι Φοῖβος ἔχει καλύβαν, οὐ μάντιδα δάφνην,
> οὐ παγὰν λαλέουσαν, ἀπέσβετο καὶ λάλον ὕδωρ.

> Go and tell the king: fallen is the elaborate hall,
> no longer does Phoibos have his shrine, nor the prophetic laurel,
> no longer the voiced spring; extinguished is the babbling water.

[45] Traditionally delivered to the Emperor Julian the Apostate by Oribasius but perhaps a forgery of the later fourth century A.D: Kedrenos 1.532; *Anthologia Graeca* 687; T. Gregory, "Julian and the Last Oracle at Delphi," *GRBS* 24 (1983) 355–66, with earlier references; A. Markopoulos, "Kedrenos, Pseudo-Symeon and the Last Oracle of Delphi," *GRBS* 26 (1985) 207–10.

CHAPTER 3

Daidala in Classical and European Literature

BY THE END OF the archaic period, the epic root δαιδαλ- had become specialized to a number of poetic and ritual functions, emphasizing properties in narrative, aesthetics, and cult. Once established, these dimensions hardly multiplied in classical and later poetry but were only repeated and refined with variations, often with a deliberately archaizing effect.

Aeschylus uses such a word only once in his surviving plays, where it enjoys an effect exaggerated by its artificial isolation. In the closing play of the *Oresteia* trilogy, Apollo pleads Orestes' case with the chorus of Furies by reminding them of Klytemnestra's gruesome deed (*Eumenides* 631–35):

> ἀπὸ στρατείας γάρ νιν ἠμποληκότα
> τὰ πλεῖστ' ἄμεινον' εὔφροσιν δεδεγμέη
> δροίτῃ, περῶντι λουτρὰ, κἀπὶ τερμάτι
> φᾶρος περεσκήνωσεν, ἐν δ' ἀτέρμονι
> κόπτει πεδήσασ' ἄνδρα δαιδάλῳ πέπλῳ.

> For him, back from the campaign having won
> more things, better than worse, receiving with glad heart
> in the bath, at the edge of the tub,
> she pitched the robe like a tent, and trampling the man
> in its endless folds, the much-decorated robe, she cut him down.

The adjective represents a new formation (δαίδαλος instead of δαιδάλεος) typical of the poetic versatility of the word. In the context of the trilogy, these five lines recapitulate the elaborate prelude to murder in *Agamemnon* 930–75 and its ghastly execution, offstage. Throughout the play, from before Agamemnon's arrival home to the aftermath of the crime, the robe prepared for him by his wife is a dominant, even oppressive motif (cf. Figure 7).[1] It accumulates a profusion of motifs in all three plays. First introduced

[1] On the imagery of robe/net: E. Vermeule, "The Boston Oresteia Krater," *AJA* 70 (1966) 4, 6–7, 10–12, 20–21; A. Lebeck, "Imagery and Action in the Ores- teia," in *The Oresteia* (Washington, D.C., 1971), 59–73; A. Prag, *The Oresteia: Iconography and Narrative Traditions* (Warminster, 1985), 80–81, pl. 3;. E. Flin-

as πετάσματα, a "passage paved with purple" (πορφυρόστρωτος πόρος) for the triumphant returning king (909–10), it alarms Agamemnon as something foreign, barbarian, and an ἐπίφθονος πόρος (918–21) or "path provoking envy" which he fears to tread (923–25):

> ἐν ποικίλοις δὲ θνητὸν ὄντα κάλλεσιν
> βαίνειν ἐμοὶ μὲν οὐδαμῶς ἄνευ φόβου·
> λέγω κατ' ἄνδρα, μὴ θεόν, σέβειν ἐμέ.

> As a mortal, to tread colored cloths
> is something not without fear, for me.
> I say to honor me as a man, not a god.

Klytemnestra dwells with malicious pleasure on its splendid color and decoration (958–65), and Agamemnon finally yields to her flattery and his arrogance. Only Kassandra sees it vividly as the "net of Hades" (1115) and a trap (μηχάνημα) for the royal bull (1125–29), before the deed; afterward, Klytemnestra boasts of the success of her trap, calling the robe an ἄπειρον ἀμφίβληστρον, or "endless dragnet" (1382), as well as a πλοῦτον εἵματος κακόν or "wealth of woven evil" (1383), an oxymoron fulfilled now that the evil hidden in the robe's richness emerged in the slaughter. A similar juxtaposition, καλὸν κακόν, disguised the evil inside Pandora's beauty (*Theogony* 585) and is common to many poetic phenomena ultimately called δαιδάλεος, and the cumulative descriptions of the robe in the *Oresteia* almost make the adjective inevitable.

In the *Choephoroi*, Orestes and Elektra revive the motif of the robe and the same image of a net cast around a victim (ἀμφίβληστρον, the same word used at *Agamemnon* 1382) in their lament.[2] Later, Orestes displays the robe itself on stage, as evidence and justification for his revenge: no expression seems to satisfy its evil. He calls it μηχάνημα, δεσμόν ἀθλίῳ πατρὶ, and (997–1000):

> τί νιν προσείπω, κἂν τύχω μάλ' εὐστομῶν;
> ἄγρευμα θηρός, ἢ νεκροῦ ποδένδυτον
> δροίτης κατασκήνωμα; δίκτυον μὲν οὖν.
> ἄρκυν τ' ἂν εἴποις καὶ ποδιστῆρας πέπλους.

> What should I call it, and still speak well?
> A hunting trap for game, or shroud for a corpse,
> a shower curtain, finally a net.
> Call it a trap, as a robe entangling the feet.

When the expression δαιδάλεος πέπλος finally appears in *Eumenides* 635, the adjective recapitulates the peculiar confrontation of splendor and horror that made it such an

---

toff, "The Treading of the Cloth," *QUCC* 25 (1987) 119–30.

[2] *Choephoroi* 491–98; A. F. Garvie, *Choephoroi* (Oxford, 1986), on lines 491–92.

obsession in earlier scenes. The combination of qualities thus characterized repeats those in Pandora's appearance, the coffin-cradle of Perseus, the weapon whose loss almost cost Peleus his life, and other narrative equipment singled out by δαιδάλεος. Rose's translation of the Aeschylean phrase as "fatal robe" best captures the dramatic properties of this garment, a motif elaborated if not invented by Aeschylus and which absorbed vase painters in a manner reflecting contemporary drama, much as did the chest of Perseus (Figure 7).[3] In recalling the robe long after its moments on stage, the adjective δαιδάλεος apparently has the power to remind the audience of the appearance of the robe and its fatal role in the tragedy. Years later, Euripides honors the motif in similar language in his Atreid dramas. Elektra alludes to the ἄπειρον ὕφασμα ("endless weaving") and δολίοις ἕρκεσιν ("deceitful snare") with which her mother killed her father (*Orestes* 25; *Elektra* 155), phrases that revive the same imagery, without the critical adjective.

Euripides does use variants of δαιδάλεος in a manner traditional to epic poetry, on two occasions. In his *Hekabe*, the chorus of captive women anticipates its fate in Greek hands (444–82). Among the future homes they fear, Athens occupies a prominent choice, no surprise in an Attic drama (466–71):

> ἢ Παλλάδος ἐν πόλει
> τᾶς καλλιδίφρου Ἀθαναίας ἐν κροκέῳ πέπλῳ
> ζεύξομαι ἄρματι πώλους, ἐν
> δαιδαλέαισι ποικίλλουσ' ἀνθοκρόκοισι πήναις, . . . ;

> or in the city of Pallas
> Athena of the beautiful throne, on a saffron peplos
> shall I yoke the foals to the chariot
> embroidering [them] in elaborate threads worked with flowers, . . . ?

Their vision mixes epic and Athenian ritual (much as in *Iliad* 6.269–310) as they contemplate the task of embroidering a scene of Athena's chariot and team on her peplos, a work of art over which Athenian girls toiled for four years before its presentation to the image of Athena Polias.[4] A Gigantomachy scene is described on the peplos in some ancient sources, and seems intended in this passage where Athena is visualized in a

---

[3] Vermeule, in *AJA* 70 (1966) 4, 7, 19, 21, on the motif as an invention of Aeschylus and its impact on vase painters; O. Touchefeu, "Agamemnon," *LIMC* I:1, 271–72, nos. 88–89, for early classical illustrations. Fitzgerald's translation of Homeric δόλον (*Odyssey* 4.92) as "web" has Homer anticipate the Aeschylean motif.

[4] On the *peplos*, see scholia to Euripides, *Hekabe*

468; Aristophanes, *Birds* 827, *Knights* 563; Lucian, *Nigrinus* 53; Pollux, 7.50; *IG* II² 1034, 98/7 B.C. on the ἐργαστῖναι, Strattis Frag. 30. For the ceremony on the Parthenon frieze, see W. Gauer, "Was geschieht mit dem Peplos?" in *Parthenon-Kongress Basel*, 1:220–29. T. Schäfer, "Diphroi und Peplos auf dem Parthenon: Zur Kultpraxis bei den Panathenäen," *AthMitt* 105 (1987) 185–212.

chariot—that is, in battle. In the Homeric prototype for this scene, Hekabe selects such a πέπλος from among her Sidonian treasures, those παμποίκιλα ἔργα (6.289) brought back by Paris from a Levantine detour on his leisurely return to Troy with Helen. Hekabe's votive selection was (294–95):

> ὅς κάλλιστος ἔην ποικίλμασιν ἠδὲ μέγιστος
> ἀστὴρ δ᾽ ὣς ἀπέλαμπεν. ἔκειτο δὲ νείατος ἄλλων.

> The one that was most beautiful and greatest of the wovens
> and it shone like a star. It lay there, last of all.

This Homeric robe attracts a cluster of epic compliments: to its size and decoration and its Sidonian manufacture, all properties traditional to epic praise and typically compounded in the poet's efforts to do justice to an offering worthy of Troy's chief goddess. But one epithet is conspicuously absent: δαιδάλεος. In Euripides' exploitation of the passage for his Trojan women and their Athenian goddess, he borrows ποίκιλος (as a verb) and adds δαιδάλεος. Other epic passages may have contributed to the ode in the *Hekabe*: the "arming" of Hera in *Iliad* 14 provides the verb ζεύξομαι (178–79) that figures in *Hekabe* 469 and the noun form δαίδαλα represents the handiwork of Athena adorning Hera, like the πολυδαίδαλος ἱστός on which she instructs Pandora (*Works and Days* 64). In a single phrase, Euripides pays homage to epic characterizations of Athena, Hera, and Pandora, as well as to the quality of the Panathenaic peploi of his day.

Euripides indicates the same affection for epic language in another choral passage, in the parodos of the *Iphigeneia in Aulis* (216–26):

> ὁ δὲ διφρηλάτας ἐβόατ᾽
> Εὔμηλος Φερητιάδας,
> ᾧ καλλίστους ἰδόμαν
> χρυσοδαιδάλτους στομίοις
> πώλους κέντρῳ θεινομένους,
> τοὺς μὲν μέσους ζυγίους,
> λευκοστίκτῳ τριχὶ βαλιοὺς
> τούς δ᾽ ἔξω σειροφόρους,
> ἀντήρεις καμπαῖσι δρόμων,
> πυρσότριχας, μονόχαλα, δ᾽ ὑπὸ σφυρά
> ποικιλοδέρμονας.

> And the charioteer cried out
> Eumelos, the son of Pheretos,
> whose handsome horses I saw
> with reins decorated with gold,

> driven with the goad,
> the ones yoked in the middle
> flecked with white foam on their mane,
> those yoked outside, the trace horses,
> at the opposite end of the racecourse,
> with shining manes, solid in hoof, and
> dappled under the fetlock.

The women of Chalkis, admiring the assembled Greek forces, dwell on Eumelos driving his χρυσοδαίδαλτοι Thessalian horses, presumably arrayed in elaborately decorated harness, much as cavalry equipment earned such adjectives in Homer (*Iliad* 17.448) and Pindar (*Pythian* 5.36; frag. 102). The adjective, a coinage unique to Euripides except for in mock prayer by a lovesick young man in Aristophanes (*Ekklesiazousai* 972), is of the variety indulged by Bacchylides, as in his χαλκοδαιδάλοισιν ἄσπισιν (frag. 2.2; see Chapter 2). Its appearance in a lyric passage of Attic drama reinforces the association of such words with lyric and epic language.

A third passage in Euripides uses the word δαίδαλον to praise a heroic weapon with a rich mythological pedigree: the club of Herakles. In a sentimental review of family memories before a dreaded end, Herakles' wife, Megara, reminds each of the hero's offspring of his father's legacy to him (*Herakles* 460–75). The eldest son was to receive Argos, the second son, Thebes and its traditional motif, the club (467–71):

> σὺ δ᾽ ἦσθα Θηβῶν τῶν φιλαρμάτων ἄναξ
> ἔγκληρα πεδία τἀμὰ γῆς κεκτημένος,
> ὡς ἐξέπειθες τὸν κατασπείραντά σε·
> ἐς δεξιάν τε σὴν ἀλεξητήριον
> ξύλον καθίει δαίδαλον, ψευδῆ δόσιν.

> You were to be lord of chariot-loving Thebes
> acquiring my inherited fields of the earth
> thus you persuaded him who sired you;
> in your right hand he used to put the protector,
> the elaborate wood, as a pretend gift.

Although the manuscript offers δαιδάλου (Δαιδάλου), the restoration of δαίδαλον makes better syntactic and narrative sense than "a false gift of Daidalos," as argued in the latest commentary on the tragedy.[5] In terms of Euripidean vocabulary, the word demonstrates tragic use of traditional language for magic weapons and for those with a

---

[5] Restored by Hermann; G. Bond, *Euripides' Herakles* (Oxford, 1981), 186; cf. the restoration of the adjective instead of the proper noun at Pindar *Nemian* 4.59 (pp. 47–48). The transmission of the name in manuscripts could well have been influenced by the legend and reputation of the craftsman in later times.

narrative history, as in epic and lyric diction. For δαίδαλος celebrates the club's famous adventures in the hands of Herakles, for whom it eventually functions as an identifying attribute in art. As a ψευδὴς δόσις to his young son, it represents a brief loan without heroic consequences. Like the ashen spear of Achilles, only a hero can wield it, and that hero has now disappeared with the club, not expected to return. Thus the ambiguities often marked by δαιδαλ- are vivid here, where Megara mourns an end soon to be reversed, and the club is doubly false in that she believes it has failed the hero, but in truth it will survive along with him. As in so many poetic passages, δαίδαλος marks a symbol rich in history and an immediate instrument in a dramatic setting.

The traditional uses of δαιδαλ- in Greek drama are powerful but few, given the extant corpus of Attic tragedy and comedy and the dramatic potential of these words. Sophokles, for example, never employed such words in his preserved works. But the vitality of these words is by no means diminished by the classical period, for they flourish in Hellenistic and classicizing poetry as a powerful allusion to epic and literary tradition. For Theokritos, such words epitomize a tribute to Homeric language and setting. In his first idyll, the famous κισσύβιον, Greek poetry's most explicit compliment to the analogy of art and verse, attracts a predictable δαίδαλμα (1.32–33):

> ἔντοσθεν δὲ γυνά, τι θεῶν δαίδαλμα, τέτυκται,
> ἀσκητὰ πέπλῳ τε καὶ ἄμπυκι.

> And inside the cup a woman, some marvel of the gods, is shaped,
> wonderfully wrought, complete with peplos and headband.

In this lavish description laced with motifs from epic forerunners—the shield of Achilles, the shield of Herakles, the manufacture of Pandora—one would expect epic diction to be lavished on a cup of largely imaginary properties.[6] It is the figure of the woman that is singled out as τι θεῶν δαίδαλμα, "some creation of the gods," in a phrase that evokes Hesiod's Pandora most vividly, as the ultimate artifice of the gods. The concentration of δαίδαλα surrounding her manufacture in Hesiod (see Chapter 1) and the debt of Theokritos and the Alexandrians, in general, to the poetry of Hesiod makes this a familiar relationship.[7]

Two other variations on the theme of δαίδαλα appear in the poems of Theokritos. In the epithalamion for Helen (Idyll 18), her skill at the loom is praised among the other attributes that make her Λακεδαίμονι κόσμος, "the toast of Sparta" (32–34):

[6] D. Halperin, Before Pastoral: Theocritus and the Ancient Tradition of Bucolic Poetry (New Haven, 1983), devotes an entire chapter to "Three Scenes on an Ivy-Cup," 161–89; bibliography on the κισσύβιον, 161 n. 50. Decades of comparison to Hellenistic relief vessels and other forms of Greek vases have left this cup better understood as a literary artifice.

[7] Halperin, Before Pastoral, 245–48; E. Simon, Pergamon und Hesiod (Mainz, 1975), on the influence of Alexandrian Hesiodic scholarship on Hellenistic iconography.

> οὐδέ τις ἐν ταλάρῳ πανίσδεται ἔργα τοιαῦτα,
> οὐδ' ἐνὶ δαιδάλεῳ πυκινώτερον ἄτριον ἱστῷ
> κερκίδι συμπλέξασα μακρῶν ἔταμ' ἐκ κελεόντων.

And no one produces such works from her knitting basket
nor cut a more closely woven cloth from the tall warp-threads
having woven it with the shuttle on the intricate loom.

Once again, the epic dimensions of this passage are explicit. In the *Odyssey* the queen of Sparta has a gold and silver knitting basket (τάλαρος) on wheels (4.131–32). Helen is introduced at the loom in the *Iliad*, weaving the story of the Trojan War as it unfolds around her, in an extraordinary passage where one would expect δαίδαλα (3.125–28).[8] The art of weaving distinguishes not only heroines like Helen and Penelope but artifices like Pandora, who learns from Athena πολυδαίδαλον ἱστὸν ὑφαίνειν (*Works and Days* 64), and respectable Athenian women as candidates for the privilege of weaving the Panathenaic peplos. The agreement between δαιδάλεος and ἱστός in the lines of Theokritos is closest to Hesiodic diction, both in the words themselves and in the emphasis on weaving as a necessary skill for an eligible bride.

The third use of δαιδαλ- in Theokritos applies it to a weapon, a traditional epic subject for the epithet. In the story of baby Herakles and his infant triumph over the two snakes (*Idyll* 24), Amphitryon springs up in the night at the alarm and arms himself, in a vignette abbreviated from epic arming scenes (42–45):

> δαιδάλεον δ' ὥρμασε μετὰ ξίφος, ὅ οἱ ὕπερθεν
> κλιντῆρος κεδρίνου περὶ πασσάλῳ αἰὲν ἄωρτο.
> ἤτοι ὅ γ' ὠριγνᾶτο νεοκλώστου τελαμῶνος,
> κουφίζων ἑτέρᾳ κολεόν, μέγα λώτινον ἔργον.

And he sprang up with his elaborate sword, the one that
always hung above the cedar bed from a peg.
Indeed he reached out for his newly woven quiver,
lifting up the scabbard with the other [hand], a great work of lotus.

As Gow points out in his commentary, the epic adjective is more common for armor itself rather than for a weapon like a sword, but at least since Pindar (*Nemean* 4.59) it qualifies weapons as well. Other elements of Amphitryon's gear are praised in description with formulaic compliments (μέγα ἔργον) but as an arming scene this passage is somewhat ironic, if not comic. For the infant hero has already defended himself against

---

[8] A. Bergren, "Helen's Web: Time and Tableau in the *Iliad*," *Helios* 7 (1980) 19–34; P. Klindienst Joplin, "The Voice of the Shuttle is Ours," *Stanford Review* of Literature 1, no. 1 (1984) 25–53, on women, weaving, and poetry; G. Kennedy, "Helen's Web Unraveled," *Arethusa* 19 (1986) 5–14.

the two snakes, without the help of his father or elaborate weapons. In this passage, δαιδάλεος fulfills its epic potential for ambiguity here, in that it promises powers in a weapon ultimately useless to the course of the narrative.

Such studied applications of epic words and functions perpetuate themselves in the works of classicizing poets of the Hellenistic and Roman periods, even generating a tradition of *daedala* in Latin literature. In later Greek poetry, forms of δαιδαλ- are naturally copious in archaizing epic like the *Dionysiaka* of Nonnos, where all forms of the root—δαιδάλεος, δαιδάλλω, δαίδαλμα, δαίδαλον, and πολυδαίδαλος—proliferate in association with armor, furniture, vessels, and textiles.[9] In hexameter, the adjectival form not only qualifies objects traditionally "daedalic," such as jewelry, but conveys a sense of the old-fashioned in art as well as archaism in poetry.[10] Similar words are common as archaisms in Manetho (2.320, 4.438, 6.421) and Quintus of Smyrna (1.141), but a few late uses reflect classical themes. These include Lucian's description of the statue of Knidian Aphrodite as a δαίδαλμα of Parian marble (*Amores* 13), introducing an episode where the statue inspires physical desire and even a passionate embrace that leaves its stain on the statue (15–16). This "magic" power indicates a classical topos appropriate to Daidalos (see, Chapter 8), not just an archaizing epithet. Poetic δαίδαλα are even present in the prose of Clement of Alexandria (*Protrepticus* 31; *Stromateis* 7.846), an author also concerned with the nature of statues and idolatry, without ever mentioning Daidalos himself.[11]

The religious function of *daidala*, as cult epithets or nouns for votives, appears simultaneously with their poetic functions around fifteen times in the Palatine Anthology.[12] In the same corpus, the artist's name, praised with an epithet as ἥρως, serves as a model for the skill of a painter named Kimon (*Anthologia Graeca* 16.84), in a poetic tradition kept alive since *Iliad* 18. In Latin, adjectives and common nouns formed on *daedalum* and *daedalus, -a, -um* are popular, especially in their more sophisticated metaphorical applications. Lucretius, for example, calls *tellus daedala* (1.7.228; cf. 5.234) as well as *carmina* (2.505), speech (*verborum daedala lingua*: 4.551), and statues (5.1451). Venantius invents a *Daedalicus manus* (10.11.17).

---

[9] W. Peek, *Lexikon zu den Dionysiaka des Nonnos*, vol. 1 (Hildesheim, 1968), 349–50; vol. 3 (Hildesheim, 1974), 364–65. A typical target for these words is the necklace of Harmonia (5.136): inspired by Penelope's gift from a suitor (*Odyssey* 18. 291ff.; see Chapter 1, text and n. 53), made by Hephaistos, and fateful in the future of Kadmos and his bride.

[10] As in the δαιδάλεοι χλιδῶνες of the Samians who also wear golden τέττιγες: Asios, frag. 13, Athenaeus, 12.525. C. M. Bowra, "Asius and the Old-fashioned Samians," *Hermes* 85 (1957) 393–94.

[11] *Protrepticus* 2.21P, 4.40P–43 P (note Eupalamos,

Dipoinos, and Skyllis), 4.44–45P; *Stromateis* 1.163.4–164.4, 5.14.717. Donohue, *Xoana*, 127–28, 132–33, 202–4, on Clement and his theories of idolatry developed under the influence of Jewish polemical scholarship in Alexandria.

[12] Adjectival forms for dedications: e.g. πολυδαί-δαλον δέπα (6.332), δαιδαλοέντα τρίποδα (6.344), or a καλὸν δαίδαλον for Arsinoe made by the gem-cutter Satyrios (9.776); δαιδαλόχειρ (6.204), δαιδα-λέη χείρ (9.826), and δαιδαλέοιο τεχνᾶς in metaphorical applications to artistry, also to raw materials χρυσὸς πολυδαίδαλος (11.332) as in *Odyssey* 13.11.

These self-conscious archaisms are accompanied by references to Daidalos himself, often in one and the same work. In the Greek Anthology, where poetic adjective forms are common, the artist appears as ἥρως Δαίδαλος (16.84). In the most celebrated example, Vergil calls Circe *daedala* (*Aeneid* 7.282), a predicate that conjures up all the baleful qualities of the word in an epithet for a witch, but he also devotes a long ekphrasis to the legend and art of Daidalos in Book 6 (14–23).[13] In this vivid pageant displayed at a turning point in the epic and career of Aeneas, Daidalos appears as both architect (6.19: *posuit immania templa*) and as artist who decorates the doors of his monument with figural scenes, involving relief or inlay work in gold (6.22: *effingere in auro*). Both talents could be derived from his achievement in *Iliad* 18, where architecture and figural scene are both conjured up in the word χορός. Other details of the passage allude to Homeric conventions, such as the expression *remigium alarum* (6.19), which maintains the poetic imagery of wings for oars promoted in Greek poetry.

In other words, Vergil's tribute to Daidalos could be inspired by the Greek epic tradition, alone, uncomplicated by classical and Hellenistic biography and art criticism (see Part III). In passages such as these, the eminently poetic nature of the traditions surrounding Daidalos still dominates and survives independently of academic speculation on sculpture and sculptors. In Latin literature at its most Greek moments, the coexistence of poetic vocabulary for art and the personification of those qualities is faithful to the original juxtaposition in Homer and to the circumstances of the artist's resurrection in classical thought (Part III).

The figure of Daidalos (*Daedalus*) held special appeal for Latin authors as a symbol of Greek art and as an artist who migrated to Italy in legend, and was popular in art in Italy since the fifth century (see Chapter 7). Thus his persona in Latin poetry, much as in Roman art, focuses on the invention of wings and the flight with Ikaros.[14] In particular, it is Ovid's allusions to the craftsman, his wings, and his flight with Ikaros, that survive antiquity with the greatest popularity in the Renaissance and modern times. In addition to the detailed story told in the *Metamorphoses* (8.183–235), the myth enters the discussion of another winged figure, Amor, whom the poet fancies himself capturing as Minos failed to capture Daidalos (*Ars Amatoria* 2.19–98). Finally, Ovid's exile inspired thoughts of other artists escaped from inhospitable political regimes and a longing for

[13] H. Rutledge, "Vergil's Daedalus," *CJ* 62 (1967) 309–11; "The Opening of *Aeneid* 6," *CJ* 67 (1971–1972) 110–15; J. Zarker, "Aeneas and Theseus in *Aeneid* 6," *CJ* 62 (1967) 220–26; Haft, "The Myth That Crete Became," 157–67; duBois, *History, Rhetorical Description and the Epic*, chap. 2; W. Fitzgerald, "Aeneas, Daedalus and the Labyrinth," *Arethusa* 17 (1984) 51–65. M. Paschalis, "The Unifying Theme of Daedalus' Sculptures on the Temple of Apollo Cumanus (Aen.

6.20–33)," *Vergilius* 32 (1986); M. J. Putnam, "Daedalus, Virgil and the End of Art," *AJP* 108 (1987) 173–98. Cf. Juvenal, 3.25; Silius Italicus, 12.85–103.

[14] Ovid, *Metamorphoses* 8.159; Horace, *Odes* 2.20.9–16: R. Carruba, "The White Swan and Daedalian Icarus," *Eranos* 80 (1982) 145–49. Roman painting: von Blanckenhagen, *RömMitt* 75 (1968) 106–43; P. Green, "The Flight Plan of Daedalus," *EchCl* 23 (1979) 30–35.

wings, this time for return (*Tristia* 2.105–6; 3.8.5–16; cf. 1.1.90 and 3.4.21). It is this romantic form of Daidalos and his son that survives in European art and literature.[15] Like all myths, that of Daidalos evolved as human interest did. Thus the story of flight captured the Christian imagination, once only angels and the Neo-Platonic soul (cf. Plato, *Phaedrus* 249d) sported wings. The modern exploration of flight maintains a fascination with the myth to the point of its reenactment as an experiment in human-powered flight.[16] The role of Daidalos as forger and sculptor, and his even more remote origins in early Greek poetry and mythology derived from Near Eastern traditions, wane as his aeronautical talents captivate the modern imagination. But the versatility of his talents promises future evolution of his story to keep pace with human ingenuity and inventions.

[15] N. Rudd, "Daedalus and Icarus (i) From Rome to the End of the Middle Ages," and "Daedalus and Icarus (ii) From the Renaissance to the Present Day," in *Ovid Renewed*, ed. C. Martindale (Cambridge, 1988), 1–54. C. F. Ahern, Jr., "Daedalus and Icarus in the *Ars Amatoria*," *HSCP* 92 (1989) 273–96, on exiled Ovid's identification with Daidalos.

[16] See *National Geographic* (July 1988) for a project sponsored by MIT and United Technologies, which completed a human-powered flight from Crete to Thera on April 23, 1988; G. Dorsey, *The Fullness of Wings: The Making of a New Daedalus* (New York, 1990).

· PART II ·

Daidalos and

Kadmos

CHAPTER 4

Da-da-re-jo and *Kothar-wa-Hasis*: From Ugarit to the Aegean

THE QUEST FOR THE ORIGINS and significance of Daidalos and δαίδαλα in the first chapter traced their earliest manifestations to Homeric poetry and its afterlife. But prehistoric epigraphic evidence—Late Bronze Age tablets in pre-Homeric Greek syllabic script—offers an ancestor for Daidalos in the Aegean tradition. Moreover, literary texts from Late Bronze Age Syria document a contemporary phenomenon and suggest a Near Eastern source for the Greek craftsman-god. The convergence of the Aegean and the Levant in a close and sustained pattern of commercial contacts supports an environment for intellectual transmission. Ultimately, the kinship of Daidalos and Kothar reflects shared traditions that promoted the emergence of Iron Age culture in the Eastern Mediterranean.

The language of Mycenaean Greek confirms the origin and survival of δαίδαλα as exclusively poetic words, independent of technical meanings. The evidence is negative: no trace of the adjective, verb, or common noun forms of this root survive amid the many detailed descriptions of furniture, jewelry, armor, and equestrian equipment that correspond to Homeric δαίδαλα. This absence is hardly a surprise, given the great distance between a bureaucratic shorthand devoted to itemized inventories, and the poetic world of objects never seen but praised. Even the eloquent Ta furniture tablets from Pylos, rich in -εσσα and -ειος adjectives that specify component details and in passive participles in -μενος that admit the role of the invisible craftsmen, ignore the root popular in poetry. Modern editors of the documents compare these tablets, in vocabulary and content, with the description of Penelope's chair in *Odyssey* 19.53–62, conspicuous for its absence of δαιδαλ- words and introduction of a foreign (?) craftsman, Ikmalios.[1] These thirteen tablets are home to "the longest extant Mycenaean sentences" (twenty-three consecutive words) and a sprinkling of rare verbs, the passages closest to "prose" in Mycenaean Greek as well as to the descriptions of artifacts in the earliest Greek po-

---

[1] *DMG*, 332–34; Lacroix, "Ikmalios"; J. Probonas, Ἡ Μυκηναικὴ Ἐπικὴ Ποίηση μὲ Βάση τὰ Μυ-κηναϊκὰ Κείμενα καὶ τὰ Ὁμηρικὰ Ἔπη (Athens, 1980), 23–27.

etry. But although the objects described—vessels, furniture, and other household equipment—are as lavish as any in Homeric passages, their details are confined, syntactically, to adjectival formations and instrumentals. The careful composition of many of these epigraphic descriptions obeys a hierachy of materials and motifs closer to poetic ἔκφρασις than to equivalent descriptions in cuneiform inventories, but never allow for ornamentation. The most elaborate objects are inlaid with gold, silver, ivory, and colored stone, decorated with figural motifs: Ta 642 describes a nine-foot stone table decorated with gold, silver, and varieties of blue stone (*a-ja-me-na a₂-ro-u-do-pi ku-wa-no-qe pa-ra-ke-we-[qe ku-ru-so qe] e-ne-wo-pe-za*) and another inlaid with ivory pomegranates and helmets. Tablet Ta 707 describes a throne or stool (θρᾶνυς) inlaid with figures of men and lions: *ta-ra-nu ku-te-se-jo a-ja-me-no e-re-pa-ti-jo a-di-ri-ya-pi re-wo-pi-qe*; it resembles closely works attributed to Daidalos and Hephaistos, as in epic poetry (*Odyssey* 7.86–94, 11.609–16; Hesiod, *Theogony* 581–84). A striking parallel to these Mycenaean descriptions involves an altar attributed to Daidalos (Scylax, *Periplous* = *Geographici Graeci Minores* 321): ἐν δὴ τῷ βωμῷ εἰσι γεγραμμένοι ἀνδρ[ιάν]τες, λέοντες, δελφῖνες. Δαίδαλον δέ φασι ποιῆσαι. This painted or incised decoration on an archaic monument is faithful to the Homeric repertoire of the artist, elsewhere eclipsed by the reputation of classical sculpture.[2]

This world of art in Mycenaean palaces introduces the Near Eastern connection central to this second part of the book. Not only are materials (ivory, semiprecious blue stone) and techniques like inlay native to Cyprus and the Levant, in the Late Bronze Age and early Iron Age, but the motifs—human figures, lions, and palm trees—appear in Oriental art and in descriptions of Phoenician survivals.[3] If δαιδάλεος ever had a technical denotation in prehistoric Greek, it had disappeared by the Mycenaean phase of the language, even though it may have already entered the poetic domain. It is important to emphasize that this distinction reflects genre rather than chronology: the same scribes who recorded ivory footstools for palace accounts could have heard, if not sung, the praise of such artifacts as δαιδάλεος in performances of poetry in the same palace.[4] But no epigraphic inventory would preserve such adjectives, just as classical

---

[2] G. Roux, "Pindare, le prétendu trésor des Crétois et l'ancienne statue d'Apollon à Delphes," *REG* 75 (1962) 375–78; parallels exist in Mycenaean furniture panels, especially in ivory. A rare survival of such early furniture is suggested in the chair attributed to Daidalos on the Akropolis of Athens (Pausanias, 1.27.1; but see Chapter 10).

[3] See p. 83, on κύανος; and Chapter 1, n. 49, on the ivory throne from Salamis, Cyprus, decorated with panels of sphinxes and palm trees, fit for the hand of Ikmalios and the seat of Penelope (*Odyssey* 19.53–59).

It is probably Phoenician, like the bronze stands created for King Solomon by Hiram of Tyre and decorated with figures of animals, monsters, and plant symbols like the *tîmôrah* or palm capital: 1 Kings 6.23–26, 29–35; 7.36. In literary parallels from Ugarit, Kothar's gifts for Athirat include vessels with animal friezes (?): *CTA* 4.2, 40–43.

[4] A. Hurst and Fr. Bruschweiler, "Descriptions d'objets à Pylos et dans l'Orient contemporain," in *Colloquium Mycenaeum*, 65–80, on the similarity of descriptions in Linear B to poetic ἔκφρασις.

inscriptions recording sanctuary property never reproduce the epithets that proliferate in contemporary dedications or vase inscriptions. Thus the Linear B tablets shed poor light on the life of ordinary δαιδαλ- words in the Bronze Age, since their epigraphic nature excludes them from expressions that survive only in poetry.

In contrast to this silence on technical δαίδαλα, a place suggests the name of Daidalos himself. It does not appear among the dozens of personal names (which constitute two-thirds of Mycenaean Greek vocabulary) for armorers, carpenters, weavers, dyers, unguent boilers, and other artisans essential to civilized life in a Mycenaean palace.[5] Instead, Daidalos appears in a tantalizing context: as eponym for a place-name, and in a way that suggests a sanctuary. Among the Knossos tablets listing offerings to various divinities, offerings of oil are twice destined for a certain *da-da-re-jo*.[6]

The form *da-da-re-jo* (with a locative ending, "-*de*") can be read either as Δαιδαλεῖον, a denominative appellation implying an actual personal name, or Δαιδάλεον, more directly an outgrowth of the adjectival form. The most recent arguments support the former reading, understood as "the [shrine] of Daidalos."[7] Killen sees the -*e-jo*- formations as Mycenaean forerunners of the personal possessive suffix derived from personal names but admits that *da-da-re-jo* enters his argument largely on the strength of its later etymological associations.[8] In other words, modern acquaintance with the post-Homeric personality of Daidalos and his connection with Knossos encourages a translation of "*da-da-re-jo*" as "the place of Daidalos" and thence the morphological identity of "*e-jo*" as a possessive suffix, once the name is accepted.

Divorced from Killen's linguistic argument, which easily supports other Mycenaean possessive adjectives in -*e-jo*- but should perhaps exclude *da-da-re-jo* as evidence, the place-names unfortunately fail to illuminate the historicity of an early Daidalos. That there was a shrine to Daidalos near Knossos during Mycenaean occupation presumes that a figure who entered the Greek tradition as a figure of speech was already wor-

[5] Mycenaean onomastics: O. Landau, *Mykenisch-griechische Personennamen* (Göteborg, 1958), 260; A. Morpurgo Davies, "Terminology of Power and Terminology of Work in Greek and Linear B," in *Colloquium Mycenaeum*, 87–108.

[6] Fp 1 + 31,3; Fs 723; Fs 32, Fp 18,1; *DMG*, 128, 305–307. M. V. Cremona, D. Marozzi, E. Scafa, and M. Sinatra, *La toponomastica Cretese nei documenti in Lineare B di Cnosso. SMEA* 69 (1978) 65, 120–21; Gérard-Rousseau, *Mentions religieuses*, 51; Canciani, *ArchHom II: N. Bildkunst*, 2, 73 n. 319, for fuller bibliography; J. K. McArthur, *The Place-Names of the Knossos Tablets*, *Minos* suppl. 19 (Madrid, 1985), 19–20; F. R. Adrados, ed., *Diccionario micénico* (Madrid, 1985), 148–49, s.v. *da-da-re-jo*.

[7] *DMG*, 128; Ruigh, *Grec mycénien*, 263; L. A. Stella, "Testimonianze di santuari Cretesi in testi Cnossi in Lineare B," in *Second Cretological Congress*, 253, 260–61: "luogo sacro e forse un tempio." S. Hiller, "Amnisos und das Labyrinth," *ZAnt* 31 (1982) 68, 71–72; "Mykenische Heiligtümer: Das Zeugnis der Linear B–Texte," in *Sanctuaries and Cults*, 115. Canciani, *ArchHom II: N. Bildkunst*, 2, 319, for whom *da-da-re-jo* assures that Daidalos is "fest in der späten Bronzezeit verankert."

[8] J. T. Killen, "Mycenaean Possessive Adjectives in -*e-jo*," *Transactions of the Philological Society*, Oxford (1983) 70. I am grateful to Petar Ilievski for this reference and for a copy of the article.

shiped in the Late Bronze Age, much as he may have enjoyed a sanctuary in Athens by the late sixth century B.C. (see Chapter 9). Reluctant to accept this consecration without further proof, some scholars have discouraged any connection with later traditions, on both linguistic and archaeological grounds.[9] But alternative readings that avoid the craftsman while retaining his attributes are equally treacherous. Gérard-Rousseau, for example, renders the expression as "une place bien travaillé," "un endroit artistement ouvré par l'homme ou par la nature, sans qu'il s'agisse nécessairement d'un sanctuaire."[10] While this would satisfy the word's meaning in epic poetry, no testimonia can demonstrate when δαιδάλεος entered Greek poetic vocabulary, relative to the date of the Linear B texts from Knossos. So Gérard-Rousseau's reading, while preferable to one that certifies Daidalos as the object of a Bronze Age cult at Knossos, presumes a morphological and semantic identity for the word that is equally dependent on external evidence and unverifiable.

The most sensible pronouncement on Mycenaean *da-da-re-jo* has been offered by Kerenyi, who rejects entirely the derivation from a personal name and prefers a toponym derived from "die regelrechte und bezeugte adjektivische Weiterbildung des Grundadjektivs."[11] This prudent reading, from a scholar receptive to the sensational in Greek myth, draws support from classical place-names formed on the same root, including a place called Δαίδαλα in Crete, attested by Stephanus of Byzantium (cf. cities with the same name in Lykia and the Rhodian Peraia: Livy, 37.22; Strabo, 14.2.2, 3.2), and the site of the Attic deme of Daidalidai (Chapter 10). While these toponyms could have been inspired by the legend of Daidalos the artist, just as fourth-century sculptors took their names from him, contemporary evidence for the legend exists, unlike in the Bronze Age. But Kerenyi's view uncouples *da-da-re-jo* from etymologies based on historical mythology and emphasizes that the word is fundamentally a place-name, like many other enigmatic ones in Mycenaean Greek.

In conclusion, the syllabic phenomenon of *da-da-re-jo-de* is of limited value for clarifying the background to the Homeric craftsman, or indeed the semantic values of any δαιδαλ- words. It remains a place-name and, from its context alone, may be a sanctuary, but one whose ritual identity may not necessarily be embodied in its name. Moreover, as a toponym at Cretan Knossos under Mycenaean occupation, it could well be a pre-Mycenaean place-name adopted by the Greeks and whose original meaning bore no relation to Homeric δαίδαλα. Its strongest link to *Iliad* 18 is the association with Knossos, and it is not impossible that the χορός attributed to Daidalos and the place, "*da-da-re-jo*," are one and the same. But Homeric and Mycenaean forms, in this case,

[9] Linguistic reservations (Householder and Nagy, *Greek: A Survey of Recent Work*, 19): "Without the corroboration of internal analysis, projection of any Linear B item forwards or backwards in time . . . becomes tenuous at best." Cf. Renfrew, in *Archaeology of Cult*, 400.

[10] Gérard-Rousseau, *Mentions religieuses*, 51.

[11] K. Kerenyi, "Möglicher Sinn von *di-wo-nu-so-jo* und *da-da-re-jo-de*," in *Primo Congresso Internazionale del Micenologia*, 1021–26.

are incapable of mutual reinforcement or contradiction, since their chronological and etymological relationships are uncertain. While the same root could account for both epic and epigraphic phenomena, a prehistoric place-name is no more helpful than a classical one in explaining the origin of δαιδάλεος in poetry and mythology. Not until the archaic and classical period do adjectives in δαιδαλεῖος derive explicitly from the Homeric craftsman's name, as in Euripides' usage (frag. 372, Nauck; see Chapter 3). The Knossos tablets do contribute implicit support to the tradition that the earliest attested home for Daidalos is Crete. Otherwise, the place called *da-da-re-jo* by Mycenaeans at Knossos and associated with divine offerings or property must remain a tantalizing corollary to the poetic phenomenon of Daidalos.

What makes this prehistoric candidate for the craftsman figure more substantial emerges from his contemporary world, not only in Crete but outside the Aegean. As already determined, Daidalos makes his debut in Greek literature as such a close companion of the god Hephaistos that he only exists in Homer as a shadowy figure in a simile who serves to praise the work of Hephaistos (Chapter 1). Happily, the name of Hephaistos is also attested in Mycenaean Greek and at Knossos, although in a form as poorly supportive of his divine status as *da-da-re-jo* is for Daidalos. The name *a-pa-i-ti-jo*, "Hephaistios," belongs to either a person or represents a festival, if not the name of a month, and presumes the existence of **a-pa-i-to*, **Haphaistos*.[12] Assuming *a-pa-i-ti-jo*, like *da-da-re-jo*, is a theophoric name, Hephaistos would find a place in the Mycenaean pantheon along with the other gods who anticipate their classical personalities. Unfortunately, his own name does not appear independently in any Linear B religious archives with those of other Greek gods. Some scholars compare this absence to the lack of a historical cult of Hephaistos in Crete or Messenia and assume that tablet-poor Athens, his exclusive home in classical times, might be hiding his name in undiscovered evidence.[13] However, this craftsman-god could well have been reappropriated in classical Athens in the same manner, and for the same reasons, that the city adopted Daidalos (see Chapter 10). In epic poetry and mythology, Hephaistos was associated with Lemnos, probably for the sake of its volcanic metal sources.[14] His metalworking apprenticeship in a sea cave with the Nereids (*Iliad* 18.397–404) may reflect the earliest phase of Aegean mining and metallurgy, attested in caves.[15] At least one ancient source asso-

[12] Kn L 588 NP; *DMG*, 127, 352ff.; P. Kretschmer, "Die vorgriechischen Sprach- und Volksschichten," *Glotta* 30 (1943) 115–17; Ruigh, *Grec mycènien*, 157 n. 130; Gérard-Rousseau, *Mentions religieuses*, 34–35; Stella, *Tradizione micenea*, 119–24.

[13] Gérard-Rousseau, *Mentions religieuses*, 51; Delcourt, *Héphaistos*, 191; Brommer, *Hephaistos*, 3.

[14] *Iliad* 1.593; *Odyssey* 8. 294; W. Burkert, "Jason, Hypsipyle, and New Fire at Lemnos," *CQ* 20 (1970) 1–16; *contra* Ph. Forsyth, "Lemnos Reconsidered,"

EchCl 28 (1984) 3–14.

[15] H. Gropengiesser, "Siphnos, Kap Agios Sostis: Keramische Prähistorische Zeugnisse aus dem Gruben- und Hüttenrevier," *AthMitt* 101 (1986) 1–39; J. Lesley Fitton, "*Esse quam videri*. A Reconsideration of the Kythnos Hoard of Early Cycladic Tools," *AJA* 93 (1989) 31–39, reattributes the so-called "Kythnos" hoard to the island of Naxos, probably from the cave of Zeus, where recent excavations by K. Zachos have produced copper axes in Final Neolithic levels.

ciates him with Mount Ida on Crete (Diodorus 5.66.1–80), home of the invention of ironworking (by the Daktyls, according to the Marmor Parium), and there may be a confusion with a Cretan cult in the Homeric reference to a priest of Hephaistos with a son called Ἰδαῖος (*Iliad* 5.9–11). Others have connected the appearance of his name with the emergence of the artisan class of *ka-ke-we*, χαλκῆες, bronze-workers with a privileged status in the Mycenaean palace economy.[16] Connections between bronze industry and sanctuaries were once claimed from Linear B records, but the references to *ka-ko na-wi-jo*, "temple bronze," and *po-ti-ni-ja-we-jo ka-ke-we*, "bronze-workers of the goddess," do not necessarily make smiths sacred, in the view of recent scholarship.[17]

In concluding a discussion of Bronze Age Daidalos and Hephaistos, it is important to stress that neither name appears directly as the name of a god, or in epigraphic contexts associated with craftsmanship. One could argue for an independent derivation of name and cult for both of the craftsmen figures in historical times. Instead, the comparative evidence of a Late Bronze Age tradition active in an area of the Near East in close contact with Crete suggests not only parallels but cognate manifestations and potential sources for both Mycenaean names and their divine associations. The mythological poems preserved in the cuneiform archives of Ugarit (modern Ras Shamra) have long been familiar, if insufficiently explored, as rich comparative material for Greek literature.[18] Tales of heroic narrative and stories involving multiple pantheons of gods and goddesses provide paradigms and parallels for Greek traditions. As Walcot stresses, Greek and Ugaritic literature may only share common sources older than both (e.g., from the Hurrian tradition); the tablets from Ugarit may only be the closest in time, geography, and transmission to their Aegean counterparts.[19] A comparison of *da-da-re-jo* and *a-pa-i-ti-jo* with

[16] Stella, *Tradizione micenea*, 121; DMG, 352–59; M. Lejeune, "Les forgerons de Pylos," *Historia* 10 (1961) 409–34; L. R. Palmer, *The Interpretation of Mycenaean Greek Texts* (Oxford, 1963), 279–89; Eckstein, *ArchHom II: L. Handwerk*, 1, 27–29. Carlier, *La royauté en Grèce*, 108–10, plots the relationship of the *pa-si-re-u* officials and bronze-workers, who appear to have had greater independence than their female counterparts, the textile workers (see n. 5). For Near Eastern bronze smiths in palaces, see M. Heltzer, "Royal Economy in Ancient Ugarit," in *State and Temple Economy in the Ancient Near East*, 459–96.

[17] A. Leukart, "Autour de *ka-ko na-wi-jo*: quelques critères," 183–87, and S. Hiller, "*Ka-ko na-wi-jo*. Notes on Interdependences of Temple and Bronze in the Aegean Bronze Age," in *Colloquium Mycenaeum*, 189–95. Knapp, *Copper Production and Divine Protection*. Cf. recent caution on the model of the "temple state" economy in the ancient Near East: B. Foster, "A New

Look at the Sumerian Temple State," *JESHO* 24 (1981) 225–41.

[18] Gordon, "Homer and Bible"; cf. his "Poetic Myths and Legends from Ugarit," *Berytus* 25 (1977) 5–133; P. Walcot, "The comparative study of Ugaritic and Greek literatures," *UF* 1 (1969) 111–18; 2 (1970) 272–75; and 4 (1972) 129–32. Stella, *Tradizione micenea*, 369–91. Many comparative studies depend on dubious linguistic correlations and ignore more profound and intimate relations of theme and genre: e.g. G. Dossini, "Ugarit, Homère et la culture mesopotamienne," *AAAS* 29–30 (1979–1980) 207–11.

[19] Walcot, *UF* 1 (1969) 115, agreeing with R. D. Barnett (review of *Hesiod and the Near East*, by P. Walcot, *JHS* 88 [1968] 152) that poems like Hesiod's *Theogony* presume "some set of Oriental poems as yet undiscovered, combining Babylonian, Anatolian and Phoenician elements together"; cf. West, *JHS* 108 (1988) 169–70.

their Near Eastern counterparts helps demonstrate how early, prolonged, and thorough was the impact of Oriental literature on the Greek tradition.

The Ugaritic and Phoenician assembly of gods commanding separate functions and domains, offerings and ritual occasions, provides the closest model for the Greek pantheon now attested in Mycenaean tablets.[20] The transmission of many of these concepts through poetic or ritual formulas includes expressions like those describing Baal as "rider of the clouds," inherited by Zeus as νεφεληγερέτης, "gatherer of the clouds."[21] These gods travel by air (often on wings) or on the backs of donkeys, much as in Greek mythology.[22] Multiple deities at Ugarit even manifest a collective divinity paralleled at Knossos in the Linear B formula, pa-si te-o-i-si (πᾶσι θεοῖς). Their Ugaritic relatives are not only contemporary but likewise survive in the Iron Age Levant in Semitic expressions for the "family of gods."[23]

As in Greek literature since the epic tradition, the Ugaritic pantheon is served by a craftsman god resembling Hephaistos, who performs similar functions for his fellow deities in the manufacture of jewelry, weapons, furniture, and dwellings. His name, Kothar-wa-Hasis, appears in various forms some forty-five times in the extant texts of Ras Shamra, primarily in the narrative poems about Baal, Keret, and Aghat.[24] His name(s) and epithets are multiple and expressive of various aspects of craftsmanship, with demonstrable cognates not only in Ugaritic but in related Semitic languages as well as in some Greek survivals. His chief appellation, Kothar, has connections with an entire family of Semitic words derived from ktr, ranging from a hapax legomenon in the Hebrew Bible (Psalm 68.7) to a toponym in the Koran.[25] Most recently argued is the kinship with Akkadian kašāru, a verb meaning to restore or repair.[26] Occasionally, materials specified

---

[20] E. Th. Mullen, The Assembly of the Gods: The Divine Council in Canaanite and Hebrew Literature (Missoula, Mont., 1980). J.-M. de Tarragon, Le culte à Ugarit (Paris, 1980), chap. 6.

[21] M. Weinfeld, " 'Rider of the Clouds' and 'Gatherer of the Clouds,' " JANES 5 (1973) 421–26; Stella, Tradizione micenea, 368–91; Dombrowski, Europa, examines the transmission of names, epithets and legends from Ugarit to Greece.

[22] M. Smith "Divine Travel as a Token of Divine Rank," UF 16 (1984) 359; J. Wiesner, "Der Gott auf dem Esel," AA (1969), 531–45, esp. 542, for gods arriving on donkeys; could the "return of Hephaistos" to Olympos (on a mule) derive from the image of a craftsman-god on donkey-back, on a house-call for his divine colleagues?

[23] J. Nougayrol, Ugaritica 5 (1968) 42ff., on the Ugaritic "collège des dieux" (e.g. in RS 20.24, the "Pantheon text") and its connections to the Mari pantheon. Teixidor, Pagan God, 14, discusses survivals in Phoenician expressions such as "all the holy ones" (Arslan Tash), the "whole family of gods" (Karatepe; Byblos) which survive until Persian times. Pa-si te-o-i-si: Gérard-Rousseau, Mentions religieuses, 170–72.

[24] Gordon, Homer and Bible, 53–55; Gaster, Thespis, 154, 164–65; P. Xella, "Il dio siriano Kothar," in Magia, 111–25. Smith, "Kothar," for citations, abbreviations, and translations used in this chapter.

[25] Multiple readings of Semitic three-consonantal roots with variable vocalizations are especially abundant for ktr: "In attempting to discuss this particular Semitic root, one is overwhelmed by an embarrassment of riches." Lichtenstein, JANES 4 (1972) 105–6; A. van Selms, "The Root k-t̠-r and its Derivatives in Ugaritic Literature," UF 11 (1979) 739–44; Smith, "Kothar," 51–84.

[26] Smith, Kothar, 51–84, defends this derivation, although his name for Kothar, "Skillful One," would

in Akkadian texts describing such repair are of metal, and the cognates of *ktr* most attractive for comparison to Daidalos are other Semitic words involving metal.[27] For example, a theophoric name, *ksrmlk* or "servant of *Kothar*" appears as the personal name of an Akkadian silversmith at Ugarit, not unlike the manner in which the names and patronymics derived from Daidalos are adopted by Greek sculptors (see Chapter 9). This group of words compares with one of the plausible etymologies for δαιδαλ- words, also involving metal. At one time, it was even argued that Kothar's debut coincided with the introduction of gold and silver metallurgy at Ugarit in the second millennium B.C.[28] As in Greece, the earliest imagery of craftsmanship celebrated those who worked metal (Frontispiece; cf. Figure 2). Happily, Kothar now has a divine forerunner earlier in the second millennium: tablets from Ebla (Tell Mardikh) in central Syria document a deity related to Kothar in etymology and mythology, called *Ka-ša-lu* or *Ka-ša-ru*.[29] The earliest myths about the first craftsman-gods and their magical powers probably arose with the first miracles of technology—the extraction of copper, the firing of clay—and the legacy of Kothar may be as old as those first experiments in metal. In Late Bronze Age Ugarit, the chief craftsman-figure was naturally, if not etymologically, linked to the most glamorous art form. Thus the artifacts produced by Kothar—weapons, furniture, and vessels—are not only made of metal, but the gifts for the goddess Athirat are specified as gold and silver. In the Baal epic, Kothar is sent to his bellows and tongs to produce them (*CTA* 4.1.21–44 = *KTU* 1.4, I. 21–44):[30]

> Prepare, please, a present for Lady Athirat of the Sea,
>> a gift for the creatress of the gods.
> The Clever One [*hyn*] went up to the bellows,
>> the tongs were in the hands of *Hasis*;
> He poured silver, he cast gold,
>> he poured silver by the thousands [of shekels],
>> he cast gold by the ten thousand [bars];
> He cast a canopy and a reclining couch,
>> a divine dais worth twenty thousand [shekels],

agree with more than one etymology for *ktr*. A. Van Selms, "The Root k-*t*-r and Its Derivatives in Ugaritic Literature,"*UF* 11 (1979) 739–44, prefers an etymology related to binding and captivity. The connection once argued between Kinyras, king of Cyprus (*Iliad* 11.20), and κιθαρις, the Greek lyre (Brown, *JSS* 10 [1965] 197–219), need no longer be maintained: Baurain, *Onomata* 5 (1980) 7–12, and *BCH* 100 (1980) 277–308. However the kinship of Kothar with the founder hero of Kythera is attractive, given the island's Phoenician connections (Chapter 5).

[27] M. Dietrich and O. Loretz, "Zur Ugaritischen

Lexikographie (II)," *Orientalistische Literaturzeitung* 62 (1967) 541–42, cite Akkadian, e.g. *kušartu*, *kušāru*, and *kušru* (II), "ein grosser Kultgegenstand aus Metall" (cf. *kušartu*), possibly "ein Beschlag?" according to the *Akkadisches Handwörterbuch*.

[28] J. Obermann, *Ugaritic Mythology*, 14, 48. Cf. Frontisi-Ducroux, *Dédale*, 45–51.

[29] A. Archi, "Les dieux d'Ebla et les dieux d'Ugarit," *AAAS* 29–30 (1979–1980) 170; Smith, *Kothar*, 37, 40–42.

[30] Gibson, *Canaanite Myths and Legends*, 55–56. Text and translation of Ugaritic passages cited in this

> a divine dais covered with silver,
>> laminated with a layer of gold;
> A divine throne with seat in gold,
>> a divine stool covered with electrum [tin?],
> divine sandals with straps
>> which he has plated with gold
> a divine table filled with figures
>> creatures of the foundations of the earth
> a divine bowl shaped like one from Amurru,
>> shaped like one from Yamanu,
> where there are tens of thousands of wild oxen.

The craftsman-god receives divine instructions to move to his forge and hammer out a series of objects in metal, praised in as many ways as poetic language can muster. The entire passage is too close to the Homeric episode where Hephaistos makes a new set of armor for Achilles, at the request of the goddess Thetis (*Iliad* 18.368–81, 468–82; see Chapter 1), for coincidence. The Homeric figure of Thetis retains older traditions of a divine creator-goddess (see n. 50), reminiscent of Athirat's title (*qnyt*) in this passage. Moreover, Kothar's repertoire of bribes for Athirat incorporates other epic δαίδαλα: couches (cf. *Iliad* 24. 597), thrones and footstools (*Iliad* 18.390; *Odyssey* 10.315) decorated vessels and jewelry with natural motifs (*Odyssey* 19.225–31; Hesiod, *Theogony* 581–84). The prominence of metal in both Greek and Semitic descriptions of art could only reflect a similar preoccupation with precious metals in the Late Bronze Age; but other factors encourage a more direct relationship between these literary conventions. In terms of Kothar's name, his practice as a metallurgist supports a connection between *ktr* as a root related to metal, partly through the support of the Homeric parallels.

Elsewhere in Ugaritic literature, parallel manifestations of *ktr* in divine names—the *ktrt* goddesses and [the] *ktrm*—are the most problematic and least helpful in clarifying the meaning of Kothar, since they are likewise personifications derived from the same semantic root. The *kotharat* goddesses display creative talents similar to the craftsman-god's, but deploy them in nature, not culture, as goddesses of birth (as will be explored). Most illuminating, as in the study of Homeric Daidalos where related words in the same corpus clarified the nature of his name (Chapter 1), are adjectival and adverbial forms. In the opening tablet preserved from the Keret epic, one-third of his family (children or wives?) died "*ktrm*." This has been rendered as "in childbirth" (if wives), "at birth" (if offspring), but most probably emphasizes a healthy condition in nature as related adjectives praise culture.[31] The other use of adverbial *ktrm* is applied to the

---

chapter based on Gibson, with improvements courtesy of Mark Smith and Francis Deblauwe.

[31] Ginsberg first connected *ktrm* with *ktrt*, the god-

desses of childbirth (see n. 47) and was followed by Gordon and others, until Gaster compared the expression with Syriac *kušrâ* and suggested "in full washing of Athtar in the underworld (*CTA* 2.3.23). Text and context allow three possible readings, as "skillfully [they will wash me]", "the *ktrm* [skillful ones?] will wash me," or "Kothar will wash me."[32] The word *mktr* expresses the result of a verbal form and seems to mean "skilled work" ("the works of Kothar"). It is specifically applied to works of art made by Kothar as gifts for Athirat, the sea goddess, in the Baal epic (*CTA* 4.1.4–44). Upon instructions of the other gods, Kothar prepares gold and silver furniture and vessels to win Athirat's agreement for the construction of a house for Baal (the passage describing their manufacture will be discussed shortly). The goddess is delighted and exclaims at the magnificence of the gifts (*CTA* 4.2.26–31 = *KTU* 1 4.2. 27–33):

> When Athirat saw [the work] of silver,
>> the work of silver and the sh[ine] of the gold,
> Lady A[thirat] of the Sea was glad,
>> she [called] to her lad:
> "See the skilled work [*mktr*], even, [. . .],
> O fisherman of Lady Athira[t of the Sea]."

As Smith argues: "The exegesis of *mktr* as 'skilled work' serves to define more precisely the meaning of PN [personal name] Kothar as 'skilled worker.' "[33] Thus the verbal expression *mktr* suggests the same relationship to *ktr* that "daidalic" work (e.g., δεδαιλμένο) displays toward its eponymous craftsman, Daidalos (Chapter 1). In fact, the Greek and Ugaritic word groups behave in remarkably similar ways as techniques of poetic narrative. Here, *mktr* abbreviates the work of *ktr* just as δαιδάλεος and its compound forms cluster around the manufacture of the armor of Achilles, and a revival of the word later (e.g., *Iliad* 19.13, 19, 369–91) serves to recall an entire passage (see Chapter 1). Even the ambiguous properties manifested by "daidalic" creations in Greek poetry are shared in Ugaritic literature. The bow and arrows made by Kothar and brought to Danel for his son, Aqhat (*CTA* 17.5 = *KTU* 1.17. V, 2–33), ultimately bring death and sorrow to the royal house. The goddess Anat covets the weapons, tries to bribe them away from Aqhat, and kills him for their sake. Mourning, famine, and crime (Pagat's murder of Anat's hit man) fall on Danel's kingdom, ultimately a result of Kothar's weapons.[34] The armor forged by Hephaistos and compared with the work of Daidalos carried

---

bloom, healthy" (debate summarized by Smith in "Kothar").

[32] M. Smith, "The Magic of Kothar, the Ugaritic Craftsman God, in KTU I. VI.49–50," *RB* 91 (1984) 377–80, prefers the last reading, but a nonnoun form seems preferable.

[33] Smith, "Kothar," 64. His defense is essential and eliminates other readings of *mktr* as the epithet of a

minor god (Van Selms, *UF* 11 [1979] 739–44) or as "marvelous gifts" (Coogan, *Stories from Ancient Canaan*, 98) that obscure its relationship to Kothar, as do many translations of Greek "daidalic" words.

[34] D. R. Hillers, "The Bow of Aqhat: The Meaning of a Mythological Theme," in *Orient and Occident*, 71–80; H. P. Dressler, "Is the Bow of Aqhat a Symbol of Virility?" *UF* 8 (1976) 217–20; S. Parker, "Death and

the same narrative burden, in its role in the deaths of Patroklos, Hektor, and Achilles (*Iliad* 18–23; see Chapter 1). Thus the function of each word, Greek and Semitic, within its literary context encourages the comparative method, on an intertextual level, and the analysis of *ktr* reveals the tip of an iceberg of agreements between Ugaritic and Greek literature.

Like Hephaistos and Daidalos, Kothar also works in materials other than metal, such as wood, and his other names and epithets indicate his wide range of skills. As architect and carpenter, he is summoned to supervise the construction of Baal's house after Anat tells Baal (*CTA* 4.5 = *KTU* 1.4 V, 95–97):

> Build a palace of silver and gold,
> a palace of pure lapis lazuli.

The palace of Alkinoos, king of the Phaiakians in mythical Scheria, was built by Kothar's Aegean equivalent and features the same combination of precious materials (*Odyssey* 7.86–94):

> χάλκεοι μὲν γὰρ τοῖχοι ἐληλέατ᾽ ἔνθα καὶ ἔνθα,
> ἐς μυχὸν ἐξ οὐδοῦ, περὶ δὲ θριγκὸς κυάνοιο·
> χρύσεαι δὲ θύροι πυκινὸν δόμον ἐντὸς ἔεργον·
> ἀργύρεον δ᾽ ἐφ᾽ ὑπερθύριον, χρυσέη δὲ κορώνη.
> χρύσεοι δ᾽ ἑκάτερθε καὶ ἀργύρεοι κύνες ἦσαν,
> οὓς Ἥφαιστος τεῦξεν ἰδυίῃσι πραπίδεσσι
> δῶμα φυλασσέμεναι μεγαλήτορος Ἀλκινόοιο,
> ἀθανάτους ὄντας καὶ ἀγήρως ἤματα πάντα.

> For the walls were of bronze, this side and that,
> from the threshhold to the center, and around a frieze of blue stone,
> and golden doors enclosed the well-built house.
> And silver was the lintel above, gold the handle below it
> and golden dogs stood on both sides,
> whom Hephaistos made, with his clever skills,
> guarding the home of great-hearted Alkinoos,
> immortal and ageless for all days.

Gold and silver adorn both palaces, and even lapis lazuli is suggested in the mysterious blue material expressed by κύανος, never used elsewhere in Homer as a material noun, and identified by archaeologists either as lapis lazuli or as blue glass paste.[35] The

---

Devotion: The Composition and Theme of Aqhat," in *Love and Death in the Ancient Near East. Essays in Honor of Marvin H. Pope*, ed. J. Marks and R. M. Good (Hamden, Conn., 1987); Smith, *Kothar*, 351–76.

[35] Brown, *JSS* 10 (1965) 203–4; Eckstein, *ArchHom II: L. Handwerk*, 1, 40–41; Fittschen, *ArchHom II: N. Bildkunst*, 1, 22–23. *Ku-wa-no* and *ku-wa-no-wo-ko*-i (*κυανουργοί* or "kuano-workers") both appear in Linear B

silver dogs are not matched in the prescription for Baal's palace, but as guardians of the Phaiakian palace door they suggest Near Eastern animals flanking temple and palace doors, as well as dogs in Mycenaean frescoes in throne rooms, as found at Pylos.[36] In the landscape of the imagination, Greek epic poetry was enriched by Oriental details, just as Odysseus sets his false tales in plausible landscapes in Crete, Phoenicia, and Egypt. The respective roles of native craftsman-gods also share similarities, when Homeric and Canaanite poetry are juxtaposed. In this passage, Hephaistos is represented like a Near Eastern craftsman in the service of gods, in the fashion of artisans who serve kings, as Hiram of Tyre and his Phoenicians work for King Solomon in the Hebrew Bible (1 Kings 5–7). Eventually, Hephaistos appears in action near the throne of Zeus in scenes in Greek art. In one such example, from sixth-century Athens, he may be joined by Daidalos, if the running figure of Ikaros belongs to the same scene (Figure 9). In one of the earliest versions of the birth of Athena, on a vase from Tenos (Figure 14e), one craftsman (lame?) squats near the throne of Zeus, more like a midwife boiling water in a tripod cauldron while another (Daidalos?) floats above. In the context of the Homeric world, the service of Hephaistos for the Phaiakians suits their near-divine status as relatives of the Kyklopes (*Odyssey* 6.3–6). The only other homes Hephaistos builds in epic poetry, including the bedroom of Hera (*Iliad* 14.166–69, 338–39), are for the Olympian gods (*Iliad* 1.606–8), each of whom enjoys such a heaven-built home as a privilege of the pantheon. As suggested (n. 22), the "return" of Hephaistos to Olympos, on the back of a mule, to dissolve his anger and the trap for the goddess Hera, suggests the summoning of a craftsman to the divine palace for emergency services, just as craftsmen were called to build a new palace for Baal. For the same divine housing allowance apparently was distributed among the Ugaritic family of gods, according to Baal's complaint to El and Asherath (*CTA* 3.5. E 46–47, 4.4. 50–51; restored at 4.1. 10–12):

> Lo, Baal has no house like the gods,
>> nor a court like the sons of Athirat.

Thus, in his architectural as well as metallurgical skills, Kothar overlaps in function and techniques with Hephaistos and his relationship to Homeric gods, and is praised for similar qualities. He also occupies a similar role in the pantheon of gods, at least in poetry if not in cult.[37]

---

inventories, and blue glass as a raw material was apparently being imported to the Aegean in the fourteenth century (on the Ulu Burun ship; see Chapter 5).

[36] Faraone, *GRBS* 28 (1987) 257–80; E. Akurgal, *The Art of Greece: Its Origins* (New York 1970), 69–109, on Neo-Hittite animal reliefs and column bases; I. Winter, "Art as Evidence for Interaction: Relations be-

tween the Assyrian Empire and North Syria," in *Mesopotamien und seine Nachbarn*, 1:355–82, on Neo-Assyrian versions and possible Middle Assyrian forerunners. Pylos: M. Lang, *The Palace of Nestor at Pylos II. The Frescoes* (Princeton, 1969), pls. 133, 137, color plate P.

[37] In a mutilated passage from the Keret epic where the gods assemble for the king's wedding to Hurriya

Common as the second half of Kothar's name is the expression ḥss, meaning "Wise One." In Mesopotamian literature, this adjective accompanies the god Ea in the *Enūma Eliš*; in its intensive form *atra ḥasīs* or "exceeding in wisdom," it praises Utnapishtim in the Gilgamesh epic (Tablet XI.187) and serves as opening line (and convenient title) of the most celebrated Akkadian poem.[38] So closely linked are the two parts of Kothar's double name, "Skillful-and-Wise," that they even evoke a dual pronoun (*hmt* in *CTA* 17.5, 20) and once appear without their conjunction (*KTU* 1.123), to the confusion of later interpreters not familiar with Semitic parallelism. In Greek poetry, such dual expressions are also applied to pairs of deities (e.g., Κράτος Βία τε: Aeschylus, *Prometheus Bound* 12), but the occasional independence of the two names in Ugaritic poetry allowed them to be understood as two separate personalities, by nonnative readers, a misunderstanding that will be examined. The second name, however, merely repeats and intensifies the god's skill as craftsman, and appears once as an independent name for the god, much the way "Daidalos" first appears in connection with Hephaistos.

In addition to Kothar-and-Hasis (in Gaster's charming rendering, "Sir Adroit-and-Cunning"), he is also praised as ḥrš yd—"Clever Craftsman" or "Skilled Artisan"—and as *hyn*, "Deft One." The former expression, a common term for craftsmen at Ugarit, is composed of a root with rich connotations in the language of Greek and Near Eastern craftsmanship. Ḥrš has relatives in Akkadian, where *harāšu* means "to bind, put together," and an analogy in Greek, where the verb ἀραρίσκω likewise means to assemble or put together and is personified in the names of Greek craftsmen like Harmonides (*Iliad* 5.60), if not Homer himself.[39] The closest etymological and semantic relative of the Ugaritic term is Phoenician ḥrš, meaning "artisan"; the Hebrew word for "smith," *ḥaraš* (*ḥoreš*) demonstrates how metallurgy, as always, dominated ancient technology.

The fourth and final term for the Ugaritic craftsman god is *hyn*, meaning "clever" or "deft," which appears four times in the company of Kothar's other names. The praise of a divine craftsman for various forms of wisdom is traditional in related literature. The Biblical pair of craftsmen, Bezalel and Oholiab, are endowed by God with "ability and intelligence, with knowledge and all craftsmanship" for a range of skills in metal, masonry, and woodworking clearly related to Canaanite tradition (*Exodus* 31.2). In Greek epic, Hephaistos is praised not only for his craftmanship but with intellectual epithets

---

(*CTA* 15.2.5 = *KTU* 1.15 II, 5), Kothar appears as one of the wedding guests, much as Hephaistos attends the wedding of Peleus and Thetis in archaic Greek poetry and art.

[38] Smith, "Kothar," 85–90, on this epithet and other double names in the Ugaritic pantheon.

[39] Smith "Kothar," 91ff.; Heltzer, in *State and Temple Economy in the Ancient Near East*, 484–94, on ḥrš for craftsmen in the Ugarit tablets. The Greek words as-

sume a root **ar-* and are already common in Mycenaean: Chantraine, *Dictionnaire Étymologique*, 110–11 s.v. ἅρμα; Eckstein, *ArchHom II: L. Bildkunst*, 1, 20. On the origin and significance of Homer's name as a formation from ὁμοῦ plus ἀραρίσκω, see summary in Nagy, *Best of the Achaeans*, 297–300; Vermeule, in *Troy and the Trojan War*, 86–87 (cf. name of Daidalos, Chapter 1).

appropriate to Odysseus. He is πολύφρονος, "very wise," κλυτόμητις, "renowned in wisdom," πολύμητις, "rich in wisdom," ἰδυίῃσι πραπίδεσσιν,"with knowing heart," and so are his pupils (e.g., a worker in gold is praised as ἴδρις at *Odyssey* 6.232–34 = 23.159–61). In hexameter the epithets of Hephaistos often represent the craftsman alone, without his proper name, as when περικλυτὸς ἀμφιγυήεις in final position identifies him (after a bucolic diairesis, e.g. at *Iliad* 18.383, 462, 587, 590).[40] In Ugaritic, the equivalent terms likewise complement and substitute for Kothar in formulaic ways traditional to the techniques of parallelism in Semitic poetry. His main persona, for example, *Kothar-wa-Hasis*, appears most frequently as a single expression, but the two components of the name are divided between two lines that repeat the same idea, in Near Eastern poetic tradition. In the Aqhat epic, for example, the arrival of the crafts-man-god is noticed by Danel (*CTA* 17.5. = *KTU* 1.17 V, 10–11):

> He saw Kothar coming,
> > He saw Hasis approaching.

When the craftsman departs, a similar pair of verses divides his names into parallel, repeated expressions (31–33):

> Kothar departed for his tent,
> > Hayyan departed for his dwelling.

When Kothar is fetched to forge gifts for Athirat as a prelude to building a house for Baal, the messengers are instructed (*CTA* 3.6.18–24; cf. *KTU* 1.1.3. 2–5):

> At the feet of Kothar bow low and fall,
> > prostrate yourself and honor him;
> and say to Kothar-wa-Hasis,
> > repeat to Hayyan, of skillful hands (*ḫrš yd*),
> "Message of [Baal] the Conqu[eror] . . ."

On several occasions, ancient and modern interpreters of the Ugaritic texts must have misunderstood these pairs of terms as two, if not four, separate craftsmen. The misun-derstanding may have stimulated traditions of craftsmen pairs, perhaps encouraged by collaboration between related technologies: potter and painter, architect and engineer, or any tradition where master and apprentice work together. In Philo's account, for example, Χουσώρ and his brother appear in a list of half a dozen inventors of civilized arts, suggesting how formulaic these figures had become by the Hellenistic period. Whether all manifestations of creative pairs in the literary record can be traced to the

---

[40] On the mysterious adjective ἀμφιγυήεις, see H. Humbach, "ἀμφίγυος and ἀμφιγυήεις," in *Studi linguistici in onore de Vittore Pisani* II (Brescia, 1969), vol. 2:569–78, for an interpretation as "double-armed" or "armed with a double axe."

same source, and whether they derive from parallelism in Near Eastern poetry alone, would be difficult to defend. But the phenomenon of Daidalos may well originate in such expressions, as will be argued.

Kothar's names might well be multiplied by the discovery of more texts; his talents, and his domains, are amply represented. In addition to his manufacture of weapons, gold and silver objects, and architecture, a case has been made for his skills as a magician. In providing two clubs for Baal in his battle against the sea, Kothar names the weapons in a ceremony that suggests a spell is cast over them and that their task (conquering Sea) will be accomplished by magic (*CTA* 2.4.11–15 = *KTU* 1.2 IV, 11–23):

> Kothar fashioned two weapons,
>> and he proclaimed their names:
> "You, your name is Yaggarish ("Driver?").
>> Yaggarish, drive Yamm!
> Drive Yamm from his throne,
>> [Na]har (River) from his seat of dominion.
> May you dance in the hands of Baal,
>> Like a vulture in his fingers.
> Strike Prince Yamm in the back,
>> [Jud]ge River between the hands (= on the back)."

The weapon performs as instructed but fails to overcome Baal's enemy, whereupon Kothar charms the other club in a set of nearly identical verses, christening the second weapon *Ayyamarri* ("Expeller") with greater success.[41] Obermann observed the magic properties of Kothar's work and words, in this passage; other Ugaritic sources (god lists equating local deities with Akkadian ones) compare Kothar with figures like Ea, the Mesopotamian god of magic (RS 20.24, 15). More recently, scholars have compared this episode with the description of Kothar's Phoenician successor, Chousor, whom Philo claims λόγους ἀσκῆσαι καὶ ἐπῳδὰς καί μαντείας (*FGrH* 790 F 2.11, from Eusebius, *Praeparatio Evangelica* 1.10.11).[42] However, many intervening centuries prevent these two sets of testimonia from supporting each other, directly. Philo's translation of Sanchuniathon could well reflect a learned interpretation of the same (or related) passage, not independent evidence for Kothar's status as magician. But as a metallurgist, he inspired the kind of awe reserved for magicians and shares with other craftsmen skilled with metalworking a legendary association with magic.[43] In the Near East in the Late Bronze

---

[41] G. Rendsburg argues for an ancient illustration of these weapons in action: "UT 68 and the Tell Asmar Seal," *Orientalia* 53 (1964) 448–52.

[42] J. Obermann, "How Baal Destroyed a Rival: A Mythological Incantation Scene," *JAOS* 67 (1947) 195–208; A. Kapelrud, *Baal in the Ras Shamra Texts* (Copen-

hagen, 1952), 85; Gaster, *Thespis*, 161–63; Smith, "Kothar," 397–41.

[43] "Magic" smiths in the Greek tradition include the Sintians (*Odyssey* 8.294), the Kabeiroi, the Telchines and Daktyls of Crete, and Daidalos himself (Chapter 8). They often share suspiciously similar

Age, metalworking is either associated with sanctuaries (i.e., on Cyprus at Kition and Enkomi) or seems to be accompanied by sacrifices performed at specific stages of metallurgy.[44] This close association of religion with metallurgy encouraged the intimacy of cult with craft, and hence the proliferation of mythological figures—the Telchines, Daktyls, and other mischievous and mobile spirits of metal—and of magic powers for metallurgists.

Outside of this widespread and predictable connection between metal and magic, other evidence for Kothar's magic powers is not overwhelming. His "prediction" that Baal will win eternal kingship from his battle with Yam (CTA 2.4.7–10) hardly makes the craftsman a prophet. The claim introduces the christening of the weapons and sounds more like a guarantee from craftsman to customer. In two similar passages, the craftsman guarantees delivery of his goods to those who have ordered them—inadequate qualifications for prophetic powers. In the last line of a speech otherwise lost, he assures Danel that he will deliver bow and arrows (CTA 17.5.2–3). When Kothar advises Baal to include a window in his new house and offers to make it, the offer is rejected, but the craftsman insists: "You will heed my words, O Baal" (CTA 4.6.2, 15). Later the god changes his mind and asks for a window, whereupon the craftsman laughs and reminds him: "Baal the Conqueror, didn't I tell you: 'You will recall my words, Baal?' " (CTA 4.7.23–25). Surely these passages belong to the tradition of craftsman performing skills not commanded by other gods and make Kothar no more of a magician than they would other divine or mortal artisans. His relative, Daidalos, also becomes a "magician" in classical Athens (see Chapter 8), through an expansion of metaphor into anecdotes.

His connections with other Ugaritic mythological figures and functions are somewhat more mysterious, as in his appearance as ḥbr or "companion, familiar," of Shapsu in CTA 6.6.48–49. In a related expression, a group of celebrants with Rapiu are called ḥbr kṯr ṯbm, "the goodly companions of Kothar," in RS 24.252. Smith compares these uses of ḥbr with Ras Ibn Hani 78/20 to derive a meaning such as "charmer" or "spellbinder" for CTA 6.6.48–49 and interprets RS 24.252 as "those good ones divined by Kothar, i.e. the Rephaim."[45] Elsewhere in Ugaritic literature, parallel manifestations of kṯr in divine

---

powers of incantation (the Telchines, e.g., practice τάς τε ἐπῳδὰς καὶ τελετὰς καὶ μυστήρια: Diodorus, 5.64). Gaster, Thespis, 161–63; Delcourt, Héphaistos, 165–70 (on Völund/Wieland in Northern mythology, 121–22); P. Realacci, "I Telchines, 'Maghi' nel segno della trasformazione," in Magia, 197–206. Wertime, JFA 10 (1983) 447, on metal and magic: "It was a matter of constant astonishment to the ancients that such totally different forms of matter could be achieved by the application of heat to often not dissimilar earthy matrices."

[44] Knapp, Copper Production and Divine Protection,

rejects a religious connection, but see Frisch and others, Kamīd el-Lōz 6, 181–82; in Iron Age Thessaly: see my Chapter 5, n. 73.

[45] Smith, "Kothar," 397–410, 441–45; Y. Avishur, "The Ghost-Expelling Incantation from Ugarit (Ras ibn Hani 78/20)," UF 13 (1981) 16, 22–23, on ḥbr meaning "to bind." Musical instruments in the verses immediately preceding ḥbr kṯr ṯbm in RS 24.252 do not identify the "companions of Kothar" as musicians, especially since kṯr's connection with a presumed Semitic root of κίθαρις has been rejected: Smith, "Kothar," 76–77, 441–45.

names—the *ktrt* goddesses and the *ktrm* (?)—are the most problematic and least helpful in clarifying the meaning of Kothar, since they are likewise personifications derived from the same semantic root. The word *ktrm* could yield "skillfully" but is more commonly read as a masculine plural noun, "the *ktrm*" (male wedding attendants?), or simply as the name of Kothar (one of the wedding guests?).[46]

The most intriguing extension of Kothar's powers involves a separate set of deities with related functions in the (re)productive life of Ugarit and its pantheon. A group of goddesses, the *ktrt* or "skilled ones," have been interpreted as both guardians of marriage and childbirth and as singers or musicians.[47] Creative and abundant interpretations of these figures depend heavily on variant etymologies and parallels outside the Ugaritic corpus in particular, a Biblical *hapax legomenon* (Psalm 68:7), and the determination of scholars to make the Ugaritic evidence solve the Hebrew problem. The *ktrt*'s appearances in Ugaritic are limited to the Aqhat epic and the wedding poem of Nikkal and Yarih. In the former, the *ktrt* are entertained as guests of Danel for seven days, as a prelude to his conception of a son (CTA 17.2.26–41). Their name and function, presumably "the skillful ones," are accompanied and perhaps specified by a parallel verse praising them as *bnt hll* ("daughters of joyful noise"?) and *snnt* ("swallows" according to Viroulleaud and Gaster). Elaborate connections with music are adduced through reading the *hbr ktr tbm* (RS 24.252) as musicians and the performance of ἐπῳδαί by Kothar's Phoenician successor, Χουσώρ (to be discussed). Context is a better guide to the identity of the *ktrt*: their visit to Danel rewards him with the conception of a son immediately thereafter (as far as the broken tablet allows us to understand, with its fragments of verses suggesting sex and gestation). Moreover, their other appearance in Ugaritic mythology supports their function as goddesses of fertility and childbirth. At the marriage of Nikkal and Yarih, the *ktrt* serve as bridesmaids and are both numbered and named (CTA 24 = KTU 1.24, 6–7, 12, 15, 40–47).[48] Seven of them (a number that complements their seven-day visit with Danel) bear names personifying attributes of marriage and bridal gifts, appropriate to their context and function (KTU 1.24, 40–50). Their associations with childbirth are reinforced by their use in alphabetic cuneiform incantations on tablets from Arslan Tash and Beth Shemesh, thought to be amulets for protection against the dangers of childbirth.[49] Their numbers reappear in figures such

---

[46] Gaster translates "in full vigor" according to the etymology which relates *ktr* to Akkadian *kašāru* (rather than, e.g., *kušūru*). Van Selms, *UF* 11 (1979) 739–44, classifies *ktrm* as a masculine plural noun, just as he prefers *mktr* as the epithet of a minor god.

[47] Ch. Virolleaud, "Hymne phénicien au dieu Nikal et aux déesses *kosarot* provenant de Ras Shamra," *Syria* 17 (1936) 213ff.; Th. Gaster, "The 'Graces' in Semitic folklore. A Wedding-song from Ras Shamra," *JRAS* (1938) 37ff.; B. Margalit, "The *Kosarot/Ktrt*: Pa-

troness-Saints of Women," *JANES* 4 (1972) 53–61, and responses: M. Lichtenstein, "Psalm 68.7 Revisited," ibid., 97–112; Margalit, "Of Brides and Birds: A Reply to M. Lichtenstein," ibid., 113–117. Smith "Kothar," appendix 1, pp. 466–72.

[48] W. Herrmann, *Yarih und Nikkal und der Preis der Kutarat-Göttinnen* (Berlin, 1968); Margalit, *JANES* 4 (1972) 53–61, 113–17.

[49] W. F. Albright, "The Beth-shemesh Tablet in Alphabetic Cuneiform," *BASOR* 173 (1964) 51–54.

as the seven Titanides or Artemides attested by Philo of Byblos as daughters of Astarte (*FGrH* 790 F 2 = Eusebius, *Praeparatio Evangelica* 1.10.24).

According to the interpretation argued by Margalit and sustained by Smith, Kothar's female namesakes preside over reproduction, or the creation of life in nature, as he provides a divine authority for the world of craftsmanship. This collaboration of male and female creators recalls how Thetis retains her residual divine function in the *Iliad*. In Orientalizing literature of the Greek world, Alkman compares Thetis with a bronze craftsman in describing her demiurgic role in the creation of matter, while Empedokles' Aphrodite (Love) participates in the creation of men as clay statues.[50] The distribution of labor between the world of nature and that of culture is as old as the division of gender itself, and is expressed in manifold ways throughout world cultures.[51] The extreme vision of this phenomenon identifies a male obsession with art as compensatory or competitive creation, a substitution for the reproductive role monopolized by women and envied by men. When Athena models a horse or participates in workshops (Figures 59–61), only her status as a virgin goddess (who denies maternity: Aeschylus, *Eumenides* 736–38) allows her to perform a man's task, sculpture. Anecdotes about the animation of statues by their male creators simulate the act of giving birth denied to men. Legendary paradigms for this phenomenon in antiquity include God's creation of Eve from Adam's rib (Genesis 2.21–24), the concoction of Pandora by Hephaistos and other gods (Hesiod, *Theogony* 570–612), the animation of statues by Daidalos (Chapter 8), and Pygmalion's transformation of his statue.[52] The Ugaritic equivalent to Pandora appears in the Keret epic, when El creates Shataqat, a female healing deity, to cure Keret's illness (*CTA* 16.5 = *KTU* 1.16, V, 26–30):[53]

> [I] myself shall perform magic and sh[all] create,
>> I shall create a female being able to cast out the [dis]ease,
>> to expel the illness!

---

[50] According to an allegorical commentary on Alkman's fragment 5 (= *PapOxy* 2390, col. III, lines 18–19: G. Kirk, J. E. Raven and M. Schofield, *The Presocratic Philosophers*, 2d ed. [Cambridge, 1983], 47–49, no. 40), the poet compares τὴν φύσιν τῆς τοῦ χαλκοῦ ὕλης, ἣ δὲ Θέτις τ[ῆς] τοῦ τεχνίτου. M. West, "Three Presocratic Cosmogonies," *CQ* 57 (1963) 154; G. Most, "Alcman's 'Cosmogonic' Fragment," *CR* 101 (1987) 1–18, derives Thetis's role as demiurge from her supervision of the ὁπλοποιία in *Iliad* 18. L. Slatkin, "The Wrath of Thetis," *TAPA* 116 (1986) 1–24, on her cosmic potential; on Thetis and her Near Eastern counterpart(s), Tethys and Athirat, see Burkert, *Orientalisierende Epoche*, 88–90. Cf. Aphrodite's role as cosmic creator in Empedocles (frags. 62–95: M. R. Wright, *Empedokles. The Fragments* [New Haven, 1985], 217–18).

[51] See Sherry Ortner's classic essay: "Is Female to Male as Nature Is to Culture?" in *Women, Culture and Society*, ed. R. Rosaldo and L. Lamphere (Stanford, 1974), 67ff. G. Lerner, *The Creation of Patriarchy* (Oxford, 1986), 145–46, 151–52, 180–86 (Genesis).

[52] Warner, *Monuments and Maidens*, 213–40, on male/female expressions of creativity, from Pandora to Pygmalion.

[53] According to Gordon, El "animates two effigies that become his wives" in analogy to the magic maidens of Hephaistos: "Homer and Bible," 54, no. 144.

> He filled his p[alms] with the best of loam,
>> he pinched off clay such as [is used by the potter.]

The use of clay, the emphasis on male creation of a female being, and the function of the new creature—both helpful and harmful—belong to those Near Eastern traditions that reappear in Greece, in the creation of Pandora, *femme fatale*, and of Athena, born of a male but without a mother, assisted by male and female midwives-craftsmen (Figure 13). Within the Ugaritic world, the relationship between Kothar and the *kotharat*—single, masculine versus plural, feminine expressions of creative powers—finds a supportive parallel in the carpenter god, Ilish(a), and his wives, the carpenter-goddesses. In the same section of the Keret epic, after the king has fallen ill (*CTA* 16.4 = *KTU* 1.16, IV, 2–13), El summons Ilish and his wive(s), before creating his creature, Shataqat, to save the king. In three sets of verses (repeating El's instructions, the words of his messenger, and El's greeting), Ilish is hailed as:

> Ilish(a), the carpenter-god,
> Ilish, the carpenter of Baal's house,
> and his wives, the carpenter-goddesses.

Because the Baal epic casts Kothar, not Ilish, as the carpenter of the house of Baal (*CTA* 4.5–4.7), this reading must be reconciled with the creation of Baal's house. If *ngr* means "carpenter" rather than steward or servant, either Ilish is a collaborator of Kothar's or he represents an alternative form of his name and personality, as suggested by some scholars.[54] In either case, however, a male artisan-god is accompanied by female complements and assistants to his creative skills, like the ἀμφίπολοι or female servants of Hephaistos in the *Iliad* (18.470–420).

Many of these accessories to divine creation survive in the extraordinary scene on a seventh-century relief pithos from Tenos, which shows an unusual version of the birth of Athena (Figures 13, 14).[55] Alternative Greek theogonies—the birth of Zeus from Ge, the birth of Athena from Metis—have been proposed to account for its unconventional features. The newborn deity (Figure 14b) appears nude to some and must be male, it is argued, or holds the wrong attribute (a branch?) for Athena; the seated figure on a throne giving "birth" from the head (Figure 14b) is hard to identify as Zeus: he or she faces front rather than profile right, appears more female than male with a short, Hathor-style haircut and a "skirt" like a chiton. The attendant figure with an ἄρπη

---

[54] Nougayrol, *Ugaritica* 5 (1968) 61, compares *ilš* with *hyn* as "divinités secondaires-artisanes" derived from Kothar's epithets.

[55] Discovered by N. Kontoleon, " Ἡ Γέννησις τοῦ Διός," *KChr* 15–16 (1961–1962) A:282–93; "Die frühgriechische Reliefkunst," *AE* (1969) 228–36;

F. Brommer, "Die Geburt der Athena," *JRGZM* 8 (1961) 72–73 (birth of Athena from Metis); E. Simon, "Die Geburt der Athena auf der Reliefamphora in Tenos," *AK* 25 (1982) 35–38; E. Condoléon-Bolanacchi, "À propos de l' 'amphore de la naissance' de Xoburgo (Ténos)," *AK* 27 (1984) 21–24.

(sickle or surgical knife) to the left, where one would expect Hephaistos, is female; but if she is Eileithyia (Figure 14c), then the figure seated at a cauldron to the right makes far too modest a figure to be Hephaistos, and competes with an airborne man (Figure 14d: Daidalos?).

The debate about this scene and its lack of agreement with Greek iconography are solved with a Near Eastern image (Figure 15): on an Egyptianizing cylinder seal found at Bronze Age Byblos, the figure of a ruler-god on a throne suggests an origin for this un-Hellenic Zeus.[56] Although this seal may never have been seen by a Greek artist before burial beneath the temple at Byblos in the Late Bronze Age, like the one from Beth Shean (Figure 16), duplicates may still have circulated then or centuries later, proliferating images that inspired Greek artists trying to tell Greek tales. The confrontation between these two images epitomizes the complications of understanding early Greek art: much of it cannot be understood from Greek conventions alone. Like the demons under the handles of a Protoattic krater in Berlin, assigned numerous functions in Greek art (protosatyrs, etc.) before being recognized as reflections of Phoenician monsters seen on metal bowls, the original home for such creatures was in the East.[57]

The last attribute of Kothar to be considered here reveals a paradox of East-West relations: no sooner has one discovered an Oriental home for a Greek convention in art, cult, or poetry than it betrays an Aegean association of its own. One connection of Kothar that has been parlayed into a divine function derives from his occasional titles, *bn ym*, "son of the sea," and *bnm 'dt*, "son of the confluence." Despite the fact that Kothar actually helps Baal defeat Yamm with special weapons, some have tried to extend his own powers to the sea, on the basis of these titles but largely supported by attributes of related Greek and Phoenician deities.[58] For example, Kothar's Phoenician successors, Οὔσωος and Χουσώρ, invented essential maritime tools and techniques such as the fishhook, line, and bait and the seagoing raft (Philo, *FGrH* 790 F 2 = Eusebius, *Praeparatio Evangelica* 1.10.10). More compelling than these marine skills, which are shared with all the other inventors in Philo's catalogue, are Greek traditions calling the Telchines ὑγρονόμοι or "water wardens" (Nonnos, *Dionysiaka* 14.17–40), υἱοὶ θαλάττης, "sons of the sea" (Diodorus, 5.55), or παῖδες θαλάσσης "children of the

[56] P. Montet, *Byblos et l'Égypte: Fouilles 1921–24* (Paris, 1928), 62–68, fig. 20, pl. XXXIX, no. 42; "Les Égyptiens à Byblos," *MonPiot* 25 (1921–1922) 248–54; H. Goedicke, "A Cylinder Seal of a Ruler of Byblos of the Third Millennium," *MDAIK* 19 (1963) 1–6, with responses by W. F. Albright, in "The Eighteenth Century Princes of Byblos and the Chronology of Middle Bronze," *BASOR* 176 (1964) 44–46 and H. Goedicke, "The Cylinder Seal of a Ruler of Byblos Reconsidered," *JARCE* 5 (1966) 19–21. I am grateful to Hans Goedicke and Antonio Loprieno for advice on this seal.

[57] Morris, *Black and White Style*, 61–62, pl. 13; cf. P. Blome, "Phönizische Dämonen auf einem attischen Krater," *AA* (1985), 573–79.

[58] Smith, "Kothar," 105–73, on Kothar's maritime powers, assuming that Phoenician Chousor is represented by Triton in a Hellenistic treaty (Polybius, 2.42): M. L. Barré, *The God-List in the Treaty between Hannibal and Philip V of Macedonia: A Study in the Light of the Ancient Near Eastern Treaty Tradition* (Baltimore, 1983), 84–86.

sea" (Eustathius ad *Iliad*, 771). These poetic designations are more closely related to each other than the rationalistic reductions of them to historical inventions, represented in Philo's (Sanchuniathon's) account. Moreover, the ascription of a maritime seat to a divinity is formulaic in Near Eastern conceptions of divinity: compare "the roots of the sea are his throne" (Job 36:31). Kothar's titles belong with his "homes" in Kaphtor and Egypt: in a world that imports raw materials and transports finished products, not to mention their manufacturers, such titles are probably too formulaic for specific powers.

These last two "homes" associate the Ugaritic craftsman-god explicitly with "Kaphtor" (Crete?) and Egypt. When Kothar is fetched by gods in need of his services, he is mentioned in connection with two distant locales in particular. Twice in the Danel epic, when served by the king and his wife (*CTA* 17.5 = *KTU* 1.17 V, 20–21 and 30–31), Kothar is referred to as "Lord of all divine Memphis" (*b'l ḥkpt*). In other poetic expressions repeated several times (e.g., at *CTA* 1.3 = *KTU* 1.1 III, 1–2; *CTA* 3.6. 15–16) and sometimes alternating with his other names, he is described thus:

> *kptr ks'u ṯbth:*
>
> *ḥkpt 'arṣ nḥlth:*
>
> Kaphtor is the throne of his dwelling
>
> Memphis is the land of his inheritance

In the same epic passage where all three of his foreign domains are invoked (*CTA* 17.5. 2–33), Kothar also has a "divine home," a "tent" like other gods (32–33), whither he departs once his mission is accomplished. This suggests that his claims to Egypt and "Kaphtor" are cult titles, like the traditional *bn ym* ("son of sea") and *bnm 'dt* ("son of the confluence"). Thus neither locale makes him a god native to the Aegean or to Egypt, rather than to Ugarit, but the two expressions are poetic indications of Late Bronze Age industry and trade.

Relations between Egypt and the Levant were close and constant, according to historical and archaeological sources linking the extended Levantine coast through the Via Maris traffic (Map 2).[59] As a North Syrian compliment to the monuments and cults of Egypt, an "inheritance" at Memphis could simply indicate the artistic influence and political dominion of Egypt in the coastal Levant in the Late Bronze Age. But a specific cult connection enriches this relationship beyond an ornamental epithet, for Kothar's closest relative in the Egyptian pantheon resides at Memphis. Kothar's Phoenician and Greek descendants, Chousor and Hephaistos, were identified with Ptah, whose name and cult produced the Egyptian name for Memphis (*ḥwt-k3-ptḥ, ḥt-ka-ptaḥ*, "abode of Ptah"). Kothar's Ugaritic attributes suggest how early this process of syncretism was at work.[60] This connection with Egypt therefore feeds into the origins of the *interpretatio*

---

[59] Smith, *Interconnections*, chap. 1; Helck, *Beziehungen Ägyptens zu Vorderasien*; Smith, "Kothar," 182.

[60] B. Holmberg, *The God Ptah* (Lund, 1946); Dombrowski, *Europa*, 187 n. 42; Smith, "Kothar," 102,

Graeca of the Levantine evidence. Not only does Kothar's connection to Ptah–Memphis anticipate his relationship with Hephaistos, but the "home of Ptah," *Ḥkptḥ*, is what the Greeks learned to call Egypt (Αἴγυπτος).[61] In other words, it may have been through the Levant in the Bronze Age that speakers of Greek, from the Aegean, learned the name of Egypt, just as their experience of Egypt was channeled from the Levant. Αἰ-γύπτ(ι)ος was already current in the language of Homer and in Mycenaean Greek at Knossos (Db 1105), and the same process may have brought Kothar to the Aegean.

The latter relationship is indicated by his other domicile, *kptr*. The identity of Kaphtor has been accepted as Crete, based on the appearance and attributes of the Keftiu in New Kingdom tomb paintings and Near Eastern references, which extend from the third millennium B.C. through the third century A.D.[62] As early as the reign of Zimrilim (ca. 1780) at Mari on the Euphrates, merchants from "Kaptar" acquired tin from the Near East and apparently turned it into weapons (described as "Kaptarite work") inlaid with precious materials like gold and lapis lazuli. In Eighteenth Dynasty Egypt, "Keftiu ships" and men bring exotic goods and artifacts—metal, vessels including Aegean-look-ing rhyta, and ivory—from abroad. The Aegean world, in general, seems to be the source of these references and representations, rather than a specific place such as Crete.[63] References to Kaphtor and its luxury industries are concentrated in the great international age of the Aegean Bronze Age, its latest phase (ca. 1500–1200 B.C.), and agree with the record of luxury goods found in Aegean palaces and tombs. In four-teenth-century Ugarit, Egypt and the Aegean were natural frames of references for lux-ury arts in metal, both for their production and their distribution. Ugaritic mythology reflects this international market of luxury artifacts dominated by metals, whose mobile craftsmen carried tools and materials on Keftiu ships, and any serious industrial enter-prise began with importing materials and metallurgists. The mechanics, agents, and consequences of this exchange will be examined in Chapter 5, where the archaeological record reveals the relationships that must have inspired expressions describing Ugaritic craftsmen as "Lord of Memphis" and "enthroned at Kaphtor."

On a literary level, Kothar's connection with Kaphtor intensifies his close relationship with Hephaistos. Their epithets, creations, and specialties overlap too closely for coin-

104–5, argues that *b'l ḥkptḥ* indicates "an ancient rec-ognition of the similarities of these two gods of crafts."

[61] Astour, *Hellenosemitica*, 88; J.-E. Dugand, "A pro-pos de Σαλαμίς," in *Salamine de Chypre*, 94 n. 106, cf. review of *CAH* II.1 by Muhly, *JAOS* 97 (1977) 66; Smith, *Kothar*, 102 n. 249. Cf. the Greek word Νεῖ-λος, derived from an Eighteenth Dynasty Egyptian word: H. Goedicke, "Νεῖλος: An Etymology," *AJP* 100 (1979), 69–72.

[62] Strange, *Caphtor/Keftiu*, argues that Caphtor = Cyprus; cf. Knapp, *JFA* 12 (1985) 231–50; cf. I. Vin-

centelli, "Appunti sulle nuove proposti di localizza-zione di Caphtor/Kefitu," in *In Memoria di Piero Mer-iggi*, *SMEA* 24 (Rome, 1984) 263–69. Wachsmann, *Ae-geans in the Theban Tombs*.

[63] Thus argued Virolleaud (*Ugaritica* 5 [1968] 570) in calling *kptr* "la Crète ou, plus généralement, [le] monde égéen ou préhellénique," which agrees with the status of the Aegean as a trading rather than po-litical presence in the Near East, and the inheritance of Keftiu activity by Canaanites and Phoenicians (see Chapter 5).

cidence, but the question of influence and its direction can be argued both ways. Hellenists tend to view the Levantine formula as "a notable tribute to Daedalus and his colleagues."[64] More specifically, Cyrus Gordon and those eager to demonstrate a Semitic population on Crete and its repercussions for Levantine culture claim that *Kothar-wa-Hasis* is "essentially a reflex of a Cretan prototype" and represents the "strong artistic influence of Crete" back to the Near East.[65] From the perspective of the Greek pantheon, the Ugaritic craftsman-god suggests an *interpretatio Syriaca* of Hephaistos, and the suggestion of Hephaistos's cult, through his name, at Mycenaean Knossos (Kn L58, NP) would prove that Kothar's identification with Hephaistos begins in the Late Bronze Age. Yet the Ugaritic texts presumably antedate the final literary conception of Hephaistos in Homer, where the Greek god makes a gold and silver krater for Phaidimos, king of the Sidonians (*Odyssey* 4.615–17 = 15.117–18), in an *interpretatio Homerica* of the god Kothar. The only mortals for whom Hephaistos produces his divine creations are Phoenicians, as if Greek poets returned the compliment that enthroned Kothar at Kaphtor, by establishing clients for Hephaistos in the Levant.[66]

A third scenario explaining the kinship of Kothar and Hephaistos has both craftsmen share a common tradition, manifest in the eastern Mediterranean literary *koine* of the Late Bronze Age. This would replace the model of "influence" with a more fruitful and accurate view of the Orientalizing experience as a two-way street, in keeping with the mutual praise in Greek and Levantine poetry implied by their references to "Phoenician" and "Kaptorite" art, respectively.[67] This explains why, for example, a fresco from Mycenae with a "goddess of grain" finds its closest parallel in an ivory pyxis from Syria, whose deity already wears Aegean dress (Chapter 5, n. 39). They illustrate the Mycenaean and Canaanite poles of the two-way exchange, whose link lies in the poetics analyzed in Part I. It is the phenomenon of Daidalos that illuminates the relationship between Kothar and Hephaistos as an aspect of the assimilation of East by West.

The name of Daidalos personifies qualities that appear elsewhere as adjectives; in fact, he developed in the process of composition, whereby all other possible forms of his name had been exhausted in the Homeric description of the shield of Achilles (as argued in Chapter 1). His existence also depends heavily on the personality of Hephaistos and other artists like Harmonides (*Iliad* 5.60) and even Athena (*Iliad* 14.179), in that poetically versatile forms of δαιδαλ- cluster in passages devoted to these other craftsmen. In the Ugaritic tradition related to Greek epic poetry, multiple names express qualities confined to adjectives in Homer, and behave with sufficient independence from each other so as to suggest separate personalities for each epithet or title. The clearest

---

[64] Thus West in *Early Greek Philosophy and the Orient*, 29 n. 4, although he represents *kptr ks'u ṯbth* as a "palace and workshop in Crete."

[65] Gordon, "Homer and Bible," 95 no. 141 (cf. no. 38); *Minos* 3 (1955) 126.

[66] Wiesner, *AA* (1968) 172–73; Stella, *Tradizione mi-*

cenea, 123. J.-E. Dugand, in *Salamine de Chypre,* 94, points out that "Phaidimos" translates Semitic *PL'* (cf. Hebrew *Pallu'* in Genesis 46.9), which would reinforce the Levantine contact behind this passage.

[67] Stella, *Tradizione micenea,* 368–91; Burkert, *Orientalisierende Epoche,* 106–10.

expression of this misunderstanding is in Philo's translation of Sanchuniathon's account of the Phoenician generations of inventors, where *Kothar-wa-Hasis* has been split into Χουσώρ and his "brother," plus a related figure, Οὖσωος.[68] The latter appears as the great-uncle of Chousor and is credited with the adaption of animal skins for clothing, the first (dug-out?) sea craft, and the earliest cult practices (stelai and libations). His great-nephew, Χουσώρ, invented iron and its working with his (unnamed) brother. By himself, he pronounced magic words in the form of λόγους καὶ ἐπῳδὰς καὶ μαντείας, "stories and songs and prophecies," and contributed many inventions to seafaring: the fish-hook, line, bait, and the raft, on which he was apparently the first to sail. Philo equates him explicity with Hephaistos (εἶναι δὲ τοῦτον τόν Ἥφαιστον) although only metallurgy is common to both craftsmen, and the glamorous metals of the Late Bronze Age (gold, silver) have been replaced by the raw material that gave the Iron Age its name. These major differences suggest that Chousor may have inherited little more than his name from Kothar. Although worshiped posthumously (as if to reconcile his status with Hephaistos), he has lost trappings of his divinity, as well as his poetic personality, in the euhemeristic transmission. He has also gained marine powers all too common among the other Phoenician inventors; Ousoos shares with Sydyk the development of seafaring, for example. Even his magic spells are common for other mythical metallurgists like the Daktyls, who are called γόητες and invented mystery rites as well as the working of iron (Strabo, 10.3.22), much as Chousor did for the Phoenicians. In short, too many of Chousor's qualities reflect Hellenistic euhemerism for them to substantiate the Ugaritic legend of Kothar.

Since the decipherment of the Ugaritic texts, most scholars have recognized the division of *Kothar-wa-hasis* into multiple personalities beginning in the Bronze Age, according to Philo or his source, Sanchuniathon. Not all agree that the figure of Οὖσωος is derived from *ḥss*, Kothar's other half, because the etymological relationship is less explicit than between Χουσώρ and Kothar.[69] Within the account of Philo (or Sanchuniathon) alone, pairs of craftsmen are repeated throughout half a dozen generations. Hypouranios and Ousoos are succeeded by Agrieus and Halieus ("Hunter" and "Fisher") before Chousor and his brother, in the next generation by Τεχνίτης and Γήινος Αὐτόχθων ("Earthborn Native"), followed by Agros and Agrotes, two farmerheroes, and finally by Misor and Sydyk. The last two are the father of pairs familiar in the Greek world as craftsmen, healers, and seafarers (e.g., the Kabeiroi and the Dioskouroi) but also personify *ṣdq* and *mšr*, Semitic concepts of justice and righteousness.[70]

[68] Philo of Byblos = *FGrH* 790 F 2, 9–14; Attridge and Oden, *Philo of Byblos*, 45, 82, 84; Baumgarten, *Philo of Byblos*, 142–43, 162–70; Smith, "Kothar," 473–76.

[69] O. Eissfeldt, *Taautos und Sanchuniathon* (Berlin, 1952) 39; Attridge and Oden, *Philo of Byblos*, 82–83

and Baumgarten, *Philo of Byblos*, 163–64, prefer the Biblical Azael as an ancestor for Οὖσωος, while others point to a district of Tyre called "Uzu."

[70] Baumgarten, *Philo of Byblos*, 175; Attridge and Oden, *Philo of Byblos*, 85 nn. 74–77; see Chapter 5, on Kabeiroi in Greece. Weinfeld, in *Mesopotamien und*

Chousor and his "brother," Ousoos, reflect the Greek rationalization of early legends about craftsmen into historical inventors arranged into categories and generations. But in between Kothar and Chousor, twin craftsmen or pairs in Hebrew, Greek, and Roman literature could represent intermediate stages in the legacy of Kothar. As noted, the closest descendants of Canaanite and Homeric craftsmen are a pair named by the Hebrew God to build his tabernacle and his equipment (*Exodus* 31.1–11). Bezalel and Oholiab, of the tribe of Dan, are endowed by God "with all craftsmanship, to devise artistic designs, to work in gold, silver and bronze, in cutting stones for setting, and in carving wood, for work in every art." Following the completion of the religious structures this pair of craftsmen are joined by their pupils, and God once again inspires them, this time to pass on their skills (35.30–35): "And he has inspired him to teach, both him and Oholiab the son of Ahisamach of the tribe of Dan. He has filled them with ability to do every sort of work done by a craftsman or by a designer or by an embroiderer in blue and purple and scarlet stuff and fine twined linen, or by a weaver—by any sort of workman or skilled designer." The talents and techniques of Kothar, Hephaistos, and the semantic range of δαίδαλα are embraced in this Biblical concept of an early Iron Age craftsman, whose talents in wood, textiles, metalworking, and jewelry are the most highly valued. Before Daidalos evolved into a vehicle for classical and philosophical values (see Part III), he belonged to this artistic sphere, much as the Mycenaean world shares more with the Near East than with its classical heritage. Subtler than in Biblical literature are classical characterizations of craftsmen that allude to a tradition of sons, pairs, and pupils. Among craftsmen who worked in pairs—as father and son or master and apprentice—some of the earliest are associated with Crete, an area involved with the Levant in both the Bronze and Iron Ages (see Dipoinos and Skyllis, Chersiphron and Metagenes, etc., discussed in Chapter 6). Eventually, Daidalos himself acquired both a son, Ikaros, and a nephew-apprentice, Talos or Kalos (see Chapter 9). But the literary contribution to this dual tradition could well derive from the Bronze Age.

The distance between the Ugaritic and Phoenician versions, compounded by the intrusion of Hellenistic concepts and Greek translations, prevents tracing, or even presuming, these intermediate stages with confidence. But the relationship of Daidalos to Hephaistos suggests that refractions and misunderstandings of the northwest Semitic craftsman's literary dimensions began as early as the Bronze Age. For the name and qualities expressed by Homeric *daidala* duplicate the poetic relationship of *ktr* and *mktr* as if Daidalos were a formation parallel to one or more of Kothar's appellations. The uncertain etymology of *dal-* prevents a definite equation with *ktr*, *ḥss*, or *hyn*, specifically: any one of them could have inspired the Greek equivalent, Δαίδαλος, whose meaning, "Skillful One," conveys much the same sense as Kothar and his other names

---

seine Nachbarn, 513 n. 15, compares *ṣdq* and *mṣr* with Hesiod's (ἰθείας δίκας and ἰθυδίκῃσι ἀνδράσι: *Works and Days* 225–26, 230).

in Ugaritic. Thus Daïdalos would be an *interpretatio Homerica* of Kothar or his other names, perhaps the result of an epic collision with a craftsman already native to the Aegean and its poetic tradition.

This Hellenization included a translation of a Semitic word into a Greek equivalent, although neither word displays an etymology clear enough for appreciation. But transmission through a calque, a process crucial to the interaction of Near Eastern and Greek culture, is amply attested in Greek as early as Homeric poetry. Happily, it is also concentrated in those expressions that point to the Orient. The name of the Sidonian king, Phaidimos, has been compared with Semitic names with the same meaning, "illustrious" or "shining" (see n. 66). The most significant of all of these translations is the name of the Phoenicians themselves, a Greek rendition of "Red" or "Purple" people that duplicates Semitic "Canaan."[71] In other words, next to transliterations of place-names like *ḥkptḥ* into Αἴγυπτος and loanwords for products like sesame and cumin, gold and linen, certain Near Eastern names and terms were understood in their native meanings by Greeks and translated into Greek equivalents. Dombrowski has recently emphasized this distinction by identifying the Greek name and figure of Europa as a translation of the name of the Ugaritic goddess, ʿAnat, rather than a transliteration of Semitic ʿereb. In his appendix on the related translation that produced Φοινίκη, he comments on the neglected phenomenon of Greek *Lehnübersetzungen*, which he defines "Wiedergaben fremder Namen durch solche eigenen, die etwa den gleichen Sinn hatten und auf wirklich oder vermutlich ähnliche Weise gebildet worden waren."[72] This secondary level of transmission requires either a native interpreter capable of explaining the word to a speaker of Greek, or a Greek capable of understanding the foreign word through a minimal command of the foreign language. Since the Middle Bronze Age, interpreters are attested at Mari for merchants from "Kaptar," and a modicum of bilingual communication must have governed certain commercial transactions throughout the long history of East-West exchange. That such linguistic interaction ultimately included intellectual exchange is borne out by the comparative evidence of Ugaritic and Homeric poetry and the close similarities between Aegean and Near Eastern religion since the Late Bronze Age (see Chapter 5). The climax of this intellectual encounter would seem to be the invention and transmission of the alphabet, which presumes a level of *Stadt-* and *Schriftkultur* far beyond superficial commercial relations.[73]

---

[71] M. Astour, "The Origin of the Terms 'Canaan,' 'Phoenician' and 'Purple',"" *JNES* 24 (1965) 346–70; Muhly, *Berytus* 11 (1970) 24–35; Edwards, *Kadmos*, 56–58, 94–98; Dombrowski, "Eine weitere griechische Lehnübersetzung: Φοινίκη," in *Europa*, 163–66. Some still prefer an association with palm-trees, based on po-ni-ki-jo in Linear B: Billigmeier, *Kadmos*, 58–62; J. Melena, "*Po-ni-ki-jo* in the Knossos Ga Tablets," *Minos* 14 (1973) 77–84; C. Murray and P. War-

ren, "*Po-ni-ki-jo* among the Dye-plants of Minoan Crete," *Kadmos* 15 (1976) 40–60; E. D. Foster, "*Po-ni-ki-jo* in the Knossos Tablets Reconsidered," *Minos* 16 (1977) 52–66.

[72] Dombrowski, *Europa*, 163. On Semitic loanwords transliterated into Greek, see E. Masson, *Recherches sur les plus anciens empruntes sémitiques en Grec* (Paris, 1967); Billigmeier, *Kadmos*, 46–71.

[73] Burkert, *Orientalisierende Epoche*, 29–35, 36–42, on

In terms of the Late Bronze Age, the world of the Ugaritic texts lies midway between the Mari archives and the first Greek alphabets. The excavations at Ras Shamra have revealed a community where such intellectual transformations took place (Chapter 5), and elements from its literature have been accepted as the source for Aegean counterparts. If goddesses like Anat, along with her consort Baal, in his form as a bull, are migrating to Crete as Europa and Zeus, then the transformation of Kothar into Greek "Daidalos" belongs to a congeries of Near Eastern arrivals. Daidalos even preserves the association with Crete that Kothar enjoyed in the form of a "throne at Kaphtor," for his Homeric equivalent designs for a Cretan princess descended from Anat/Europa, Ariadne.

In his post-Homeric life, Daidalos continues to shadow Hephaistos. Weapons crafted by Hephaistos are described as δαιδάλεος (*Aspis* 237–317; Pindar, *Nemean* 4.59–60), and the two artists substitute for each other in different versions of the same myth.[74] In early Greek art, both craftsmen (?) seem to attend the birth of Athena (Figure 13, 14d and, by implication, in Figure 9). Late in the classical period, Daidalos wears the outfit of Hephaistos and substitutes for him in a duel with Ares, where only the inscription identifies Daidalos (Figure 11).[75] In cult, the next milieu where the two craftsmen converge is in classical Athens, where they become major figures of local cult and Daidalos becomes a descendant of Hephaistos ([Plato] *Alkibiades* 1.121. a1; see Chapter 10). So successful was the transformation of Daidalos into a historical craftsman that commentators on his debut in the *Iliad* expressed consternation that the work of a god (Hephaistos) could be compared with that of a mere mortal (Daidalos).[76]

In conclusion, Ugaritic and Mycenaean sources corroborate a Near Eastern origin for a Late Bronze Age Daidalos, a cult figure (at least at Knossos) competitive with Hephaistos and still respected in epic poetry. That a deity representing art should have made

---

the background to the Greek adoption of the alphabet; Morris, in *Challenge of* Black Athena, 43–44, on the neglect of the calque in studies of East-West influence. Cf. Gordon, *Berytus* 25 (1977) 129, on the intellectual community at Ugarit.

[74] For example, Theseus escapes from the labyrinth either with a thread provided by Daidalos, or a crown made by Hephaistos: Delcourt, *Héphaistos*, 159–62; F. Brommer, "Theseus-Deutungen," *AA* (1982) 69–88. Kris and Kurz, *Legend, Myth and Magic in the Image of the Artist*, 68–69, both describe Attic Daidalos as a "double" of Hephaistos, apparently following C. Robert (*RE* IV, 1955; *Archäologische Märchen*, 11–12 n. 1); Schachermeyr, *Rückerinnerung*, 132, calls him "der irdische Doppelgänger eines Hephaistos."

[75] A black-figure vase from the Athenian Acropolis

(601) shows fragments of winged feet labeled "Ἴκαρος" (Figure 9). Unless the artist has misnamed Hermes, whom one might expect at the birth of Athena, Ikaros, if not his father, Daidalos, was present at the miracle performed by Hephaistos. Beazley, *JHS* 47 (1927) 224–26, suggested that Daidalos appeared in the same scene, appropriately on a vase made and dedicated for a patroness of craftsmanship, Athena. Daidalos appears as Hephaistos on a phlyax vase from Bari (Figure 11), London (Br. Museum F 269): A. D. Trendall, *Phlyax Vases. BICS* suppl. 19 (1967) 52 no. 81; Delcourt, *Héphaistos*, 93–94 n. 5.

[76] Nicanor (in Venetus Graecus 822: Erbse, *Scholia Graeca in Homeri Iliadem*, 4:564–65) discusses others' complaints that the simile in *Iliad* 18.591–92 is δύσφημον, μᾶλλον δὲ ἀπρεπές as γελοίως: see Chapter 1, n. 25.

an official impact on the Mycenaean pantheon at Knossos reflects the nature of Aegean relations with the Levant. Archaeology and mythology attest to the mobility of craftsmen and especially of metallurgists. Bronze traveled cast as ingots and as scrap, and was accompanied by tools and smiths, according to the contents of the Late Bronze Age Gelidonya wreck. Bronze- and ironworkers like the Telchines practiced island hopping just as tinkers and potters still do, and must have spread their tales with their trade.[77] Centuries of exchange in resources, techniques, and artifacts inspired mutual respect of exotic art in both locales, from "Kaptarite work" in eighteenth-century Mari to the work of πολυδαίδαλοι Phoenicians in Homeric Greece. If Kothar had a throne at Kaphtor, its Mycenaean name was the "Daidaleion." The relation between the two gods epitomizes the sophisticated and intellectual exchange between East and West that included mutual admiration of each other's arts. How Kothar became Daidalos requires understanding the archaeological patterns that reveal human interaction in Mediterranean history.

[77] Ch. Kardara, "The Itinerant Art," in *Primo Congresso Internazionale del Micenologia*, 222–27.

CHAPTER 5

From Bronze to Iron: Greece and Its Oriental Culture

AEGEAN AND LEVANT IN THE BRONZE AGE

THE LEVANTINE BACKGROUND of Daidalos bridges not only Orient and Aegean but helps narrow an artificial "gap" between the second and first millennia B.C., encouraged in modern scholarship. Understanding his background requires alternatives to the traditional periodization and classification of ancient cultures, particularly regarding the intercourse of East and West. The kinship of Kothar and Daidalos not only reintegrates what was once a common culture but highlights the foundation of that relationship—traffic in commodities.

The history of maritime connections in the ancient Mediterranean is a long, rich, and complex story of strategies for the exchange of natural resources.[1] The earliest seaborne voyages traceable in the Aegean, in Mesolithic times, involved the procurement of a raw material (obsidian). Their circumstances—limited coastal navigation, individual enterprise, and the quest for specific minerals—remained characteristic of ancient Mediterranean exploration.[2] Recent arguments even make agriculture, once the vanguard of the Neolithic "revolution," a response to the incentive of trade, developed for surplus to compete for newly available commodities.[3] The earliest "colony" attested in the Aegean, an Early Minoan settlement on Kythera, was probably dispatched for the sake of mineral resources in Lakonia, the same reasons, in the form of different metals, that drew Phoenicians there many centuries later.[4] The first contacts between Crete and the

---

[1] H. Müller-Karpe, ed., *Zur geschichtlichen Bedeutung der frühen Seefahrt*, Kolloquien zur allgemeinen und vergleichenden Archäologie 2 (Munich, 1982). See Maps 1 and 2 for sites discussed in this chapter.

[2] Obsidian from the island of Melos reached Franchthi Cave in the Argolid: C. Perlès, "Des navigateurs méditerranéens il y a 10,000 ans," *La Recherche* 10 (1979) 82–83; R. Torrence, *Production and Exchange of Stone Tools: Prehistoric Obsidian in the Aegean* (Cambridge, 1986).

[3] C. Runnels and Tj. van Andel, "Trade and the Origins of Agriculture in the Eastern Mediterranean," *JMA* 1 (1988) 83–109, with debate in *JMA* 2 (1989) 139–56, 297–302.

[4] J. Yakar, "Cythera and the Ancient Near East," *Anatolica* 4 (1971–1972) 133–37, for the Aegean's earliest Orientalia (Old Babylonian seal and a Fifth Dynasty stone bowl); J. N. Coldstream and G. L. Huxley, ed., *Kythera: Excavations and Studies* (London, 1972); S. Morris, "Lakonian Marble in the Bronze

Near East followed the same lure of metals.[5] Current discoveries of tin in the Taurus mountains of south-central Anatolia contribute to the picture of the coastal Levant as chief market for copper from Cyprus and tin from Anatolia, as well as to the background of Old Assyrian colonization in southeast Anatolia.[6] By the Middle Bronze Age, Aegean entrepreneurs evidently reached Mari on business trips, communicating through interpreters, and Minoan palace workshops were transforming imported materials into "Kaptarite work."[7] Cyprus was a critical stage, if not source, in the traffic of metal from East to West, but the Aegean's primary destination was the Levant, as in the Iron Age.[8] In fact, Cyprus and the Levant shared with the Aegean a satellite status with the Near East, and their histories must be traced outside the epigraphic horizons of its empires. For example, the confusion generated by the collapse of the Old Babylonian Dynasty at Mari, the rise of the Hittites, and the Hyksos invasions of Egypt actually promoted a Cypriote role in the copper trade and intensified Aegean relations with Cyprus.[9]

The Late Bronze Age (1500–1200 B.C.) ushered in the most significant phase of Aegean relations with the Near East, an "international age" of lasting intellectual and social exchanges as well as commercial transactions linking the Aegean with Hittite, Egyptian, and Mesopotamian empires. Figures called "Keftiu" bring tribute in Egyptian records and representations; their images resemble those in Aegean paintings, they carry Aegean objects, and they come from the "Islands in the Middle of the Sea."[10] These pic-

Age," *AJA* 86 (1982) 278; Morris, in *The Minoan Thalassocracy* 61, 111; Morris, "Hollow Lakedaimon," *HSCP* 88 (1984) 9. Phoenicians and metal in Lakonia: Drews, *AJP* 100 (1979) 46 n. 9.

[5] H. Klengel, "Near Eastern Trade and the Emergence of Interaction with Crete in the Third Millennium B.C.," *SMEA* 24 (1984) 7–19; H.-G. Buchholz, "Das Metallhandel des zweiten Jahrtausends im Mittelmeerraum," in *Society and Economy in the Eastern Mediterranean*, 187–228.

[6] K. Aslihan Yener, "The Archaeometry of Silver in Anatolia: the Bolgardağ Mining District," *AJA* 90 (1986) 469–72; "Tin in the Turkish Taurus Mountains," *Antiquity* 61 (1987) 220–26. Old Assyrian colonies in Anatolia: Curtin, *Cross-Cultural Trade*, 67–70.

[7] Strange, *Caphtor/Keftiu*, 90–91, texts E 33–36 from Mari; Kantor, *Aegean and the Orient*, 74–75. A. Malamut, "Syro-Palestinian Destinations in a Mari Tin Inventory," *IEJ* 21 (1971) 31–38, on the "man from Caphtor" trading in tin at Mari through an interpreter (*ta-ar-ga-ma-an-num*, "dragoman": Mari A.1270). Oriental/izing art in Middle Bronze Age Crete: S. Peirce, "Syrian Influence on Middle Minoan Art," *AJA* 84 (1980) 226; E. Møller, "A Re-evaluation

of the Oriental Cylinder Seals found in Crete," and I. Strøm, "Middle Minoan Crete: Re-Consideration of Some of Its External Relations," both in *Interaction and Acculturation in the Mediterranean* ed. J. Best and N. de Vries (Amsterdam, 1982), 85–103, 104–23.

[8] R. Merrillees, *Trade and Transcendence in the Bronze Age Levant*, SIMA 39 (Göteborg, 1979), 5–11. Y. Portugali and B. Knapp, "Cyprus and the Aegean: A Spatial Analysis of Interaction in the 17th–14th Centuries B.C.," in *Prehistoric Production and Exchange*, 44–78; Knapp, *JFA* 12 (1985) 231–50.

[9] D. Saltz, "The Chronology of the Middle Cypriote Period," *RDAC* (1977) 51–69; T. Stech, "Copper and Society in Late Bronze Age Cyprus," in *Prehistoric Production and Exchange*, 100–105; cf. Knapp, *Copper Production and Divine Protection*, 70–73, on Cypriote culture (1700–1400 B.C.) and the demand for copper; *JFA* 12 (1985) 249–50, and with Portugali in *Prehistoric Production and Exchange*, 44–78. Cf. the fate of Phoenicians after the Late Bronze Age (nn. 84–90).

[10] Wachsmann, *Aegeans in the Theban Tombs*, for a recent survey of Keftiu in Egyptian art; Strange, *Caphtor/Keftiu* (on literary testimonia), locates the Keftiu on Cyprus, not Crete.

torial images and their names are not a demographic record of Bronze Age merchants: they do not guarantee that Keftiu are specifically Cretans or any other ethnic group, rather than a variable consortium of merchants and entrepreneurs. While this consortium no doubt included Aegean interests, products, and markets, the focus of trade remained the coastal Levant, the pivot point of contact between the Aegean and Egypt. The term "Keftiu" may have indicated foreign seafarers the way "Phoenicians" did for the Greeks (see the following section) or "Iavan" in Assyria, and probably included Levantines. Port of origin, destination, and cargo identified such traders to foreign eyes, more than the ethnic affiliation of their crew.[11] Despite its modern imprecision, "Keftiu" may be an accurate as well as convenient description of the ancient partnership of Aegean and Levant in maritime commerce of the Late Bronze Age.

The most eloquent testimony to Keftiu trade between the Aegean and the Near East emerged in two Bronze Age shipwrecks excavated off the Lykian coast of Turkey. The first one discovered, which sank off Cape Gelidonya around 1200 B.C., contained a cargo of bronze and copper ingots, scrap, and tools, along with other evidence for industry and trade in metals, attributed by the excavator to the Levant.[12] Transmission of techniques, at least in the Iron Age, was partly the responsibility of imported workmen, and the contents of the Gelidonya wreck (tools, scrap, and ingots) suggest itinerant craftsmen of the kind associated with "Kaptor" in Near Eastern sources. The more recent discovery, still under excavation off Ulu Burun near the city of Kaş on the Lykian coast, sank about two hundred years earlier (in the late fourteenth or early thirteenth century, according to its Mycenaean and Egyptian artifacts), with an even more spectacular cargo.[13] Luxury items of gold, ivory, faience, glass, amber, and silver, along with exotic φάρμακα (jars of frankincense, orpiment, fig-medicine), bring to life scenes of tribute and offering in Egyptian tomb paintings of the period, but these are mere trinkets compared with the primary, motivating cargo of copper and tin ingots. A ship like this might have collected its cargo at a Levantine port such as Ras Shamra, could have called at Cyprus, even started from Egypt, and was probably bound for the Aegean. On the basis of the wreck's contents, Bass reconstructs a highly plausible counterclockwise circle of trade that linked Egypt, the Levant, and the Aegean for many centuries and in

[11] Pace Knapp's emphasis on ethnicity (JFA 12 [1985] 244). Bunnens, L'expansion phénicienne, 15–21, on Bronze Age Keftiu as background to Phoenician trade; A. Altman, "Trade between the Aegean and the Levant in the Late Bronze Age: Some Neglected Questions," in Society and Economy in the Eastern Mediterranean, 229–37, on the Levantine role.

[12] G. Bass, Cape Gelidonya: A Bronze Age Shipwreck, TAPS 57 (Philadelphia, 1967); J. F. Muhly, T. S. Wheeler, and J. R. Maddin, "The Cape Gelidonya Shipwreck and the Bronze Age Metals Trade in the

Eastern Mediterranean," JFA 4 (1977) 353–62; for a redefense of the Levantine role, see G. Bass, "Cape Gelidonya and Bronze Age Maritime Trade," in Orient and Occident, 29–38; but in Challenge of Black Athena, 111–12, he admits that new finds of Mycenaean stirrup jars near the wreck mean the ship "may or may not be Canaanite."

[13] Excavation reports: Bass, AJA 90 (1986) 269–96; National Geographic 172, no. 6 (1987) 693–733; Pulak, AJA 92 (1988) 1–37; AJA 93 (1989) 1–29. Also Morris, in Challenge of Black Athena, 42–45.

which eastern Mediterranean merchants—Keftiu, Canaanite, or Phoenician, depending on the historical setting—played the primary role.[14] The anonymous crew of the Kaş wreck could be Aegean, Cypriote, or Levantine, and most likely included some of each, as on Egyptian ships in the Amarna period or on the ships of Tyre whose loss was lamented in Ezekiel 27.[15]

The mixed contents of the Kaş wreck defy theories of Canaanite or Aegean "monopolies" on Bronze Age trade with the Levant, but illuminate the Keftiu phenomenon and its effects in the eastern Mediterranean. For example, such vessels could have brought the hoard of lapis lazuli in lumps and seals to Boiotian Thebes, a windfall in cargo from the Levant. Discovered in 1963, these seals revived the role of the Near East in Bronze Age trade, along with the authenticity of the Theban myth of Kadmos.[16] In their definitive publication, the lapis objects are called a diplomatic gift to a Mycenaean ruler of Thebes from a Kassite king of Babylon, via Cyprus.[17] The cuirass worn by Agamemnon was such a gift from Kinyras of Cyprus, probably a Levantine king of the Late Bronze Age (Iliad 11.15–46; see Chapter 1, nn. 15–17); in the Iron Age, Amasis of Egypt and Polykrates of Samos revived such exchanges. But the interpretation proposed for the Theban seals presumes a greater importance than Aegean dynasts—as opposed to their markets and products—held among Near Eastern rulers. It also leaves unexplained how other miscellaneous objects found with the seals (agate beads and stamp seals, faience, ivory, and raw lapis) reached the same destination with finished products fit for a king. In addition, many of the seals were reworked or covered with gold foil, apparently in Cyprus, probably intermediate to their Syrian and Mesopotamian origins.[18] The faience plaques of Amenophis found at Mycenaean sites probably made their way to the Ae-

[14] Bass, AJA 90 (1986) 85–96; National Geographic 172, no. 6 (1987) 698–99, for map of Eastern Mediterranean trade; Weinstein, in Bass and others, AJA 93 (1989) 24–29, on indirect trade between Egypt and the Aegean in the Late Bronze Age.

[15] As Merrillees once argued for the Gelidonya wreck in Trade and Transcendence in the Levant, 8. Knapp, JFA 12 (1985) 244, argues for "a multi-dimensional, complex network of exchange conducted by both royal and private merchants," citing an internationally staffed ship in Amarna letter 27. Ezekiel 27 describes ships built of four kinds of wood, outfitted with sails of imported linen and purple, rowed by men from Sidon and Arward, with pilots from Zemer, and Byblite shipwrights, but owned by Tyre.

[16] These seals turned Thebes into a Babylonian colony (B. Hemmerdinger, "La colonie babylonienne de la Kadmée," Helikon 7 [1967] 232–40; cf. his "Trois notes. I: Kadmos, II. Emprunts du grec mycénien à L'akkadien, III. L'infiltration phénicienne en Béotie,"

REG 9 [1966] 698–703) or "a commercial depot for Canaanites"; J. Sasson, "Canaanite Maritime Involvement in the Second Millennium B.C.," JAOS 66 (1966) 126–38. Others still denied "Phoenicians" in the Bronze Age Aegean: Muhly, Berytus 11 (1970) 19–64; Edwards, Kadmos, 131–37; Morris, in JMA 3 (1990) 58–60.

[17] E. Porada, "The Cylinder Seals Found at Thebes in Boeotia," AfO 28 (1981) 1–70, esp. 68–70.

[18] Cf. Mitannian seals found in Greece as casual arrivals, not official gifts: I. Pini, "Mitanni-Rollsiegel des 'Common Style,' " PZ 58 (1983) 114–26. Other objections to Porada's interpretation: Edwards, Kadmos, 131–34; G. Mylonas, Mycenae and the Mycenaean Age (Princeton, 1965), 204 n. 68, attributes the seals to an "antiquarian . . . wanax." S. Symeonoglou, The Topography of Thebes (Princeton, 1985), 227, has "little doubt that they came to Thebes as the commodity lapis lazuli"; Morris, JMA 3 (1990) 58–60.

gean by similar means, without requiring the kind of relationship that the Pharaoh cultivated with Syrian and Kassite rulers.[19] The Kaṣ wreck, like the treasures found at Thebes and Mycenae, includes equally "official" foreign objects, such as seals and scarabs, but many were recut, deliberately damaged, or found with scrap, as if part of a secondhand cargo in precious materials.[20] Tomb robbers or looters of sanctuaries could have sold them to "Keftiu," who brought them to the Aegean in secondhand trade. The fortuitous discovery of imported Oriental seals and jewelry with their raw materials illustrates the dynamics of Orientalizing exchange. Foreign products and exotic materials were turned into "Kaptarite" work throughout the second and first millennium, whether as Egyptian stone bowls "improved" in Crete, cylinder seals recut in Cyprus, or Oriental bronze reliefs applied to Greek sculpture in the seventh century B.C.[21] Transforming imported novelties into native traditions was apparently what Greeks enjoyed and excelled at, whether in the Bronze Age or the Iron Age.

Thanks to these two Bronze Age ships, archaeologists and historians can better imagine the exchange that inspired expressions praising an Ugaritic craftsman-god as "Lord of Memphis" and "enthroned at Kaphtor." Keftiu ships circulated materials and techniques of craftsmanship, especially in those luxury arts in which their craftsmen-gods specialized. Itinerant metalworkers—like the Telchines, who discovered iron on Cyprus, then migrated to Crete, Rhodes, and Thebes (Strabo, 10.3.7, 14.2.7; Pausanias, 9.19.1)—may have traveled on ships such as these in the Bronze Age and continued to do so after the collapse of Near East–based networks.[22]

However such discoveries refine our understanding of Orientalizing art, our objective is poetry, whose travels leave more delicate traces. The context and contacts involved in the encounter between East and West must have included an intellectual dimension to sponsor the profound and lasting cultural impact observed in literature and religion.

[19] E. Cline, "Amenophis III and the Aegean: A Reassessment of Egypto-Aegean Relations in the 14th Century B.C.," *Orientalia* 56 (1987) 1–36, makes the faience plaques a diplomatic gift like the Theban seals: cf. P. Haider, "Zu den ägyptisch-ägäischen Handelsbeziehungen zwischen ca. 1370 und 1200 v. Chr. I: Das Handelssystem," *MBAH* 7, no. 2 (1988) 12–26, and "II: Handelsgüter und Handelswege," *MBAH* 8, no. 1 (1989) 1–28; G. Hölbl, "Zur kulturellen Stellung der Aegyptica in der mykenischen und frühgriechischen Welt," *Forschungen zur ägäischen Vorgeschichte. Das Ende der mykenischen Welt*, ed. E. Thomas (Cologne, 1987), 123–42.

[20] See comments by Collon and Weinstein in *AJA* 93 (1989) 12–26.

[21] Cf. worked and unworked ivory found on Cyprus (*RDAC* [1969] 40–41; pl. v, 4; *RDAC* [1985] pls.

XI, 6; XIV, 5) and in seventh-century burials at Carthage: S. Lancel, "Ivoires phénico-puniques de la nécropole archaique de Byrsa, à Carthage," in *Studi Fenici e Punici*, 687–92; J. Phillips, "The Minoanization of Aegyptiaca" (paper presented at ASOR meetings, November 1989), on the Cretan market in Egyptian stone bowls; see Chapter 6, n. 15, for an Oriental bronze cauldron stand remade into a Greek *sphyrelaton* statue.

[22] Gordon, in *Aegean and the Near East*, 136–43; Chr. Kardara, "The Itinerant Art," in *Primo Congresso Internazionale di Micenologia*, 222–27; Catling, *RDAC* (1984) 69–91; P. Zaccagnini, "Patterns of Mobility among Ancient Near Eastern Craftsmen," *JNES* 24 (1983) 245–64. I discuss the Phoenician survival of this tradition later in this chapter.

Here, too, the Kaş wreck suggests an early route for the most Oriental of all Greek imports, the alphabet. To philologists and epigraphers, the most exciting find from the wreck is a folding wooden tablet on ivory hinges with traces of wax, stowed in one of the large storage vessels that served as "china barrels" full of pottery and miscellaneous items.[23] What letters and language it once served are open to speculation, and subject to epigraphic persuasions. Scholars have argued for a Canaanite protoalphabet as early as the fourteenth century, including Greek acquaintance with that alphabet long before the first Greek alphabetic inscription in the eighth century.[24] Greek etymology demonstrates that the word for such a writing tablet, δέλτος, was borrowed from the Near East along with the object, as if circumstances of learning and literacy accompanied the Greek adoption of the Semitic alphabet.[25] It seems unlikely that such a portable, casual tablet served formal archives using syllabic or cuneiform scripts. It is much more attractive to imagine it covered with Καδμήια γράμματα, according to the implied pattern of early, frequent, but casual and dispersed dissemination of the alphabet by Phoenicians and their forerunners.[26] The Ulu Burun tablet may be no more responsible for the dissemination of the alphabet to Greece than the Teke bowl, three centuries later (see Chapter 6), but neither is it any less important. If this tablet sank before it reached the Aegean, others may have survived the journey along with teachers of letters, and contributed to the reputation of Kadmos. It is a pleasant coincidence to find such a tablet so close to Lykia, which inspired at least one scholar to reexamine the Bellerophon episode in the *Iliad*, with its lead tablet covered with σήματα λυγρά, as an Oriental story.[27] At the very least, the tablet introduces the promise of literacy to the exchange between the Levant and the Aegean.

Without such connections, it would be possible to leave the relationship at the level of objects, in gifts or sales to "men from Kaptor" more interested in unloading copper or acquiring tin than in listening to poetry or learning about gods. The writing tablet on

[23] Reported by C. Pulak in *AJA* 92 (1988), 33; cf. Bass, *National Geographic* 172, no. 6 (1987) 730–31. The presence of orpiment, an arsenical compound mixed with wax on the writing tablet, in the same shipment (*AJA* 91 [1987] 278; *AJA* 92 [1988] 11; *AJA* 93 [1989] 10–11) suggests writing materials were to be delivered at one of the ship's destinations.

[24] Bernal, *Black Athena*, 427–33, and "On the Transmission of the Alphabet to the Aegean before 1400 B.C.," *BASOR* 267 (1987) 1–19, and *Cadmean Letters*, summarizes earlier arguments by Stieglitz, Naveh, Mendenhall, Millard, and McCarter, for a Canaanite linear alphabet, to which add G. Lundin, "Ugaritic Writing and the Origin of the Semitic Consonantal Alphabet," *Aula Orientalis* 5 (1987) 91–99, and W. C. Watt, "The Byblos Matrix," *JNES* 46 (1987) 1–14.

[25] Burkert, in *Greek Renaissance*, 52, claimed "the δέλτος is as old in Greece as the alphabet" (cf. his *Orientalisierende Epoche*, 33) before the Ulu Burun tablet was found; Morris, in *Challenge of* Black Athena, 44.

[26] G. Mendenhall "The Inscription from Çatal Hüyük in the Plain of Antakya," *Kadmos* 14 (1975) 48–63; W. Johnstone, "Cursive Phoenician and the Archaic Greek Alphabet," *Kadmos* 17 (1978) 151–66; Naveh, *Early History of the Alphabet*, 175–86. Bernal, *Cadmean Letters*, argues for a date of transmission before 1400 B.C.

[27] R. Bellamy, "Bellerophon's Tablet," *CJ* 84 (1989) 289–307, calls the Bellerophon episode "unmistakably Oriental," comparing it to Biblical literature, and citing the tablet from the Kaş wreck (p. 292, n. 8).

its way to the Aegean could have carried any one of Ugarit's languages or scripts, and archaeological evidence from Ras Shamra itself demonstrates the other end of this intellectual network shared by the two craftsmen-gods, *Kothar-wa-Hasis* and Ἥφαιστος ὡς Δαίδαλος, as Greeks may have misunderstood the double name of the Canaanite craftsman. Although no Aegean names or scripts (other than Cypriote) have been identified in tablets at Ugarit, Minoan imports and "men from Kaptor" in the Middle Bronze Age port are succeeded by a dramatic increase in Aegean imports in the fourteenth and thirteenth centuries B.C.[28] Some of the most intriguing and intimate connections in the archaeological record appear in the context of cult. As a recent analysis argues: "The significance of Ugarit for the history of religion rests to no little degree on the way in which its strategic location led to the interaction of religious elements from varying cultures, thus providing us with a partial prism for perceiving the spectrum of the religious world of the Middle and Late Bronze Ages."[29]

This interaction left traces in artifacts and architecture as well as tablets. Aegean rhyta and their imitations are as popular as Syrian and Cypriote versions in sacred deposits, which include private *Kultvereine* and the houses of "priests" apparently familiar with foreign rituals and their paraphernalia. Copious in these private cult contexts are tablets in several languages: Ugaritic, Akkadian, and Hurrian texts with hymns and divinations constitute the private library of one eccentric priest called Agaptari.[30] The rooms of his house produced Mycenaean rhyta, a local imitation of a lion's head rhyton dedicated to Resheph, models of lungs and livers used for divination, a mug with a mythological scene, a libation tube or stand common in Levantine cults, gold bowls for libation, and ivory fragments of the head of a deity. Perhaps this well-equipped diviner was also well traveled, if he practiced the itinerant trade welcomed and admired in Greece (*Odyssey* 17.383), and helped introduce many Oriental practices to Greek religion.[31] His cult collection serving a variety of beliefs and practices was not unique in a city with documents in seven languages and five scripts (where someone must have invented the alphabet in exasperation, if for no other reason). Recent excavations reopened at Ugarit since

---

[28] M. Astour, "Ugarit and the Aegean: A Brief Summary of the Archaeological and Epigraphic Evidence," and E. Linder, "Ugarit: A Canaanite Thalassocracy," in *Orient and Occident*, 17–27, 31–42; cf. A. Caubet, "Ras Shamra et la Crète," in *La Syrie au Bronze Recent*, 17–22, and other essays.

[29] P. Miller, "Aspects of the Religion of Ugarit," in *Ancient Israelite Religions*, 54. Cf. J.-M. de Tarragon, *Le culte à Ugarit* (Paris, 1980), on testimonia; A. Caquot and M. Sznycer, *Ugaritic Religion*, Iconography of Religions 15, no. 8 (Leiden, 1980), for illustrations.

[30] O. Eissfeldt, "Kultvereine in Ugarit," *Ugaritica 6* (1969) 187–95; J.-C. Courtois, "La maison du prêtre

aux modèles de poumon et de foies d'Ugarit," *Ugaritica 6* (1969) 91–119; C. Schaeffer, "Contexte archéologique de date du rhyton léontocéphale de la maison d' Agaptari," *Ugaritica 7* (1978) 149–54; E. Lipiński, "The Socio-Economic Condition of the Clergy in the Kingdom of Ugarit," in *Society and Economy in the Eastern Mediterranean*, 133–35.

[31] Burkert, in *Greek Renaissance*, and *Orientalisierende Epoche*, chap. 2, on "East-West Magic and Medicine." Cf. West, *Early Greek Philosophy and the Orient*, 239–42, on the Magi who fled Persia and may have influenced the religion of Ionia; *JHS 108* (1988) 171–72.

1978 have revealed a cult complex christened the "sanctuary of the rhytons" with the same kind of evidence for Ugarit's colorful variety of international beliefs.[32] This modest shrine—a single room with platform, benches, and "altar"—was crammed with exotica such as Syrian and Mycenaean rhyta, an ivory pyxis, a miniature bronze tripod, and other equipment common to Levantine, Cypriote, and even Aegean shrines. This private cult installation provides a more intimate alternative to the official temple of Baal and Dagon on the akropolis of Ugarit, an archaeological counterpart to "l'omniprésence des dieux à Ougarit" reinforced in the texts.[33] In other private contexts, hoards of bronze figurines help identify the house of an artisan-smith involved in the production of "smiting gods" in bronze covered with gold or silver foil, a type not only numerous in the Near East but found at a number of Aegean sanctuaries.[34]

Excavations promise more of these domestic shrines, along with Aegean rhyta and vessels as exotic or prestige dedications in sanctuaries of Syria and Palestine.[35] Ugarit was not the only Levantine city with an international population and contacts in the Late Bronze Age. Beth Shean, for example, was home to an Egyptian garrison, produced Egyptianizing art (anthropoid sarcophagi, cylinder seals: Figure 16), and imported as well as produced "Philistine" and local Mycenaean pottery. Byblos enjoyed similar international connections, art, and population, and its finds shed light on Greek motifs (Figures 13–15). But Ugarit was the chief port city of Canaanite Syria, as well as the home to cuneiform literature, which contributed to the *koine* inherited by the Homeric corpus (Chapter 4). Objects like the gold plaque with a Canaanite goddess found in the Kaş wreck may have been obtained in such Syrian ports, items that influenced Greek cult and iconography.

What encourages close scrutiny of these Levantine contexts is the simultaneous appearance of related cult practices and objects—animal sacrifice, platforms or benches and idols, male and wheel-made figurines—in the Aegean in the Late Bronze Age. Re-

[32] A. Caubet et al., "Ras-Shamra-Ougarit 1978–1980," *Syria* 59 (1982) 182–91; A. Caubet et al., "Ras-Shamra-Ougarit (1981–1983)," and M. Yon, "Ras-Shamra-Ougarit," *Syria* 60 (1983) 201–24, 288–90; "Sanctuaires d'Ougarit," in *Temples et Sanctuaires*, 48–50.

[33] Yon, *Syria* 60 (1983) 288; cf. "Sanctuaires d'Ougarit," in *Temples et Sanctuaires*, 37–50, esp. 43–47, on the akropolis temples (excavated by Schaeffer and still to be published in detail).

[34] For excavated figurines, see Schaeffer *AAAS* 11–12 (1961–1962) 191, fig. 6, and *AfO* 20 (1963) 206 fig. 21; Negbi, *Canaanite Gods in Metal*, 135 nos. 1327, 1442; cf. H. Seeden, *The Standing Armed Figurines in the Levant*, PBF I.1 (Munich, 1980), 102–6. For a critical review of these figurines as "archaeological or-

phans" difficult to correlate with deities in religious texts, see J. Muhly, "Bronze Figurines and Near Eastern Metalwork," *IEJ* 30 (1980) 148–61; P.R.S. Moorey and St. Fleming, "Problems in the Study of the Anthropomorphic Metal Statuary from Syro-Palestine before 330 B.C.," *Levant* 16 (1984) 67–90; Knapp, *Copper Production and Divine Protection*, 7–9.

[35] Yon predicts additional shrines in unexcavated urban quarters and compares the tower complex at Minet el-Beida, the harbor of Ras Shamra: for excavation report, see Schaeffer, *Syria* 13 (1932) 2–10. Aegean vases and rhyta: V. Hankey, "Imported Vessels of the Late Bronze Age at High Places," in *Temples and High Places*, 108–17; U. Zevulun, "A Canaanite Ram-Headed Cup," *IEJ* 37 (1987) 88–104.

cent discoveries and arguments make Mycenaean religious iconography as well as ritual late and Oriental, with healthy survivals into Iron Age forms.[36] The citadel of Mycenae, for example, incorporated the archaeology of cult into a complex of buildings near the citadel wall, separate from the palace. This context—among private houses instead of official, public, or palatial structures—recalls Ugarit, whose dispersed and diverse collections of religious paraphernalia indicate an informal but widespread distribution of religious interest outside of official cults. The cult area at Mycenae includes a building with frescoes and a libation channel, facing an open court with a plastered altar, originally excavated by Tsountas in the nineteenth century.[37] More recently excavated is the cult area found by Taylour, including rooms decorated with frescoes representing several divine figures.[38] In one fresco, a "goddess" carries stalks or tails and resembles Near Eastern deities from Late Bronze Age Syria.[39] A collection of grotesque wheel-made terracotta "idols" from an adjacent room are eccentric among Mycenaean figures, and are likely to be votives rather than cult images. Their closest ancestors come from the Near East, and they survive in Iron Age Cyprus (Figures 23, 24) and the Punic world.[40] The examples from Mycenae may provide an important link between examples East and West, Bronze Age and Iron Age in this genre.

At Tiryns, the lower citadel had a small shrine with "cult bench" built against the fortifications added in the thirteenth century; its finds include Mycenaean idols, male figurines, and *Cypriaka*.[41] The Mycenaean sanctuary at Epidauros, on the peak later sacred to Apollo Maleatas, shows a significant divergence from Minoan forms and kinship with Near Eastern and later Greek religion, especially in the domain of burnt sacrifice.[42]

[36] Coldstream, *Deities in Aegean Art*, 8–10, and S. Langdon, "The Return of the Horse Leader," *AJA* 93 (1989) 185–215 (cf. *AJA* 91 [1987] 296) on the evolution of Greek religious imagery; Negbi, *Levant* 14 (1982) 179–82, on smiting gods and Greek deities; cf. H. Gallet de Santerre, "Les statuettes de bronze mycéniennes au type dit du 'Dieu Reshef' dans leur contexte Égéen," *BCH* 111 (1987) 7–29.

[37] Reinvestigated by Wace in 1950, thereafter by G. Mylonas, ·Τὸ Θρησκευτικὸν Κέντρον τῶν Μυκηνῶν, *PAA* 33 (Athens, 1972). For the frescoes, see I. Kritseli-Providi, οἱ Τοιχογραφίες τοῦ Θρησκευτικοῦ κέντρου τῶν Μυκηνῶν (Athens, 1982).

[38] W. Taylour, "New Light on Mycenaean Religion," *Antiquity* 44 (1970) 270–80; *The Mycenaeans* (London, 1983), 49–61.

[39] N. Marinatos, "The Fresco from Room 31 at Mycenae: Problems of Method and Interpretation," in *Problems in Greek Prehistory*, 246–47. She is frequently compared with the Syro-Aegean "Mistress of Animals" on an ivory pyxis from Minet el-Beida (Cold-stream, *Deities in Aegean Art*, 8); cf. the Canaanite goddess on a gold plaque from Lachish (C. Clamer, "A Gold Plaque from Lachish," *Tel Aviv* 7 [1980] 152–62); R. Hestrin, "The Lachish Ewer and the 'Asherah,' " *IEJ* 37 (1987) 212–23.

[40] A. Moore, "The Large Monochrome Terracotta Figures from Mycenae: The Problem of Interpretation," in *Problems in Greek Prehistory*, 219–28. Wheel-made figures of this type appear as "mourning pots" in Middle Kingdom Egypt, are common in Late Bronze Age and archaic Cyprus (Figures 23, 24), and survive in the Punic West: J. Ferron and M. E. Aubet, *Orants de Carthage* (Paris, 1974), 155–65.

[41] K. Kilian, "Zeugnisse Mykenischer Kultausübung in Tiryns," in *Sanctuaries and Cults*, 49–58; French, in Renfrew, *Archaeology of Cult*, 273. *Cypriaka* include terracotta figurines, wall brackets, copper ingots, and bronze working in its new IIIC phase: *ARep* (1983–1984), 23–25.

[42] V. Lambrinoudakis, "The Mycenaean Sanctuary of Apollo Maleatas at Epidauros," in *Sanctuaries and*

The sanctuary at Epidauros also produced a bronze "mask" for a bull, restored by the excavator as a large rhyton. It may indicate instead that sacrificial victims had their heads decorated in precious metal, as their horns were gilded in Homeric Greece (*Odyssey* 3.5–8) and in Canaanite rites, or that a bull's mask was worn by men in other rites.[43] Two shrines from the Cycladic islands substantiate these Mycenaean cult installations as innovations of the Late Bronze Age, under Levantine influence. Bronze figurines and masks of gold foil, male terracotta figurines, imported faience, shell and glyptic, even a tortoise-shell lyre are Aegean novelties in a series of small shrines with benches and platforms at Phylakopi on Melos, similar to those at Mycenae and Tiryns.[44] Near Eastern imports to Melos like the bronze "smiting" god match those found in sanctuaries at Delos, Tiryns, and Sounion; this Oriental figure became Greek centuries later, in statues of gods in action like the early classical bronze from Artemision (Figure 41). In other convergences between Bronze Age cults East and West, the assembly of terracotta statues from the temple at Ayia Irini on Keos resembles votive practices active in Iron Age Cyprus, vivid in the crowd of statues found around the altar at Ayia Irini on Cyprus (Figures 24a, b).[45]

Appreciating these discoveries requires suspending the separation of Bronze and Iron Ages in classical scholarship. The role of Cyprus and Crete in the Orientalization of Greece involves two islands not only early and eager to receive Near Eastern innovations but conservative in maintaining them. Thus Iron Age temples like Dreros may be the best Aegean parallels for Bronze Age shrines, while practices alive in archaic Cyprus help interpret Mycenaean ones in the Aegean. The periodization of Greek culture has discouraged such associations, but the dimensions of the Orientalizing experience, like the span of cultures offered by Homeric poetry, deserve a synoptic view of the two millennia. Chronology also complicates the geographical "source" of these parallels. In

Cults, 59–63; R. Hägg, "Degrees and Character of Minoan Influence on the Mainland," in *The Minoan Thalassocracy*, 120–21, and "Mycenaean Religion: The Helladic and Minoan Components," in *Linear B: A 1984 Survey*, ed. A. Morpurgo Davies and Y. Duhoux (Louvain, 1985), 203–5. Cf. B. Bergquist, "The Archaeology of Sacrifice: Minoan-Mycenaean versus Greek. A Brief Query into Two Sites with Contrary Evidence," in *Early Greek Cult Practice*, 21–34, for a provocative analysis of Kato Symi and Epidauros (cf. Vermeule, *ArchHom V. Götterkult*, 12, 59). Apollo "Maleatas" has been connected with Cape Malea (Astour, *Hellenosemitica*, 306), both from Phoenician *malaḥ* = "height?"

[43] Lambrinoudakis, in *Sanctuaries and Cults*, 63, fig. 9; Sasson, in *Orient and Occident*, 153 n. 10, on wooden statuettes from Mari with gilded horns; Exodus 32, with Cassuto's commentary. See Chapters 5, 6, on the wearing of *bucrania* in Near Eastern and Greek ritual.

[44] Renfrew in *Sanctuaries and Cults*, 30–32; *Archaeology of Cult*, esp. 302–59, 405–43. His emphasis on "continuity" neglects the role of the Near East: for example, comparison of Syrian statuettes to the Dreros *sphyrelata* may reflect common Near Eastern origins more than their "continuity": see Chapter 6. See Negbi (n. 48) for a Near Eastern cult at Phylakopi.

[45] M. Caskey, *Keos II.1. The Temple at Ayia Irini. The Statues* (Princeton, 1986). SCE 2: figs. 277–81, pls. 228–30, plans xxviii–xxix, and J. Connelly, "Standing before One's Own God. Votive Sculpture and the Cypriot Religious Tradition," *BA* 52, no. 4 (1989) 210–18, for Cypriote parallels; Ferron and Aubet, *Orants de Carthage*, 159–65, for Punic and other examples.

the Levant—at Qasile and Ekron, for example—architecture and artifacts are associated with Philistine culture and compared with Mycenaean sanctuaries, even attributed to Aegean immigrants with an appeal to the "Captorite" origin of the Philistines in the Bible.[46] The discrepancy in date—Philistine sites belong to the twelfth century, most Aegean shrines destroyed or abandoned near the close of the late thirteenth century—defends the reverse influence, from West to East, or at least earlier forms survive in the Aegean. On Cyprus, altars and other religious installations are compared with Aegean and Near Eastern traditions, some traced to the Aegean, while sites like Kition are called both Mycenaean and Phoenician.[47] In the Aegean, putative home of these innovations, their appearance is attributed to the Orient: one Near Eastern scholar has posited a "bilingual cult" in the double shrine at Phylakopi and elsewhere, shared by Aegean and Semitic deities.[48] Aegean scholars are less inclined toward Near Eastern and Cypriote parallels, but there are exceptions among experts.[49] Perhaps the rubric of the "Sea Peoples," diverse in ethnicity and inclusive of several populations that shared these traditions, best describes the agents of these innovations. This allows for a fruitful understanding of these phenomena as symptomatic of the Late Bronze traffic in culture, which included cult.

In the afterlife of this exchange, many elements of Canaanite religion manifest in Late Bronze Age Syria and Palestine are mirrored in the Aegean as Greek religious rites and terms, much as they are inherited in Phoenician culture and even in Hebrew Yahwism.[50] The Agia Triada sarcophagus from Crete (Figures 19a, b) represents in its shape

[46] T. Dothan, *The Philistines* (New Haven, 1982), 63ff., 237–51, 257; A. Mazar, *Explorations at Tell Qasile. Part One. The Philistine Sanctuary: Architecture and Cult Objects*, QEDEM 12 (Jerusalem, 1980), 61–73; *Part Two*, QEDEM 20 (Jerusalem, 1985). M. Burdajewicz, "À propos des temples philistins de Qasileh," *RB* 93 (1986) 222–35. T. Dothan, "Ekron of the Philistines," *BAR* (January–February 1990) 26–36, esp. 30–34, on Aegean influence. *Contra* J. Schäfer, "Bemerkungen zum Verhältnis mykenischer Kultbauten zu Tempelbauten in Kanaan," *AA* (1983) 551–58.

[47] E.g. J. Webb, "Late Cypriote Altars and Offering Structures," *RDAC* (1977) 112–32; cf. Renfrew, *Archaeology of Cult*, 435–36, on features that appear later (i.e., after 1200 B.C.) in Cyprus than the Aegean. V. Karageorghis, *Kition, Mycenaean and Phoenician*, PBA 49 (London, 1973), and discussion in *Temples and High Places*, 106–7. Cf. essays in *Cyprus between the Orient and the Occident*.

[48] Negbi, *BSA* 83 (1988) 339–57, esp. 346–57, and "A Canaanite Figurine in Late Minoan Crete," in *Fourth Cretological Congress*, 363–66, for a similar cult

in the Patsos cave on Crete after 1200 B.C. Cf. B. C. Dietrich, "Some Foreign Elements in Mycenaean Cult Places and Figures," in *Linear B: A 1984 Survey*, 227–39.

[49] E. French, in Renfrew, *Archaeology of Cult*, on terracottas (p. 277) and their Near Eastern and Cypriote parallels (pp. 412–13, 435–36), to which add Cypriote pottery (T. D. Atkinson and others, *Excavations at Phylakopi on Melos* [London, 1904], 158–59). In "Mycenaean Figures and Figurines, their Typology and Function," in *Sanctuaries and Cults*, 173, she admits that the "amazing growth in popularity of figures on the mainland not paralleled on Crete in LH IIIA could be influenced from the Near East."

[50] Th. Gaster, "The Service of the Sanctuary: A Study in Hebrew Survivals," in *Mélanges Dussaud*, 2:577–82, on sacrificial terminology, including "to perform sacrifice," *'asah* (Greek ῥέζειν); cf. *bêt* and νάος, *bāmāh* and βωμός (Burkert, *Greek Religion*, 87 n. 43). J. Sasson, "The Worship of the Golden Calf," in *Orient and Occident*, 151–59: burnt offerings, dance and athletics, responsal singing, and cult images in

and in its decoration an aggregate of imported practices.[51] Its scenes of animal sacrifice, libation, music, votive offerings, even statues and shrines are closer to classical Greek traditions than to Minoan ones, despite the local style of the painting. The same site and period featured a shrine unfamiliar in Minoan architecture, which agrees with Near Eastern and Greek mainland plans.[52] The equivalent installation at Knossos, the Shrine of the Double Axes, lies outside the palace, as at Mycenae, Tiryns, and Hagia Triada. The Knossos shrine, built in the Late Minoan IIIA1 period, is identical to the mainland and Cretan examples of the period, in its shape and contents. A "cult bench" faces the door of the small, rectangular room and carries votives such as figurines and horns of consecration with cuttings for double axes.[53] These installations date to the Mycenaean period on Crete, and must represent the adoption of the same new religious practices that inspired the shrines on the mainland and in the Cyclades.

Such influence could have spread via Cyprus, which welcomed a large Levantine and Mycenaean community at the end of the Bronze Age, and whence cults and crafts spread to Greece. The closest parallels for the Ugaritic shrines are on Cyprus, in sanctuaries at Kition and Enkomi where a deity with strong Levantine associations occupies an industrial sanctuary with metalworking and cult practices side by side.[54] Several innovations in Greek cult forms, practices, and iconography may have been transmitted first to Cyprus in the "Canaanite diaspora," then to Greece by Phoenicians, either from Cyprus or directly from the Levant.[55] Phoenician deities who experienced an *interpretatio*

Canaanite cult; J. P. Brown, "The Sacrificial Cult and Its Critique in Greek and Hebrew (II)," *JSS* 25 (1980) 1–21; A. Hultgard, "The Burnt-Offering in Early Jewish Religion," and M. Ottosson, "Sacrifice and Sacred Meals in Ancient Israel," both in *Gifts to the Gods*; 83–91, 133–36, B. Janowski, "Erwägungen zur Vorgeschichte des israelitischen šelāmîm-Opfers," *UF* 12 (1980) 251–53. Teixidor, *The Pagan God*, chap. 2, on Phoenician religion and its Canaanite antecedents. W. Dever, "A Survey of the Archaeological Evidence for Religion and Cult in Late Bronze–Iron I Syria-Palestine," in *Ancient Israelite Religions*, 222–37. G. Mylonas, "Contribution to the Religion of the Achaeans," in *Mycenaeans in the Eastern Mediterranean*, 101–4; D. Rupp, "Reflections on the Origins of Greek Altars," in *The Greek Renaissance*, 107.

[51] Vermeule, *ArchHom V. Götterkult*, 12 n. 18, and "Kadmos and the Dragon," 184, on its Egyptian and Near Eastern elements (first noted by Paribeni, *MonAnt* 19 [1908] 68 n. 1); cf. the Tanagra larnakes and their Near Eastern connections: Vermeule, *Aspects of Death*, 69–78; T. Dothan, "A Female Mourner Figurine from the Lachish Region," in *W. F. Albright Al-*

bum, Eretz-Israel 9, ed. A. Malamat (Jerusalem, 1969), 43–47, 135.

[52] Excavated in 1903: L. Banti, "I Culti Minoici e Greci de Haghia Triada," *ASAA* 3–4 (1941–1943) 10–74. B. Rutkowski, *The Cult Places of the Aegean* (New Haven, 1986), 162–67. Agia Triada has also produced a Late Bronze Age fresco with scenes of animals being led to sacrifice: S. Immerwahr, *Aegean Painting in the Bronze Age* (University Park, Penn., 1990), 102, 181.

[53] Rutkowski, *Cult Places*, 128–49; Evans, *POM*, 2:338, fig. 190.

[54] O. Masson, "Remarques sur les cultes chypriotes à l'époque du Bronze Recent," in *Mycenaeans in the Eastern Mediterranean*, 110–21; Knapp, *Copper Production and Divine Protection*, 6–23; S. Dalley, "Near Eastern Patron Deities of Mining and Smelting in the Late Bronze and Early Iron Ages," *RDAC* (1987) 60–66. Also see references in n. 47.

[55] Carter, *AJA* 91 (1987) 355–83, and in *Early Greek Cult Practice*, 89–98, on the transmission of Near Eastern masks, poetry, and ritual via Cyprus across the Dark Ages; E. Puech, "Le rite d'offrandes de cheveux

Graeca via Cyprus include Adonis, Aphrodite, and even forms of Apollo. Apollo Amyklaios began as Semitic *Mkl*, was worshiped on Cyprus as Apollo-Mkl, transported by Phoenicians to Gortyn (and perhaps Kommos) as Apollo Amyklaios, and moved in with Hyakinthos in Lakonia.[56] Others were introduced to Greek religion by characters like Thaletas from Gortyn, the Cretan town of Levantine ancestry that worshiped Apollo Amyklaios and used Near Eastern masks in its rites for Athena (see Chapter 6, nn. 28–31). Like those who brought mystery rites from Sparta to Crete, Thaletas migrated to Sparta with the ὑπερχορῆμα, a dance form of Near Eastern origin.[57] More vividly, gods who wear horns in Canaanite and Cypriote iconography (Figure 22) were explained in the Greek myth of the Minotaur (Chapter 6). Inherited as "the bull of Jacob" title of God in Biblical Hebrew, this zoomorphic god became a monster in the Greek tradition, the product of an unnatural union between bull and woman more familiar in the Levant. Indirect testimonia and archaeological representations suggest the acknowledgment in antiquity of Oriental elements in Greek literature and religion.[58]

The most unusual of eastern innovations in religion enjoys recent and dramatic evidence. A Late Minoan IB house at Knossos has produced human bones belonging to four young children, aged eight to twelve, with unmistakable signs of butchery among vessels, which suggests consumption—that is, cannibalism.[59] It is impossible to ignore mythology when evaluating this bizarre assembly, which recalls tales of Cretan taste for human victims. Most notorious is the story of the Athenian compensation for the murder of Androgeos, exacted by Minos in the form of seven youths and seven maidens from Athens, until Theseus slew the Minotaur and liberated Athens from this gruesome tribute (Plutarch, *Theseus* 15–19). This mythological tale is amplified by reports that as-

---

d' après une inscription phénicienne de Kition vers 800 av. notre ère," *RSF* 4 (1976) 11–21, for an Oriental custom thereafter common in Greece (Burkert, *Greek Religion*, 70).

[56] Aphrodite: Burkert, *Greek Religion*, 152–56; S. Ribichini, *Adonis* (Rome, 1981). Apollo Amyklaios: Burkert, *Grazer Beiträge* 4 (1975) 51–79; R. F. Willetts, "What's in a Name?" in *Relations between Cyprus and Crete*, 235–40; *contra* E. Lipiński, "Resheph Amyklos," in *Studia Phoenicia*, 4:87–99. M. Schretter, *Alter Orient und Hellas* (Innsbruck, 1974), 151–73, for Near Eastern aspects of Apollo as healer (e.g. Smintheus, Hekatos/Hekatebolos, etc.). B. C. Dietrich, "Tradition in Greek Religion," in *The Greek Renaissance*, 87 (incl. Aphrodite and Astarte). "Apollo Karneios," may have a Syrian home, "Karne" (Astour, *Hellenosemitica*, 140) and a Cypriote relative, "Apollo Keraeatas": K. Hadjioannou, "On the Identification of the Horned God of Engomi-Alasia," in *Alasia* 1, ed. C.F.A. Schaeffer (Paris, 1971), 33–42; Knapp, *Copper*

Production and Divine Protection, 14.

[57] Sasson, in *Orient and Occident*, 158–59; on Thaletas of Gortyn, see Chapter 6. His name could be Cypriote or Levantine: cf. "Kyprothales" on a bowl from Cyprus (Markoe, *Phoenician Bowls*, 175–76) and Thales of Miletus, of Phoenician descent (Herodotus, 1.170).

[58] Particularly from Cyprus, where Theophrastos and Asklepiades claim that sacrifice was invented (Porphyry, *De Abstinentia* 2.26, 4.15): Burkert, *Grazer Beiträge* 4 (1975) 51–79, and *Greek Religion*, 47, 51, 62, 108, 167.

[59] P. Warren and others, "Human Bones from a Late Minoan IB House at Knossos," *BSA* 81 (1986) 333–88; cf. in *Sanctuaries and Cults*, 155–67; *Minoan Religion as Ritual Action* (Göteborg 1988), 7–9. D. Hughes, "Human Sacrifice in Ancient Greece: The Literary and Archaeological Evidence" (Ph.D. diss., Ohio State University, 1986), 28–38, doubts "cannibalism" is indicated.

sociate Cretans with human sacrifice. Plutarch himself (*Theseus* 16) cites Aristotle's testimony (from his *Constitution of the Bottiaeans*) that the Cretans once sent their firstborn to Delphi in fulfillment of a vow. Euripides attributes "banquets of raw meat" (ὠμο-φάγαι δαῖτες) to the mysteries of Idaian Zeus (in his *Cretans*, cited by Porphyry, *De Abstinentia* 4.19), and the peculiarities of Cretan sacrifices apparently justified an entire treatise on the topic (by Istros of Crete, also cited by Porphyry, 2.56). Among those Cretans responsible for sacrificing children, Istros names the Kouretes, who offered their infants to Kronos in a rite reflected in the myth of the Birth of Zeus (Chapter 6, n. 21). Kronos provides another link to Canaanite, Phoenician, and Punic practices behind these "Cretan" customs and other Greek tales of the sacrifice of children. It was Kronos, according to Diodorus (20.14.4–7; cf. Sophokles, *Andromeda* frag. 126 Radt), who received infant sacrifices at Carthage and at Rhodes (Porphyry, 2.54), and El/Kronos who first sacrificed his only son in the *aition* for this custom, in time of war (Philo of Byblos, *FGrH* 790 F 3b).

These references indicate Greek acquaintance with a Semitic custom widely disseminated in the ancient Mediterranean. The rite of offering one's children to the gods, often the firstborn son, was called *mlk* or *molek* in Biblical Hebrew (cf. Punic *molk*) and was common in the Punic world. A special infant cemetery called *tophet*, after the one in Jerusalem, was devoted to this rite in North Africa (Carthage), Sicily (Motya and Selinos), and Sardinia.[60] Its Bronze Age, Canaanite origins survive in a Ugaritic prayer that vows the offering of a firstborn son to the chief god of the city, and in Egyptian representations of Syrian cities under siege where children's bodies are lowered off the walls, an image that may have survived in the Homeric tradition as the death of Astyanax.[61] As with many Canaanite rites, infant sacrifice survived the demise of Ugarit primarily in Biblical prohibitions, but also was practiced on historical occasions during the siege of cities (2 Kings 3:27). The bones from Knossos may be a dubious attestation for its practice in Bronze Age Greece, but other sources testify to its dissemination west by Levantines, in the period when the population of the Aegean began building shrines

---

[60] L. Stager, "Carthage: A View from the Tophet," in *Phönizier im Westen*, 155–56; L. Stager and S. Wolff, "Child Sacrifice at Carthage: Religious Rite or Population Control?" *BAR* 10 (January–February 1984) 31–51. S. Brown, *Late Carthaginian Child Sacrifice and Sacrificial Monuments in Their Mediterranean Contexts* (Sheffield, 1990). E. Lipiński, "Sacrifices d'enfants à Carthage et dans le monde sémitique oriental," in *Studia Phoenicia*, 6:151–62. *Pace* G. Heider, *The Cult of Molek* (Sheffield, 1985), *molek* is a technical term and not a Northwest Semitic deity: see review by S. Olyan and M. Smith, *RB* 94 (1987) 273–75. The rite is also represented on the archaic monument from

Pozo Moro in Iberia: see Chapter 7, n. 41.

[61] A. Herdner, "Une prière à Baal des Ugaritains en danger," *CRAI* 1972 (1973), 693–703; B. Margalit, "Why King Mesha of Moab Sacrificed his Oldest Son," in *BAR* (November–December 1986) 62–63, 76 (RS 24.266, V, 9–19). The Karnak relief with the siege of Ashkelon by Ramses II shows such a scene: A. Spalinger, "A Canaanite Ritual Found in Egyptian Reliefs," *Journal of the Society for the Study of Egyptian Archaeology* 8 (1978) 47–60. S. Morris, "The Sacrifice of Astyanax: Near Eastern Contributions to the Fall of Troy," forthcoming.

and sacrificing animals. As in the Biblical proscription of this rite under the reforms of Yahwism, the rite of infant sacrifice in Greece was rejected in practice—but remembered in mythology. Every city-siege legend includes the sacrifice, or self-sacrifice, of royal children to save a nation—Iphigeneia at Aulis, the daughters of Erechtheus in Athens, Menoikeus of Thebes, Makaria at Marathon. A practice abhorred and punished by the gods is buried in a Greek mythological cycle of murder, retribution, and divine vengeance. Thus the tribute Athens paid Crete arose from a murder that brought on plague and war, only to be expiated by human sacrifice (Plutarch, *Theseus* 15–16). If Kothar was adopted in Crete as Δαίδαλος in the Late Bronze Age, other Canaanite traditions apparently accompanied his migration, but survived in mythology in unmistakably Greek ways.

This comparison of selected religious and cultural practices in the Late Bronze Aegean makes more plausible the reception of Near Eastern motifs in poetry, including the metamorphosis of Kothar into Daidalos. The transmission of religious beliefs and practices from East to West must have resembled the migration of metallurgy, and even the adoption of the alphabet: the process was not so much incremental but rather repeated in independent and informal encounters, whose consequences were never identical. Only such a model explains, for example, the variety of early Greek alphabet scripts as well as the duplication of Near Eastern cults and deities in different locales.[62] As suggested from the domestic contexts of cult in Mycenaean settlements, the world of itinerant Homeric δημιοεργοί should be the model for the understanding of early Greek Orientalizing culture, not the Amarna and Boghazköy archives or their Iron Age successors. Like the oral tradition itself, that culture, especially its religion, was continuous from the Bronze Age through the Iron Age, justifying the use of the term "early Greek" to embrace the second and first millennia. The epigraphic definition of historical periods creates an artificial "Dark Age," which must then be "reconciled" with the "inconsistencies" of more faithful records of that continuity, poetry and archaeology.[63]

The most crucial figure among the four categories of δημιοεργοί listed in *Odyssey* 17 (382–85) is the ἀοιδός or poet, immodestly praised by Homer more generously than the other craftsmen, by an entire line (17.385). Only poetry could have brought Greece its Near Eastern expressions like the "wine-dark sea," or that mysterious memory of a

---

[62] Greek regional scripts reflect various "stages" of the Semitic system and defy a single, uniform or official adoption: Mendenhall, *Kadmos* 14 (1972) 60–61; W. Johnstone, *Kadmos* 17 (1978) 151–66; B.S.J. Isserlin, "The Antiquity of the Greek Alphabet," *Kadmos* 22 (1982) 151–63; and Naveh, *Early History of the Alphabet*. Even Diodorus admitted that the Greeks kept reinventing the alphabet, during a period of widespread illiteracy (5.57.5; see Chapter 13). On the dispersal of Near Eastern gods, see n. 56; cf. the "gradualist" evolution of Greek religion during the Dark Ages defended in Renfrew's *Archaeology of Cult.*

[63] Morris, in *Challenge of* Black Athena, 48–49; see also P. Kalligas, "Hero-Cult in Early Iron Age Greece," in *Early Greek Cult Practice*, 229–34, on the newly brilliant tenth and ninth centuries, largely thanks to Lefkandi and Knossos.

Canaanite formula, "the word of the tree and the whisper of the stone."[64] Other epic motifs took their origin in foreign images, not formulas, and may have traveled with objects, but settled in poetry. Thus the story of the return of the Homeric king, in the *Odyssey*, borrowed contests for kingship from the prowess of Egyptian Pharaohs who claim to drive arrows through bronze (Figure 16).[65] A curious Egyptianizing cylinder seal from Bronze Age Byblos (Figure 15) became the bizarre composition on a relief pithos from Tenos (Figures 13, 14; see Chapter 4, nn. 55, 56). As in scenes of infant sacrifice, which became the pitiful death of Astyanax (n. 61), Greek artists saw Near Eastern motifs, most frequently on small portable objects that traveled as trinkets, and applied them to a Greek story. Like their Levantine colleagues in craftsmanship who turned Egyptian motifs into new arrangements, Aegean artists and poets were seduced by exotica, but felt compelled to make them familiar. The introduction of Near Eastern themes into Greek poetry was related as well as similar to the adoption of visual motifs—hence the virtue and necessity of a synoptic view. Together they make Homeric Greece synonymous with "die orientalisierende Epoche der griechischen Kultur."[66] Bronze Age Aegean frescoes point to an early form of narrative, whose poets and poetry must have survived just as luxury arts in bronze and ivory outlasted the palaces that sponsored them.[67] In short, Homer's citation of, and compliment to, Daidalos may be one survivor of an eastern Mediterranean *koine* in art and culture of the Late Bronze Age. Its Iron Age survival begins in Homer:

> Μέντης Ἀγχιάλοιο δαΐφρονος εὔχομαι εἶναι
> υἱός, ἀτὰρ Ταφίοισι φιληρέτμοισιν ἀνάσσω.
> νῦν δ᾽ ὧδε ξὺν νηΐ κατήλυθον ἠδ᾽ ἑτάροισι
> πλεών ἐπὶ οἴνοπα πόντον ἐπ᾽ ἀλλοθρόουσ᾽ ἀνθρώπους
> ἐς Τεμέσην μετὰ χαλκόν, ἄγω δ᾽ αἴθωνα σίδηρον.

---

[64] C. Gordon, "The Wine-Dark Sea," *JNES* 37 (1978) 51–52. For the Ugaritic origin of ἀπὸ δρυὸς οὐδ᾽ ἀπὸ πέτρης (*Iliad* 20.126; *Odyssey* 19.163; cf. περὶ δρῦν καὶ περὶ πέτρην: Hesiod, *Theogony* 35), see West, *Theogony*, 167–69; M. Smith, "Baal's Cosmic Secret," *UF* 16 (1984) 295–98; Burkert, *Orientalisierende Epoche*, 109 n. 24. Orientalia in other heroic themes and poetic formulas: Stella, *Tradizione micenea*, 362–91; West, *JHS* 108 (1988) 169ff; W. Albright, "Some Oriental Glosses on the Homeric Problem," *AJA* 54 (1950) 162–76; S. Levin, "Anomalies of Homeric Greek Clarified by Semitic Parallels," in *Europa*, 194–203.

[65] Burkert first compared the Bronze Age cylinder seal from Beth Shean, Israel, to the Homeric contest of the bow (*Odyssey* 21.393–421): "Von Amenophis II zur Bogenprobe des Odysseus," *Grazer Beiträge* 1

(1973) 69–78; P. Walcot, "Odysseus and the Contest of the Bow: The Comparative Evidence," *SMEA* 84 (1984) 357–69; W. McCleod, "The Bow and the Axes," in *Studies Presented to Sterling Dow*, 203–10.

[66] Burkert, *Orientalisierende Epoche*, 114, although largely confined to the Neo-Assyrian Empire, while West dates these exchanges before 1100 B.C. and the demise of Canaanite poetry with the fall of Ugarit: *JHS* 108 (1988) 169–72; Morris, in *Challenge of Black Athena*, 45–46.

[67] S. Morris, "A Tale of Two Cities: The Miniature Frescoes from Thera and the Origins of Greek Poetry," *AJA* 93 (1989) 511–35; N. Yalouris, "Ein Schlachtengemälde im Palast des Nestors," *AthMitt* 104 (1989) 41–48, compares frescoes from Pylos to passages in *Iliad* 7 and Mycenaean *diptera/poro*.

I call myself Mentes, son of bold Anchialos,

and I rule over the Taphians, lovers of oars.

Now I have come here with my ship and my companions

sailing over the wine-dark sea toward men of foreign speech

bound for Temesos after bronze, while I carry shining iron.

—Odyssey 1.180–84

The final frontier of this eastern Mediterranean *koine* extended west beyond the Aegean to Italy,[68] Sardinia,[69] and Spain,[70] where metal resources attracted explorers, craftsmen, and settlers from Cyprus and the Levant (see Map 1). This new westward route included the Aegean, according to Italian finds from Crete, including the western part of the island, home to something of a revival in the Late Bronze Age.[71] The novel and ultimate goal of this expanded metallurgical network may have been iron, which shows up sporadically in the Bronze Age and is prized as a prestige item in literature of the second millennium.[72] Although far more plentiful and more easily extracted than copper or tin, iron involved technological challenges (higher smelting temperature), which may have discouraged its common use even after its discovery. This discovery may

[68] A. M. Sestieri, "The Metal Industry of Continental Italy, 13th to 11th Century B.C., and Its Connections with the Aegean," *ProcPS* 39 (1973) 383–424; L. Vagnetti, "Mycenaean Imports in Central Italy," in *Mycenaeans in Early Latium*, ed. E. Peruzzi (Rome, 1980), appendix 2. 151–67; F. Lo Schiavo, E. Mac-Namara, and L. Vagnetti, "Late Cypriote Imports to Italy and Their Influence on Local Bronzework," *PBSR* 53 (1985) 1–71; M. Marazzi, S. Tusa, and L. Vagnetti, ed., *Traffici micenei nel Mediterraneo* (Taranto, 1986); L. Vagnetti, in "Cypriote Elements beyond the Aegean in the Bronze Age," *Cyprus between the Orient and the Occident*, 201–16.

[69] M. Becker, "Sardinia and the Mediterranean Copper Trade: Political Development and Colonialism in the Bronze Age," *Anthropology* 4 (1980) 91–117; M.-L. Ferrarese Ceruti, "Documenti micenei nella Sardegna meridionale," in *Ichnussa. La Sardegna dalle origini all'età classica*, ed. Atzeni and others (Milan, 1981), 605–12; F. Lo Schiavo, L. Vagnetti, and M. L. Ferrarese Ceruti, "Micenei in Sardegna?" *Acc Linc* 35 (1980) 371–93; Lo Schiavo, "Copper Metallurgy in Sardinia during the Late Bronze Age: New Prospects on Its Aegean Connections," in *Early Metallurgy in Cyprus*, 271–83; D. Ridgway, "Sardinia and the First Western Greeks," and M. Dothan, "Šardina at Akko?" in *SSA*, 2:173–85, 105–15; M. L. Ferrarese Ceruti, L. Vagnetti, and F. Lo Schiavo, "Minoici, Micenei, e Ciprioti in Sardegna nella seconda metà del

II. Millennio a. C.," *SSA*, 3:7–37; D. Ridgway, in *Greek Colonists and Native Populations*, 65–69.

[70] J. C. Martín de la Luz, "Die erste mykenische Keramik von der Iberischen Halbinsel," and Ch. Podzuweit, "Bemerkungen zur mykenischen Keramik von Llanete de los Moros, Montoro, Prov. Córdoba," both in *PZ* 65 (1990), 49–52, 53–58; Podzuweit has these sherds arrive via Sardinia.

[71] B. Hallager, "Crete and Italy in the LM III period," *AJA* 90 (1986) 293–305; cf. "A New Social Class in Late Bronze Age Crete: Foreign Traders in Khania," in *Minoan Society: Proceedings of the Cambridge Colloquium, 1981*, ed. O. Krzyszowska and L. Nixon (Bristol, 1983), 111–19; Y. Tzedakis, *AAA* 3, no. 1 (1970) 111–12, and report in *AJA* 91 (1987) 305–6, on western Crete (cf. n. 75). L. V. Watrous, "A Preliminary Report on Imported 'Italian' Wares from the Late Bronze Age Site of Kommos on Crete," *SMEA* 27 (1989) 69–79; L. Vagnetti, "A Sardinian Askos from Crete," *BSA* 84 (1989) 355–60, for Iron Age survivals. D. Ridgway, in *Greek Colonists and Native Populations*, 69.

[72] Waldbaum, *From Bronze to Iron*, 17–23, on iron before 1200 B.C.; S. Kosak, "The 'Gospel of Iron,' " in *Kaniššuwar. A Tribute to Hans Güterbock on his Seventy-Fifth Birthday*, ed. H. Hoffner and G. Beckman, Assyriological Studies no. 23 (Chicago, 1986), 125–35, on iron in Hittite inventories as a rare, perhaps ceremonial item, as in Homer (*Iliad* 23.850).

have been an accident of bronze working, as a by-product or residue of the iron-rich silicates used in extracting copper from sulfide ore.[73] Greek legends about "double mines" of copper and iron in locales where geology supports their coexistence, such as Euboia (Strabo, 10.1.9, 447c), may reflect such accidents and collaboration in metallurgy. Legend also claims that both Crete and Cyprus were home to the invention of iron-working in antiquity, discovered by the Daktyls on Mount Ida but also in western Crete at Aptera (Diodorus, 5.64.5), alternatively on Cyprus, according to another source which names three legendary craftsmen, Akmon, Kalmis and Damnameneus (schol. Apollonius Rhodius, 1.1129; Clement, *Stromateis* 1.16.75; cf. Strabo, 14.653.7). More-over, both Cyprus and Crete are rich in iron ores and evidence for early ironworking.[74] One suspects this resource, rather than copper and bronze working, behind the pros-perity of western Crete in the Late Bronze Age, and the intensity of its contacts with Cyprus into the Geometric period.[75] In addition to artifacts, linguistics support Aegean and Cypriote interest in western sources of iron as early as the second millennium. For the Semitic root that produced Latin *ferrum* (iron) must have reached Italy long before the first millennium, according to a recent linguistic analysis.[76] What may have brought Italian and Cypriote finds to western Crete in the Late Bronze Age, and helped export western Cretan stirrup jars throughout the Aegean and sarcophagi to Tanagra, was Le-vantine-initiated traffic for iron, not necessarily Aegean activity. East-central Greece is nearest and next richest to Crete in iron, and the prosperity of LH IIIC sites in central Greece (Lefkandi, Perati) may be related to prospection for iron.[77] Provenance studies

[73] Thus Wertime speculated in *Coming of Age of Iron*, 12–17 (cf. J. A. Charles, "The Coming of Copper and Copper-Based Alloys and Iron: A Metallurgical Sequence," in *Coming of Age of Iron*, 151–81, and Wer-time, *JFA* 10 [1983] 451–52), an "accident" now at-tested in the Bronze Age Levant (Frisch and Mans-feld u. Thiele, *Kamīd el-Lōz* 6, 160–80) and in Iron Age Thessaly: K. Kilian, "Weihungen aus Eisen und Ei-senverarbeitung im Heiligtum zu Philia (Thessa-lien)," in *The Greek Renaissance*, 131–47, esp. 146.

[74] T. Stech, J. Muhly, and R. Maddin, *RDAC* (1985) 195–202; Snodgrass (pp. 285–95) and Varoufakis (pp. 315–24) in *Early Metallurgy in Cyprus*; cf. Metalloge-netic Map of Greece (see n. 127), text, 182–84, 207–17, on the millions of tons of iron extracted today from these areas.

[75] Kanta, *LM III Period in Crete*, 199–200, 217–28, 290–313; L. Vagnetti, "Testimonianze di metallurgia Minoica dalla zona di Nerokourou (Kydonias)," *SMEA* 84 (1984) 155–71; M. Popham, "Connections between Crete and Cyprus between 1300–1100 B.C.," and Y. Tzedakis, "Cypriote 'Influences' in the Geo-

metric Pottery of Western Crete," both in *Relations be-tween Cyprus and Crete*, 178–91, 192–98; for a geologi-cal approach, see K. Zervantonakis, "Συμβολὴ τοῦ ὀρυκτοῦ πλούτου τῆς Κρήτης στὴν ἀναπτύξη τοῦ πολιτισμοῦ τῆς ἀρχαιοτῆτας," in *Fifth Cretological Congress*, 1:123–24, on copper, iron, and mixed sul-fides in Crete. Copper and bronze: Z. Stos-Gale and N. Gale, "Chemical and lead isotope analyses of Mi-noan bronzes from Nerokorou, Crete," *SMEA* 84 (1984), 169–71; Watrous, *SMEA* 27 (1989) 69–79.

[76] G. Rendsburg, "Semitic PRZL/BRZL/BRDL, 'Iron,'" *Scripta Mediterranea* 3 (1982) 59–60, fig. 1, ar-gues that triliteral *brz produced *bhers-om to *fers-om to *ferrum*, unlike the later quadriliteral form (*brzl) cir-culated by the Phoenicians as far as Spain and Eu-rope. On iron in Etruria, see *L'Etruria mineraria. Atti del XII Convegno Nazionale di Studi Etruschi, 1979*, ed. G. Camporeale (Milan, 1981) esp. M. Gras, "L'Etrurie minière et la réprise des échanges entre l'Orient et l'Occident: Quelques observations," 315–22.

[77] Kanta, *LM III Period in Crete*, 290–97, on lar-nakes; 300–301, on Cretan stirrup jars exported to

may identify the sources of copper and clay in metal and ceramic artifacts found in the West, but their carriers could be Levantine, as easily as Cypriote, Aegean, or Italian.[78]

The first book of the *Odyssey* introduces this world where iron and copper travel the Mediterranean, sometimes in opposite directions on the same ships. When Athena disguises herself as a visiting stranger on Ithaka, in the passage just quoted, she masquerades as a merchant of metal, bearing iron from an imaginary country of seafarers to a place famed for copper where men speak an alien tongue. Whether she travels east or west, her journey is plausible: "Mentes the Taphian" could bring iron from Spain or Sardinia toward Cyprus for exchange with copper, or carry a similar cargo in the opposite direction, like the Gelidonya ship. If $T\varepsilon\mu\acute{\varepsilon}\sigma\eta\varsigma$ derives from Semitic (*t*)*mss*, "foundry, forge," Athena's destination need not only be Tamasos on Cyprus but any port or city dealing in ingots, just as Biblical Tarshish, Cilician Tarsus, and Iberian Tartessos all indicate a mine.[79] When iron and its sources entered the technological network of the Late Bronze Age, they established eastern Mediterranean contact with the West critical in the formation of urban culture in the first millennium.

This vision of Mediterranean activity makes it easier to understand how trade survived disintegration at the end of the Bronze Age, in particular at the end of the thirteenth century. Egyptian archives report disruptions in the form of foreign aggressors of various names and types, often collected under the name of the "Sea People(s)."[80] Hittite and Ugaritic letters document battles at sea and on land, famine, siege, and blockades; in the Aegean, extra protection against aggression and siege is installed at palatial centers like Tiryns, Mycenae, and Athens. These anticipated and actual disas-

---

Porto Raphti and Perati, near Laureion mines; 326, on iron finds in LM IIIC; on the iron ores of northeast Boiotia, see n. 179.

[78] As argued by R. Tylkot in "The Sea Peoples in Sicily, Sardinia, and Etruria: A Re-examination of the Archaeological and Textual Evidence in Light of Recent Research," at the Archaeological Congress in Baltimore, January 1989. Provenance studies have not identified traders, only cargo: L. Vagnetti and R. Jones, "Towards the Identification of Local Mycenaean Pottery in Italy"; and N. Gale and Z. Stos-Gale, "Recent Evidence for a Possible Bronze Age Metal Trade between Sardinia and the Aegean," both in *Problems in Greek Prehistory*, 335–84.

[79] Dugand, "À propos de Salamis," in *Salamine de Chypre*, 85–86. According to radiocarbon dates, the Tamasos mines on Cyprus were not opened until ca. 664 B.C. (Buchholz, in *Early Metallurgy in Cyprus*, 321) but the name was in circulation much earlier. The Etymologicum Magnum glosses $T\acute{\alpha}\varphi\iota\iota\iota$ (s.v.) to in-

clude pirates who traveled with Kadmos (Edwards, *Kadmos*, 30–31, 37), a reference that encouraged E. Oberhummer, *Phönizer in Akarnanien. Untersuchungen zur phönizischen Kolonials- und Handelsgeschichte mit besonderer Rücksicht auf das westliche Griechenland* (Munich, 1882), to identify "Taphians" with Phoenicians in northwest Greece.

[80] F. Schachermeyr, *Die ägäische Frühzeit*, vols. 3–5 (Vienna, 1979–1980), for archaeology and history from the thirteenth to the eleventh centuries B.C.; H. Tadmor, "The Decline of Empires in Western Asia ca. 1200 B.C.E.," in *Symposia*, 1–14; Strange, *Caphtor/ Keftiu*, 156–65 (Cyprus); Sandars, *Sea Peoples*; Muhly, "The Role of the Sea Peoples in Cyprus during the LC III Period," in *Cyprus at the Close of the Late Bronze Age*, 39–55. See essays by G. A. Lehmann, T. Dothan, and G. Hölbl, in *Griechenland, die Ägäis und die Levante*; M. Mann, *The Sources of Social Power* (Cambridge, 1986), 1:184–89.

ters culminate in destruction or abandonment of major urban and archival centers in the Mycenaean, Hittite, and Canaanite world in the decades before and after 1200 B.C.

The agency of outside invasion by new arrivals was long a convenient explanation for the widespread and thorough devastation of Bronze Age life, and appropriate to the variety of ethnic newcomers in historical references. More popular recently (i.e., more congenial to systems theory) and more accurate is the recognition of troublemakers like the Sea Peoples as a symptom, not a cause of Late Bronze Age disruptions. Internal factors—overexploitation of resources, an overspecialized economy, faction between royal and rural populations—could have strained palace-based economies in the Aegean and the Levant, making them vulnerable to inside and outside disruptions.[81] Such conditions invited independent profiteers in a variety of regional manifestations, as both indigeneous, disadvantaged social classes and newly arrived opportunists. This model recognizes aspects of the same phenomenon in the activity of pirates in the coastal Levant including Phoenicians, the rise in status of nomads like the Arameans in Syria-Palestine, and the Aegean appearance of local *Hirtenstämme* and new arrivals like the "Dorians" (speakers of northwest Greek). Egypt's eleventh-century "Tale of Wenamun" and the tall tales in the *Odyssey* about piracy, kidnapping, thieves, and mercenaries illustrate a true *Zeitalter der Wanderungen*, when authority over a wider territory has declined but local enterprise still flourishes. Poor in historical records and inscribed accounts of imperial bureaucracy and trade, these times were busy and profitable for independent entrepreneurs, who reorganized trade networks to their own advantage and maintained opportunities for artisans and merchants. This milieu actually encouraged agents like the Keftiu and Canaanite traders, whose activity assisted the re-formation of urban cultures in several locales. For only in Egypt and Mesopotamia does the structure of empire revive in the early Iron Age. In most areas—the coastal Levant, North Syria, and the Aegean—smaller, independent city-states develop, among which the Kingdom of Israel and the Greek polis command the greatest notoriety, thanks to the Hebrew Bible and classical literature. The common constitutional pattern of these states evolved between 1200 and 800 B.C. largely because of, not despite, an imperial vacuum.

In the Levant, these local states and their urban culture survived the disintegration of larger political units, and the critical dimensions of their Iron Age culture were established in the Late Bronze Age. In Palestine, literary and archaeological sources agree on the arrival of the "Peleset," the Biblical "Philistines," with material culture that included

---

[81] Sandars, *Sea Peoples*, 183–84, 197–202; Knapp, *Copper Production and Divine Protection*, 96–100; M. Liverani, "The Collapse of the Near Eastern Regional System at the End of the Bronze Age: The Case of Syria," in *Centre and Periphery in the Ancient World*, ed. M. Rowlands, M. Larsen, and K. Kristiansen (Cambridge, 1987), 66–73. Cf. the collapse of the Roman Empire and the Classic Maya from "ecological, demographic and social stress" in Hodges, *Dark Age Economics*, 5, citing Renfrew; N. Yoffee and G. Cowgill, ed., *The Collapse of Ancient States and Civilizations* (Tucson, 1988); J. A. Tainter, *The Collapse of Complex Societies* (Cambridge, 1988).

Mycenaeanizing pottery and Aegean-like cults, and Biblical claims as "Kaptorite."[82] Their culture transmits that Late Bronze Age *koine* common to the Aegean and the Levant, including novelties in cult forms and scripts.[83] Farther north in the coastal Levant, the destruction of an archival center like Ugarit overshadows the survival of other Canaanite cities.[84] Similarly, among the Phoenician cities, some actually profited from the collapse of powerful states such as Ugarit and Egypt, and experienced a period of prosperity.[85] Specialized industries in smaller luxury arts, in particular bronze and ivory, maintained their forms and themes into the early Iron Age, thanks to the survival of δημιοεργοί and the transmission of their talents within families.[86]

From the westward perspective, this expansion of Levantine craftsmen and merchants later known as Phoenicians actually begins in the Late Bronze Age in the form of a "Canaanite diaspora."[87] The first wave of this diaspora, Levantine refugees on Cyprus in the twelfth century and earlier, represents the first "Phoenician" occupation of

---

[82] T. Dothan, *The Philistines* (New Haven, 1982); "Some Aspects of the Appearance of the Sea Peoples and Philistines in Canaan," in *Griechenland, die Agäis und die Levante*, 99–120; add essays by Singer, Mazar, Raban, and Dothan in *Society and Economy in the Eastern Mediterranean*. Cf. A. Giboa, "New Finds at Tel Dor and the Beginning of Cypro-Geometric Pottery Import to Palestine," *IEJ* 39 (1989) 204–18.

[83] W. F. Albright, "Northeast Mediterranean Dark Ages and the Early Iron Age Art of Syria," in *Aegean and the Near East*, 144–64; M. Dothan, "Ashdod at the End of the Late Bronze Age and the Beginning of the Iron Age," and Y. Shiloh, "Iron Age Sanctuaries and Cult Elements in Palestine," both in *Symposia*, 125–34, 147–57; G. W. Ahlström, "An Archaeological Picture of Iron Age Religions in Ancient Palestine," *Studia Orientalia* 55 (1984) 117–45. See especially the sanctuary at Tell Qasile (n. 46) for activity from 1200 to 1000 B.C. and the essays by Peckham, McCarter, Tigay, and Dever in *Ancient Israelite Religions*.

[84] The port of Ugarit, Minet-el-Beida, outlasted its neighbor, as did other Syrian cities like Ras ibn-Hani (Muhly, in *Ebla to Damascus*, 261–270) while cities like Megiddo essentially "remained Canaanite during the Early Iron Age" (Muhly, *IEJ* 30 [1980] 155); A. Kempinski, "The Overlap of Cultures at the End of the Late Bronze Age and the Beginning of the Early Iron Age," in *N. Avigad Volume, Eretz-Israel* 18 (Jerusalem, 1985), 399–407.

[85] Sidon conquers Tyre after the fall of Ugarit (Helck, *Beziehungen*, 42), while Kamīd el-Lōz still flourishes in the twelfth century: Muhly, in *Ebla to*

Damascus, 267–69; P. Corbett, "Thither Came the Phoenicians," *Scripta Mediterranea* 3 (1982) 73, calls the period between the Hittite and Assyrian empires the "Golden Age" of the Phoenicians; the Levant "never had a Dark Age" (Ridgway, in *SSA*, 2:175).

[86] Ivories: Lagarce, "Le rôle d' Ugarit dans l'élaboration du repertoire iconographique Syro-Phénicien du 1er millénaire av. J-C.," in *Studi Fenici e Punici*, 547–61; J.-Cl. Poursat, "La tradition mycénienne en Orient: Ivoires mycénisants et ivoires orientaux archaiques," in *Le rayonnement grec: Hommages à Charles Delvoye* (Brussels, 1982), 69–76; H. Liebowitz, "Late Bronze II Ivory Work in Palestine: Evidence of a Cultural Highpoint," *BASOR* 265 (1986) 3–24, distinguishes ivories of the northern and southern Levant as in the Iron Age. Bronzes: J.-Cl. Courtois, "L'industrie du bronze à Ugarit (Syrie du Nord) à l'âge du Bronze récent et ses prolongements à Chypre à l'époque du transition Bronze/Fer," in *Jahresbericht des Instituts für Vorgeschichte der Univ. Frankfurt, 1975. Geschichte des 13. u. 12. Jhts.*, ed. H. Müller-Karpe (Frankfurt, 1976), 24–32; Catling, *RDAC* (1984) 69–91 and Negbi, *Tel Aviv* 1 (1974) 159–72; Matthäus and Muhly, in *Bronzeworking Centres of Western Asia*, 333–37; R. Laffineur, "Der Zusammenhang von Mykenischen und Frühgriechischen in der Goldschmiedekunst," in *Forschungen zur ägäischen Vorgeschichte*, 73–92.

[87] Over twenty years ago, Culican identified Bronze Age sources of Punic colonization among "Sea Peoples" and "Philistines": "Were all these *sensu lato* Phoenicians (i.e. Orientals) and is it to them

the island.[88] A familiar route along the south (Amathus) and west (Maa-Palaeokastro and Pyla-Kokkinokremos) coast of Cyprus supported new communities called military, more plausibly mercantile.[89] This route then passed by both coasts of Crete, according to Phoenician pottery from Kommos and Knossos. This first stage of "Phoenician" westward traffic may have contributed to the Late Bronze Age prosperity of Aegean sites near iron like Chania, Lefkandi, and Perati, and an increase in population by a factor of five on Rhodes (Ialysos) in the twelfth century.[90] Common to many of these sites still prosperous after 1200 B.C. is the presence of iron (and of the forests to process it), often near other metal ores, which complements the predominance of metallurgists attested epigraphically. That this was not a diaspora of refugees but of entrepreneurs, in pursuit of new resources and markets, appears in their sophisticated burial gifts (iron swords, knives) and in inscribed gold and silver artifacts, which follow a trail of Phoenician metallurgists and their apprentices and offspring through Cyprus, Crete, and Italy.[91] Thus the dispersal of Bronze Age culture to new trading and industrial centers follows familiar trade routes as far west as Italy but includes new interest in iron ores, and involves Levantines as the prime entrepreneurs with local natives, including Greeks, as collaborators.

---

the early tradition of western settlement belongs?" in "Aspects of Phoenician Settlement in the Western Mediterranean," *Abr-Nahrain* 1 (1959–1960) 54; cf. Bunnens, *L'expansion phénicenne*, 15–21; Negbi, *Levant* 14 (1982) 179–82.

[88] Catling, *Cyprus and the West* 21–22, on the culture of Cyprus (more Levantine than Aegean) after 1200 B.C; essays in *Salamine de Chypre*; Negbi, *Levant* 14 (1982) 179–82, to which add V. Karageorghis, *Palaeo-paphos-Skales: An Iron Age Cemetery in Cyprus* (Konstanz, 1983), 370–406, and essays in *Cyprus between the Orient and the Occident*; A. Snodgrass, "Cyprus and the Beginnings of Iron Technology in Early Greece," in *Early Metallurgy in Cyprus*, 285–95; V. Cook, "Cyprus and the Outside World during the Transition from the Bronze Age to the Iron Age," *OpAth* 17 (1988) 13–32. See n. 103 on the eleventh and ninth centuries, with N. Coldstream, "Early Greek Pottery in Tyre and Cyprus: Some Preliminary Comparisons," *RDAC* (1988) 33–44.

[89] V. Karageorghis, "Deux avants-postes militaires de la fin du XIIIe siècle av. J.-C. à Chypre," *CRAI* (1982) 704–24; cf. V. Karageorghis and M. Demas, *Pyla-Kokkinokremos. A Late 13th C. B.C. Fortified Settlement* (Nicosia, 1984); E. Vermeule, *AJA* 89 (1985) 359–60, calls them commercial.

[90] Muhly (cited in n. 98) 50: "An essentially Bronze Age culture continued to survive in the Aegean at a number of sites." Kanta, *III Period in Crete*, 318–22, on the vitality of postpalatial, rural Crete. In addition to Lefkandi's important LH IIIC pottery, seventeen copper "bun" ingots found off Kyme date around 1500 B.C., early evidence for Euboian metal trade: Sackett and others, "Prehistoric Euboea: Contributions Toward a Survey," *BSA* 61 (1966) 75–76. S. Iakovides, *Perati* (Athens, 1970), 110–11, on the latest Mycenaean culture of Lefkandi and eastern Attika. C. Macdonald, "Problems of the Twelfth Century B.C. in the Dodecanese," *BSA* 77 (1986) 125–51.

[91] E. Masson and P. Åström, "A Silver Bowl with Canaanite Inscription from Hala Sultan Teke," *RDAC* (1982) 72–76, (found in a twelfth-century well); P. Bordreuil, "Cuneiform non-alphabétiques non-canoniques II. À propos de l'épigraphie de Hala Sultan Tekke," *Semitica* 33 (1983) 7–15. Puech, *RB* 90 (1983) 366–95. Cf. the continuity of bronze workshops (Chapter 1, n. 20) and the role of ironworking specialists in trade diasporas (Curtin, *Cross-Cultural Trade*, 18). For Iron Age successors of these workshops in Cyprus, Greece, and Italy, see Markoe, *Phoenician Bowls*; also Chapter 6, n 48.

A subtle and fascinating relationship between history and technology is involved in the role of iron in these Late Bronze Age events and the succeeding centuries. While a shortage of copper or tin is no longer blamed for the rise of iron metallurgy as an industry producing tools and weapons, difficulty in procuring and distributing the components of bronze, with the greater fuel efficiency of iron, may have encouraged the refinement of iron technology.[92] In turn, the application of ironworking to functional artifacts (e.g., tools and weapons, rather than prestige items) then played a second critical role in the next stage of the Levantine network: the rise and expansion of the Assyrian Empire, examined in the next section.

It is under conditions like these that the rise of Greek urban culture, if not of the polis itself, should be contemplated, along the lines of "protourban" collaborative networks that developed between Mediterranean entrepreneurs and a native elite in Iron Age Europe.[93] The role of foreign contacts and commercial enterprise in the development of early Iron Age communities is far more vivid, for reasons both ancient and modern, outside of Greece. Areas like Sardinia, Iberia, and Europe were free of the Greek heritage of Mycenaean culture, which dominated memory and poetry in the Aegean. Nor did they develop formal hostilities with their foreign partners as Greeks did, in a way that suppressed alien culture as the Greeks revised their attitude to the Orient, after the Persian wars (see Part IV). Finally, modern research outside of Greece has developed far more progressive theories and models for the evolution of culture, unencumbered by classical scholarship that inevitably puts Aristotle before archaeology.[94]

To begin the history of Greece in 776 B.C. may be dismissed as a nineteenth-century convention, yet still characterizes the most recent and theoretically sophisticated scholarship.[95] More useful new studies of early Greek culture have borrowed perspectives

---

[92] A. Snodgrass, *The Dark Age of Greece* (Edinburgh, 1971), 231, 251; Waldbaum, *From Bronze to Iron*, 65, 71; and *AJA* 91 (1987) 285, on fuel efficiency; V. Piggott, "The Innovation of Iron: Cultural Dynamics of Technological Change," *Expedition* 25 (1982) 20–25; Muhly (cited in n. 98) 46–48; Wertime, *JFA* 10 (1983) 445–52.

[93] Wells, *Culture Contact and Culture Change*, 97ff., and *Farms, Villages and Cities*, esp. 94–124; D. Rupp, in "*Vive le Roi*: The Emergence of the State in Iron Age Cyprus," in *Western Cyprus*, 156 n. 87. Mann *The Sources of Social Power*, 1:191–230, on "Phoenicians and Greeks: decentralized multi-power-actor civilizations."

[94] As in Coldstream's essays *Aristotle and Archaeology* and "Dorian Knossos and Aristotle's Villages," in *Aux origines de l'Hellénisme*. For parallel developments in Europe, see Wells, *Culture Contact*; Hodges,

Dark Age Economics, for a similar process (collapse of a major empire and rise of urban culture). For Phoenician influence on local urbanism outside of Greece, see Niemeyer, *JRGZM* 31 (1984) 1–93; Semmler, in *Phönizier im Westen*, 309–35 (Iberia) and Barrecca, in *SSA* 2:152–62.

[95] On the modern "fabrication" of ancient Greece, see Bernal, *Black Athena*, esp. chap. 6, and my response in *Challenge of Black Athena*, 48–49. The obsession with the eighth century and with the polis persists in, e.g., *The Greek Renaissance*; A. Snodgrass, *Archaeology and the Rise of the Greek State* (Inaugural Lecture, Cambridge, 1977); Fr. de Polignac, *La naissance de la cité grecque: Cultes, espaces, et société aux VIIIe–VIIe siècles av. J.-C.* (Paris, 1984). W. Gawantka, *Die sogennante Polis* (Stuttgart, 1985), for a critical view.

from Bronze Age archaeology or the Near East. For example, Near Eastern terminology for Greeks ("Ionians" among the Assyrians; the Biblical "Jawan" with their "vessels of bronze": *Ezekiel* 27.13) reveals the continuity of Aegean life in different periods: both "Keftiu" and "Iavan" live "in the middle of the islands." Many traditions identified as "Greek"—chariotry and hoplite warfare, funeral games, seafaring, hunting and athletics, dance and music—already exist in the Mycenaean world. For reasons like these, the origins of Greek urban culture begin before 1200 B.C., with a demise, not highpoint, in the fifth century.[96] The polis arose not in the eighth century, but from the recently dissolved Mycenaean world, enriched by new arrivals from the East, who included δημιοεργοί talented in various skills, from metal to magic and poetry. The world of "early Greece"—the world of Homer—is neither Bronze Age nor archaic but both, nor is it more Greek than it is Oriental. This reformulation not only discards traditional periodization but recasts social and ethnic dimensions, more determined by craftsmen, technicians, and the elite entrepreneurs who employed them than by political constructs assumed from other and later cultures. In such a world, it is no surprise to find Daidalos alongside Hephaistos, as Kinyras of Cyprus is a contemporary and equal of Agamemnon. From his Canaanite ancestor, Kothar, to his sons and pupils in Crete, Daidalos spans this early "Greek" culture as a paradigm of its continuity and its Orientalism.

GREEKS AND PHOENICIANS IN THE MEDITERRANEAN

The term "Phoenician" therefore refers to a category of people
involved in certain recognisable activities rather than to a single
ethnic group, e.g. in the Homeric poems, all traders are
"Phoenicians."

—S. Frankenstein, in *Power and Propaganda*, 288

[96] E. Rystedt, "Mycenaean Runners—Including *Apobatai*," in *Problems in Greek Prehistory*, 437–42; W. Decker, "Der mykenische Herkunft des griechischen Totenagons," in *Forschungen zur ägäischen Vorgeschichte*, 201–30; Van Effenterre, *La cîté grecque*; add E. Vermeule and V. Karageorghis, *Mycenaean Pictorial Vase Painting* (Cambridge, Mass., 1982), for other Late Bronze Age motifs (musicians, dancers, hoplites). H. E. Stier, "Probleme der frühgriechischen Geschichte und Kultur," *Historia* 1 (1950) 195–230, treats Greek history as continuous from 1200 B.C. to the Persian Wars and questions "was im archaischen Hellas eigentlich nicht aus dem Orient herstammte" (p. 227). In art: R. Hampe and E. Simon, *The Birth of Greek Art from the Mycenaean to the Archaic period* (London, 1980); D. Levi, "Continuità della tradizione micenea nell'arte greca arcaica," in *Primo Congreso Internazionale del Micenologia*, 185–215; Laffineur, in *Forschungen zur ägäischen Vorgeschichte*, 73–92.

It should be clear by now that, as usual, ancient historical reality
was much more complex than modern theories. For example, just
what is meant by a "Greek" in the period from the twelfth to the
tenth century B.C.?"

—G. Mendenhall, *Kadmos* 14 (1975) 53 n. 17

The next critical stimulus for the emergence of Greek urban culture involved fresh interaction with the Orient. The directions, locations, and dimensions of Levantine trade and traffic established in the Bronze Age Aegean survived the catastrophes that closed the millennium. Long before ninth-century Tyrian colonies on Cyprus and at Carthage, Levantine imports reached Cyprus, Rhodes, Crete, Athens, and Euboia in the Aegean and even Spain.[97] Whether in faience, ivory, tin bronze, perfumed oil and its containers, scripts syllabic and alphabetic, or mythological literature, Greece never lost its taste for Oriental luxuries or the means to acquire them. When Odysseus meets "Phoenicians" on Crete in one of his false tales (*Odyssey* 14.300), he could have done so in the twelfth century, the eighth century, or any time in between. Understood as a revival, or survival, of Late Bronze Age Canaanite maritime trade, the Phoenicians do not "appear" or "arrive" in the West as much as they remain there, retaining their contacts with minerals and markets even when demand dwindles.

New customers appeared soon, once again in the East. The rise of the Neo-Assyrian Empire encouraged war and commerce in the eastern Mediterranean, supporting Phoenician expeditions for metal and timber, eventually colonies. Novel iron technology found its first market in weapons, originally among the Philistines, more widely among the Assyrians.[98] In this traditional arrangement, Levantines neither emigrated as refugees from imperial power, nor were they crippled by tribute, but enjoyed a profitable relationship with resources and raw materials.[99] Phoenician explorers, manufacturers,

[97] Niemeyer, *JRGZM* 31 (1984) 1–94, on Phoenician activity in the Mediterranean prior to ninth-century Assyrian expansion.

[98] R. Pleiner and J. K. Borkman, "The Assyrian Iron Age: The History of Iron in the Assyrian Civilization," *PAPhS* 118 (1974) 228–313; J. Muhly, "How Iron Technology Changed the Ancient World—And Gave the Philistines a Military Edge," *BASOR* 8, no. 6 (1982) 40–50. Cf. the role of iron in Africa: S. Barnes and P. Ben-Amos, "Benin, Oyo, and Dahomey: Warfare, State Building and the Sacralization of Iron in West African History," *Expedition* (Winter 1983) 5–14. The uses of iron include agricultural (plowshares), military (weapons, horse and chariot gear), and in

dustrial (as a mordant in dyeing, perhaps in the production of "Phoenician" purple?).

[99] W. Culican, "Almuñecar, Assur and Phoenician Penetration of the Western Mediterranean," *Levant* 2 (1970) 28–36; Bunnens, *L'expansion phénicienne*; M. T. Larsen, "The Tradition of Empire in Mesopotamia," and S. Frankenstein, "The Phoenicians in the Far West: A Function of Neo-Assyrian Imperialism," both in *Power and Propaganda*, 75–103, esp. 98–101, and 263–94; P. Garelli, "Remarques sur les rapports entre l'Assyrie et les cîtés phéniciennes," in *Studi Fenici e Punici* 61–66; J. Elayi, "Les cîtés phéniciennes et l'empire assyrien d'Assurbanipal," *RAss* 77 (1983) 45–58; M. B. Rowton, "War, Trade and the Emerging

and merchants set up "gateway communities," defined as "specialized trading centers
. . . at strategic nodes where the production or flow of raw materials and goods can be
controlled and where local exchange systems overlap with interregional systems."[100]
The dynamics of these settlements are clearest in Cilicia, Cyprus, Italy, and Iberia, at
ports near rivers or otherwise linked to inland communities for collaboration in metal
exploration.[101] In the Near East, Levantine interests of the Bronze Age—when copper
and tin attracted Assyrians, then Canaanites, to Anatolia—are reproduced by Phoenician explorers of iron.[102] Moving west, Cyprus may have been the first home to iron
technology in the Late Bronze Age and continued to attract Levantine entrepreneurs. A
new route west, along the south coast of Cyprus and Crete, was active by the eleventh
century, the first phase of the early and long-lived Phoenician communities beginning
with the colony called "new town" (Qarthadast) at Kition.[103]

Because these centuries are so fertile for Greek culture, their dynamics and personnel
linking Greece with the Levant are critical, yet obscured in Semitic and Greek epigraphy
and archaeology. Phoenician and North Syrian styles need the same careful distinction
outside the Levant that they have received at home; script and dialect in early Semitic
inscriptions in the west are sometimes Aramaic, not Phoenician.[104] In the coastal Le-

Power Center," in *Mesopotamien und seine Nachbarn*,
1:187–94; Niemeyer, *JRGZM* 31 (1984) 1–93, esp. 89;
Burkert, *Orientalisierende Epoche*, 12, 15–19. E. Linder,
"The Khorsabad Wall Relief: A Mediterranean Sea-
scape or River Transport of Timbers?" *JAOS* 102, no.
6 (1986) 273–81, for Phoenician transport of timber to
Assyria. Mann, *The Sources of Social Power*, 184–93,
on Phoenician enterprise.

[100] Knapp, *JFA* 12 (1985) 249 n. 165 (describing
Toumba tou Skourou in Cyprus); cf. his article in *Prehistoric Production and Exchange*. Compare emporia in
the rise of European urban culture: Hodges, *Dark Age
Economics*, chap. 3.

[101] Markoe, *Phoenician Bowls*, 125–26. In Spain,
Phoenicians exchanged oil and pottery for metal:
Pseudo-Aristotle, *De Auscultationibus Mirabilis* 135;
Pseudo-Scylax, *Periplous* 112; Gill, *BSR* 56 (1988) 1–12
(see Chapter 7). North Africa: M. Ponsich, "Terri-
toires utiles du Maroc punique," in *Phönizier im Westen*, 429–44, esp. 442–44, on "Les fleuves, moyens de
pénétration," and remarks by Riis and Shefton, 256–
57; Stucchi (cited in n. 160) 73–84. Bunnens, *L'expansion phénicienne*, 391, notes how well-defined local
cultures, such as Etruria and Greece, only accommodated Phoenicians as private settlers for commercial
purposes without the later, formal Punic colony.

[102] G. Kestemont, "Le commerce phénicien et l'ex-

pansion assyrienne du IXe.–VIIIe. siècle," *OrAnt* 11
(1982) 143, compares relations between North Syria
and Cilicia in the Bronze Age (Ugarit and Ura) and
those in the early Iron Age (Tyre and Karatepe). Cf.
I. Winter, "On the Problems of Karatepe," *AnatStud*
29 (1979) 138–40, for Phoenician interests in Cilicia.

[103] Bunnens, *L'expansion phénicienne*, 348–58;
O. Masson and M. Sznycer, *Recherches sur les Phéni-
ciens à Chypre* (Geneva, 1972); E. Gjerstad, "The
Phoenician Colonization and Expansion in Cyprus,"
RDAC (1979) 230–54; V. Karageorghis, "New Phoe-
nician Discoveries in Cyprus," in *Studi Fenici e Punici*,
173–77; M. Sznycer, "Salamine et les Phéniciens," in
Salamine de Chypre, 123–29; Markoe, *Phoenician Bowls*,
6–8. Bikai, *Phoenician Pottery of Cyprus*, and "Trade
Networks in the Early Iron Age: The Phoenicians at
Palaepaphos," in *Western Cyprus*, 125–28 (also see nn.
88, 89).

[104] Ivories: I. Winter, "Phoenician and North Syr-
ian Ivory Carving in Historical Context: Questions of
Style and Distribution," *Iraq* 38 (1976) 1–22; "Is there
a South Syrian Style of Ivory Carving in the Early
First Millennium B.C.?" *Iraq* 43 (1981) 101–30; cf. in
Lakonia (Carter, *Greek Ivory-Carving*, 152–56) and
Crete (Sakellarakis, *L'Antro Ideo*, 28–35, figs. 7–9).
Epigraphy: H. Lozachmeur, "Sur la bilingue gréco-
araméenne d' Agçakale," *Semitica* 25 (1975) 97–102;

vant, Phoenicians, Greeks, and Cypriotes cannot be distinguished with confidence from material evidence. Greek "colonies," once identified by Greek pottery as the hallmark of Greek expansion, belong to their Levantine context. Al Mina, in particular, no longer dominates the modern imagination as a Greek haven in the East and the home of the alphabet. In recent views, it represents a Syrian port (perhaps for Tell Tayinat) and reflects more about Assyrian expansion than Greek colonization.[105] Other Phoenician sites in Syria and Lebanon—Tell Sukas, Sarepta, Umm el' Amed—display Levantine culture whose "Greek influence" may be exaggerated.[106] Greek pottery and even coins abroad could represent Cypriote transmission or objects returned with Phoenicians exploring the Aegean, as in ancient testimonia where Phoenicians carry Attic pottery (e.g., Pseudo-Scylax, *Periplous* 112).[107] In turn, communities in Greece, Italy or Spain could have been as Phoenician as Kition or Sarepta, particularly where Phoenicians arrived first according to foundation dates—in the eleventh century at Gades and in Sardinia. This makes the Greek colonizing movement of the eighth century one of those lessons, like the alphabet, that Hellenes learned from the Levant (see Chapter 7). West of Greece, native populations added a third ingredient to the cooperative, later competitive, relationship between Greeks and Orientals.[108]

These ambiguities are epitomized on Cyprus: an island Levantine in locale but stubbornly Aegean in script, with a population both Aegean and Canaanite in the Late

G. Garbini, "Un iscrizione aramaica a Ischia," *PdP* 33 (1978) 143–50; F. de Salvia, "Un aspeto di Mischkultur Ellenico-Semitica a Pithekoussai (Ischia): I pendagli metallici del tipo a Falce," in *Studi Fenici e Punici*, 89–95; D. Ridgway on the Levantine identity of Ischia's settlers (Aramaean, Phoenician, or Cypriote?) in *SSA*, 2:178–79.

[105] D. Saltz, "Greek Geometric Pottery in the East: The Chronological Implications" (Ph.D. diss., Harvard University, 1978), 1–73; Helm, " 'Greeks' in the Neo-Assyrian Levant," 78–86; J. Elayi, "Al Mina sur l'Oronte à l'époque Perse," in *Studia Phoenicia*, 5:249–66; A. J. Graham, "The Historical Interpretation of Al Mina," *DHA* 12 (1986) 51–65, and *CAH* III.3, 93; Morris, in *Challenge of* Black Athena, 49–50. J. N. Coldstream, "Early Greek Visitors to Cyprus and the Eastern Mediterranean," in *Cyprus and the Eastern Mediterranean*, 90–96; Boardman *OJA* 9 (1990) 169–90.

[106] P. J. Riis, "Griechen in Phönizien," in *Phönizier im Westen* 237–60; Muhly, in *Ebla to Damascus*, 269–70; P. Corbett, "Thither Came the Phoenicians," *Scripta Mediterranea* 3 (1982) 74–78, 84–88, calls Hellenization of Phoenician cities largely a Roman phenomenon; cf. Elayi, *Pénétration grecque*.

[107] Riis, in *Phönizier im Westen*, 237–55 (Cypriote

carriers); cf. O. Masson, "Pélerins chypriotes en Phénicie (Sarepta et Sidon)," *Semitica* 32 (1982) 45–49; J. Teixidor, *JNES* 46 (1987) 74, prefers Phoenicians, as does Gill *BSR* 56 (1988) 1–12; Helm, " 'Greeks' in the Neo-Assyrian Levant," 70–93; Coldstream, in *Cyprus and the Eastern Mediterranean*, 90–96. On Greek coins as silver bullion, see C.F.A. Schaeffer, "Une trouvaille de monnaies archaïques grecques à Ras Shamra," in *Mélanges Dussaud*, 461–87; Elayi, *Pénétration grecque*, chap. 2.

[108] Ischia: G. Buchner, in *Phönizier im Westen*, 277–98; Frankenstein, in *Power and Propaganda*, 278, on "the interrelationship of Phoenician and Greek trading ventures in the Central Mediterranean"; M. G. Amadei Guzzo, "Fenici e Aramei in Occidente nell' VIII sec. A.C.," in *Studia Phoenicia*, 5:35–47. Iberia: C. R. Whittaker, "The Western Phoenicians: Colonisation and Assimilation," *PCPhS* 200 (1974) 58–79; J. Kirkin, "Phönizer und Spanier. Zum Problem der kulturellen Kontakte," *Klio* 63 (1981) 411–21; Gill, *BSR* 56 (1988) 1–12; M. Semmler, "Zur Problematik des orientalisierenden Horizonts," in *Phönizier im Westen*, 326, tackles the "vast and complex panorama of provincial Phoenician and autochthonous art."

Bronze Age, then home to a Phoenician colony. Its art and inscriptions defy experts and suggest a mixed community.[109] North Syrian burial customs appear on Cyprus since the ninth century, much as they do in Crete (see Chapter 6). Innovations in ashlar masonry and its decorative elements, probably Levantine in origin, appear first in Cyprus at Phoenician Kition, with a more lasting impact in the Aegean in early Greek architecture.[110] In Levantine terms, this building tradition is inherited from Canaanites in Phoenicia and Palestine, exported to Cyprus, and eventually to the Aegean. Aspects of Semitic cult practices—sacrifice involving altars and bucrania—survive into archaic Cyprus, where they lie intermediate, in period and locale, to the Levant and Greece. Developments in sculpture and metallurgy survive the Bronze Age in a Cypriote context, perhaps through the residence of Semitic craftsmen (see nn. 114, 115). In short, the island of Cyprus, with a Phoenician colony at Kition and material clues elsewhere, substantiates a Levantine presence more faintly visible at Aegean sites and anticipates their complexity. Literary testimonia for a Cypriote role in "Phoenician" expansion westward are scarce, beyond Dido's disputed stop at the island for a shipment of brides, en route from Tyre to Carthage.[111] But inscriptions, bronzes, and pottery found in Italy, Sicily, and Sardinia (Chapter 7) suggest Cypriotes in Levantine communities in the West, survivors or renovators of the island's Bronze Age contacts (see nn. 69, 70, 78). Trading posts in Egypt such as Marsa Matruh, full of Late Bronze Age pottery from Cyprus, the Near East, and the Aegean, are predecessors of special cities like Naukratis where Psammetichos I welcomed "Greek and Phoenician" merchants, many of whom must have hailed from Cyprus.[112] The early Iron Age cemetery at Knossos held pottery

[109] E.g: A. Dupont-Sommer, "Une inscription phénicienne archaique recemment trouveé à Kition (Chypre)," *Mémoires de l'Académie des Inscriptions et Belles-lettres* 44 (1970) 1–28, now considered Greek: Cross, in *Temples and High Places*, 106; L. Stager, in *Phönizier im Westen*, 274. Cf. Buchner, in *Phönizier im Westen*, 291, for Semitic graffiti from Ischia first read as Greek.

[110] N. Sandars, "Some Early Uses of Drafted Masonry around the Levant," in ΦΙΛΙΑ ΕΠΗ, 1:67–73. Cf. E. Stern, "Phoenician Elements in the Architecture of Tell Mevorakh," in *Excavations at Tell Mevorakh. Part One. From the Iron Age to the Roman Period,* QEDEM 9 (Jerusalem, 1978), 71–75; Y. Shiloh, *The Proto-Aeolic Capital and Israelite Ashlar Masonry,* QEDEM 11 (Jerusalem, 1979); G. and O. van Beek, "Canaanite-Phoenician Architecture: The Development and Distribution of Two Styles," in *Y. Aharoni Memorial Volume, Eretz-Israel* 15 (Jerusalem, 1981), 70–77; I. Sharon, "Phoenician and Greek Ashlar Con-

struction Techniques at Tel Dor, Israel," *BASOR* 267 (1987) 21–42. For transmission of these techniques to Crete and Anatolia, see C. Ratté, *AJA* 93 (1989) 274 (see n. 200), and my Chapter 6 on Gortyn.

[111] Justin, 18.5.1–5; cf. Servius on *Aeneid* 1.443. Bunnens, *L'expansion phénicienne*, 299–303, calls this too late and too Roman, but admits the Nora Stone as possible evidence for Cypriote Phoenicians in Sardinia. Cf. A. M. Bisi, "Κυπριακά," in *Contributi allo studio della componente cipriota della civiltà punica* (Rome, 1966); and C. Baurain, "Le rôle de Chypre dans la fondation de Carthage," in *Studia Phoenicia*, 6:15–27.

[112] Diodorus Siculus, 66.8, 67.9; recent excavations at Marsa Matruh: D. White, *JARCE* 23 (1985) 51–84, and *JARCE* 26 (1989) 87–114; Naukratis: W. Davis, "Ancient Naukratis and the Cypriotes in Egypt," *GöttMisz* 35 (1979) 13–23; "The Cypriotes at Naukratis," *GöttMisz* 41 (1980) 7–14, on Cypriote pottery in Egypt before the Saite settlement.

under Cypriote influence and a Phoenician-inscribed metal bowl of Cypriote shape.[113] North Syrian and Phoenician impetus for Greek monumental sculpture may well have taken place through the intermediary of Cyprus.[114] In the domain of metallurgy, Crete and Cyprus belonged to the same network connecting resources and craftsmen since the Late Bronze Age.[115] Practical elements that certify this exchange are manifest in Cretan terminology for weights and measures, borrowed from Cyprus.[116] Legal terms show a similar pattern, according to an inscribed term from Crete corroborated by a lexicographer's gloss.[117] Ceramic, bronze, and perfume industries of the early Iron Age must have flourished through collaboration between Cypriotes and Cretans, according to oil vessels manufactured on Crete in close imitation of Cypro-Phoenician ones. Once established, a Greco-Oriental community on Crete and its industries (see Chapter 7) continued to acquire supplies and inspiration via Cyprus.[118] As late as the Hellenistic period, Phoenicians on Rhodes and Kos still display cult and civic connections to Cyprus and their homeland, although epigraphers have doubted their relationship to early archaic merchants.[119] Each such overlap means that "Phoenician" or North Syrian effects in the Aegean are potentially from Cyprus, rather than the Levant.[120]

[113] J. N. Coldstream, "Some Cypriote Traits in Cretan Pottery, 950–700 B.C.," in *Relations between Cyprus and Crete*, 260–62; "Knossian Figured Scenes of the Ninth C. B.C.," in *Fourth Cretological Congress*; *RDAC* (1984) 122–39. For Cypriote white slip from Rhodes, Thera, Melos, see Edwards, *Kadmos*, 180 n. 196.

[114] Adams, *Orientalizing Sculpture*, 30–31; B. Lewe, *Archaische Grossplastik auf Zypern* (Frankfurt, 1975), on Cyprus as transmitter of Egyptian influence on early Greek sculpture, esp. after Amasis's conquest of the island (Herodotus, 2.182); G. Markoe, "Egyptianizing Male Votive Statuary from Cyprus: A Re-examination," *Levant* 22 (1990) 111–22; Carter, *Greek Ivorycarving*, 33–34, and *Beginning of Greek Sculpture*. Also see Chapter 9.

[115] Catling *RDAC* (1984) 69–91; "Copper in Cyprus, Bronze in Crete," and N. Platon, "L'exportation du cuivre de l' ile de Chypre en Crète," and M. Yon, "Chypre et la Crète au XIe siècle," all in *Relations between Cyprus and Crete*, 69–75, 101–10, 241–48. Iron replaced copper, and western Crete with Mount Ida eclipsed Knossos, as early as the thirteenth century: see essays by Popham and Tzedakis in *Relations between Cyprus and Crete* and others in *Cyprus between the Orient and the Occident*.

[116] The word πελεκύς appears in Cretan vocabulary as a standard of weight common also to Cyprus: V. Karageorghis, "Pikes or Oboloi from Crete and

Cyprus," in *Antichità Cretesi*, 2:168–72. A rare form for ἡμίσυ is glossed as Cypriote (Bechtel I.448, s.v. ἡμίνα) and appears in Cretan inscriptions: *LexGort* 2.49, 8.4; *SIG* 525, 13. Niemeyer, *JRGZM* 31 (1984) 62–64, on Levantine terms and measures in the West.

[117] ἀκεύοντος (*LexGort* 2.17–18), cf. Hesychius, s.v. ἀκεύε = τηρεῖ. Κύπριοι.

[118] Coldstream, *RDAC* (1984) 122–39. See analyses of bronzes by Rolley and others (see Chapter 6, n. 15). Markoe, *Phoenician Bowls*, 110–17; Muhly, in *Bronzeworking Centres of Western Asia*, 338–39.

[119] P. M. Fraser, "Greek Phoenician Bilingual Inscriptions from Rhodes," *BSA* 65 (1970) 31–36. A tombstone (Rhodes Museum, PBE 1233) commemorates Ἡρακλίδης Κιτιεύς a "servant of Melkart" and native of Kition. Cf. D. Michaelides and M. Sznycer, "A Phoenician Graffito from Tomb 103/84 at Nea Paphos," *RDAC* (1985) 249–56, for a Phoenician metal founder named on a proto-Rhodian amphora of the Hellenistic period; see n. 134 for bilingual inscription from Hellenistic Kos.

[120] Helm, " 'Greeks' in the Neo-Assyrian Levant," sees Eastern trade "largely, if not exclusively, in the hands of merchants from Cyprus (and probably the Levantine coasts as well)" and calls "Cypro-Phoenicians" such traders in the Aegean (p. 126); cf. Bernal, *Black Athena*, 427.

Near Eastern scholars disclaim confidence on these distinctions, a lesson to Hellenists. Frankenstein's useful definition of "Phoenicians" (quoted previously) admits an
ambiguous origin for much Levantine material in Greece and will be used here for con-
venience. It includes Phoenicians, Aramaeans, or North Syrians from Cyprus or the
Levant, but could even include native members of a Phoenician workshop, community,
or family. This admits a long and fertile exchange between East and West, including
Greek communities of the Aegean, which flourished primarily outside formal colonization, Greek or Phoenician. Debated models of "cultural pluralism" and "mutual acculturation" assume an original, or ultimate, product: cultures conveniently labeled Greek,
Punic, Iberian, or Italian.[121] Such definitions only became a Western concern after
Greeks defeated Persians and still perplexes *Hellenosemitica*, as in the question posed by
a Semitic epigrapher (quoted at the opening of this section).[122] The more emerges in
excavation—currently in Crete, Euboia, and Ischia—the more difficult it becomes to answer his question, and the more futile to ask it. The case of the Phoenicians helps illustrate how the period called "Orientalizing" extends from the Bronze Age to late antiquity, and remains better understood as a dimension of Greek culture rather than a
phase.

Despite the absence of formal, historical Phoenician "colonies" in the Aegean, as in
Cyprus or the West, their artifacts are manifest since at least the tenth century. Modern
reluctance to recognize Phoenicians in the Greek world has recently yielded to archaeological evidence and a critique of scholarship.[123] Geology, history, and archaeology
demonstrate how comparing resources, artifacts, and traditions can point to Phoenicians at specific sites in the Aegean. Greek sources acknowledge Phoenicians either
through myth, as in the wanderings of Kadmos and his family, or in actual references
to their historical activity in Greece, beginning with Homer and Herodotus. These testimonia are often localized where resources might have attracted them, particularly local
iron ores in use by the ninth century.[124] Finally, Oriental or Orientalizing luxury artifacts

[121] Corbett, *Scripta Mediterranea* 3 (1982) 81. Cf. the
essays in *Studia Phoenicia*, vols. 3–5, esp. C. Baurain,
"Portées chronologiques et géographiques du terme
'phénicien,' " in *Studia Phoenicia*, 4:7–28. Boardman
prefers "Levantine" to "Phoenician," which he finds
"overprecise and too loosely employed by scholars
today" (pp. 10–11 in "The Lyre Player Group of
Seals. An Encore," *AA* [1990] 1–17).

[122] G. Mendenhall, "The Inscription from Çatal
Hüyük in the Plain of Antakya," *Kadmos* 14 (1975) 53
n. 17; p. 61 on early writing long before "any political
entity that can be called 'Greek' in the classical
sense."

[123] Bunnens *L'expansion phénicienne*, 6–9. Bernal,

Black Athena, 359–99 and "The Return of the Iron Age
Phoenicians" in scholarship (pp. 426–27), now restored to pre-Aryan models of the nineteenth century (e.g., Max Dunker's "Die Phöniker in Hellas,"
in *Geschichte des Altertums* [Leipzig 1881] 42–55).
E. Van 't Dack, "Les Phénicisants et nous," in *Studia
Phoenicia*, 5:1–18.

[124] Varoufakis, in *Early Metallurgy in Cyprus*, 318–
22. Cf. Drews, *AJP* 100 (1979) 46 n. 9, on iron in Lakonia; Bakhuizen, *Chalcis-in-Euboea*, 45–56; Crete:
Faure, *Ulysse le Crétois*, 92–94, to which add Kommos
(for notice of iron found in excavations, see *Hesperia*
53 [1984] 283, pl. 55, d-e; 60, b).

or cult practices point to Phoenicians in the same metal-rich areas: Thasos, Euboia and Boiotia, Lakonia, Crete, and Rhodes. This coincidence of cult and craft maintains the chief dimensions in the Daidalos tradition; it is a related myth, the travels of Kadmos in search of Europa, that follows closely the traces of Phoenicians exploring the Aegean. A tour of his stopping points will introduce the case of Crete, home of Daidalos, in the next chapter.

> "The river brings iron to the sea like a secret wedding gift by the
> groom to his bride. But the sea desiring to make her gift public
> crushes it on the beach in the form of sand in full view to all."

—Niketas Magistros (tenth century A.D.)

Although the lure of metals has been cited throughout this chapter as the chief catalyst for Levantine contact with Greeks, a more detailed description of those involved in Phoenician exploration of the Aegean is overdue. The importance of these mineral sources cannot be exaggerated in understanding Levantine settlement in Greece; they have rarely been consulted by archaeologists except when supported by ancient testimonia, as in the case of Thasos (see nn. 185–88).[125] Levantine interest in Aegean ores is best understood in terms of "polymetallism," a term congenial to both geological realities and ancient anecdotes.[126] If copper, then iron, drew Easterners to Greece's many islands and shores, a chief source of these and other valuable minerals was mixed sulfide ores formed by deep tectonic and hydrothermal activity.[127] These deposits are rich in copper, lead, silver, gold, and iron; chief occurrences of such deposits that drew Phoenicians were in western Crete, Lakonia and the Cyclades, the "Laureiotiki" region of eastern Attika, southern Euboia and Boiotia, and Thrace.[128] Critical to the Phoenicians

[125] Most archaeologists (e.g., Desborough, in *Essays: Fitch*, 34, 38–39) only notice ancient molds; Coldstream, for example, denies Euboia the same attractions as Thasos, calling Greece "poor in raw materials, especially in most metallic ores": in *Phönizier im Westen*, 262, 266 (despite iron on Euboia: see n. 168). Drews (cited in n. 141) is one of the few classicists to invoke geology; P. Faure, "Les minerais de la Crète antique," *RA* (1966) 45–78, and in *Fourth Cretological Congress*, 50–168, notes Cretan iron ores near settlements, without the Phoenician connection.

[126] Photos, *Extractive Iron Metallurgy*, 62ff.; cf. Strabo on Euboia's "double mine" of copper and iron" (10.1.9: 447c). Adjacent timber resources, as in Thasos and Thrace, may have provided an added attraction.

[127] See the Metallogenetic Map of Greece and its explanatory volume, 123–47; A. Papastamatakis, Ἡ ἐκμεταλλεῦσις τοῦ ὀρύκτου πλούτου τῆς ἀρχαίας Ἑλλάδος (Athens, 1975). Recent research by the Max-Planck Institut in Pernicka, *JRGZM* 34, no. 2 (1987) 607–714. On the formation of these deposits, see B. C. Papazachos and G. A. Papadopoulos, "Deep Tectonic and Associated Ore Deposits in the Aegean Area," in *Proceedings of the VI. Colloquium on the Geology of the Aegean Area* (Athens, 1977), 1071–80; N. Gale and S. Stos-Gale, *RDAC* (1985) 92–93.

[128] N. G. Melidonis, Ἡ γεωλογία τῆς νήσου Ἀνάφης. Γεωλογικαί καί Γεωφυσικαί Μελέται 8:3 (Athens, 1963), 300, on the distribution of sulfide ores at these locations. Formations in Cyprus are similar enough to have lent experience to those ex-

and to their customers, the Assyrians, were the iron ores plentiful in western Crete, Lakonia, Euboia, and Thasos.[129] As in Sicily, Iberia, and Cilicia, Phoenician settlements or trading posts were also located on shipping routes where access to resources could be organized with local cooperation, preferably on the coast or an offshore island, as Thucydides observed (6.2.6). In addition, local factories bottling perfume and ointment, made from Oriental recipes and ingredients, were established to produce "imported" goods for exchange. But far more valuable to the Levant were deposits in the western Mediterranean, Etruria, Sardinia, and Spain. Although closer, the Aegean offered but a staging post en route to Tartessos.[130]

Beginning with those sites closest to the Levant, the presence of Phoenicians in the Dodekanese was a literary phenomenon supported in the nineteenth century, now enriched by archaeology. The Levantine connections of this area begin in the Bronze Age, when Cypriote pottery found on Rhodes complements the discoveries from the shipwrecks found south of Lykia. In subtler evidence, Mycenaean pottery from Rhodes found in the western Peloponnese and the Adriatic suggests that Levantines bound for Sicily and Italy stopped in the eastern Aegean on a trip west.[131] Was this Canaanite traffic inherited by "Phoenicians" who left pottery in the ninth century on Kos, then ran a local industry in perfume and its containers?[132] Rhodes supported the same industry in the early period, then imported Phoenician ivories and silver bowls, bronze protomes, Syrian harness decoration, Cypriote sculpture, seals and tridacna shells, and other characteristic Oriental luxuries.[133] Moreover, these islands continued as home to

---

ploring the Aegean: cf. G. Constantinou, "Geological Features and Ancient Exploitation of the Cupriferous Sulphide Orebodies of Cyprus," in *Early Metallurgy in Cyprus*, 13–23; Bunnens, *L'expansion phénicienne*, 6–9; A. Mousoulos, "Συμβολὴ στὴ μελέτη τῆς θειούχου μεταλλοφορίας τῆς νήσου Κύπρου," in ΦΙΛΙΑ ΕΠΗ, 2:335–58.

[129] Metallogenetic Map and explanatory volume, 175–76, 190–91. Varoufakis, in *Early Metallurgy in Cyprus*, esp. 320. Curtin, *Cross-Cultural Trade*, 18, on iron production and trade diasporas.

[130] Coldstream, in *Phönizier im Westen*, 261–75, devises a model with Rhodes and Crete as "staging posts" for ultimate goals such as Athens and Euboia (p. 264); M. Baslez, "Le role et la place des Phéniciens dans la vie économique des ports de l'Égée," in *Studia Phoenicia*, 5:267–86. See also Mazzarino's (*Fra Oriente e Occidente* [Florence, 1947]) reconstruction of the Phoenician route along the islands to the West, with Crete as a pivotal point.

[131] This scenario is barely considered in T. Papado-

poulos and R. Jones, "Rhodiaka in Achaea," *OpAth* 13 (1980) 225–35; T. Papadopoulos, "The Dodecanese and the Western Peloponnese in the Late Bronze Age: Some Thoughts on the Problems of Their Relations," or in P. Åström, "Relations between Cyprus and the Dodecanese in the Bronze Age," both in *The Archaeology of the Dodecanese*, ed. S. Dietz and I. Papachristodoulou (Copenhagen, 1988), 73–75, 76–79.

[132] Coldstream, "The Phoenicians of Ialysos," *BICS* 16 (1969) 2–8, and in *Phönizier im Westen*, 268–69, with earlier literature (von Bissing, Culican); compare the influx of population at Ialysos in the twelfth century (n. 90).

[133] Boardman, *Greeks Overseas*, 62–63, 65–66, 69–72, 74; Coldstream, *BICS* 16 (1969) 2–8, and in *Phönizier im Westen*, 269; M. Martelli, "La stipe votiva dell'Athenaion di Jalysos: Un primo bilancio," in *Archaeology of the Dodecanese*, 104–20. Markoe, *Phoenician Bowls*, 124–27 on Oriental bowls from Rhodes; Carter, *Greek Ivory-Carving*, chap. 2, on couchant-animal ivories from Rhodes; V. Webb, *Archaic Greek Faience*

Phoenician speakers long after 700 B.C., not only for the faience and unguent industry but as a significant community into Hellenistic times.[134] No wonder allusions to the Levant are sprinkled through sources on Rhodes, especially in the context of cult. Legendary craftsmen made their home on the island, like the Telchines, renowned as teachers, magicians, and inventors of statues, and their patrons Apollo Telchinios at Lindos, Hera Telchinia at Lindos and Kameiros, and Nymphs named after the Telchinians (Diodorus, 5.55). Levantine residents installed a Semitic cult, Zeus Ataburios, the Greek equivalent of Baal Tabor, on a Rhodian peak, and offered human sacrifices to Kronos, elsewhere Greek equivalent to El (Porphyry, *De Abstinentia* 2.54).[135] The temple of Athena at Lindos received thousands of *Aegyptiaka* in offerings; it was also alleged a foundation of Danaos, from Egypt (Diodorus, 5.58). Kadmos is said to have founded the temple of Poseidon at Ialysos, which he left under the supervision of Phoenicians, according to local historians, who also maintain that the Phoenicians fortified Ialysos and held Rhodes until besieged by Greek invaders.[136] Finally, Diodorus also records a dedication by Kadmos: a bronze cauldron with Phoenician letters (5.58), like the tripods with Καδμήια γράμματα seen by Herodotus at Thebes (5.59). These sanctuaries where foreign objects outnumber Greek ones are numerous in East Greece, most notably Samos (Figure 25). Their imported votives can be dismissed as exotica dedicated by Greeks; more recent studies suggest an international clientele typical of the archaic period.[137]

Thus the evidence from Rhodes indicates imports and industry, onomastics and traditions appropriate to Semitic craftsmen, with a distinct emphasis on religion as the sphere where influence survived. Whether Bronze Age connections or new reasons attracted them is a question relevant to all their Aegean points of contact. Although Rhodes is not as rich in iron as other Aegean islands, iron slag is reported from a Hel-

(Warminster, 1978), 5–10, on Rhodian faience; M. McClellan, "Core-Formed Glass from Dated Contexts" (Ph.D. diss., University of Pennsylvania, 1984), 21, and A. M. Bisi, "Ateliers phéniciens dans le monde égéen," in *Studia Phoenicia*, 5:225–38, for resident Eastern glass-makers on Rhodes.

[134] Athenaeus, 8.360e; Fraser, *BSA* 65 (1970) 31–36, on Phoenicians on Hellenistic Rhodes; Ch. Kantzia, ". . . ΤΙΜΟΣ ΑΒΔΑΛΩΝΘΜΟΥ [ΣΙΔ]ΩΝΕΣ ΒΑΣΙΛΕΩΣ. Μία δίγλωσση ἑλληνική-φοινικική ἐπιγραφή ἀπό τήν Κῶ," and M. Sznycer, "La partie phénicienne de l'inscription bilinguie gréco-phénicienne de Cos," both in *Deltion* 35A (1980) 1–16, 17–30.

[135] Billigmeier, *Kadmos*, 65–66, accepts "Ataburios" as the only Semitic toponym in Greece, rejecting others proposed by Gordon and Astour. W. Helck, "Ein

Indiz früher Handelsfahrten Syrischer Kaufsleute," *UF* 2 (1970) 35–37. See Chapter 6 on infant sacrifice.

[136] *FGrH* 532 (3) = Polyzelos of Rhodes (cf. *FGrH* 521 F6 in Athenaeus, 260D–361B); *FGrH* 523 F1 = Zenon of Rhodes in Diodorus Siculus, 5.58.1–3; Ergias of Rhodes, *FGrH* IIIB, 513 F1; Diktys of Crete 4.4. Edwards, *Kadmos*, 30, 78, 81, 101; Billigmeier, *Kadmos*, 94. Lindian temple chronicle (*FGrH* III B, no. 532 F1; B 3, L 16–18).

[137] I. Kilian-Dirlmeier, "Fremde Weihungen in griechischen Heiligtümern vom 8. bis zum Beginn des 7. Jhdts. v. Chr.," *JRGZM* 32 (1985) 215–54; I. Strøm, "Greece Between East and West, 10th–8th Centuries B.C: Evidence from the Sanctuaries," paper delivered at *Greece between East and West: 10th–8th Centuries B.C.*, March 15, 1990, Institute of Fine Arts, New York.

lenistic metalworking site, and its phosphorous content points to a source on Crete.[138] Minerals on the mainland opposite Kos and Rhodes, in the Halikarnassos peninsula, may have been more significant for Levantine interests in the Dodekanese. Recent research has identified both ancient slag and mines, the latter in use until the twentieth century, near the site of ancient Myndus (Gümüşlük, whose modern Turkish name indicates a connection with silver).[139] The proximity of these minerals, oxidized sulfides visible as surface ores, to Levantine-looking settlements on islands offshore, characterizes the Phoenician presence in the Aegean and throughout the western Mediterranean. Thus Rhodes may have functioned as gateway to mainland minerals, as did Kythera and Thasos, as well as a stop on the route west. Carian mines might have helped attract the Athenians who left Protogeometric pottery there, unless entrepreneurs from the Levant traveled to Laureion as well as Caria.[140] The latter could have dedicated objects like the Syrian bronze horse-harness piecemeal at two Greek sanctuaries, to Hera on Samos (Figure 25; see n. 198) and to Apollo on Euboia (n. 172), perhaps on a trip that visited both islands.

Thus one direction for Near Eastern sailors arriving in the Aegean was directly north along the coast of Asia Minor, perhaps en route to the richer minerals of inland Anatolia (e.g., Sardis) and of northern Greece. Proceeding westward, the next point of Levantine settlement was Crete, whose metal resources, imported and local Orientalia, and legendary material deserve separate discussion (Chapter 6). As argued previously, Cretan prosperity in the latest Bronze Age may reflect the first exploitation of iron, especially in western Crete, and must have continued to attract Phoenicians. Italian pottery and later a Sardinian askos (see n. 71) make the island a stopover on a Levantine route to the West since the Bronze Age. From Crete, ships proceeded north toward the Cyclades and Thrace or west toward Lakonia. The sea voyage to the southern Peloponnese for minerals had been made as early as the third millennium, by Minoan explorers of Lakonian minerals (see n. 4). As Drews observed, it was probably iron that drew Phoenicians to southern Lakonia, according to modern geology and ancient testimonia.[141] An-

[138] Varoufakis, in *Early Metallurgy in Cyprus*, 318. Ancient testimonia on Rhodian sources of lead (Pliny, *Naturalis Historia* 34.175; Dioskourides, 5.103) have not been confirmed in modern exploration: Pernicka, *JRGZM* 34, no. 2 (1987) 647.

[139] G. A. Wagner and others, "Geochemische und isotopische Charakteristika früher Rohstoffquellen für Kupfer, Blei, Silber und Gold in der Türkei," *JRGZM* 33 (1986) 723–52, esp. 724–25; Pernicka, *JRGZM* 34, no. 2 (1987) 645–48.

[140] V. Desborough, *Protogeometric Pottery*, (Oxford, 1952) 218–22, including a tomb from Assarlik associated with gold, iron, and silver; Ç. Özgünel, *Carian*

Geometric Pottery (Ankara, 1979), 102–3; A. Snodgrass, *The Dark Age of Greece* (Edinburgh, 1971), 157–58, 236–37; R. Catling, "Protogeometric Vases from Amorgos in the Museum of the British School," *BSA* 84 (1989) 177–85, connects Euboian and Rhodian pottery in the Cyclades with traffic across the Aegean.

[141] Drews, *AJP* 100 (1979) 46 n. 9, citing a U.S. geological pamphlet of 1955; cf. the Greek Metallogenetic Map (text, pp. 178–79, nos. 156–73); cf. p. 145, nos. 112–17, for related mixed sulfide deposits; A. J. Holladay, "Spartan Austerity," *CQ* 27 (1977) 116. Pernicka, *JRGZM* 34, no. 2 (1987) 659. Varoufakis, in *Early Metallurgy in Cyprus* 319 fig. 2, claims both "rich

cient sources connecting the Phoenicians with Lakonia concentrate on Kythera, the island also called "Porphyroussa," as if the Phoenicians made it famous for their purple industry (Aristotle, cited by Stephanos of Byzantion on Πορφύρουσσα). The cult of Aphrodite Ourania on Kythera, the oldest in Greece (Pausanias, 3.21.1), was founded by the Phoenicians (Herodotus, 1.105), and the island's name derived from Semitic names according to ancient and modern arguments.[142] In Lakonia proper, Oriental influence dominates in minor arts since the eighth century, in such distinctive media as terracotta masks, ivories, and marble perirrhanteria.[143]

Several factors require Phoenicians resident in Lakonia to account for these Orientalizing traits, beginning with the conspicuous lack of Oriental imports that forces one to imagine local craftsmen. Then, more profound influence survives in cultural institutions, especially in religion. Artemis/Ortheia, Apollo Amyklaios and Karneios, and their rites can be traced to the Near East; in politics, the celebrated Spartan constitution reminded Aristotle of Carthage and shares enough with Cretan ones to indicate a common source: why not Levantine citizens?[144] Lakedaimon's Dorian identity, with a stable

---

haematite deposits of high purity" and evidence for ancient mining: Y. Bassiakos, "Ancient Iron Metallurgy in Laconia," in *New Aspects of Archaeological Science in Greece. Fitch Lab Occasional Papers no. 3* (Athens, 1988), 54–58; D. Kiskyras, "Ὁ ὀρυκτός πλοῦτος τῆς Μάνης καί γενικώτερα τῆς Λακωνίας," Λακωνικαί Σπουδαί 9 (1988) 117–32. Lakonian iron was praised in antiquity (Daimachus, *FGrH* 65 frag. 4) and may have inspired the legendary "iron coinage" of Lykourgos (R. Halleaux, "La monnaie de fer de Lycurge et le problème des acides en chimie antique," in *Stemmata. Mélanges de philologie, d'histoire et d'archéologie offerts à Jules Labarbe* [Liège, 1987], 451–57, a reference I owe to Ken Sheedy).

[142] Stephanus of Byzantium, s.v. Κύθηρα, attributes the name to "Kytheros, son of Phoinix" (cf. Eustathius, *Iliad* 10.268 on "Kytheros the Phoenician"); V. Bérard, *Les Phéniciens*, 2:207–10, derives "Kythera" from Semitic *keter* ("crown"); cf. Astour, *Hellenosemitica*, 143; Bernal, *Black Athena*, 382. Brown, *JSS* 10 (1965) 197–219, invokes the same root (*ktr*) responsible for Kothar (Chapter 4); *contra* G. Morgan, "Aphrodite Cytherea," *TAPA* 108 (1978) 115–20. On purple murex, see Huxley, in J. N. Coldstream and G. Huxley, *Kythera: Excavations and Studies* (London 1972), 36–37; Markoe, *Phoenician Bowls*, 126, n. 186. "Phoinikous" was one of the ancient names of the city's harbor (Xenophon, *Hellenica* 14.8.7–8; cf. the modern name of a beach on the east coast ("Φύρι᾽ Ἄμμος"),

named for its iron sands or purple trade? The island's colorful reputation may indicate ancient iron ores, not purple mollusks: Kiskyras, Λακωνικαί Σπουδαί 9 (1988) 128, on Kythera's iron-rich mineral springs. E.J.W. Barber, *Prehistoric Textiles* (Princeton, 1990), 238–39, on mineral mordants for dyeing purple in Phoenician industry.

[143] Carter, *Greek Ivory-Carving*, and *AJA* 91 (1987) 355–83; *AJA* 93 (1989) 355–78; J. Carter and S. Whitney, "Isotopic Analysis of Gray Marble Perirrhanteria," *AJA* 92 (1988) 276 and "Isotopic Analysis of Seventh-Century B.C. Perirrhanteria," in *Classical Marble: Geochemistry, Technology, Trade*, ed. N. Herz and M. Waelkens (Dordrecht, 1988), 419–31; Carter, *The Beginning of Greek Sculpture*; Markoe, *Phoenician Bowls*, 117–18. E. Langlotz, *Studien zur nordostgriechischen Kunst* (Mainz, 1975), 9, calls Lakonia "fast eine Provinz des Ostens."

[144] Carter, *AJA* 91 (1987) 381, and "Masks and Poetry in Early Sparta," 89–98, on Spartan and Near Eastern rituals, including possible survivals of Phoenician human sacrifice (Pausanias, 3.16.9–11; cf. Porphyry, *De Abstinentia* 2.55.4 and Hughes, "Human Sacrifice," Drews, *AJP* 100 (1979) 44–58, on the Spartan, Cretan, and Carthaginian constitutions; cf. Oliver, *Demokratia*, 56, and A. Snodgrass, *Archaic Greece* (London, 1980), 32, 90, for Phoenician influence on the Greek polis.

population and constitution admired by Greeks and Europeans, has obscured its Semitic origins until recently. As on Crete, the disintegration of its Orientalizing culture suggests its very sources, when the decline of local industries like ivory carving coincides with the defeat of the Assyrian Empire around 600 B.C.[145] But some Spartans still proclaimed their kinship with the Jews in the Hellenistic period.[146]

Phoenician involvement in the central Aegean repeats the Lakonian pattern, including the role of resources. The island of Thera, some sixty miles north of Crete, is usually considered a Spartan colony in the archaic period and infrequently associated with Phoenicians. But it offers a surprising concentration of evidence, beginning with its minerals. Along with its neighbor to the east, Anaphe, Thera is a major source of those mixed sulfide deposits of hydrothermal origin that produced copper, lead, and iron, the latter in unusually high concentration.[147] The resources available on both islands may explain certain legends connecting them with the Levant. For example, according to Herodotus (4.147), Thera's settlement was founded by Membliaros, son of a Phoenician and follower of Kadmos but also the eponym of "Membliaros," the island eventually named Anaphe (Stephanos of Byzantion, s.v. Ἀνάφη; cf. schol. Pindar, Pythian 3.88c). His descendants occupied Thera for eight generations before the advent of the Spartan colony, as in western Mediterranean settlements where Greeks followed Phoenicians (Chapter 7).[148] Material culture supports these testimonia for Phoenicians on Thera. Phoenician pottery in shapes typical for Aegean (and western Mediterranean) contact communities appears in graves on Thera.[149] One of these graves produced gold jewelry identical to examples from the Idaian Cave on Crete accepted as Oriental.[150] Such finds

[145] Carter, Greek Ivory-Carving, 163–73, 225–62, 290–92, traces the dispersal of ivory craftsmen to new Panhellenic centers (e.g. Delphi, Ephesos) in the sixth century; cf. absence of Spartan poets after seventh-century figures like Alkman and Tyrtaios.

[146] Bernal, Black Athena, 109–10, on King Areios's letter to Jerusalem (1 Maccabees 12.20–22; Josephus, Antiquitates 226, Vita 427); Cl. Orrieux, "La parenté entre Juifs et Spartiates," in L'étranger dans le monde grec, ed. R. Lonis, (Nancy 1988), 169–91; cf. S. Spyridakis, "Notes on the Jews of Gortyna and Crete," ZPE 73 (1988) 171–75.

[147] Melidonis, " Ἡ Γεωλογία τῆς νήσου Ἀνάφης," esp. 281–300; hydrothermal ores on Thera discussed by K. Böstrom and others in Thera and the Aegean World III (papers delivered at Thera congress, September 1989); cf. Metallogenetic Map and text (p. 147, no. 141, 142: 4,000 tons of sulfide lead and zinc ores, and 15,000 tons of limonite; cf. p. 182 n. 198).

[148] For a Phoenician derivation of "Membliaros"

from Mem-bli-'ar, see M. Astour, "Greek Names in the Semitic World and Semitic Names in the Greek World," JNES 23 (1964) 197–98, although he argues for a West Semitic presence on the island before 1500 B.C.: Hellenosemitica, 113–28. On the antiquities of Anaphe, see H. von Gaertringen, Thera (Berlin, 1899), 1:351–58; foundation legends of Thera, pp. 142–49.

[149] E. Pfuhl, "Der archaische Friedhof am Stadtberge von Thera," AthMitt 28 (1903) 228, pls. XIX:8, 11, XX:4–5, XXII:4; cf. W. Culican, "Phoenician Oil Bottles and Tripod Bowls," Berytus 19 (1970) 5–16; "Sidonian Bottles," Levant 7 (1975) 145–50; cf. Coldstream, RDAC (1984) 122–39, for these containers on Cyprus and Crete.

[150] Pfuhl, AthMitt 28 (1903) 228, pl. v:15 (grave 89: 109). Beyer, Dreros und Prinias, 51, calls the Theran jewelry "wohl Kretisch." New examples from the Idaian Cave: Sakellarakis, in Early Greek Cult Practice, 181; L'Antro Ideo, 27, fig. 6.

are joined by faience objects, including a pyxis from the same grave, elsewhere a clear sign of the same network connecting Cyprus, Rhodes, and Crete with some western sites.[151] In fact, Cretan pottery and metal finds, including shapes characteristic of the Levantine workshops identified in central Crete, dominate imports in the Sellada cemetery, and cease abruptly in the early sixth century, with the disintegration of the Aegean network after the decline of Assyria. As on Thasos, local responses to these minor arts included some of the first experiments in monumental Greek sculpture (*kouroi*) in marble.[152] Their funerary function was confirmed by the discovery of a pair of marble feet embedded in rock in the Thera cemetery. This context for such early statues is a reminder that the votive function of kouroi may be a later development in Greek culture, leaving early Aegean kouroi more closely related to other archaic Mediterranean statuary under Oriental influence.[153]

Nor is Oriental influence on Thera lacking in cult, where Kadmos is alleged to have founded the altars of Poseidon and Athena (Theophrastos, schol. Pindar, *Pythian* 4.11). Archaeology offers other Near Eastern elements in cult: an infant burial on Thera produced the same masks that indicate on Cyprus, Crete, Samos, Rhodes, and at Sparta a Near Eastern ritual complex.[154] This encourages a closer look at the unusual "gymnopaidia" rituals attested at the city of Thera, in the Apollo Karneios sanctuary. This cult figure was imported from Sparta and may derive from a Cypro-Levantine deity (see n. 56). His Theran temenos features some of the earliest rock-cut inscriptions in Greece, in letter forms closely related to those from Sparta, Crete, and nearby Melos, also visited by Phoenicians (Festos and Stephanus of Byzantium, s.v. Ἀνάφη).[155] Whether related through geography or a cognate community, or both, these scripts are also faithful to the Semitic canon and have persuaded some scholars, classical and Near Eastern, of an Aegean home for the alphabet.[156] As a Spartan colony, Thera shares cult and culture

[151] Pfuhl, *AthMitt* 28 (1903) 238, fig. 81, from grave 89; Webb, *Archaic Greek Faience*, 44, no. 178, plus two aryballoi on display (Thera Museum inv. nos. 1093, 1094). Recent archaic finds from the same cemetery include Rhodian, Cretan, and Ionian pottery and two (Cypriote?) bronze rod tripods: *BCH* 99 (1975) 683–84, fig. 203; *BCH* 103 (1979) 605.

[152] N. Kontoleon, "Theräisches," *AthMitt* 73 (1958) 117–39; Richter, *Kouroi*, 45, no. 18a–d, figs. 97–102; A. Brookes, "The Daedalic Sculpture of Thera," *AJA* 85 (1981) 187.

[153] *ARep* 12 (1966) 18, fig. 31; B. Ridgway, "Mediterranean Comparanda for the Statues from Monte Prama," *SSA*, 2:64 (see Chapter 7, n. 44) for comparanda from Punic Sardinia. Recent discoveries of stone statuary in the early Iron Age cemetery at

Eleutherna in Crete by N. Stambolides (*BSA* 85 [1990] 398–400) support the funerary origins of Greek sculpture, defended by Carter in her forthcoming *Beginning of Greek Sculpture*.

[154] Reported in N. Zapheiropoulos, *Praktika* (1965) 184, pl. 227a (*Praktika* [1974], pl. 227a); cf. Carter, *AJA* 91 (1987) 359 (infant burials are characteristic contexts for these masks elsewhere in the Mediterranean, e.g. on Samos: U. Sinn, in *Early Greek Cult Practice*, 98).

[155] Graffiti: Jeffery, *LSAG*, 316–19, 323, pls. 61–62 (*IG* XII.3, 536–37, 540, 543, 573, 767).

[156] S. Mazzarino, *Fra Oriente e Occidente* (Florence, 1947), traces Phoenicians along this "route of the alphabets" via Crete, Thera, and Melos; *LSAG*, 316–17 (Therans learned their letters from Crete); M. Guarducci, *Epigrafia Graeca* (Rome, 1967) 1:347; F. Cross,

with Cretan institutions, including homoerotic rituals.[157] But the most explicit religious transplant from the Orient is the cult of Apollo Asgelatas on Anaphe, attested in inscriptions (*IG* XII. 3.248 = *LSCG*, 129; cf. the Ἀσγελαῖα festival: *IG* XII 3.249). Burkert's brilliant connection of this cult epithet with the Babylonian healing deity, *Azugallatu* (Gula of Isin), would make the god on Anaphe a direct witness to Oriental healing practice in Greece.[158] Typically, the cult acquires a Greek foundation legend, one that attributes the origins of the cult to the returning Argonauts.[159]

Additional sources support Phoenicians on Thera, via Crete. Battos, the Theran founder of Cyrene in Libya, had as mother a Cretan princess from Axos, near the Idaian Cave and probably home to a Levantine community (see Chapter 6). The foundation of Cyrene was assisted by Korobios of Itanos on Crete, a purple-fisher whose home and profession point to a Phoenician identity (Herodotus, 4.151–53). Recent study of Greeks in Libya before the foundation of Cyrene implies that minerals of inland North Africa attracted them.[160] Perhaps Phoenicians accompanied or even inspired the first Greek trips to Libya, as they apparently introduced Greeks to the metals of Etruria, Sardinia, and Spain. Finally, an enigmatic passage in Tacitus has Semitic refugees flee from Crete to Libya, a reference tempting to associate with the decline of archaic communities in Crete around 600 B.C. and an exodus to Punic territories farther west (*Histories* 5.2): "Iudaeos Creta insula profugos novissima Libyae insedisse memorant, qua tempestate Saturnus vi Iovis pulsus cesserit regnis."[161] The mixture of archaic pottery found in

---

"Early Alphabetic Scripts," in *Symposia*, 111, comments on "the marked concentration of archaic features in these scripts." Naveh, *Early History of the Alphabet*, 178, 185, concludes that Cretans and Therans were the "first Greeks to employ the alphabetic unity." For a new view, see Bernal, *Cadmean Letters*, 126.

[157] K. J. Dover, *Greek Homosexuality* (London, 1978), 122–24, 195. Although common to Sparta and Crete, these rites of male initiation to adulthood are not "Dorian," for they have Bronze Age Cretan antecedents and Hellenistic descendants: R. B. Koehl, "The Chieftain Cup and a Minoan Rite of Passage," *JHS* 106 (1986) 99–110; Plato, *Laws* 636a; Echememos, frag. 1, and Timaios, frag. 144, on the Cretan origins of pederasty implied by the myth of Minos and Ganymede. *IG* XII.3 350, 354, 355, 371, name "Koures" as well as Zeus: Verbruggen, *Le Zeus crétois*, 183–86, on Zeus and Koures on Thera and in Crete. Hellenistic love stories with survivals of Cretan traditions: Conon, *Diegesis* 16 and Strabo, 10.14.12 (Promachos and Leukokomos).

[158] Burkert, "Itinerant Diviners and Magicians," in *Greek Renaissance*, 118; *Orientalisierende Epoche*, 75–76; "Oriental and Greek Mythmaking," in *Interpreting Greek Mythology*, 24. According to U. Wilamowitz (*Isyllos von Epidauros*, [Berlin 1886], 93), who inspired Burkert, "Asklepios" might even be involved in this Oriental derivation.

[159] Conon, *Diegesis* 49; Callimachus, *Aetia* frags. 7.19, 21; Apollonius Rhadius, 4.1694 ff; Apollodoros, 1.139 (9.26). A. Henrichs, "Three Approaches to Greek Mythography," in *Interpretations of Greek Mythology*, 247, 269 n. 11, 270 n. 20.

[160] S. Stucchi, "Problems Concerning the Coming of the Greeks to Cyrenaica and the Relations with their Neighbors," *MeditArch* 2 (1989) 73–84; Bakhuizen, *Chalcis-in-Euboea*, 26 n. 79, on iron ores of North Africa. M. Fantar, "L'impact de la présence phénicienne et de la fondation de Carthage en Méditerranée occidentale," in *Studia Phoenicia* 6:9–11, on Phoenician expansion and colonization as an example to Greeks.

[161] R. R. Stieglitz, "The Letters of Kadmos: Mythol-

Libya includes wares from Crete, Thera, and Melos, perhaps a complement to Tacitus's account of the exodus of Levantines from the Aegean to North Africa as well as to that of Herodotus.[162]

The islands of Thera and Anaphe, sources of attractive minerals, were also convenient stops for Phoenicians (Cypriotes) headed for the riches of the northern Aegean. The next goals of such a route, aimed at Thasos and its peraea, would be eastern Attika, Euboia, and Boiotia, related in geography, geology, and material culture. The Laureion ores are Greece's richest mineral source outside of Thrace. Exploited since the Final Neolithic period, they may have become newly attractive in the age of iron, as early as LH IIIC according to prosperity attested at Perati and Lefkandi.[163] If the Protogeometric boom in Athens and its early Oriental contacts mean the minerals of Laurion attracted Levantine explorers, then Thorikos should have eclipsed it.[164] Instead, eastern Attika kept closer affinities with Euboia and the Cyclades than with the plain of Athens, as in prehistoric times, with an independent culture in later Orientalizing eras (the seventh century).[165] Only after Kleisthenic *synoikismos* and the exploitation of new Laureion silver veins in the early fifth century do the fortunes of Athens reflect its minerals.

The iron and copper ores of central Euboia attracted ancient comment and modern exploration, however disputed their relationship to the toponym Χαλκίς.[166] The name may have inspired some false etymologies such as *"aere ibi primum reperto"* (Pliny, *Naturalis Historia* 4.63–64), the claim that the Chalkidians were the first to make or wear bronze armor (Strabo, 10.3.6, 19.), and the name "Chalcedon" for its legendary kings. Ancient testimonia on copper have been dismissed for lack of confirmation, but bronze working is implied at Lefkandi in tenth-century finds, with copper reported near Chalkis and in southern Euboia.[167] Even more plentiful is Euboia's iron ore, visible in

ogy, Archaeology and Eteocretan," in *Fourth Cretological Congress*, 615.

[162] G. Schauss, "Greek Trade along the North African Coast in the Sixth Century B.C.," *Scripta Mediterranea* 1 (1980) 21ff.; cf. his *The Extramural Sanctuary of Demeter and Persephone at Cyrene, Libya. Final Reports, Volume II. The East Greek, Island and Laconian Pottery* (Philadelphia, 1985), 96–107; Stucchi *MeditArch* 2 (1989) 73–84, and "Die archaischen griechischen Vasen und die Kyrenaika: Importe, Imitationen und Einflüsse—Ein Überblick," in *Ancient Greek and Related Pottery*, 139–43, on Greek pottery in Libya.

[163] Geology: Metallogenetic Map, 142–43, nos. 101–9; 176, nos. 138–42, for iron and other ores at Laureion, less known than its silver; Pernicka, *JRGZM* 34, no. 2 (1987) 657–59; Stos-Gale and Gale, *SMEA* 84 (1984) 170.

[164] Coldstream, in *Phönizier im Westen*, 263–66;

Snodgrass, *Dark Age of Greece*, 231–33.

[165] Desborough, in *Essays: Fitch*, 34–35; cf. Sakellariou (cited in n. 178). Morris, *Black and White Style*, on the anomaly of Athens in the Orientalizing period; pp. 99–100, on Sounion, Thorikos, Brauron in the archaic period.

[166] Bakhuizen, *Chalcis-in-Euboea*, 58–64; the debate continues in A. Mele, "I Ciclopi, Calcodonte e la metallurgia calcidese," with response by Bakhuizen, "Le nom de Chalcis et la colonisation chalcidienne," in *Nouvelle contribution*, 9–33, 163–74.

[167] Metallogenetic Map (text p. 208, no. 51) for copper; cf. G. Marinos and W. Petraschek, Αἱ μεταλλοφόροι φλέβες Καρυστίας Εὐβοίας (Athens, 1955), although Bakhuizen cites C. Guernet, *Géologie de la region de Chalkis (Eubée)*. Γεωλογικὰ χρονικὰ Ἑλληνικῶν χωρῶν (1966), 307–13, on the lack of copper at Chalkis. *Lefkandi I*, 93–97; Board-

the mountains northeast of Chalkis and the Lelantine plain for open-cast mining.[168] Hence its ancient reputation for ἔργα σιδήρου (Callimachus, frag. 701; cf. ἄριστοι ἐκεῖ σιδηρουργοί, Eustathius on Dionysius, *Periegeta* 764).[169] Greek legend associates miraculous metals and metallurgists with this island, from a magic "double mine" of bronze and iron (Strabo, 10.1.9, 447c) to the reputation of Χαλκίδικαι σπάθαι (Alcaeus, frag. Z34, 7) and the Εὐβοικὸν ξίφος, αὐτόθηκτον (Aeschylus, frag. 703). Other resources of interest to Phoenicians on Euboia were purple-producing mollusks (Aristotle, *Historia Animalium* 5.15); did murex, mines, or Phoenicians give the island the name "Porphyra" (Strabo, 447), as with Kythera?

If resources attracted Levantine visitors to Euboia, they were remembered as Ἄραβες who arrived with Kadmos (Strabo, 10.1.8) and "Dryopes" who settled at Karystos, then went to Cyprus (Diodorus, 4.37.2). The ancestors of the Gephyraeans of Eretria, whose Athenian branch included Harmodios and Aristogeiton, are descended from companions of Kadmos (Herodotus, 5.57; Strabo, 9.2.10). Mythological figures connected to the wanderings of Kadmos and Io include Euboia in their travels (Hesiod, frag. 296).[170] Most curious of all are references to Kouretes in connection with Euboia, as the children of the eponymous nymph, Chalkis (Strabo, 10.3.6, 19). These legendary figures occupy the domains of cult and metallurgy in Crete, where they have plausibly been connected with Levantine activity in both domains at the Idaian Cave (see n. 157; also Chapter 6). To find them familiar in the home of Kadmos (Korinna, frag. 654.i.12–18) and in Euboia enriches their Oriental connections.

Recent archaeology on Euboia has dispelled Greece's "Dark Age," through an extensive network of Iron Age burials at Lefkandi and Eretria, with evidence for monumental architecture as early as the tenth century.[171] The cemeteries clustered near the iron ores of the Lelantine plain testify to continuity in craftsmanship and imagination, but also in Orientalia: gold jewelry, faience, ivory, bronze tripods, and other unmistakable signs of Phoenician (or Cypriote) provenance.[172] That these luxuries were not all imports is sug-

---

man, *Greeks Overseas*, 42–43, fig. 15, on foundry debris, including a tripod-leg mold.

[168] Bakhuizen, *Chalcis-in-Euboea*, 45–57 (45–49, on Chalkis). They are estimated at 30 million tons: Metallogenetic Map and text, 175–76, nos. 129–36, and 190–91, nos. 31–41; Pernicka, *JRGZM* 34, no. 2 (1987) 659.

[169] Ancient testimonia: Bakhuizen, *Chalcis-in-Euboea*, pts. II.1 (swords, etc.), 2 (ore deposits), and 4 (smiths); D. L. Page, *Sappho and Alcaeus* (Oxford, 1955), 218–19.

[170] West, *Hesiodic Catalogue of Women*, 145–46, 149–52, on the Oriental associations of Euboian legends; *JHS* 108 (1988) 172, for a "Euboian" Odyssey.

[171] *Lefkandi* I; M. R. Popham, L. H. Sackett, and E. Touloupa, "The Hero of Lefkandi," *Antiquity* 56 (1982) 169–74, and "Further Excavations of the Toumba Cemetery at Lefkandi, 1981," *BSA* 77 (1982) 213–48; P. Themelis, "Die Nekropolen von Lefkandi-Nord auf Euboea," in *Griechenland, die Ägäis und die Levante*, 145–60; M. R. Popham, P. A. Calligas, and L. H. Sackett, "Further Excavations of the Toumba Cemetery at Lefkandi, 1984 and 1986: A Preliminary Report," *ARep* 35 (1988–1989) 117–29; R. Catling and I. Lemos, *Lefkandi II. The Protogeometric Building at Toumba 1: The Pottery* (Oxford, 1990).

[172] V. Karageorghis and L. Kahil, "Témoignages Eubéens à Chypre et Chypriotes en Eubée," *AK* 10

gested by a jeweler's hoard buried at Eretria before 700 B.C. and the clay mold for a tripod leg found at Lefkandi (see nn. 125, 167); the same kind of craftsmen buried with the tools of their trade on Crete may have been active on Euboia.[173] In fact, the entire assembly of material from central Euboia—including the distribution of cemeteries and their urban implications—resembles closely the picture around Knossos examined by Coldstream (see Chapter 6). The similarity of material culture in these early communities derives from their common foundation in the marketing of metals and manufacturing of perfume, and perhaps from common demographic ingredients (Levantine entrepreneurs) with consistent patterns of settlement. The modern tendency to identify "Euboians" in Syria, Cyprus, Crete, Ischia, and even Euboia itself may be a mistake. Euboians sought rich iron ores in Etruria and North Africa west of Utica, as Phoenicians from Crete and Thera migrated to Libya (see nn. 160–62).[174] Those who initiated this network of trade and settlement were not Greek, but Levantine, and the culture they helped sponsor was too mixed to call Greek.[175] The presence of Phoenician pottery in the Aegean *before* Greek (Euboian) pottery appears in Cyprus or the Levant means that traffic may have flowed from the East, before it did in the other direction. One anticipates the discovery of Semitic inscriptions on Euboia, given the presence of Near Eastern immigrants suggested in testimonia and archaeology. In the meantime, Lefkandi's wealth of Levantine material has inspired philologists to revive the Oriental origins of Greek epic, and even to postulate a "Euboian" Odyssey (see n. 170).

The nearby island of Skyros must have welcomed similar craftsmen or their luxury products, according to spectacular gold jewelry in its Iron Age tombs.[176] These finds

(1968) 133–35; Coldstream, in *Phönizier im Westen*, 261–72, for the new Toumba finds (over 10,000 faience beads, a bronze situla of Egyptian provenance, and other exotic grave goods). Popham and others, *BSA* 77 (1982) 247, and *ARep* (1988–1989) 118–19, on their Near Eastern, especially Cypriote, connections; Markoe, *Phoenician Bowls*, 125 n. 179. Cf. A. Charbonnet, "Le dieu aux lions d' Eretrie," *ASAA* 8 (1986) 117–56.

[173] P. Themelis, "An 8th-Century Goldsmith's Workshop at Eretria," in *Greek Renaissance*, 157–65. Gold: Bakhuizen, *Chalcis-in-Euboea*, 85 (cf. Strabo, 5.4.9, 247c, on gold from Pithekoussai, the Euboian colony on Ischia); *Lefkandi I*, 461–64, for gold jewelry and gold ores in southern Euboia (cf. Metallogenetic Map, text p. 229, nos. 149–51).

[174] Pseudo-Scylax, *Periplous* 111, names "many Naxian" islands (?), a harbor called Pithekoussai and an island with a city called Euboia, opposite Psegas, a city west of Utica: H. Treidler, "Eine alte Ionische Kolonisation in numidischen Afrika—Ihre histor-

ische und geographische Grundlage," *Historia* 8 (1959) 257–83; rejected by Bakhuizen, *Chalcis-in-Euboea*, 25–26, as Euboian colonies in the eastern Magreb. Buchner, in *Phönizier im Westen*, 297 n. 40; Desborough, *Essays: Fitch*, 27–40.

[175] See Desborough, in *Essays: Fitch*, 25–42, and D. Ridgway, in *SSA*, 2:175, and "The First Western Greeks and Their Neighbors 1935–1985," in *Greek Colonists and Native Populations*, 61–72, for "Euboean pioneers" who may not be Greek; Graham, *DHA* 12 (1986) 59, on misnamed "Euboean emporia."

[176] I. Papadimitriou, "Ausgrabungen auf Skyros," *AA* (1936) 228–34; V. Desborough, "A Group of Vases from Skyros," in ΣΤΗΛΗ, 55–58, and in *Essays: Fitch*, 36, 39; *Lefkandi I*, 286; I. Lemos and H. Hatcher, "Protogeometric Skyros and Euboea," *OJA* 5 (1986) 323–37; E. Sakellarakis, in *Early Greek Cult Practice*, 234. P. Kalligas, "Ἡ ἀρχαῖα Σκύρος," in Ἴδρυμα Ν. Π. Γουλανδρή: Διαλέξεις 1986–1989 (Athens, 1990), 82–88.

could be dismissed as indirect evidence of Levantine contact, were it not for substantial iron ores on Skyros.[177] Euboia's neighbor, Boiotia, also offers rich iron sources but the opposite in Oriental evidence: it exceeds Skyros and Euboia in testimonia on Levantine immigrants, but is poorer in Orientalia of the early Iron Age. Sakellariou has argued that eastern Attika, Euboia, and Boiotia formed part of the same cultural and perhaps political landscape between 1100 and 700 b.c.[178] What may have made them a single community were their metal ores and their Levantine occupants, much as a similar material culture (larnax burials) connects Tanagra and western Crete as provinces rich in iron centuries earlier (see n. 77). In all the discussion of Kadmos, no one has noticed why he chose to settle in Boiotia, although legends credit him with tell-tale achievements such as the invention of bronze working at Thebes (Hyginus, *Fabellae* 274). No wonder a Boiotian poet is the first to mention the Idaian Daktyls and devote a poem (Hesiod, frag. 282) to those magicians of metal, who also discovered iron on Crete and were active on Samothrace. Other legendary craftsmen like "Telchinias" emigrate from Cyprus to Boiotia (Pausanias 9.19.1) and contribute to major arts like temple building. No doubt the migration of the Gephyraioi from Chalkis to Tanagra, and eventually to Athens (Herodotus, 5.57), followed an iron master, especially if their name was once Semitic, as Astour argues. Their descendants keep furnaces at Larymna alight today with iron extracted from eastern Boiotia, more properly the landscape along the Euripos coast, which includes ancient Lokris and modern Phthiotis.[179] Unfortunately, Boiotian burials do not match those of Lefkandi, although sanctuaries like Kalapodi in Phokis, rich in Late Bronze and Iron Age activity, produced plentiful bronze and iron finds.[180] The legend of Kadmos is better sought at Thebes when iron became a major factor in

[177] The Metallogenetic Map of Greece reports ores that produced half a million tons of iron (from nickel ores rich in iron at 46%): pp. 184–86, 190 n. 29. cf. iron pyrite (p. 197 no. 46); I. Papastamatiou, "Παραρτηρήσεις τινὲς ἐπὶ τῆς γεωλογίας καὶ μεταλλογενέσεως τῆς νήσου Σκύρου," *Deltion of the Geological Society* 4 (1961) 219–38.

[178] Sakellariou, "La situation politique en Attique et en Eubée de 1100 à 700 av. J.C.," *REA* 48–49 (1976–1977) 11–21, esp. 16; C. Talamo, "Alcuni Elementi Euboici in Beozia in Eta Arcaica," in *Nouvelle contribution*, 35–49.

[179] Bakhuizen, *Chalcis-in-Euboea*, 51–57; Metallogenetic Map (text), 184–90, nos. 5–29, for the ores around Mount Ptoon and in eastern Lokris. W. E. Petraschek, "Die Eisenerz und Nickelerzlagerstätten von Lokris in Ost-Griechenland," in *The Mineral Wealth of Greece*, no. 3 (Athens, 1953), 83–169; W. Siegl, "Mineralogische Untersuchung der Eisenerze von Lokris und Skyros," *Geological and Geophysical Studies* III.2 (Athens, 1954). S. C. Bakhuizen, "On Boiotian Iron," in *Second International Conference on Boiotian Antiquities, Montreal, 1973* ed. J. M. Fossey and A. Schachter, *Teiresias* suppl. 2 (Montreal, 1979), 19–20; E. Photos, "The Question of Meteoritic Versus Smelted Nickel-rich Iron: Archaeological Evidence and Experimental Results," *World Archaeology* 203 (1989) 405.

[180] Varoufakis, in *Early Metallurgy in Cyprus*, 320 (iron at Kalapodi); R. Felsch and others, *AA* 102 (1987) 1–99 (162: iron weapons). Continuity in minor arts: M. Krogalska, "Late Mycenaean Tradition in Boiotian Archaic Terracottas," in *Primo Congresso Internazionale di Micenologia*, 228–31. The perirrhanterion from the Ptoon sanctuary (Richter, *Korai*, 29, no. 9, figs. 49–52) is a link to the Orientalizing art world of Lakonia, Samos, etc.: see the references to Carter cited in n. 143.

early Greek culture, not during the Late Mycenaean period.[181] Those Καδμήια γράμματα reported by Herodotus (5.58) could have been Phoenician (if not Cypriote or Aramaic?) letters on tripods perhaps from Cyprus, centuries later than the cuneiform seals or Linear B tablets most recently compared with this passage. It was the early first millennium that introduced the cult of the Kabeiroi, the Semitic "Great Gods," to Thebes as Kadmos did to Samothrace, and probably the eccentric festival of the Daidala related to Near Eastern rituals involving processions with images, robes, and sacred trees.[182] The best contemporary witness to Levantine influence on early Boiotia is still Hesiod, as Sanchuniathon admits in his comments on Greek appropriation of Phoenician mythology (Philo, frag. 2, D = Eusebius, *Praeparatio Evangelica* 1.10.40–41).[183] But even the city's most celebrated poem, the epic cycle story of the Seven against Thebes, may be closely modeled on Babylonian poetry and Assyrian magical traditions.[184]

The northern Aegean offered the richest mineral opportunities for Levantine entrepreneurs, especially if one believes that the "Chalkidike" got its name from its minerals and not from hypothetical colonists from Chalkis (Strabo, 10.1.8, 447c). Evidence from Thasos fits the pattern familiar in other Phoenician settlements (Kythera, Ischia), where an offshore island lies convenient to mainland and inland resources. The Strymon valley, in the Thracian peraea opposite Thasos, is the largest source of gold, iron, and other precious metals in the entire Aegean, in the form of mixed sulfide deposits weathered in river sands, as well as ores in the Σκαπτὴ Ὕλη mountains.[185] Thasian minerals appear

---

[181] Astour, Edwards, and Billigmeier see Kadmos active in Mycenaean Thebes; the *myth* of Kadmos is probably archaic (Vermeule, "Kadmos and the Dragon," 177–88). S. Symeonoglou, *The Topography of Thebes* (Princeton, 1985), 64–83; A. Schachter, "Kadmos and the Implications of the Tradition for Boiotian History," *La Béotie antique*, ed. P. Roesch and others (Paris, 1985), 145–53. As Burkert points out (citation in n. 184, p. 40), Oidipous's grandfather and link to Kadmos, La(m)bdakos, can hardly predate the introduction of the letter "lambda" with the Phoenician alphabet: M. Jameson, "Labda, Lambda, Labdakos," in *Corinthiaka*, 4. See Chapter 13 on the classical legend of Kadmos.

[182] Kabeiroi: Astour, *Hellenosemitica*, 155–56, on their Semitic derivation, observed centuries ago by Scaliger; Billigmeier, *Kadmos*, 73. Cf. their Phoenician relatives (Philo of Byblos: Eusebius, *Praeparatio Evangelica* 1.10.14, 38). Schachter, *Cults of Boiotia*, 2:88–96, etc. On the Daidala festival and its Near Eastern qualities, see Chapters 2, and 6.

[183] See n. 170; P. Walcot, *Hesiod and the Near East* (Cardiff, 1966); West, *Theogony*, 1–31, and *JHS* 108

(1988) 172; M. Weinfeld, in *Mesopotamien und seine Nachbarn*, 513 n. 15. Hesiod's performance in a poetry festival at Chalkis involves Boiotia in the cultural landscape envisioned by Sakellariou, *REA* 48–49 (1976–1977) 11–21.

[184] W. Burkert, "Seven against Thebes: An Oral Tradition between Babylonian Magic and Greek Literature," in *I Poemi epici rapsodici non omerici e la tradizione orale*, ed. C. Brillante, M. Cantilena, and C. O. Pavese (Padua, 1981), 29–49.

[185] Photos, "Early Extractive Iron Metallurgy"; H. J. Unger and E. Schütz, "Pangaion. Ein Gebirge und sein Bergbau," and Ch. Koukouli-Chrysanthaki, "Die frühe Eisenzeit auf Thasos," both in *Südosteuropa zwischen 1600 und 1000 v. Chr. Prähistorische Archäologie in Südosteuropa* 1, ed. B. Hänsel (Berlin, 1982) 145–72, 199–243; E. Photos, H. Koukouli-Chrysanthaki, and G. Gialoglou, "Extractive Iron Metallurgy on Thasos and the East Macedonian Mainland," in *Science in Archaeology*, ed. R. Jones and H. Catling, Fitch Lab Occasional Papers 2 (Athens, 1986), 43–47; D. Samsaris, "Les mines et la metallurgie de fer et de cuivre dans la province romaine de Macédoine," *Klio*

chiefly in titanium-rich haematite sands, a source of iron readily available on the sea-shore and convenient to seafarers like the Phoenicians. These ores were probably known and used in the eleventh and tenth centuries B.C., according to finds from Tha-sos, Macedonia, and Thrace, and remained significant in Ottoman and modern times.[186] Related sulfide ores of iron and gold available in the minerals' oxidation zone were also mined in the island's mountainous interior.[187] At least one such (extractive) mine has been discovered in the ancient city of Thasos itself, on the acropolis.[188]

Herodotus reports both a Phoenician cult of Herakles (Melqart: 2.44) on the island and Phoenician exploitation of Thracian and Thasian mines (6.47). Strabo adds that Kadmos discovered the Pangaion gold sources in the Thracian peraea of the island (14.5.28, C 280; cf. Pliny, *Naturalis Historia* 7.56; Clement, *Stromateis* 1.16.75). Given these promises, archaeologists have expected full-fledged Phoenician settlements with mining activity and a sanctuary. Unlike in Spain, the archaeological evidence for Phoe-nicians from Thasos is surpassed by its legends and minerals. The coastal and alluvial availability of iron, celebrated in the Byzantine passage at the head of this section, may not have required a substantial settlement for processing metal ores, only "collecting expeditions" of the type envisaged for obtaining obsidian from Melos since Mesolithic times. But Phoenicians may have left their mark on the island in other ways. For ex-ample, the sanctuary of Herakles excavated by the French is neither early nor Levantine enough to substantiate Herodotus's claim for a Phoenician cult. However, earlier levels (the late seventh century) are under new excavation, and the possibility of some Phoe-nician influence on its late archaic temple is now admitted.[189] Outside of the Herakleion, North Syrian and Phoenician ivories (Figure 26) and glass beads represent early if spo-

69 (1987) 152–62; G. A. Wagner and G. Weisgerber, ed., *Antike Edel- und Buntmetallgewinnung auf Thasos. Der Anschnitt* Beih. 6 (Bochum, 1988). The Metallo-genetic Map of Greece and text (pp. 123–33) list fifty-four sulfide deposits in coastal Thrace and Thasos, plus silver from Thasos (p. 17) and gold (pp. 210–14). Iron ores on Thasos are estimated at 20 million tons (pp. 168–69, nos. 60–77); in 1962 the German steel in-dustry (Krupp) produced 300 tons of iron a day there. On the minerals of the Chalkidike and its name, see Bakhuizen *Chalcis-in-Euboea*, 14–15; Per-nicka, *JRGZM* 34, no. 2 (1987) 654–57.

[186] Photos, "Early Extractive Iron Metallurgy," esp. 25ff., on Thasos and its ores, intrusive between gneiss and the island's other famous commodity, marble. Thasian specialists in metallurgy were re-cruited as ἐπιστάτεις at the Laureion mines in the late classical period and defected to the Goths' gold industry in the fourth century A.D.

[187] G. A. Wagner, E. Pernicka, W. Gentner, and H. Gropengiesser, "Nachweis antiken Goldbergbaus auf Thasos: Bestätigung Herodots," *Naturwissenschaf-ten* 66 (1979) 613, and "Ancient Gold Mines on Tha-sos," *Naturwissenschaften* 68 (1981) 263–64; M. Varelidis, E. Pernicka, and G. A. Wagner, "Die Goldvorkom-men von Thasos," in Wagner and Weisgerber, *Edel-und Buntmetallgewinnung*, 313–20.

[188] A. Muller, "La mine de l'acropole de Thasos," in *Thasiaca, BCH suppl.* 5 (1979) 315–44; A. Muller and T. Kozelji, "La mine d'or de l'acropole de Thasos," in Wagner and Weisgerber, *Edel- und Buntmetallgewin-nung*, 180–97.

[189] Bunnens, *L'expansion phénicienne*, 360–61, for full bibliography (Pouilloux, Bergquist, etc.) on the sanc-tuary of Herakles; for the latest excavations, *BCH* 109 (1985) 881–84; *BCH* 110 (1986) 802–806; J. de Courtils and A. Pariente, "Excavations in the Herakles Sanc-tuary at Thasos," in *Early Greek Cult Practice*, 121.

radic imports to the sanctuary of Artemis.[190] Imports like these, comparable with signs of local Levantine interests on Rhodes, also inspired local translations into monumental sculpture and architecture. Lions appear on limestone reliefs in a "North Syrian" style, the island boasts several examples of Aeolic "leaf" capitals (Figure 27), and even the famous unfinished marble calfbearer (Figure 28) belongs to a long tradition of animal-bearing figures in the Near East.[191] Other Thasian sculpture, such as the portal reliefs of Herakles as archer and other gods, maintain Near Eastern traditions of figures flanking gateways; the marble votive reliefs from the "Prytaneion" show worshipers approaching a shrine with a seated goddess, a Greek version of Oriental conventions also imitated in Sparta and Crete.[192] The frequency of names like Κάδμος and Ἡρακλείδης in classical inscriptions (cf. Pausanias, 5.25.12), and of Semitic place-names like Ainyra and Koinyra, support survivals in traditions, if not genealogy.[193] Certain cult regulations on the island—most notably, the prohibition against pork and the sacrifice of pigs (IG XII, suppl. 414)—suggest Semitic influence on Greek religious practices, as they do on Crete (Chapter 6). Moreover, the cult of Herakles as a city god, along with the tradition of figures in relief on city gates as in North Syrian cities, is highly unusual in the Greek world, outside of Herakles Alexikakos. It maintains the Levantine tradition of a god as protector of the city: Melqart, "Lord of the City," and his Greek counterpart, Herakles, protected new Phoenician settlements throughout the Mediterranean, just as the Greek cult of a city goddess (Athena Polias) enjoyed Near Eastern antecedents.[194] Finally, the

[190] Ivories reported in BCH 83 (1959) 775, fig. 1 (Figure 26); cf. F. Salviat, "Lions d'ivoire orientaux à Thasos," BCH 86 (1962) 95–116; Boardman, Greeks Overseas, 62 fig. 32, with a near twin from Crete (Sakellarakis, L'Antro Ideo, 44 fig. 29); Carter, Greek Ivory-Carving, 33, 89. Glass-paste bead, in the shape of a human head, from the Artemision: BCH 109 (1985) 877–78, fig. 4 (from a fourth-century well): M. Seefried, Les pendentifs en verre sur noyau des pays de la Mediterranée antique (Rome, 1982), type C 1.

[191] First pointed out upon discovery by C. Picard in his report: BCH 45 (1921) 120–21, no. 5; cf. A. Parrot, "Le 'Bon Pasteur:' À propos d'une statue de Mari," in Mélanges Dussaud, 171–82. Cf. North Syrian parallels, e.g. the ibex-bearer from Carchemish (E. Akurgal, The Art of Greece: Its Origins [New York, 1970], 113, fig. 81, pl. 34 a). For the Orientalizing lion reliefs (mid-seventh to early sixth century in date), see B. Holtzmann, "Deux reliefs orientalisants de Thasos," in Archaische und klassische griechische Plastik, 2:73–77. Betancourt, Aeolic Style, 88–91, for the capitals.

[192] Bonnet, Melqart, 349, pl. 11, fig. 34, compares

the relief of Herakles the archer (now in Istanbul) with those at Zinjirli. The cult relief from Thasos (now in Malibu) resembles, in iconography and function, the Prinias stelai (Lembesi, Οἱ Στῆλες τοῦ Πρινιᾶ, 66–70, and in Carter, Beginning of Greek Sculpture, forthcoming).

[193] J. Pouilloux, Thasos. Recherches sur l'histoire et les cultes de Thasos (Paris, 1954), 1:311–17 (IG XII.8, 273, 5; 436); "La Fondation de Thasos: Archéologie, littérature, et critique historique," in Rayonnement grec. Hommages à Charles Delvoye (Brussels, 1982), 92–94; for further Phoenician elements, see F. Salviat and J. Servais, "Stèle Indicatrice Thasienne trouvée au Sanctaire d'Aliki," BCH 88 (1964) 278–84; F. Salviat, "Lions d'ivoire orientaux à Thasos," BCH 86 (1962) 108–9 n. 7.

[194] P. Xella, "Le polythéisme phénicien," in Studia Phoenicia, 4:35–37, on Phoenician city cults, especially that of Melqart; Bonnet, Melqart, 346–71, on Thasian cults; see Chapter 7, n. 62, on Herakles/Melqart cults. Pork as sacrificial meat was forbidden in the cult of the Nymphs and Apollo on Thasos (IG XII.8, 358); also noted by H. Matthäus, in Wagner and Weisger-

attraction of Parian colonists to Thasos could have followed Phoenician exploration for metals, if Greek ventures abroad followed Levantine entrepreneurs.

An important analogy to Thasos in terms of metals, cults, and legends is the island of Samothrace. Various traditions have Kadmos introduce its mysteries of the Great Gods (Hellanikos, *FrGH* 1 no. 4 F23) or at least become an initiate (Diodorus, 5.48). One story has him meet his bride, Harmonia, at a festival here, as well as lose his mother, Telephae (Demagoras of Samos: schol. Euripides, *Phoenician Women* 7; Mnaseas, *FrGH* III 154 frag. 28). The "Great Gods" themselves derive their name from Semitic *kbr* (as mentioned in n. 182). Kinship with a Boiotian cult of Levantine origin argues for a Semitic contribution to new cults at Samothrace, corroborated by ancient equations between the Kabeiroi and the Daktyls at Samothrace (Diodorus, 5.64.4; cf. Philo in Eusebius, *Praeparatio Evangelica* 1.10.14), another connection to Thebes, Crete, and other locales associated with metalworkers. Geology, once again, justified Levantine interest in this island. It belongs to the same sulfide deposit formations that attracted Phoenicians to Thasos and Thrace, and iron in its magnetic form even played a role in the Samothracian cult, presumably for its "magic" properties.[195]

Finally, it remains to consider the coast of Asia Minor as a significant sphere of Levantine activity, and not only as a predictable link in a maritime route from the southeastern Aegean to the north, as in the Persians' expansionist campaign. A focal point in legend as in history is Miletos, home not only to the greatest seafarers, merchants, and colonizers of the archaic Greek world but to wise men of Phoenician ancestry like Thales (Herodotus, 1.170). The testimony of Herodotus could be dismissed as mere Greek admiration of the Orient, expressed through the attribution to sages of an Eastern pedigree or sojourn among foreign wise men. However, grounds for taking Thales' ancestry more seriously have also been admitted,[196] and he is not the only Ionian with Near Eastern connections. Kadmos gave his name to an early historian of Miletos (Diodorus, 1.37.3) and to the citizens of Priene (called Καδμεῖοι according to Hellanikos), and the Phoenicians installed a cult of Melqart at Erythrai (Pausanias, 7.5.5–8). Several areas of coastal Asia Minor were known as Φοινίκη, including Lydia (Stephanus of Byzantium, s.v. Ἴος), home to the gold of the Paktolos, and Caria, whose mineral deposits (in the

---

ber, *Edel- und Buntmetallgewinnung*, 18–19. See Chapter 5 on city goddesses in the Late Bronze Age Aegean.

[195] Sulfide deposits: Melidonis, Γεωλογία τῆς νήσου Ἀνάφης, 300. Iron: Metallogenetic Map (text, p. 125, n. 5; p. 163, n. 4); cf. *Etymologicum Magnum*, s.v. Μαγνῆτις, Lucretius, 6.1044–47 for praise of Samothracian magnetic iron. Cult: S. Guettel Cole, *Theoi Megaloi. The Cult of the Great Gods at Samothrace* (Leiden, 1984), 130; Pliny, *Naturalis Historia* 33.1.23;

Billigmeier, *Kadmos*, 107–11; Samsaris, *Klio* 69 (1987) 161–62, on iron in cult at Samothrace.

[196] B. Soyez, "Le phénicien Thalès et le synoecisme de l'Ionie," *AntClass* 43 (1974) 74–82, includes other testimonia about Phoenicians in Ionia. W. F. Albright, "Neglected Factors in the Greek Intellectual Revolution," *PAPhS* 116 (1972) 225–42, and West, *Early Greek Philosophy and the Orient*, on Near Eastern sources of Ionian philosophy.

Halikarnassos peninsula: see n. 139) may have been attractive to Phoenicians. No wonder the Milesians laid claim to the invention of the alphabet (*FrGH* 1 F20); the eastern Aegean is one of those locales that called inscribed letters τὰ Φοινικήια (*SIG*³ 38, 40, from Teos) and applied the title φοινικογράφος to magistrates (*IG* XII.2, 96–97, from Mytilene).

Complementing these literary and epigraphical testimonia are archaic Orientalia found in Ionia, primarily Cypriote and Phoenician imports at sanctuaries: Ephesos, Miletos, and more recently, Erythrai and Smyrna (Bayrakli), have produced the kind of imports and imitations in bronze, ivory, and faience, common at the sanctuary of Hera on Samos.[197] More than just occasional imported trinkets dedicated by admiring Greeks, some bear inscriptions from Oriental patrons. A bronze horse-bridle from Samos (Figure 25) whose blinker was found at Eretria was inscribed with the name of the ninth-century king of Damascus, Syria; such objects may have been dedicated as well as transported by foreigners.[198] Cypriote sculptures and terracottas number in the thousands on Rhodes and Samos, and a life-sized example was dedicated at the sanctuary of Athena at Old Smyrna (Bayraklı).[199] Monumental responses to Oriental imports appear in the flowering of archaic East Greek sculpture and architecture, including Aeolic capitals and a new style of drafted masonry inspired if not executed by Levantine craftsmen.[200] Beyond Orientalia predictable at major sanctuaries, Cypriote terracottas are frequent finds at towns along the Knidos and Halikarnassos peninsulas.[201] Some of these complement

[197] A. Bammer, "Spuren der Phöniker im Artemision von Ephesus," *AnatStud* 35 (1985) 103–8, on Phoenician ivories and cult practices (horse, dog, and donkey sacrifices) at Ephesos; cf. R. Lebrun, "Anatolie et le monde phénicien du IXe au IVe siècle av. J.C.," in *Studia Phoenicia*, 5:23–33; E. Lipiński, "Phoenicians in Anatolia and Assyria (9th–6th centuries B.C.)," *OLP* 16 (1985) 81–84; *The Anatolian Civilizations* (Istanbul, 1983), 2:18–38, for Oriental/izing finds from Erythrai, Bayrakli (Smyrna), Ephesos, and Miletos, the latter rich in bronzes: a griffin protome, shield with lion's-head boss, North Syrian plaque (W. Schiering, "Bronzescheibe mit Reliefvenzierung," *IstMitt* 18 [1968] 149–56), and (Phoenician) *Aegyptiaka*: C. Weikert *IstMitt* 7 (1957) 126–32; cf. Boardman, *Greek Overseas*, 113, fig. 130.

[198] H. Kyrieleis and W. Röllig, "Ein alt-orientalischer Pferdeschmuck aus dem Heraion von Samos," *AthMitt* 103 (1988) 37–75; A. Charbonnet, *ASAA* 8 (1986) 117–56, for the blinker from Eretria. Kilian-Dirlmeier, *JRGZM* 32 (1985) 215–54.

[199] An estimated two thousand such statues have been found at Lindos and the Heraion on Samos: G. Schmidt, *Samos VIII. Kyprische Bildwerke aus dem Heraion von Samos* (Berlin, 1968); E. Gjerstad, "The Cypro-Archaic Life-Size Terracotta Statue Found in Old Smyrna," in *Tenth International Congress of Classical Archaeology, Izmir 1973*, ed. E. Akurgal (Ankara, 1978), 2:709–13.

[200] Betancourt, *Aeolic Style*, 50–57 on capitals and bases from western Asia Minor; V. Karageorghis, "The Relations between the Tomb Architecture of Anatolia and Cyprus in the Archaic Period," in *Tenth International Congress of Classical Archaeology, Izmir 1973*, 1:361–77; C. Ratté, "Lydian Masonry and Monumental Architecture at Sardis," *AJA* 93 (1989) 274; see n. 110, on Phoenician drafted masonry. On East Greek sculpture, see J. Pedley, *Greek Sculpture of the Archaic Period: The Island Workshops* (Mainz, 1976), 46–59; newer finds in *Archaische und klassische griechische Plastik*, 1:1–91.

[201] W. Radt, "Kyprische Terrakotten auf der Halikarnassischen Halbinsel," *Siedlungen und Bauten auf der Halbinsel von Halikarnassos unter besonderen Berücksichtigung der archaischen Epoche, IstMitt* Beih. 3 (Tübingen, 1970), 265–72; A. Johnston and V. Wilson, "Cypriaka from Datça," *BICS* 25 (1978) 33–34.

Knidian elements on Cyprus and at Naukratis to suggest a regular route that included Egypt, Cyprus, and East Greece, marked by a trail of East Greek pottery. The change from predominantly Euboian and Attic pottery in the Levant, between 1000 and 700 B.C., to a period (the seventh and sixth centuries) when East Greek imports become more numerous, suggests a major reorientation in trade patterns to an East Greek center. A new metallurgical perspective on these contexts might compare them with Rhodes, Euboia, Crete, and Thasos, in terms of local Levantine visitors keen on metal sources. It is not surprising that the Milesians became the great explorers of the Black Sea and Egypt, and knew about places like Sardinia (Herodotus, 1.170). Like the Euboians, they learned quickly and well from the Phoenicians, and took over as the leading merchants and mercenaries in the sixth-century Aegean once the Phoenicians transfer their interests to the western Mediterranean after the fall of Tyre.

These Aegean sites close a full circle of Phoenician-generated industry and commerce active between the eleventh and the sixth centuries, from the decline of Mycenaean palaces until the Persian wars. The kinship and vitality of these regional centers belie the modern concept of a "Dark Age," as if major cultural activity in Greece was dormant between Homeric times and classical Athens. Without writing, monuments, or other media deemed a sufficient index of history, these ages look "dark" to modern eyes. In reality, these five centuries may have been dominated by Levantine enterprise in which the Greeks played willing apprentices and partners, in marriage as well as commerce. During these centuries, they absorbed innovations in religion, poetry, and politics that manifest themselves in the transformations known as archaic art and culture.

A major disruption in this Aegean network coincides with the rise of Babylon and its conquests in the Near East. With the fall of Nineveh (612 B.C.) and, after a long siege, of Tyre (ca. 574 B.C.), the Phoenician network lost its eastern terminus with Assyria; Greek response to these events is reflected in their awe at Nineveh's fate (Phokylides, frag. 4). In the first half of the sixth century, the scarcity of Greek pottery in the Levant may indicate a loss of conveyors: this is when representations of "hippo" ships (Phoenician transport vessels) disappear in the Assyrian world.[202] Levantine opportunism rapidly found new markets: as merchants and mercenaries, the Phoenicians turned to a new master, Egypt, while their Mediterranean network migrated to North Africa and the Punic West, from the Aegean.[203] The Greeks, always their brightest pupils, apparently copied them with a similar shift to newer markets: Egypt, the Black Sea, North Africa, the West (e.g., Massalia, founded ca. 600 B.C.). The sixth century is the age of the great Panhellenic sanctuaries and their patronage by tyrants like Polykrates, the Kypselids, and even Athenian aristocrats who named their sons after Egyptian and Lydian kings and cultivated close ties with Oriental monarchs, even modeled their im-

---

[202] P. Corbett, "Thither Came the Phoenicians," *Scripta Mediterranea* 3 (1982) 77; E. Linder, "The Khor-sabad Wall Relief," *JAOS* 106 (1986) 278 n. 49.

[203] A. di Vita, "Libia," in *L'espansione fenicia*, 77–98.

age after them (Figure 36).[204] Eventually, two generations later, both Greeks and Phoenicians found a new Near Eastern master and patron in Persia, whose policies encouraged local entrepreneurship and the autonomy of local cultures. That very master ultimately brought them into conflict with each other, at Salamis, but the Athenian mythification of this event suppresses the fact that Greeks and Phoenicians both served in the Persian fleet, as they had with the Egyptians and the Assyrians. The early Phoenician evidence in the Aegean thus encourages an examination of archaic Greek history from the Near Eastern perspective: not from compensatory classical legends about early Greek tyrants and lawgivers, composed centuries after the archaic period, but from contemporary archaeology and from richer sources in the Near East.

In this early age of mixed populations exchanging techniques, stories, and family ties, each of those communities may have involved the same kind of more profound exchange in social and political institutions that can be detected on Crete. Against the background of a major industry exploiting Aegean resources for an eastern market, the dimensions of Phoenician presence in Greek areas represent far more than an assembly of imported trinkets (ἀθύρματα) and exotic tales. Particularly in Lakonia and Crete, early developments in epigraphy and constitutional law-codes institutionalized relations between Levantines and Greeks. The legacy of these early communities survived but was preserved in times when the Levant had become an enemy, and its contributions to early Greek culture suppressed. This selective examination of Aegean sites provides an introduction to the situation on Crete and, ultimately, clarifies the dimensions of Daidalos. For the evidence appears earliest and most generously on Crete, thanks to its resources, its prehistoric relations with the Levant, and its prominent location on the new Levantine route westward.

---

[204] An Athenian may have named his son "Psamatichos" as did Periander, tyrant of Corinth: E. Brann, *The Athenian Agora VIII: Late Geometric and Protoattic Pottery* (Princeton, 1962), 54, no. 194, pl. 10; cf. review by J. M. Cook, *Gnomon* 34 (1962) 823; Boardman, *Greeks Overseas*, 141–53, for Egyptian names and traditions adopted by Greek artists and aristocrats.

CHAPTER 6

Daidalos in Crete

KAPTOR AND ITS CULTURE

τέταρτον δὲ γένος συμμιγῆναί φασιν εἰς τὴν Κρήτην
μιγάδων βαρβάρων τῶν διὰ τὸν χρόνον ἐξομοιωθέντων τῇ
διαλέκτῳ τοῖς ἐγχωρίοις Ἕλλησι.

And the fourth population to intermingle in Crete they say to
be a mixture of barbarians who adopted in the course of time
the language of native Greeks.
—Diodorus, 5.80.2

CRETE'S LONG HISTORY of contact with the Near East throughout the second millennium made the island a natural home for Daidalos, until Athenians repatriated him in the fifth century. During a lengthy and fruitful relationship with the East, Crete may have been called Kaptor, a place where Kothar had a "throne" (see Chapter 4). The classical transformation of Kothar/Daidalos epitomizes the experience of early Greek art and culture: dispersed, diverse, and deeply Oriental for many centuries, then aggressively appropriated by Athens after the Persian wars. The island's intimacy with the East experienced modern neglect, between the powerful command of "Minoan" Crete on the European imagination, and the quest for signs of "preclassical" art in the first millennium. The archaeology of Crete during the transitional centuries is either treated as Subminoan, a survival of Bronze Age palatial culture, or as "Protogeometric" with an acute case of premature Orientalization.[1] For example, the island is almost reprimanded for developing a full-blown Orientalizing style (in pottery) without the decent interval of a Geometric phase.[2] This early Orientalizing decorative style bears the cum-

---

[1] E.g., J. C. Clough, "Untersuchung zum Archaismus an kretischen Gefässen und Kleinplastiken aus Ton und Bronze des 8. u. früh. 7. Jhts. v. Chr." (Ph.D. diss., Munich, 1972); U. Naumann, *Subminoische und protogeometrische Bronzeplastik auf Kreta*, AthMitt Beih. 6 (Berlin, 1976); Blome's *Bildwelt Kretas*; or B. Hayden, "The Development of Cretan Architecture from the LMIIIA through the Geometric Peri-

ods" (Ph.D. diss., University of Pennsylvania, 1981); C. Verlinden, *Les statuettes anthropomorphes crétoises en bronze et en plomb, du IIIe. millénaire au VIIe. siècle av. J.-C.* (Louvain-la-Neuve, 1984); Lembesi, Σύμη Βιαννοῦ I, mainly pursue traditional styles and phases.

[2] J. N. Coldstream, "A Protogeometric Nature Goddess from Knossos," *BICS* 31 (1984) 94: "How illogical it might seem that the Cretans should have

bersome name of "Protogeometric B" despite its most ungeometric, ornamental nature, which coexists with Attic Middle Geometric styles, often on the same vase.[3] Efforts to trace motifs to Minoan survivals often discover more immediate sources of inspiration in the East, not the past.[4] Elsewhere in Greece, the early Iron Age has emerged as an independent rather than a transitional period, with its own "Iron Age" phases instead of "sub-" or "proto-" parasites on earlier and later styles.[5] This chapter will focus on Crete's sustained Orientalizing experience during the age when iron determined that relationship—from the twelfth century until about 600 B.C.—as background for a new perspective on the mythology of Crete, including Minos and Daidalos.

As proposed previously, the iron resources of Crete may have attracted Levantine attention even after catastrophes struck the Near East and the Aegean around 1200 B.C. (see Chapter 5, nn. 75–77, 175). These resources help explain why western Crete, in particular, was still adopting Near Eastern forms such as the larnax in the Late Bronze Age, and developing them into a local industry exported to Boiotia, a sister province equally rich in iron. Iron-bearing stones are reported on Mount Ida in antiquity by Pliny (*Naturalis Historia* 37.130), who also attributes the discovery of iron by the "Daktyls" on Mount Ida on the authority of Hesiod, as if the primacy of Cretan ironworking was familiar in Boiotia, an area endowed with similar metal ores.[6] These resources not only inspired legends about Daktyls, Kouretes, and Daidalos himself but determined the location of Iron Age [*sic*] cities in Crete (Map 1, inset), as observed by Faure.[7] Settlements represented by cemeteries in the Knossos area, the Mesara plain (Gortyn and Kommos), around the bay of Mirabello from Dreros to Itanos, and the slopes of iron-rich Mount Ida share a pattern of interaction with the Orient. These areas of Crete apparently stayed in contact with Cyprus through Subminoan and Protogeometric times and never stopped "Orientalizing." Their Eastern contacts merely retracted, then revived with the new network supplying Assyria with iron (as traced in Chapter 5). For several centuries, resident craftsmen from the Near East (North Syria and Phoenicia) may have practiced their skills in Crete.

---

been toying with freehand orientalising motifs before they had formed a proper Geometric style!"

[3] As analyzed by Coldstream, " 'Bilingual' Greek Amphorae from the North Cemetery of Knossos," in ΕΙΛΑΠΙΝΗ, 335–39.

[4] Despite its title, J. N. Coldstream's "Some Minoan Reflexions in Cretan Geometric Art," in *Studies in Honour of T.B.L. Webster*, ed. J. Betts, J. T. Hooker, and J. R. Green (Bristol, 1988), 2:23–32, concludes that Oriental sources, especially Cyprus, are dominant by the ninth century.

[5] E.g. at Tiryns: Kilian, in *Problems in Greek Prehistory*, 199; cf. A. Papadimitriou, "Bericht zur früheisenzeitliche Keramik aus der Unterburg von Tiryns:

Ausgrabungen in Tiryns 1982/83," *AA* 103 (1988) 227–43. The phenomenon of "Sub-Mycenaean" continues to attract debate: P. A. Mountjoy and V. Hankey, "LH IIIC Late Versus Submycenaean. The Kerameikos Pompeion Cemetery Reviewed," *JdI* 103 (1988) 1–37.

[6] Pliny, *Naturalis Historia* 7.197: "*ferrum [invenisse] Hesiodus in Creta eos qui vocati sunt Dactyli Idaei*," and the Suda registers a poem περὶ τῶν Ἰδαίων Δακτύλων among the works of Hesiod (frag. 282).

[7] "Nouvelles localisations des villes crétoises," *KrChr* 17 (1963) 16–23; "Les minerais de la Crète antique," *RA* (1966) 45–78; "Les mines du roi Minos," in *Fourth Cretological Congress*, 1:150–68.

After the decline of Bronze Age palatial culture, related areas remained active on a more modest level. Thus the north-south plain and slopes of Central Crete, between Mount Ida and the peak of Dikte, were occupied during the transition to an iron-based economy. Northern Mount Ida dominates Crete's Oriental/izing culture in the first millennium, with a cult cave on the north slope associated with nearby cities (Axos, Eleutherna), including Knossos.[8] It was metal artifacts from the Idaian Cave that first announced the possibility of foreign craftsmen in Crete with a role in Orientalizing art and cult. When first discovered one hundred years ago, the bronze shields from the Idaian Cave were taken for Phoenician or Cypriote work based on Assyrian prototypes.[9] Scholars gradually introduced the possibility of native Greek craftsmen instead, until the manufacturerers became fully Hellenized in official literature.[10] Although Kunze's thorough analysis purported to settle lingering doubts by claiming the shields as certifiably Cretan, Dunbabin took the bold step of reassigning them to Oriental craftsmen, immigrants to Crete who thereafter trained Greek apprentices.[11] The fate of these shields in modern scholarship follows a pattern in classical attitudes toward the Orient.

One hundred years later, votive bronzes from Mount Ida—vessels, tripods, and especially the shields—remain the most dramatic evidence for Levantine activity in Crete.[12] The workshop that produced the special tympanon shields for the Idaian Cave disappears in the seventh century, but is succeeded by specialists in bronze armor (helmets, mitras, and cuirasses) dedicated at regional sanctuaries in Crete and at Panhellenic sanctuaries (Figure 33).[13] The dynamics of these metal workshops are suggested by a recent analysis of Greek and Oriental bronzes in terms of their tin and alloy contents.[14] Scientific results agree with technical evidence from workshop sites like Olym-

---

[8] Faure, *RA* (1966) 63, on the limonites of Mount Ida, artifacts such as the large iron wheel from the Idaian Cave (E. Fabricius, "Alterthümer auf Kreta II. Die idäische Zeusgrotte," *AthMitt* 10 [1885] 68), and the cave's relationship to Axos. Pilgrimage from Knossos to the Idaian Cave: Plato, *Laws* 625b.

[9] Verbruggen, *Le Zeus crétois*, 71–75, on the early excavations; *Creta Antica*, 53–56; F. Halbherr, "Scavi e trovamento nell'antro di Zeus sul Monte Ida in Creta," *Museo Italiano di antichità classica* 2 (1888) 689–766, on the first season (1885); P. Orsi, 769–904, on the shields; E. Kunze, *Kretische Bronzereliefs* (Stuttgart, 1931), 1–4.

[10] A. L. Frothingham, Jr., "Early Bronzes Recently Discovered on Mount Ida in Krete," *AJA* 4 (1888) 431ff–49; cf. H. Brunn, *Griechische Kunst-geschichte* (Munich, 1893), 1:90ff., called the resident workshop "Cypriote"; revived by Canciani and others. See Blome, *Bildwelt Kretas*, 15, for summary of scholarship.

[11] Dunbabin, *Greeks and Their Eastern Neighbors*, 41, followed by Boardman, *Cretan Collection in Oxford*, 138, 151; Canciani, *Bronzi orientali*, 13, 18, and "Éléments chypriotes dans les bronzes crétois pendant la période orientalisante," in *Relations between Cyprus and Crete*, 269–78 (Cypriote). Blome, *Bildwelt Kretas*, 15–16, and Markoe, *Phoenician Bowls*, 110–16, agree that the shields were made in Crete but under the influence of imported models if not masters.

[12] Boardman, *CAH* III.3, 225–27; Markoe, *Phoenician Bowls*, 110–17, 123–24.

[13] Hoffman, *Early Cretan Armorers* (hoard from Afrati/Arkades and related Cretan bronze work, including the mitra from the Schimmel Collection illustrated in Figure 33); Boardman, *Cretan Collection at Oxford*, 141.

[14] S. Filippakis, E. Photos, Cl. Rolley, and G. Varoufakis, "Bronzes grecs et orientaux: influences et apprentissages," *BCH* 107 (1983) 111–32; E. Magou, S. Philippakis, and Cl. Rolley, "Trépieds géomè-

pia, where Oriental bronze repoussé reliefs were locally repaired and reworked into a sphyrelaton statue.[15] Trace elements and technical analysis agree with the stylistic features that first indicated Orientals at work in Crete; all point to a steady supply of materials from the Near East and constant imitation, by Greek craftsmen, of Oriental artifacts. Their Oriental origin may even have survived in an ancient *termus technicus*, according to one of its etymologies. Hesychius provides the following gloss of a word critical to Greek perceptions of the Orient:

κάδμος· δόρυ. λόφος. ἀσπίς. ΚΡΗΤΕΣ

kadmos: "spear, crest, shield," among the Cretans.

Apparently Cretans may have used the word κάδμος as a common noun for certain aspects of weaponry. Since the seventeenth century, philology accepts the name of Kadmos as a Greek equivalent of Semitic "QDM," meaning essentially "the easterner" or "Oriental."[16] The expression Καδμήια γράμματα in fact indicates that the adjective was used interchangeably with Φοινικήια to describe the letters of the Greek alphabet. The adjective καδμήια is no more denominative than δαιδάλεα, and need not be derived from Kadmos and his legendary role in the transmission of the alphabet. Instead, both name and adjective derive from the same term for "eastern," just as Daidalos personifies but does not explain the origin of words related to his name. If the common noun κάδμος is derived from the Semitic root and is used to describe Oriental novelties as well as newcomers, the Cretan application of the word to certain types of metal weaponry means that the Greeks themselves may have identified such artifacts, by name, as Oriental.[17] The role of these shields in hiding infant cries (birth of Zeus, or death of sacrificed infants? [n. 21]) makes them Eastern in cult terms, as well. This unusual convergence between style, ritual, scientific analysis, and nomenclature in neglected testimonia provides encouragement, if not a methodological model, for detecting not only Orientalia manifest to the modern eye but their acknowledgment in antiquity.

---

triques de bronze," *BCH* 110 (1986) 121–36.

[15] *Deltion* 17 (1961–1962) Chr. 115, pls. 129, 130; P. Bol, *Antike Bronzetechnik. Kunst und Handwerk antiker Erzbilder* (Munich, 1985), 102–3, fig. 64.

[16] Burkert, *Orientalisierende Epoche*, 7 n. 3, citing Edwards, *Kadmos*, 78–79 n. 72: Billigmeier, *Kadmos*, 73–74, on the three-consonantal root, which means "that which is before, in front" and indicates the east in a culture oriented [sic] to the rising sun (cf. Hebrew *qedem*, *qadmoniot*). An alternate Indo-European derivation favored by Boisacq, Frisk, and many classicists presumes a root related to κέκασμαι: Edwards, *Kadmos*, 78–79; Dombrowski, *Europa*, 111 nn. 359–66

(cf. the double derivation, Greek and Semitic, for "Europa," discussed in these passages subsequently).

[17] Edwards, *Kadmos*, 79 n. 72, cautions that "it is by no means certain that the proper name Κάδμος has the same origin [as the common noun κάδμος]." A. Schachter "Kadmos and the Implications of the Tradition for Boiotian History," in *La Béotie antique*, ed. P. Roesch and others, (Paris, 1985), 151–52, cites Hesychius's gloss and compares the Theban "Kadmos" to the Argive "Aspis," as names for citadels that resemble shields.

Renewed investigations at the Idaian Cave are increasing its repertoire of Orientalia annually, with bronze, gold, ivory, faience, and amber artifacts.[18] The cult use of the cave can be traced back to the Early Bronze Age and lasts through Subminoan times into the Protogeometric period.[19] Complementary finds at the sanctuary of Aphrodite at Axos suggest occupation since LM III, then a rise in the quantity and quality of material culture matching the evidence from the cave, as if the city and the cult of Zeus flourished, in close partnership, from the ninth to the sixth centuries.[20] Mount Ida is also home to the "throne" of Zeus as well as his "birthplace" and the site of related infant sacrifices in myth, was sacred as the locale for Minos's converse with Zeus, and imported cult figures like Herakles Daktylos, associated with Tyre.[21] The communities associated with cave/cult and iron ores demonstrate a pattern typical for early Crete. In art, imported and local Orientalia stimulate monumental versions of figures in limestone, the first "Daedalic" statues.[22] Axos developed an early law code like other Cretan cities, and may have profited in legend from its proximity to Mount Ida, where Minos acquired the laws from Zeus (Plato, *Laws* 624b). In the seventh century, its population was active in Aegean commerce and colonization: the mother of Battos, the Theran founder of Cyrene, was from Axos, and another Theran, a merchant named Themision, was a resident of this city (Herodotus, 4.151–53). Like their cousin Korobios of Itanos, a purple-fisher from eastern Crete who led the Therans to Cyrene (Chapter 5), these figures represent a class of merchants and explorers who inherited the Bronze Age network of the Keftiu, with all its Levantine connections.

The south coastal plain of the Mesara was home to the palace of Phaistos, a "villa" complex at Agia Triada, and a harbor town at Kommos in the Bronze Age.[23] The harbor site continued to attract Levantine interests in the Dark Ages, possibly as a port in metal

[18] Sakellarakis, annual reports in *Praktika* (1980–1983); *Ergon* (1984) 106–11, pls. 114–52 (1985) 78–87; *L'Antro Ideo*, 19–48; Ἀρχαιολογία 15 (1985) 753, figs. 142–45.

[19] Sakellarakis, *L'Antro Ideo*, 24–27, and *Early Greek Cult Practice*, 173–93. Verbruggen, *Le Zeus crétois*, 71–99, 140, on the cult of Idaian Zeus.

[20] Axos: Kanta, *LM III Period in Crete*, 201; D. Levi, "I bronzi di Axos," *ASAA* 13–14 (1930–1931) 43ff. Hoffmann, *Early Cretan Armorers*, 21–25, 28–33); *Creta antica*, 65–67; G. Rizza, "Le terracotte di Axos," *ASAA* 45–46 (1969) 211–302; Davaras, *Statue von Astritsi*, 37. Verbruggen, *Le Zeus crétois*, 97–99 (on Axos's role in the cult).

[21] Verbruggen, *Le Zeus crétois*, 75–99; C. Grottanelli, "Eracle Dattilo dell' Ida: Aspetti Orientali," *OrAnt* 20 (1982) 201–8. C. Tzavellas-Bonnet, "Melqart, Bès et l'

Héraclès Dactyle de Crète," in *Studia Phoenicia*, 3:231–40. S. O'Bryhim, "Hesiod and the Curetes," *APA Abstracts, 1990*, 185), on infant sacrifice and the Idaian Cave. On Minos and Zeus, see Chapter 6.

[22] Davaras, *Statue aus Astritsi*; Adams, *Orientalizing Sculpture*, 35ff., for the statues from Eleutherna and Astritsi; Blome, *Bildwelt Kretas*, 46, pl. 20, 1–2; M. Sipsie-Eschbach, "Bemerkungen zum Torso aus Astritsi," *AA* (1982) 487–91; Stambolides, *BSA* 85 (1990) 398–400, on new limestone statues from Eleutherna cemetery.

[23] *Creta Antica*, 121–201, for Italian excavations at Phaistos and Hagia Triada; J. Shaw and others, *A Great Minoan Triangle in South Central Crete: Kommos–Hagia Triada–Phaistos, Scripta Mediterranea* 6 (1985), and reports in *Hesperia* 1977–1982, 1984, and 1986 on Kommos.

traffic. Its early Iron Age sanctuary resembles a Phoenician one in plan and imports, and might have honored an imported Oriental god like Apollo Amyklaios.[24] The triple-pillar shrine and small bench-and-hearth temples called "Cretan" are familiar in the Levant, as at Tell Sukas.[25] Their Near Eastern cult forms first appear in Late Minoan Crete (e.g., at Hagia Triada: Chapter 5, n. 53) and have therefore been hailed as surviv-als of Minoan culture, but could represent continuous contact with the Near East. The series of new shrines at Kommos draw attention to older discoveries of early temples at nearby Phaistos. An archaic shrine with Orientalizing votives sits on Geometric remains southeast of the palace; an early Doric limestone capital with petals carved on the echi-nus may belong to another, built over the west court of the palace.[26] A third temple found on the Phalandra hill resembles those from Prinias and elsewhere, with a single "hearth" room with interior columns and prostyle porch.[27]

Variations of these Orientalia in pottery and architecture come from nearby Gortyn, chief city of the Messara in Greek and Roman times.[28] In Orientalizing times, the sanc-tuary of Athena on the acropolis produced the city's richest archaeological finds, from bronzes and their clay imitations to ritual objects reminiscent of the Near East (masks similar to those from Sparta), but also Crete's earliest limestone relief sculpture and temples.[29] For historians, none of these shares the reputation of the city's archaic law code, itself a witness to the lasting effect of the Orient on Greek culture.[30] Testimonia

[24] Copper ingot in Bronze Age levels at Kommos: T. Stech, in *Prehistoric Production and Exchange*, 100–105. V. Watrous and others, discussion in *Scripta Mediterranea* 6 (1985) 13–18. Cf. seventh-century iron ingot: *Hesperia* 53 (1984) 283; *BCH* 108 (1984) 833–35, fig. 183, and Levantine pottery with parallels from Halikarnassos, Rhodes, and Cyprus: *Hesperia* 53 (1984) 278–79. Apollo Amyklaios is attested at Gortyn and postulated at Kommos: Willetts, in *Relations be-tween Crete and Cyprus*, 240, citing Shaw, *Hesperia* 47 (1978) 152–54. M. Shaw, "A Bronze Figurine of a Man from the Sanctuary at Kommos, Crete," in ΕΙΛΑΠ-ΙΝΗ, 371–82, for a figure with Near Eastern features, and "Two Cups with Incised Decoration from Kom-mos, Crete," *AJA* 87 (1983) 441–52, for local imita-tions of Oriental metal vessels.

[25] J. Shaw, "A Phoenician Shrine at Kommos," *AJA* 91 (1987) 297; "Phoenicians in Southern Crete," *AJA* 93 (1989) 165–83. Cf. P. Riis, "Tell Sukas," in *Phönizier im Westen*, 246–49, fig. 11; Muhly, in *Ebla to Damascus* 269–70. The bronze bull found on the Kommos altar has a parallel in Israel: A. Mazar, "The 'Bull Site'—An Iron Age I Open Cultic Place," *BASOR* 247 (1982) 27–42. For an alternate view of such temples, see

Samuelsson (cited in n. 33).

[26] L. Pernier, "Memorie del Culto di Rhea a Phaes-tos," in *Saggi di storia antica e di archeologia offerti a Giu-lio Beloch* (Rome, 1910), 241–53; V. La Rosa, "Capitello arcaico da Festos," in *Antichità Cretesi*, 2:136–48.

[27] D. Levi, "Gli scavi à Festos negli anni 1958–1960," *ASAA* 23–24 (1961–1962) 462–67; *Festos e la Ci-viltà Minoica*, vol. 1, Incunabula Graeca 60 (Rome, 1976), 599–602, fig. 965.

[28] *Creta antica*, 69–116, for the history of excavations and bibliography.

[29] Rizza and Scrinari, *Gortina*; *Creta Antica*, 111–14. Seated statue: Adams, *Orientalizing Sculpture*, 25; Blome, *Bildwelt Kretas*, 45, pl. 19:3. The temple is built of large gypsum blocks, has a tripartite interior and exterior limestone reliefs with three figures: Rizza and Scrinari, *Gortina*, 50, pls. 3–4; Blome, *Bildwelt Kretas*, 48, pl. 20:4; Carter, *The Beginning of Greek Sculpture*.

[30] It survives in an early classical copy rebuilt into an early Roman theater: *Creta antica*, 73–81; R. F. Wil-letts, *The Law Code of Gortyn* (Berlin, 1967), and *CAH* III.3, 237–48.

on Gortyn present personalities like Thaletas, who introduced ritual music and dance to Greece, specifically to Sparta, where ritual forms like the masks of Ortheia (Chapter 5, n. 143) show a similar debt to the Orient. The city's religious life must have been as sophisticated as its early civic institutions, and as evocative of Near Eastern culture. The city is also rich in legend and cult, and in representations of myth.[31] It is one of the sites in Crete associated with Europa, for whom the Hellotia festival with wreath and tree is celebrated, and it also contributes to the Knossian genealogy of Minos and Daidalos, who married a Gortynian woman in some legends.

Halfway between Gortyn and Knossos lies Prinias, sharing the southeast slopes of Ida with Gortyn and equally precocious in its development of monumental sculpture and architecture. Twin buildings on the akropolis resemble shrines at Kommos and Phaistos, but exceed them in their monumental form and sculptural decoration. Stone orthostates with sculpted reliefs of armed warriors on horseback (Figure 30) and grazing deer may have formed an orthostate course along the exterior walls of "Temple A." An elaborate lintel bearing two seated goddesses above, a frieze of panthers on its face, and a third female figure on the soffit, spanned the temple's door forming a transom.[32] The form of Crete's unusual early temples, in part a Subminoan survival, makes more sense in the Levant, especially with relief sculpture so evocative of North Syria.[33] Unique to Prinias is a series of limestone stelai with incised figures of women and warriors, found built into the akropolis but probably used as funerary markers (Figure 31). The new Iron Age cemetery under excavation at Eleutherna (n. 22), with its built stone enclosures incorporating free-standing and relief sculpture, makes the Prinias stelai more likely to be funerary, not votive. Their technique of manufacture suggests the same curious "translation" from toreutic or incised metal into soft stone observed in Bronze Age sculpture (the Shaft Grave stelai) and characteristic of the way metallurgy anticipated archaic sculpture.[34]

[31] E.g. Rizza and Scrinari *Gortina*, pl. XXXII, 212; Burkert, "Oriental and Greek Mythology: The Meeting of Parallels," in *Interpretations of Greek Mythology*, 28–29 (molded clay plaque of Oriental type with "Oresteia" scene), and in *Early Greek Cult Practice*, 87, for Europa's festival at Gortyn.

[32] G. Rizza, "Nuove richerche sulla Patela e nel territorio di Priniàs: Relazione preliminare degli scavi de 1969," *CronArch* 8 (1969) 7–32, and in *Creta antica*, 227–34; Beyer, *Dreros und Prinias*, for the most "North Syrian" reconstruction of the sculpted orthostates with an early date (ca. 700); cf. Adams, *Orientalizing Sculpture*, 68–78 (ca. 600); Blome, *Bildwelt Kretas*, 47–48, pl. 20:3.

[33] Even Beyer, *Dreros und Prinias*, 66–70, calls Dreros "Subminoan"; S. Stucchi, "Questioni relative al

Tempio A di Prinias ed al formarsi degli ordini dorico e ionico," in *Antichità Cretesi*, 2:89–119. The best parallel for a small temple on a peak with altar and terrace may be at Tell Sukas in Phoenicia: P. Riis "Griechen in Phönizien," in *Phönizier im Westen*, 246–49, fig. 11; Muhly, in *Ebla to Damascus*, 270. Cf. Dreros: Burkert, *Greek Religion*, 89. E. Samuelsson, "Greek 'Hearth-Temples': An Alternative Interpretation," *AJA* 92 (1988) 279–80, considers Crete's Iron Age temples to be civic dining-rooms, like prytaneia.

[34] Lembesi, Ὀι Στῆλες τοῦ Πρινιᾶ, 62–70, pl. I, 38–39, and in *Antichità Cretesi*, 2:120ff., for their reconstruction; Adams, *Orientalizing Sculpture*, 41ff.; Blome, *Bildwelt Kretas*, 48–49. Vermeule, *Greece in the Bronze Age*, 90–94, on comparable Bronze Age techniques; cf. the bronze gorgoneion from Dreros and

These later archaic achievements in sculpture and architecture at Prinias are linked to a settlement that begins in Geometric times and shows Oriental connections as explicit as those at Knossos. Some five hundred meters northwest of the akropolis of Prinias lies a cemetery where 680 burials took place between the thirteenth century and the destruction of Prinias at the inevitable Cretan terminus around 600 B.C.[35] The burials include cremations laid in rock-cut pits and inhumations in tholoi or rectangular chambers cut in rock, complete with dromos, and lined with ashlar blocks, or in rectangular chambers built of rubble, against a tumulus. The latter combine inhumation and cremation (the head is buried separately, only the body is cremated) and their offerings are characteristic of early Cretan Orientalizing art in painted pithoi, terracotta figurines, and gold ornaments.[36] Most unusual are eighteen burials of animals, including a team of horses sacrificed in connection with funerary rites and burials of smaller animals such as dogs, highly evocative of Oriental ritual.[37]

This continuous, prosperous, and sophisticated (Orientalizing) community at Prinias compares closely, especially in pottery and jewelry, with the Iron Age history of Knossos, whose remains stem predominantly from burials. Hundreds of graves include Minoan tholos and chamber tombs still used during Subminoan and Protogeometric times, from the eleventh century through the archaic period.[38] Cremation appears in this community in the tenth century, then prosperity revived the level and quality of luxury imports, including Levantine metalwork, by the ninth century. Local industry imitating exotica, specifically perfumed ointment and its containers, appears near the time of its companion industries on Rhodes and Euboia.[39] The most glamorous of these local industries was in gold, according to a set of jewelry and a "jeweler's hoard" buried in a reused tholos tomb at Khaniale Teke near Knossos.[40] According to Boardman, the de-

its limestone counterpart: BCH 60 (1936) 251, fig. 20, and 270–74, pl. xxix.

[35] G. Rizza, "Gli scavi di Prinias e il problema delle origini dell'arte greca," in Un decennio di ricerche archeologiche. Quaderni de la ricerca scientificà 100 (Rome, 1978) 1:85–137; "Prinias nelle fasi geometrica e orientalizzante," ASAA 61 (1983) 45–51; "La Necropoli di Siderospilia," in Creta Antica, 238–56.

[36] Rizza, in Creta Antica, 250–56; "Ceramiche figurate di Prinias," in Antichità Cretesi, 2:153–60.

[37] G. Rizza, "Tombes de chevaux," in Relations between Crete and Cyprus, 294–97, for their eastern Mediterranean connections; cf. L. Day, "Dog Burials in the Greek World," AJA 88 (1984) 21–32 (Crete and Cyprus, to which now add Ashkelon in Israel). For survivals of these practices in Sicilian tombs: G. Rizza, "La necropoli di Butera e i rapporti fra Sicilia e Creta in età protoarcaica," Kokalos 30–31 (1984–

1985) 65–70.

[38] Boardman calls archaic Knossos "a city of the dead" (CAH III.3, 229). For a synthesis, see Coldstream, "Dorian Knossos and Aristotle's villages," in Aux origines de l'Hellénisme, 312–22; The Formation of the Greek Polis: Aristotle and Archaeology, 20–22.

[39] Coldstream, in Phönizier im Westen, 268–69; RDAC (1984) 122–39.

[40] Boardman "The Khaniale Teke Tombs, II," BSA 62 (1967) 56–75, esp. 63–67; cf. earlier report in BSA 57 (1962); Cretan Collection in Oxford, 131–38 (shields and Teke jewelry); "Orientalen auf Kreta," in Dädalische Kunst, 14–25; CAH III.3, 222–26; Coldstream, in Phönizier im Westen, 267–68. However, other scholars (e.g., Lembesi, BSA 82 [1975] 173–75; Beyer Dreros und Prinias, 49, 50; Blome, Bildwelt Kretas, 12) have reclaimed these finds as Greek works.

ceased was an immigrant artist in a workshop active on Crete for over a century, responsible for the jewelry found in the Idaian Cave as well as in another Knossian cemetery at Fortetsa. These Cretan finds can now be compared with earlier experiments in gold jewelry from Attica and Euboia to reconstruct a scenario whereby Greek artists might have learned from Oriental masters.[41] An expansion of the settlement area around Knossos toward the coast, as indicated by new cemeteries distant from the palace area and not just reused Minoan tombs, has been connected with the foundation of a new harbor in the ninth century.[42] As at Kommos, the harbor town of a Bronze Age palace-area outlives the palace, to become a critical Iron Age nexus with the expansion of Phoenician trade in response to the Assyrian Empire.

The Khaniale Teke finds are complemented by other metal finds from cemeteries around Knossos, such as the bronze belt from Fortetsa with its "Assyrianizing" scene of a city siege.[43] A limestone relief from the same site and one from Khania in western Crete duplicate the scene on this belt so closely as to reinforce the mutual debt of both areas to the sphere of Assyrian influence, perhaps through Syrian craftsmen or their art.[44] Bronze and stone reliefs reinforce the technical relationship between Orientalizing metal relief work and archaic monumental limestone imitations, suggested in the Prinias stelai. Even more impressive, and more Oriental, is a large limestone head from the sanctuary of Zeus Thenatas at Amnisos, a port of Knossos. Details such as the large cavities for inlaid eyes of a different material anticipate local Cretan style with over-large eyes called "Daedalic" but derived from Syrian conventions.[45] The unusual architecture of the sanctuary, with a monumental terrace or altar and large stone eagles on pillars (?), adds to the picture of early archaic experiments in Orientalizing architecture on Crete, home of legendary builders in addition to Daidalos.[46]

[41] P. Themelis, "An Eighth-century Goldsmith's Workshop from Eretria," in *The Greek Renaissance*, 157–65 (Chapter 5, n. 173). Coldstream, in *Phönizier im Westen*, 264–68, on Greek apprenticeship: "Men do not suddenly copy the art of complete strangers through casual imports" (p. 272). G. Falsone, "La coupe phénicienne de Fortetsa, Crète: Une reconsideration," in *Studia Phoenicia*, 5:181–94.

[42] As suggested by Coldstream in "Dorian Knossos and Aristotle's Villages," in *Aux origines de l'Hellénisme*, 317; see further on Amnisos.

[43] Fortetsa belt: J. Brock, *Fortetsa: Early Cretan Tombs near Knossos*, BSA suppl. 2 (Cambridge, 1957), 134–35, pls. 115, 168; Blome, *Bildwelt Kretas*, 7, 10–12, pl. 3:1–2; Adams, *Orientalizing Sculpture*, 13. Related to these is the bronze relief found in 1900 at Kavousi by Harriet Boyd (*AJA* 5 [1901] 147–48; Blome, p. 11, fig. 3), a site in eastern Crete now under reexcavation:

excavation reports by Coulson, Day, and Gesell, *Hesperia* 52 (1983) 389–420; 54 (1985) 327–55; 55 (1986) 355–87; 57 (1988) 279–301.

[44] Adams, *Orientalizing Sculpture*, 8–13, concluding that: "Oriental immigrants . . . must have arrived on several occasions and from various parts of the Assyrian-dominated Near East" (p. 13, also appropriate to the transmission of the alphabet); cf. Blome, *Bildwelt Kretas*, 7–8, fig. 2, pl. 3:1–2, dates reliefs and belt (along with the Dreros statues) to the late eighth century; Carter, *The Beginning of Greek Sculpture*.

[45] *Praktika* (1936), 83 fig. 2; *AA* (1937) 224, fig. 1 (found in Roman levels). Adams, *Orientalizing Sculpture*, 5–6, attributes its inlaid eyes and massive style to "a workman from Iron Age North Syria, east Anatolia, or Urartu."

[46] Excavation reports in *Praktika*, 1930–1938; S. Marinatos, "Ἐπὶ τὰ ἴχνη τοῦ Χερσίφρονος καὶ Με-

Oriental connections on Crete were dramatically escalated over a decade ago by the discovery of a bronze bowl inscribed in Phoenician letters, found in a reused Minoan tomb (Tomb J) in the Teke cemetery of Knossos. Attic pottery in the tomb and Semitic letter forms date bowl and burial in the early ninth century, its letter forms perhaps as early as 1000 B.C., making the Teke bowl the earliest Phoenician inscription in the West outside Sardinia.[47] If we assume this personal possession inscribed with the name of its Semitic owner was buried with him, the Teke bowl, like the jeweler's burial from the same cemetery, shows Oriental immigrants lived and died in Crete around the turn of the millennium. It also belongs to a scattered corpus of inscribed Oriental bowls that document the migration of Semitic craftsmen throughout the Mediterranean.[48] Most important, the Teke inscription means that the Semitic alphabet was in circulation in the Aegean around 1000 B.C., although the earliest Greek adoption of such a writing system cannot be presently dated before the later eighth century.[49]

Epigraphers east and west have long suspected that the Greek alphabet grew from long periods of experimentation and adaption, not a sudden innovation.[50] Crete enjoys several claims to be the first home of the Greek alphabet. Local historians and lexicographers attest to the island's reputation for early writing (Dosiadas, *FGrH* 458 F6, 468 F 1; Photios, Suda s.v. Φοινικεῖα γράμματα), and modern comparisons of early Cretan

ταγένους ἐν Ἀμνυσῷ," *KrChr* 7 (1953) 258–66. K. Davaras and O. Masson, "Cretica: Amnisos et ses inscriptions," *BCH* 107 (1983) 383–401. New investigations make this site more likely to be the main port of Knossos: J. Schäfer and others, "Neue Forschungen der Universität Heidelberg in Amnisos, 1983–85," in ΦΙΛΙΑ ΕΠΗ, 3:44–82. Schäfer's reluctance to admit Oriental influence in Late Bronze Age Aegean architecture (*AA* [1983] 551–57; Chapter 5, n. 45) would not encourage comparisons to Syria and Phoenicia.

[47] Reported by H. Catling, *ARep* (1976–1977), 11–14; M. Sznycer "L'inscription phénicienne de Tekke près de Cnossos," *Kadmos* 18 (1979) 89–93; F. Cross, "Newly Found Inscriptions in Old Canaanite and Early Phoenician Scripts. II: An Archaic Phoenician Inscription from Crete," *BASOR* 238 (1980) 15–17, and "Phoenicians in the West: The Epigraphic Evidence," in *SSA*, 2:118, 125–26 n. 12. Boardman, *Greeks Overseas*, 37, fig. 6; Coldstream, in *Phönizier im Westen*, 263, 271–72. Earlier dates for Attic Protogeometric would reconcile epigraphy and pottery: cf. Saltz, "Greek Geometric Pottery in the East," 288, and A. Yannai, "Raising the Dates of Greek Protogeometric?" *AJA* 86 (1982) 292.

[48] G. Falsone, "La coupe phénicienne de Fortetsa,

Crète. Une reconsidération," in *Studia Phoenicia* 5:181–94. Bronze Age forerunners: see Chapter 5, n. 91. Italy: Markoe, *Phoenician Bowls*, 72–74; M. Heltzer, "A Recently Discovered Phoenician Inscription and the Problem of the Guilds of Metal-casters," and R. Barnett, "Phoenician and Punic Arts and Handicrafts: Some Reflections and Notes," both in *Studi Fenici e Punici*, 119–23, 18–26. At least one silver bowl probably made in Italy is inscribed with the name of its maker: B. d'Agostino and G. Garbini, "La patera orientalizzante da Pontecagnano riesaminata," *StEtr* 45 (1977) 51–62.

[49] O. Murray, *Early Greece* (Sussex, 1980), 91–94; Naveh, *Early History of the Alphabet*, 184: "The antiquity of the Greek alphabet is not a question of epigraphy alone; it is also, and primarily, a historical issue."

[50] Naveh, *Early History of the Alphabet*, 175–86; B. Isserlin, "The Antiquity of the Greek Alphabet," *Kadmos* 22 (1982) 151–63. For a Bronze Age claim: M. Bernal, "On the Transmission of the Alphabet to the Aegean before 1400 B.C.," *BASOR* 267 (1987) 1–19; others dismiss the Teke bowl: R. Wachter, "Zur vorgeschichte des griechischen Alphabets," *Kadmos* 28 (1989) 19–78. See Chapter 5, nn. 25–28, for other discoveries and scholarship.

letter scripts with Phoenician inspire confidence in these claims.[51] Similarities include punctuation, such as "paragraph" divisions, as well as letter forms and agree with the tradition that Crete learned its letters first. For example, the closest equivalent to the Phoenician *yod* appears in the Dreros law code, Cretan digamma resembles Semitic *waw* (*ICr* 4.1–40, from Gortyn), and a right-to-left direction in writing persists in this area into the fifth century, as if Semitic influence were persistent.[52]

Not only morphology points to close and early testimony on Crete with Phoenician letters and their users. Just as most Greeks called the alphabet "Phoenician letters" and attributed their invention or adoption to Kadmos and his Phoenicians, Cretans knew those who could write as ποινικασταί, "phoenicianizers," as if the practitioners of early letters as well as the letters themselves associated with Phoenician origins. On a bronze mitra allegedly from Arkades (Afrati) reused as a plaque for an inscription around 500 B.C., one Spensithios is established as ποινικαστάς of the city. Special privileges were accorded him and his descendants, in exchange for his duties: ποινικάζειν δὲ πόλι καὶ μναμονεύϜεν τὰ δαμόσια . . . τά τε θιήια καὶ τἀνθρώπινα, to "record for the city and remember the city's [decisions] . . . both sacred and secular."[53] The office held by Spensithios has been equated with that of the γραμματεύς at Athens, but his title implies that it was Phoenicians, in Greek areas, who first adopted their letters to a new language and lent their names to letters and their execution. Moreover, his office compares closely with that of Near Eastern secretaries (to be discussed), and it has been argued that he enjoys special status as a foreign worker, not as a citizen.[54] According to the date of the Teke bowl, Greeks could have learned to call the letters of the alphabet Φοινικεῖα γράμματα and the art of writing ποινικάζειν as early as the ninth century, long before they adopted the practice themselves. In fact, a long period when writing was the domain of Phoenicians, alone, before Greek imitation, might help perpetuate such terms.

The city alleged as the provenance of the Spensithios decree, Arkades, produced quantities of Oriental imports and imitations in a cemetery distinctive in burial customs. Boardman, who emphasized the Oriental significance of the Teke jewelery deposit, also

[51] Jeffery, *LSAG*, 310; R. F. Willetts, "Some Characteristics of Archaic Cretan Writing," and Jeffery, "'Αρχαῖα γράμματα: Some Ancient Greek Views," both in *Europa*, 320–31, esp. 326; 152–66.

[52] Willetts and Jeffery in *Europa*, 320–31, 152–66; A. R. Millard, "The Canaanite Linear Alphabet and Its Passage to the Greeks," *Kadmos* 15 (1976) 130–44. W. Johnstone, "Cursive Phoenician and the Archaic Greek Alphabet," *Kadmos* 17 (1978) 151–66.

[53] L. H. Jeffery and A. Morpurgo Davies, "Ποινικαστάς and ποινικάζειν," *Kadmos* 9 (1970) 118–56; A. Raubitschek, "A Mitra Inscribed with a Law," in Hoffman, *Early Cretan Armorers*, 47–49. Attempts to

reduce these words to color terms (G. Edwards and R. Edwards, "Red Letters and Phoenician Writing," *Kadmos* 13 [1974] 48–57) or judicial ones (A. J. Beattie, "Notes on the Spensithios Decree," *Kadmos* 14 [1975] 8–41, argues for a derivation from ποινή) have been defeated: G. P. Edwards and Ruth B. Edwards, "The Meaning and Etymology of ποινικαστάς," *Kadmos* 16 (1977) 131–40; cf. Edwards, *Kadmos*, 23, 112.

[54] H. Van Effenterre, "Le contrat du travail du scribe Spensithios," *BCH* 97 (1973) 31–46; *contra* C. Gorlin, "The Spensithios Decree and Archaic Cretan Civil Status," *ZPE* 74 (1988) 159–65.

first drew attention to burial practices at Arkades, eccentric even within the spectrum of Cretan variations.[55] A form of secondary cremation, sometimes in double vessels, takes exception to the local tradition of cremation or inhumation in tholoi and chambers. The closest parallel for these curious burials in seventh-century Crete, where one vessel is stacked inside another, comes from North Syria, according to Boardman, specifically the Yunus cemetery of Carchemish. Claiming that people do not imitate alien burial customs as readily as decorative motifs, Boardman identified the occupants of the Afrati graves as North Syrians, perhaps even migrants from the Carchemish area after its destruction by the Assyrians.[56] Although scholars now hesistate to identify changes in burial customs with ethnic affiliations, other Mediterranean cemeteries where Phoenicians, Greeks, and natives intermarry and interbury in this period demonstrate similar patterns.[57] Other grave goods from Arkades point to the East, such as Cypro-Phoenician bronze bowls, and this area of Crete also specialized in clay imitations of exotic metalwork found earlier and elsewhere in Crete.[58] The city's chief sanctuary and source of the bronze armor (considered later) had a set of buildings probably meant to display this armor, otherwise eccentric to Greek sacred architecture. Monumental architecture of Oriental inspiration is indicated in a stone palm capital of Egyptianizing style built into a tholos tomb (Figure 29).[59]

Thus the Arkades cemetery demonstrates not only Levantine influence but a distinction in genre, rites, and imports from Knossos or Eastern Crete. This pattern agrees with the implications in epigraphy and monumental art of a constant but varying relationship with the Orient, whose immigrants arrived from several Near Eastern locales, settled in different ways and interacted with local culture along lines outside formal or political colonization. This discontinuity in immigration, with different ethnic, cultural, and linguistic groups arriving from a variety of Levantine centers over several centuries,

[55] Boardman, BSA 62 (1967) 58, 63, compared the burial of the gold ornaments in two pits below the Teke tomb floor with a Near Eastern foundation deposit rather than a Greek burial (R. S. Ellis, Foundation Deposits in Ancient Mesopotamia [New Haven, 1968]). Arkades: Boardman, CAH III.3, 225; in Dädalische Kunst, 20–23; graves investigated and published by D. Levi, "Arkades," ASAA 10–12 (1927–1929) 78–400. M. A. Rizzo, "Arkades," in Creta antica, 257–63; Cf. Near Eastern–type foundation deposits also at Gortyn: Rizza and Scrinari, Gortina, 24–25; Burkert, in Greek Renaissance, 118.

[56] Boardman, in Dädalische Kunst, 21–22, figs. A-F; Greeks Overseas, 60, fig. 31. On the cemetery and chronology of Carchemish, see Bienkowski (cited in n. 57) 81 and I. Winter, "Carchemish ša kišad Puratti," AnatStud 33 (1983) 177–97 (190ff. on defeat by Assyrians in 717 and 700 B.C.).

[57] Cf. the Phoenician cemetery at Khaldeh (Beirut, Lebanon) for similar cremations in amphorae with flat dishes as covers: R. Saidah, Bulletin du Museé de Beyrouth 19 (1966) 51–90; Semmler, in Phönizier im Westen, 322, on Phoenician cremations in Iberia; Buchner, in Phönizier im Westen, 290–96. On cremation and population, see A. Snodgrass, The Dark Age of Greece (Edinburgh, 1971), 14–46; P. Bienkowski, "Some Remarks on the Practise of Cremation in the Levant," Levant 14 (1982) 79–89.

[58] Levi, ASAA 10–12 (1927–1929) 308–11, 372–80, figs. 408, 491; Markoe, Phoenician Bowls, 167–69; Rizzo, "Arkades," in Creta antica, 257–63. Blome, Bildwelt Kretas, 42–44, pl. 19:1–2 .

[59] Levi, ASAA 10–12 (1927–1929) 107, fig. 206; 451, fig. 58b; Boardman, Greeks Overseas, 143, fig. 170 compares it with an Egyptian capital; cf. Cretan Collection at Oxford, 147.

left a Near Eastern impact on Greek culture rich in variety but difficult to classify, much less predict.

In eastern Crete, the bay of Mirabello attracted Oriental interest for two resources attested in archaeology and testimonia. The iron ores respected in the name of "Cape Sidero," the easternmost point where Itanos was established, have been noted by Faure as significant to settlement and the name of the founder-hero, Itanos, is associated with metallurgical discoveries.[60] The purple (murex) species whose extraction kept Korobios the Cretan not only prosperous but well traveled (Herodotus, 4.151) was an active industry on the island of Kouphonissi, as in Libya where Korobios led the Therans.[61] Phoenician settlement is explicit in legend, where the eponymous founder of Itanos is identified as the son of "Phoinix" in inscriptions (*ICr* III.4, 76, 78) and the city is attested as a Phoenician foundation by Stephanus of Byzantium (s.v. Ἴτανος). Although he could have derived this claim from the name "Phoinix," many other Cretan cities seem to bear this name (*ICr* II, 16, 191ff.; 20, 22ff.), also invoked as a sacred witness at Dreros in a sixth-century inscription (*ICr* I.9.84ff., no. I, 30–31, A). The latter document also depicts a curious scene of a two-handled vessel (?) between two Ionic-looking columns; it has been compared with Bronze Age representations, like the libation-pouring scene on the Hagia Triada sarcophagus.[62] But a Near Eastern pillar cult could have inspired both Bronze and Iron Age representations, instead of a case of "continuity" where a Minoan tradition is privileged above potential Near Eastern sources. The connection of a hero with an Eastern name, "Phoinix," to an Orientalizing cult and motif (pillars) suggests an *interpretatio Graeca* of an Oriental convention in the convergence of name and image. Itanos himself, Korobios the purple-fisher, and local landmarks may bear Hellenized Semitic names, according to a few interpreters.[63] The site of Itanos has not produced explicit Levantine evidence as early as in central Crete, but eastern Crete has been less well explored.[64]

[60] Faure, *RA* (1966) 161, on iron near Siteia; cf. Zervantonakis (Chapter 5, n. 75); A. J. Reinach, "Itanos et l'*inventio scuti*," *RHR* 61–62 (1910) 226–27.

[61] Kouphonissi's murex deposits date to the Middle Bronze Age: R. Bosanquet, "Excavations at Palaikastro," *BSA* 9 (1902–1903) 276–77; "Dicte and the Temples of Dictaean Zeus," *BSA* 40 (1939) 70–72; N. Papadakis, "Ἀνασκαφικὲς ἐρευνὲς στὸ Κουφονῆσι Σιτείας," in *Fifth Cretological Congress*, 273–75. D. Reese, "Palaikastro Shells and Bronze Age Purple-dye Production in the Mediterranean Basin," *BSA* 82 (1987) 204; "Industrial Exploitation of Murex Shells: Purple-dye and Lime Production at Sidi Khrebish, Benghazi (Berenice)," *Libyan Studies* 11 (1979–1980) 79–93. This resource might have helped attract Levantines to Crete, especially if known since the Midroussa) name of Kythera is related to Lakonia's

attractions for the Levant: Chapter 5, n. 141.

[62] H. Van Effenterre, "Une copie grecque d'une fresque minoenne?" *CRAI* (1960) 117–27; "Le culte de Phoinix à Dréros," *BCH* 85 (1961) 553–68.

[63] V. Berard, *Les Phéniciens et l'Odyssée*, 337, derived Itanos from West Semitic (Hebrew *etan*: Amos 5:24); R. Dussaud, "L'influence orientale en Crète," *Syria* 18 (1937) 233, and "Itanos," *Syria* 26 (1949) 394–95, also identifies "he who (belongs) to the people of Itanos" in a Punic inscription from Hadrumetum; Astour, *Hellenosemitica*, 140–41, on Semitic derivations for Itanos, Korobios (*qorob*?), and Cape Salmone (< *Salmon*? Judges 9:48; Psalm 68:15). Cf. St. Alexiou, "Une nouvelle inscription de Panormos-Apollonia en Crète," in *Aux origines de l'Hellénisme*, 323–27, for an archaic name, "ΘΑΔΙΟΣ," possibly Semitic.

[64] Itanos: See excavation report by J. Deshayes,

The sanctuary of Zeus at Palaikastro, a coastal city south of Itanos, has produced more Orientalia than Itanos itself. Its most celebrated document, an inscribed Hellenistic hymn to Diktaian Zeus involving the Kouretes, seems to illustrate the story depicted on an Idaian Cave shield.[65] The Greek hymn has always been cited as a Hellenic text "illustrated" on the Orientalizing shield from the Idaian Cave: Near Eastern looking "genius" figures with raised cymbals drown out Rhea's birth pangs in order to conceal the birth of Zeus from his father, Kronos, identified as the central figure. Instead the story of the birth and accession of Zeus, cognate with the Near Eastern myth of Kumarbi, may have drawn details from scenes like those on the shield, not directly associated with the birth of a challenger-god in Oriental antecedents. This link between image and story duplicates a pattern suggested earlier in this chapter, where Near Eastern motifs on portable arts contribute to Greek narratives later seen in poetry (Plates 13–18). Before the Hellenistic period, the cult of Zeus at Palaikastro may have displayed more Oriental features, like his cults elsewhere in Crete—at Amnisos, for example (see n. 46). Its archaic phases were rich in Orientalia, such as bronze shields and monumental art forms like architectural terracotta revetments, and the sanctuary suggests an early archaic life characteristic of the sanctuaries of Sparta.

Of all the archaic shrines on Crete, the "temple" at Dreros best illustrates the influence of Near Eastern social and legal practices on early Crete. The akropolis was the site of an early archaic building similar to those of Prinias in plan (without its limestone sculpture) and probably equally Levantine in form.[66] North Syrian art may also have inspired the trinity of hammered bronze statues found in association with the temple. These early and experimental images have been attributed to Near Eastern immigrants and compare closely to miniature figures from Crete.[67] Considered prototypes of Greek σφυρήλατον or "hammer-driven" bronze sculpture, these statues of bronze foil are actually closest to Syrian limestone figures covered in gold and silver foil.[68] Although

BCH 75 (1951) 201–9, for Geometric and archaic sherds. For a recent discovery with Near Eastern connections, see C. Davaras, "Une tombe à voûte en Crète orientale," in Aux origines de l'Hellénisme, 297–310.

[65] Palaikastro: excavation reports in BSA 7–12 (1901–1906) and BSA suppl. 1 (1923); Hymn to Zeus: R. C. Bosanquet and G. Murray, BSA 15 (1908–1909) 339–65 (ICr III.2.2); Verbruggen, Le Zeus crétois, chap. 5, 101–11, with earlier bibliography (West, Guarducci, etc.); Markoe, Phoenician Bowls, 82–83, pl. 168. For an alternate view of the Kouretes myth as an aition for infant sacrifice, see O'Bryhim, APA Abstracts, 1990, 185.

[66] In reporting on Dreros, S. Marinatos, BCH 60 (1936) 234–35, emphasizes its Minoan features but his

analogy (fig. 16), the Shrine of the Double Axes at Knossos, compares with Near Eastern shrines (above, Chapter 5, n. 53). Cf. Beyer, Dreros und Prinias, 13–18, for a new study that still stresses its "Subminoan" form (cf. Burkert, Greek Religion, 89). E. Thomas, "Kretisch-Mykenische und Frühgriechische Kultbänke," in Kolloquium zur Ägäischen Vorgeschichte, ed. W. Schiering (Mannheim, 1987), 91–97.

[67] Boardman, Cretan Collection in Oxford, 137ff.; Lembesi, in Οἱ Στῆλες τοῦ Πρινιᾶ, 87ff., and Blome, Bildwelt Kretas, 12–15, 78–80, pl. 4:1–2; cf. a miniature kriophoros in gold from the Teke graves: pp. 10–13, fig. 5.

[68] As noted by Renfrew in discussing the Syrian bronzes with gold "heads" from Phylakopi (Archaeology of Cult, 302, 441). Even the massive limestone

oft-cited as the earliest certifiable Greek cult images and found in situ, the bronze statuettes were not excavated under archaeological supervision but broken in an accidental
discovery by local farmers; they have only been restored on the "bench" in the temple.[69]
The closest analogies for this type of shrine with benches date to the Late Bronze Age
Aegean, a parallel usually emphasized for the sake of Minoan "continuity" but which
should also be appreciated for its Levantine legacy.[70] Nor is their identification with the
Greek deities Leto, Apollo, and Artemis assured, although Apollo was eventually worshiped at Dreros. Relatives of the Dreros statues—gold miniatures from the Idaian Cave
and monumental limestone reliefs from Gortyn—are formulaic in early Cretan religious
imagery but not necessarily members of a Greek pantheon.[71]

What accompanied, if not inspired, such new religious forms in art were new cult
practices, among the richest but most complex of Oriental influences on early Crete.
This Eastern debt survives in myth as in cult, and should be integrated with suggestions
from the archaeological record. The modern view favors the Minoan factor in survival,
rather than the Oriental heritage common to Late Bronze and early Iron Age culture on
Crete (as in the cult of Phoinix at Dreros and its temple: see n. 62). Religious influence
from the East was active since the Late Bronze Age, when religious iconography in the
Aegean was closely connected to the eastern Mediterranean, and thereafter survived on
Crete in better health than elsewhere. The Greeks themselves remembered Crete for its
contributions to religion, claiming that its natives invented τιμὰς καὶ θυσίας καὶ τὰς
περὶ τὰ μυστήρια τελετὰς (Diodorus, 5.77), all of which appear first in the Levant.
In legend, the Telchines of Crete were renowned not only for their art but for their
invention of divine images (Diodorus, 5.55.2), and were thought to practice τάς τε
ἐπῴδας καὶ τελετὰς καὶ μυστήρια (5.64). The island was the birthplace of Zeus, home
to priests for Delphi (Homeric Hymn to Apollo 388–544) and of Cretans like Epimenides
who purify Athens (Athenaion Politeia 1; Diogenes Laertius, 1.10.110). Certain Cretan

---

head from Amnisos may have been covered with
metal foil: Adams, Orientalizing Sculpture, 5–6, pl. 1.
Near Eastern parallels include the bronze "smiting"
figurines like those from Phylakopi, Tiryns, Sounion,
but also more distant Orientalia: J. Makkay, "Archaeological Examples of Gold-Masked Statue and Mace,"
Orientalia 56 (1987) 69–73 (on a text from Sultantepe,
with parallels from Hittite literature and archaeology). The σφυρήλατον technique may have survived in Sparta, where it is attributed to pupils of Dipoinos and Skyllis or Daidalos: Pausanias, 3.17.6.

[69] Statues reported by S. Marinatos, BCH 60 (1936)
220, 224; Romano, "Early Greek Cult Images,"
284–93.

[70] Thus Marinatos, BCH 60 (1936) 234–35, compares

the Dreros temple with the Shrine of the Double
Axes at Knossos; Renfrew, Archaeology of Cult, 241,
compares Phylakopi's Late Bronze Age shrine with
Dreros's.

[71] Blome, Bildwelt Kretas, 80, cautions against
equating these Cretan triads with Greek deities. Cf.
Rizza and Scrinari, Gortina, 251–52; Th. Hadzisteliou-
Price, "Double and Multiple Representations in
Greek Art and Religious Thought," JHS 91 (1971) 48–
69, for Egyptian parallels, or C. Schaeffer, "Triade
hittite sur un pendentif en electrum de Ras Shamra,"
Ugaritica 3 (1956) 94–95. F. Brommer, "Gott oder
Mensch," JdI 101 (1986) 49, suggests the Dreros fig-
ures are votives, not divine images.

practices suggest a Semitic heritage, such as the "worship" of the pig (Athenaeus, 10.375/6 = Agathokles of Babylon) or even sacrifice to it, at Praisos (Athenaeus, 4.203), comparable with the prohibition against pork in sacred laws from Thasos (Chapter 5, n. 188). Pigs are often offered in Punic contexts in association with infant sacrifice (see the Pozo Moro relief: Chapter 7, n. 42), a tradition that may have been practiced on Crete in the Late Bronze Age and survived in the legend of human tribute to the Minotaur (Chapter 5). Foundation deposits (e.g., at Gortyn, Arkades; see n. 55) recall Near Eastern practices, as do the burials of animals at Prinias, Kavousi, and Knossos (n. 37). The tradition of δημιοεργοί who practiced religious as well as artistic specialties seems closely linked on Crete, such that these innovations may have migrated, together, from the Orient.

A second critical sphere of Oriental influence in Crete determined that most fundamental and famous of the island's developments: laws. Cretan law codes were among the earliest and most abundant as well as the most admired in the Greek world, such that sages and lawgivers from other states—especially Lykourgos of Sparta—traditionally visited Crete for inspiration.[72] The antiquity of law codes in the Near East and their similarities to early Cretan law first encouraged comparison.[73] The fact that Crete also learned how to write down such laws from Levantine practitioners of the alphabet reinforces the hypothesis: were function and form of the alphabet adopted under similar circumstances and from the same sources?[74] For specific Near Eastern legal and religious expressions formalizing political decisions passed into the Greek epigraphic tradition from the Near East, and they appear first in Crete. In particular, the formulaic heading θεοί has been traced to Near Eastern curse formulas found on Babylonian boundary stones and funerary markers (kudurrus).[75] The early law code from Dreros rendered this expression in its full and original form, restored as θίος ὀλοίον, or "may the god destroy," a Greek equivalent of the Semitic imprecation common on boundary stones

[72] Jeffery, LSAG, 310–14; R. Willetts, in CAH III.3, 234–48; R. Willetts, "Cretan Law and Early Greek Society," and G. Manganaro, "Epigrafia e istituzioni di Creta," both in Antichità Cretesi 2:22–31, 39–58; M. Gagarin, Early Greek Law (Berkeley, 1986), 81–86.

[73] By Boardman in "Orientalien auf Kreta," in Dädalische Kunst, 22–25, citing M. Mühl, Untersuchungen zur altorientalischen und althellenischen Gesetzgebung, Klio Beih. 29 (1933). Cf. S. Segert, "Form and Function of Ancient Israelite, Greek and Roman Legal Sentences," in Orient and Occident, 161–65, esp. 163, for Hebrew parallels; M. Smith, "East Mediterranean Law Codes of the Early Iron Age," in H. L. Ginsberg Volume, Eretz-Israel 14 (Jerusalem, 1978) 38–43; Weinfeld, in Mesopotamien und seine Nachbarn, 2:491–538,

for a comparison of the reforms of Nehemiah and Solon. Gagarin, Early Greek Law, 126–29, 132–35, rejects Near Eastern influence on Greek law codes as "possible, but unlikely" (p. 136).

[74] On the relationship between law and literacy, see H. Immerwahr, "Early Greek Literacy: The Evidence of Written Law," AJA 90 (1986) 178–79; J. Goody, The Logic of Writing and the Organization of Society (Cambridge, 1986), chap. 4, "The Letter of the Law."

[75] R. Pounder, "The Origin and Meaning of Theoi in Greek Inscription Headings" (Ph.D. diss., Brown University, 1975), 83ff.; "The Origin of θεοί as Inscription-Heading," Studies Presented to S. Dow, 243–50.

since the Kassite period. Transmission of the formula from Mesopotamia to Crete was probably the work of Aramaeans or Phoenicians, for they left similar versions of the formula on North Syrian temples and Cypriote tombs. Independent of this epigraphic argument, visual motifs on *kudurrus* have been compared with Orientalizing griffin protomes, which would mean that the same monuments influenced other aspects of early Greek culture.[76] Another inscription from Dreros, bilingual in Greek and Eteocretan, contains phrases that have been compared with the description of the Tabernacle in Exodus 26.3, a further link between Greek and Near Eastern sacred architecture if not specifially between Daidalos and Bezalel.[77]

Another link between Cretan writing, law, and the Orient is established in the Spensithios decree. The ποινικασταί who "remembered" and "recorded" civic decisions in early Cretan communities played roles more familiar in Near Eastern judicial contexts, where scribes often inherited their office and the kind of responsibilities and privileges accorded Spensithios in Crete.[78] During Sennacherib's campaigns against Judea in the reign of Hezekiah, the Assyrian king sends three officials—the Tartan, Rabsaris, and Rabshakeh—to Jerusalem. Instead of the king himself, three complimentary officials— Eliakim the household overseer, Shebnah the secretary, and Joah the recorder—met them and asked to negotiate in Aramaic rather than in the language of Judah (in Hebrew: 2 Kings 18.18, 26, 37; cf. Isaiah 36.3, 22). Similar offices and combinations of "recorder" and "scribe" are attested under David (2 Samuel 8.16, 20.24; and 1 Chronicles 18.15), Solomon (1 Kings 3), and Josiah (2 Chronicles 34.8). Not only the two offices as γραμματεύς and "rememberer" (Hebrew *mazkîr*; cf. ὑπομνήματο) but their close involvement with public policy in the community are all functions inherited by Spensithios. With many of these practical aspects, the concept of a legal code as well as its permanent record could have been introduced to Crete through Near Eastern example or with immigrants establishing communities similar to those in the Levant. An encouraging and instructive analogy for this process is the Old Assyrian colonization of Anatolia, where "the use of the Assyrian language with its inherent scribal and legal traditions must have paved the way for conceptual influence by Assyrian colonists."[79]

The contents of the archaic Cretan law codes imply a delicate balance between the different elements of a mixed population in early Crete, with further parallels to the Assyrian colonies in Anatolia and other Near Eastern contexts. A double-inscribed stele from Lyttos in a mixed dialect excludes ἀλλοπολιάται from the city, on one face, and

---

[76] N. Smith, "Near Eastern Origins for Griffin Protomes on Cauldrons?" *AJA* 90 (1986) 186.

[77] J. Dus, "The Dreros Bilingual and the Tabernacle of the Ancient Israelites," *JSS* 10 (1965) 54–58.

[78] H. van Effenterre, "Le contrat de travail du scribe Spensithios," *BCH* 97 (1973) 31–46; Edwards and Edwards, *Kadmos* 16 (1977) 136; Burkert, *Orien-*

talisierende Epoche, 30–35. Goody, *Logic of Writing*, 41, on the hereditary and privileged status of scribes in Israelite kingdoms.

[79] Kl. Veenhof, "The Old Assyrian Merchants and Their Relations with the Native Population of Anatolia," in *Mesopotamien und seine Nachbarn*, 1:152–53.

allots land for the κοινωνία and the σύγκρισις on the other.[80] The famous Gortyn law code provided special rights for children of mixed marriages, as if intermarriage had created complex problems for inheritance.[81] Similar provisions regulating dual status among citizens are characteristic of mixed populations (e.g. in Sparta, the Lipari islands, and in Hellenistic cities with Levantine residents).[82] The guarantee of rights among different groups may arise in mixed communities for practical reasons more often than for principles of equality. Even the distinction so cherished in classical Greek thought between ἐλεύθερος and δοῦλος first appears in the Gortyn law code.[83] In other words, it may have been coexistence of social groups or rival claims to property or legal rights among them that encouraged principles of equality and of "Greek" democracy, just as Greek colonization, for example, introduced equitable land distribution among settlers. In this scenario of constitutional evolution through conflict before ideology, Crete was remembered as an early and progressive innovator among Greek communities, but it may have acquired this status because it was the most mixed in population.

The analogy of the Assyrian colonies, and the archaeology of Levantines in Crete, depicts collaboration between foreign merchant-manufacturers and a local elite in terms of status or skills. The latter's power and prestige were enhanced by the relationships they developed with foreign entrepreneurs who offered opportunities for exchange of local resources with exotic prestige items. This arrangement common in early European communities of the Iron Age is a highly fruitful model for understanding the rise of Greek archaic aristocracy, who identified strongly with members of foreign royalty by adopting their names and ideology, as early as the seventh century.[84]

This social effect, along with the alphabet, belongs to the latest and most profound influences that the Orient had on the developing urban culture of Greece. The experience of Crete and its influence on other early Greek constitutions encourages a closer comparison of Solon's reforms with Near Eastern ones. The rise of hendiadystic concepts like "justice and righteousness" in the Near East (Phoenician ṣdq mšr and Biblical mšpṭ wṣdqh: Genesis 18.19; Isaiah 9.4, 16.5; Jeremiah 23.5, 33.15) has been compared

---

[80] H. and M. Van Effenterre, "Nouvelles lois archaïques de Lyttos," *BCH* 109 (1985) 157–88.

[81] *ICr* VII.1–10. Residence and status were matrilineal at Gortyn, a tradition it is tempting to associate with a Semitic heritage. Cf. Kleenhof, in *Mesopotamien und seine Nachbarn*, 1:150–53, for similar legal provisions in a community of Assyrians and Anatolians practicing intermarriage.

[82] T. Figueira, "The Lipari Islanders and Their System of Communal Property," *CA* 3 (1984) 179–206. Cf. the arrangements in Assyrian colonies: Curtin, *Cross-Cultural Trade*, 67–70. See M.-F. Baslez, "Les communautés d'Orientaux dans la cîté grecque: Formes de sociabilités et modèles associatifs," in *L'é-*

tranger dans le Monde Grec, ed. R. Lonis (Nancy, 1988), 134–58.

[83] As noted by Raaflaub, *Entdeckung der Freiheit*, 19 n. 70. The Athenian "discovery" of this distinction was also encouraged by contact with non-Greek cultures (as after the Persian wars): see Chapter 11.

[84] Cf. P. Wells, *Culture Contact and Culture Change* and *Farms, Towns and Villages*, 102–16, for Mediterranean influence on European elite and Europe's urban culture. Greek adoption of foreign elite names and images: see Chapter 5, n. 204. Markoe, *Phoenician Bowls*, 75–86, on Orientalia among wealthy Etruscans; Gunter, "Models of the Orient."

with Hesiod's ἰθείας δίκας (*Erga* 225–26, 230), equally "royal" in their application, whether to King David (2 Samuel 8.15) or to Hesiod's βασιλεῖς. Moreover, these intellectual developments accompanied practical measures extended by royal decree to relieve the pressure of debts, taxes, and enslavement on the poor. Specific and striking agreements with Greek phrases and practices deserve close scrutiny. The remission of debts or ṣmt maṣa declared by Nehemiah as governor of Judah (426–24 B.C.) translates literally as σεισαχθεῖα or "shaking off of burdens," and the details of Nehemiah's reforms—remission of debts, restoration of mortgaged property, liberation of enslaved debtors (Nehemiah 5; cf. Jeremiah 23.33–39) overlap closely with those of Solon. Both Nehemiah (5.12; 10.1, 26) and Solon (*Athenaion Politeia*. 6.1) adjure their people to keep the law, and both established new codifications.[85] If, when, and how a transmission of concepts and phrases took place is a complex question. Comparison of Solon and Nehemiah depends on later witnesses: Aristotle (or the author of the *Athenaion Politeia*) and Plutarch for testimonia on Solon and the latter's poems, and the "Chronicler" author of Nehemiah, in the fourth or third centuries B.C. Later cross-fertilization could explain "Oriental" elements accumulated by the tradition of Solon as a legislator and lawgiver, rather than early archaic influence from the Near East on his practices. For example, Diodorus may exaggerate the debt of Hellenic institutions to Eastern prototypes, when he compares Solon's σεισαχθεῖα to the early Egyptian example of Bocchoris (717–711 B.C.; Diodorus, 1.79. 3.64; 98.1). On the other hand, modern scholarship may have underestimated, if not denied, the extent of such Oriental influence. Religious practices and communal institutions are not adopted casually or for superficial reasons, but classicists have been late to accept the idea of more profound transformations.[86] The presence of Oriental residents influenced more than motifs and media, metallurgy and minor arts: an immigrant population penetrates the fabric of society and religion and determines changes in beliefs, practices, and institutions throughout social and religious life.

Among these, the early Greek polis itself, sponsor of early law codes, may derive far more from non-Greek sources than classical scholarship has recognized, although Aristotle did. His celebrated comparison of the Spartan constitution (in particular, its dyarchy) to that of Crete and Carthage highlights the Phoenician background of these cities.[87] In Greek tradition, a pair of heroes tracing their ancestry to Herakles are in-

---

[85] Weinfeld, in *Mesopotamien und seine Nachbarn*, 1:499–501, on Solon and Nehemiah. John Herington suggests that the ἀξώνες that displayed Athenian laws (Immerwahr, *AJA* 90 [1986] n. 74) might derive from polygonal cylinders of Near Eastern cuneiform inscriptions.

[86] Bernal, *Black Athena*, on scholarly resistance to the Orient. Levin, in *Europa*, 194, on classicists' "mistrust of Semitic influence" in fear of "bibliolatry and

Phoenicomania. . . . They acknowledge some specific borrowings—notably of the alphabet—which they think can be attributed to slight or casual intercourse. For they do not readily conceive of any association between Greeks and Semites so intimate that notable and not superficial features of one society transmitted to the other."

[87] Drews, *AJP* 100 (1979) 45–58, advances this bold argument; cf. A. Snodgrass, *Archaic Greece* (London,

voked to explain the unusual dual monarchy maintained in Sparta. "Herakles" may hide his Phoenician counterpart, Melqart, for officials at Sidon and Tyre attest to a system of government close to the early Greek polis.[88] If parallel civic forms can be integrated with the archaeological evidence for Oriental immigrants and their effects on urbanization, new political institutions may be an additional Eastern legacy to Greece.

Thus archaeology and anthropology expand the picture of early Crete to suggest activity more Levantine than Greek, which thrived as long as the network that kept it alive—the Assyrians and their appetite for iron. Archaic Cretan culture disappears, almost literally, around 600 B.C., when scores of cities seem to have been abandoned, and even the contents of sanctuaries are reduced to a trickle of finds.[89] All the Iron Age cemeteries of Knossos were abandoned, and its Demeter sanctuary is barely active until the late fifth century. After centuries of local creativity, Cretan achievements in Orientalizing bronzes do not outlast the early archaic armor, "heavily dependent on Peloponnesian models," in the early sixth century.[90] Most dramatic is the finale of Crete's early experiments in monumental limestone sculpture and architecture, which have no direct successors in the marble schools of the Cyclades.[91] Religious architecture on Crete maintains archaic forms into the Hellenistic period, as if isolation from innovation, not just religious conservatism, prevailed after major emigration of artists.[92] The designers of Crete's early archaic buildings and statutes apparently found new markets and media elsewhere, according to literature and archaeology. Celebrated Cretan artists like Dipoinos and Skyllis, "sons" or "pupils" of Daidalos, migrate to the Peloponnese (Pausanias, 2.15.1), while architects and engineers like Chersiphron and Metagenes from Knossos are soon employed on colossal temple projects in Ionia (Vitruvius, 10.2.12; Pliny, *Naturalis Historia* 7.125). Legendary craftsmen like the Telchines migrate to Rhodes, and even

---

1980), on early Greek and Phoenician cities (pp. 31–32, 90, 121); Van Effenterre, *La cîté grecque*, 42.

[88] Drews cites Diodorus 16.45.1 for Sidon, Josephus, *Contra Apionem* 155–58 for Tyre; for suspiciously "democratic" civic decisions taken by Punic and Phoenician cities, see M. Sznycer, "L'assemblée du peuple dans les cîtés puniques d'après les temoignages epigraphiques," *Semitica* 25 (1975) 47–68; S. Moscati, in *Accademia Nazionale dei Lincei. Atti dei Convegni Lincei*, 39, 45ff., 53ff. D. van Berchem, "Sanctuaires d'Hercule-Melqart. Contribution à l'étude de l'expansion phénicienne en Mediterranée," *Syria* 41 (1967) 73–109; Bonnet, *Melqart*.

[89] Demargne, *Crète dédalique*, chap. IV.4: "La Crète du VIe siècle: L'arrêt brusque de la renaissance crétoise"; N. Kontoleon, "Παρατηρήσεις εἰς τὴν δαιδαλικὴν τέχνην τῆς Κρήτης," in *Third Cretological Congress*, 153; Boardman, *CAH* III.3, 223, 230–33; *Cretan Collection at Oxford*, 148–49. Robertson, *History of*

Greek Art, 30, claims Crete's abrupt decline at the end of the seventh century does not revive until Theotokopoulos (El Greco).

[90] Boardman, "Archaic Finds at Knossos," *BSA* 67 (1962) 29; Hoffmann, *Early Cretan Armorers*, 41–46, "Chronology." Coldstream, "Dorian Knossos and Aristotle's Villages," in *Aux origines de l'Hellénisme*, 321, calls the sixth century the true "Dark Age" of Crete: cf. Coldstream, *Knossos. The Sanctuary of Demeter* (London, 1973), 182; Prinias: Rizza and Scrinari, *Gortina*, 92–97.

[91] Adams, *Orientalizing Sculpture*, 2; see review of Démargne, *La Crète dédalique*, by Dunbabin, *Gnomon* 24 (1952) 195–97; Boardman, in *Fourth Cretological Congress*, 43–47.

[92] In his forthcoming handbook of Greek architecture, Frederick Cooper analyzes a number of "early" temples on Crete, beginning with Olous, which may be archaizing or archaistic (postclassical).

lawgivers like Epimenides visit Athens in time to purify the city after Kylon's murder and assist Solon design his reforms (*Athenaion Politeia* 1; Diogenes Laertius, 1.10.110). At some point, Crete exported religion as well as craftsmanship and constitutional reforms. Epimenides was equally celebrated for introducing mysteries abroad (Porphyry, *De Abstinentia* 4.19 = Euripides, *Cretans* frag. 472; Athenaeus, 7.282) as he was for his constitutional genius, and various Daktyls established the altar of Zeus at Olympia (Herakles Daktylos: Pausanias, 2.31.10) and the Olympic Games (Pausanias, 5.7.6–10). Cretans were enlisted as priests of Apollo at Delphi (*Homeric Hymn to Apollo* 388–544) and even introduced Demeter to eastern Attika, perhaps as merchants relocating to Euboia and Boiotia if not as holy men (*Homeric Hymn to Demeter* 122–28). In the archaeological record, these legends may be reflected, if not inspired by, the export of Cretan bronzes to major Greek sanctuaries, along with their manufacturers.[93]

Among merchants and manufacturers, emigration absorbed the population elsewhere, probably as a response to Crete's economic collapse and the decline of opportunities on the island. The most conspicuous example of this historic migration is the foundation of Cyrene around 600 B.C. by Therans and Cretans (Herodotus, 4.151–53; cf. Tacitus, 5.2), a date confirmed by Cretan pottery in North Africa.[94] The arrival of Samians, later Aiginetans, in western Crete (Kydonia: Herodotus, 3.57–59) implies that Aegean Greeks appropriated Cretan opportunities in resources and trade after Levantine networks relocated toward the west. Other points of Phoenician settlement in the Aegean may have been affected, as well, although none as dramatically as Crete. Lakonia lost its ivory carvers after the seventh century, some to cheaper materials available locally (e.g., bone) and some to new markets elsewhere. Meanwhile, Sparta's sculptors migrated elsewhere in search of employment.[95]

Explanations for this disintegration range from natural disasters and internal warfare or invasion by other Greeks, to cultural failures.[96] It is far more likely that Babylon's defeat of Assyria and siege of Tyre had an indirect but drastic effect on the "gateway communities" of Crete, which lost their Oriental sponsor. The fall of Nineveh im-

---

[93] E.g. J. Marcadé, "Un casque crétois trouvé à Delphes," *BCH* 73 (1949) 421–36; E. Kunze, "Ein kretisches Meisterwerk des 7. Jhdts. vor Chr. in Olympia," in *Second Cretological Congress*, 196–97; Hoffman, *Early Cretan Armorers*, 50–53, for dedications of Cretan armor from Olympia and Delphi. While votive armor could be booty captured on Crete by other Greeks (Samians, Aiginetans), vessels are also concentrated in these sanctuaries: Markoe, *Phoenician Bowls*, 205–6 (G4).

[94] Boardman and Hayes, *Excavations at Tocra, 1963–65. Part I: The Archaic Deposits*, *BSA* suppl. 4 (1966) 14, 78–79; cf. *Part II: The Archaic and Later Deposits*, *BSA* suppl. 10 (1973) 36–37, 73. Cf. Chapter 5, nn. 160–62.

[95] Carter, *Greek Ivory-Carving*, 287–92, on archaeological evidence and testimonia (e.g., the sculptors Dorykleidas, Theokles, and Medon) and *AJA* 93 (1989) 374–76, on ivory and bone (e.g., the career of the artist Hegylos). If Sparta's iron resources had attracted Phoenician traders serving Assyria in the first place, their disappearance around 600 B.C. agrees with the evidence from Crete.

[96] A war with Sparta (Pausanias, 2.21.3), for example, has been blamed for the decline of Crete; Boardman, *CAH* III.3, 230, suggests a climatic or physiological disaster; N. Kontoleon, *Aspects de la Grèce préclassique* (Paris, 1970), 85–87, blamed the lack of a true *polis* in Crete for inhibiting its development of

pressed the Greek imagination (Phokylides, frag. 4) but must have had a far more devastating effect on the Aegean economic sector in trade with the Orient. The dissolution of the Phoenico-Aramaean network after the fall of the Assyrian Empire affected Crete more dramatically and irrevocably than any other province of Greece, perhaps precisely because it was so intimately (and economically) a province of the Orient. Ezekiel's lament for the city of Tyre (27.27) mourns losses apparently experienced indirectly by Crete after the fall of Assyria:

> Your riches, your wares, your merchandise,
>> your mariners and your pilots,
> Your caulkers, your dealers in merchandise,
>> and all of your men of war who are in you,
> with all your company that is in your midst,
>> sink into the heart of the seas
>> on the day of your ruin.

The colorful and wealthy array of men and merchandise recited in poetry and prose (27.3–25; cf. Joel 3.6) may include a reference to Greeks, if "Jawan" represent "Ionians."[97] Their exchange of metals and men with Tyre confirms the Homeric picture of Phoenician traffic in metal vessels and captives or slaves, and reminds classicists of the other commodity attractive to Levantine markets: chattel, whether kidnapped or purchased. The fall of Tyre and other cities of the coastal Levant to Babylon apparently was reflected in the Aegean, where Crete experienced a devastating blow to its material prosperity, similar to that experienced in other communities in the Mediterranean enriched by Phoenician trade. In Etruria, the abrupt end to Oriental imports in the early sixth century has been traced to the same event: the Babylonian destruction of Tyre and a shift to western Mediterranean Punic trade patterns, with "Carthage's taking the lead in the mercantile empire."[98] This change in external relations resembles other patterns, such as in the early European communities first stimulated by Mediterranean trade in the archaic period. Once the Greeks decreased their interest in European resources or diverted it via Massalia, that network disintegrated, to be replaced by connections up the Adriatic and through the Po valley.[99]

As suggested in the conclusion to Chapter 5, this interpretation of trade patterns within the Aegean and abroad provides a new background for contemplating the archaic period (sixth century) in Greece. The activity of mixed Levantine-Greek enterprise

---

archaic culture; Blome, *Bildwelt Kretas*, 108 "Kreta hat sich künstlerisch in der Ausbildung der dädalischen Tektonik erschöpft"; Verlinden, *Les statuettes*, 172.

[97] E. Lipiński, "Products and Brokers of Tyre according to *Ezekiel* 27," in *Studia Phoenicia*, 3:213–20; cf. his "The Elegy on the Fall of Sidon in Isaiah 23," in

H. L. Ginsberg Volume, Eretz-Israel 14 (Jerusalem, 1978) 79–88; Niemeyer, *JRGZM* 31 (184) 90.

[98] J. MacIntosh Turfa, "International Contacts: Commerce, Trade and Foreign Affairs," in *Etruscan Life and Afterlife*, ed. L. Bonfante (Detroit, 1986), 68.

[99] P. Wells and L. Bonfante, "West-central Europe

is inherited by the Greek elite, and may have contributed to the rise of tyrants in various states, while interstate commerce, as it were, became the dominion of Panhellenic sanctuaries and their controlling leagues. Crete did not participate in this new world except by exporting its specialists, and hence the island's political and economic importance did not revive until the Hellenistic and Roman periods. Precisely for this dormancy in culture, Crete, like Sparta, invited foreign fantasies disparaging or romanticizing its culture. The island's absence at the battle of Salamis established its lack of prestige in the classical period, and opened it to the vilification applied to Minos. As usual, the earliest witnesses, in poetry and art examined in the next section, are far more benign to the Cretan past, free from the prejudice of classical revision.

MINOS AND MOSES

Τί γὰρ ἐστι Πλάτων ἢ Μωυσῆς ἀττικίζων;

For what else is Plato except Moses speaking Attic Greek?

—Numenios of Apamaea (Clement, *Stromateis* 1.22.150.1)

The fate of archaic Crete represents an eccentric and isolated version of the Orientalizing experience in Greece, intensified by the island's early, continuous, and thorough contact with the Near East. Several centuries of this intimate and profound exchange produced innovations in art that did not evolve into Panhellenic archaic and classical patterns, for history turned its back on Crete after 600 B.C. Instead, the effects of early contact survived in legend: Greek memory helps modern discoveries illuminate the particular experience of Crete, rescuing the Orientalizing period from its marginalized status as an archaeological phase. The challenge of this chapter is to correlate the complexity of Cretan early Iron Age art with its mythological and ritual traditions. The comparison of the Idaian shield and the Palaikastro hymn in the previous section suggests that many early scenes in Crete remained close to Levantine parallels before integration into Greek religion. Myth and ritual were not the only two partners in the dialogue of Greek religion; art was often a vital third participant. Cult practices millennia old found new representations just as they inspired new etiologies, rarely codified as a fixed set of tales or beliefs. The story of Daidalos exemplifies this process, building epic episodes onto a rich iconographic tradition, repeatedly crystallized in a particular historical occasion and setting.

and the Mediterranean: The Decline in Trade in the   Wells, *Culture Contact and Culture Change*, 102.
Fifth Century B.C.," *Expedition* 21 (1979) 18–24; cf.

Archaeology has forged modern perspectives on Crete, and the discoveries summarized in the preceding section discourage a sentimental hold on the "Minoan" past. A Levantine component in early Crete is manifest already, however subtle, in epic poetry. Cited primarily as the home of Idomeneus in the *Iliad*, in the *Odyssey* the largest island in the Aegean provides a locale for adventures real and fictional.[100] An informal account of Crete inside a tale-within-a-tale—Odysseus's false adventures in Crete, as narrated to Penelope—makes Crete a highly urbanized, polyglot society, an island of ninety to a hundred cities with at least six different ethnic and linguistic groups: ἄλλη δ᾽ ἄλλων γλῶσσα μεμιγμένη (*Odyssey* 19.177). The detailed census that follows, although often dismissed as interpolation, names Achaians, Eteocretans, Kydonians, Pelasgians, and even Dorians, in their only appearance in the Homeric corpus. Few of these proper names can be equated with culture or language groups, a common problem in Homeric philology. The Pelasgians, for example, are associated elsewhere in Homer with Aeolis and Thessaly; are the Kydonians colonists from Samos (Herodotus, 3.44) or native to Crete (cf. *Odyssey* 3.292)? Do the Dorians correspond to their early Iron Age counterparts who settled Crete, or only Knossians? "Achaians" are too common in epic terminology to represent a specific group, such as the Mycenaean occupants of Knossos or their descendants. Most intriguing of all are the enigmatic Eteocretans, Crete's earliest inhabitants (Diodorus calls them ἀρχαιότατοι and αὐτόχθονες: 5.64.1), associated with eastern Crete both in non-Greek inscriptions as yet undeciphered and in history (Strabo locates them in the Praisos area: 10.4.6). Scholars have made them Minoan or Anatolian descendants and have rendered their documents into a number of known languages, none decisively.[101] The Semitic connection has been argued with more publicity than others, but presumes too many acts of faith, such as accepting Minoan Linear A as Semitic and then the Eteocretans as exclusive descendants of those who spoke it.[102] Some letters and words compare closely to Semitic ones, and the coincidence of early Phoenician traits with local Linear B survivals suggests fertile ground for the home of the first alphabet in Eteocretan territory. For eastern Crete, defined by ancient sources and the distribution of inscriptions as Eteocretan, was also home to Oriental contacts and experiments.[103] Without linguistic confirmation, Eteocretan remains an elusive language, one of several language groups in Crete in the historical period, and its speakers

[100] Haft, *The Myth That Crete Became*, 2–107; Faure, *Ulysse le Cretois*; C. Emlyn-Jones, "True and Lying Tales in the Odyssey," *GR* 33 (1986) 1–10.

[101] Yves Duhoux, "Les Etéocrétois: Esquisse d'une acculturation," in *Interaction and Acculturation in the Mediterranean*, I, 171–76; "Les Etéocrétois et l'origine de l'alphabet grec," *AntClass* 52 (1982) 287–94; *L' Étéocrétois: Les textes—la langue* (Amsterdam, 1982).

[102] C. Gordon, "The Dreros Bilingual," *JSS* 8 (1963)

76–79; Astour, *Hellenosemitica*, 144, 346–47; R. Stieglitz, "The Letters of Kadmos: Mythology, Archaeology and Eteocretan," in *Fourth Cretological Congress*, 606–16, esp. 609ff.; *Archaic Scripts from Crete and Cyprus*, ed. J. Best and F. Woudhuizen (Leiden, 1988), 1–29; Bernal, *Black Athena*, 77 n. 16.

[103] Duhoux, *AntClass* 52 (1982) 290; see the previous section for Oriental influence in Eastern Crete.

of uncertain origin, beyond the likelihood that they are not Greek. In summary, Homer's roll call of Crete agrees with its early inscriptions, rich in dialects and provisions for foreigners (ἀλλοπολιάται).[104]

No Levantine people are identified in Odysseus's description of Crete, and the Phoenicians one might expect here are active but mobile elsewhere in epic poetry. Craftsmen in the *Iliad* (23.740–45), they are praised in the *Odyssey* as renowned in seafaring (ναυσικλυτοί: 15.415), as merchants both cunning (πολυπαίπαλοι: 5.419) and greedy (τρῶκται), and as professional slave traders: they kidnapped the infant Eumaios and his mother (15.403–84). Phoenicians help Odysseus escape from Crete in the tall tale he spins for Athena (*Odyssey* 13.272–73), so their traffic carries them to the island in the Greek imagination, if not in reality.[105]

It is not the Phoenicians, but the portrait of Minos that suggests Levantine elements in the culture of Crete, in the conclusion of this passage (*Odyssey* 19.178–79):

> τῇσι δ᾽ ἐνὶ Κνωσός, μεγάλη πόλις, ἔνθα τε Μίνως
> ἐννέωρος βασίλευε Διὸς μεγάλου ὀαριστής

> And in it lies Knossos, the great city, where Minos
> used to rule for nine years, the intimate of great Zeus.

In a landscape of a hundred cities, Knossos reigns as the central urban unit and Minos as its master, the only Homeric king (βασιλεύς) to command the verb form for ruling, and father to an equally powerful son, Deukalion, "lord of cities and men" (*Iliad* 13.454). A fragment of Hesiod describes the same arrangement, where Minos rules the surrounding cities (frag. 144 = [Plato], *Minos* 320D):

> ὃς βασιλεύτατος γένετο [ἔσκε κατα-] θνητῶν βασιλήων
> καὶ πλείστων ἤνασσε περικτιόνων ἀνθρώπων
> Ζηνὸς ἔχων σκῆπτρον, τῷ καὶ πολέων βασίλευεν.

> He who was most kingly of mortal kings
> and used to lord over the greatest number of men dwelling around,
> holding the scepter of Zeus, with which he also ruled over cities.

This bouquet of epic compliments echoes many Homeric ones: βασιλεύτατος is an expression of rank accorded Agamemnon alone in the *Iliad* (9.69), while the scepter of Minos reflects the one he wields in judgment over the dead (*Odyssey* 11.598). The additional measure of Minos's power, that he "lorded over many men dwelling around,"

---

[104] G. Neumann, "Zu einigen kretischen Personennamen," in *Studies Palmer*, 255–59; A. Scherer, "Personennamen nichtgriechischer Herkunft im alten Kreta," *FuF* 39 (1965) 57–60; J. Chadwick, "Some Observations on Two New Inscriptions from Lyktos," in ΕΙΛΑΠΙΝΗ, 329–34, on non-Doric elements.

[105] J. Muhly, "Homer and the Phoenicians," *Berytus* 19 (1970) 19–64; Carter, *Greek Ivory-Carving*, 21–23.

has been enthusiastically adduced as archaic evidence for the classical tradition of his "thalassocracy." Yet the passage does not specify that his subjects inhabit the Aegean islands or other territories separated from the royal seat by water, and related terms such as περίοικοι in Lakedaimon refer to surrounding lands, not islands. Euripides seems to interpret Hesiod's reference as a *land* empire within Crete, by presenting his tragic Minos in Homeric phrases: "ruling Crete, land of a hundred cities" (ἀνάσσων | Κρήτης ἑκατομπτολιέθρου: *Cretans* frag. 476.3–4: cf. *Iliad* 2.649) as well as transmitting his Levantine parentage in calling him "son of Phoinix-born [Phoenician?] Tyrian, child of Europa" (Φοινικογενοῦς παῖ τῆς Τυρίας | τέκνον Εὐρώπας: frag. 476.1–2; cf. *Iliad* 14.321). And Aristotle's remark on those who still obey the laws of Minos in Crete calls them περίοικοι, as if Aristotle shared visions like Hesiod's of the territory around Knossos, in analogy to the Spartan model, which he often compared with Crete's. Despite the classical promotion of his legendary thalassocracy, the Cretan king's primary domain, in the classical imagination, remained a thickly settled island of Crete, not the Aegean. Only in political mythology, not the poetic vision of Euripides, does Minos acquire a naval empire fit to compare with that of the Phoenicians (Strabo, 1.3.2, 48) and, deliberately, that of Athens (Chapter 12).

Finally, the last phrase in Hesiod's verses, τῷ καὶ πόλεων βασίλευε, "with this [scepter] he also used to rule cities," suggests a supplement to Minos's rule over the περικτίονες, as if he controlled both urban and rural populations with a scepter he only wields in the underworld, elsewhere in Homer (*Odyssey* 11.598). The very passage in Plato that cites Hesiod's verses substantiates this integration of country and city, in the words of the philosopher himself. The Cretan heroes, Talos and Rhadamanthys, divide their domains between country and city, whereby the brother of Minos serves as νομοφύλαξ κατὰ τὸ ἄστυ and the giant as νομοφύλαξ κατὰ τὴν ἄλλην Κρήτην (Plato, *Minos* 321C).

It is tempting to seek the source of these poetic impressions in the archaeological record of early Iron Age Crete. In contrast to the gradual *synoikismos* of mainland Greek cities, Knossos exhibits a strongly nucleated phase of urbanization as early as the seventh century.[106] This precocious urban evolution is common in areas where culture contact is a catalyst for rapid change, and at Knossos, contact with the Levant is an obvious factor. Comparative evidence teaches that contact between foreign and native populations often stimulates local industries, social stratification, and protourbanism, in strikingly similar fashion.[107] Certainly by 1000 B.C. the presence of Cypro-Phoenicians is sug-

---

[106] N. Coldstream, "Dorian Knossos and Aristotle's Villages," in *Aux origines de l' Hellénisme*, 312–22, and *The Formation of the Greek Polis: Aristotle and Archaeology*, 20–22, for a reconstruction of settlement patterns around Knossos and the sea from the early

cemeteries. Cf. Van Effenterre, *La cîté grecque*, 143–45, for a focus on a different period in this area.

[107] Cf. Phoenicians and natives in Iberia: I. Semmler, in *Phönizier im Westen*, 309–32; G. Chamarro, "Survey of Archaeological Research in Tartessos,"

gested by the inscribed Teke bowl (see n. 48), and that its effects might be reflected in the epic vision of Crete is plausible. Against this historical scenario, Minos's epic attributes reveal wider correspondences with the earliest conceptual definition of an urban community, under specific stimulus from the Orient.

In Minos's brief and controversial (interpolated, to some) appearance in Odysseus's glimpse of the Underworld, he is identified as the son of Zeus (*Odyssey* 11.311) and Europa, the daughter of Phoinix. His parents represent that union between the chief god in the form of a bull and a desirable goddess named for her "Beautiful Face" whom the Near East knew as Baal and Anat.[108] As a Levantine princess captured or lured from Tyre to Crete and mother to a local dynasty, Europa is an image appropriate to the Late Bronze and early Iron Age history of Crete. Like Dido, she accompanies, as it were, a Levantine stream westward through the Mediterranean, in the late second and early first millennium B.C. Europa is already acknowledged as the "daughter of Phoinix" in epic poetry (*Iliad* 14. 321–22; cf. Hesiod, *Ehoiai* frag. 141.7–8, M-W), "the mythical expression of the fact that the Phoenicians sailed over the whole Mediterranean, from Phoenicia (Φοῖνιξ) via Crete (Μίνως) to the far west" where Rhadamanthys, her other son, rules the Elysian fields.[109] Europa is not the eponymous heroine of Europe until after the Persian wars (e.g., see Aeschylus, *Prometheus Bound* 734) and even then Herodotus points out how inappropriate her name is for a continent where she never set foot (4.45). Her unnatural union repeats itself in the next generation in Pasiphae's desire to mate with a bull, a revival of the bovine union between god and female that becomes, in Greek mythology, an occasion for Daidalos's most challenging commission. Images of females with or on bulls are more common in Greek art than within the domain of Europa alone and suggest a pattern of divine iconography where Europa forms one specific tale.[110] Thus through his parentage (a Phoenician mother) as well as in the na-

---

AJA 91 (1987) 231. Greeks and Hallstatt Europe: Wells, *Culture Contact and Culture Change*. See C. Renfrew, "Trade as Action at a Distance: Questions of Integration and Communication," in *Ancient Civilization and Trade*, ed. J. Sabloff and C. C. Lamberg-Karlovsky (Albuquerque, 1975), 3–59, for trade as a stimulus for other changes, via the "multiplier effect."

[108] Dombrowski, *Europa*, argues for this derivation of "Εὐρώπα," a translation of Anat's name and similar to other Greek epic praise of feminine beauty (e.g., βοῶπις) rather than a transliteration of Semitic *'ereb* as implied by Hesychius, s.v. Εὐρώπη. Cf. G. R. Steward, "Europe and Europa," *Names* 9 (1961) 79–90. A. Anselin, *Le mythe d' Europe. De l'Indus à la Crète* (Paris, 1982); Burkert, *Greek Religion*, 64. Bovine features persist in Hebrew formulas (e.g., the "bull of Jacob") and iconography: see the odd couple from the Sinai, Yahweh and his Asherah, depicted in graffiti and vase-paintings from Kuntillet 'Ajrud: W. Dever, "Asherah, Consort of Yahweh?" *BASOR*, 255 (1984) 21–37; Coogan, McCarter, in *Ancient Israelite Religions*, 21–37, 146–47; also see my nn. 132ff.

[109] H. Vos, "Europe—Europa," *Lampas* 3 (1970) 135–45; cf. his review of R. Edwards's *Kadmos* in *Mnemosyne* 36 (1983) 233. Cf. G. Huxley, *Minoans in Greek Sources* (Belfast, 1968), on the genealogy of Minos as a mixture of Greeks and Phoenicians in Crete.

[110] W. Technau, "Die Göttin auf dem Stier," *JdI* 52 (1937) 76–103; E. Zahn, *Europa und der Stier* (Königshausen, 1983); M.-C. Villanueva Puig, "Sur l'identité de la figure féminine assise sur un taureau dans la céramique attique à figures noires," in *Images et société en Grèce ancienne*, ed. C. Bérard, Chr. Brun, and A. Pomari (Lausanne, 1984), 131–43, a reference I

ture of his conception and even in his wife's sexual encounters, Minos appears in Crete, and in Greek legend, as Phoenician as the δημιοεργοί who told his tale.[111] No wonder he was remembered as a stranger (ξένος τῆς νήσου: Strabo, 4.8, 477) and as an "Asian" (Plato, *Gorgias* 523e)—and no wonder he made such a convenient enemy for Athenian Theseus, after the Cretans failed to show at Salamis (Chapter 11).

The persona of Minos also incorporates trappings of kingship foreign in origin, as the figures of mythological kings like Priam are assimilated to Oriental despots like the Great King of Persia (Chapters 11 and 13). His royal prerogatives in Homer include divinely sanctioned kingship and the power to sit in judgment, characteristics of Near Eastern rulers before they reached Greece. In his Homeric guise, Minos appears as judge as well as king, albeit as judge among the dead "wielding a golden scepter while dispensing laws among the dead" (χρύσεον σκῆπτρον ἔχοντα θεμιστεύοντα νέκυσσιν· *Odyssey* 11.569), a function that helped promote his classical reputation as a lawgiver. Subtler but more profound connections to the Orient are implied in the extraordinary line with which Odysseus closes his portrait of Crete (*Odyssey* 19.179). Minos is not described as the son of Zeus but as his ὀαριστής. Best rendered as "confidant" or "familiar" of the king of the gods, the term is reserved elsewhere in Homeric poetry for conjugal, sexual intimacy (*Iliad* 14.216; cf. *Homeric Hymn to Hermes* 58) or for a bond in battle (*Iliad* 13.291; 17.228), relationships that do not exclude each other in ancient Greece. Scholiasts on *Odyssey* 19.179 gloss ὁμιλητής for this expression, perhaps to circumvent the sexual overtones. The closest Greek equivalent to this relationship between god and lawgiver exists in the *Homeric Hymn to Zeus* (23.1–3), where the king of the gods is described as seated next to Themis, sharing private words with her: ὅστε Θέμιστι ἐγκλιδὸν ἑζομένη πυκινοὺς ὀάρους ὀαρίζει. Themis hears intimate words from Zeus in the process of becoming, like Minos, a divinely inspired lawgiver. To express this communication between mortal and god necessary for the divine dispensation of laws to men, the term ὀαριστής finds its closest parallel in the Biblical relationship between Moses and Yahweh, who communicate in similar terms of intimacy (Exodus 33.11; cf. Numbers 12.8; Deuteronomy 34.10): "Thus the Lord used to speak to Moses, face to face, as a man speaks to a friend."[112]

This friendship between Moses and the Hebrew God dominates Greek and Roman conceptions of Moses, remembered as the *familiaris dei* in learned literature as well as popular sources, such as magical papyri.[113] The sexual overtones of this intimacy, how-

owe to Judy Barringer; M. Robertson, "Europa," in *LIMC* IV.1; on Syrian forebears, see C. Schaeffer, *Ugaritica* 3 (1956) 94–95; also see n. 72.

[111] Schachermeyr, *Rückerinnerung*, 281–90, observes how "quasi-Levantine" is the genealogy of Minos in literature, and how free of any "genuine Minoan" [sic] traditions.

[112] M. Smith, " 'Seeing God' in the Psalms: The Background to the Beatific Vision in the Hebrew Bible," *CBQ* 50 (1988) 171–83.

[113] E.g., in the *Historia Augusti* 5.2.4–5; in the Jewish Sibylline oracles and in Philo Moses, 1.1156; *PGM* III.1508–9, XII.92–94. See J. Gager, *Moses in Greco-Roman Paganism*, SBL Monograph 16 (Nashville, 1972),

ever unintentional or misunderstood, are not only maintained but emphasized for the sake of love charms, according to demotic magical papyri where the relationship between God and Moses is invoked to empower a similar relationship between humans. The relationship between Minos and Zeus is given a similar interpretation along quasi-sexual lines, according to the meanings of the Greek word ὀαριστής and its maintenance through equivalents like συνουσία ("intercourse"?) or the verb φοιτάω (suggesting frequency and intimacy) in Plato (Laws 624b).

Critical to the Homeric relationship between Minos and Zeus is the initial word in the same hexameter line, the enigmatic expression ἐννέωρος, "nine years." Ancient and modern commentators have struggled with its ambiguities. Presumably, it indicates that Minos ruled for nine years, after nine years, or at the age of nine (like the giants at Odyssey 11.311, or the ox at Odyssey 10.19) However, if the adjective agrees with ὀαριστής more closely than with the verb, as Plato understood (Minos 319b–c; Laws 624b), it somehow qualifies Minos's intimacy with Zeus as a periodic event marked by nine-year intervals. Scholiasts on this line have Minos spend nine years on Ida, separated from men composing laws to be certified by Zeus, but admit that others connect the expression with nine years of rule, or with nine years of education by Zeus.[114] Such Hellenistic opinions, postdating the Septuagint prepared under Ptolemy II (Philadelphos), could betray the influence of the Hebrew tradition, just as Moses became a θεσμοθέτης of the Jews (Longinus, 9.9), presumably in analogy to Minos the νομοθέτης (Plutarch, Theseus 16), and Strabo has Minos issue προστάγματα like Biblical "commandments." For the Biblical account, composed in the archaic period but set in the Late Bronze Age, has Moses secluded with God on Mount Sinai, in a cloud, for forty days and nights, both for the first consultation (Exodus 24.15) and for the second visit to replace the broken tablets (34.28). During this period of seclusion, reinforced by ritual abstention from food and drink, the fundamentals of Israelite religion (ultimately of Judaism and Christianity) are established as a covenant between the Jews and Yahweh. The Jewish people are to become "a kingdom of priests and a holy nation" honoring God with sacrifice, offerings, and a ritual setting (Exodus 19.6–30).

Most of the ritual prescriptions of Hebrew religion (further specified in Leviticus and Numbers), including their general contractual nature as a covenant between god and man, are shared by Greek religion. The probability that their Canaanite antecedents were introduced to the Late Bronze Age Aegean, probably under Near Eastern auspices (Chapter 5), suggests that the agreement remembered between Minos and Zeus had

---

22, 140–46. Cf. M. Stern, *Greek and Latin Authors on Jews and Judaism* (Jerusalem, 1974), 3:38–41. The similarity between Moses and Homeric Minos was noted as early as van Leeuwen's commentary on the Odyssey (1917; cf. W. B. Stanford's commentary on Odyssey 19.179).

[114] Ephoros, at Strabo, 10.4.8; F. J. Tritsch, "The Judgement of Minos," in *Third Cretological Congress*, 1:354–60, Glenn Morrow, *Plato's Cretan City* (Princeton, 1980), 23–24.

religious tenets as well as legal ones. Other witnesses to Crete's role in introducing sacrifice, mystery rites, divine images, and honors (see previous section) may reflect the same heritage, for the island acquired an exclusive reputation for religion, as in law. If Minos represents the import of Near Eastern law codes to Crete, he also accompanied the religious practices and imagery that transformed the Aegean in the Late Bronze Age. To the synoptic vision of Diodorus (1.94.1–2) and Strabo (16.2.38), parallels between Moses and Minos, to whom Diodorus adds Lykourgos and Apollo, were manifest. The language used in their comparisons of these figures betrays a conscious juxtaposition: as just noted, Strabo calls the laws Minos got from Zeus "προστάγματα," as if received as divine orders like "commandments." But the Homeric line makes a common heritage early, not just a coincidence, and when Diodorus has Kadmos emigrate from Egypt when Danaos does (5.58), he supports the origins of this convergence in the Late Bronze Age.

This densely packed phrase in Homer could be a slim survival of a whole world of laws and rites common to Greece and the Near East in the Late Bronze Age, explored in the convergence of Mycenaean and Canaanite culture behind Daidalos and Kothar. Minos and Moses may be another pair like the two craftsmen, the Hebrew figure spanning the Exodus until the Exile, the Homeric king, like his client, Daidalos, a bridge across the Dark Ages. And like Daidalos's impact on archaic and classical Greek art and ritual, Minos's Homeric guise already participates in early Greek law. For example, one application of poetry to practice, like the migration of δαιδάλεος to Greek religion, is anticipated in the Greek equivalent of Hebrew "forty days and forty nights," ἐννέωρος, a formulaic epithet based on the number nine popular in dactylic poetry.[115] The epic expression could be explained through poetic diction alone, and the interval of nine years is formulaic throughout Greek tradition. In mythology, for example, one legend relevant to Minos and Crete specifies nine years as the interval at which tribute was exacted from Athens in the form of seven youths and maidens (Plutarch, *Theseus* 15; for a discussion of this story as a transformation of Semitic infant sacrifice, see Chapter 5). This pattern could have inspired the constitutional conventions considered later, rather than explaining them. But the Homeric description of Minos in periodic intercourse with Zeus suggests early Greek legal terminology. Configurations of nine (or, reckoned inclusively in the Greek system, ten years) crop up in early Greek constitutions, whether as the number of magistrates in Athens or Olympia, or as the number of years for holding such offices. On Crete itself, a cycle of ten years was required between holding successive terms as κόσμος, according to the Dreros law code, where the number of local officials was expressed as οἱ δέκα τῆς πόλεως. A period of ten years elapsed for the trial of Solon's laws at Athens, a decade during which he went into voluntary

---

[115] C. B. Anderson, "Cycles of Nine," *CJ* 50 (1954–1955) 131–38.

exile (Plutarch, *Solon* 25). Any coincidence between Cretan and Athenian laws could only be reinforced by the lessons Solon is said to have learned from Epimenides (Plutarch, *Solon* 12).

The most striking coincidence between Homeric ἐννέωρος and early Greek kingship comes from Sparta, described in Plutarch's life of Agis (11). In the third century, an unusual ceremony termed simply τὸ σημεῖον, "the sign," is invoked to settle a dispute between the two kings, Leonidas II and Agis IV (243–242 B.C.). On a moonless night, the ephors of Sparta watch in silence for a falling star, whose appearance leads to a trial of the Spartan kings περὶ τὸ θεῖον and a suspension of their powers until an oracle confirms their right to rule.[116] This rare procedure implies a vote of confidence in reigning kings, guided by ritual observances including consultation of astral phenomena and oracular sources. Although no occasion other than this third-century recourse is attested historically and its regular use is unlikely, Plutarch indicates its periodic use at regular intervals with a temporal phrase, δι᾽ ἐτῶν ἐννέα, "every ninth year." The kinship between the constitutions of Crete and Sparta, acknowledged in antiquity as in modern opinion, supports the resemblance of this procedure and its timing to Homer's description of the kingship of Minos. The phrase ἐννέωρος βασίλευε may reflect early Iron Age constitutional practices, with revolving offices or temporary magistracies of the type guaranteed by the Dreros inscription, and, like other features of Cretan and Spartan constitutions, could point to the Near East.

These passages have only been discussed together in the context of comparative religion, as examples of the ritual renewal of kingship traditional in primitive societies.[117] But their coincidence suggests more than an anthropological analogy, especially when substantiated by other ancient evidence on Minos. In Aristotle's lost *Constitution of the Cretans*, the philosopher and political scientist reports that Minos revised the laws of Crete every ten years (frag. 611, Rose). While probably an attempt to synthesize *Odyssey* 19.179 with historical Cretan procedures, Aristotle's Homeric exegesis suggests the most constructive direction for understanding the legends surrounding Minos. Like other political panoramas set in imaginary passages in epic, contemporary reality may have been a more immediate source of inspiration for the poet when called upon for more "spontaneous" material (cf. the discussion of the Shield of Achilles in Chapter 1).

Other aspects of Minos partake in the same Levantine heritage. His brother, Rhadamanthys, is praised as a δίκαιος ἀνήρ (Plato, *Minos* 318d) and shares his brother's reputation for justice (Plato, *Laws* 625d) as well as its administration in the underworld (*Odyssey* 4.564). The names of both Minos and Rhadamanthys have been associated

---

[116] H. W. Parke, "The Deposing of Spartan Kings," *CQ* 39 (1945) 106–12; Carlier, *La royauté en Grèce*, 294–96. Verbruggen, *Le Zeus crétois*, 84 n. 64, mentions a possible connection between Homeric ἐννέωρος and

the Spartan ritual, without pursuing it.

[117] E.g., J. Frazer, *The Golden Bough*, 3d ed. (London, 1920), 4:70; see Stanford's commentary on this line.

with Egyptian etymologies: the former with the name of the legendary first lawgiver and Pharaoh of Egypt, *MNA*, variously rendered in Greek as Μῖν (Herodotus, 2.4, 99), Μήνης (Manetho = Eusebius, *FGrH* II 538, 539), Μήνας (Diodorus, 1.43, 45), or Μιναῖος (Josephus, *Antiquitates* 8.155–57). Like other Egyptian images, names, and concepts, *MN* may have reached the Aegean via North Syria, according to theophoric names from Ugarit honoring *MN* (*Min/Man*).[118] His brother's un-Greek name, Ῥαδάμανθυς, has been compared with an Egyptian compound, **Rdi M(a)ntw*, or "Month gives."[119]

However disputed these etymologies, that of Minos, in particular, suits his nature as a founding figure in Cretan civilization and provides an etymology where no convincing Greek one exists. Egyptian sources also match the origin of other words and legends that migrated to Crete from Egypt, most notably the Labyrinth. Whether Egyptian or Aegean in name, the behavior of the two brothers belongs in the Levant. Rhadamanthys serves as νομοφύλαξ κατὰ τὸ ἄστυ (Plato, *Minos* 321c) in a manner suspiciously resembling that of Aaron, brother of Moses, who serves as his spokesman and head priest (Exodus 4:14, 7, 27–30). It was Rhadamanthys who invested the "king" of Delos (Diodorus, 5.79), as if legitimating the link between ritual, kingship, and law embodied in Minos. In fact, the two brothers share a regency not unlike legendary and historical Spartan kings, a tradition of dyarchy now traced to Phoenician origins (by Drews; see n. 87).

The function of Rhadamanthys is also shared by Talos, the bronze giant built by Hephaistos for Minos (Ἡφαιστότευκτον: Simonides, frag. 204) and who also serves as his νομοφύλαξ (Plato, *Minos* 321c):

> ὁ γὰρ Τάλως τρὶς περιῄει τοῦ ἐνιαυτοῦ κατὰ τὰς κώμας,
> φυλάττων τοὺς νόμους ἐν αὐταῖς, ἐν χαλκοῖς γραμματείοις ἔχων
> γεγραμμένους τοὺς νόμους, ὅθεν χαλκοῦς ἐκλήθη.

> For Talos travels through the towns three times a year,
> guarding the laws in them, holding the laws written on
> bronze writing tablets, for which reason they are called "brazen."

While a certain portion of this tale obviously derives from the brazen reputation of the giant, Talos, his image as legal guardian provides insight for early Iron Age developments on Crete. The emphasis on a periodic "refresher" in current laws, broadcast to the rural communities of Crete and enforced by written code, calls to mind the services of Spensithios in political communities in eastern Crete where he serves as ποινι-

---

[118] B. Mazar, "A Genealogical List from Ras Shamra," *Journal of the Palestine Oriental Society* 16 (1936) 153; J. Tigay, "Israelite Religion: The Onomastic and Epigraphic Evidence," in *Ancient Israelite Religions*, 164–65. Cf. A. Braune, *Menes-Moses-Minos* (Essen, 1988), and S. Morenz, "Traditionen um Menes," *ZaeS* 99 (1972) x-xvi.

[119] Bernal, *Black Athena*, 63–64.

κασ τάς and μνάμων —scribe and "reminder." The occasional "reminder" of the laws, like Minos's periodic renewal of them on Mount Ida, or Solon's moratorium on any revisions to the law code for ten years, is traditional to the Hebrew covenant's sabbatical renewal (Leviticus 25, Deuteronomy 15). Moreover, the institution of a law code, in Crete as well as in Israel, involved two dimensions: proclamation or φήμη, as in Hebrew prophecy, then νόμοι, the written law code itself (Plato, *Laws* 625b), as Hebrew law is codified in the books of the Bible called "the writings."

The figure of Minos, cherished as a modern symbol of prehistoric Crete and the eponym of that culture, exhibits too many archaic attributes for the Bronze Age. His Near Eastern parentage attributes him to that complex of mythological figures who represent what the Aegean received from the Levant in the second millennium, as a social and legal counterpart to the artisan figure of Daidalos. The arts of civilization in its literal (i.e., civil, or urban) sense became a conscious preoccupation in Greek culture as early as 1200 B.C. If the origins of the polis have their roots in the Late Bronze Age, as many now recommend (Chapter 5), then figures like Minos serve as Moses did, a symbol of the origins of Iron Age communities with legal and religious institutions.

Later perspectives on Minos, including his association with infant sacrifice or cannibalism, evolve with Greek attitudes toward the past and the Orient. In the fifth century, Athenian sponsorship of Theseus as a new national hero forces Minos into the position of enemy of Athens, a negative image encouraged by his description as ὀλοόφρων at *Odyssey* 11.322. The classical promotion of Solon as legendary lawgiver for Athens helped undermine Minos and could reflect the same attempt to locate the origins of Greek institutions in Athens that removed Daidalos from Crete to Athens (Part IV). This revised view of Minos could not entirely suppress his reputation as a lawgiver, however, for he was still praised as a just ruler (βεβασιλευκὼς νομιμώτατα: Diodorus, 5.78, 79). Conflict and compromise between these simultaneous views made the "defense of Minos" a popular *topos* in later literature (e.g., in Strabo, 10.4.8; Plutarch, *Theseus* 16). Classical conservatives (including Plato and Aristotle) helped restore his reputation along with admiration for the conservative constitutions of Sparta and Crete.

More influential on the modern "Minoan" image was the epoch of its discovery. As an historian put it: "Minoan civilization is the only great civilization created in the twentieth century."[120] The modern Minos helped resurrect a European vision of its own past even before the excavation of Knossos. As Priam served to personify prehistoric remains at Troy and Agamemnon at Mycenae, the name of Minos was immediately applied to Middle Bronze Age discoveries at Knossos, and has unfortunately been retained.[121] In fact, no classical source on Minos confirms a civilization comparable to "Mi-

[120] C. Starr, "Minoan Flower Lovers," in *Minoan Thalassocracy*, 9.

[121] W. McDonald, *Progress into the Past: The Redis-* *covery of Mycenaean Civilization* (New York, 1967), 113–69 (Evans first called his discoveries "Mycenaean" before competition with the mainland en-

noan" Crete—the emphasis is rather on a large number of smaller cities (not a limited number of palatial units controlling rural territories), a concern for justice not attested in Aegean prehistory, and other factors more appropriate to early Iron Age Greece than to a Bronze Age palace. A romantic attachment to the unanticipated culture of Bronze Age Crete has exaggerated "Minoan" elements in the material and literary culture of Crete in archaeological scholarship for the sake of continuity, to demonstrate Greece's (and Europe's) link to a glamorous past. Modern affection for prehistoric Crete, whose discovery (just after the liberation of Crete from Turkish rule) took place during a strong drive for Greek roots, has overestimated this past and signs of its "revival" or "renaissance."[122] Moreover, European eagerness to identify roots as old as possible for Greek civilization, as if in competition with the discovery of Mesopotamian prehistory, precipitated notions of cultural continuity.[123] Eventually, this reconstituted culture of Crete was invoked to claim that Greek sources on "Phoenicians" reflected Aegean, not Near Eastern populations. The newly discovered frescoes of men with dark red skins (now recognized as a convention in art, not an ethnic attribute) were applied to an etymology of "Phoenicians" as "Redmen."[124] Only rarely has a scholar recognized that a so-called Minoan or Eteocretan element "has largely been conjectured from some of the stranger Orientalizing works which owe more to individual invention than to any direct transmission of Minoan forms."[125] An objective view of "Minoan" culture has only recently become a concern in scholarship.[126]

If early sources on Minos reveal origins later and more Levantine than Middle Bronze Age Crete, the latter remains surprisingly distant from the classical Greek imagination. Despite this discrepancy between testimonia and prehistory, mythology about Crete assumed to reflect a vivid but confused memory of Bronze Age civilization, whose palaces left tales of a bewildering "labyrinth" and whose many representations of bulls and acrobats survived in images of creatures half-bull, half-man.[127] As with Minos,

---

couraged an exclusive terminology for Crete). Bernal, *Black Athena*, 385–87. Cf. Faure, *Ulysse le Crétois*, 264–69, on Minos Kalokairinos "au prénom prédestiné" (one of the first explorers of Knossos no doubt helped attach his name to the palace).

[122] As in Demargne's subtitle for *La Crète dédalique: Études sur les origines d'une renaissance*; Willetts, in *CAH* III.3, 234, on the "legacy of a famous past" and its "remarkable renaissance"; Beyer, *Dreros und Prinias*, 66–70, calls Orientalizing Dreros "die Personifikation des Subminoischen Erbes" (p. 70); Blome, *Bildwelt Kretas*, 105–8, on the survival of Minoan motifs.

[123] As emphasized by Evans in his inaugural lecture as president of the Hellenic Society: "These are the days of origins" (in McDonald, *Progress into the*

Past, 164). Cf. M. Herzfeld, *Ours Once More: Folklore, Ideology and the Making of Modern Greece* (Austin, 1982), on Greek folklore and "continuity" in modern Greece.

[124] Edwards, *Kadmos*, 56, 87–88, 95, 112, traces the history of this theory from its archaeological proponents (Evans, Hall) to its philological enthusiasts (Fick 1905, etc.).

[125] Boardman, *Cretan Collection at Oxford*, 132.

[126] See *Minoan Society. Proceedings of the Cambridge Colloquium, 1981*, ed. O. Krzyszowska and L. Nixon (Bristol, 1983), especially papers by S. Crawford, J. Cherry, and L. Nixon; cf. J. Bintliff, "Structuralism and Myth in Minoan Studies," *Antiquity* 58 (1984) 33–34.

[127] By 1932 such connections were "generally ac-

other legends of Crete have been too readily applied to the island's Bronze Age remains without reference to the Orient, and these include Daidalos. His Cretan adventures remained most colorful and popular, peopled by figures attested in the same Homeric tradition: Minos, Ariadne, and Theseus. But those episodes linked to Knossos—the manufacture of a wooden cow for Pasiphae and their offspring, the Minotaur, the design of the Labyrinth, and the escape with wings—have found no prehistoric support, and are even absent from epic poetry. They do not appear until the archaic period, are celebrated in classical drama, and synthesized in Hellenistic mythography.[128] As Nilsson noted many years ago, it is curious and significant that "reminiscences of Minoan Crete are found in Attic myths only."[129] In the network of stories involving Daidalos with Minos, Ariadne, and Theseus, themes and images can be identified in the archaic period, followed by an important recasting of the tale in fifth-century Athens, in the historical milieu that sponsored new myths and in fact created Greek history (Part IV).

The Minotaur begins in representations of heroes fighting creatures half-bull, half-man, formulaic images with anonymous performers in the Late Geometric period.[130] It is important to stress the distinction between the preoccupation with bulls in Bronze Age Aegean art—in protome or rhyton form, leaping with acrobats, or being led to sacrifice (as on the Pylos vestibule fresco)—and the composite image of a bull-headed human.[131] The source of this "bull of Minos," a term only compounded as "Minotaur" after 400 B.C., is probably a misunderstanding of images of gods in the shape of bulls or men wearing bull's masks in ritual, attested in Cyprus and the Near East but imported into Aegean ritual (Figures 20–24).[132] The wearing of horns characterizes both

knowledged": Nilsson, *Mycenaean Origin of Greek Mythology*, 176 (170–80 on "Minoan" legends). Schachermeyr, *Rückerinnerung*, 281–90, stresses the historicization of myth on Crete and the attempt to reconcile Minos and Theseus.

[128] Huxley, *Minoans in Greek Sources*, traces the progressive synthesis of such traditions.

[129] *Mycenaean Origin of Greek Mythology*, 180, attributing this coincidence to factors of migration, based on theories now obsolete.

[130] E. Young, "The Slaying of the Minotaur. Evidence in Art and Literature for the Development of the Myth, 700–400 B.C." (Ph.D., diss. Bryn Mawr College, 1972), 63–83.

[131] For an intriguing anticipation of the Greek conflation of bull and man in Mycenaean visions of Minoan bull-leapers, see N. Schlager, "Minotauros in der Ägäischen Glyptik?" in *Fragen und Probleme der bronzezeitlichen ägäischen Glyptik*, ed. I. Pini, CMMS Beiheft 3 (1989), 225–39. Chr. Vogelpohl, "Minotauros und Stiermensch: Überleben Kretisch-myken-

ischer Formen oder orientalischer Einfluss?" paper delivered at "Das Ende der Mykenischen Welt," Cologne, 1987 (unpublished).

[132] Burkert, in *Greek Renaissance*, 99, and *Greek Religion*, 65 n. 94, 371–72 nn. 78–80. Cf. V. Karageorghis, "Notes on Some Cypriote Priests Wearing Bull-masks," *HThR* 64 (1971) 261–70; "Some Eleventh-Century Clay Masks from Kition," in *Studies T.B.L. Webster*, ed. J. L. Betts, J. T. Hooker, and J. R. Green (Bristol, 1988), 2:65–67. A. Hérmary, "Statuette d'un 'prêtre' masqué," *BCH* 103 (1979) 734–41. Masks are now attested in Late Bronze Israel, worn by a dancer with a musical instrument on a clay plaque: A. Biran, "The Dancer from Dan, the Empty Tomb and the Altar Room," *IEJ* 36 (1986) 168–73. See Carter, *AJA* 91 (1987) 355–83, on Near Eastern masks and ritual imported to Greece; G. Markoe, "The Rise of Phoenician Art," *BASOR* 279 (1990) 15–16. For Near Eastern gods with bull's-horns or heads, see the basalt stele of Baal-Hadad with the head of a bull (now in Damascus: J. Gray, *Near Eastern Mythology* [New York,

divine images like the horned god of Enkomi, probably Apollo Karneios (see Chapter 5, n. 57), or the ram-headed figure of Baal-Hammon on a throne from the sanctuary at Meniko (Figure 22). Unlike Baal, El is the god who receives infant sacrifice among non-Greeks in the form of Kronos (at Carthage: Diodorus, 20.14.4–7), implying that more than one Near Eastern cult was transformed by the Greek imagination. The characterization of gods in the form of a bull has a long history in the Near East, where it is attested in Ugarit, Phoenicia, and Israel, and may have reached the Aegean from the Levant via Cyprus in the Late Bronze Age. Biblical survivals of this divine iconography include the appellation of God as the "bull of Jacob," the Semitic counterpart for the "bull of Minos" who eventually become the "Minos-bull." Zeus still wears gilded horns in Orphic visions: "ταύρεα δ᾽ ἀμφοτέρωθε χρύσεα κέρατα."[133] Bovine headgear is also appropriate to mortals ministering to such a cult figure or performing stories about them in ritual drama. Figurines of men donning bulls' masks (Figure 21) or wearing them in ritual scenes match terminology for such mortal servants, called "Kerastai," or "Horned Ones" on Cyprus. The practice of wearing bull's horns in a ritual setting is suggested by an alternate reading of qeran (qeren) at Exodus 34.29, 35, the passage describing how Moses is transformed by his encounter with Yahweh. The preferred meaning, followed by the Septuagint, is that the face of Moses "was glorified" or "shone" (δεδόξασται in Greek). However, the word qeran can also mean "became horned," and the Jerome Bible resurrects this reading by translating the verb as cornuta esset.[134] In support of this reading in the Hebrew Bible, some scholars have imagined that Moses actually wore a ritual mask with horns, in analogy to Canaanite practices.[135] Whether original to the intention of the Hebrew phrase or not, Jerome's translation determined the European image of Moses wearing horns, most celebrated in the sculpture of Michelangelo.[136] Given the kinship between Moses and Minos considered already, it is at least possible that a bull's head, or horns, characterized an encounter between man and god in a source common to the story of Moses and the mythology of Minos and the

1988], 70; cf. p. 78 for the same god striding on a stele, wearing a horned crown) or the stele of seated El with horned crown from Ugarit (Ebla to Damascus, 299, no. 151).

[133] O. Kern, Orphicorum Fragmenta, (Berlin, 1922) 168–69, line 14; dismissed by M. L. West, The Orphic Poems (Oxford, 1983), 240, as the result of "some Hellenistic syncretism" in the Rhapsodic Theogonies, a late compilation.

[134] J. Sasson, "Bovine Symbolism in the Exodus Narrative," Vetus Testamentum 18 (1968) 380–87; W. Propp, "The Skin of Moses' Face—Transfigured or Disfigured?" CBQ 49 (1987) 375–86.

[135] E.g., H. Gressmann, Mose und seine Zeit (Göttin-

gen, 1913), 246–47 n. 7; A. Jirku, "Die Gesichtsmaske des Mose," ZDPV 67 (1945) 43–45; E. Auerbach, Moses (Amsterdam, 1953), 154–59; K. Jaros, "Des Mose 'strahlende Haut,'" ZAW 88 (1976) 275–80; "The Shining of Moses' Face: A Case Study in Biblical and Ancient Near Eastern Iconography," in The Shelter of Elyon. Essays in Honor of G. W. Ahlstrom, ed. B. Barrick and J. R. Spencer, JSOT suppl. 31 (Sheffield, 1984), 159–73.

[136] R. Mellinkoff, The Horned Moses in Medieval Art and Thought (Berkeley, 1970); "More about Horned Moses," Jewish Art 12–13 (Jerusalem, 1986–1987) 184–98.

Minotaur. Even without Moses, some ritual performer as bull-man based on Near Eastern cult was incorporated into Greek myth as a new form of monster appropriate to the tradition where heroes fight composite creatures. The pattern is familiar: as with infant sacrifice, a rite rejected by Greek religion survives as a story appropriate to the heroic tradition, both cases here (bull-god and human sacrifice) glorifying Theseus. Minos and his "bull" share a Near Eastern legacy of the Late Bronze Age, independent of Middle Bronze Age tradition of bulls in art on Crete.

The Minotaur's parents, Pasiphae and her bull-consort, are hard to find before the fifth century, when drama (notably Euripides' *Cretans*) made them popular. The origin of the story, as mentioned previously, derives from legendary encounters between gods-as-bulls and women, common in Near Eastern images and myths. From a convention of divine/mortal mating tales, the story was made specific to a succession of characters in Cretan tradition, where it served to link other bovine hybrids like the "Minotaur" to a plausible set of parents. Representations as well as full accounts of the marvelous contraption made by Daidalos are late, and the story piqued the interest of Roman painters, Christian authors, and modern artists.[137] As a wheeled artifice designed to deceive gods and men, the theme is a trope on other marvelous contraptions in legend, such as the wooden horse of Troy, but difficult to substantiate before the version elaborated by Euripides. The tradition presumes that Daidalos was known for talents outside of sculpture by the fifth century, and thus joins the evidence for the Labyrinth in its architectural and near-magical dimensions.

That perennial favorite for "continuity," the labyrinth, may appear in Mycenaean Greek as *da-pu-ri-to* on a Knossos tablet and as a motif on a Pylos tablet.[138] The earliest λαβύρινθος in Greek literature is Egyptian, not Cretan, and appears in a fifth-century source, Herodotus's description of Egypt (2.148), without reference to Crete. Diodorus and Pliny reconcile the Cretan and Egyptian constructions through a visit to Egypt by Daidalos, the same trip that exposed him to the manufacture of statues, Egyptian style

---

[137] On Pasiphae, see Frontisi-Ducroux, *Dédale*, 137–41. Ancient sources: Plato, *Minos*; Diodorus, 4.77; Apollodoros, 3.1.4; Clement, *Protrepticus* 4; ancient representations: Philostratos, *Imagines* 1.167, and in Roman wall paintings: J. Nyenhuis, "Daidalos et Ikaros," *LIMC* III.1, 313–21; D. A. Birmingham, "Masson's Pasiphae: Eros and the Unity of the Cosmos," *ArtB* 69 (June 1987) 279–94, a reference I owe to Jody Maxmin.

[138] J. H. Heller, "A Labyrinth from Pylos," *AJA* 65 (1961) 57–59 (PY Cn 1287); KN Gg 702: *da-pu-ri-to-jo po-ti-ni-ja*, a place-name associated with a Potnia or goddess who receives one jar of honey. C. Gallavotti,

"Labyrinthos," *PdP* 12 (1957) 161–76, reproduces the arguments of the Etymologicum Magnum, which glosses Δαιδάλειον as the Labyrinth and the work of Daidalos. In his suggestion, *da-da-re-jo* "allude forse alla costruzione artistica del Palazzo," of which *da-pu-ri-to* would be a specific part. Gérard-Rousseau, *Mentions religieuses*, 56–58; C. Gallini, "Potinija Dapuritojo," *Acme* 12 (1959) 149–76; P. Scarpi, "Daidalos e il Labyrinthos," *BIFG* (1979) 194–210. Stefan Hiller, "Amnisos und das Labyrinth," *ZAnt* 31 (1982) 63–72, argues that both *da-da-re-jo* and *da-pu-ri-to* are probably cult sites near Knossos.

(Diodorus, 1.96–97; Pliny, *Naturalis Historia* 36.19.85). Its etymology could likewise be Egyptian, too; certainly it bears no incontrovertible relationship to the Lykian double axe and its name, λάβρυς, as assumed for years.[139] An Egyptian etymology first proposed in 1872, which compares the Greek word with *lapi-ro-hun-t* (*R-pr-n-hnt*) or "Temple on the Mouth of the Sea" to account for both Egyptian *aition* and Greek word, has been recently revived by Stieglitz.[140] As Minos represents a Hellenized *Menes* from Egypt, so his labyrinth may have been imported from Egypt, too. Certainly the modern identification of this word with the architectural form of Cretan Middle Bronze Age palaces rests on no explicit ancient association. Instead of a palace for Minos, ancient traditions locate monuments such as the "house of Rhea" at Knossos, home of her children, the Titans (Diodorus, 5. 66). Such legends suit the tendency to attribute megalithic prehistoric remains to earlier races of giants, the way the Cyclopes were given credit for Mycenaean citadel walls (Pausanias, 2.16.4). The figure of Rhea is also more appropriate to images of Bronze Age "goddesses" than to the image of Minos, mature rulers being infrequent in "Minoan" art.

The visual history of the labyrinth as it evolves into the meander/maze begins in the early archaic period with a curvilinear motif linked to legend, although not to Crete.[141] An intriguing source for this type of motif is the prehistoric spiral, which appears on a Boiotian black-figure skyphos as the thread of Ariadne, in a related Cretan episode (Figure 10a).[142] The central figure of the scene encircling the cup is Theseus slaying the Minotaur, flanked at the left by a diminuitive Ariadne, holding the proverbial thread that will lead the hero to safety. To the right of Theseus are superimposed two rows of draped figures, seven male and seven female (with white faces, feet), all clad in himatia and garlanded (Figure 10b). Their number naturally recalls the Athenians rescued by Theseus from the Minotaur (Plutarch, *Theseus* 15). This archaic juxtaposition of monster, victims, and hero suggests the tradition was established by 550 B.C., as hinted in frag-

[139] Evans, "Knossos Excavations, 1903," *BSA* 9 (1902–1903) 111, and *POM* 3:283; G. Pugliese Caratelli, "Labranda e Labyrinthos," *RAAN* (1939) 285–300, already recommended "una maggiore prudenza" in comparing Λαβύρινθος and Λάβρανδα. Cf. P. Faure, *Fonctions des cavernes crétoises* (Paris, 1964), 166–73 (compares λαύρα, λαυρεῖον?).

[140] R. Stieglitz, "Labyrinth: Anatolian Axe or Egyptian Edifice?" in *Coins, Culture and History in the Ancient World: Numismatic and Other Studies in Honor of Bluma L. Trell* (Detroit, 1981), 195–98, based on H. Brugsch, "Das altägyptische 'Seeland,' " *ZaeS* 10 (1872) 89–91, and Bernal, *Black Athena*, 64, for *R-pr-n-hnt*.

[141] Its earliest extant appearance is on an Etruscan vase of the mid- to later seventh century, where the inscribed word, "truia," connects it with Troy: J. P. Small, "The Tragliatella Oinochoe," *RömMitt* 93 (1986) 63–96. Compare the earliest representations of Daidalos, also Etruscan: Chapter 7.

[142] Louvre MNC 675, from Tanagra, the "Rayet skyphos"; A. Waiblinger, *CVA Louvre 17 (France 26)* (Paris, 1974), pl. 29; Beazley, *JHS* 47 (1927) 222–23; Frontisi-Ducroux, *Dédale*, fig. 1; Kokalakis, "Icarus," 25–30. This spiral has also been called a stylized flower (by C. Robert: *RE*, 4:2000) and compared with the motif of the labyrinth: Frontisi-Ducroux, *Dédale*, 144.

ments of Hesiod's *Catalogue of Women* (frag. 140–45). Armless beneath her cloak like the dancers in two rows on the same cup, Ariadne proffers a spiral at the end of a line curving down and out from her chest, perhaps simulating her missing arm (Figure 10a). The spiral is assumed to be the artist's convention for thread or ball of string, an element required by the narrative but uncommon in archaic visual repertoire. This visual ambiguity could reflect the process of improvisation familiar in archaic art, when stories long familiar in poems are first translated into visual formulas, and vice versa. More intriguing is the idea that the Bronze Age motif of the spiral survived in artifacts and memory, then grew into the story of a coil of string complete with a mythological *aition* for its popularity. In other words, the representation of Ariadne's thread as a spiral may be more than an improvisation: the artist may deliberately have invoked a Bronze Age motif as a Minoan insignia for a story set in Crete. Conversely, the survival of the motif may have encouraged the tale of the thread, a process common in the Greek transformation of prehistoric and Near Eastern formulas into human story. Its resemblance to the labyrinth motif, or rather as a curvilinear complement to the meander-square maze, provided mutual encouragement to the two shapes and their tales.[143]

However spiral and thread are related, Ariadne's attribute allows one of those rare communications between prehistoric artifacts and archaic mythology. This process, where motif precedes myth, also helps explain variant attributes with which Ariadne rescues Theseus, such as the luminous wreath or garland that illuminates the hero's escape from the labyrinth. The first literary source on the wreath is Pseudo-Eratosthenes (*Katasterismoi* 27.5; cf. Hyginus, *Astronomia* 2.5, for Amphitrite as well as Ariadne). The motif is current in the visual arts in the early archaic period, according to its description on the chest of Kypselos (Pausanias, 5.19.1), but is difficult to identify in surviving scenes before black-figure pottery. A recent study of Greek wreaths includes the speculation that the χορός in *Iliad* 18.590, gift of Daidalos to Ariadne, could have been confused with circular motifs in the visual arts and contributed to the legend of a wreath or garland, luminous enough if made of precious metal.[144] The correlation between different motifs begins in antiquity—for example, with a scholiast's comment on *Iliad* 18.590—that the dance steps of the χορός imitate the labyrinth, an explanation that betrays an attempt to synthesize works attributed to Daidalos. Χορός, spiral, and garland share the theme of circularity, vivid in antiquity in the gloss of Hesychius (χορός· κύκλος, στέφανος), as well as close associations with Crete.[145] Wreath and garland, like

[143] Frontisi-Ducroux, *Dédale*, 141–44, on the visual and symbolic analogy between the two forms.

[144] Blech, *Studien zum Kranz*, 259–67, esp. 261, on Ariadne. On thread, wreath, and ring, see F. Brommer, "Theseus-Deutungen, II," *AA* (1982) 69–82.

[145] Eckstein, *ArchHom II:L. Handwerk*, 1, 7, and

Blech, *Studien zum Kranz*, 262, on an illuminating χορός, if ἀσκέω can mean "to light someone's way." On other modern juxtapositions of the various motifs, see Duchemin (cited in n. 151); Frontisi-Ducroux, *Dédale*, 141–50.

the spiral, are survivals of Minoan-Mycenaean iconographic motifs, all worn, carried, or held by women.[146] These garlands survived in Greek ritual, and particularly in Crete (on a stele from Prinias: Figure 31), in ritual scenes and as attributes of Cretan deities (?) like Diktynna, Eileithyia, and Europa.[147] In myth, Ariadne and her wreath are surely a survival of prehistoric female figures engaged in ritual activity, transformed into a mythological paradigm to serve a new master, Theseus. Ariadne and her magic aids—wreath, thread, and ring—suit a similar pattern. The visiting hero's "rescue" of a native princess is exclusive to no single tradition but is especially appropriate to a culture where women figured prominently in representations of ritual and ceremony.[148]

Another motif in the story of Theseus and Ariadne, the ring with which Theseus demonstrates his kinship with Poseidon and superiority to Minos, incorporates Bronze Age and archaic realia into classical symbolism. The ring is first attested in the early classical period, in Bacchylides's *Ode* 17 (60–62) and in Mikon's painting in the Theseion (Pausanias, 1.17.3); the motif was encouraged by the Delian League but inspired by earlier traditions. The extravagant gold jewelry of Aegean prehistory, in particular its gold rings with narrative and ritual intaglio designs, did not entirely disappear from Greek view, thanks to tomb robbers, heirlooms, and memory. Yet such δαίδαλα also revived with new prosperity in the archaic period and acquired new narrative powers as the magic ring in tales of kings and gods.[149] Elements that contribute to this aspect of the tale include folk tradition—the magic recovery of objects cast into the sea—and symbolic ritual, the casting of objects into the sea on the swearing of oaths (see Chapter 12).

In the early archaic period, thread, wreath, and ring all figure in the tradition linking Theseus, Daidalos, and Ariadne in a Cretan scenario, composed of uneven survivals embroidered into a poetic matrix. As with the Minotaur, Theseus and Ariadne are prematurely identified in any couple holding a wreath or departing by ship. By the sixth century, the Athenian hero and his Cretan bride appear in a developed visual narrative,

---

[146] Blech, *Studien zum Kranz*, 282; P. Warren, "The Fresco of the Garlands from Knossos," in *L'iconographie minoenne*, BCH suppl. 11 (1985) 187–208. M. Caskey, "Ayia Irini, Kea: The Terracotta Statues and the Cult in the Temple," in *Sanctuaries and Cults*, 132 nn. 16–18, and *Keos II: The Temple at Ayia Irini. Part I: The Statues* (Princeton, 1986), 36–37, for garlands worn by terracotta figures from a Bronze Age temple, and their relationship to later Greek practice (e.g., Athenaeus, 15.678d–688c).

[147] Representations collected by Blech, *Studien zum Kranz*, 452–53; in *L'iconographie minoenne*, Warren, 205–6. Wreaths on stelai from Prinias (Lembesi, Οἱ Στῆλες τοῦ Πρινιᾶ, 66–70) and in dance scenes (e.g., mitra from Rethymnon: Hoffman, *Early Cretan*

Armorers, 25–26 pl. 46, 1). Carter, in *Early Greek Cult Practice*, 94–96, for wreaths and marriage in Lakonia.

[148] M. Nilsson, The *Minoan-Mycenaean Religion and Its Survival in Greek Religion*, 2d ed. (Lund, 1968), 523–28, *Mycenaean Origin of Greek Mythology*, 172–74. N. Marinatos, *Art and Religion in Thera* (Athens, 1984), chaps. 6, 8.

[149] Polykrates, Amasis, and the ring: Herodotus, 3.39–43; J. Labarbe, "Polycrate, Amasis et l'anneau," *AntClass* 53 (1984) 15–34. This ring (σφρηγίς) was the work of Theodoros, the renowned craftsman of Samos (according to Pausanias, an emerald; Pliny, *Naturalis Historia* 37.4, calls it a sardonyx) and presumably engraved with an intaglio design for sealing purposes.

as on the François vase, equipped with motifs such as ring, thread, or wreath.[150] The classical transformation of this legend (Chapter 12) incorporates the chief actors into a new political, even moral, version emphasizing the role of Athens.

The classical period also welcomes a rash of labyrinth motifs in the form of meander-based designs, on red-and black-figure vases inspired by drama.[151] The most explicit reference to Crete is on the classical and later coinage of Knossos, where circular, rectangular, and cruciform meanders indicate the original home of the labyrinth.[152] Thereafter it appears in Atthidographers' accounts of the adventures of Theseus (Pherekydes, Philochoros, and Kleidemos), where it is already contaminated by Athenian interests. By the Hellenistic period, the word shows active meanings in poetic, ritual, and mythological contexts (Callimachus, *Delian Hymn* 311i: γναμπτὸ ἔδος σκολιοῦ λαβυρίνθου). Apollodoros, first to call Daidalos an architect, identifies the λαβύρινθος as "the one made by Daidalos" (3.15.8,6). His description of it as an οἴκημα καμπαῖς πολυπλόκοις πλανῶν τὴν ἔξοδον, "a house with many-winding curves misleading [from] its exit" is strongly reminiscent of a fragment of Sophokles (Nauck, 34): οἴκημα καμπαῖς πολύπλοκος and may derive from that dramatist's *Daidalos*. Eventually the term *labyrinth* describes parts of Greek monumental architecture, according to the building accounts from Hellenistic Didyma, which refer to an element called λαβύρινθος, in the context of more technical terms for parts of the temple such as θυροῖα, μεσοτοιχός, and an ἄβασις.[153]

A conspiracy of circumstances—the survival of structures and images from prehistoric Crete, first impressions of monumental architecture abroad, and the need for a narrative explaining both—encouraged the tale of the Labyrinth in the early archaic period. If the foreign element suggested by Herodotus is genuine, this myth participates in those Greek claims to native authorship of forms learned abroad. In the mythological account of this experience, Daidalos is expected to account for both Bronze Age creations and Iron Age innovations, and ultimately to justify the latter as a legacy of the former, rather than as a development stimulated by non-Greek sources.

While Theseus and Ariadne are linked in the visual arts in the archaic period, the figure and story of Daidalos, rare in archaic and classical Greek art, make a solitary but significant appearance with Theseus, Ariadne, and the Minotaur on the Rayet skyphos. The sum of its individual eccentricities—the portrayal of the young Athenians who in-

[150] A. Stewart, "Stesichoros and the François Vase," in *Ancient Greek Art and Iconography*, ed. W. Moon (Madison, 1983), 53–74; F. Brommer, "Theseus-Deutungen," AA (*1982*) 69–88, on the relative roles of thread, ring, and wreath.

[151] P. Wolters, *Darstellung des Labyrinths* (Vienna, 1907); R. Eilmann, *Labyrinthos* (Athens, 1931); P. Lehmann Williams, "The Meander Door: A Labyrinthine Symbol," in *Studi Luisa Banti*, ed. G. Becatti and others (Rome, 1965), 215–22. M. Duchemin, "Le thème

du héros au labyrinthe dans la vie de Thesée," *Kokalos* 16 (1970) 30–52. On Theseus in early fifth-century literature and art, see Chapter 12.

[152] Frontisi-Ducroux, *Dédale*, pl. VIII.

[153] A. Rehn and R. Harder, *Didyma vol. 2: Die Inschriften* (Berlin, 1958), nos. 25–27, passim; J. C. Montego, "Note on the Labyrinth in Didyma," *AJA* 80 (1976) 104–6; H. W. Parke, *The Oracles of Apollo in Asia Minor* (London, 1985), 216–17.

spired the mission of Theseus, Ariadne waiting patiently to lead out Theseus after his triumph over the monster, a figure in flight, and the mystery of the mounted man—suggests an unusual experiment, perhaps a Boiotian approximation of an Attic tradition.[154] On the reverse of the vase, a warrior mounted on a galloping horse, bears an unknown relationship to the exploits of Theseus (Figure 10c). Is he Peirithoos? Minos in pursuit? or Daidalos himself? This cavalier is followed by a curious airborne figure placed horizontally just beneath the right handle attachment, his head and shoulders hovering above the tail of the moving horse (Figure 10d). This anthropoid aloft is naked except for a belt, and wears wings for arms; the vase is badly damaged near his head, which appears neckless and bearded. The flying figure has no visual precedent in archaic art, unless he borrows his pose and placement from birds in Lakonian cavalry scenes or hapless monsters.[155] The identification as Ikaros remains the most attractive.[156] That the figure is falling, rather than still in successful flight, seems indicated by his folded (rather than extended) wings, and in his resemblance to other mythological figures near death (like the decapitated Medusa on the Polyphemus Painter's name vase, the Eleusis amphora). This would then be the earliest Ikaros (or Daidalos) in Greek art represented in flight and fall; the awkward join of head and shoulders, the clumsy pose aloft, suggest the artist invented this figure, with such details as the belt a conscious embellishment.[157] If this is Ikaros, tantalizing is the implied presence of Daidalos, represented by his son and his invention—wings—but still as shadowy a figure as he is in literature before the fifth century. Elsewhere, the airborne pair are attested in isolation, as on the early classical Etruscan bulla (Figure 8). Whether the winged figure is Daidalos or Ikaros, this archaic scene would not only illustrate wings and flight but would incorporate them into the Cretan cycle represented by Theseus, Ariadne, and the Minotaur.

As often in Greek myth, both visual and literary sources are a likely inspiration for this portion of the tale, and several point to Crete. A connection to Crete is already implied in the belt of Ikaros, that article of attire essential to archaic Cretan male (and female) figures.[158] Images of craftsmen, sometimes winged or wearing winged footwear,

[154] Its Attic proportions, scale, and size as well as narrative mean some still hesitate to call the vase Boiotian; possibly "l'artiste s'inspire des modèles antiques qu'il enjolie de détails:" A. Waiblinger, CVA Louvre 17 (France 26), 32.

[155] Beazley, JHS 47 (1927) 222 n. 4, on Lakonian parallels; for this phenomenon in Protoattic and Protocorinthian, see Morris, Black and White Style, 37–38 nn. 4–5.

[156] Beazley, JHS 47 (1927) 222–23; Kokalakis, "Icarus," 25. For other early representations of Ikaros, see Akropolis 601 (Figure 9), etc., in Nyenhuis, "Daidalos et Ikaros," LIMC III.1, 316–19. E. Simon, "Frühe Bilder des fliegenden Daidalos," forthcom-

ing, prefers Daidalos here.

[157] Compare Nessos on the Protoattic amphora by the New York Nessos Painter (Morris, Black and White Style, pl. 14), an early centaur type plagued by apparent deformities (both legs on one side of his equine body, a neckless head and beard) that betray an experimental phase.

[158] I. Raubitschek and T. Raubitschek, "Der kretische Gürtel," in Wandlungen, 49–52; Boardman, in Fourth Cretological Congress, 44, 46–47. The belt is probably a North Syrian convention (H. Seeden The Standing Armed Figurine in the Levant [Munich, 1980], 134) and shows up as far away as Sardinia, on archaic stone statuary (see Chapter 7, n. 44).

contribute to a popular tradition of demon-artists with magic powers, including wings, a common attribute of gods and heroes in Greek art.[159] On the seventh-century Cycladic pithos where Athena is born from the head of Zeus, not only the two Olympians but the female birth-attendant on the left, the seated craftsman to the right, and the fragmentary figure in the air above him all wear wings (Figures 13, 14). Cretan representations of pairs of winged figures (Figure 33), including those of "bound captives with wings," an invitation to the story of two craftsmen held prisoner, are especially prolific and naturally provocative for the tradition of a figure like Daidalos. They may well have stimulated the stories, but most resist firm identification with the Cretan craftsman.[160] Like early scenes from Crete where Theseus and Ariadne, or Europa and the bull, are identified with enthusiasm by scholars, such Greek mythological correspondences are premature, particularly in Crete. These creatures are better understood as an Orientalizing phenomenon inspired by Near Eastern images (Figure 32), without Greek associations yet.[161] Despite Crete's rich iconographic tradition of early Iron Age art, little of it can be coordinated with conventional Greek narrative or cult. Cretan images, prehistoric as well as archaic, enriched the tradition of Daidalos and other winged craftsmen, including those in black-figure vase painting eventually labeled Ikaros.[162] Ironically, Crete was not directly or originally involved in developing the image of Daidalos, which responded rather to historical attitudes elsewhere in Greece. If many creatures, or all gods, wear wings lightly in Greek art, only certain provinces were home to poets who made up stories about how they got their wings, it appears. Nilsson pinpointed this paradox in observing that much of Minoan legend is Athenian in origin (see Chapter 13).

Outside of iconography, Crete contributed to an intriguing variation on the tradition of "wings" invented by Daidalos. One of the *xoana* attributed to Daidalos in Roman

[159] S. Papaspyridi-Karouzou, "Un Πρῶτος Εὑρετής dans quelques monuments archaiques," *ASAA* 8–10 (1946–1948) 36–46; N. Gialouris, "Πτερόεντα πέδιλα," *BCH* 77 (1953) 293–321. C. Hart, *Images of Flight* (Berkeley, 1988), 95–119, on Near Eastern and Greek wings for deities; M. Smith, "Divine Travel," *UF* 16 (1984) 359, on Canaanite air traffic (see Chapter 4, n. 22).

[160] Hoffman, *Early Cretan Armorers*, 35–36, fig. 6; Beyer, *Dreros und Prinias*, 70, Blome, *Bildwelt Kretas*, 69–70 (on "Europa,") 75–76 nn. 86–87. A. Lembesi, "Τελετουργία καὶ μύθος στὶς Κρητικὲς παράστασεις τοῦ 7ου αἰ.," ΕΙΛΑΠΙΝΗ, 125–38, on the lack of mythological narrative in early Cretan art. Cf. the cut-out plaque from Afrati (Arkades): D. Levi, "Arkades," *ASAA* 10–12 (1927–1929) 28, fig. 8; 31 (D); Boardman, *Cretan Collection in Oxford*, 48 n. 1, pl. 16

(Ikaros); C. Kardara, "Some Remarks on Two Early Cretan Bronzes," *AAA* 2 (1969) 216–18, and in *Second Cretological Congress*, 186–88, identifies this figure as a bound Daidalos, captive of Minos, but its sources are surely Near Eastern, like the Old Babylonian seals with pairs of winged captives (cited by Astour, *Hellenosemitica*, 271–72) or the bound captive in Egyptian art transmitted via Phoenicia (Kardara, *AAA* 2 [1969] 216–19).

[161] Basalt stele found at Aleppo: W. Orthmann, *Untersuchungen zur späthethitischen Bildkunst* (Bonn, 1971), 54, pl. 4, Aleppo 1. I am grateful to Ulla Kasten and Michael Morris for obtaining an illustration. Astour, *Hellenosemitica*, 194–95 n. 6, and 271–72, for a Near Eastern derivation of "Ikaros."

[162] Karouzou, *ASAA* (1946–1948) 36–46; Kokalakis, "Icarus."

times was a statue of Herakles at Thebes in Boeotia (Pausanias, 9.11.2), dedicated as well as made by the craftsman. This bequest was intended to express thanks for a favor rendered Daidalos by Herakles: the rescue and burial of the body of Ikaros on the island that bore his name thereafter, after the fatal flight from Crete. In this version, however, wings are not mentioned: instead, Daidalos invented sails for the ships he built for his escape, by means of which he "outsailed the oars of Minos's fleet." An Attic story may lie behind this version: according to Kleidemos, Daidalos escaped from Crete by boat (merchant ship) and was pursued by Minos in warships, a scenario suitable to maritime politics of the fifth century (cited in Plutarch, *Theseus* 19; see Chapter 12). In the same tradition, he is credited with a major innovation in the history of seafaring, the introduction of the airborne trap of cloth with which ships capture wind and its power to move transport. Throughout the history of Greece, sails were literally the wings of man, and the language of early Greek poetry makes this explicit. The ships of the Phaiakians are admired by Athena for being "as swift as wing or thought" (*Odyssey* 7.36), although as protégées of her enemy, Poseidon, their nautical powers may be more intimidating than reassuring to the hero of the poem. At *Odyssey* 11.125 (= 23.272), oars are described as "wings for ships," in a portrayal of landlocked peoples without such civilized amenities, to whom Odysseus must spread the gospel of Poseidon. The most vivid equation between sails and wings was proffered by Hesiod, in a context celebrating the Aiginetans as the first practitioners of seafaring (frag. 205):

> οἵ δή τοι πρῶτον τεῦξαν νέας ἀμφιελίσσας,
> πρῶτοι δ᾽ ἱστία θέσαν νεὼς πτερὰ ποντοπόροιο.

> They were the first to build ships, curved on both ends,
> and they first put up sails, the wings of a seagoing ship.

The anecdote in Pausanias suggests that sails and wings, once equivalent in poetry, became substitutes in the catalogue of inventions by Daidalos.[163] His other creations acquired wings in poetry, in the context of being praised in many forms of δαιδαλόεις. The armor of Achilles is the most celebrated work of art to experience this transformation (*Iliad* 19.386; see Chapter 1). The constellation of poetic δαιδαλ- words that illuminated the hero's armor during its manufacture reappear when he puts it on, in Book 19 (e.g., lines 13, 19). His actual entry into battle (19.365–85) is formulaic in its detailed praise of epic armor, but culminates in an unusual event, once the last element (his helmet) is in place (19.386): τῷ δ᾽ εὖτε πτερὰ γίγνετ᾽, ἄειρε δὲ ποίμενα λαῶν. The suit of armor grows wings and lifts the hero, the best of the Achaeans and the one who achieves immortality, into the air, as if its powers exceeded mere poetic praise and ac-

---

[163] Hart, *Images of Flight*, 89–93, on the connection between wings and sails, or travel by air and travel by sea, in the Greek imagination.

quired life—as did the works of Daidalos. For the metaphor of movement used to praise art in early and poetic modes becomes reality in the fifth century, when statues gain faculties of sight, speech, and autokinesis (see Chapter 8). As the works of Daidalos acquire such magic powers in the Greek imagination, the power of flight, enjoyed by select gods and heroes, was a natural addition to his accomplishments.

These vivid images in poetry and the power of metaphor may well have conspired with the vision of winged figures in early art to encourage a tradition that Daidalos invented wings. Several scenarios are possible to imagine: poetic metaphor may have endowed practical inventions like sails with the quality, ultimately the reality, of wings. Or the story of wings worn in art, then "invented" in legend by early and magical craftsmen, may have been reduced or rationalized to a more plausible and practical invention, such as sails. In such a process, the Greek imagination is both victim and benefactor of Greek reason, and neither deserves full credit or blame, as far as the testimonia allow. Other nautical refinements ascribed to Daidalos include the ship's mast and sail-poles (according to Kleidemos, in Plutarch, *Theseus* 19, Phanodikos, and Servius at *Aeneid* 4.14). Many scholars reduce all these "inventions" to rationalized explanations of "wings," but a healthy proportion of them may reflect Greek memory of prehistoric seafarers from Crete. For one fact abides throughout stories about Daidalos: his link to Crete, and the association with an island reputed for its thalassocracy is no accident. The exact nature of Minoan (Middle and Late Bronze Age) expansion throughout the Aegean is still a controversial topic; the idea was conceived under the influence of classical and modern theories of naval supremacy.[164] The convergence of archaeological and literary evidence guarantees that Minoan culture had reached many Aegean settlements outside Crete and that ships were largely responsible for this diffusion. However, the milieu that forged a naval empire for Minos in myth was building its own empire, in classical reality (see Part IV).

These visual elements attested in representations of Daidalos and his son testify to an activity in popular narrative that developed independently of his poetic adjectives. In such diversification, an inherited poetic tradition fed by Oriental iconography evolved a new landscape of myth, including the invention of wings. Those wings took him west, to the "greatest" Greece of all, where his persona first served to justify Hellenism against the claims of barbarians.

[164] See *Minoan Thalassocracy* for archaeological evidence and debate on Crete's reputation for seafaring, unchallenged until the Persian wars (see Part IV). J. Warzeski, "Minoan Cultural Hegemony and the Myth of the Minoan Thalassocracy" (M.A. thesis, Yale University, 1985), 1–4, on Mahan and modern theories of naval history, which encouraged modern conceptions of Minoan sea power. (Compare how early archaic Aigina monopolized seafaring and hence earned the praise of Hesiod: Morris, *Black and White Style*, 92–115.)

CHAPTER 7

Daidalos in Sicily:
Greeks and Phoenicians
in the West

ᾤκουν δὲ καὶ Φοίνικες περὶ πᾶσαν τὴν Σικελίαν

And the Phoenicians used to live all around Sicily.

—Thucydides, 6.2.6

Phoenixque multus habuit hos pridem locos.

And the Phoenician used to inhabit many of these places,
before.

—Avienus, *Ora Maritima* 440

THE FIRST DAIDALOS in ancient art identified by an inscription appears at a great distance from Athens and Crete: in Italy. In many legends the flight of Daidalos and son took them to Magna Graecia, where this episode in their adventures became especially popular, eventually in Roman painting.[1] An Etruscan gold bulla in early classical style displays a winged craftsman in squatting "flight" (in profile, with their feet tucked up underneath the body) on each face (Figures 8a, b).[2] Both figures wear the short chiton traditional as craftsman's garb; one carries a saw and adze, the other a double axe and carpenter's (T-) square. The former is identified as TAITΛE in letters

[1] P. von Blankenhagen, *RömMitt* 75 (1968) 106–43; E. Richardson, "The Story of Ariadne in Italy," in *Studies in Classical Art and Archaeology*, 189–95; cf. Kokalakis, "Icarus," 26 (Daidalos on Etruscan gems). The earliest inscribed Daidalos now appears on an Etruscan bucchero olpe of the mid-seventh century from Cerveteri: E. Simon, "Frühe Bilder des fliegenden Daidalos," forthcoming.

[2] Now in Baltimore: Walters Art Gallery 57.371 B; G.M.A. Hanfmann, "Daidalos in Etruria," *AJA* 39 (1935) 189–95; Becatti, *Oreficerie antiche*, 186, fig. 316, pl. 78; Frontisi-Ducroux, *Dédale*, pl. II, fig. II; Kokalakis, "Icarus," 26. T. Döhrn, *Etruskische Kunst* (Mainz, 1982), 22–23; *Gold Jewelry. Craft, Style and Meaning from Mycenae to Constantinople*, ed. T. Hackens and R. Winkes (Louvain, 1983), 109–111, no. 28.

above his head, the other as VIKAPE, with an initial digamma, the Etruscan equivalents of Daidalos and Ikaros. The letters run right to left and feature other archaisms (the digamma) conspicuously un-Attic, suggesting that this legend reached Etruria at an early date and via a Dorian route—Corinth or even Crete itself have been suggested. However they reached the West, Daidalos and his son appear with similar instruments in gems and sculpture from Etruria. With the tools of their trade (if not of their own invention: Pliny, *Naturalis Historia* 7.198) in hand, the two craftsmen arrive, like Demaratus of Corinth, to import Greek art to the West, where legend associates Daidalos with a host of ἔργα.

According to this Etruscan view, carpentry became paramount among the skills attributed to Daidalos in the West; architecture, in the broadest sense, dominates the Western legends, and even maintains a special claim in Etruria. Pliny's descriptions of Etruscan tombs, like that of Lars Porsenna at Clusium (derived from Varro: *Naturalis Historia* 36.19.4) which included a "labyrinth" in its basement, encouraged the Renaissance claim that the "Daedalic" art of architecture had been born in Italy.[3] The adventures and achievements of Daidalos in the West are a blueprint for the evolution of mythological traditions in conjunction with history and art, and anticipate his treatment in Athens examined in the second half of the book.

A rich component of Daidalos's career in Magna Graecia involves Sicily, where his experiences form a sequel to his misadventures in Crete. Either his assistance to Theseus in escaping the labyrinth or his invention of Pasiphae's seduction trap provoked the displeasure of Minos and a flight into exile.[4] In this version, the invention of wings and the fall of Ikaros take place when father and son escape from Crete to Sicily, unlike the Attic stories that narrate this flight from Athens to Crete (Chapter 8), or the Ikarian *aitia* that have Daidalos flee Crete for the mainland. The last-named flight probably appeared first in the history of mythography, although two versions already competed in the fifth century (Kleidemos, *FGrH* 323 frag. 17, from Plutarch, *Theseus* 19.8). How, why, and when Sicily entered the story involves Aegean contact with Sicily for over a thousand years.[5]

In the version recorded by Diodorus, Daidalos finds a new royal patron in the West, Kokalos of Kamikos (Inykos, according to Pausanias, 7.4.6) and produces a new series of wonders, this time marvels of engineering and architecture. Daidalos was pursued by Minos from Crete but had already made himself popular enough in his new home

[3] F. Borsi, "Leon Battista Alberti e l'*Etruria sacrum*," in *Fortuna degli Etruschi*, ed. F. Borsi (Milan, 1986), 36; M. Vickers, "Imaginary Etruscans: Changing Perceptions of Etruria since the Fifteenth Century," *Hephaistos* 7–8 (1985–1986) 158 n. 23.

[4] First in Herodotus, 7.170; fullest account in Diodorus (4.77–79). Cf. Pausanias, 7.4.7, Apollodorus,

1.12–15; Zenobius, Hyginus, etc. Bérard, *Colonisation grecque*, 417–29; Sjöqvist, *Sicily and the Greeks*, 3–9; Prinz *Gründungsmythen*, 138–49.

[5] Prinz, *Gründungsmythen*, 147, argues that the flight from Crete to the mainland, with its *aition* for the island of Ikaros, predates the Sicilian stories.

to gain accomplices in the form of his host's daughters, a replay of his relationship with Ariadne. Minos's clever stratagem tricks Daidalos into revealing his identity with a challenge that the designer of the labyrinth cannot resist: the task of threading a string through a snail's shell (Apollodoros, *Epitome* 1.14–15). Forced to release Daidalos to Minos, Kokalos receives the Cretan king as a guest and treats him to a bath at his daughters' hands—a welcome tradition for epic heroes (eg., *Odyssey* 4.47–50; 19.317). Enlisted by Daidalos, the daughters manage to scald their unwelcome guest to death in hot water, "une cure thermale inversée" borrowed from Daidalos's reputed introduction of thermal baths elsewhere in Sicily.[6] Minos was buried in a special structure with his bones interred below, a temple to Aphrodite above, as described by Diodorus. The tomb was disassembled in the early fifth century and the bones of Minos returned to Crete by Theron, the dynast of Akragas in the fifth century (Diodorus, 4.79.4).

The historical setting of this postscript, the death of Minos, is classical and suspect, for it betrays the same political purposes that claimed and moved the bones of heroes in similar disputes over territory and power.[7] In this case, the return of the bones is invoked as a theme in interpolis negotiations and recriminations about participation and resistance in the Persian wars. Herodotus's account of Daidalos in Sicily, although it ignores Minos's gruesome end and the dispute over his remains, is already a political myth. For it adjoins Cretan consultation of the Delphic oracle on the eve of the Persian invasion, and justifies their abstention from the Greek cause. The oracle reminded them (they claim) that other Greeks did not help them avenge the death of Minos, despite Cretan response to Agamemnon and the expedition to Troy.[8] Thus Herodotus's account, and with it the earliest evidence for a Sicilian Daidalos, is already entangled with the Athenian manipulation of early Greek history occasioned by the Persian wars (see Part IV).

Theron's interest in the remains of Minos, like the story of the bones of Orestes or Theseus, may have drawn its plausibility from a venerated tomb, of archaic or prehistoric date, in the area of Akragas. Archaeologists have been eager to connect its description with structures emergent in Crete, such that Evans readily named one of his discoveries at Knossos the "Temple Tomb" for its resemblance to Diodorus's description of Minos's tomb.[9] As with other connections claimed between traditions and prehistoric

---

[6] Frontisi-Ducroux, *Dédale*, 176. Herodotus, 7.160, merely specifies a βιαῖος θάνατος for Minos, elaborated in later accounts known to Apollodoros, Tzetzes, Ovid, Strabo (279), schol. Pindar, *Nemean* 4.95; Diodorus, 4.79.

[7] S. Spyridakis, "Salamis and the Cretans," *PdP* 31 (1976) 345–55; cf. Prinz, *Gründungsmythen*, 147–49. Herodotus, 1.68 (bones of Orestes); Kimon and the bones of Theseus (Plutarch, *Theseus* 36; *Kimon* 8): see Chapter 12; A. Snodgrass, "Les origines du culte des héros dans la Grèce antique," in *La mort, les morts dans les sociétés anciennes*, ed. G. Gnoli and J.-P. Vernant (Naples, 1982), 107–19.

[8] H. B. Mattingly, "Athens and the Western Greeks, ca. 500–413 B.C.," in *Annali del Istituto Italica di Numismatica* 12–14 (1965–1967) suppl. 1 (Rome, 1969) 201–22; Spyridakis, *PdP* 31 (1976) 345–55; Boardman, *CAH* III.3, 233.

[9] Evans, *POM* 4:959–61; K. Lehmann-Haupt, "Das Tempel-Grab des Priester-Königs zu Knossos," *Klio*

remains, modern arguments defending them must yield to the historical setting that inspired the mythological elements. Theron's classical diplomacy probably accounts for the renown of the tomb. His political motives probably involved better relations with local Sicilians and with western Greeks, to be promoted by a noble and pious gesture. The episode is suspiciously dependent on the Congress of Gela and the question of Sicilian unity.[10] Theron's character was distinguished not only through birth and wealth but also "through his generosity toward the many": καὶ τῇ πρὸς τὸ πλῆθος φιλαν-θρωπίᾳ. His piety reconciled the legendary past with contemporary political unity much as may have the historian who transmitted the legend.

Most of the elements of Daidalos's Sicilian adventures, including his creations, can be traced to similar preoccupations in the historical period. In Magna Graecia, material relics inspired legends of epic heroes' activity in the West, stories that provided a historical precedent for Greek settlements. The most celebrated such legend linking the Greek heroic past with the settlement of Italy involves Aeneas, but other Homeric heroes—Diomedes, Philon, Ktetes, Epeios—were linked to tombs and artifacts in Sicily and South Italy.[11] In the context of these heroic traditions, the adventures of Daidalos in Sicily can be traced to the same Iron Age quest for historical claims and familiar heroes in a new land.[12] This explanation covers those works attributed to his hand as well. In Sicily he is credited with the fortifications of Kamikos, a water dam in the Megara Hyblaia region, thermal baths at Selinos, and a precarious platform for Aphrodite's temple on the akropolis of Eryx, none of which are attested in archaeology.[13]

Only two of his Sicilian creations recall his traditional (epic) talents in the realm of minor arts and metallurgy. The most exotic is a replica of a golden ram, or honeycomb, for Erykian Aphrodite, περιττῶς εἰργασμένον καὶ τῷ κατ᾿ ἀληθεῖαν [κηρίῳ, κριῷ] ἀπαρεγχειρήτως ὡμοιωμένον: "cunningly wrought and moreover resembling a true [honeycomb? ram?]"(Diodorus, 4.78.5). Because the manuscript permits "ram" (κριόν) next to "comb" (κηρίον), the exact nature and material of this object are in doubt. But two of its qualities—its gold materials and lifelike properties (praiseworthy realism)—suit Daidalos the epic craftsman, and modern discoveries of gold jewelry have been eagerly compared with this reference (see nn. 24, 25). The second Sicilian δαίδαλον is

25 (1932) 169–96; Becatti, RömMitt 60–61 (1953–1954) 31–32, and Sjöqvist, Sicily and the Greeks, 3–9, disconnect the legend from prehistoric remains.

[10] M. J. Fontana, "Terone e il TAPHOS di Minosse: uno squarcio di attività politica siciliota," Kokalos 24 (1978) 201–19, suggests that Diodorus's source may have been Antiochos of Syrakuse, who began history of Sicily with the legendary king, Kokalos, and concluded with the Congress of Gela. Cf. Bérard, Colonisation grecque, 437–50; F. W. Walbank, "The His-

torians of Greek Sicily," Kokalos 15 (1969) 476–97; Pearson, Greek Historians of the West, 11–33, 55.

[11] Holloway, Italy and the Aegean, 97–106, on these traditions and their historical connections. For the link between Aeneas and Daidalos, see Vergil, Aeneid 6. 14–32; also Chapter 3.

[12] G. Gianelli, Culti e miti della Magna Grecia (Florence, 1963); Prinz Gründungsmythen, 148–49; Holloway, Italy and the Aegean, 101–2.

[13] Diodorus, 4.78; Sjöqvist, Sicily and the Greeks, 4.

far more conventional to his epic repertoire. A distant source, the Lindian temple chronicle, records a bronze krater once given as a ξείνιον by Daidalos to Kokalos, thereafter to Athena Lindia by the tyrant Phalaris of Akragas, presumably a descendant of Gela's Rhodian colonists.[14] As a guest gift from visiting artist to host, it was also presumably thought to be made by Daidalos, but is associated with the craftsman primarily through historical conditions rather than as a tribute to his art. The krater, an epic as well as archaic type of gift or dedication, functions as a historical link between Cretan founders and Sicilian colony, much as do other works attributed to Daidalos to be discussed. Dedicated by a tyrant of Akragas, the krater must have played a role in his local political negotiations among native and Greek Sicilians similar to that represented by the bones of Minos in Theron's reign or the statue from Omphake in that of Antiphemos. Thus the krater at Lindos (presumably inspired by an archaic bronze one, in the tradition of those sent by Sparta to Sardis, or from Lydia to Delphi) is a predictable archaic gift or dedication and hardly contributes to an understanding of Daidalos, his adventures, and his art.

Unlike the career of Daidalos in Athenian and postclassical sources (see Part III), sculpture is conspicuously absent from his creations in Sicily, except in one reference. Pausanias mentions an ἄγαλμα taken to Gela by its founder, Antiphemos, from the neighboring city of Omphake (8.46.2; 9.40.3, 4, where more than one statue is mentioned). Like tombs claimed to belong to heroes in territorial disputes, these statues are intimately linked to the historical legends attendant on early Greek colony foundations. Cretan colonists assured their claim to Gelan territory, previously occupied by Greek settlers without a formal colony, by "reappropriating" statues made by their fellow Cretan, Daidalos.[15] Control of the cult, more importantly than its statues, legitimized Greek claim to the area, in the way early sanctuaries determined political disputes of the archaic period.[16] In terms of Daidalos's works, it may be significant that only the founding of Gela, the single colony with a Cretan connection, invoked his activity as sculptor, although for religious and political purposes rather than through his reputation as an artist. As Holloway admits, "The notion of pre-Greek and non-Greek images in Italian

---

[14] Lindos Temple Chronicle = *Syll.*³ 725, C, 21–28; C. Blinkenberg, *Lindos II. Inscriptions* (Berlin, 1941), 171.

[15] H. Wenkter, "Die Ktisis von Gela bei Thukydides," *RömMitt* 63 (1956) 129–39, esp. 134: "Das bedeutet, die Kultbilder des Daidalos, kretischer Besitz, werden zu einer kultischen Sicherung des Anspruchs der kretischen Griechen auf das Gebiet von Gela gemacht." Cf. Sjöqvist, *Sicily and the Greeks*, 9, citing Freeman, Pais, Parieti, and other nineteenth-century scholars who reached the same conclusion. Graham,

CAH III.3, 165, assumes "colonization was achieved by force."

[16] Wenkter cites numerous parallels for this phenomenon; Snodgrass, in *La Mort*, esp. 116. See various essays in *Santuari e politica nel mondo antico*, ed. M. Sordi (Milan, 1983), including a discussion of the statues of Damia and Auxesia and the early war between Athens and Aigina (Herodotus, 5.82): M. Ciccio, "Il santuario di Damia e Auxesia e il conflitto tra Atene ed Egina (Herod. V, 82–88)," 95–104; Morris, *Black and White Style*, 110–19.

shrines is not implausible"; locally venerated wooden or other cult images could have inspired a claim for Daidalos's craftsmanship just as they did in Crete, and for the same reasons, given Gela's foundation by Cretans.[17]

As in the Cretan traditions on Daidalos (Chapter 6), archaeological discoveries have refueled modern confidence in the historicity of the legends. Daidalos's classical, Athenian (Chapter 9) reputation as a sculptor and discoveries of statuary in Sicily have encouraged Italian scholarship on Sicilian art under his name, for several generations. The first such "Daedalica Siciliae" by Paolo Orsi appeared sixty years ago and focused on two early archaic sculptures in limestone and terracotta in the Syracuse Museum.[18] At this early date, Cretan antiquities had only begun to emerge and Löwy's seminal articles had barely launched the modern "Daedalic" style, yet Orsi used the expression "l'arte dedalica" freely and in distinction from "Daedalica," the collective noun coined from Daidalos's name.[19] Orsi felt confident in defining the early Sicilian school of sculpture from these examples, and connected their evolution to mainland works in the following manner: "La testa di Laganello, e poche altre scolture che ora citeremo, rilevamo, quali piu di quell'arte che fu dedalico-cretese nelle sue prime origini, poscia cretese-peloponnesica e da ultimo dedalico-siceliota" (p. 145). If pupils of Daidalos like Dipoinos and Skyllis spread Daedalic art to the Peloponnese, then Cretan and Peloponnesian settlers brought it to the Sicilian colonies, a view Orsi shares with other modern scholars (see Chapter 7). Title and tradition of "Daedalica Siciliae" were maintained in subsequent literature by Gabrici, Arias, and Meola, tailored to limestone and terracotta discoveries from Sicilian sites.[20] An unexpected boost for Daidalos's Sicilian authenticity materialized with the discovery of wooden statuettes preserved in a spring sanctuary at Palma di Montechiaro near Akragas, in 1934.[21] The description of Daidalos's statues by Dio-

[17] Holloway, *Italy and the Aegean*, 100; Dunbabin, *Western Greeks*, 112, assumes such statues are genuine works of Daidalos, imported from Crete; Bérard, *Colonisation grecque*, 425, sees a local *xoanon* for Kokalos. Rizza, *Kokalos*, 30–31 (1984–1985) 70, identifies Butera as ancient Omphake.

[18] P. Orsi, "Daedalica Siciliae," *MonPiot* 22 (1916) 131–62.

[19] On Löwy and later scholarship, see Chapter 9. G. Vallet and F. Villard, "Megara Hyblaea VIII. Remarques sur la plastique du VIIe siècle," *MEFRA* 76 (1964) 25, point out that Orsi actually used the term *daedalica* long before the style had been defined.

[20] E. Gabrici, "Daedalica Selinuntia," *MAAN* 5 (1924) 3–18, focused on terracotta reliefs from Selinus; in "Daedalica Siciliae II," *ASNP* (1937) 129–41, Arias claimed to succeed Orsi's original article; cf. his "Contributi alla storia dell' arte dedalica nella Magna Grecia e nella Sicilia," *RAI* 4, 3, 5 (1943) 212–33. E. Meola's *Terracotte Orientalizzante di Gela*, *Mon Ant* 48 (Rome, 1971), was subtitled *Daedalica Siciliae, III.* Cf. G. Rizza, "Dedalo e le origini della scultura greca," *CronArch* 2 (1963) 1ff.

[21] G. Caputo, "Tre xoana e il culto di una sorgente sulfurea in territorio geloo-agrigentino," *AccLinc* 37 (1938) 585–684, in their first and definitive publication, readily assimilated them to current theories of *xoana* and the "Daedalic" style. Richter subdivided them in style and therefore date: *Korai*, 35, no. 31, figs. 109–12 (late seventh century); 43, nos. 53 and 54, figs. 175–82 (first quarter of the sixth century), but they are probably contemporary and all sixth-century. Donohue, *Xoana*, 215–16. On the Palma sanctuary, see E. de Miro, "La Fondazione di Agrigento e l'ellenizzazione del territorio fra il Salso e il Platani," *Kokalos* 8 (1962) 128–35.

dorus and Pausanias and the artist's alleged presence in this area of Sicily were promptly authenticated on the basis of these statuettes. Even the enigmatic place-name, *Daedalium*, preserved in a late itinerary on this area, has been identified with the modern site of Palma on the strength of the wooden δαίδαλα found there.[22]

The reasoning of Caputo and of those who accept these statuettes as proof of Daidalos's activity in Sicily rests on a chain of weak links familiar in scholarship assimilating archaeological finds with legends about Daidalos (see Chapter 9). The statuettes are equated with *xoana*, then compared with the style of Daidalos's literary oeuvre and to the literary tradition of the statues from Omphake ascribed to Daidalos by Pausanias. Such arguments are as ill-founded as those linking other early archaic artifacts, from Crete and elsewhere, with the name and the legend of Daidalos. The discovery of wooden statuettes from Samos in more recent years demonstrates the sophistication and wide distribution of archaic sculpture in wood.[23] The Palma examples represent a local expression of an archaic Greek type, perhaps inspired by Rhodian and Ionian imports.

Other minor arts, outside of sculpture, attract attention as substantiations of "Daedalic" art in Sicily.[24] The "golden honeycomb" for Erykian Aphrodite listed by Diodorus recalls Homeric δαίδαλα. A set of gold jewelry and decorated bowls discovered in tombs at Sant' Angelo Muxaro, some fifteen kilometers from Akragas, once provoked great interest in reviving the Sicilian Daidalos.[25] But both rings and bowl are now recognized as archaic works in a local Orientalizing style, neither Bronze Age Minoan (as the rings were once called) nor relevant to Iron Age Crete and a later persona of Daidalos.

If anything, the results of modern archaeology in Sicily demonstrate developments unanticipated in the literary tradition of Daidalos's adventures. The island's "Daedalic" sculpture is later than that in the same style from Greece, hence more properly a sub-

[22] E. De Miro, "Influenze cretesi nei santuari ctonî dell' area geloo-agrigentina," in *Antichità Cretesi*, 2:207, on the other hand, identifies *Daedalium* as a foundation by Cretan colonists in the tradition of the Knossian *da-da-re-jo*, on architectural rather than sculptural grounds. Caputo (n. 21) proposes a more sensible ancient identity for the Palma sanctuary in a malodorus spot (i.e., sulphurous spring) near Gela called "Gelonium stagnum . . . quod taetro odore abigit proximantes" (Solinus 5.21–22): *AccLinc* 37 (1938) 679–84; *NSc* 19 (1965) 185–89, Suppl., "Palma di Montechiaro (Agrigento)—Daedalium."

[23] D. Ohly, "Neue Holzfunde aus dem Heraion von Samos. Befund und Rekonstruktion der Hera-statuette," *AthMitt* 82 (1967) 89–99; G. Kopke, "Neue Holzfunde aus dem Heraion von Samos" *Ath Mitt* 82

(1967) 100–116; H. Kyrieleis, "Archaische Holzfunde aus Samos," *AthMitt* 95 (1980) 87–147; Donohue, *Xoana*, 216–18.

[24] Arias, *RAI* 4, 3, 5 (1943) 212–33; Dunbabin, *Western Greeks*, 241, on marble lamps, probably Cycladic imports and not native "Daedalic."

[25] P. Orsi, "La necropoli di S. Angelo Muxaro," *AAP* 17 (1932) 7 fig. 32; Becatti, *Oreficerie antiche*, 183–84, nos. 302a, b; 303a, b; Sjöqvist, *Sicily and the Greeks*, 6–9; R. D. Barnett, "The Nimrud Bowls in the British Museum," *RSF* 2 (1974) 19, calls the bowl from the tomb group "a local Sicilian version of a Phoenician original." Cf. Markoe, *Phoenician Bowls*, 214–15. For genuine Phoenician jewelry from Sicily, see W. Culican, "Phoenician Jewelry," *Berytus* 22 (1973) 37, 39.

Daedalic phase (or, in Ridgway's expression, "Lingering Daedalic"), and more heavily influenced by Ionian areas of East Greece (including Rhodes, a Dorian city) than by "Dorian" elements as Jenkins defined the Daedalic style.[26]

Outside of the statue of Omphake (Pausanias, 9.4.7), the bulk of Daidalos's alleged creative activity in Sicily involved architecture and engineering projects of massive and impressive scale. Sicilian architecture of the first millennium may have been a powerful stimulus to stories about Daidalos, just as Greek sculpture revived him in Athens. Temple building at Greek colonies in the West in the archaic and classical periods was prodigious for the sheer number of projects, often side by side, the ambitious scale of several colossal temples, and their experimental features.[27] City planning and defensive engineering flourished as well, and these visible records of western Greek achievements helped make Daidalos primarily an architect, rather than a sculptor, in Sicily.[28] An additional factor was the role of immigrant craftsmen in this development, including some who fled inhospitable or unprofitable regimes in Ionia for better opportunities in booming Magna Graecia.[29]

Tales about Daidalos in the West may have been encouraged by cultural developments outside art and architecture. Poets and philosophers from Pythagoras to Aeschylus and Plato found new and eager patrons at the courts of western tyrants.[30] Such archaic and classical patterns of emigration no doubt fed the tradition of Daidalos in Sicily by providing a paradigm for the flight of a craftsman from one royal patron to another. This paradigm suits the original, Oriental persona (Chapter 4) of a craftsmen who travels among the gods and works on commission for divine, as for royal, patrons.

However, many scholars have maintained that his adventures derive from monumental prehistoric structures in the West, or "prove" that the legends of Daidalos and Minos in Sicily reflect genuine Greek memories of Bronze Age contact with the West.[31] Colos-

---

[26] Jenkins, *Daedalica* (see Chapter 9); Ridgway, *Archaic Style*, 22–26; Vallet and Villard, *MEFRA* 76 (1964) 25–42, is valuable for its conservative conclusions—for example, on the lack of seventh-century sculpture in Sicily. On Ionic elements in Sicily, see Barletta, *Ionic Influence in Archaic Sicily*.

[27] R. R. Holloway, "Architect and Engineer in Archaic Greece," *HSCP* 73 (1960) 281–90; F. Winter, "Tradition and Innovation in Doric Design I: Western Greek Temples," *AJA* 80 (1976) 139–45; Barletta, *Ionic Influence in Archaic Sicily;* D. Mertens, *Der Tempel von Segesta und die Tempelbaukunst des griechischen Westens in klassischer Zeit* (Mainz, 1985).

[28] Becatti, *RömMitt* 60–61 (1953–1954) 30–33; F. Winter, *Greek Fortifications* (Toronto, 1971) 29 n. 59; Sjöqvist, "Greek Civilization in Sicily," in *Sicily and*

the Greeks, 61–67.

[29] Holloway, *HSCP* 73 (1960) 281–90, on architect-engineers like the son of "Knidiedes," whose name was inscribed on the stylobate of the temple of Apollo at Syracuse. H. Engelmann, "Die Bauinschrift am Apollonion von Syrakus," *ZPE* 44 (1981) 91–94, reads κἐπικλε στύλεια· καλὰ ἔργα; M. Guarducci, "Ancora sull'epigrafe del tempio di Apollo a Siracusa," *AccLine* 37 (1982) 13–20, prefers ἐπίηλε στύλεια.

[30] Dunbabin, *Western Greeks*, 298–99; C. J. Herington, "Aeschylus in Sicily," *JHS* 87 (1967) 74–85.

[31] The classic statement of this view was T. J. Dunbabin's "Minos and Daidalos in Sicily," *BSR* 16 (1948) 1–18; cf. E. Manni, "Minosse ed Eracle nella Sicilia dell'età del bronzo," *Kokalos* 8 (1962) 6–29; G. Caputo

sal prehistoric structures no doubt encouraged tales about Daidalos, and may account for the tradition that has him accompany Aristaios's settlement of Sardinia.[32] But the architectural links are the weakest. Sardinian rock-cut nuraghi only resemble Minoan tholoi in a superficial manner, and their connection to Crete is at best a legendary association with the labyrinth motif. The "Temple Tomb" at Knossos fulfills neither of its names, but may be a residential villa (see n. 9). The fortifications of Erice (Eryx) are classical and later, despite the area's connection to Daidalos (see subsequent discussion, with n. 48). Place-names like "Minoa" and the legend of King Kokalos, whom the Greek imagination sought to connect with Aegean heroes, were the primary sources of inspiration.[33] But the overwhelming role of historical circumstances in the formation of these legends persuaded most scholars to decline any connection with prehistoric Aegean pottery in the West, until the recent and dramatic discoveries discussed in Chapter 5. In the Late Bronze Age, relations between Italy and the Aegean now appear richer and more complex than previously suspected, and specifically involve Crete, the home of Daidalos, and the island of Sardinia. The most prolific contact is documented at the end of the Late Bronze Age through ceramic and metallurgical evidence linking Cyprus, Crete, and the West.[34] In the dramatic transformation and transmigration of the Mediterranean metals trade at the end of the Late Bronze Age, iron replaced copper, and West replaced East, as primary resource and region. The island of Sardinia, for example, seems to have attracted enterprising Levanto-Cypriotes in the Late Bronze Age, according to pottery and ingots that suggest this western island suddenly appeared more lucrative and safer to Eastern merchants.[35] The archaic and classical reputation of Sardinia as the "largest island in the world" (Herodotus, 1.170, 5.106, 6.2) and its interest for Athenian imperial ambitions may derive from the prehistoric period when its resources and isolation attracted Mycenaean entrepreneurs and refugees from Late Bronze Age troubles.[36]

---

on "architettura dedalica," *Kokalos* 10–11 (1964–1965) 99–116; M. Marazzi, *Egeo ed Occidente alla fine del II millennio a.C.* (Rome, 1976), 81–120.

[32] Daidalos in Sardinia: Diodorus, 4.29; Pausanias, 10.17.3; Servius on Virgil, *Aeneid* 6.20. Bérard, *Colonisation grecque*, 417, 425, 436–37; Becatti, *RömMitt* 60–61 (1953–1954) 33; Frontisi-Ducroux, *Dédale*, 174 n. 20; J. M. Davison, "Greeks in Sardinia: The Confrontation of Archaeological Evidence and Literary Testimonia," in *SSA*, 1:68–70.

[33] Thus Sjöqvist, *Sicily and the Greeks*, 6–9.

[34] Chapter 5, nn. 69–78; in this network, Mycenaean pottery even reached Spain (n. 70).

[35] L. Vagnetti, 'L'Egeo e Cipro," and F. Lo Schiavo and D. Ridgway, "La Sardegna e il Mediterraneo oc-

cidentale allo scorcio del II millenio," both in *La Sardegna nel Mediterraneo tra il secondo e il primo millennio a.C.* (Cagliari, 1986), 359–67, 391–412; articles by Lo Schiavo and Merkel on "Sardinian Metallurgy," in *SSA*, 2:229–71; M. L. Ferrarese Ceruti, L. Vagnetti, and F. Lo Schiavo, "Minoici, Micenei, e Ciprioti in Sardegna nella seconda metà del II. millenio a. C.," in *SSA*, 3:7–37; Chapter 5, n. 69.

[36] R. J. Rowland, Jr., "The Biggest Island in the World," *CW* 68 (1975) 438–39; Davison, "Greek Presence in Sardinia: Myth and Speculation," in *SSA*, 2:190–95, and "Greeks in Sardinia," *SSA*, 1:71–81; L. Breglia Pulci, "La Sardegna arcaica tra tradizioni euboiche ed attiche," in *Nouvelle contribution*, 61–95.

The identity of the merchants, metallurgists, traders, and shippers who trafficked with the western Mediterranean since the Late Bronze Age, as in the eastern situation (Chapter 5), defies ethnic specificity. They included successors of the "Keftiu" and ancestors of Homer's Phoenicians, Canaanite migrants from Ugarit and Cyprus, and their Aegean apprentices and colleagues. Epigraphic evidence suggests guilds of metal casters inherited by successive generations, and as a Near Eastern metallurgist transplanted to Crete (Chapters 4–6), Daidalos is perfectly at home as a prehistoric wanderer to the West.

As in the Cretan stories about Daidalos, or the Boiotian myths of Kadmos, the Sicilian Daidalos has prehistoric roots but a historic cast. The western wanderings of Daidalos, originally a specialist in metallurgy, may well derive from prehistoric exploration of minerals. But the historical factors stimulating the legends are still post-Homeric and not merely a memory of Mycenaeans in the West. The main contribution made by new prehistoric evidence of Aegean and Levantine contact with the West is an advanced understanding of those patterns of interaction examined earlier, for the Aegean and Levant itself (Chapter 5 and 6). The critical catalyst for the legend lay in history itself, and in its retroactive manipulation for political purposes. No less an authority than Thucydides himself, in his famous excursus on the Greek colonies in Sicily with which he introduces the fateful Athenian expedition, provides the critical insight (6.2.6):

> ᾤκουν δὲ καὶ Φοίνικες περὶ πᾶσαν μὲν τὴν Σικελίαν ἄκρας τε ἐπὶ τῆς θαλάσσης ἀπολαβόντες καὶ τὰ ἐπικείμενα νησίδια.

> For Phoenicians were also living all around the coasts of Sicily and on the very shore, having seized even the islands lying opposite the coast.

According to this classical account, the Phoenicians preceded the Greeks in the settlement of coastal Sicily and its offshore islands. Until the most recent discoveries and scholarship, the testimony of Thucydides could not easily be reconciled with the available evidence. It has usually been dismissed as a mistaken extension of Punic expansion historically confined to western Sicily and post-Geometric times, at the earliest.[37] However, recent increase in both archaeological activity and in the recognition of Phoenician elements in early finds from the western Mediterranean has altered this perspective radically. The evidence begins in the Bronze Age, when refugees and entrepreneurs from the eastern Mediterranean move their markets west (Chapter 5). As the descendants of those merchants, Phoenicians in the west can now be attested as early as the

---

[37] E.g., Graham, *CAH* III.3 (1980), 95: "No evidence has been found anywhere in Sicily for Phoenician settlements which antedate the arrival of the Greeks." Davison, "Greek Presence in Sardinia," *SSA*, 2:188. A. Snodgrass, "Greek Archaeology and Greek History," *CA* 4, no. 2 (1985) 204, even cites this passage as an example of false colonization stories.

ninth century, near the time claimed for their arrival in ancient sources.[38] In several areas, four in particular (Sicily, Sardinia, Italy, and Spain), Phoenicians were active in the production of luxury goods to exchange for local resources, long before the Greeks arrived. However, later Greek sources claimed Hellenic priority or identity for sites actually settled earlier, if not exclusively, by Levantine entrepreneurs. An examination of the three best-documented cases of such "compensatory Hellenization" among the four areas mentioned leads to a finer appreciation of how and why Daidalos arrived in Sicily (the fourth locale of Phoenician settlement and Greek claims).

The most thoroughly documented and analyzed contrast between Phoenician priority and Greek counterclaims involves the Iberian peninsula, strictly speaking beyond the world of Daidalos but not the reach of Herakles. Spain was the goal of some of the earliest and most distant Phoenician travels, according to ancient memory and modern archaeology.[39] Strabo records a Phokaian colony, Μαινάκη at the mouth of the river (?), the modern Rió de Vélez near significant deposits of iron, some ten navigable kilometers upriver. His account stands in direct conflict with discoveries at this locale and with testimonia of an earlier date. For the mouth of the river attracted a Phoenician settlement (Toscanos) in the eighth century B.C., rich in Greek and Near Eastern finds linking the local community to Italy and the Aegean. Abandoned in the sixth century B.C., Toscanos shows no signs of reoccupation until the Roman imperial period, except for a Punic settlement on the opposite bank of the river with an outpost to the southwest. This archaeological record agrees beautifully with a Roman itinerary, the *Ora Maritima* of Rufus Festus Avienus, derived from an archaic Greek source. Avienus, or his archaic predecessor, never mentions the Phokaian presence on the Spanish coast, not even the archaic coastal site of Emporion (Ampurias) northeastward from Toscanos. Instead, he admits that (440): *"Phoenixque multus habuit hos pridem locos."*

This original and correct identification of local occupation may date to a period contemporary with the life of the settlement, or near its end in the sixth century B.C. Etymology may support the Levantine identity of the early settlement, if the name Mainake derives from a Semitic word, as scholars of Near Eastern languages have suggested.[40]

---

[38] Dunbabin, *Western Greeks*, 326–54, on early and friendly relations between Greeks and Phoenicians in Sicily. V. Tusa, "La Questione Fenicio-Punica in Sicilia," *Eretz Israel* 8 (1967) 50–57, and "Sicilia," in *L'espansione fenicia*, 175–91; "La presenza fenicio-punica in Sicilia," in *Phönizier im Westen*, 95–112; S. Moscati, "Fenici e Greci in Sicilia: Alle origini di un confronto," *Kokalos* 30–31 (1984–1985) 1–22; V. Tusa, "Sicily," in *The Phoenicians*, 186–205. H.-G. Niemeyer, "The Phoenicians in the Mediterranean: A Non-Greek Model for Expansion and Settlement," in *Greek Colonists and Native Populations*, 469–89.

[39] H. Schubart, "Phönizische Niederlassungen an der Iberischen Südküste," in *Phönizier im Westen*, 207–31 (cf. B. Shefton, 338–68); J. Cirkin, "Phönizier und Spanier. Zum Problem der kulturellen Kontakte," *Klio* 63 (1981) 411–21. J. G. Chamarro, "Survey of Archaeological Research on Tartessos," *AJA* 91 (1987) 197–232. Add Mycenaean pottery from Córdoba: Chapter 5, n. 70.

[40] A full account in H.-G. Niemeyer, "Auf der Suche nach Mainake: Der Konflikt zwischen literarischer und archäologischer Überlieferung," *Historia* 29 (1980) 165–89, and "Die phönizische Niederlas-

Only in the classical period—the earliest witness being Ephoros, who calls this site Μασ-
σαλιωτική—did Greek sources associate the ruins with Phokaians, rather than Phoenicians. Barring possible confusion between Φωκαική and Φοινική, non-Greek monumental ashlar ruins may have been mistaken for Greek ones by a Hellenistic geographer,
according to Niemeyer. Knowledge of other Phokaian colonies farther north, reinforced
by the size and reputation of Massalia and its expansion southward along coastal Lan-
guedoc, would have encouraged a claim for Phokaians. Furthermore, the historical conflict between Phokaians and Phoenicians, which culminated in the battle at Alalia (Herodotus, 1.165–66), might have helped promote a Phokaian claim to territory actually
Phoenician.

The modesty of Greek influence in Spain until the classical period is underscored by
the subtle Levantine flavor of its monumental sculpture and architecture. Even the ar-
chaic and classical sculpture called "Phokaian" looks less Greek than it does Syrian and
Anatolian with respect to the faces and figures.[41] The Pozo Moro cemetery in inland
Spain features a pillar monument with relief sculptures that look as if transplanted from
North Syria in the ninth or eighth centuries. Its ritual and mythological scenes reflect
Near Eastern literature and cult practices such as the sacrifice of a pig and an infant to
a double-headed monster, in the presence of figures wearing animal masks.[42] As the
Canaanite rite of infant sacrifice survived faintly in myth in Crete, or in deformed ritual
in Sparta (Pausanias, 3.16.9–11), it was still commemorated in art in Spain, if not celebrated in act. Thus the art and archaeology of Iberia suggests the kind of Phoenician
settlements, attracted to mineral resources, also found in the Aegean. Without the collision with a strong native tradition in material culture in Crete and elsewhere, Levantine style retains a more characteristically Punic flavor in Spain, for a longer period. But
ancient (and modern) sources on these settlements have promoted the Greek component, whether in myth, style, or etiology.

Niemeyer's analysis, and the general incongruence between literature and archae-

---

sung Toscanos: Eine Zwischenbilanz," in *Phönizier im
Westen*, 185–206. Röllig and Treumann derive Mainake from *mnqe/mnqeh*, or from *menaha/mainacha/me-
nacha*, and most recently *maka*, more appropriate to
the kappa in Greek, rendering "empty place" =
"place of rest," "new foundation" or "free harbor,"
rather than "military camp": Niemeyer, *Historia* 29
(1980) 179 n. 59, 186–89, and W. Röllig in *Phönizier im
Westen*, 370. Bunnens, *L'expansion phénicienne*, 244–46,
on Avienus; Snodgrass, *CA* 4, no. 2 (1985) 203–4, on
Mainake.

[41] J. M. Blasquez and J. Gonzales Navarette, "The
Phokaian Sculpture of Obulco in Southern Spain,"
AJA 89 (1985) 61–69; cf. M. Almagro-Basch, "L'ori-

gine de l'art ibérique à la lumière des récentes découvertes," *RA* (1977) 275–82; W. Trillmich, "Early Iberian Sculpture and 'Phocaean Colonization,' " in
Greek Colonists and Native Populations, 607–11.

[42] M. Almagro Basch, "Los relieves orientalizantes
de Pozo Moro (Albacete)," *Trabajos de Prehistoria* 35
(1971) 251–71; "Pozo Moro y el influjo fenicio en el
periodo orientalizante de la Peninsule Iberica," *RSF*
10 (1982) 231–72; "Pozo Moro. Un monumento fune-
rario iberico orientalizante," *MadrMitt* 24 (1983) 177–
293. On the relationship of this monument to the *molek* rite of infant sacrifice, see Th. Heider *The Cult of
Molek* (Sheffield, 1985), 189–92.

ology in Spain, are matched by a similar configuration of evidence and identical conclu-sions in the case of Sardinia. Its attraction for entrepreneurs from the eastern Mediter-ranean can now be traced to the Late Bronze Age (Chapter 5). This large island rich in copper and iron sources was explored by Phoenicians as early as the date one allows for the Nora Stone, but certainly by the ninth century, according to conspicuous amounts of Levantine pottery.[43] Monumental sculpture develops on the island in the seventh century in the form of large-scale limestone statues of warriors and athletes, derived from bronze statuettes the way the first sculpture in Greece suggest miniature or metal prototypes.[44] Greek material in Sardinia, on the other hand, appears late and scantily, and probably had traveled no farther than from Greek colonies in Sicily and Italy, rather than reflecting a more distant and influential source of interest (see n. 47). Yet Greek sources of the fifth and fourth centuries embroider elaborate legends involv-ing the island, clearly "una rielaborazione di un cospicuo materiale mitologico."[45] Ac-cording to Bondi's comparison of the sources to the archaeological record, a tradition largely Attic "distorted a series of dates, in such a way as to make certain Phoenician colonies of the southwest coast of Sardinia appear to be Greek foundations."[46] Davison (n. 32) pinpoints Athenian interests in western wealth during the late fifth century—culminating in the Sicilian expedition of the Peloponnesian War—for the introduction of Daidalos to Sardinian history, first attested in Diodorus (4.30). At the instigation of Iolaos,

καὶ τὸν Δαίδαλον ἐκ τῆς Σικελίας μεταπεμψάμενος, κατεσκεύασεν ἔργα πολλὰ καὶ μεγάλα μέχρι τῶν νῦν καιρῶν διαμένοντα καὶ ἀπὸ τοῦ κατασκευάσαντος Δαιδάλεια καλούμενα. ᾠκοδόμησε καὶ γυμνάσια μεγάλα τε καὶ πολυτελῆ, καὶ δικαστήρια κα-τέστησε καὶ τἆλλα τὰ πρὸς τὴν εὐδαιμονίην συντείνοντα.

And having sent for Daidalos from Sicily, he built many great works which have survived until now and are called "Daidaleia" from his construction of them. He built not only gym-nasia, large and elegant, but he also established law courts and the other things promoting well-being.

---

[43] Niemeyer, in *Phönizier im Westen*, 370; Bondi (cited in n. 45); F. Cross, "Phoenicians in the West: The Early Epigraphic Evidence," in *SSA*, 1:117–30, dates the Nora Stone to the eleventh century; *contra* W. Röllig, in *Antidoron. Festschrift Thimme*, ed. D. Metzler and others (Karlsruhe, 1983), 125–30; cf. M. Dothan, "Šardina at Akko?" *SSA*, 2:105–15, for connections between Sardinia and the Levant in My-cenaean IIIC; O. Negbi, "Early Phoenician Presence in the Western Mediterranean," in *SSA*, 3:247–50; E. Acquaro, "Sardinia," in *The Phoenicians*, 210–25.

[44] C. Tronchetti, "Nuragic Statuary from Monte Prama," *SSA*, 2:41–59; B. Ridgway, "Mediterranean Comparanda for the Statues from Monte Prama," *SSA*, 2:61–72, finds closer parallels on Cyprus than in Etruria (cf. L. Bonfante, "The Etruscan Connection," in *SSA*, 2:73–83).

[45] S. F. Bondi, "Osservazioni sulle fonti classiche per la Colonizzazione della Sardegna," *Saggi Fenici* 1 (1975) 49–66.

[46] Bondi, in *Phönizier im Westen*, 370 (my transla-tion).

That this legend was an extension of Daidalos's adventures in Sicily is indicated by its Sicilian authority (Diodorus, or his source, Timaeus), by the fact that Daidalos is "summoned" from his legendary duties in Sicily, and in archaeology, where some of the first Hellenic elements (e.g., terracotta figurines, pottery) are related to Sicilian equivalents.[47] In Diodorus's account, the first sentence describing his Sardinian works implies monuments of prehistoric proportions and fame that attracted the name Δαι-δάλεια much as did "Cyclopean" walls. Bronze Age nuraghi inevitably suggest themselves as structures likely to inspire legend and name, but the rest of Diodorus's description suggests another direction. Large and luxurious gymnasia, law courts, and "others promoting εὐδαιμονίη" are not only remote from prehistoric associations but introduce a Daidalos unheard of elsewhere: a designer of civic buildings. Such achievements on Sardinia complement those on Sicily: contributions to the life of a Greek city, structures for leisure and justice to match his defensive and hydraulic installations claimed on Sicily.

These western Greek activities, once again, are explicitly "colonial" in inspiration, a symbolic imposition of the Greek way of life and thought on alien territory. But, as implied in the account of the statues removed from Omphake to Gela, a natural element of chauvinism colors these legends, introducing a Greek priority where others were present earlier. If native Sicels did not precede Greeks at most places in Sicily, other immigrants may have—in particular the Phoenicians. At Eryx, for example, Daidalos's improbable engineering works must be reconciled with the city's Punic history and classical fortifications.[48] Even his elaborate gold "honeycomb" for the Aphrodite sanctuary at Eryx (possibly a Punic goddess, since Astarte of Eryx was worshiped at Carthage) suggests gold Orientalizing work, like the discoveries in the Sant' Angelo Muxaro tombs.[49] Thus Greek sources on Daidalos's activity at the site present a weaker case than does the Levantine evidence.

The site of Heraklea Minoa, an archaic Greek colony founded from Selinos, demonstrates Phoenician/Punic finds and perhaps even a Semitic name long before its Hellenic identity.[50] Its Greek name celebrates two Aegean heroes as if to certify, doubly, Greek

---

[47] As noted by Moscati, in *Fenici e Punici in Sardegna* (Milan, 1968), although more recent evidence and analysis include Etruscan and South Italian origins for Greek pottery in Sardinia (Davison, in *SSA* 1:73–77).

[48] A. M. Bisi, "Scavi e richerche alle fortificazione puniche di Erice," *Kokalos* 14 (1968) 307–15.

[49] See n. 25. S. Moscati, "Centri artigianili fenici in Italia," *RSF* I (1973) 37–52. D. Harden, *The Phoenicians* (London, 1971), 80, on Astarte of Eryx at Carthage.

[50] Tusa, in *Phönizier im Westen*, 98, cites Punic am-

phoras, Tanit signs, symbols, and letters, from E. Miro, "Heraklea Minoa. Scavi eseguiti negli anni 1955–57," *NSc* (1958) 283 nn. 33–34, fig. 51; Culican, in *Phönizier im Westen*, 110, on its Phoenician and Punic pottery. Its Semitic name may have been *Ras MLQRT* or "Cape of Melqart (Herakles)," especially if Minoa place-names in the Aegean mean a promontory? Another Semitic name that compares with the Greek colony's name is *Malcara* (Bérard, *Colonization grecque*, 424).

claims extending to the heroic past.[51] Its foundation legends replicate those of Herakles and Daidalos in their competition with Phoenicians in the West. The Spartan "Dorieus" fails to found Greek colonies in Punic North Africa and in Sicily, where he revives the Greek claim to Eryx through Herakles but loses his life; it is his descendants who founded Heraklea Minoa.[52] Minos's other Sicilian connection, the city of Kamikos imagined to be near the Cretan colonies of Gela and Akragas, likewise yields evidence of early Phoenician influence, in the Orientalizing metalwork from the Muxaro tombs (n. 25). The stylistic interpretation of the gold workmanship, now to be compared with new discoveries at Knossos and Lefkandi, is corroborated by the exclusive presence of Phoenician pottery in the same necropolis and the conspicuous absence of Greek equivalents.[53]

The effect of these recent views recommends a closer look at ambiguous finds from the Gela area, such as the earliest "Greek" import there, actually a Cypriote Bichrome IV cup of the seventh century.[54] The same ware appears in Etruria (Pontecagnano), Campania (Cumae), Spain (Toscanos), Sardinia, and elsewhere in Sicily, all places associated with Phoenicians.[55] While it could well have reached Gela via Rhodes or Crete, the colony's founding cities, its distribution elsewhere at Phoenician sites, and the Phoenician presence on Cyprus, allow Cypro-Phoenicians an equal if not dominant role in bringing the ware to Gela. Even Cretan pottery in the West, found widely outside the island's single colony, Gela, could represent Phoenician traffic rather than Greek.[56] Greek pottery from Gela antedating its historical foundation date has been hailed as evidence of an earlier οἴκησις ("settlement"), suggesting why Thucydides uses ἔκτισαν and ἔποικοι ("founded" and "residents") instead of ᾤκισαν and ἄποικοι ("settled" and "colonists") to describe the early settlement of Gela.[57] Likewise, burial customs identi-

[51] Manni, *Kokalos* 8 (1962) 6–29; E. Sjöqvist, "Heracles in Sicily," *Acta Instituit Romani Regni Suediae* 22 (1962) 117–23.

[52] Dunbabin, *Western Greeks*, chap. 11; A. Schenk, "Dorieus," *Historia* 9 (1960) 181–215; G. Mastruzzo, "Osservazioni sulla spedizione di Dorieo," *Sileno* 3 (1977) 129–47; Boardman, *Greeks Overseas*, 215; Davison, "Greek Presence in Sardinia," in *SSA*, 1:189.

[53] W. Culican, in *Phönizier im Westen*, 110 (red-ware jugs).

[54] P. Åström, "Coppi Ciprioti provenienti da Gela," *Kokalos* 14 (1968) 332–33. Cf. P. Orlandini, "Le più antica ceramica greca di Gela e il probleme di Lindioi," *CronArch* 2 (1963) 50–56.

[55] Etruria: Markoe, *Phoenician Bowls*, 146; Toscanos: Schubart, in *Phönizier im Westen*, 231 and *MadrMitt* 9 (1968) 86 fig. 6; G. Maas-Lindemann, *MadrForsch* 6

(1983) 955–57. Sardinia: see Chapter 5, nn. 69, 78.

[56] F. G. Lo Porto, "Vasi Cretesi e pseudocretesi in Italia," in *Antichità Cretesi*, 2:172–88; Graham, *CAH* III.2, 95. Cretan art in Etruria: E. Löwy, "Daedalica Etruriae," *StEtr* 4 (1930) 97–100; L. Bonfante Warren, "Riflessi di Arte Cretese in Etruria," in *Studi Luisa Banti*, ed. G. Becatti and others (Rome, 1965), 81–87. Compare how Lakonian pottery in South Italy could represent Samians who stopped at Gythion rather than Spartans themselves: R. M. Cook "Die Bedeutung der bemalten Keramik für den griechischen Handel," *JdI* 74 (1959) 114–23; "Archaic Trade: Three Conjectures," *JHS* 99 (1979) 153–54.

[57] H. Wenkter, "Die *Ktisis* von Gela bei Thukydides," *Röm Mitt* 63 (1956) 129–39; Barletta, *Ionic Influence in Archaic Sicily*, 239–64.

fied as "Cretan" in Sicily could indicate North Syrian or Phoenician habits long adopted by Crete as native.[58]

Once Phoenician settlement, rather than forerunners of the Greek colony, is considered, a scenario of Levantine exploration, settlement, and influence as a prelude to the formal Greek colony can be imagined. In the early centuries of western Mediterranean exploration, as in the Aegean, communities of Greeks and Phoenicians appear to have cohabited peacefully and productively to the point of intermarriage, exchange of burial customs, joint industrial ventures and communications in letters. Such a situation is most plausible, even vivid, when documented epigraphically, as at Ischia.[59] At this Euboian colony, one of the earliest and farthest north in western Greece, imports of Greek and Levantine origin match early inscriptions in Greek and Aramaic (some on the same vessels) that make the site a new candidate for the home of the Greek alphabet.[60] Hellenic prejudice lingers in the tendency in modern scholarship to label those Phoenicians present μέτοικοι, skilled craftsmen in Greek service, whereas the original commercial and industrial initiative could well be a sign of Levantine enterprise.[61] The nature of these early communities is elusive, yet all-important to the development of social and cultural institutions that eventually epitomize Greek civilization (as suggested in Chapters 4–6).

Only in the archaic and classical periods, with the rise of Carthage and its Punic establishments, did Greeks and Phoenicians experience division and conflict. These historical hostilities account for a certain measure of pro-Greek revisions of early colonial history in regions where rival claims to common interests were involved.[62] This pattern—early cooperation dissolving into classical confrontations, producing abiding attitudes in literature—repeats itself wherever Greeks and non-Greeks coexisted in the archaic Mediterranean world. On Crete, the figure of Minos was admired, then reviled, during the Athenian Empire, and the figure of Daidalos served to appropriate the culture of early Crete into an Athenian past. In the West, the same figure asserted Greek

---

[58] Rizza and Moscati in *Kokalos* 30–31 (1984–1985) 65–70, 1–22, on the kinship between Butera and Crete; see, Chapter 6, nn. 55–57, on Levantine burial customs in Crete.

[59] G. Buchner, in *Phönizier im Westen*, 277–306, in section of the Cologne conference entitled "Phönizier und Griechen: Partnerschaft und Konkurrenz." Mysterious graffiti from Segesta, in Sicily, deserve a review in this context: A. Ambrosini, "Italica o Anatolica la Lingua dei Graffiti di Segesta?" *Kokalos* 14 (1968) 168–77, at one point suggests either Asia Minor, Cyprus, or Crete as the most plausible origin (p. 173).

[60] Buchner and Coldstream, in *Phönizier im Westen*,

290–96, 269–71; S. Segert, *The Origin of the Greek Alphabet* (Los Angeles, 1977), 3.

[61] For example, D. Ridgway, "Sardinia and the First Western Greeks," in *SSA* 2:173–85, identifies early enterprise in Iberia, Italy (Ischia), Sardinia, and the Levant under the rubric of "Euboian"; could it represent Euboian pottery along the trail of Phoenician activity? See now his *L'Alba della Magna Graecia* (Milan, 1984), reviewed by L. Bonfante, *AJA* 91 (1987) 151.

[62] As concluded by E. Manni, "Sémites et Grecs en Sicile jusqu'au Ve. siècle av. J.C.," *Bulletin de l'Association Guillaume Budé* (1974) 63–84. I am grateful to David Jordan for this reference.

claims and culture over "barbarian" ones, only after the classical confrontation between Greek and Punic forces. In this scenario, Daidalos played a handy role: his name attached itself with ease to monuments and their legends so that, like Herakles, his adventures grew in step with Greek ambitions westward.[63] Moreover, his cultural value as a Greek hero of the arts who preceded the banner of barbarism also served a classical desire to see Greeks first and foremost in the development of civilization. All these patterns trace themselves more fully and profoundly in the homeland of Greek chauvinism: Athens.

[63] U. Täckholm, "Tarsis, Tartessos und die Säulen des Herakles," *OpRom* 5 (1965) 142–200; D. Van Berchem, "Sanctuaires d' Hercule-Melqart: Contribution à l' étude de l' expansion phénicienne en Mediterranée," *Syria* (1967) 73–109, 307–38; A. Brelich, "Herakles, Melqart, Hercules e la peninsola Iberica," in *Minutal. Saggi di Storia delle Religioni* (Rome, 1974), 111–32; C. Jourdain-Annequin, "Héraclès en Occident. Mythe et histoire," *DHA* 8 (1982) 227–82. Greeks and Phoenicians beyond the Pillars of Herakles [*sic*]: B.S.J. Isserlin, "Did Carthaginian Mariners Reach the Island of Corzo (Azores)? Report on the Result of Joint Field Investigations Undertaken on Corzo in June, 1983," *RSF* 12 (1984) 31–46; J. Fernandez Juraldo, "Die Phönizier in Huelva," and P. Cabeira and R. Olmos, "Die Griechen in Huelva," both in *MadrMitt* 26 (1985) 49–60, 61–79; Davison, "Greek Presence in Sardinia," in *SSA*, 1:187–92.

DAIDALOS

AND ATHENS

· PART III ·

The Reincarnation of

Daidalos

CHAPTER 8

Magic and Sculpture

T HE NAME VASE of the Foundry Painter spans the ancient biography of the artist Daidalos as perceived in early classical Athens, the focus of the latter half of this book. The interior (Figure 1) presents Hephaistos making armor for Achilles, watched by Thetis, the hero's mother: this occasion gave birth to Daidalos in Homeric poetry (*Iliad* 18. 590–92; Chapter 1). The exterior of the cup (Figure 58) is devoted to the manufacture of bronze statuary, the monumental art in which Athens excelled during the period of the cup's manufacture, and the medium with which Daidalos became associated during the same decades. Contemporary with the deployment of poetic δαί-δαλα in classical tragedy (Chapter 3) was a far more important and innovative development in classical literature: the reappearance of the eponymous figure of Daidalos himself, in a guise partially derived from his poetic cognates but remote from his fleeting persona in Homer. The personification of Daidalos as a mythological artist was closely tied to historical events in Athens, which eventually claimed him as a native son.

Attic drama is the first genre since epic poetry that preserves both poetic words formed on δαιδαλ- and the name of the artist himself, beyond the incidental allusions to him in archaic literature. His adventures form the main subject of lost plays bearing his name as title, like the *Daidalos* of Sophokles (frag. 191–204, Kassel-Austin: probably a satyr play) and comedies by Aristophanes (frags. 184–97), Plato (frags. 19–20) and Euboulos (frags. 21–22). Related dramas include the *Kamikoi* of Sophokles (frags. 323–27 Radt) and the *Kokalos* by Aristophanes (frags. 359–71), both devoted to the Sicilian adventures of Daidalos, the *Minos* (frag. 407) by Sophokles and Euripides' *Cretans*, apparently set in Crete. According to Clement of Alexandria (*Stromateis* 6.752), the comedies by Plato and Aristophanes entitled *Daidalos* overlapped considerably in content (τὰ ἀλλήλων ἀφαιροῦνται), as if the legend was popular to the point of becoming repetitive. Crucial to classical conceptions of Daidalos was the role of Minos as antagonist: the Cretan figure once revered as lawgiver and ruler eventually became a frequent antagonist in classical tragedy (ὁ τραγικώτατος μῦθος: Plutarch, *Theseus* 16).[1] The dynam-

---

[1] On Cretan myths in Attic tragedy, see K. Reckford, "Phaedra and Pasiphae: The Pull Backward," *TAPA* 104 (1974) 319–28; Haft, *The Myth That Crete Be-* *came*, 162, 231–35 n. 89; P. Ghiron-Bistagne, "Phèdre ou l'amour interdit," *Klio* 64 (1982) 29–49; Kokalakis, "Icarus," 115–20. Cf. Chapter 6.

ics of this antagonism that made Daidalos an Athenian hero will be explored in Chapters 10–13; this section will investigate the dimensions of Daidalos, the artist.

The substance of Attic dramas about Daidalos addressed local historical manifestations of his legend; the surviving fragments of these lost plays indicate precious little about the artist beyond an emphasis on his Sicilian adventures (Chapter 7) as a sequel to those in Crete. That the artist's talents at this point emphasized architecture is implied in phrases praising builders' skills, such as τεκτόναρχος μοῦσα (quoted from the Sophokles play by Pollux, 7.117 = frag. 159 Radt) and the verb ἀρχιτεκτονεῖν from the drama by Aristophanes (cf. Hesychius, s.v. τεκτονουργὸς = ἀρχιτέκτων). Other talents tailored to Sicilian episodes, notably the famous trick with the sea snail, first appear in these dramas (Sophokles, *Kamikoi* frag. 324 Radt; cf. Apollodoros, 1.14). In the absence of complete dramas, later epitomes and collations by mythographers embroider these classical scraps into a complicated chain of adventures in Athens, Crete, and Sicily, well stocked with local personalities.

The Athenian connection, new since epic and archaic poetry, is introduced at least as early as Sophokles' *Kamikoi*, whose fragment 323 implies an *aition* for Perdix and her sanctuary on the Akropolis (Chapter 10). But even Sicily may have entered the story via Athens, no surprise in a period when Athenian ambitions expanded west to include Magna Graecia. One of the earliest testimonia to Athenian preoccupation with Daidalos in Sicily appears in Herodotus's digression on Crete's absence from the battle of Salamis (7.170; see Chapter 7, n. 8). The Cretans justified this absence by citing past grievances against fellow Greeks (7.171). The Delphic oracle reminded them, they claimed, how other Greeks refused to help them avenge the death of Minos in Sicily, while the Cretans responded to Menelaos's expedition to Troy and suffered on behalf of Helen's husband. Valuable information emerges from this meager passage: in the aftermath of the Persian wars, the legends of Minos and Daidalos were located three generations before the expedition to Troy, linking epic to recent history in the same chain of causation argued in the opening paragraphs of Herodotus's work. Thus one aspect of the revival of Daidalos in classical times—his western Greek adventures—was inspired by a convergence of regional and historical interests: in this case Crete, Sicily, and the Persian wars. Obedience to historical concerns is characteristic of the shape taken by myth in the classical period, and the case of Daidalos introduces a phenomenon to be explored more fully in the book's fourth part.

Meanwhile, other Athenian sources attest to another new contemporary concern, Daidalos's activity as sculptor and architect. A cluster of testimonia implicates poets, philosophers, and artists alike in this new *topos*, making it difficult to determine whether his renascense as an artist was sponsored in serious, professional circles of sculptors and philosophers, or through popular exaggerations of his legendary talents.[2]

---

[2] Thus E. Kunze, in "Zu den Anfängen der griechischen Plastik," *AthMitt* 55 (1930) 141, describes one reference as "gleichfalls zum literarischen τόπος gewordenen, vielleicht von Euripides oder von der Kö-

Both these traditions, learned and light-hearted, might reflect a more official promotion of his persona under the same historical circumstances that elevated Hephaistos to a leading Attic cult. Under these auspices, the figure of Daidalos reappears in Greek literature, when new intellectual preoccupations encouraged a reconstruction of his epic personality. The discussion that follows will examine imagery in poetry and prose that evokes the authority of Daidalos, its possible connections to a more learned and technical branch of debate, and the sum of these implications for the classical image of the artist.

A major proportion of classical references to Daidalos and his art are humorous, whether in comedies and satyr plays or in philosophy. They extend a metaphor made literal into a visible phenomenon, especially amusing on stage: the animation of statues as a metaphysical, aesthetic, and ultimately comic phenomenon. One reason the dramatic stage made an important contribution to the classical obsession with sculpture was the popularity of the sanctuary as a setting for Greek tragedy, hence frequency of statues on stage.[3] Episodes of supplication, prayer, purification, oracular consultation, and crucial encounters took place among altars and statues, according to illustrations of drama.[4] Ritual interaction with statues in tragedy inevitably inspired parodies in satyr plays and comedy, where conversant and active statues became a popular *topos*.[5] Many of the comic effects of this *topos* were no doubt transmitted in stage action now lost, and what was once a visual gag has become an artificial problem for scholarship. Among these jokes, Daidalos may have been particularly popular precisely because his oeuvre was conveniently vague, and his reputation for magic statues securer than for attested works.

The earliest such testament is in a satyr play by Aeschylus called *Theoroi* or *Isthmiastai*.[6] In a scene set in a sanctuary, the satyrs exclaim at the sight of what seem to be their own portraits (frag. 78, 6–7, 11–17):

> 6 εἴδωλον εἶναι τοῦτ᾽ ἐμῇ μορφῇ πλέον
> τὸ Δαιδάλου μ[ί]μημα φωνῆς δεῖ μόνον.
>
> . . . .
>
> 11 εὐκταῖα κόσμον ταῦτ[α] τῷ θεῷ φέρω
> καλλίγραπτον εὐχάν.
> τῇ μητρὶ τῇμῇ πράγματ᾽ ἂν παρασχέθοι·

---

modie angeregten, Sokratischen Witz in Plato's *Menon* herausgesponnen."

[3] R. P. Winnington-Ingram, "A Religious Function of Greek Tragedy: A Study in the Oedipus Coloneus and the Oresteia," *JHS* 74 (1954) 16–24; M. Kuntz, "Setting and Theme in Greek Tragedy" (Ph.D. diss., Yale University, 1985), 44–45, on cult settings and their dramatic appeal. Cf. Stewart, *Greek Sculpture*, 141–42, on the effects of "living" gods on stage.

[4] E.g. Aeschylus's *Suppliant Women* and *Eumenides*, Sophokles' *Oidipous at Kolonos*, and Euripides' *Hippolytos*, *Iphigeneia in Tauris*, and *Ion* are examples of surviving plays with episodes in sanctuaries or near statues. T.B.L. Webster, *Monuments Illustrating Tragedy and Satyr Play*, BICS suppl. 20 (London, 1967); Romano, "Early Greek Cult Images," 455–64.

[5] Kassel, *ZPE* 51 (1983) 1–12.

[6] PapOxy 2162: *Oxyrhynchus Papyri* 18 (London,

ἰδοῦσα γάρ νιν ἂν σοφῶς.
15   τρέποιτ' ἂν .†ἀξιάζοιτό θ' ὡς
δοκοῦσ' ἔμ' εἶναι, τὸν ἐξ-
ἔθρεψεν. οὕτως ἐμφερὴς ὅδ' ἐστίν.
εἶα δὴ σκοπεῖτε δῶμα ποντίου σεισίχθο[νος
κἀπιπασσάλευ' ἕκαστος τῆς κ[α]λῆς μορφῆς[
ἄγγελον, κήρυκ' [ἄ]ναυδον, ἐμπόρων κωλύτορ[α
ὅς γ'] ἐπισχήσει κελεύθου τοὺς ξένο[υς] φ[

This image full of my form
this imitation of Daidalos lacks only a voice.
I bring these [as] a well-won ornament to the god,
      a well-made votive.
It would challenge my own mother!
      For seeing it she would clearly
      turn and [wail]
      thinking it to be me, whom she raised.
      So similar is it [to me].
Come now consider the home of the marine god, the earth-shaker
and nail up each one [of you] a messenger of your fine shape
a herald unheard, a restraint on travelers
who might hold back strangers from the road.

The nature of the εἴδωλον ("image") is not clear, nor is the role of Daidalos, in its genitive case. These portraits could be painted, as implied by καλλίγραπτον, sculpted, or even molded satyr-head antefixes, in Fraenkel's imaginative suggestion.[7] Presumably the εἴδωλον was visible on stage and its impact comic or grotesque, an apotropaic face likely to frighten one's own mother. The exact meaning of τὸ Δαιδάλου μίμημα is unclear: "the likeness by Daidalos," "the imitation of a work by Daidalos," less likely a "portrait of Daidalos," are all possible.[8] The original editor of the papyrus even identified Daidalos as the second speaking role in the play, a character who enters carrying iron equipment for the athletes and thus might be a craftsman (lines 86–87):[9]

1941) 14–22; Aeschylus frag. 276 = Radt, frags. 78a 6–7. H. Lloyd-Jones, *Aeschylus*, vol. 2 (Cambridge, Mass., 1961), 541–46. Sutton, *Greek Satyr Play*, 29–33; Hallett, *JHS* 106 (1986) 75–78; S. De Angeli, "Mimesis e Techne," *QUCC* 28 (1988) 27–45, esp. 31–35. Stewart, *Greek Sculpture*, 142.

[7] E. Fraenkel, "Aeschylus: New Texts and Old Problems," *PBA* 28 (1942) 244–45 (rejected by Radt, who finds ἐπιπασσάλευειν, line 19, more suitable for nailing up votives); Lloyd-Jones, *Aeschylus*, 2:547–

48; Philipp, *Tektonon Daidala*, 28, prefers portraits of satyrs.

[8] Lloyd-Jones, *Aeschylus*, 2:547, cf. 551 ("this likeness by the Skillful One"); Sutton, *Greek Satyr Play*, 30 ("Daedalus-wrought likeness"); Hallett, *JHS* 106 (1986) 76 ("this Daedalus reproduction").

[9] This character is probably another athlete, not an artist, and satyrs are portrayed in both guises in vase paintings: Sutton, *Greek Satyr Play*, 129–31, 134–36; Simon, in *Eye of Greece*, 31–33.

ἐγὼ [φέ]ρω σοι νεοχμὰ [ταῦτ] ἀθύρματα
ἀπὸ σκεπάρνου κ᾽ ἀκμ[ονος ν]εόκτιτα.

I carry for you these novel treasures,
newly acquired from anvil and hammer.

What is most vivid in the description of these εἴδωλα now obscure is their extraordinarily resemblance to life: "full of my shape," "all they need is a voice" to come alive. This quality, the power to imitate life, dominates all classical references to the works of Daidalos and most ancient speculation about his art. This first view of Daidalos attests to a fascination with human images near life, in a generation when sculpture itself aspires to those qualities, and this metaphor has even been attributed to contemporary impressions of early classical statuary.[10] According to this interpretation, Aeschylus's satyrs do not admire particular masks or props, but are astonished by the development of lifelike poses, gestures, and expressions achieved by early classical sculptors. Like the modern reading of a vase painter's taunt, ὡς οὐδέποτε Εὐφρονίος, this argument applies modern stylistic judgment of Greek art to ancient testimonia, as if Athenians of Aeschylus's day registered the same critical response to early classical statues as in modern sensibilities. However debated its interpretation, this passage marks a critical development in classical culture: the emergence of art, especially sculpture, as an intellectual medium, subject to theoretical as well as technical treatises, the source of modern art criticism.[11] For example, the representation of movement preoccupies recent discussions of classical sculpture, but this topic derives from ancient literature, including some comments by sculptors.[12] Their thought and work may even have been influenced by philosophical theories, according to some recent arguments.[13] More generally, praise of art as "lifelike" is an important chapter in the history of pre-Platonic as well as Platonic art criticism.[14] In the early classical period, this dialogue between life and art accompa-

[10] Hallett, JHS 106 (1986) 76–78, drawing on G. Else, "Imitation in the Fifth Century," CP 53 (1958) 78, and G. Sörbom, Mimesis and Art: Studies in the Origin and Early Development of Aesthetic Vocabulary (Stockholm, 1966), esp. 41–53.

[11] P. Bruneau, "Situation méthodologique de l' histoire de l'art antique," AntClass 44 (1975) 425–87, esp. 446–54, "Les artistes," on the origins of the history of art in the fifth century.

[12] B. Fehr, Bewegungsweisen und Verhaltensideale: Physiognomische Deutungsmöglichkeiten der Bewegungsdarstellungen an griechischen Statuen des 5. u. 4. Jh. v. Chr. (Bad Bramstedt, 1979); I. Kleemann, Frühe Bewegung. Untersuchungen zur archaischen Form bis zum Aufkommen der Ponderation in der griechischen Kunst

(Mainz, 1986); Leftwich (cited in n. 13).

[13] I. Mark, "The Gods on the East Frieze of the Parthenon," Hesperia 53 (1984) 289–342, attributes the design of the Parthenon's sculpture to the influence of Protagoras; G. Leftwich, "Opposition in the Canon of Polykleitos" (Ph.D. diss., Princeton University, 1987), associates the sculpture and theories of Polykleitos with Pythagorean "opposites"; Hallett, JHS 106 (1986) 82–84, attributes early classical innovations to a premeditated compromise between naturalism and monumentality.

[14] Sörbom, Mimesis and Art, 41–77, "Mimesis and Works of Art before Xenophon and Plato"; Philipp, Tektonon Daidala, 4–41, on art in archaic and classical literature.

nies the emergence of sculpture as a significant and symbolic art form beyond its archaic architectural and votive tradition, in response to the new purposes of art. History played one major role in the animation of art through action and allegory (as will be explored in Chapter 11). Others attribute innovation to developments within art alone (see, nn. 6–12), while a third type of explanation focuses on a new conception of the divine, expressed in cult images.[15] It is no coincidence that the same period also witnessed speculation on Daidalos and turned him into a sculptor, or that sources in philosophy and poetry played as vital a role as art.

The discourse on voice and animation in the inanimate sustains itself through the fifth century. Decades later, Euripides extends the imagery of Aeschylus in reference to Daidalos, in the same play that revived the poetic adjective δαιδάλεος in a choral lament (*Hekabe* 470). Later in the play, Hekabe despairs of her power to persuade Agamemnon (836–40):

> εἴ μοι γένοιτο φθόγγος ἐν βραχίοισι
> καὶ χερσὶ καὶ κόμαισι καὶ ποδῶν βάσει
> ἢ Δαιδάλου τέχναισιν ἢ θεῶν τινός,
> ὡς πάνθ᾽ ὁμαρτῆ σῶν ἔχοιτο γουνάτων
> κλαίοντ᾽, ἐπισκήπτοντα παντοίους λόγους.

> If only I had a voice in my arms
> and my hands and my hair and my footsteps
> either through the arts of Daidalos or through some divine agency
> so that in unison they could clasp your knees
> crying, invoking every argument.

In this impassioned appeal, Hekabe desires the powers of speech to animate her entire body—arms, hands, hair, and limbs—to give her cause more eloquence than words alone. Such a feat can only be performed through "the arts of Daidalos or one of the gods," that is, through magical powers bestowed on inanimate objects by the gods or divine craftsmen, in particular by Daidalos. This plea elaborates a figure of speech where an inanimate object comes alive by speaking, in the same illusion that Aeschylus applies to εἴδωλα. A specific form of representational art may not be necessary to either passage: Hekabe does not imagine herself as a statue so much as she longs for multiple and articulate voices to speak throughout her body.[16] Such a metaphor belongs to po-

---

[15] D. Willers, "Zum Hermes Propylaios des Alkamenes," *JdI* 82 (1967) 37–109; "Archaistische Plastik als Problem der Klassischen," in his *Zu den Anfängen der archaistischen Plastik in Griechenland. AthMitt* Beih. 4 (Berlin, 1975) 66–70; review by E. Harrison, *Gnomon* 53 (1981) 496–98. F. Brommer, "Gott oder Mensch,"

JdI 101 (1986) 37–53. Donohue, *Xoana*, 30–32; Freedberg, *Power of Images*.

[16] S. Murnaghan, "Body and Voice in Greek Tragedy," *Yale Journal of Criticism* 2 (1988) 23–43, on "replacing the body's adventures with forms of speech" (p. 23) in classical drama.

etry but also enters philosophical speculation of the fifth century. For example, Empedokles imagines the ancestors of men and women as τύποι (itself an artistic form) before
the addition of voice or language, "neither cry nor any innate voice for men:" οὔτ᾽
ἐνοπὴν οὔτ᾽ αὖ ἐπιχώριον ἄνδρασι γῆρυν (frag. 62 = Simplicius, *Physica* 381.29):[17]
Euripides' version of this image emphasizes the divine addition of voice, in a literal
manifestation of "spirit," to animate physical matter. It anticipates the identification of
the divine with the powers of speech, as in Demokritos's definition of the names of the
gods as ἀγάλματα φωνοέντα, "statues with voices" (68 B 142).

That the τέχναι Δαιδάλου invoked by Hekabe were eventually associated with
sculpture is clear from the scholiast on this line, who identifies Daidalos as a maker of
statues that move and speak (τὸν Δαίδαλον φασὶ ποιεῖν εἴδωλα, καὶ μετὰ τὸ
πληροῦν αὐτὰ ποιεῖν κινεῖσθαι καὶ φθέγεσθαι). In support he quotes another passage by Euripides, from the satyr play *Eurystheus* (frag. 188), where statues move and
emit sound (ὅτι δὲ ἐκινεῖτο καὶ προίει φωνήν, αὐτός τε Εὐριπίδης ἐν Εὐρυσθεῖ
λέγει):

> Οὐκ ἔστιν, ὦ γεραιέ, μὴ δείσῃς τάδε.
> τὰ Δαιδάλεια πάντα κινεῖσθαι δοκεῖ
> βλέπειν τ᾽ ἀγάλμαθ᾽, ὧδ᾽ ἀνὴρ κεῖνος σοφός.

> Don't be afraid, old man, it's nothing.
> All the statues of Daidalos appear to move
> and see, so clever is the man.

The context must be a comic situation like the one in the satyr play by Aeschylus,
where a character on stage (here, an old man) has been frightened by a lifelike work of
art, specifically a statue. He is reassured with the explanation that "Daidalic" statues,
explicitly the work of Daidalos, only appear to move and see, such is the artist's skill,
expressed by σοφός. The word is used here in its archaic and technical sense, yet also
participates in the language of classical philosophy, where σοφός and δοκεῖ address
questions of appearance and reality, wisdom and its false illusions. In the fourth century, Daidalos is still remembered for those qualities; Minos is said to have kidnapped
him for the sake of his σοφία (Xenophon, *Memorabilia* 4.2.32).

Euripides introduces one of the first, as well as one of the few, genuine possessive
adjectives formed from the name of Daidalos, a formation also conjectured for Mycenaean *da-da-re-jo* but not explicit until this satyr play. It bears no relationship in morphology or meaning to those poetic adjectives (Chapter 1) expressing qualities anterior
to the personification as a craftsman. But it anticipates the modern adjective "Daedalic"

[17] M. Wright, *Empedocles. The Fragments* (New Haven, 1985) 217–18. Pollitt, *Ancient View of Greek Art*,
272–84, for ancient testimonia on τύποι (including

Empedokles, frag. 62, p. 258, where τύποι is identified as a "crude form, rough shape"); cf. *AJA* 88
(1984) 419.

as a denominative formation, restricted in meaning to a modern category in sculpture (Chapter 9). In ancient usage, Hesychius reports the same adjective in, appropriately enough, Aristophanes' *Daidalos* (frag. 194). He defines Δαιδαλεῖα, citing Aristophanes, as "the statues made by Daidalos, bound in order not to run away" (τὰ ὑπὸ Δαιδάλου κατασκευασθέντα ἀνδριάντα ὡς διὰ τὸ ἀποδιδράσκειν δεδεμένον). The craftsmanship of Daidalos has here exceeded metaphor; his statues are so "animated" that they must be bound in place to prevent escape, a popular joke extended from a figure of speech. In a variation on this joke, a statue (of Pan?) disappears and the skills of Daidalos are assumed to have removed it, in a comic fragment also quoted in a scholion to Euripides' *Hekabe* (838). In the words of a mystified character, the disappearance of a bronze statue is attributed to the magic of Daidalos (Kratinos, *Thracians*, frag. 75 Kassel-Austin; cf. Euripides, *Eurystheus* frag. 372 N):

A: ⟨Πανίσκον ἥκων⟩ δεῦρο μαστεύων τινά
    [codd: πανὶ κακὸν]
B: πότερα χαλκοῦν ἢ ξύλινον
      ⟨ἢ⟩ καί ⟨τι⟩ χρύσεον προσῆν;
A: οὐδαμῶς ξύλινος ἐκεῖνος,
B: ἀλλὰ χαλκοῦς ὢν ἀπέδρα. πότερα Δαιδάλειος ἦν; ἤ τις ἐξέκλεψεν αὐτόν;

A: Here comes [a statue of Pan] looking for something [wicked]
B: (Is it) bronze or wood
    or was it even gold?
A: Not at all: that one is wooden.
B: But even though it's bronze, it ran away. Was it made by Daidalos? Or did someone steal it?

In other comic episodes, statues walk and talk on stage, as in a comedy of Plato (frag. 188) where a statue of Hermes himself answers an actor who demands:

              οὐκ ἐρεῖς; οὗτος τίς εἶ; λέγε ταχύ. τί σιγᾷς;
(HERMES):   Ἑρμῆς ἔγωγε Δαιδάλου φωνὴν ἔχων
            ξύλινος βαδίζων αὐτόματος ἐλήλυθα.
            Won't you speak? Who are you? Tell me at once. Why are you silent?
(HERMES):   I am Hermes with a voice from Daidalos
            made of wood (but) I came here by walking on my own.

Three attributes now formulaic are claimed by this statue of Hermes: speech, autokinesis, and the handiwork of Daidalos. In this scene, the statue seems to have appeared on stage in a manner curious or sudden enough to require explanation, for which the name of Daidalos suffices.

In philosophical contexts that admit a sense of humor—the conversations of Sokrates—the same kind of joke also serves, usually as metaphor for argument. In discussing "true opinions" (αἱ δόξαι αἱ ἀληθεῖς) in Plato's *Meno* (97), Sokrates introduces the behavior of statues so lively as to require bonds: ὥστε οὐ πολλοῦ ἄξιαί εἰσιν, ἕως ἄν τις αὐτὰς δήσῃ αἰτίας λογισμῷ. Sokrates forgives Meno for not understanding the superiority of ὀρθὴ δόξη to ἐπιστήμη on the basis of his origin, Thessaly, a place lacking statues of Daidalos: ὅτι τοῖς Δαιδάλου ἀγάλμασιν οὐ προσέσχηκας τὸν νοῦν· ἴσως δὲ οὐδ᾽ ἔστι παρ᾽ ὑμῖν ("because you have not turned your mind to the statues of Daidalos. Maybe there are none in your home").

MENO: Πρὸς τί δὲ τοῦτο λέγεις;

SOKRATES: ὅτι καὶ ταῦτα, ἐὰν μὲν μὴ δεδεμένα ᾖ, ἀποδιδράσκει καὶ δραπετεύει, ἐὰν δὲ δεδεμένα, παραμένει.

MENO: Τί οὖν δή;

SOKRATES: Τῶν ἐκείνου ποιημάτων λελυμένον μὲν ἐκτῆσθαι οὐ πολλῆν τινὸς ἄξιόν ἐστι τιμῆς, ὥσπερ δραπέτην ἄνθρωπον—οὐ γὰρ παραμένει— δεδεμένον δὲ πολλοῦ ἄξιον· πάνυ γὰρ καλὰ ἔργα ἐστί.

MENO: Why do you say that?

SOKRATES: Because, unless bound, they run away and escape, but if they are fastened down, they remain in place.

MENO: What of it?

SOKRATES: Once one of his creations is loosed, it is not worth much value as a possession, like an escaped slave, for it does not stay in place. But a secured example is worth much, for they are entirely beautiful works.

Sokrates' familiar manner assumes the same acquaintance with "living statues," at least among Athenians, as in comic references. That the joke was exclusively Athenian, and not just through the lopsided survival of classical literature, is supported by Sokrates' pardon of a Thessalian visitor for not knowing the works of Daidalos: "Maybe you don't have any of them [in Thessaly]" (97d.7). The expression implies that works attributed to Daidalos were actually, if not exclusively, present in Athens, and familiar to the local imagination.[18] This would help explain frequent references to the artist's reputation in the works of Plato. In the *Euthyphro*, Sokrates compares the words of Euthyphro to the works of Daidalos (11.c.1–4), to explain why Euthyphro's arguments (τὰ ἐν τοῖς λόγοις ἔργα) "run away and do not wish to stay where one places them" (ἀποδιδράσκει καὶ οὐκ ἐθέλει μένειν ὅπου ἄν τις αὐτὰ θῇ). The language of philosophy

[18] In the second century A.D. Pausanias reports many statues of Daidalos on his travels, and Nicanor knows a sufficient number to understand the simile at *Iliad* 18.591: (Erbse, *Scholia Graeca in Homeri Iliadem*, 4:565); in Attica, however, Pausanias sees only a stool by Daidalos (1.27.1: see Chapters 10 and 13).

freely applies the behavior of mobile statues to elusive argument, as in Euthyphro's response accusing the clever Sokrates of the same slippery statements (11.d.1): ἀλλὰ σύ μοι δοκεῖς ὁ Δαίδαλος. To dramatize Euthyphro's instable arguments, Sokrates protests that even Daidalos does not make the works of others move, preferring "immobile arguments" (ἀκίνητοι λόγοι) to the σοφία of Daidalos, the latter as proverbial as the wealth of Tantalos (*Euthyphro* 15b.6; cf. Euripides, *Hekabe* 840).

These humorous references to statues with human powers strike a chord particular, if painful, to the city of Athens. One would expect statues of herms, especially, to provoke interaction on stage, and at least one was attributed to Daidalos (Plato, frag. 188). The theme culminates tragically in the final joke played on Greek statues, the mutilation of the Herms in 415 B.C., which became implicated in the Athenian disaster in Sicily.[19] Paranoia following defeat sought "conspiracy" in what must have been a drunken prank, even though earlier, harmless mutilations performed under the influence of wine and youth were recalled (ἄλλων δὲ ἀγαλμάτων περικοπαί τινες πρότερον ὑπὸ νεωτέρων μετὰ παιδίας καὶ οἴνου γενενημέναι· Thucydides, 6.27). The frequency of such defacements is suggested in a graffito sketch of two goblins defacing a herm, on an Attic black-glazed vase found in the workshop of Pheidias at Olympia (Figure 34).[20] Its interpretation as an apotropaic workshop scene, where two demons who bedevil craftsmen are shown defacing the guardian of their workshop in the manner of votive offerings displayed in a sculptor's workshop (Figure 58), seems largely determined by the findspot, a sculptor's workshop. A more mischievous purpose may lie behind this casual scene, if the two figures are mutilating a herm (one holds aloft, triumphantly, the fruit of the prank: a severed phallus?) in accordance with an Attic tradition. Some ten years later, the political suspicions against those who played the prank in Athens put an end to such activity, but the joke lingers on in comedy, where herms on stage exposed themselves to obscene derision.

Finally, a fragment of Philippos quoted by Aristotle (attributed by Themistios to Euboulos, frag. 22), completes the corpus of comic references to Daidalos and links them to philosophical speculation, his other sponsor in fifth-century Athens. In discussing motion as a function of the relationship between body and soul (*De Anima* 1.3, 406b, 15–22), Aristotle compares the theories of Demokritos, for whom the soul empowers movement in the body, with a comic poet's joke on Daidalos:

[19] Thucydides, 6.27–29, with Dover's commentary; Andokides, *On the Mysteries*, 34–46. R. Osborne, "The Erection and Mutilation of the Hermai," *PCPhS* 11 (1986) 47–73. O. Murray, "The Affair of the Mysteries: Democracy and the Drinking Group," in *Sympotica*, ed. O. Murray (Oxford, 1990), 151. For a radical view of the mutilation as revenge by frustrated Athenian feminists, see E. Keuls, *The Reign of the Phallus* (New York, 1985), chap. 16.

[20] A. Mallwitz and W. Schiering, *Olympische Forschungen V. Die Werkstatt des Pheidias in Olympia* (Berlin, 1964), 237–47, fig. 68, pl. 79; E. Harrison, *Agora XI: Archaic and Archaistic Sculpture* (Princeton, 1961), 141 n. 241. For related classical humor about herms, see the representation of a herm sporting a votive pinax on his phallus, in a fourth-century mosaic from Arta: *Deltion* 31 (1976) B.2, 201 pl. 147; *ARep* (1984–1985) 35–36, fig. 47.

φησὶ γὰρ τὸν Δαίδαλος κινουμένην ποιῆσαι τὴν ξύλινην Ἀφροδίτην, ἐγχέαντ᾽ ἄργυρον χυτόν.

They say that Daidalos made mobile his wooden statue of Aphrodite, by pouring molten silver (quicksilver) into it.

The joke embellishes the popular theme of "moving statues" with obscene overtones implied by the verb κινεῖν, a "primary obscenity" in Old Comedy.[21] In the proximity of such a familiar lewd reference, the verb ἐγχέω acquires suggestive properties, especially when its receptacle is a statue of Aphrodite, well-known object of physical passion on the part of mortals.[22] Byzantine commentators on this passage imagine how Daidalos made hollows in the statue for pouring in quicksilver, in the most literal interpretation in terms of postclassical theories of *theiurgy* and *stoicheiosis*, the animation of images by the injection of liquids or insertion of substances.[23] Modern misunderstanding of this passage has credited Demokritos with the first serious discussion of Daidalos and his art (see n. 37). It is Aristotle, not Demokritos himself, who compares a philosophical statement with a joke from comedy, applying the image of quicksilver as a metaphor for the soul's action on the body. Elsewhere, Aristotle's only reference to Daidalos in his own words (rather than in paraphrase of a comic reference) suggests a far more traditional source for speculation on the sculptor and his statues. In imagining αὐτό-ματα instruments that would eliminate the need for slaves, he makes the following comparison (*Politics* 1.4):

> For if each instrument were able to accomplish its own task, either in obedience or anticipa-tion [of others], like the [works of] Daidalos or the autokinetic tripods of Hephaistos which, as the poet says, "of their own accord entered the assembly of the gods," then in the same manner, shuttles would weave and plektra play the lyre on their own, master builders would not need apprentices, nor masters, slaves.

A broad range for the skills of Daidalos is implied in the phrase τὰ [ἔργα τοῦ] Δαι-δάλου, in keeping with other classical expressions for his oeuvre (e.g., Plato, *Republic* 529). Moreover, this passage derives the wide domain of his talents largely from epic poetry, in a coordinated reference to Daidalos and the tripods of Hephaistos not only suggestive of Homer but specific to *Iliad* 18. Aristotle's conception of Daidalos in this simile is a direct inspiration from epic poetry alone: independent of contemporary *topoi* on statues in drama and philosophy, classical authors equated objects praised as δαί-

[21] J. Henderson, *The Maculate Muse* (New Haven, 1975), 5, 64, 151–53 (no. 206); as a common pejorative in the vocative for pathics: pp. 209, 218.

[22] See the anecdote about Praxiteles' Aphrodite of Knidos: Pliny, *Naturalis Historia* 35.64.5; Lucian, *Erotes* 13–15. Warner, *Monuments and Maidens*, 213–40, on erotic interaction with female statues, from Pan-dora to Pygmalion; Freedberg, *Power of Images*, esp. chaps. 12 and 13, for sexual arousal by images.

[23] Paraphrases of this passage in Aristotle, by Phi-loponos and Themistios, are discussed in Donohue, *Xoana*, 165–66, 179–83, nos. 153 and 363; Freedberg, *Power of Images*, 87–89.

δαλα, δαιδάλεος, πολυδαίδαλος with δαιδαλεῖα—the works of Daidalos. For in *Iliad* 18 and elsewhere, it is such artifacts that are praised as αὐτόματα or endowed with life, not the only work Homer attributes to Daidalos himself—the mysterious χορός created by the activity of ἀσκεῖν. Most post-epic speculations on Daidalos and his art, the subject of this chapter, derive from learned interpretations or rationalizations of the poetic family of δαίδαλα, assembled in Part I and reviewed here.

Epic conventions praising artifacts in poetry invoke the role of legendary, divine, or exotic craftsmanship and δαιδαλ- qualities, whose effect is the animation in objects, the illusion of life. *Iliad* 18 is the richest source of such expressions in their full range, convening Hephaistos, Daidalos, every variant of δαιδαλ- words, and the power of movement in art. First to display such autokinetic powers are the magic tripods of Hephaistos invoked by Aristotle (*Politics* 1.4). Like Helen's wheeled basket of gold and silver (Odyssey 4.125–35), they could be inspired by Near Eastern artifacts or their description, as in those cast by Hiram of Tyre for King Solomon (1 Kings 7.27–37). Even before they acquire their δαιδάλεα οὔατα, the tripods of Hephaistos inspire awe (*Iliad* 18. 375–77): they are able "to enter the divine assembly on their own and each go to its own chamber, a wonder to behold" (οἱ αὐτόματοι θεῖον δυσαίατ᾽ ἀγῶνα ἠδ᾽ αὖτις πρὸς δῶμα νεοίατο, θαῦμα ἰδέσθαι). The next wonder made by the smith-god is equal in magic, his ἀμφίπολοι (*Iliad* 18.417–20):

> χρύσεαι, ζωῆσι νεήνισιν εἰοικυῖαι.
> τῆς ἐν μὲν νόος ἐστὶ μετὰ φρέσιν, ἐν δὲ καὶ αὐδή
> καὶ σθένος, ἀθανάτων δὲ θεῶν ἄπο ἔργα ἴσασιν.
>
> Golden girls, like unto living maidens,
> in whom is a mind with wits, and in whom a voice
> is and strength, and they know works from the immortal gods.

These divine creatures—whether servants, imaginary creations, or both—not only move, but their likeness to ζωαὶ νεηνίαι ("living creatures") endows them with νόος, φρένες, αὐδή, and σθένος: human powers in mind, voice, and strength. The fascination with αὐτόματα in classical philosophy, especially in Aristotle, derives from imaginary creatures like these, prototypes for Plato's puppets.[24] Specific creations by Daidalos—the giant, Talos, in particular—epitomize the magic power of his statues, as a man

---

[24] *De Motu Animalium* 701b, 2–10: M. Nussbaum, *De Motu Animalium* (Princeton, 1978), 347, and "The Text of Aristotle's *De Motu Animalium*," HSCP 80 (1976) 146–52. Cf. *Metaphysics* 983a.15. Puppets (and a puppet show) are implied in Plato's cave: *Republic* 514b; cf. *Laws* 1.644d–45c, 7.804b. On animated statues, see A. Stewart, "When Is a Kouros Not an Apollo? The Tenean 'Apollo' Revisited," in *Corinthiaca*, 63–64 n. 42. Kallistratos, *Ekphrasis* 8, attributes the motion of Daidalos's statues to μηχαναί; cf. H. von Hesberg, "Mechanische Kunstwerke und ihre Bedeutung für die höfliche Kunst des Hellenismus," *MarbW* (1987) 47–72; Freedberg, *Power of Images*, 36, and passim.

of metal who functions as guardian of laws.[25] Ultimately, classical attitudes toward statuary as an imitation of life, including those works attributed to Daidalos, have their roots in such poetic praise of art. Comparative as well as internal evidence makes these passages critical to the evolution of the myth of artist-as-magician, common in traditions also found outside Greece.[26]

In the *Iliad*, figures on the Shield of Achilles "converse like living creatures" (μίλενν δ' ὥς τε ζωοὶ βροτοί) and furrows of earth darken as if ploughed, "although [only] of gold" (χρυσείη περ ἐοῦσα), as if overcoming the limitations of inanimate material. Several δαίδαλα in the *Odyssey* demonstrate similar powers for animals in art, most vividly on the famous gold brooch in which Penelope recognizes evidence of her husband's safe existence (*Odyssey* 19. 226–31). Many marveled at this daidalon, that "even though made of gold, the dog kept his grasp on the fawn | but it kept struggling, in vain to escape from its paws" (ὡς οἱ χρύσειοι ἐόντες ὁ μὲν λάε νεβρὸν ἀπάγχων, | αὐτὰρ ὁ ἐκφυγέειν μεμαὼς ἤσπαιρε πόδεσσι). Although less explicit a metaphor for art come alive, this artifact inspires the same sense of wonder at the conflict between its artifice and its life: θαυμάζεσκον ἅπαντες, in the words of Odysseus himself—as θαῦμα ἰδέσθαι expresses more generally elsewhere. The concessive use of the participle, ὡς . . . χρύσειοι ἐόντες (cf. χρυσείε περ ἐοῦσα at *Iliad* 18.549), "although only of gold," emphasizes the contradiction between inanimate material and the vitality of figural art, more vividly, if naively, than the more common ζωῆσι . . . εἰοικυῖαι, "like living creatures." Beyond awe, fear can be inspired by epic art, when animals in art are so lifelike as to frighten observer and poet. The gold τελαμών of Herakles, glimpsed by Odysseus in his peep into the underworld, ends in a plea inspired by such a sentiment (*Odyssey* 11.609–14):

χρύσεος ἦν τελαμών, ἵνα θέσκελα ἔργα τέτυκτο,
ἄρκτοι τ' ἀγρότεροί τε σύες χαροποί τε λέοντες,
ὑσμῖναί τε μάχαι τε φόνοι τ' ἀνδροκτασίαι τε.
μὴ τεχνησάμενος μηδ' ἄλλο τι τεχνήσαιτο,
κεῖνον τελαμῶνα ἑῇ ἐγκάτθετο τέχνῃ.

It was a gold scabbard, where wondrous deeds were worked,
bears and wild boars and lions with glaring eyes
and fierce battles and man-slaughtering murders.

---

[25] Talos: Simonides, frag. 568 (Page) and Pausanias 8.53.5 (created by Hephaistos); Delcourt, *Héphaistos*, 160–62; Frontisi-Ducroux, *Dédale*, 125–34. Sutton, *Satyr Play*, 155, compares classical αὐτόματα to the figure of Talos in Sophokles' *Daidalos* or *Pandora* (frags. 160–61, Kassel-Austin).

[26] Philipp, *Tektonon Daidala*, 4–18 on descriptions of art in early Greek literature; R. S. Bluck, *Plato's* Meno (Cambridge, 1961), 410, on poetic sources of theories about statues in motion. Kris and Kurz, *Legend, Myth and Magic in the Image of the Artist*, on Hephaistos and Daidalos in their Indo-European context.

May the artist who applied his art to that scabbard
not make any other one!

Here the θέσκελα ἔργα are so vivid as to frighten even a hero of vast experience and provoke the fervent outburst: "May the artist never repeat such work!"[27] The belt itself can be compared with Mycenaean weapons, but its closest parallels are not provided through archaeology but within the epic corpus itself, in Pandora's crown. The dazzling interior of the palace of Alkinoos, whose description owes elements to Canaanite poetry and its Hebrew legacy (Chapter 4; cf. 1 Kings 6–7), includes magic creatures that attract these formulaic phrases for art. The gold and silver dogs guarding the palace, made by Hephaistos, are described as ἀθανάτους ὄντας καὶ ἀγήρως ἤματα πάντα (Odyssey 7. 91–94): "immortal and ageless for all time." These wonderful animals, kin to the Mycenaean dogs painted around the throne room at Pylos, are made of gold and silver, the result of a collaboration between the poet's imagination and the craftsmanship of Hephaistos.[28] They are joined, a few lines later, by golden attendants kin to those who assist Hephaistos at home in Iliad 18 (Odyssey 7.100–103): χρύσεοι . . . κοῦροι, "golden young men" who hold torches to light the banquet halls. These extraordinary creatures, like Hellenistic λυχνοῦχοι or Victorian lamp brackets more than any ancient illuminating fixture, are exclusive to neither Bronze nor Iron Age and more at home in the poetic imagination.[29] They join a significant group of anthropoid figures in epic poetry, including the ἀμφίπολοι of Hephaistos and creatures more directly suggestive of artificial humans—namely, statues. The divine figures of Ares and Athena on the shield of Achilles come closest to statues (Iliad 18.516–19):

ἦρχε δ᾽ ἄρα σφιν Ἄρης καὶ Παλλὰς Ἀθήνη,
ἄμφω χρυσείω, χρύσεια δὲ εἵματα ἕσθην,
καλὼ καὶ μεγάλω, σὺν τεύχεσιν, ὥς τε θεώ περ,
ἀμφὶς ἀριζήλω. λαοὶ δ᾽ ὑπ᾽ ὀλίζονες ἦσαν.

And with them led Ares and Pallas Athena,
both of them golden, and their clothing was gold,
large and beautiful in their armor, being gods,
both of them larger than life, but the people below were smaller.

What distinguishes these figures is their size, their costly material (gold bodies in gold raiment), scale, and visibility, qualities that anticipate archaic and classical statues of

---

[27] Philipp, Tektonon Daidala, 12, 72, on this description, unusual for its lack of verbs in lines 611–12 (cf. descriptions of art in Linear B: Chapter 4) and for its attitude toward an anonymous artist.

[28] Faraone, GRBS 28 (1987) 257–80; also see Chapters 1 and 4.

[29] U. Jantzen and R. Tölle, "Beleuchtungsgeräte," in ArchHom II: P. Hausrat, 84; Canciani, ArchHom N. "Bildkunst," 35. Compare the cherubim adorning the temple of Solomon: 1 Kings 6–7.

gods, especially cult images. Their epic context in passages studded with δαιδαλ-words, particularly in *Iliad* 18, helped inspire classical admiration of movement and "life" in the statues of Daidalos, as well as his reputation for images laden with religious powers. Human personalities in the Homeric poems, as well as artificial creatures, attract such life-giving embellishments. When Athena transforms Odysseus the beggar into his true self and improves him, whether for Nausikaa or for his wife, she makes him into a statue (*Odyssey* 6.229–35):

> τὸν μὲν Ἀθηναίη θῆκεν Διὸς ἐκγεγαυῖα
> μείζονά τ᾽ εἰσιδέειν καὶ πάσσονα, κὰδ᾽ δὲ κάρητος
> οὔλας ἧκε κόμας, ὑακινθίνῳ ἄνθει ὁμοίας.
> ὡς δ᾽ ὅτε τις χρυσὸν περιχεύεται ἀργύρῳ ἀνὴρ
> ἴδρις, ὅν Ἥφαιστος δέδαεν καὶ Παλλὰς Ἀθήνη
> τέχνην παντοίην—χαρίεντα δὲ ἔργα τελείει—
> ὡς ἄρα τῷ κατέχευε χάριν κεφαλῇ τε καὶ ὤμοις

> And Athena, born from Zeus made him
> taller and broader in appearance, and poured down
> thick curly hair on his shoulders, like hyacinth flowers,
> as when some man pours gold around silver,
> a clever one, whom Hephaistos and Pallas Athena
> taught every craft—he accomplishes pleasing works—
> thus she shed grace around his head and shoulders.

Odyssey 23.156–62 repeats these lines very closely and perhaps deliberately; on both occasions Odysseus is being dressed up as a false bridegroom, once for his flirtation with Nausikaa, here for his second wooing of his wife.[30] In both instances the goddess improves his size and stature, makes his hair darker or curlier (depending on whether "hyakinthine" refers to tight curls or blue-black luster) and endows him with χάρις, that quality of grace bestowed on both men and art, especially helpful for seduction (as in Hera's ἀπατή of Zeus in *Iliad* 14.183: see, Chapter 1). The simile in *Odyssey* 23 borrows the τέχνη and value system (gold and silver) of prehistoric metalwork for the beautification of Odysseus, but the comparison employs a sophisticated figure of speech. Life imitates art, in that the appearance of a mortal man is compared with the artificial beauty of man-made metalwork. Such a simile inverts the formulaic praise of art—the brooch Odysseus wears, for example, that writhes with life "even though made of gold"—as revealed in its corollary. Once the goldworker is invoked—a χρυσοχόος like Laerkes who gilds the horns of a sacrificial bull (*Odyssey* 3.425)—the role

---

[30] Philipp, *Tektonon Daidala*, 35–36, on this passage and its poetic afterlife. Murnaghan, *Disguise and Rec-* ognition, 92–97 (Nausikaa) and chap. 4, "Penelope."

of divine patrons follows: thus Hephaistos and Athena are praised for their role in his craft. The result is that Athena's transformation of Odysseus is compared with that of a goldworker, a craftsman in turn endowed by herself, in overlapping figures of speech not uncommon in paratactical composition.

All these passages praising beauty in nature and art—whether metalwork, born-again heroes, or the wardrobe of the gods—culminate in the most dazzling epic creature of all, Hesiod's Pandora. In keeping with her name, she has it all: divine artists (Athena and Hephaistos) as dressers, χάρις, and δαίδαλα (*Theogony* 578–84; cf. Chapter 1):

> ἀμφὶ δέ οἱ στεφάνην χρυσέην κεφαλῆφιν ἔθηκε,
> τὴν αὐτὸς ποίησε περικλυτὸς ἀμφιγυήεις
> ἀσκήσας παλάμῃσι, χαριζόμενος Διὶ πατρί.
> τῇ δ᾽ ἐνὶ δαίδαλα πολλὰ τετεύχατο, θαῦμα ἰδέσθαι,
> κνώδαλ᾽, ὅσ᾽ ἤπειρος πολλὰ τρέφει ἠδὲ θάλασσα,
> τῶν ὅ γε πόλλ᾽ ἐνέθηκε—χάρις ἀπελάμπετο πολλή—
> θαυμάσια, ζῴοισιν ἐοικότα φωνήεσσιν.

> And around her head she placed a golden crown
> which he himself had made, the famous all-clever one,
> working it with his hands, pleasing Zeus the father
> and he placed on it many *daidala*, a wonder to behold,
> wild beasts, as many as the earth and the sea support
> of these he placed on many—and much grace shone forth—
> wondrous creatures, like unto living voices.

Unlike the apotropaic gear of Herakles (*Odyssey* 11.609–14), Pandora's outfit is not meant to frighten but to charm, hence the animals in gold are δαιδάλεα rather than σμερδαλέος. Prominent among the vocabulary praising her κόσμος are the powers of speech and life: ζῴοισιν ἐοικότα φωνήεσσιν is an expression derived from Homer and inherited by archaic poetry. The participation of the gods in her manufacture, and her "daidalic" crown, became popular in classical art (Figure 50). Pandora's parthenogenesis and its motifs cap the tradition of inanimate creatures come alive in epic poetry. While these references cannot certify the existence of monumental sculpture during Hesiod's lifetime, they only anticipate forms not yet manifest in the archaeological repertoire of the time of the poems, the way poetic expressions like ἑκατόμπεδον migrate from hexameter to monuments (Chapter 2). But they embody a conceptual foundation common to art and poetry that helped inspire divine images, sustained in the tradition that Pheidias created images from Homeric models.

Phrases like Hesiod's outlive epic poetry into the language of Pindar, for example, praising the art of Rhodes, particularly sculpture (*Olympian* 7.52):

αὐτὰ δὲ σφίσιν ὤπασε τέχναν
πᾶσαν ἐπιχθονίων Γλαυκ-
    ῶπις ἀριστοπόνοις χερσὶ κρατεῖν.
ἔργα δὲ ζωοῖσιν ἑρπόν-
    τεσσί θ' ὁμοῖα κέλευθοι φέρον·

And the gray-eyed goddess granted them
every art, to surpass all mortal men
with their hands, makers of masterpieces,
and all their roads displayed works
like unto living creatures.

Pindar's sophisticated and self-conscious use of this poetic formula finds its popular counterpart among archaic artists in casual comment on figures in action. For example, on a black-figured band-cup decorated with animal fights by Neandros, informal dipinti express pleasure at how "a lion got this boar, yes he did, well done."[31] The inscription focuses on live combat, on the result or effect of art, not the craftsmanship that created the illusion of action; it expresses the same awe, at eye level, that Pindar introduces as a poetic simile in praise of art. A third archaic dimension where figural art has a voice is represented by inscribed votive statuettes bearing a voice in letters, like "Daidaleia" of Mazi (Figure 5). Greece's earliest epigraphers supplied the "voice" missing from art forms nearly alive; when manufactured objects were dedicated to divine purposes, cult supplied what art had not. When Hekabe makes her impassioned plea for a voice in all her limbs (Euripides, *Hekabe* 838), the image closest to her metaphor is that of archaic inscriptions claiming divine attention in the first person, often in letters running up and down the legs of statuettes.[32] This archaic convention lasts into the classical image of "talking statues" and survives in the Hellenistic dialogue epigram (e.g., Callimachus, frag. 114) and in Roman satire (Horace, *Ode* 1.8; Propertius, 4.2), entering the repertoire of ancient παροιμίες (Bekker, *Anecdota Graeca* I.240.16. s.v. Δαιδάλου ποιημάτων, Tzetzes I.19.536–41, s.v. Τὰ δὲ δαιδάλεια).

Only in the fifth century did these independent conventions in poetry, ritual, and art converge in a conscious attempt to articulate the powers of life and art. The two strains, poetic and popular, are joined in the fifth century by a third, the philosophical contemplation of motion and life, itself a descendant of pre-Sokratic speculation on the nature of life. That sculptors as well as philosophers and poets also contributed to this debate emerges in traditions surrounding the fifth century's most celebrated work of art. An explicit epic debt exists on the part of classical sculptors according to the tradition that

[31] Boston, MFA 61.1073: J. D. Beazley, *Paralipomena*, 2d ed. (Oxford, 1971), 69; Vermeule, *Aspects of Death*, 91, fig. 11.

[32] M. Burzazechi, "Oggetti parlanti nelle epigrafi greche," *Epigraphia* 24 (1962) 3–54; Kassel, *ZPE* 51 (1983) 1–12. Stewart, in *Corinthiaca*, 63–64 n. 42.

Pheidias inspired himself from Homer's Zeus (citing *Iliad* 1.527–30) in creating the cult statue for the temple at Olympia (Strabo, 8.354).[33] The same self-conscious tribute to the epic tradition is in fact embodied in the ensemble of the Athena Parthenos, as suggested in the discussion of Hesiod's Pandora (Chapter 2). Her base is decorated with figures illustrating the birth of Pandora, epic poetry's ultimate "statue" creation as well as one in which Athena played an important and "daidalic" role.[34] The connection from Pandora to the Parthenos is intriguing if one assumes a conscious, even ironic intent on the part of Pheidias. It implies a compliment subtler and more arrogant, in his comparison of himself to the collaborative efforts of all the gods and the guiding design of Athena and Hephaistos, than the self-portrait that anecdote attributes to his design on the shield (see Chapter 9). Yet it agrees with the tradition that Homer inspired Pheidias for his other celebrated cult image, the Zeus of Olympia, and demonstrates how epic poetry was a source for sculptors as well as tragedians in the fifth century, both of whom may account for the popularity of the Pandora story in classical vase painting.[35] Ultimately, Pandora's classical revival owes more to influences other than to Pheidias, his vanity, or his sense of humor. Her reconstitution makes her a female equivalent of Erichthonios, son of the craftsman Hephaistos and "father" of the newly autochthonous Athenians. She embodies at once the birth of monumental figural art and the origins of the Attic race, a myth promoted by classical Athens like the figure of Daidalos himself.[36]

This detailed review of the poetic language of art suggests the primary source for the classical resurrection of Daidalos: the extension of a metaphor into the articulation of statues. To recapitulate, figural art is praised for its "life" in early poetry; in a century dominated by sculpture, statues became the primary medium for this metaphor, although it also animated paintings that deceived men and animals, as in fourth-century anecdotes about the rivalry of Parrhasios and Zeuxis (Pliny, *Naturalis Historia* 35.64). A comic twist on this tradition makes statues come alive, answer back, and interact with humans, in activity encouraged, if not inaugurated, on stage.

But poetry and its inversions in comedy tell only part of the story. The third dimension behind the classical persona of Daidalos is the most elusive but potentially the most serious: was there formal recognition of Daidalos as a historical sculptor in the fifth century? One modern argument claims such a convergence of legend and art in the lost work of Demokritos, as paraphrased by Aristotle.[37] As presented earlier, Aristotle jux-

[33] Pollitt, *Art of Greece*, 70–74; *Ancient View of Greek Art*, 97 n. 2, 210, 214; *Art and Experience*, 99–100. Hallett, *JHS* 106 (1986) 79 n. 1.

[34] Fehr, *Hephaistos* 2 (1980) 113–25, and *Hephaistos* 3 (1981) 70–72, on the birth of Pandora as an analogy to the creation of the Athena Parthenos. On the myth of Pandora in fifth-century Athens, see Chapter 12, with n. 54 for recent identifications and reconstruc-

tions of this base.

[35] Webster, *Monuments*, 150–51; Simon, in *Eye of Greece*, 145–47.

[36] Loraux, *Les enfants d'Athena*, 84, 94, 122–25, 153, 252, 276; also see Chapter 12.

[37] B. Schweitzer, "Daidalos und die Daidaliden in der Überlieferung," in his *Xenokrates von Athen* (Halle, 1925), 20–31, from K. Reinhardt, "Hekataios

taposed the theories of Demokritos with comic antics attributed to Daidalos and his statues (Philippos, frag. 22), distinguishing neatly and conveniently between the two strands of the Daidalos tradition, in philosophy and comedy. The confusion of the two separate strands invented a lost work of Demokritos discussing art in the context of cultural evolution. The philosopher's interest in art is attested in the titles of lost works such as περὶ ζωγραφίας ("On Painting") and in his reputation for experience in all the arts (περὶ τεχνῶν πᾶσαν εἶχεν ἐμπειρίαν: Diogenes Laertius, 9.37). But this passage cannot provide conveniences such as the lost source for Diodorus's discussion of Daidalos, and scholars have gradually isolated the original misunderstanding.[38] It seems best to eliminate Daidalos from Demokritos's theories of cultural evolution, especially since a preoccupation with statues by Daidalos in other sources predates the philosopher's writings. Turning to Plato, only once does Sokrates discuss the style of Daidalos's statues (except for his generous compliment, πανὺ καλὰ ἔργα, in the *Meno*), and he does so in the context of rhetorical criticism, a familiar occasion for ancient art history.[39] In the *Hippias Major*, Sokrates' target is the successful sophist, Hippias of Elis. In a critique of old-fashioned philosophy, Sokrates compares a hypothetical resurrection of Bias of Priene (in a predictable pun, Βίας ἀναβιοίη) with a revival of the works of Daidalos (*Hippias Major* 282.a.1):

γέλωτ᾽ ἂν ὄφλοι πρὸς ὑμᾶς, ὥσπερ καὶ τὸν Δαίδαλόν φασιν οἱ ἀνδριαντοποιοί, νῦν εἰ γενόμενος τοιαῦτ᾽ ἐργάζοιτο οἷα ἦν ἀφ᾽ ὧν τοὔνομ᾽ ἔσχεν, καταγέλαστος ἂν εἶναι.

It would appear laughable to you, just as the sculptors say that Daidalos, if he were now alive and made such works as were those which gave him his name, would be a joke.

Such an appeal to the realm of art to develop a point about rhetorical style is a textbook example of art criticism as a by-product of literary theory. It is reinforced by the explicit comparison with which Sokrates prefaces his invocation of Bias and Daidalos (281.d.4):

ὥσπερ αἱ ἄλλαι τέχναι ἐπιδεδώκασι, καί εἰσι παρὰ τοὺς νῦν δημιουργοὺς οἱ παλαιοὶ φαῦλοι, οὕτω καὶ τὴν ἡμετέραν τῶν σοφιστῶν τέχνην ἐπιδεδωκέναι φῶμεν καὶ εἶναι τῶν ἀρχαίων τοὺς περὶ σοφίαν φαύλους πρὸς ὑμᾶς;

---

von Abdera und Demokrit," *Hermes* 47 (1912) 492–513. According to Schweitzer (p. 27), "Daidalos ist von Democritus schon aus dem Mythenhimmel herabgezogen und zu einem archaischen Meister gemacht worden."

[38] A. T. Cole, *Democritus and the Origins of Greek Anthropology*, APA monographs 25 (Cleveland, 1967), 11–13; Pollitt, *Ancient View of Greek Art*, 79, 109 n. 19,

appeals to Spoerri's rebuttal to Schweitzer; Philipp, *Tektonon Daidala*, 53, points out pre-Demokritean sources on Daidalos, such as the papyrus fragment of Aeschylus's *Theoroi* (see nn. 6–8) not known to Schweitzer; Kassel, *ZPE* 51 (1983) 1–12, isolates Schweitzer's critical error and its afterlife.

[39] Pollitt, *Ancient View of Greek Art*, 32–49, 60–61.

Just as the other arts have advanced, and the older ones now appear poor among today's artists, in the same way our present art, that of the sophists, may we say has advanced and those of old involved with wisdom now appear poor?

In terms of the style of Daidalos, this judgment contrasts sharply with Sokrates' praise of his καλὰ ἔργα in the *Meno*. But the celebrated irony of Sokratic pronouncements, especially in dialogues where he is leading a victim to confusion, prevents serious conclusions in terms of art history and criticism. The substance of the reference is that the statues of Daidalos would appear καταγέλαστον to contemporary eyes. This reflects an attitude common throughout Greek and Roman art criticism, where "the art of Pheidias represents the supreme achievement of Greek sculpture,"[40] such that older works would appear ludicrous in comparison with those of the master. At the same time, the informal authority cited by Sokrates implies an element of radical irreverence toward the works of Daidalos among artists. It appears that his statues enjoyed no small measure of popularity, to which sculptors took bold exception in expressing professional admiration or preference for a classical style. Sokrates's source implies: "Despite the nobility/antiquity of the works of Daidalos, anyone who made them today would appear old-fashioned to the point of ridicule, such has sculptural style changed." Pausanias adheres to this classical sentiment in admiring the statues of Daidalos in the second century A.D., despite their primitive appearance (2.4.5; see, Chapter 9), and the judgment passed on by Sokrates through Plato simply provides a (late) classical pedigree for this sentiment.

What makes this passage intriguing is the reference to the testimony of sculptors: ὥσπερ φασιν οἱ ἀνδριαντοποιοί. It allows one to imagine comments on the style of Daidalos in some classical source, perhaps even the existence of technical or aesthetic treatises by sculptors known to Sokrates and Plato, to which reference could be made in this informal manner. Without positing formal lectures by sculptors on their craft, one could imagine an oral tradition by which masters taught pupils in some manner that also informed the general public. Whatever (if any) its precise meaning, the reference to the authority of statue makers on Daidalos implies that contemporary artists discussed his style as old-fashioned. How "old" they made Daidalos is unclear: whether an archaic kouros, or an older cult image, looked laughable in the fifth century cannot be determined, and the reference sheds no light on the presumed life-span of Daidalos.

Other passages in Plato indicate the historical age of Daidalos, as imagined by classical Athenians. In the *Ion*, Sokrates discusses ἀνδριαντοποιία in terms of three legendary sculptors—two from the epic tradition (Daidalos and Epeios) and one of archaic pedigree: Theodoros of Samos. In the *Laws* (677d), the sculptor is a contemporary of Orpheus and Palamedes, removed in time by at least a thousand years to the company

---

[40] Ibid., 61 (cf. Hallett, *JHS* 106 [1986] esp. 79, n. 1).

of other legendary artists and inventors. These two references imagine Daidalos in epic and heroic time, while other passages place him, if not in more recent generations, firmly in Attic history. For the legend of Daidalos the sculptor not only developed in classical Athens, it made him an Athenian, a refinement that makes Sokrates' praise of his works as "entirely beautiful works" (πανὺ καλὰ ἔργα) quite appropriate, if chauvinistic. In the *Euthyphro's* discussion of slippery λόγοι, Sokrates reveals his personal interest in Daidalos: he calls him an ancestor, ὁ ἡμετερὸς πρόγονος (11.b.9). Elsewhere, Sokrates claims the same kinship in tracing his own ancestry to Hephaistos and Zeus, via Daidalos (in the pseudo-Platonic *Alkibiades* 1.121a.1). Originally associated with Lemnos or Crete (see Chapter 4), Hephaistos became an Athenian favorite by the fifth century, their craftsman-patron and even ancestor (παῖδες Ἡφαίστου describes Athenians in Aeschylus, *Eumenides* 13).[41] Daidalos became an Athenian as a result of similar cultural appropriations in the fifth century, and his epic association with Hephaistos through *Iliad* 18 no doubt helped him share in the migration of Hephaistos. In the *Ion* (533.a.7), Sokrates calls Daidalos the son of Metion, a specific link in the long-range ancestry from Daidalos to Hephaistos and Zeus. Metion is one of several "fathers" bestowed on Daidalos by Athenian tradition, among other names equally complimentary to craftsmanship ("Palamaon" and "Eupalamos," Pliny's *Eucheir*), all dependent on the lineage of Erechtheus.[42] Sokrates' own whimsical claim to descent from Daidalos may reflect either his father's profession as λιθουργός (a member ex officio of the "Daidalidai"), or Sokrates' membership in the deme "Daidalidai" (see Chapter 9) or both. Sokrates' "kinship" with Daidalos helps account for some of his affection for the mythological figure in argument, through nepotism. Its source and authority involve the broader question of the origins of Daidalos's Athenian connections (Part IV).

By the time Plato wrote the *Republic*, the figure of Daidalos reiterates the philosopher's rejection of traditional craftsmanship, however impressive, in his pursuit of ἀλήθεια and συμμετρία. In discussing the latter, Sokrates recommends study of the stars, "just as if someone should find diagrams carefully designed and made by Daidalos or some other artist or painter" (529d.6–530: ὁμοίως ὥσπερ ἂν εἴ τις ἐντύχοι ὑπὸ Δαιδάλου ἢ τινὸς ἄλλου δημιουργοῦ ἢ γραφέως διαφερόντως γεγραμμένοις καὶ ἐκπεπονημένοις διαγράμμασιν). Sokrates argues that, however "beautiful in terms of execution" is the draughtsmanship of venerated artists, whether by Daidalos "or some

---

[41] *Odyssey* 6.233; Solon, frag. 12.49; Delcourt, *Héphaistos*, 193–203, on the craftsman ignored in cult until fifth-century Athens: see Chapter 12. Loraux, *Les enfants d'Athèna*, 28–30; N. Robertson, "The Riddle of the Arrephoria at Athens," *HSCP* 87 (1983) 288. Compare the fate of Epimenides of Crete who becomes the Athenian culture-hero, Bouzyges: Shapiro, *Kernos* 3 (1990) 341.

[42] Plato's source is shared by Pherekydes (schol. Sophokles, *Oidipous at Kolonos* 472) and repeated by Diodorus (4.76), who compromises by making Metion son of Eupalamos, a relationship reversed by the tradition found in Apollodoros (3.15.8) and other mythographers: Frontisi-Ducroux, *Dédale*, 90–94; see Chapter 10.

other craftsman or painter," it would be "absurd to examine seriously the truth in them" (κάλλιστα μὲν ἔχειν ἀπεργασίᾳ, γελοῖον μὴν ἐπισκοπεῖν ταῦτα σπουδῇ ὡς τὴν ἀλήθειαν ἐν αὐτοῖς). This passage involves the complex issue of Plato's views on art, as a phenomenon to be admired but incapable of providing greater truths.[43] The simile compares Daidalos to other unnamed figures, including painters, without chronology, in a passage ultimately less useful, historically, than in the *Hippias Major* where the works of Daidalos are invoked for their antiquity. Together, the two references do not guarantee that Daidalos was perceived exclusively as sculptor: ἔργα is unhelpfully broad, while the passage in the *Republic* is more plausible for a painter of geometric figures than a sculptor. Unlike the claim to "living statues" exploited on stage and in other Platonic dialogues (*Meno, Euthyphro*), Daidalos here belongs with painters, and elsewhere when Plato invokes an unnamed artist as author of κινούμενα and ἔνεργα ἔργα (*Timaeus* 19b), he has a painter (ζωγράφος) in mind. Pliny knew Daidalos as the son of a painter called "Eucheir" ("Handy-man:" a rendering of Eupalamos? *Naturalis Historia* 7.205). If Daidalos has gained a new home by the fifth century and increased his reputation, his craftsmanship is barely more precise than in Homer.

In retrospect, classical testimonia on Daidalos are meager in biographical information, especially if one excludes later commentary on these passages, and he is barely more "historical" an artist than in the *Iliad*. When his origins are specified, Daidalos belongs to the remote mythological past, a contemporary of epic figures like Orpheus, Palamedes, and Epeios, or is associated with archaic but near-legendary artists like Theodoros of Samos (in Plato's *Ion*). The personification of δαιδάλεος is either a descendant of Hephaistos (as in Plato, *Alkibiades* 1.124) or the peer of the smith-god and other divine craftsmen, as in passages where he is juxtaposed with unspecified "other gods" (e.g., in Euripides' *Hekabe*, Plato's *Hippias Major* and *Republic*, and Aristotle's *Politics*). In one highly personal reference where Sokrates claims him as ancestor (Plato, *Alkibiades* 121.4), Daidalos is the son of an Athenian, Metion, and has been incorporated into Attic genealogy (Chapter 9). The weakness of Daidalos's casual bond to sculpture is manifest in those references where he is associated with painting or other works, and in his lack of a clear chronological home. Only three statues are attributed to him in classical sources: a wooden statue of Hermes (Plato Comicus, frag. 188), a wooden Aphrodite "injected" with mercury (Philippos or Euboulos), and a bronze statue (Kratinos, *Thracians* frag. 74), each more appropriate to its immediate dramatic context than to any particular type, medium, or style. The only comments on style make the works of Daidalos old-fashioned by classical standards but rich in magic or comic effects. Plato, through the mouthpiece of Sokrates, exploits its extension, the theme of runaway statues, in a manner more proper to comedy than philosophy, while Aristotle balances the comic effects of Daidalos's work with serious speculation about motion.

[43] Pollitt, *Ancient View of Greek Art*, 31–49.

This limits evidence for serious discussion of Daidalos to Sokrates' phrase, ὥσπερ φασι οἱ ἀνδριαντοποιοί (*Hippias Major* 282.a.1), which allows primarily for a discussion of contemporary (e.g., Pheidian) style by sculptors, not necessarily an allusion to Daidalos as sculptor. Only ironic sources mix serious speculation on movement and the art of Daidalos, as when Euripides calls the artist σοφός in praising the life of his statues with an ambiguous compliment. In other words, there is scant trace of a "historical" sculptor named Daidalos in fifth-century sources, in contrast to the learned and confident references to such a creature in later scholia and comments on these passages. Even the antiquarian interests of the fifth century that fed theories and styles of classical sculpture did not yet, it appears, incorporate the legend of Daidalos into the evolution of archaic sculpture as Diodorus and others did. This image of an archaic sculptor, complete with pupils, pedigree, and idiosyncratic style, developed under different intellectual conditions, in the world of Hellenistic and modern scholarship.[44]

[44] Becatti, *RömMitt* 60–61 (1953–1954) 34–35, recommends separating classical sources on Daidalos from Hellenistic theories about early Greek art, as did Carl Robert in 1890, and Philipp (in *Dädalische Kunst auf Kreta*).

CHAPTER 9

The "Daedalic" Style

A LITERARY TRADITION of "living art," derived from poetic conventions come alive for comic and philosophical purposes, evolved in close association with the name of Daidalos in fifth-century Athens. Eventually this tradition was rationalized into a historical personality and style. So convincing was the reconstitution of an actual sculptor that Homer's simile, comparing the work of a god (Hephaistos) with that of a mere mortal (Daidalos) confounded readers by the Hellenistic period.[1] The emergence of a historical sculptor explored in the previous chapter derived from four different components of ancient art criticism: popular, literary, and philosophical and professional. Three of these are active in the classical era, in comedy, satyr play, and Sokratic humor, the literary in tragedy, and the philosophical in Sokrates' references to the oeuvre and style of Daidalos. A more professional treatment is implied by Sokrates' allusion to "what the sculptors say," but most of this component emerged under the special conditions that fostered the rise of professional art criticism, in the Hellenistic period.[2]

Significantly enough, Daidalos does not appear in Pliny's chapters on the history of art as a sculptor, much as the artist is absent from inscriptions.[3] Since many of Pliny's sources, and indeed many of the earliest "professional" treatises on the arts, were technical essays by practicing artists,[4] the omission of a figure with remote and poetic sources is no surprise. Instead, Daidalos does appear in the second major tradition of ancient Greek art history, arising later than Pliny's sources and preserved in comparanda to the history of rhetoric in the prose of Quintilian and Cicero.[5] The source common to these two Latin writers concentrated on the classical achievement of Pheidias as the culmination of Greek sculptural style, in preference to the fourth-century Sikyonian tradition of Lysippos favored by "Xenokrates" and Pliny. A single reference to Daidalos

[1] Scholiasts on *Iliad* 18.590–92 (Erbse, *Scholia Graeca in Homeri Iliadem*, 4:564–66) attempt to explain how a god could be praised through comparison to a mortal. K. Snipes, "Literary Interpretation in the Homeric Scholia: The Similes of the *Iliad*," *AJP* 109 (1988) 196–222.

[2] Pollitt, *Ancient View of Greek Art*, 73–84, includes the lost writings of Demokritos (p. 106 n. 1) as an

earlier possibility, based on Schweitzer's mistaken theory (see Chapter 8, n. 38); Bruneau, *AntClass* 44 (1975) 425–87.

[3] A coincidence noted by C. Robert, *Archäologische Märchen*, 10.

[4] Pollitt, *Ancient View of Greek Art*, 11–25, 73–81.

[5] Ibid., 73, 81–84.

appears in Cicero's *Brutus*, where the evolution of sculpture is compared with that of rhetoric (18.71). In concluding a passage packed with artists of the fifth and fourth centuries (Kanachos, Kalamis, Myron, Polykleitos, Zeuxis, Polygnotos, Apelles, etc.), Cicero considers antecedents of the classical style, on the grounds that "nihil est enim simul et inventum et perfectum." As a paradigm for the origins of the various arts, the achievement of poets before Homer is defended along with those of the early Latin pioneer, Ennius, whose own verses apologized for the lack of learned poetry in his tongue. In supporting the primitive origins of Latin poetry, Cicero compares Livius Andronicus's translation of the *Odyssey* to an *opus Daedali*, while admitting Livius' own *fabulae* unworthy of reading twice:

> nam et Odyssia Latina est sic tamquam opus aliquod Daedali et Livianae fabulae non satis digna, quae iterum legantur.

> For even the Latin *Odyssey* is as some work of Daedalus and the fables of Livius not sufficiently worthy, that they should be read again.

In this brief testament critical to the ancient chronology of Greek sculpture, Daidalos is hardly closer to being a historical personality than when Plato or Aristotle groups him with Hephaistos, Orpheus, Palamedes, and Epeios (Chapter 8). Daidalos is, in fact, conspicuously absent from Cicero's concise survey of classical sculptors immediately preceding this passage, and only surfaces as a paradigm for a primitive stage of art. The expression *opus Daedali* does not even specify sculpture, and is just as ambiguous as ἔργα Δαιδάλου in Greek sources, as well as equally faithful to his epic range of skills.

Daidalos the sculptor emerges, instead, in brief comments on classical literature, primarily in scholia to references in tragedy and philosophy, then in miracle catalogues (e.g., of Palaiphatos), and in proverbial and lexical literature extending into the Christian era.[6] The fullest account appears in the early books of Diodorus Siculus on Sicilian history, in close connection with the Sicilian adventures of Daidalos (4.76–79; Chapter 7). The sculptor is introduced as an Athenian and the son of Erechtheus, son of "Metion" and grandson of "Eupalamos," those suspiciously appropriate names for a family of craftsmen (see Chapter 8). His skills include a great deal more than sculpture:

> In natural ability he far surpassed all other men, both in the art of building and in the manufacture of statues and in stoneworking. And having become the inventor [εὑρετής] of many techniques in art, he made wondrous works [ἔργα θαυμαζόμενα] in all parts of the inhabited world. In the making of statues he so far surpassed all others that later generations told tales about him, that his statues resembled live men. For they see and walk and on the

---

[6] Overbeck, *Schriftquellen*, 11–17, conveniently assembles the ancient sources on the art of Daidalos, without his adventures. A. Henrichs, "Three Approaches to Greek Mythography," in *Interpretations of Greek Mythology*, 242–77.

whole maintain such a disposition in their whole body, that the artificial creature seems to be a living creature [ἔμψυχον ζῷον]. As the first to give them eyes and make them move their limbs, making them extend their limbs, it is reasonable that he was admired among men. For the artists before his time used to make statues with closed eyes, and with arms at rest and close to their sides.

Diodorus continues with an account of Daidalos's Athenian, Sicilian, and Cretan adventures, punctuated by his most spectacular designs—Pasiphae's cow contraption, wings for himself and Ikaros, and engineering projects for his Sicilian hosts. Diodorus's only other reference to Daidalos as sculptor, in another passage, compares the style of his statues with that of the Egyptians (1.97.6):

τόν τε ῥυθμὸν τῶν ἀρχαίων κατ᾽ Αἴγυπτον ἀνδριάντων τὸν αὐτὸν εἶναι τοῖς ὑπὸ Δαιδάλου κατασκευασθεῖσι παρὰ τοῖς Ἕλλησι.

The style of old statues in Egypt is the same as those made by Daidalos among the Hellenes.

This crucial comparison has encouraged the modern identification of Daidalos as an archaic sculptor and of his works as kouroi, those Greek statues most suggestive of Egyptian ones.[7] Stylistic comparison of archaic Greek statues to Egyptian ones encouraged the same claim to similarity made by Diodorus, to derive the origins of Greek sculpture from Egypt. It has been argued that the Saite canon in sculpture was known and copied by Greek sculptors.[8] But kinship between Egyptian and Greek sculpture seems more manifest in the sixth century than the seventh, when the first statues and reliefs were made. Moreover, Greek sculpture in Egypt shows insufficient influence from native traditions, and the "Greek" presence there may be confined to Cypriotes.[9] These revisions agree with a general shift in scholarly interest to the Near East—Cyprus, Phoenicia, and Syria—as a more likely source of Aegean statue types and techniques.[10] These recent trends in scholarship discourage the use of archaeological evi-

---

[7] For ancient testimonia on Daidalos in modern scholarship, see Donohue, Xoana, 179–88; typical of the modern consensus is Ridgway, Archaic Style, 27–33, who interprets ῥυθμός to include "movement," not just "pattern" (cf. Pollitt, Ancient View of Greek Art, 218, 225, on ῥυθμός).

[8] E. Guralnick, "Proportions of Korai," AJA 85 (1981) 269–80; "Profiles of Korai," AJA 86 (1982) 173–82; "The Proportions of Kouroi," AJA 82 (1978) 461–72; Hurwit, Art and Culture of Early Greece, 194–97.

[9] W. Davis, "Ancient Naukratis and the Cypriotes in Egypt," GöttMisz 35 (1979) 13–23; "The Cypriotes at Naukratis," GöttMisz 41 (1980) 7–19; "Egypt, Samos and the Archaic Style in Greek Sculpture," JEA 67 (1981) 61–81; cf. Guralnick, AJA 85 (1981) 270.

Cypriote contact with Egypt began in the Bronze Age (e.g., at Marsa Matruh: Chapter 5, n. 112).

[10] Cook, JHS 87 (1967) 27–29; B. Lewe, Studien zur archaischen kyprischen Plastik (Frankfurt, 1975), argues that even Egyptian traits in Cypriote sculpture are transmitted via Syro-Palestine; cf. Kaulen, Daidalika, 174–83; G. Markoe, "Egyptianizing Male Votive Statuary from Cyprus: A Re-examination," Levant 22 (1990) 111–22; Morris, JMA 3 (1990) 61. Carter, Beginning of Greek Sculpture, defends the Levantine (North Syrian) origins of Greek statuary in limestone, before marble. As far away as Punic Sicily, Egyptian(izing) statues travel under Phoenician auspices: V. Tusa, in The Phoenicians, 192.

dence to interpret the passage in Diodorus, which must be understood within its historical and literary context. Nor should this passage be invoked to defend the superficial similarity in statue types as a historical phenomenon.[11] Rather than comparing Egyptian statues with Greek kouroi, Diodorus could be expressing (or merely transmitting) the judgment that the works of Daidalos occupy the same venerated position in the history of Greek art that ancient Egyptian ones do. In other words, the reference to Egypt betrays an antiquarian interest in establishing the age of a statue type, by claiming the same high antiquity for the works of Daidalos that the Greeks admired in Egyptian culture since their first contact.[12] This attitude is implicit in the kind of language with which Diodorus introduces the sculptor (4.76–79). Expressions that emphasize myth and the miraculous, invention and wonder (εὑρετής, θαυμαζόμενα, δοκεῖν εἶναι, and μυθολογῆσαι) maintain the reputation of his works as wonders and his identity as legendary, or at least remote, in the world of Hellenistic learning. In his choice of language Diodorus merely reaffirms ironic or exaggerated anecdotes from classical drama and philosophy, without the intermediary of a scholarly source or learned treatise.

Diodorus's description of the artist's innovations assumes that earlier artists made statues without eyes or extended limbs. The historian, or his source, seems to have matched classical praise of Δαιδαλεῖα, full of allusions to movement and speech, to a suitable equivalent chosen from the corpus of statues extant—and admired—in the Hellenistic period. This explanation is repeated consistently, in the scholia to classical sources and in later discussions of a lexicographical and critical nature. These variations on the themes of life expressed through movement and sight reduce a classical metaphor to physiology—that is, open eyes and mobile limbs.[13] For example, a commentator on Plato's *Meno* 367 explains:

Δαίδαλος ἄριστος ἀγαλματοποιὸς ἐπιγεγονὼς πρῶτος ἀναπετάννυσί τε τὰ τούτων βλέφαρα, ὡς δόξαι βλέπειν αὐτά, καὶ τοὺς πόδας, ὡς νομίσαι βαδίζειν, διίστησι. καὶ διὰ τοῦτο δεδέσθαι, ἵνα μὴ φύγοιεν, ὡς δῆθεν ἐμψύχων ἤδη γεγονότων αὐτῶν.

[11] As warned by Cook, *JHS* 87 (1967) 24–27; A. B. Lloyd, *Herodotus Book II* (Leiden, 1975), 50–60, rejects the historicity of Daidalos but admits Egyptian elements in Greek sculpture; Hurwit, *Art and Culture of Early Greece*, 190–97. Discussions of Diodorus 1.98.5–9: R. Anthes, "Affinity and Difference between Egyptian and Greek Sculpture and Thought," *PAPhS* 107 (1963) 60–81; B. Ridgway, "Greek Kouroi and Egyptian Methods," *AJA* 70 (1966) 68–70.

[12] Compare how Pausanias believes (πείθομαι) that all statues in the time of Danaos were *xoana*, "and especially the Egyptian ones" (καὶ μάλιστα τὰ Αἰγύπτια: 2.19.3), in a similar antiquarian vision. Don-

ohue, *Xoana*, 140–47; my Chapter 13; Bernal, *Black Athena*, 39–40, 109–30 on Greek interest in Egypt (p. 111 on Diodorus).

[13] Overbeck, *Schriftquellen*, nos. 119–37, for references to the artist's style (on his life and works: nos. 74–118). These include classical writers (Euripides, Plato, Aristotle) and their scholia, later Greek literature on art and religion (Palaiphatos, Diodorus, Lucian, Philostratos, Pausanias, Aristides, Dio Chrysostom, Zenobios, Themistios) and lexicographers (Suidas, Hesychius, Tzetzes). See Kassel, *ZPE* 51 (1983) 3 n. 13; Donohue, *Xoana*, 179–88.

Daidalos, the greatest maker of statues, was the first to open their eyelids, so that they appear to see, and to separate the feet, so that they appear to walk. And because of this he bound them, in order that they might not run away, as if they were living and breathing.

The scholiast on another of the Daidalos references in Plato (*Euthyphro* 11c) expresses the same judgment in different words:

Δαίδαλος δὲ ᾿Αθηναῖος ἦν τῶν πώποτε ἀνδριαντοποιῶν περιφανέστατος· πρῶτος δὲ καὶ περισκελὲς ἄγαλμα ἐσχημάτισε τῶν πρὸ ἐκείνου κατὰ ταυτὸ συμβεβηκότα τὼ πόδε τὰ βρέτη ἐργαζομένων· ἀφ᾽ οὗ δὴ καὶ ὁ τοῦ περιιέναι καὶ κινεῖσθαι τὰ φιλοτεχνήματα αὐτοῦ ὑπὸ τῶν πολλῶν ἀνάκειται λόγος αὐτῷ.

Daidalos the Athenian was foremost among the sculptors of that time. He was also first to design a statue with legs apart, the images before that time having their limbs worked together. From that time derives the account current among many, of statues moving and walking around.

Throughout the many comments to this effect prevails a definite element of the casual and popular nature of this reputation, expressed with words like λόγος, δόξα, φήμη, ἱστορηθῆναι, νομίζειν, which emphasize opinions or explanations of poetic phenomena but no reliable sources. Nor do they imply any consistent type or style of statue. Despite specific descriptions like those by Palaiphatos (*De Incredibilis* 22: Δαίδαλος δὲ πρῶτος ἐποίει διαβεβηκότας τὸν ἕνα πόδα: "Daidalos first made [a statue] moving one leg"), which call to mind a statue like a kouros with one leg advanced, and Diodorus's comparison to Egyptian figures, most of the comments do not contribute to a consistent image. For one thing, they imply forerunners that cannot be attested; "closed eyes" never characterize a phase of Greek sculpture, even the earliest marble figurines of the Early Bronze Age being enlivened by painted features now faded to ghosts.[14] One could correlate the claim for "open eyes" with the innovation of separately inlaid eyes for bronze or ivory faces, were this not native to Syrian sculpture since the third millennium B.C. and adopted by the Greeks belatedly, if repeatedly.[15] Moreover, such a feature would have to be synchronized with the first "walking" kouroi, a separate innovation in early archaic sculpture. This second critical step [*sic*] attributed to Daidalos, the illusion of movement through extended arms and legs, would not agree with the majority of specific works attributed to the sculptor in both earlier and later times. The figures of Pan, Hermes, and Aphrodite named in classical sources as the works of Daidalos were more likely to resemble those ἀγάλματα τῶν πρὸ τούτου τεχνιτῶν, especially the wooden Hermes figure (Plato, frag. 188) who may have been an actual herm, hence pillar-shaped, without limbs.

[14] P. Getz-Preziosi and S. Weinberg, "Evidence for Painted Details in Early Cycladic Sculpture," *AntK* 13 (1970) 4–12.

[15] Carter, *Greek Ivory-Carving*, 253 n. 196, on inlaid eyes. Cf. W. Déonna, "Les yeux absents ou clos des statues de la Grèce primitive," *REG* 48 (1935) 219–44.

A similar contradiction exists between Hellenistic descriptions and the statues attributed to Daidalos in the time of Pausanias. By that time, the concept of *xoana* preoccupied the religious, historical, and aesthetic imagination, as a stage of Greek sculpture conjectured by antiquarians and apologists, without archaeological foundation.[16] Pausanias in fact equates the two concepts in several passages where he calls some works of Daidalos ξόανα (9.40.3, 4; 2.4.5; 8.35.2; 9.11.4; see Chapter 2 for his gloss of δαίδαλα as an old term for ξόανα at 9.3.2). His description of the Aphrodite on Delos made by Daidalos (9.40.3–4) calls her

οὐ μέγα ξόανον, λελυμασμένον τὴν δεξίαν χεῖρα ὑπὸ τοῦ χρόνου· κάτεισι δὲ ἀντὶ ποδῶν ἐς τετράγωνον σχῆμα.

not a large *xoanon*, the right arm having been worn away by time. Instead of legs, the lower body ends in a rectangular shape.

Her lower body apparently ends in a pillar-like shaft of the kind reserved for herms and often represented in cult images on vases.[17] In other words, classical and Roman conceptions of the works of Daidalos correspond to those that Hellenistic writers attributed to his *predecessors*, as in the words of Themistios (*Orationes* 15.316a): Πρὸ μὲν Δαιδάλου τετράγωνος ἦν οὐ μόνον ἡ τῶν Ἑρμῶν ἐργασία, ἀλλὰ καὶ τῶν λοιπῶν ἀνδριάντων ("Before the time of Daidalos not only the statuary of herms was square, but also the [shape of] other statues").

While this contradiction is revealing of Hellenistic taste for ἀρχαϊκός, a word first used in this period to describe earlier sculptural styles, it undermines the historical veracity of a Daidalos tradition.[18] No author who comments on the technical innovations by Daidalos also names actual statues attributed to him, except Diodorus. And the latter's comparison to older Egyptian statues, which provides a rare description of statues by Daidalos, is nowhere reinforced by an attributed work. Instead, the Sicilian historian only documents the miraculous designs in engineering and architecture with local associations (Chapter 7).

Thus the learned Hellenistic comments that aimed to link literary compliments or jokes with phases of Greek sculpture focused on a stage of early Greek art that enjoyed contemporary appeal. In other fields of Greek art—not only sculpture but in architecture and painting—the classical period seems to have sponsored a taste for archaizing forms contemporary with more progressive and self-conscious developments. These

[16] H. V. Herrmann, "Zum Problem der Entstehung der griechischen Grossplastik," *AA* (1974) 636–38 [cf. in *Wandlungen* 35–40]; Donohue, *Xoana*, 60–68, 365–405, nos. 187–282, for nearly one hundred references to ξόανα in the itinerary of Pausanias.

[17] K. Schefold, "Statuen auf Vasenbilder," *JdI* 52 (1937) 30–75; Romano, "Early Greek Cult Images,"

455–64.

[18] Pollitt, *Ancient View of Greek Art*, 154–58, on the technical and stylistic dimensions of ἀρχαϊκός, to which add one of its earliest attestations in a Hellenistic inventory from Delos: *IDélos* 1426 B:I, [ἀπολλωνίσκον] ἀρχαϊκόν. Hurwit, *Art and Culture of Early Greece*, 15–32, "Archaios."

theories resemble many classical sources in deriving primarily from literature, fed by philosophical concepts of the animation of objects. Moreover, they were independent of the popular superstitions that associated the name of Daidalos with ancient images—a process that produced the attributions reported to Pausanias—and the local historical promotion of his biographical and professional data. The only such reference with a promising technical ring, Diodorus's comparison of the ῥυθμός of Egyptian and Daidalic statues, does not agree with the artist's works or style as documented by the same author.

A chronological review of attributions to Daidalos since the *Iliad* produces scattered and inconsistent references more relevant to their context than to a single artist. One of the earliest attested appears in the lost works of the archaic geographer Skylax (mentioned in Chapter 4). In his *Periplous* (*Geographici graeci minores* 321), he describes an altar of Poseidon on a Libyan headland, decorated with "painted figures, lions and dolphins: they say that Daidalos made it" (γεγραμμένοι ἀνδριάντες, λέοντες, δελφῖνες· Δαίδαλον δέ φασι ποιῆσαι). The participle γραμμένοι (from γράφω, to paint or write) has been all too readily emended to γεγλυμμένοι ("carved") to reconcile the description with sculpture, satisfying the tradition of monumental altars with relief sculpture as well as modern expectations of Daidalos as sculptor. But the verb agrees with allusions to painting in connection with Daidalos in the fifth century (e.g., Plato, *Republic* 529d; see Chapter 8). Moreover, the type of figural decoration implied is matched in descriptions of archaic works like the "throne of Apollo" at Amyklae, or could represent the inlay of precious materials, as old as Mycenaean furniture.[19] Neither bears a close relation to the free-standing statues that dominate classical and later traditions on Daidalos, but this archaic work, perhaps the earliest attested since the χορός of Ariadne, agrees with the range of anonymous δαίδαλα in poetry and of Daidalos's ἔργα in literature as late as Cicero.

The next source on the works of Daidalos belongs to the Hellenistic mythographical tradition: the colorful *Bibliotheca* attributed to Apollodoros.[20] His account dwells on the adventures of the artist in Athens, Crete, and Sicily and is presumably based on sources common to lost tragedies on this theme (Chapter 8). When he does discuss the art of

---

[19] The "throne" at Amyklai (Pausanias, 3.18.9–19.6) includes myriad mythological figures, none preserved: R. Martin, "Bathyclès de Magnésie et le 'trône' d'Apollon à Amyclae," *RA* (1976) 205–18. See Pylos Ta 708.3 and Ta 722.2 for Mycenaean furniture inlaid with ivory figures and lions; also Chapter 4. Donohue, *Xoana*, 21 n. 48, and 433, no. 329, compares the altar in Euripides, *Ion* 1403 (βωμοῦ . . . ξόανα), with the one described by Scylax and suggests both altars were elaborately decorated with

"carved ornaments of some kind."

[20] Probably compiled in the first century A.D., despite its attribution to Apollodoros of Athens (second century B.C.); its earliest source cited is Pherekydes of Athens: *Gods and Heroes of the Greeks: The Library of Apollodorus*, trans. M. Simpson (Amherst, Mass., 1976/1986), 1–2; cf. A. Henrichs, "Three Approaches to Greek Mythography," in *Interpretations of Greek Mythology*, 242–77, esp. 243, 247.

Daidalos, he barely mentions sculpture. He introduces Daidalos as an ἀρχιτέκτων, first enlisted by Pasiphae for her unusual commission, and concentrates on three celebrated designs: the wooden cow, the Labyrinth, and the invention of wings. Only twice does sculpture intrude, and then in subordination to architecture, once when Daidalos is reintroduced in his Athenian guise (3.15.8–9):

κατασκευάζει αὐτὸν [τὸν λαβύρινθον] Δαίδαλος ὁ Εὐπαλάμου τοῦ Μητίονος καὶ Ἀλκίππης· οὗτος ἦν ἀρχιτέκτων ἄριστος καὶ πρῶτος ἀναλμάτων εὑρετής.

Daidalos the son of Eupalamos, son of Etion and Alkippe, made [this] labyrinth. He was the best builder and the first inventor of statues.

The last phrase has a formulaic ring to it, claiming primacy in terms of rank and age in both monumental traditions of Greek art. According to this source, Daidalos was primarily an architect, then invented the art of sculpture, a claim in the πρῶτος εὑρετής tradition but simply another mode of formulaic praise without historical foundation.[21] Needless to say, such a claim contradicts the tradition that Daidalos first made statues move, which associates him with the archaic kouros pose rather than the earliest statues. The claim was, however, a popular one, especially in the mythographic tradition. As with other legends, Hyginus echoes Apollodoros in his statement (*Fabellae* 274) that "Daedalus Eupalami filius deorum simulacra primus fecit." The veneration of the primitive implied in popular attributions to Daidalos in the Roman period (see subsequent comments on Pausanias) belongs to the same tendency to explain what is "best" as "oldest." Other sources only praise Daidalos as ἀγαλματοποιὸς ἄριστος or περιφανέστατος (e.g., in scholia to Plato, *Republic* 7.529e, and *Meno* 367) possibly because these commentators are acquainted with his improvements on sculpture, not its invention. Once the brief Hellenistic flirtation with an archaic correspondence for the works of Daidalos disappears, the same compliments reappear in ample but poetic rather than specific terms. Thus Solinus praises him as "fabricae artis magister" (5.8) and Ovid calls him "ingenio fabrae celeberrimus artis" (*Metamorphoses* 8. 159) in a tradition that displaces his limited assocation with sculpture in favor of architecture and adventure.

If the first reference to Daidalos-as-sculptor in Apollodoros belongs to the miraculous, the second revives his classical powers to animate statues. After Herakles buries the corpse of Ikaros on the island that then acquires his name, the artist-father rewards the hero with a portrait (2.6.3):

ἀντὶ τούτου Δαίδαλος ἐν Πίσῃ εἰκόνα παραπλησίαν κατεσκεύασεν Ἡρακλεῖ ἣν νυκτὸς ἀγνοήσας Ἡρακλῆς λίθῳ βαλὼν ὡς ἔμπνουν ἔπληξε.

---

[21] A. Kleingünther, Πρῶτος Εὑρετής. *Untersuch-* (Leipzig, 1933). *ungen zur Geschichte einer Vorstellung, Philologus* suppl.

In exchange for this act, Daidalos made a statue in Pisa, closely resembling Herakles; not recognizing it one night, Herakles threw a stone at it, as if it were alive, and struck it.

This anecdote, presumably local to Pisa, plays on the comic side of Herakles the buffoon as well as on the "lifelike" reputation of the works of Daidalos. Hesychius knew this joke, probably directly from Apollodoros, and further describes the Herakles statue as wooden (s.v. πλήξαντα καὶ πληγέντα· εἰκόνα ξυλίνην ὁ Δαίδαλος χαριστήριον τῆς Ἰκάρον ταφῆς). So convincing is the portrait that its own subject, Herakles, mistakes it for an aggressor at night and attacks it. Thus the tale joins the classical anecdotes on comic, violent, or erotic interaction with statues in mistaken response to their "realistic" properties (Chapter 8), a reputation shared by paintings whose fruit attracts birds and human error (Pliny, *Naturalis Historia* 35.64). It produces a conflicting account of the artist in Apollodoros, in that the inventor of the first statues cannot also represent the innovator who improved on primitive ones at a later stage of Greek sculpture. In this overlap, the "first inventor" tradition encounters the classical "refiner," and the Cretan architect must also be a sculptor in Sicily; such contradictions are excused in a mythographic assembly.

Actual works of sculpture attributed to Daidalos appear as local claims, inspired by regional imagination without ties to a sustained oeuvre. Such works are occasionally cited in geographical and lexigraphical compilations; for example, Stephanus names an Ἄρτεμις Μονογισσηνή as a "foundation of Daidalos" (ἵδρυμα Δαιδάλου), explaining her epithet in terms of her Carian home (μεγίσσα γὰρ τῇ Καρῶν φωνῇ λίθος). After the Sicilian works attributed to Daidalos by Diodorus (see Chapter 7), the largest collection of works is also one of the latest to be assembled by a witness to the Greek world: Pausanias. His descriptions of specific statues by Daidalos agree with the contemporary report by Nicanor (on *Iliad* 18.598): Δαίδαλος δὲ πολλοὺς εἰκὸς ἑωρακέναι, or more people are likely to know works by Daidalos than by Hephaistos. In Pausanias's account of cities and sanctuaries visited in the second century of the Roman era, a total of nine works by Daidalos are cited; disparate purposes of cult and history associate them with the legendary artist. As with Pausanias's references to ξόανα, these descriptions have encouraged generally accepted theories of the history of Greek sculpture, which now deserve similar revision and rejection.

Three are associated with Crete, whose epic home for the artist (*Iliad* 18.592) no doubt encouraged the attribution of venerable cult statues to his hand. A statue of Britomartis at Olous (9.40.3) represents a specifically Cretan goddess and one whose *aedes* is venerated as a work of Daidalos by Solinus (*Collectanea rerum memorabiliarum* 2.8).[22] An

---

[22] The site has produced a double temple of Ares and "Kyprogeneia (Aphrodite)," probably of Hellenistic date with an archaic predecessor: J. Bousquet, "Le Temple d'Aphrodite et d'Arès à Sta Lenika," *BCH* 62 (1938) 386–408.

'Aθήνα παρὰ Κνωσίοις is listed as a second example of his ξόανα ἐν Κρήτῃ (Pausanias, 9.40.3–4), this time in a locale specific to his earliest manifestation (*Iliad* 18.591). The goddess's name also has possible forerunners at Bronze Age Knossos, if she corresponds to the *A-ta-na po-ti-ni-ja* (cf. Homeric Πότνι' 'Aθηναίη) in the Linear B tablets from Knossos.[23] If there is a connection, the statue known by Pausanias would be a rare Greek memory of Mycenaean religion; for the story of Daidalos, the statue's locale remains its most significant contribution.

A third work of Daidalos is attributed by Cretan colonists in Sicily, who claim that the founder of Gela, Antiphemos, captured a statue by the Cretan sculptor from Omphake, a Sicanian town and rival of Gela (Pausanias, 8.47.2). The statue did not survive the passage of time and its existence was only reported to Pausanias (9.40.4). This last work belongs to the Creto-Sicilian tradition that claimed statues by Daidalos as testimonia to territorial rights, much as the bones of heroes functioned in archaic territorial disputes. In Sicily, in particular, the reputation of Daidalos served Greek colonists in their conflict with native Sicilians and Phoenicians (Chapter 7).

Other works of Daidalos reported by Pausanias reflect his fascination with early cult images, expressed in the concept of ξόανα and a popular preoccupation contemporary with his travels. The wooden Aphrodite on Delos was cited already for its inconsistency with Daidalos's "moving statues." Described as an under life-sized ξόανον with a rectangular lower body (9.40.4), its right hand had worn away with time, a sign of age matched by its legendary link to Ariadne and Theseus in local traditions. From the Delians, Pausanias learned that Theseus dedicated it to Apollo on Delos, and Pausanias concludes that Ariadne took it from Crete, adding the Cretan element to local claims for the statue's heroic history.

Two works of Daidalos in Boiotia represent heroes of local fame. One is a statue of Trophonios, revealed only to those who consult his oracle at Lebadeia as Pausanias did (9.39.2). The other Boiotian statue is an ancient (ἀρχαῖον) ξόανον at Thebes representing Herakles (9.11.2, 9.40.3), a hero represented in two other statues by Daidalos. Corinth also claims a ξόανον γυμνόν of Herakles near the Athena Chalkinitis sanctuary by the theater (2.4.5), and one stands on the border of Messenia and Arkadia (8.35.2).

Pausanias knows of no other surviving (ὑπόλοιπα) statues of Daidalos, an apology that suggests he expected more or had heard of others no longer extant, like Omphake from Gela (8.47.2). Those he reports reflect several antiquarian traditions current at the time. One invoked legendary names to increase the reputed age and prestige of wooden images. This enthusiasm for the past colors his corpus of ξόανα, of which he lists over one hundred but attributes many to named sculptors, including classical and Hellenistic

---

[23] Kn 208 = V52; Palmer, *Mycenaeans*, 120, 131, and Gérard-Rousseau, *Mentions religieuses*, 44–45, prefer *A-ta-na* as a place-name, as it was for Athens, before it identified a goddess. N. Papahatzis, "L'origine de la déesse Athéna: Un ré-examen de l'évidence," *Kernos* 21 (1988) 79–92.

figures (Myron, Kalamis, Pheidias, and Damophon).[24] Local cult propaganda may have encouraged statues like the one of Trophonios at Lebadeia or Aphrodite at Delos to be attached to famous sculptors. No doubt the epic associations with the artist encouraged the attribution of venerated cult statues in Crete to his hand. Finally, historical purposes dating from the age of colonization helped sponsor the link between Daidalos and a statue instrumental in a territorial dispute in Sicily.

Before considering two works of Daidalos reported by Pausanias but strictly outside the repertoire of sculpture, his comments on the style of those statues are worth consideration. For they made the following impression on him (2.4.5):

Δαίδαλος δὲ ὁπόσα εἰργάσατο, ἀτοπώτερα μέν ἐστιν ἔτι τὴν ὄψιν, ἐπιπρέπει δὲ ὅμως τι καὶ ἔνθεον τούτοις.

As many statues as Daidalos made, they are somewhat odd in appearance, but something divine stands out in them.

The judgment is a classicizing one, in that it sustains the view of Daidalos's statues as outdated enough for ridicule, an opinion expressed by sculptors and philosophers in classical Athens (e.g., Plato, *Hippias Major* 282a.1; Aristotle, at Porphyry, *De Abstinentia* 2.18e; see Chapter 8). It also reveals the postclassical antiquarian in the traveler, who admires the same statues for their infusion of the divine. This pronouncement tells us almost nothing about the appearance of the statues, except that they looked unusual by Roman standards and that Pausanias sprang to their defense. The same reaction is recorded in Nikanor's comments on *Iliad* 18.591–92: he defends older works (τὰ ἔργα ἀπὸ τῶν ἀρχαιοτέρων) as "somewhat more suitable" (μᾶλλον . . . πρεπωδέστερα), especially when "commissioned (?)": ἐπιτετευγμένα. Pausanias's statement also suggests he had heard or read enough about Daidalos to develop some expectations about his art, as he had hopes of finding more surviving examples (9.40.2)—hence his disappointment upon first seeing the artist's work. His entertainment of the notion that the more "primitive" the image, the more divine, remained a popular one in the Western history of the worship of idols and theories of idolatry.[25]

Two such survivals would be hard to imagine as ἔνθεος to any eyes, for one is a piece of furniture, the other a marble relief, neither a cult image, but both faithful to the earliest testimonia on Daidalos. In his "corpus" of Daidalid works appended to the description of two statues in Boiotia (9.40.2), Pausanias compares the Homeric χορός to an actual work of art at Knossos:

καὶ ὁ τῆς Ἀριάδνης χορός, οὗ καὶ Ὅμηρος ἐν Ἰλιάδι μνήμην ἐποιήσατο, ἐπειργασμένος ἐστὶν ἐπὶ λευκοῦ λίθου.

---

[24] Pausanias on ξόανα: F. M. Bennett, "Primitive Wooden Statues which Pausanias saw in Greece," CW 10 (1917) 118–35; Donohue, *Xoana*, 140–47; Freedberg, *Power of Images*, 34–37.

[25] Freedberg, *Power of Images*, esp. chap. 2, "The God in the Image."

And the dancing place of Ariadne, the one that Homer also mentions in the *Iliad*, is made of white marble.

A second passage on another Homeric monument inspected by Pausanias, the grave of Aipytos in Arkadia, recalls the impression made by Daidalos's χορός on the poet (8.16.3):

ἐπεὶ καὶ Ἥφαιστος τὸν χορὸν ἐπὶ τῇ ᾽Αχιλλέως ἀσπίδι εἰργασμένον εἰκάζει χορῷ Δαιδάλου ποιηθέντι, σοφώτερα οὐ θεασάμενος.

Since even Hephaistos made the dancing place on the shield for Achilles resemble the dancing place made by Daidalos, having never seen a more skillful one.

The two passages are curiously exclusive of each other, separated by more than distance in place and narrative. For when citing Daidalos's effect on Hephaistos during an account of Arkadia, Pausanias does not indicate the monument he saw at Knossos, but delivers a literary comment where σοφώτερα οὐ θεασάμενος could be derived from *Iliad* 18, without autopsy of an actual work. He delivers no such direct praise to the monument itself at Knossos, Homer's praise presumably sufficing, reinforced by the periegete's own compliment, σοφός. But even without explicit description, Pausanias's report of an actual χορός in Crete, "worked in/on white marble," is significant. An epic phenomenon was identified in the second century A.D., presumably in a sculpted relief of dancers, or perhaps a painting on marble, to correspond to contemporary visualizations of Homer's χορός. Pausanias himself expresses no particular sense of contradiction between this marble χορός and the wooden ξόανα he sees elsewhere as works of Daidalos. Unless the marble scene was old-fashioned enough to agree with other ἀτοπώτερα works of Daidalos (and one thinks first of a Neo-Attic relief of dancers), the χορός he saw must have agreed with his vision of the shield of Achilles. No other authority describes such a translation of the famous χορός into material terms. The reference to white marble virtually excludes any plausible connections to prehistoric art or to any period earlier than classical times, and indeed could be accepted as accurate, before the discovery of Greece's prehistoric past.[26]

A single work of Daidalos known to Pausanias breaks with the tradition of sculpture but revives the artist's prehistoric dimensions with rare (and probably unintentional) fidelity. The fact that it comes from Athens thickens the plot with history. In the temple of Athena Polias on the Akropolis, Pausanias lists "noteworthy dedications" (ἀναθήματα ἄξια λόγου), in particular a folding stool, "a work of Daidalos": δίφρος ὀκλαδίας ἐστὶ Δαιδάλου ποίημα, followed by several items from the Persian spoils. Given

---

[26] Thus Robert, *Archäologische Märchen*, 11–12, assumes χορός was "die plastische Darstellung eines Reigens als Weihgeschenk an Ariadne," before the excavation of Knossos (Evans, *BSA* 9 [1903] 111, identified it with the west "theatral area" of the palace). Most recently, S. Lonsdale, "A Dancing Floor for Ariadne (*Il.* 18.590–92): Aspects of Ritual Movement in Homer and Minoan Religion," forthcoming.

the technical properties of Homeric δαίδαλα—which included furniture like the chest and couch of Achilles, the bed in Ithaka—a folding chair, especially if one imagines it inlaid with precious materials, comes closest of all works attested in post-Homeric sources to the style of the "original" (epic) *daidala*. Moreover, such a stool not only resembles descriptions of furniture in the Parthenon inventories but spoils from the Persian wars; in fact, as will be argued, the stool noted by Pausanias may have been an Oriental "throne" captured from the Persians but eventually attributed to Daidalos (Chapter 10). Pausanias himself expresses no sense of contradiction at the attribution of furniture and statues to the same artist, perhaps no surprise in a world where the skills of architect, sculptor, and technician often overlapped. To modern eyes, the stool by Daidalos presents a fascinating link between the two crucial sources of his legend: his epic repertoire and his Athenian reincarnation. The most "old-fashioned" artifact attributed to him, and the most Homeric, belonged to the very city that embroidered its own supplementary history and legends.

With the exception of the χορός and the δίφρος, Daidalos was admired chiefly as a sculptor in the lifetime of Pausanias, but without a trace of his classical reputation for animating statues. New historical interests and new priorities, more religious than aesthetic, shifted the focus of learning and lore to a more primitive, if partly imaginary, stage of Greek sculpture. The careful commentary of Hellenistic writers on epic and classical passages, and the specter of the kouros implied and encouraged behind those references, disappear in these later antiquarian reflections.

The ancient oeuvre of Daidalos the sculptor, however artificial, was underpinned by a network of offspring and pupils. Just as ancestors were invented for him in classical Athens, progeny multiplied in later sources. Some of these claims may have developed in Crete and derived from the impulse to link historical sculptors to legendary artists. For example, the Cretan team of Dipoinos and Skyllis is remembered by Pausanias not only as pupils of Daidalos but as his sons by a Cretan woman of Gortyn (2.15.1). As in all sources on these two artists, Pausanias only knows of works found outside of Crete, for example at Kleonai and Argos, the later home to their statues of the Dioskouroi in ebony and ivory (2.22.6). The location of their oeuvre agrees with Pliny's report (*Naturalis Historia* 36.9) that the two emigrated to nearby Sikyon, a report probably derived from Pliny's Xenokratic, pro-Sikyonian source. Pausanias further attests to the next generation of pupils, represented by Klearchos of Rhegion (3.17.6) and three Lakonian artists, Dorykleides, his brother Medon, and Theokles.[27] In turn, their pupils Angelion and

---

[27] Carter, *Greek Ivory-Carving*, 248–62, and *AJA* 93 (1989) 374–76, makes them chryselephantine sculptors, the next generation of Lakonian artists in ivory. Note that their masters, Dipoinos and Skyllis, specialized in Lakonian subjects like the Dioskouroi (Pausanias, 2.22.6). Philipp, in *Dädalische Kunst auf Kreta*, 7–8; S. Morris, "Dipoinos and Skyllis," in *Dictionary of Art* (London, forthcoming), on the pupils of Daidalos.

Tektaios taught Kallon of Aigina (2.32.5). Others claimed as pupils of Daidalos by Pausanias include Endoios of Athens, who followed his master to Crete (1.26.4), similar to legends of lawgivers (Chapter 6) in which Athens deferred to Crete for expertise in art. Smilis of Aigina, on the other hand, is a contemporary of Daidalos, according to Pausanias (7.4.4), but one who never achieved his fame in the eyes of Roman critics of the time. Passages like these seem to reflect an effort to reconcile the Athenian and Cretan traditions for Daidalos, an aspect of the wider tendency to link famous historical sculptors throughout Greece with the legend of Daidalos.

The literary tradition of "schools" of sculpture may derive from ancient workshop situations where skilled crafts were shared and transmitted to sons and apprentices, fortified by the tendency in Greek historiography to calibrate the past in generations. In the case of Daidalos, however, his lack of a stable historical context makes his position in artist genealogies dubious. Although historical sculptors took his name in the fourth century (e.g., Daidalos of Sikyon or of Bithynia), such eponymous choices presume a legendary reputation but hardly a historical one. Despite ancient and modern efforts to locate such a personality in the archaic period and link him to verifiable artists or works of art, no consistent style or setting emerges from the testimonia. The Cretan phantom of the archaic period is but a literary amalgam of prehistoric memories and early Iron Age art, yet he has given his name to a modern concept of early Greek style.

The emergence of this concept in modern times began as a literary phenomenon, then gained false credentials through archaeology. By the seventeenth century, Daidalos represented in European sculpture what a figure like Apelles meant to painting. But his figure remained a literary legend well into the nineteenth century, when scholars like Winckelmann and Brunn could only cite his reputation but concentrated on classical and Hellenistic art, the main phases preserved for Europe to appreciate.[28] When Overbeck assembled his sources on Greek artists in 1868, he included the figure of Daidalos under *Kunstheroen* (pp. 11–17) in the company of Trophonios and Agamedes, the Heliads, and others.[29] The nineteenth century, however, inaugurated new trends in archaeology and scholarship, which still maintain a dialogue on the subject of Daidalos. Especially since the liberation of Greece, the discovery of preclassical statues introduced anatomy resembling statues ascribed to Daidalos in classical and Hellenistic sources. With them, his personality and his place in the history of Greek sculpture were cre-

---

[28] Donohue, *Xoana*, 179–89, on *Kunstgeschichte* as *Künstlergeschichte*; Brunn, *Geschichte der griechischen Künstler*, 1:14–16, 25, begins with Daidalos; cf. Rumpf, *BonnJbb* 135 (1930) 75.

[29] A. Brookes's claim that Overbeck (*Schriftquellen*, 11–17), was the first to use the adjective "Daedalic" ("The Chronology of Daedalic Sculpture" [Ph.D.

diss., University of Pennsylvania, 1978], xxxv) misunderstands the German denominative for "works by Daidalos." Overbeck's heading *vordaidalische Künstler* introduces οἱ γὰρ πρὸ Δαιδάλου, not artists working in a style defined in the twentieth century as "pre-Daidalic." Likewise, *Daidaliden* refers to the sons/pupils of Daidalos, not "Daedalic" artists.

ated.[30] At the same time, refinements in sophisticated *Quellenkritik* dissolved the sources on Daidalos into discrete elements of legend, reducing his credibility as a historical personality.[31] This dialectic between discovery and theory continued into recent times. Nikandre's Artemis on Delos, for example, inspired Waldstein to defend a historical artist, in reaction to efforts like those by Robert and Petersen.[32] Compromise became a common solution to synthesize sources and statues: a "mythical" Daidalos was maintained to satisfy the epic evidence, but contrasted with a "historical" sculptor active in Crete, survived by his pupils. Meanwhile, modern historical events stimulated the second wave of scholarship on Daidalos: just as the independence of Greece opened excavations and produced archaic statues, the liberation of Crete from the Turks in 1899 led to new Iron Age discoveries and interpretations.[33] Löwy launched this movement with several pioneering articles assembling Cretan and related artifacts in a stylistic group, establishing Crete as a major *Kunstzentrum* of the seventh century and the home of Greek sculpture.[34] As Rumpf recalled in 1930: "Wie selbstverständlich hat sich die Beziehung 'daidalisch' für diese Kunst eingestellt," although he complains that such an epithet, strictly speaking, only suits works of art attributable to Daidalos, as in nineteenth-century usage.[35]

Thus the term "Daedalic" was already an informal convention by the time Jenkins institutionalized it.[36] He defends it as a "convenient and picturesque" distinction for seventh-century sculpture (p. xi), then proceeds to examine "the Dedalic style—as we shall now call it" (p. xii). His approach refined the chronological series of three groups and linked it to Protocorinthian pottery, whose figured-head aryballoi provide a neat link between sculpted heads and dated ceramic styles, although they require a leap from minor arts to monumental sculpture, no longer made easily in scholarship. Beyond such typological advancements, Jenkins concentrated on the fundamental differ-

[30] Déonna, *Dédale*, 26–28, synchronizes discoveries and scholarship (still associates Daidalos with ξόανα).

[31] Chief among these *Quellenforschungen* are Robert's *Archäologische Märchen* and Eugen Petersen's *Kritische Bemerkungen zur ältesten Geschichte der griechischen Kunst* (Ploen, 1871). Cf. Philipp, *Tektonon Daidala*, and "Daidalos: Zur schriftlichen Überlieferung," in *Dädalische Kunst*, 5–13.

[32] C. Waldstein, "Dédale et l'Artemis de Délos," *RA* (1881) 321–30. See n. 31 for Petersen; n. 28 for Brunn.

[33] Démarge, *La Crète dédalique*, 10–11, and Rizzo, in *Creta Antica*, 43–45, for bibliography and modern discoveries; cf. the modern fate of Daidalos in Sicily, Chapter 7.

[34] E. Löwy, "Spora una antichissima opera di scultura cretese," *AccLinc* 7 (1891) 601ff.; "Typenwanderung," *ÖJh* 12 (1909) 243–304; "Typenwanderung, II," *ÖJh* 14 (1911) 134. Cf. L. Pernier, "Tempi arcaici sulla Patela di Prinias. Contributo allo studio dell' arte dedalica," *ASAA* 1 (1914) 19–111, perhaps one of the earliest published uses of the term (see Chapter 7, nn. 18–20, on similar early uses by Orsi and others for Sicilian antiquities).

[35] Rumpf, *BonnJbb* 135 (1930) 76. He established three periods in Cretan-Dorian art and was followed by E. Kunze ("Zu den Anfängen der griechischen Plastik," *AthMitt* 55 [1930] 141–62, and others.

[36] Inaugurated in his "Lakonian Terracottas of the Dedalic Style," *BSA* 33 (1932–1933) 66–79, before *Dedalica*, published in 1936.

ences between Geometric and Daedalic art. He claimed a major philosophical distance between Geometric plastic art and that of the seventh century, when a canon of formulas based on fundamental principles, in a word, a *style*, appeared for the first time. "The Daedalic head is an idea": an intellectual, even mathematical conception of the human face and figure enters Greek art, hailed by Jenkins as the debut of idealism in Greek art. Translating this intellectual concept into diagnostic features, Jenkins lists "what is predictable of all Daedalic heads" (p. 16): their shallow depth with its pictorial, emphatically frontal face; a triangular outline with low, flat forehead and broad, flat-topped head; and a wiglike hairstyle. Variations occur within the latter, the decorative *Etagenperücke* (a term first coined by Poulsen), and its distribution.

On Daidalos himself, Jenkins approves Robert's judgment on the myth as an incoherent tradition but follows Kunze's defense of the term Daedalic (n. 35) as more than convenient. Daidalos's reputed activity in Crete and the Peloponnese justifies applying the epithet to seventh-century works from these areas, and Jenkins was not the first to do so (he cites Amelung, Rumpf, Buschor, and Kunze). Scholars have linked this style with confidence to Dorian regions (as in Jenkins's subtitle), encouraged by its proliferation on Crete, and even contrast the Daedalic head with Attic faces to supplement the stylistic distinction with an ethnic one.

The coherence of this style and its connection with Daidalos remain dubious. The dual allegiance of Daidalos to Athens and Crete in literary sources invalidates the "Dorian" element, which betrays more prejudice than justice, both ancient and modern. The style is defined in terms of heads and faces, and its swift and broad proliferation is even attributed to the use of molds.[37] This modern obsession with physiognomy ignores other ancient claims for "life" in the limbs of Daidalos's statues. Moreover, it privileges the specter of the *xoanon* at the expense of other phases of his alleged oeuvre.

Thus, in a series of modern appraisals stimulated by discoveries in Crete, the eponymous craftsman, his name already a personification of poetic adjectives for art, inspired a denominative epithet for art forms remote from epic δαίδαλα. Once defined, soon refined: Jenkins's chronological scheme linking miniature sculpture to monumental statues was succeeded by Kaulen's *Daidalika*.[38] Kaulen follows his chapters on style and chronology with one on history, including *Künstlergeschichte* (pp. 159–69), where "Daidaliden" precede the discussion of their master. Daidalos is now divided, with confidence, into a Minoan master-builder and an archaic sculptor, according to Rumpf's ar-

---

[37] Ridgway, *Archaic Style*, 21; the idea of a "Dorian" character is at least as old as K. O. Müller's *Die Dorier. Geschichte hellenischer Stämme und Städte*, vols. 2–3 (Breslau, 1824).

[38] Kaulen's subtitle, "Werkstätte griechischer Kleinplastik des 7. Jahrhunderts vor Chr.," expanded Jenkins's corpus to include new regions, new finds, and new media. Jenkins's four phases (Proto-, Early-, Mature-, and Late-Daedalic) were further subdivided into six, all squeezed in between 690 and 615 B.C. For recent refinements, see Brookes's dissertation ("Chronology").

guments, with some reservations expressed by Kaulen on Schweitzer's version.

Kaulen's chapter on Daidalos ends in a classic example of the modern tradition justifying a "historical" Daidalos through stylistic arguments. According to his arguments, a bronze statuette from the Athenian Akropolis (National Museum 6619) demonstrates the validity of the testimonia on Daidalos. Its provenance proves Daidalos's Attic connections, its Cretan style his link to that island, and the Egyptian "wig" confirms Diodorus's comparison to Egyptian works. The articulation of arms and legs recall literary acclaim of his powers of mobilization. Even the missing face suggests inlay technique, hence a remote connection to the epic craftsman. Finally, the statuette's style is said to represent the phase earlier than that identified by Kaulen with the master's pupils, Dipoinos and Skyllis.

While this example from Kaulen's scholarship may seem extreme, it is only an exaggeration of other technical and stylistic arguments linking the legend with discoveries. For example, admitting that the term "Daedalic" is a "convention," albeit a "misleading" one, Boardman attempts to account for the development of monumental Greek sculpture in the Cyclades rather than Crete, where literary tradition locates it.[39] As did Kaulen, he appeals to a small bronze statuette, in this instance the celebrated kouros from Delphi attributed to Crete on the analogy of sculpture from that island (Figure 35).[40] According to Boardman, this bronze expresses all the characteristics of monumental sculpture on a miniature scale, elements transferred to the home of better materials (the Cyclades with its marbles) by migrant artists like Dipoinos and Skyllis. Their memories kept alive the original Cretan role by celebrating figures like Daidalos.

Some seize on Pausanias's equation of ξόανα and δαίδαλα and see a reflection of Daidalos's style in early limestone sculptures based on wooden prototypes. For example, Ridgway accepts both the Daedalic style as defined by Jenkins *and* the artist's alleged role in conveying movement to statues, a development clearly attested exclusively outside Crete and later than the seventh century. "Ironically, this Greek innovation was attributed to Daidalos, yet it marked the rejection of the static Daedalic style."[41] The "irony" is artificial, a consequence of a "style" conceived in modern times and never reconciled with the full corpus of ancient testimonia.

---

[39] J. Boardman, "Daedalus and Monumental Sculpture," in *Fourth Cretological Congress*, 43–47. Cf. his discussion of Daidalos in *Cretan Collection in Oxford*, 158–59: "He seems a figure of little substance; a personification of the qualities implicit in his name. . . . It seems likely that the suggestive name, with its heroic overtones, was readily applied to any venerable or primitive work."

[40] Richter, *Kouroi*, figs. 14–16. For a close parallel from Crete, see the bronze kouros found in the Idaian Cave: F. Halbherr, *Museo Italiano di antichità classica* 2 (1888) 689–766, pl. 12, 1.

[41] Ridgway, *Archaic Style*, 27; G. Rizza, "Dedalo e le origini della scultura greca," *CronArch* 2 (1962) 5–49; cf. Delcourt's defense of Crete (vs. Athens) as the proper home of Daidalos, because it is the home of "arts dédaliques" (*Héphaistos*, 158); Hurwit, *Art and Culture of Early Greece*, 191–97; Lembesi, Οἱ Στῆλες τοῦ Πρινιᾶ, 112–15.

No less ingenious than the stylistic arguments are the technical solutions reconciling the literary Daidalos with early Greek art. Lacroix's solution isolates the chryselephantine technique, newly revealed in the Delphi discoveries, as the closest to prehistoric inlay works celebrated as δαίδαλα in epic and associated with Daidalos.[42] According to Lacroix, this technique transmits Minoan and Mycenaean art into the archaic period, and with it transforms Daidalos from prehistoric craftsman into archaic sculptor. The structuralist approach, which synthesizes epic vocabulary and metallurgy into a composite portrait of Daidalos, links him with the early metalworking of Crete, represented in archaeology by the Dreros statues and in legend by other craftsmen like Talos and the Telchines.[43] Finally, regional affiliations play as persuasive a role as style and technique. Independent of the persona of Daidalos, the art of early Iron Age Crete continues to attract excavation and scholarship.[44]

Scholars will (and should) continue to deplore the term "Daedalic" as inaccurate if convenient: "appellation floue, controversé et abusive."[45] Yet to campaign for its abandonment, at this point, would be pedantic and unsuccessful.[46] The ancient testimonia alone demonstrate an evolving attitude toward early Greek art, and never yield a consistent tradition of a verifiable historical artist. Once this fact is recognized, an attempt to restrict the name of Daidalos to *any* phase of Greek sculpture appears misguided. Although "Daedalic" will survive as a reference to art of the seventh century, between the Geometric and archaic styles, such Panhellenic terminology violates regional boundaries critical to this period in Greek art. Regardless of the stylistic and regional accuracy of its name, the "Daedalic" style is but the sculptural equivalent of the Orientalizing style in vase painting; it derives its forms, expressions, and even purposes from the Near East. As suggested by several scholars, a far more accurate term for early archaic sculpture would be "Orientalizing."[47] The modern convention recapitulates the ancient

[42] L. Lacroix, "À propos de découvertes récentes: La technique de l'incrustation dans l'art Créto-Mycènien," *ArchClass* 1 (1961) 251–57. Cf. Kaulen, *Daidalika*, 163–69, on "daedalic" adjectives as exclusive to inlay: Philipp, in *Dädalische Kunst auf Kreta*, 13 n. 29. Carter, *AJA* 93 (1989) 374–76, on chryselephantine sculpture.

[43] Frontisi-Ducroux, *Dédale*, 113–15, has Daidalos evolve from "ciseleur" to "artiste par excellence" and "sculpteur," a synthesis of "metallic" qualities in epic δαίδαλα and of the *sphyrelaton* technique in early Crete. Cf. her "Dédale et Talos. Mythologie et histoire des techniques," *RHR* 243 (1970) 281–96; Lembesi, Οἱ Στῆλες τοῦ Πρινιᾶ, 115.

[44] E.g., Démargne, *La Crète dédalique*; Boardman, *Cretan Collection in Oxford* (1961); the exhibit and catalogue *Dädalische Kunst auf Kreta* (1970); Adams, *Ori-*

entalizing Sculpture (1978); and Blome, *Bildwelt Kretas* (1982). Iron Age art in Crete is still emerging from active excavations: Sakellarakis, *L'Antro Ideo*; Lembesi, Σύμη Βιάννου 1.

[45] Frontisi Ducroux, *Dédale*, 19; cf. Demargne, *La Crète dédalique*, 250; Boardman, in *Fourth Cretological Congress*, 45.

[46] Thus Cook, *JHS* 87 (1967) 24 n. 1, admits its "fallacious connexion with the sculptor Daedalus," but accepts it as "convenient and clear"; Hurwit, *Art and Culture of Early Greece*, 188–90.

[47] By several students of George Hanfmann: D. Mitten in his review of Kaulen: *AJA* 74 (1970) 109; Lauren Adams in her book on Cretan sculpture, *Orientalizing Sculpture*; and Jane Carter in her forthcoming *Beginning of Greek Sculpture*.

rejection of an Oriental role by substituting the name of a Greek [*sic*] craftsmen to account for the most profoundly Oriental of Greek styles. More than an expression of stylistic traits, "Daedalic" perpetuates intellectual assumptions about the superiority of Greek art in comparison to its Eastern sources. How and why Athens launched this revision of cultural history will occupy the remainder of this book.

CHAPTER 10

Daidalos in Athens: From
the Throne of Xerxes to
the *Diphros* of Daidalos

I N PLATO'S *MENO*, Sokrates pardons a Thessalian for not heeding an allusion to the statues of Daidalos: "Perhaps you don't have any in your country" (ἴσως δὲ οὐδ᾽ ἔστι παρ᾽ ὑμῖν· 97 D). As observed earlier (Chapter 8), this represents a conscious acknowledgment among sophisticated Athenians that the legend or the joke was familiar but specific to Athens. Furthermore, it also suggests that statues attributed to Daidalos were extant in classical Athens. The same philosopher mentions Daidalos as an ancestor, twice: in the *Euthyphro* (11c–d) and in the pseudo-Platonic *Alkibiades* (1.121a), where Daidalos appears in the generations linking Sokrates with remote and famous ancestors, Hephaistos and Zeus. The fact that Plato elsewhere ranks Daidalos with epic figures like Palamedes (*Laws* 677d) and Epeios (*Ion* 533) agrees with the craftsman's legendary status in Platonic speeches by Sokrates.

Commentators on these and other classical references insert the names of Daidalos's nearer relatives into this remote genealogy, without much consistency or historical plausibility. Most commonly, Daidalos is called the son or grandson of Eupalamos and Metion, two names as obviously artificial (that is, invented for craftsmen) as his own.[1] Ultimately, Daidalos is incorporated into the line of Erechtheus through the latter's son, Metion, and it is no doubt this family that Sokrates claims to share with Daidalos, not a mythical ancestry derived from his father, the stoneworker.

Neither Metion, Eupalamos, nor their relationship to Erechtheus is attested independently of those sources on the Athenian lineage of Daidalos; therefore their existence is as dubious as their names. Moreover, while kinship with Erechtheus may appear to legitimize Daidalos by connecting him to an autochthonous and eponymous hero of Athens, modern scholarship has demonstrated how late, artificial, and politically moti-

---

[1] Overbeck, *Schriftquellen*, nos. 75–90; Frontisi-Ducroux, *Dédale*, 90–94. Eupalamos: Apollodoros, 3.15.9; schol. to Plato, *Alkibiades* 1.121, *Republic* 7.503; Tzetzes, *Chiliades*, 1.490ff., 2.884; Suda s.v. πέρδιξ· πέρδικος ἱερόν. Hyginus *Fabellae* 244, 274; Servius on *Aeneid* 6.14; Lactantius Placidus *Narrationes fabularum* *Ovidianarum* 8.3. Metion (grandfather): schol. Plato, *Alkibiades* 1.121; father: e.g., schol. to Plato, *Ion* 533; Diodorus Siculus, 4.76; Pherekydes (schol. Sophokles, *Oidipous at Kolonos* 472) and Pausanias, 2.6.5, 7.4.5. Cf. Daidalos as son of "Eucheir" the painter: Pliny, *Naturalis Historia* 7.205.

vated were the majority of Attic genealogies, including the list of kings and autochthonous heroes.[2] Thus the genealogy first attested in Plato may be no earlier than the fifth
century and Daidalos's place in the Athenian mythical past no more secure. An additional source of confusion is the profession of Sokrates' craftsman-father, Sophroniskos,
described as a "marble-worker," "marble-cutter," or "marble-carver": λιθουργός or
λιθοξόος (Diogenes Laertius, 2.18; Suda s.v. Sokrates; cf. λιθογλύφος: schol. Aristophanes, *Clouds* 773). Some have attributed the philosopher's interest in Daidalos as ancestor to this family business, confusing the tradition of "Daidalidai" or "sons of Daidalos" (a formulaic name for a guild of craftsmen) with linear descent from the
craftsman.[3] Sokrates's kinship with Daidalos derives from the same classical adoption
of the artist-hero as the Athenian versions of his adventures.

More substantial evidence for Daidalos's Athenian connections lies in the deme name
"Daidalidai," first attested in Pherekydes but which must have acquired its name by the
time of the Kleisthenic reforms. This name is not to be confused with the tradition of
"Daidalidai" or sculptors designated as honorary sons or pupils of the artist (cf. Ho-
meridae). Nor does the Attic place-name demonstrate an explicit connection with Homeric Daidalos, but probably derives from some local eponymous function. It could well
be a local version of the Knossian *da-da-re-jo*, just as Athena was worshiped at Knossos
but also in Athens. The deme, a member of the tribe of Kekrops, is one of about thirty
that bear patronymic names ending in -ιδαι. Most are relatively small (Daidalidai contributed only one bouleutic representative) and were organized by Kleisthenes around
local cult or *genos* associations. Modern opinions differ on the authenticity and authority
of such cults before the reforms, and after them.[4] This deme apparently lay north of
Alopeke, assuming it included the Δαιδαλεῖον attested epigraphically in that area.[5] In
a fourth-century πολεῖται decree, a confiscated house in Alopeke includes a house
whose boundaries are described in relation to ἡ ὁδός ἐς τὸ Δαιδαλεῖον φέρουσα καὶ
τὸ Δαιδαλεῖον, νοτόθεν: "the street leading to the Daidaleion, and the Daidaleion,
from the south." Τὸ Δαιδαλεῖον sounds like a sanctuary, presumably sacred to the

[2] Drews, *Basileus*, 86–94; Loraux, *Les enfants d'*
Athèna, chap. 1.1; M. J. Miller, "The Athenian Auto-
chthonous Heroes from the Classical to the Helle-
nistic Period" (Ph.D. diss., Harvard University,
1983), abstract in *HSCP* 88 (1984) 259–62; R. Parker,
"Myths of Early Athens," in *Interpretations of Greek*
Mythology, 187–214; Rosivach, *CQ* 27 (1987) 284–94.
Also see Chapter 13.

[3] Milchhöfer, *RE* s.v. "Sophroniskos"; cf. Robert,
Archäologische Märchen, 7.

[4] J. Traill, *The Political Organization of Attica*, *Hes-*
peria suppl. 14 (Princeton, 1975), 101 n. 100. G. Huxley, "Aristotle on the Origins of the Polis," in

ΣΤΗΛΗ, 258–64, claims many -ιδαι names were new
creations, not authentic kinship groups. G. Stanton,
"The Tribal Reforms of Kleisthenes the Alkmeonid,"
Chiron 14 (1984) 37 n. 125, argues for weaker cult en-
claves after the reforms; E. Kearns, "Change and
Continuity in Religious Structures after Cleisthenes,"
in *Crux. Essays in Greek History presented to G.E.M. de*
Ste. Croix on His 75th Birthday, ed. P. A. Cartledge
and F. D. Harvey (London, 1985), 189–207.

[5] *SEG* XII, 100, l. 11 = Athenian Agora, I 5509 (367/
6 B.C.); M. Crosby, "Greek Inscriptions: A Poletai
Record of the Year 367/6 B.C.," *Hesperia* 10 (1941) 14–
27.

eponymous hero of the deme "Daidalidai" and active in the fourth century. If Plato's Sokrates, a resident of the neighboring deme of Alopeke, has the same local *genos* or cult in mind when he describes Daidalos and Hephaistos as ancestors (*Alkibiades* 1.121), the reference in the inscription could refer to a craftsman cult.

It is important to evaluate these testimonia in isolation from each other and from their interpretations, which have combined Sokrates's "ancestry," his father's status as craftsman, and the possibility that the Δαιδαλεῖον in *SEG* XII, 100, is located somewhere relevant to a deme with a related name and that the place is a sanctuary specifically related to a cult of craftsmanship. The minimalist view allows for a local tradition healthy enough in the late sixth century to inspire a deme name. Quite possibly, this tradition was not enriched by genealogy and mythology until the classical period and may not have acquired a formal cult until the fourth century.[6] Cult and sanctuary have no Attic parallels or preclassical testimonia, and the name itself as an archaic phenomenon could share in that Panhellenic extension of poetic vocabulary to ritual names, places, and institutions, as observed in the Peloponnese and Boiotia (see Chapter 2). Even closer in morphology, although far less likely, would be a presumed prehistoric place in Attika with the same name as the Knossian *da-da-re-jo* (Chapter 4). If there was such an Attic equivalent to the phenomena considered in other archaic Greek provinces, there is no guarantee that it has anything to do with the epic Daidalos or his classical descendant, the sculptor. Three separate configurations could prevail: an archaic "Daidaleion" survived into the fourth century without connection to the personified Daidalos; a classical deme-name derived from it; a third tradition—Atthidographic (mythology/genealogy)—could have inspired the artificial ancestry of Sokrates. This third tradition appears most frequently and most colorfully in the ancient sources, providing Daidalos with a set of adventures in Athens independent of those set in Crete and Sicily.

To postclassical authors, Daidalos was indisputably Athenian by birth (γένος: Diodorus, 4.76, Pausanias, 7.4.7), presumably thanks to his respectable place in Athenian cult and topography. That genealogy provided him with his Athenian adventures, more difficult to comprehend than those in Sicily and Crete, as they make him a murderer. His most celebrated Athenian relative was his nephew Talos (Kalos), son of his sister Perdix and his pupil, then rival in the field of inventions. Talos is credited with inventing the potter's wheel, the τόρνος or compass, and the saw (Diodorus, 4.76; Apollodoros, 3.65.8). Jealous of these inventions, Daidalos killed his nephew and threw him off the citadel of the Akropolis, whereupon the boy's grief-stricken mother hanged herself (Apollodoros, 3.15.8; cf. Photios, Suda s.v. Πέρδιξ). Tried for murder by the Ar-

---

[6] J. Mikalson, *Athenian Popular Religion* (Chapel Hill, 1984), chap. 14, on rise in "religiosity" in fourth century; cf. new cults in late fifth-century Athens, of which Asklepios is the most celebrated.

eopagos, Daidalos fled to Crete and the service of Minos, whereupon (so goes the Athenian version) his Cretan adventures begin.

Several aspects of this myth, especially the nature of its ancient sources, betray its origins and motivation. The first culprit is topography, which encouraged other tales for traditional figures, like the "Hephaistion" site where Hephaistos attacked Athena (Euripides, frag. 295, Nauck). A grave of Talos was honored on the south slope of the Akropolis (Pausanias, 1.21.4), presumably near where he was pushed to his death, and a shrine to his mother, Perdix, lies nearby (Photios, Suda, s.v. Πέρδιξ). According to Pausanias's itinerary, grave and shrine must lie somewhere near the Asklepieion, since he indicates them "on the way into the Akropolis from the theater" and approaches the citadel's entrance from the theater of Dionysos. Local topographic features could account for both cult spots in terms of *aitia*. Prehistoric graves could well have stimulated the story of Talos and his fatal fall, while the etymology of Perdix from περδίκιον suggests an association with healing, conveniently provided in the nearby shrine of Asklepios.[7]

The cults for both Talos and Perdix may not be earlier than the fifth century, and as contrived as the topographic traditions that inspired them. But if such limited and late motives account for the fate and afterlife of Talos and Perdix, how did Daidalos become involved? Even if the fourth-century Δαιδαλεῖον was the site of a cult in his name, it lay near Alopeke, not the Akropolis slope, and his worship needs to be reconciled with his reputation as a murderer who fled into exile. The role of the Areopagos in his fate indicates another classical dimension, for the court's restriction to homicide cases was a recent phenomenon celebrated in other mythological crimes, most notably in the trial of Orestes (Aeschylus, *Eumenides* 470, 566–777). Daidalos's trial is first attested by Hellanikos (*FGrH* 169a: schol. Euripides, *Orestes* 1648), which confirms its classical origins, although under circumstances less chauvinistic than the tradition that moved the trial of Orestes to Athens. That is, as a crime committed in Athens, the murder of Talos is a more plausible case for an Athenian trial than those committed by Orestes.

In contrast to the Athenian cult/deme hero, the Daidalos who murdered his nephew and fled to Crete is a mythological figure ancillary to an Athenian one, Talos. Presumably, the legend of Daidalos was "attracted" to the cult of Talos to aggrandize the lat-

---

[7] Both suggestions were first made to me by Dr. Judith Binder, who was most generous with her wisdom in Athenian testimonia and topography. Mycenaean remains that became the "grave of Talos" include candidates rediscovered in later times, e.g., P. Mountjoy, "The Bronze Greaves from Athens: A Case for a LH IIIC Date," *OpAth* 15 (1984) 135–46. An additional link between Perdix and Asklepios, according to Dr. Binder, appears in the pedimental sculptures of the temple at Epidauros, where the partridge figures: N. Yialouris, in *Festschrift Brommer*, 307–9, and "Die Skulpturen des Asklepiostempels von Epidauros," in *Archaische und klassische griechische Plastik*, 2:180. Cf. the herb (περδίκιον), renamed παρθένιον after Athena's cure of the workman who fell from the Propylaia construction (*IG* I² 395; cf. Plutarch, *Perikles* 13; Pliny, *Naturalis Historia* 21.176).

ter's reputation with a legendary craftsman as ancestor. The displacement (through death) of a local, topographic hero by a figure from legend suggests how artificial and contrived was the intrusion of Daidalos into Attic tradition. The sculptor, Endoios, associated with archaic dedications and statues in Athens and elsewhere becomes an "apprentice" of Daidalos who accompanies his master's escape to Crete (Pausanias, 1.26.5). The flight of Daidalos to Crete accommodates the tradition of later adventures elsewhere and removes his pollution from Attic soil, while maintaining his Athenian origin. But Daidalos, the hero of myth, leaves behind in Athens two contradictory associations in cult: a local shrine near Alopeke and a commemoration of his crime on the Akropolis.

In addition to a possible sanctuary and a mythological/genealogical tradition, a single ancient reference claims that a portrait of Daidalos occupied a spot prominent in classical iconography: in the Amazonomachy on the shield of Athena Parthenos. A catalogue of *miracula mundi* preserved in the late antique *Liber Memorialis* 8.10 quotes Lucius Ampelius's description of the shield, "in whose center a portrait of Daidalos is fixed in such a manner that, if someone wanted to lift the portrait from the shield, the entire work would collapse" (in quo clipeo medio Daedali est imago ita colligata quam si quis imaginem e clipeo velit tollere, perit totum opus solvitur enim signum). Ampelius describes the same technical wonder about the shield of Pheidias praised by other postclassical authors: the removal of this portrait would collapse the entire shield.[8] The account of this "miracle" probably derives from the removable gold of the Parthenos, a technical triumph of its time and one useful in fiscal emergencies.[9] Both traditions—removable elements and an artist's portrait—figure prominently in Plutarch's life of Perikles (31.2–5). In this celebrated account, Pheidias is charged with embezzlement in the manufacture of the Parthenos, a charge that required the gold to be removed and weighed. One of the sources of resentment that inspired this prosecution of the artist, according to Plutarch, was the likeness of himself that Pheidias sneaked into the figures on the shield.[10] The tradition of a portrait of Pheidias is neither unique to Plutarch nor inaugurated by him, but demonstrates few signs of classical authenticity. In the most recent analysis, it cannot be traced before the Hellenistic period, and probably belongs to the anecdotal interest in the personality and biography of artists that characterized the beginnings of ancient *Künstlergeschichte*.[11]

If the likelihood that Pheidias portrayed himself on the Parthenos shield is slim, an

[8] Cicero, *Orator* 70.234, 235; *Tusculan Disputations* i.15, 34; Valerius Maximus 8.14.6, Pseudo-Aristotle's Περὶ Κόσμου 399b, *De mirabilis auscultationibus* 846a; Apuleius, *De mundo* 32 (all discussed in Preisshofen, *JdI* 89 [1974] 55–61).

[9] E.g., Thucydides 2.13; Harrison, *Hesperia* 35 (1966) 108 (esp. n. 6)–109; and "Motifs of the City-Siege on the Shield of the Athena Parthenos," *AJA* 85 (1981) 281–317. On Hellenistic fascination with re/movable parts of artworks: H. von Hesberg, "Mechanische Kunstwerke und ihre Bedeutung für die höfische Kunst des frühen Hellenismus," *MarbW* (1987) 47–72.

[10] Harrison, *Hesperia* 35 (1966) 107–33, for a perceptive analysis of the sources and motives in the case.

[11] Preisshofen, *JdI* 89 (1974) 55–61.

image of Daidalos there is even more improbable. Its existence is attested exclusively in the quotation from Ampelius, while all other sources on the Parthenos shield "portrait" involve Pheidias, who is conspicuously absent from the account of Ampelius. The most sensible solution to these sources admits that, from a distance of several centuries, Ampelius substituted the name of one celebrated artist for another.[12] The tendency to associate the two ancient artists is common in later sources, as in Menander's exclamation on the Apollo Smintheus (*Rhetor* 2.445): ποῖος Φειδίας, τίς Δαίδαλος τοσοῦτον ἐδημιούργησε ξόανον; ("What Pheidias, what Daidalos could have made this statue?") What may have encouraged the substitution in traditions about the Athena Parthenos, as Harrison suggests, is the resemblance between the miracle of removable parts and the "marvelous contrivances" attributed to Daidalos (examined in Chapter 8). In any case, a likeness of Daidalos on the Parthenos shield seems doubtful as a fifth-century reality, and his name only crept into the "portrait" tradition by accident.

Daidalos remains an attractive subject in reconstructions of classical sculpture, including elsewhere in the Pheidian Parthenon program. Martin Robertson has proposed that eight lost metopes once illustrated the myth of Daidalos in the center of the Parthenon's south side, an attractive location above the Talos cult on the slopes.[13] South metopes 13–20, preserved in Carrey's drawings and a few fragments, remain iconographic puzzles between slabs to east and west that depict a Centauromachy. Most scholarship has probed for an Attic myth in these figures[14] and thus Robertson's new interpretations maintain this tradition. He would identify craftsman and nephew in the pair of figures in slab 13, adjoining 14 with its display of the new invention, wheel-made pottery. The next pair of metopes (15 and 16) represents, in his reconstruction, Helios in his chariot as a celestial landscape element flanking Daidalos and his falling son, Ikaros. But the Cretan phase of their adventures that precipitated this flight appears in the next pair of metopes to the right, according to Robertson's interpretation, synthesizing epic, Athe-

[12] Harrison, *Hesperia* 35 (1966) 109: "The whole story seems divorced from history to such an extent that it is hardly startling to find the name of Daedalus substituted for that of Pheidias." Cf. Preisshofen, *JdI* 89 (1974) 62. Fehr, *Hephaistos* 3 (1981) 67–70, esp. 67 n. 75, prefers the bald figure as Daidalos, as does E. Simon ("Die Amazonenschlacht auf dem Schild de Athena Parthenos," *AthMitt* 91 [1976] 148).

[13] In *Studies in Classical Art and Archaeology* and in *Parthenon-Kongress Basel*, 206–8. Cf. A. Mantis, "Neue Fragmente von Parthenonskulpturen," in *Archaische und klassische griechische Plastik*, 2:72–75, for new fragments of metope 16 that match Carrey's drawings. Fehr, *Hephaistos* 4 (1982) 61 n. 40, prefers Daidalos to be the figure aloft in metope 16, if represented at all

(see n. 16).

[14] Simon, *JdI* 90 (1975) 106–20: Thessalian Centauromachy (cf. the sandals of the Parthenos: Pliny, *Naturalis Historia* 36.18) and Attic royal myth (Butes and Ixion). F. Studniczka, "Neues über den Parthenon," *NJbb* 29 (1912) 262–66: Erichthonios, the daughters of Erechtheus, and Boreas and Oreithyia. Cf. C. Praschniker, "Neue Parthenonstudien," *ÖJh* 41 (1954) 5–54; Brommer, *Die Metopen des Parthenon* (Mainz, 1967), 191ff.; J. Dörig, "Traces de Thraces sur le Parthenon," *MH* 35 (1978) 221–32: Erechtheus. For a convenient conspectus of the many interpretations of the Parthenon's south metopes see E. Berger, *Der Parthenon in Basel. Dokumentation zu den Metopen* (Mainz, 1986), 1:92–93.

nian, and "rationalizing" elements in the legend. The two archaistic "dancers" in slab 18, moving rapidly to the right in a flutter of anachronistic drapery folds, find an intriguing home in Robertson's vision. They represent the χορός made by Daidalos at Knossos in his first appearance (*Iliad* 18.592), for Robertson argues that the marble version seen by Pausanias (9.40.3; see Chapter 9) was already a familiar explanation in the fifth century. The rapid movement of the dancing maidens would be an allusion to the "moving statues" or quality of life attributed to the works of Daidalos (Chapter 8).

No small leap of faith is necessary to assimilate an ambiguous epic χορός, an anonymous classical relief only related to Daidalos in one scholar's mind, and a Roman account explaining the former in terms of a local version of the latter. To envision, in addition, the theme of "moving statues" in the iconography of the Parthenon metopes presumes a classical assimilation of epic craftsman, eponymous deme hero, Athenian murderer, and magic sculptor that is difficult to document in contemporary sources, where these elements are still discrete. Yet one is reluctant to abandon such a sophisticated synthesis appropriate to the milieu of classical Athens, when such conscious collation of traditions was practiced and illustrated. Robertson's focus on Theseus (identified on these metopes with hesitation in his first article, emphatically in the second) is especially attractive. Hyginus alone has Theseus bring Daidalos "home" to Athens, in a version (no doubt Athenian) of the legend that excludes the Sicilian component and emphasizes Athens and Crete.[15] In Robertson's interpretation, the south metopes support this tradition whereby Daidalos "was brought home by Theseus to make Athens a center of the arts."[16] Such a relationship agrees with the prominent role of Theseus in classical Athenian revision and celebration of the past, and it is through Theseus and his adventures in Crete that Daidalos developed a connection with Athens. But the presence of Theseus on the south metopes depends on Simon's identification of the triumphant figure in southwest metope 27, complementing Pentheus in metope 11 to the west.[17]

Neither this figure nor, alas, any other in the south metopes can be identified beyond conjecture, thus none can be invoked as testimonia for the image of Daidalos in classical Athens. With reluctance, no definite appearance of Daidalos in classical iconography can be ascertained, despite the popularity of his character in Attic drama (Chapter 8). Vase painting, for example, has preserved few scenes where Daidalos can be identified,

---

[15] Hyginus, *Fabellae* 40; cf. Kleidemos in Plutarch, *Theseus* 19; schol. Euripides, *Hippolytos* 884.

[16] M. Robertson, in *Parthenon-Kongress Basel*, 208. As Simon pointed out (*JdI* 90 [1975] 101), Theseus is hero in both Attic and Thessalian centauromachies, hence a frequent figure in the Parthenon sculptures as well as the Theseion paintings and on vases. Even

Fehr, *Hephaistos* 4 (1982) 61 n. 40, agrees that the incorporation of Daidalos into the Parthenon sculptures would be appropriate to the monument's celebration of art; cf. *Hephaistos* 3 (1981) 57ff., on the role of τέχναι in the Parthenon sculptures.

[17] Simon, *JdI* 90 (1975) 105 (Robertson, in *Parthenon-Kongress Basel*, 208).

most of them South Italian and later than the fifth century. In a comic scene on a phlyax vase he is labeled but otherwise indistinguishable from Hephaistos (Figure 11: see Chapter 4, n. 75). In episodes related to the flight of Ikaros, he appears on an Apulian calyx-krater where he may be supplicating Minos, and on a South Italian kotyle where he fastens the wings on his son (Figure 12).[18] The popularity of Daidalos in representations, as on stage, apparently concentrated on the comic and Sicilian aspects of his adventures, not on the heroic and mythological Athenian elements that would have inspired a set of metopes like those restored by Robertson. A deliberate synthesis of these elements did not occur this early in the history of the tradition, or in a manner that would allow an iconographic program. Nevertheless, Robertson's proposal for the Parthenon south metopes focuses on aspects of Daidalos critical to Athens: his importance to the city as a legendary craftsman, and the role of Theseus in incorporating the legend of Daidalos into Athenian history. It was in fifth-century Athens that Daidalos became a sculptor, an Athenian, a relative of Hephaistos, a protégé of Theseus, and the hero of a local community. The cognitive forces that inspired this transformation shaped not only the legend of Daidalos but the Greek sense of history and self (Part IV).

One of the works attributed to him by Pausanias deserves close attention here and forms a useful transition from his sculptural career in this chapter to his classical matrix, in the final chapter. In addition to legends, anecdotes, cult places, and family ties, a single work of art by Daidalos is attested in ancient Athens. Pausanias is the sole authority for this ἔργον, which contrasts dramatically with all the other works of Daidalos (primarily statues, as previously discussed) recorded by the antiquarian. He mentions it among other dedications in the temple of Athena Polias, identified by most scholars with the Ionic temple north of the Parthenon, known today as the Erechtheion.[19] After naming exotic statues such as a wooden Hermes dedicated by Kekrops, he notes other works worthy of mention (ἄξια λόγου), among the older ones "a folding stool, the work of Daidalos, and booty taken from the Medes—the cuirass of Masistios, who led the cavalry at Plataia, and an *akinakes* [Persian dagger] said to belong to Mardonios" (1.27.1: τῶν μὲν ἀρχαίων δίφρος ὀκλαδίας ἐστὶ Δαιδάλου ποίημα, λάφυρα δέ ἀπὸ Μήδων Μασιστίου θώραξ, ὃς εἶχεν ἐν Πλαταιαῖς τὴν ἡγεμονίαν τῆς ἵππου, καὶ ἀκινάκης Μαρδονίου λεγόμενος εἶναι).

How selective or accurate this report on the dedications in the temple is cannot be ascertained. Pausanias seems to focus on his usual favorites—the antique, exotic, and

---

[18] Apulian kotyle: Beazley, *JHS* 47 (1927) 223–24, pl. xxi, 1; South Italian kotyle: Oxford 1922.308 (cf. a volute krater, Naples 1767); Kokalakis "Icarus," 28. A. D. Trendall and A. Cambitoglou, *The Red-Figured Vases of Apulia* (Oxford, 1978), 1:21, no. 92, near the Sisyphus Painter.

[19] For recent disagreement, see K. Jeppesen, "Where Was the So-called Erechtheion?" *AJA* 83 (1979) 381–94; "Further Inquiries on the Location of the Erechtheion and Its Relationship to the Temple of the Polias," *AJA* 87 (1983) 325–33; *The Theory of the Alternative Erechtheion* (Aarhus, 1987).

miraculous (the olive tree being the only other item he describes there). The ποίημα of Daidalos is a surprise: one would expect the wooden Hermes to be attributed to Daidalos, if anything, to agree with the other works ascribed to him in classical sources and elsewhere in Pausanias (Chapter 9). Instead, Pausanias describes a folding stool as the work of Daidalos, an item of furniture common in archaic and classical Greece.[20] What is striking about its attribution to Daidalos is that it belongs to a category of δαίδαλα in the epic fashion, an article of elaborate furniture perhaps decorated with inlaid precious materials. Its name and attribution to Daidalos are presumably postepic, and therefore represent a coincidence with the epic tradition rather than a revival. This particular type of stool is unknown before the archaic period and was probably adopted by the Greeks from Egyptian and Near Eastern prototypes, like the more sumptuous throne and κλίνη.[21] Herakleides of Pontos (in Athenaeus, 12.512c) specifically associates such furniture, along with servants to carry them, with other signs of Oriental luxury (τρυφή) adopted by Athenians, such as purple garments and gold cicada brooches. The throne of Arkesilaos, on the Lakonian cup named after the king of Cyrene, illustrates not only the stool's chronological popularity but its function as an Oriental and royal attribute (Figure 36).

The context of this stool—the other dedications inside the Erechtheion—suggests another inspiration for its link to Daidalos. Pausanias next cites an item of Persian spoils: the θώραξ or cuirass of Masistios and the Persian dagger (ἀκινάκης) of Mardonios, both Persian spoils captured after the battle of Plataia, which Pausanias is surprised to find in an Athenian temple, rather than in Sparta.[22] The breastplate had astonished the Greeks at Plataia: for its gold scales could not be pierced, thanks to the hidden protection of iron ones underneath (Herodotus, 9.22), a combination of glamour and hidden strength worthy of epic praise as δαιδάλεος. The dagger also corresponds to weapons known to Athenians and stored in the buildings of the Akropolis. Some 350 of them were recorded in the Chalkotheke in an inventory of 369/8 B.C. (IG II² 1425.75–78, 395), along with private dedications of Persian vessels (lines 91–92, for a phiale called βαρβαρική, dedicated by Kleon). Gilded ἀκινάκαι appear in the Parthenon inventories of the

---

[20] O. Wanscher, *Sella Curulis. The Folding Stool. An Ancient Symbol of Dignity* (Copenhagen, 1980), 86–104; G. Richter, *The Furniture of the Greeks, Etruscans and Romans* (London, 1966), 43–46, figs. 236–49; cf. figs. 154–65, for a marble throne found in the Parthenon and decorated with a winged figure on its back—too late and too grand for a stool made by Daidalos?

[21] Wanscher, *Sella Curulis*, 86–87; Boardman, in *Fourth Cretological Congress*, 46, and *CAH* III.3 (2), 453; Becatti, *RömMitt* 60–61 (1953–1954) 29, argues that

the stool seen by Pausanias was prehistoric. H. Kyrieleis, *Throne und Klinen. JdI* suppl. 14 (Berlin, 1969), 35–41, 131–41, on Achaemenid thrones. Miller, *Perserie*, 109–11, "Spoils of the Persian Wars" (furniture). Six types of seat are listed in the Attic stelai: W. Kendrick Pritchett, "The Attic Stelai: II," *Hesperia* 25 (1956) 211–20.

[22] Herodotus, 9.80; Gauer, *Weihgeschenke*, 17, 28; Francis, in *Ancient Persia*, 81; Miller, *Perserie*, 74–157 (ἀκινάκης: 105–6 nn. 65–68; corslet: 108–9).

late fifth and fourth centuries.[23] The dagger of Mardonios, in particular, is mentioned by Demosthenes (24.129) as one of the treasures (ἀριστεῖα) stolen from the Akropolis by Glaukytes in the early fourth century B.C. Its reappearance, according to Pausanias, in the temple of Athena Polias in the second century A.D. implies that it was retrieved and returned, unless Demosthenes exaggerated the charges against Glaukytes.[24] Other votive Persian booty appears scattered through Attic inventories, an important source of Athenian familiarity and fascination with the art of the conquered, which had much the same effect on its captors as Greek art did on Rome.[25]

More intriguing for the pursuit of Daidalos is the silver-footed stool (δίφρος ἀργυρόπους) that Demosthenes mentions together with the dagger as treasures stolen from the Akropolis. Lexicographers identify this item of furniture as the seat of Xerxes from the battle of Salamis (Harpokration, Suda s.v. ἀργυρόπους δίφρος), a throne made of gold according to Plutarch's account of the battle (*Themistokles* 13.1). Such a throne, or stool, was a common accessory for Near Eastern royalty and nobility, who never moved without a servant to carry such a stool, a διφροφόρος (Athenaeus, 12.514c).[26] Lists of δίφροι and ὀκλαδίαι in the same classical inventories already cited as sources of ἀκινάκαι suggest that Persian furniture was stored as treasure there, either as booty or (as Dorothy Thompson suggested) ritual equipment or both. In addition to those cited in *IG* I³ 344–50, an early fourth-century inventory names the following (*IG* II² 1394.11–14: ἀκιν[ά]κης χρυσοῦς· ὄνυξ δακτύλιον ἔχων ἐν χαλκῇ κυλιχνίδ[ι]· δίφροι στρογγυλόποδες Γ ἀργυρό[π]ους εἰς ὑποπόδια τρία): "a golden [Persian] dagger, an onyx ring with a bronze cup; three round-footed stools, one silver-footed [stool], three footstools."

The round-footed stools, plus one distinguished by its silver feet, appear next to a gilded dagger in this inventory. Dorothy Thompson suggested that the most lavish δίφρος could have been the "throne" of Xerxes, given that "round-footed" stools sound like Persian ones. She connects them with the stools carried in the Panathenaic procession, originally as a display of triumph over the Persians, then as ritual equipment for the archon basileus and his wife.[27] A recent article by Margaret Cool Root on

[23] *IG* I³ 344, 8; 346, 8; 349, 37; 350, 8, 37; 352, 8, 37; 353, 37; repeated in 354, 355, 356, 357. *IG* II² 1394, 11–14. I am very grateful to Diane Harris, author of a Princeton dissertation on the Parthenon inventories (1990), for valuable corrections and suggestions on my discussion of Persian objects in these inventories.

[24] Thompson, in *Aegean and the Near East*, 286.

[25] *IG* II² 1607, 1610, 1613 (fourth century); R. N. Frye, *The Heritage of Persia* (Cleveland, 1963), 104; R. D. Barnett, "Median Art," *Iranica Antiqua* 2, no. 1 (1962) 77–95; A. Farkas, "Is There Anything Persian in Persian Art?" in *Ancient Persia*, 19 nn. 13–14. Miller, "Perserie," chap. 2, on spoils and chap. 4 on

Persian culture in Athens.

[26] See n. 21. For Near Eastern representations of the full ensemble, which included footstool and sunshade as well as seat, see Thompson in *Aegean and the Near East*, 287–88. F. Frost, *Plutarch's* Themistocles: *A Historical Commentary* (Princeton, 1980), 149–50, prefers the seat of Xerxes as a portable stool, not throne, to be used for descending from a wheeled conveyance.

[27] Thompson, in *Aegean and the Near East*, 286. The supporting evidence she adduces includes the διφροφόροι mentioned by Aristophanes (*Birds* 1550, *Ekklesiazousai* 730) and those depicted on the east

the relationship between the Parthenon frieze and the sculptures of Persepolis complements Thompson's identifications of Oriental traditions incorporated into Attic ritual
after the Persian wars.[28] The influence of Oriental art and ritual on classical Greek art is
manifest in other ways, notably in the proliferation of giant chryselephantine statues,
that transform the concept of the ξόανον from its archaic meaning into a cult image.[29]
Some Greek architectural forms have also been traced to Persian influence, and could
have been adopted after the Persian wars.[30] As noted elsewhere in this book, one of the
ironies of Greek defeat of Persia was the uninterrupted, even escalated, popularity of
Orientalia throughout the defense of Greek superiority that those victories generated.

Omitting the question of the role of Persian stools in Athenian ritual, a chronological
arrangement of the testimonia on Persian weapons and furniture in Athens comprising
literary sources and the Parthenon inventories suggests an interesting evolution:

1. Herodotus, 9.22.2	A golden cuirasse, plated with scales, over a pur-ple linen tunic, worn by Masistios at Plataia
2. Herodotus, 9.80.1–2	Spoils from Plataia: gold and silver tents, gilded and silver-plated couches; golden kraters and phialai and other drinking cups; gold and silver dinoi inside the baggage carts; stripped from the dead: twisted bracelets and golden daggers
3. IG I³ 344–57 (433/2–412/11 B.C.)	Persian daggers of gold; stools, couches, thrones
4. IG II² 1425, 77 (368/7 B.C.)	Iron sword, gold hilt, ivory sheath
5. IG II² 1394, 11–14 (397/6 or 396/5 B.C.)	Golden Persian dagger; silver round-footed stools (δίφροι)
6. Demosthenes, 24.129	A silver-footed stool (δίφρος) and the dagger of Mardonios (report of its theft)
7. Plutarch, Themistokles 13.1	The golden throne (δίφρος) of Xerxes
8. Pausanias, 1.27.1	A δίφρος made by Daidalos, the cuirasse of Mas-istios, and the dagger of Mardonios, all in the temple of Athena Polias

---

frieze of the Parthenon (pp. 289–90). *Contra*: Kyrieleis, *Throne und Klinen*, 140 n. 527; Diane Harris suggests that some chairs Thompson identifies as Persian could be of Greek manufacture.

[28] Root, *AJA* 89 (1985) 103–20; cf. Thompson, in *Aegean and the Near East*, 290. Root and Thompson over-
estimate the nature of "royalty" in the Greek polis
and exaggerate its similarity to Oriental despotism.
On Greek kingship, see Drews, *Basileus*, and Carlier,
La royauté en Grèce, 503–5. For other objections, see

Miller, "Perserie," 325, and *AK* 31 (1988) 88; Boardman, in *Parthenon-Kongress Basel*, 412 n. 38.

[29] As suggested by Donohue, *Xoana*, 30–32, 79.

[30] O. Broneer, "The Tent of Xerxes and the Greek
Theater," *CSCA* 12 (1944) 305–11; H. von Gall, "Das
persische Königszelt und die Hallenarchitektur in
Iran und Griechenland," in *Festschrift Brommer*, 119–
32; Vickers, *RA* (1985) 3–28, dates the Siphian treasury caryatids after the Persian wars, an argument
that has won little support.

If one assumes that the same dagger of Masistios was "returned" to the Akropolis after the speech of Demosthenes and before Pausanias's visit, the δίφρος attributed to Daidalos in the second century A.D. might well be the same one cited by Demosthenes among the stolen ἀριστεῖα. The other stools and daggers listed in the classical Parthenon inventories could likewise be Persian without having been stolen, returned, and moved, as experienced by the weapons of Mardonios and Masistios. Accepting this reconstruction makes it possible that the chair shown Pausanias was once an item of Persian booty from Plataia, if not the "chair of Xerxes" himself. The throne of the Persian king, on campaign a stool like the one on which King Arkesilaos sits (Figure 36), was an essential attribute of his image among the Greeks, as late as the fourth century (Figure 62). Only when Alexander takes his seat upon the throne of Dareios at Persepolis (Plutarch, *Alexander* 37; cf. Figure 62) has Greece defeated Persia. In narratives of the classical campaigns, Xerxes attends battles and maneuvers enthroned as a monarch, and must have been seen thus in paintings by Herodotus and others (Part IV; see Figures 36, 37, 62). Eventually his "throne," or another exotic piece of furniture and booty, could have been attributed to Daidalos, on an occasion remote enough from its manufacture to invoke the name of a legendary artist.

This migration of identity, from Oriental to prehistoric, indicates circumstances both sophisticated and naive. Inadvertently, Daidalos was resurrected under his original guise as epic craftsman and for the same purposes that δαιδάλεος adjectives served in poetry: to illustrate the exotic and miraculous in art. That a Persian chair captured in a Greek victory was eventually claimed as the work of Daidalos is both significant and suitable to Athenian experience. Since the early fifth century, Daidalos had become Atticized through local ties in family, myth, and cult. Thus the most renowned craftsman outside Olympian circles joined Athena and Hephaistos, already appropriated in classical Athens as local patrons of the arts, and even became a descendant of the latter ([Plato] *Alkibiades* 121.1.4; see Chapter 12). Having kidnapped an artist native to Cretan prehistory, the Athenian cultural appetite ultimately appropriated even non-Greek creations as the achievement of this newly native son.

Thus Daidalos joins Kadmos, an Oriental thinly disguised as a Greek to account for the origins of the alphabet in a scenario favoring Greece over the Orient (see Chapters 5 and 13). The historical forces that motivated all these naturalizations of exotic culture heroes were the same ones that brought to Athens the chair eventually attributed to Daidalos. The Persian invasion of Greece transformed Greek art history as well as the Greeks' sense of history, and the personality of Daidalos was but one figure in this pattern.

· PART IV ·

From Daidalos to

Theseus

CHAPTER 11

The Great Transformation:
History into Art

πὰρ πυρὶ χρὴ τοιαῦτα λέγειν χειμῶνος ἐν ὥρῃ
ἐν κλίνῃ μαλακῇ κατακεέμενον, ἔμπλεον ὄντα,
πίνοντα γλυκὺν οἶνον, ὑποτρώγοντ᾽ ἐρεβίνθους·
Τίς πόθεν εἰς ἀνδρῶν; πόσα τοι ἔτε᾽ ἐστί, φέριστε;
πηλίκος ἦσθ᾽, ὅθ᾽ ὁ Μῆδος ἀφίκετο;

This you must ask, lying by the fire in winter,
on a soft couch, your belly full,
drinking sweet wine, nibbling on chick peas:
"Where are you from, among men? How old are you, my friend?
And how old were you when the Mede came?"

—Xenophanes, frag. 18 (Athenaeus, 2.54e)

T HE TWO FIGURES imagined in this exchange by an Ionian philosopher, poet, and symposiast personify the intellectual and cultural adventure of this fourth and final section. Their habits are archaic, Greek, and aristocratic, but thoroughly Oriental in origin: to recline on soft couches, for example, was a refinement learned from the East, whose royal privileges became aristocratic affectations in Greece. But the question that defines one's age, manhood, and Hellenism involves the arrival of "the Mede" (in 546 B.C, in this case), perhaps the most significant intellectual event in the history of Greece. Thereafter, Oriental customs were still practiced, even increased in familiarity and popularity among Greeks, but the character and culture they represented were kept distant. This contradiction determined the dynamics of what we call classical culture, not only influencing its contents but elaborating its framework and afterlife. The role played by Athens, partly through accident, in the encounter between Greece and Persia made this city-state not only the "school of Hellas" but the catechism of Western civilization. Its lessons were didactic and influential, and included a major proportion of those cultural

values and traditions now assumed to be general and Greek. These lessons were originally dedicated not only to a cultural persuasion (the superiority of Athens) but to a
political mission: the reinforcement of Athenian power over other Greek states.

The discovery of these patterns, which gave Daidalos a new home and role, requires
tracing a transformation in material and intellectual culture, beginning with the historical events that inspired new monuments and new purposes for art. The emergence of
a new attitude toward the Orient was neither rapid nor unequivocal, and reflected the
complexities of the strategic relationships between (and among) Greek cities and their
Persian opponents. A crucial development in this process was the invention of new
myths to suit recent history, and indeed the invention of a new kind of mythology, the
medium of historical allegory. Within this framework, the figure of Daidalos exemplifies
the "great transformation," as a legend made newly Athenian and closely associated
with the new moral purposes of the figure of Theseus. In this chapter, the evolution of
these traditions in the early classical period will be traced in history, literature, and art.
Thus the "origins of Greek art" invoked in the title of this book took place twice: in the
Oriental background that inspired forms and motifs but, more important, in the conflict
with the Orient that made them Greek.

ΙΟΝΙΑ: ΟΥΔΕΝ ΟΜΟΙΩΣ ΚΑΙ ᾿ΑΘΗΝΑΙΟΙ

Throughout ancient history, the Aegean enjoyed the advantage of being the easternmost member of the Western world: close enough for fruitful contact with the Orient,
but too distant for more than a marginal role in imperial strategies exercised by Egypt,
Mesopotamia, and Anatolia (Map 2). If geography bestowed this relationship and its
benefits on Greece, as examined in the first part of this book, history transfigured it.
Mesopotamian expansion brought the Near East to Greece, eventually, in a confrontation that left an artificial distinction between "East" and "West." The events that
brought Greeks and Persians into contact and conflict began in the sixth century in
Ionia, and left their impact in verses like the one by Xenophanes just quoted.[1] In the
aftermath of these events, the years of actual Greek engagement with Persia continued
long after the battle of Plataia and even the Eurymedon and the Peace of Kallias, into
the fourth century until the Macedonian campaigns in Asia. When Alexander captures
Persepolis and the throne of Dareios (Plutarch, *Alexander* 37), the war with Persia concludes its final campaign. But its primary intellectual impact, and the focus of this chapter, occurred under Dareios and Xerxes in the early fifth century.

---

[1] The Persian wars include "not just . . . the events of 481–479 B.C. but rather the whole cycle of events from the Ionian revolt of 499 B.C. through Marathon, Thermopylae, and Salamis to Plataea" (Pollitt, in *Greek Art: Archaic into Classical*, 103), to which one could add the campaigns of Cyrus in Ionia. For a lively account of these events, see Hurwit, *Art and Culture of Early Greece*, 320–23.

The encounter that catapulted Athens to its paramount position among Greek states frustrates an objective historian. Written sources are limited and distorted by time and place, by the wisdom of hindsight and the confidence of the victor. The lack of a Persian account of this campaign, or of any Achaemenid version of Persia's own expansion, prevents any accurate reconstruction of its movements, strategies, and motives.[2] For example, the campaigns of the Persian general, Mardonios, in 492, claimed Athens and Eretria as targets of vengeance according to Greek sources; they primarily reflect an expansion of the ambitions of Dareios into Europe, a more plausible strategy.[3] In a more particular problem of bias, sources are not only exclusively Greek but specifically Athenian, and already subscribe to its political agenda of power relationships within Greece. The longest sustained account of the Persian wars, the "inquiries" of Herodotus, arranges and explains events as a progressive revelation of the emergence of Greek, and especially Athenian, superiority. This directed narrative, with its explicit privileging of Athens, helped form the Western perspective on Greece and the Orient. While recognized today, the attitude of Herodotus is typically screened for a political bias inherent in his oral and written sources or in his contemporary audience.[4] Far more influential, and more familiar to that audience, were physical testimonia—visible commemorative monuments that publicized the role of Athens—and the language deployed in political orations, such that any account of the Persian wars based on contemporary sources was inextricable from Athenian rhetoric. More than hostility to Ionians or pro-Athenian politics, the nature of these sources—public narrative, whether in painting or proclamation—determined the historiography of the Persian wars and its peculiarly dramatic structure. By the time Herodotus tackled the subject in prose, more conspicuous media—in art, rhetoric, and drama—had already cast their features.

The structure of these modes of expression, along with an implicit dedication to the promotion of Athens, emerges in the historian's first λόγος. The campaigns in Ionia constitute the first and longest act in a trilogy, succeeded by the drama that culminates at Marathon and the final act again in Asia Minor, at Mykale.[5] The beginnings of the conflict were far more casual and dispersed than in the elaborate evolution traced by Herodotus, who devoted two-thirds of his work to the prelude in Lydia and Ionia. He

[2] Lang, *Historia* 17 (1968) 24–36; K. H. Waters, "Herodotus and the Ionian Revolt," *Historia* 19 (1970) 504–8. For Persian views, see T. Cuyler Young, "480–479 B.C.—A Persian Perspective," *IrAnt* 15 (1980) 213–39. Cf. Gillis, *Collaboration with the Persians*, 1–25; Balcer, *Sparda by the Bitter Sea*, esp. chaps. 1–7, and "The Persian Wars against the Greeks: A Reassessment," *Historia* 38 (1989) 127–43.

[3] Walser, *Hellas und Iran* 34–35; J. de Romilly, "La vengeance comme explication historique dans l'oeuvre de Hérodote," *REG* 84 (1971) 314–17. To be fair to Herodotus, he admits that the punishment of

Athens and Eretria was a mere πρόσχημα (6.44.1, cf. 6.94.1: πρόφασις, cf. 7.1, 138.1), but he misidentifies the destruction of Greece as the ultimate goal of Dareios, instead of a natural [*sic*] expansion from Asia into Europe (Thrace).

[4] As in C. G. Starr, "Why Did the Greeks Defeat the Persians?" *PdP* 17 (1962) 330–31; Ch. Fornara, *Herodotus* (Oxford, 1981), 37–58; W. G. Forrest, "Herodotus and Athens," *Phoenix* 38 (1984) 1–11.

[5] Thus Else, *Origins and Early Form of Greek Tragedy*, 102, construes the histories of Herodotus. See my n. 27 on tragedy and history.

opens by claiming that the ἔργα μεγάλα τε καὶ θωμαστά of Greeks and barbarians are direct descendants of conflicts in legend, and traces the Persian Wars back to the Trojan war in a celebrated passage. Closer to recent events, the contest between the Lydian and Persian empires in Anatolia ultimately brought the Persians to coastal Asia Minor and its Greek cities, after 546 B.C. It is the Ionian revolt of 499–494 that first drew Athens, in particular, into conflict with Persia, through its dispatch of twenty ships identified by Herodotus as the ἀρχὴ κακῶν (5.97.3). The traditional modern verdict on the revolt still cherishes it as an inevitable, inspired, even heroic demonstration of Greek resistance to barbarian rule, in fidelity to the attitude of Herodotus.[6] Recent perspectives admit how much nineteenth-century European nationalism encouraged this fidelity, especially in an era preoccupied with the liberation of Greece from Ottoman hegemony. These modern and ancient prejudices suspended, the Ionian "revolt" appears less Panhellenic and ethnic in origin, more determined by internal *stasis* within Greek cities that requested Persian intervention. Archaic Ionian resistance was only the first in a long series of independent local rebellions, including the satraps' revolt of the fourth century.[7] The personal ambitions of individual tyrants (most conspicuously, Aristagoras of Miletos), the idiosyncratic relationship of each city to Persia, and the tyrants' separate responses to Miletos and Persia discouraged alliance among the Greeks of Asia. The policy of separate settlements and arrangements with Persia since 546 made a harmonious Ionian league with a coordinated strategy unlikely. The failure of the revolt deposed tyrants in the Ionian cities under Persia in favor of democratic rule, as a safer and more malleable form of local government, a result that eliminates "democracy" as a factor in Ionian resistance to Persia, largely guided by tyrants. Moreover, this system of putting down local rulers and imposing an alien "democracy," like other Oriental practices, was a technique put to good use by Athens in its classical empire.

When Athens was approached by the Ionians in 499, the city's response to the Milesian cause was not sympathy for fellow Greeks and fellow "democrats" or even the pretext offered by Herodotus (5.99): ὀφειλόμενά σφι ἀποδίδοντες, to repay a debt

[6] Concepts such as E. Meyer's "unvermeidlicher Kampf" and Bengtson's "nationaler Widerstand" are discussed by Walser, *Hellas und Iran*, 27; cf. his "Zur Beurteilung der Perserkriege in der neueren Forschung," *Schweizeriche Beiträge zur allgemeinen Geschichte* 17 (1959) 219–40. Even Raaflaub, *Entdeckung der Freiheit*, 103, still calls "freedom" a motive in the Ionian revolt, his only pre-Persian example of a concept developed later.

[7] Thus Walser's insightful analysis (*Hellas und Iran* 32). Cf. Balcer, *Sparda by the Bitter Sea*, 227–49; P. Tozzi, *La rivolta ionica* (Pisa, 1978), 134–65; D. Hegyi, "The Historical Background of the Ionian Revolt," *Acta Antiqua* 14 (1966) 285–302, and "Der Ionische Aufstand und die Regierungsmethoden Dareios I," *Altertum* 17 (1971) 142–50; J. Neville, "Was There an Ionian Revolt?" *CQ* 29 (1979) 268–75; A. Keaveney, "The Attack on Naxos: A 'Forgotten Cause' of the Ionian Revolt," *CQ* 38 (1988) 76–81; D. Graf, "Greek Tyrants and Achaemenid Politics," in *The Craft of the Ancient Historian: Essays in Honor of Chester G. Starr*, ed. J. Eadie and J. Ober (Lanham, Md., 1985), 79–123. M. Weiskopf, *The So-Called "Great Satraps' Revolt," 366–60 B.C.*, Historia Einzelschrift 63 (Stuttgart, 1989), for a critical view of events distorted in "an Isocratean panorama of barbarian turpitude."

incurred from an old alliance during the Lelantine War.[8] By the time Aristagoras arrived in Athens, having failed to win the Spartans as allies, the Athenians had already "fallen out" (διαβεβλημένοις) with the Persians (6.96.2), on account of Hippias. The exiled tyrant had won over the Lydian satrap, Artaphernes, and Athens feared the tyrant's return with Lydian or Persian power. What they dreaded was not so much the institution of tyranny but a particular tyrant responsible for the harshest reign known to Athens, after the assassination of his brother, Hipparchos, in 514 B.C. (Herodotus, 5.55, 5.62). Therefore the Athenians acted like most Greek cities toward Persia: from internal interests, here in defense against a native political enemy, the Peisistratids, despite the irony of their own recent courtship of Persia. As recently as 507/6 B.C., the Athenians themselves, under Kleisthenes, had approached the Persians for assistance against Sparta, eventually refusing the cost of Persian support: submission (earth and water) to the Great King (Herodotus, 5.73). By the time Herodotus reports these events, the reputation of Athens rested on its victory over Persia and, in retrospect, on the democracy introduced by Kleisthenes. Thus the role of Kleisthenes in diplomacy with Persia in 507/6 is tactfully played down by Herodotus, to be revived by enemies of the Alkmeonids who accused them of Medism later in the fifth century.[9] In the context of Herodotus's narrative, the pretext of a Lelantine War alliance adds an element of Panhellenic (intra-Greek?) loyalty to a response based primarily on internal concerns. With this mixture of motives—fear of Hippias tempered by support for Ionia—the Athenians sent out twenty ships, joined by five vessels from their ally, Eretria. In words echoing the fateful departure of Helen for Troy (Iliad 5.62–64), Herodotus calls these ships the ἀρχή κακῶν or "beginning of evils" for Greeks and barbarians, the origins of the confrontation whose legacy not even Herodotus suspected.

Landing in Ionia opposite Samos and marching to Sardis, the Athenians destroyed the Lydian seat of the Persian satrapy but failed to capture Hippias or take control of the city. Their hasty retreat to the sea and their disastrous defeat near Ephesos culminated in an embarrassing withdrawal from the revolt, perhaps prompted by the influence of a Peisistratid (Hipparchos) who became archon in 494 B.C. Athens' chief reward from this expedition was the formal enmity of Persia earned through the burning of Sardis. Herodotus records how the Persian king arranged to be reminded daily, at dinner, of the Athenians (Herodotus, 6.94), a story designed to dramatize the distance between Greece and Persia and the magnitude of their imbalance. Aeschylus has Atossa inquire in Persians (231):

---

[8] C. Bearzot, "La guerra lelantea e il κοινόν degli Ioni d'Asia," in Santuari e politica nel mondo antico, ed. M. Sordi (Milan, 1983), 57–81.

[9] How and Wells, appendix 18:6; Gillis, Collaboration with the Persians, 45–58; G.M.E. Williams, "The Image of the Alcmeonidai between 490 and 487/6 B.C.," Historia 29 (1980) 106–10; R. Develin, "Herodotus and the Alkmeonids," in The Craft of the Ancient Historian, 125–39 (130–33 on the shield signal).

Ὦ φίλοι, ποῦ τὰς Ἀθήνας φασιν ἱδρῦσθαι χθονός;

O friends, where on earth do they say that Athens lies?

Even after the battle of Marathon, Attika was a distant and unlikely threat to Persia, and only the motive of vengeance made their conflict seem inevitable. In Herodotus's narrative and in the Greek (Athenian) view in general, the burning of Sardis gave the Persians an excuse for revenge in invading Greece with a special target of Athens and Eretria, the two mainland cities that participated in the burning (6.44). The Athenian failure in Ionia, however, was trivial compared with what the Ionians eventually suffered. The disgrace they experienced at the battle of Lade, with its last-minute desertions and defections to the Medes, was compounded by the humiliating loss of cities and execution or deportation of populace. In the events that culminated in the battle of Lade and the destruction of Miletos, Athens was not only conspicuously absent (hence spared this disgrace) but, in the words of Herodotus (6.21) that entitle this chapter's section, embarrassed by the fate of Miletos.[10] For all these reasons, it is unlikely that Athens would have commemorated its role in the expedition in a conspicuous manner, such as on the Athenian treasury at Delphi (Figures 38, 39) or in the juxtaposition of Theseus and Kroisos on an amphora by Myson (Figure 37b).[11]

The fiction of an Ionian revolt as a resistance movement owes its inspiration, if not its very existence, to a literary and historical motive: the glorification of Athens by a counterdemonstration of Greek behavior. Thus the Ionian revolt forms a special exemplum of resistance to Persia, and the biography of Kroisos, juxtaposed in art with Athenian deeds of heroism (Figures 37a, b), became a counterlife to the heroism of Greeks. The idea of a counterhero (antagonist) is as old as Homer, where the homecoming of Odysseus draws its primary narrative tension from the failed νόστος of Agamemnon. The story of the successful return of Odysseus is rendered more acute in suspense by the counterexample of Agamemnon, whose fate initiates the *Odyssey* in the first speech of Zeus (1.28–43). The death of Aigisthos is judged ἐοικώς by Athena (1.45–46), who then introduces the uncertain fate of Odysseus as a contrast deserving of divine sympathy. Throughout the epic poem, the fate of Agamemnon is invoked repeatedly, by Nestor and Menelaos in Books 3 and 4, in the underworld settings of Books 11 and 24, and haunts the second half of the poem as a paradigm for the victim of the unfaithful wife.[12] In other words, such a technique was already organic to Greek narrative and not just a post-Persian invention of historiography, when Herodotus employed it. To a lesser de-

[10] For critical analyses of the Ionian revolt, see Tozzi, *La rivolta ionica*, esp. 213–16; D. Lateiner, "The Failure of the Ionian Revolt," *Historia* 31 (1982) 129–60; O. Murray, *CAH* IV, 461–90.

[11] As argued by Boardman in *Eye of Greece*, 12–16,

and Gauer, in *Festschrift Neutsch*, 127–128, 132. Both monuments date after 490 B.C., as Pausanias indicates for the treasury (10.11.4): see Chapter 12.

[12] Murnaghan, *Disguise and Recognition in the Odyssey*, 4 n. 3, 125–26 (see Chapter 1).

gree, the Persian campaign in Scythia also functions as a "dress rehearsal" for the invasion of Greece, but without the relative judgment on different kinds of Greek behavior.[13] The choreography of the Ionian revolt in Herodotus serves as contrast to the Athenian experience in 490 and 480/79. For example, the expedition of Mardonios to northern Greece in 492 anticipates the campaign that culminated at Marathon. A divinely dispatched storm (off Mount Athos) prefigures the storm at Artemision, invoked by the Athenians with a prayer answered by the destruction of the fleet (7.188). The source of that λόγος is clearly the sanctuary of Boreas at the Ilissos in Athens, where one can imagine the annual commemoration of the miracle with a dramatic poem, like the one created by Simonides to inaugurate ceremony and shrine.[14] This episode demonstrates two points critical to this chapter: the element of prefiguration in the Herodotean narrative of the pre-Athenian campaigns, and how the sources for those campaigns already participate in the Athenian celebration of victory.

This pattern repeats itself in other episodes of the Ionian conflict with Persia. In another scenario, the Ionian expedition to Cyprus (5.104) simulates the Persian invasion of Greece. First, internal *stasis* has already divided local Cypriotes into Medizers and resisters, the way Aigina and Boiotia's Medism encouraged their enemy, Athens, to resist. In the case of Cyprus, the king of Salamis, Gorgos, has fled to the Persians, leaving his brother, Onesilos, to revolt against Persia, with the encouragement of the Ionians: Athenian aristocrats, in particular the Peisistratids, collaborated with the enemy in similar ways. As the enemy draws near, Onesilos sends messengers throughout Ionia, like the Panhellenic appeal for a congress at the Isthmus (Herodotus, 7.172). Upon arriving, the Ionians face a choice (αἴρεσις): to fight the Persians on land or the Phoenicians by sea, a rehearsal of the challenge faced by the Athenians on land at Marathon, at sea (at Salamis) against a Persian fleet largely composed of Phoenician ships.[15] If these historical similarities are largely circumstantial, Herodotus spares no opportunity to compare the two campaigns in his use of language. Onesilos reminds them that they fight "in order that both Ionia and Cyprus be free at your hands" (ὅκως τὸ κατ᾽ ὑμέας ἔσται ἥ τε Ἰωνίη καὶ ἡ Κύπρος ἐλευθερίη), the same appeal to "freedom" imagined at the other battle of Salamis (Aeschylus, *Persians* 402–5). The Ionian response

[13] Hartog, *The Mirror of Herodotus*, 35–40, on the Scythian campaigns and how they prefigure the Persian wars in Greece.

[14] Kierdorf, *Erlebnis und Darstellung der Perserkriege*, 23–24; see Chapter 12 on Boreas.

[15] Immerwahr, *Form and Thought in Herodotus*, 245–46. Cf. other Greek battles in Cyprus in 449 B.C. (Thucydides, 1.112) and at the Eurymedon (1.100); M. Yon, "Chypre entre la Grèce et la Perse: La conscience grecque de Chypre entre 530 et 330 a.C.,"

Ktema 6 (1981) 49–56. J. Wiesehöfer, "Zypern unter Persischer Herrschaft," in *Achaemenid History*, 5: *Centre and Periphery*. Proceedings of the 1986 Groningen Achaemenid History Workshop, ed. H. Sancisi-Weerdenburg and A. Kuhrt, (Leiden, 1990), 241–52. The presence of Phoenicians on Cyprus and in the Persian fleet here may have contributed to Athenian hostility toward Phoenicians (see Chapter 13): H. J. Watkin, "The Cypriote Surrender to Persia," *JHS* 107 (1987) 154–63.

completes the poet's formula with the inevitable allusion to slavery and its memory (5.109.3): "reminding themselves what they had suffered in slavery at the hands of the Medes" (ἀναμνησθέντας οἷα ἐπάσχετε δουλεύοντες πρὸς τῶν Μήδων). Despite these admonitions and reflections, the Ionians fall short of Athenian τόλμα (cf. 3.145.13, 7.135.1; Thucydides, 1.90.1.5; 2.40.3.2). The refusal of the Ionians and their failure against the Persians on land and sea could only highlight Athenian success at a second Salamis. Likewise, those Ionians who abandon the cause after defeat are an inversion of the Aiginetan transfer of loyalty at the last minute (8.70) and the eleventh-hour arrivals of smaller cities such as Tenos (8.82). When Herodotus describes the outcome in Cyprus as the "second enslavement of Cyprus" (5.116), he anticipates the image of the successive enslavements of Ionia (6.32: once by Lydia and twice by Persia). Moreover, the Cypriotes, having been liberated once, failed to retain their freedom in a second encounter: the Athenians, having won their freedom at Marathon, reinforce it at Salamis. The very word for such "enslavement," καταδουλεύεσθαι, is not attested before Herodotus; like its complement, ἐλευθερία, it belongs to the specialized rhetoric of the Persian wars.[16] This language is also already entangled with Athenian designs on its allies, which contaminates historical narratives of pre-Persian events like this one. Any account of Greek failure against Persia not only celebrates the Athenian achievement but reproaches other Greeks and, ultimately, justifies Athenian leadership among them.

These selected examples reflect a wider system of analogy between the literary construction of the Ionian revolt and the Athenian campaigns. This surfaces particularly in the way Herodotus stages debates in councils where advice is offered and ignored.[17] For example, Hekataios of Miletos was the only Ionian to dissent from a counsel of revolt against Persia in 499. However, he did advise them that their only means to success would be to become "masters of the sea," ναυκρατέες τῆς θαλάσσης (5.36), by seizing the treasury of Apollo at Didyma and converting it into funds for war. The Ionians ignored his advice, in both ways: they resolved to tackle an enemy to whom they were hopelessly inferior, and they failed to make themselves masters of the sea or seize the treasury. No Greek familiar with the Athenian experience with Persia could fail to recall the way Themistokles persuaded his fellow citizens to spend their silver on triremes and train a navy (7.144; cf. *Athenaion Politeia* 22; Plutarch, *Themistokles* 4). Later, Herodotus condemns Aristagoras for ignoring once again the advice of Hekataios (5.126). Instead of fortifying nearby Leros, a colony of Miletos, Aristagoras sailed to Myrkinos on the Strymon in Thrace, a doomed city (donated by Dareios and fortified by Histaios: 5.23), where he lost his life in accordance with a tragic pattern. The paradigm of the

[16] G. Nenci, *Introduzione alle guerre persiane* (Pisa, 1958) 36ff.; Kierdorf, *Erlebnis und Darstellung*, 41–42 n. 2. Raaflaub, *Entdeckung der Freiheit*, 102–8, "Das Aufkommen des politischen Freiheitsbegriff in den Perserkriegen."

[17] R. Lattimore, "The Wise Advisor in Herodotus," *CP* 34 (1939) 24–35; Immerwahr, *Form and Thought in Herodotus*, 73–75. Lang, *Historia* 17 (1968) 29.

wise adviser who is not heeded extends to Persian situations: Xerxes ignores the recommendation of Demaratos to fortify Kythera in order to invade Sparta (7.235), a tactic employed to good profit by Athens in 455 and 424 (Thucydides 4.53; Pausanias, 1.27.5). Patterns like these, articulated in tragedy and painting as well as history, inspired tableaus of the kind still popular in the fourth century. On the Darius krater, the Persian king hears a Greek giving advice, below personified figures of Hellas, Asia, and Apate (Deception) who represent what happened when Persia ignored Greek advice, perhaps in the course of the Ionian revolt (Figure 62).[18]

These Ionian consultations replay their first council on the Persian question at the Panionion sanctuary at Mykale, on the occasion of their "first enslavement" by Cyrus (1.170). Herodotus reports two plans counseled by two of the "Seven Sages" of the archaic Ionian world, both rejected. Bias of Priene proposes that the Ionians sail together to Sardinia, then claimed to be "the biggest island in the world," for the sake of freedom from subjugation but also prosperity and power—one of whose criteria apparently included ruling others from the largest island in the world. A certain analogy to the strategy of Themistokles—evacuation of Athens while trusting in their naval power—allows itself, and is expanded in the next council, where the island of Lade is chosen as a site for battle much as Salamis was in 480/79 B.C. Most Athenian of all is the proposal put forward by Thales of Miletos. He advises the Ionians to establish a single council (ἐν βουλευτήριον) at Teos, in the middle of Ionia, with the other cities to function as δῆμοι with some degree of local autonomy (μῆδεν ἦσσον νομίζεσθαι). This latter proposal is particularly evocative of the *synoikismos* of Attika attributed to Theseus, as expressed in classical language and implemented in the reforms of Kleisthenes.[19] Herodotus suggests that, from the beginning, the Ionians failed to establish the kind of democracy Athens did, hence their defeat by Persia. This implication is spelled out elsewhere as an equation between ἰσηγορίη, literally "equality to speak," and military success in Athenian history (Herodotus, 5.77).[20] In the prelude to this demonstration in Ionia, the lack of a constitutional equivalent to the Athenian council incorporating the demes of Attika is explained as a conscious refusal to adopt it.

The third council during the Ionian revolt sets the stage for a campaign like the Themistoklean one for Greece in 479 B.C. (6.7). The Ionian πρόβουλοι conceive a plan expressed as an Athenian decree (βουλευομένοισι ἔδοξε) and resembling the strategy of Athens before Salamis. First, they decide how to proceed by land (πεζὸν μέν): to defend their city (akropolis) not with men but with walls, much as the mistaken Athenians

---

[18] As argued by M. Schmidt, "Asia und Apate," in ΑΠΑΡΧΑΙ. *Nuovi ricerche e studi sulla Magna Grecia e la Sicilia Antica in onore di Paolo Enrico Arias*, ed. L. Beschi and others (Pisa, 1982), 2:505–20; see Chapter 13.

[19] E.g., Thucydides, 2.15.2; Plutarch, *Theseus* 24,

for ἐν πρυτανεῖον, ἐν βουλευτήριον. See Chapter 12.

[20] Y. Nakategawa, "*Isegoria* in Herodotus," *Historia* 38 (1988) 257–75, argues that this term does not mean "free[dom of] speech" until the late fifth century.

abandon their city to the "wooden walls" and a handful of defenders (7.140–43; 8.51–53). Coordinated with this action will be an Ionian campaign at sea: a naval expedition to a small nearby island, Lade, προναυμαχήσαντας τῆς Μιλήτου, just as the engagement at Salamis saved Athens. Meanwhile, exiled Ionian tyrants are dispatched by the Persians (intimidated by the size of the Ionian fleet) to win over the rebels (6.9.2–6.11), just as the Peisistratids attempt to extract a surrender from the Athenians (8.52.2). Even Dionysios, the Phokaian general, is cast as a forerunner of Themistokles. First, he rouses the Ionians with a stirring speech full of predictable phrases about the choice between freedom and slavery (6.11.2). Then he tries to train the Ionians at nautical maneuvers: after one grueling week, the Ionians mutiny, abandon their ships for life in tents, and refuse to take further orders. This demonstration of the inferiority of the Ionian character is staged as a deliberate contrast to the hardy heroism that "saved" Athens, and Greece; the connection between climate and character is one theme that devolves from the analysis of the Persian wars (Chapter 13). The Ionian rebellion encourages the desertion of the Samians to save their property (6.13), with the exception of eleven trireme crews who disobeyed their generals and hence were honored as ἄν-δρες ἀγαθοί with an inscribed stele in the Samian agora. This monument was presumably the source of this episode consulted by Herodotus, in the same way that Athenian commemorative monuments recording the city's performance against the Persians became historical documents (Chapter 12).

The entire episode, the battle of Lade, was a disgrace to the Greek nations of Ionia. Defeat by sea brought on the fall of Miletos, the slaughter of its male population, the enslavement of women and children, and the plundering of the very sacred treasury (Didyma) that Hekataios had advised the Ionians to save by converting it into war funds (Herodotus, 5.36). The capture of Miletos is followed by the council and escape of the Samians to Sicily (6.22–25), the occupation of Caria (6.25.2), the fall of Chios, Lesbos, and Tenedos in the next year, and mop-up campaigns around the Hellespont (6.31–43). Enter, Miltiades (6.34): with this figure, Herodotus introduces the next λόγος in his account, or the "second act" of the drama, which introduces Athens, the expedition of Dareios, and the campaigns under Mardonios that culminate in Marathon.

The fate of Miletos, and of Ionia, serves as backdrop for the account of the Persian encounter with Greece and Athens. Narrative devices such as speeches, councils, and oracles are deployed anew in an account rich in epic and tragic patterns. The explicit comparison of Ionia and Athens casts the Ionian revolt as a literary as well as political phenomenon and an inversion of the triumph of Athens. It also contributes to the rhetoric of Athenian imperialism: Ionian failure to resist Persia is exploited by Athens in its claim to leadership through a defensive alliance against that enemy. Both dimensions, literary and political, characterize Herodotus's closure of the Milesian disaster, with its explicit comparison between the lack of sympathy among the Sybarites for the fate of

Miletos and the emotional demonstration displayed by Athens (6.21). Sybaris failed to return kindness by mourning for Miletos, unlike the Ionian city's respect of a long-standing ξεινίη, after Kroton's capture of Sybaris in 510 B.C. In contrast to this insensitivity, says Herodotus in an informal asyndeton: "οὐδέν ὁμοίως καὶ Ἀθηναῖοι: "not so at all the Athenians" (in no way did the Athenians behave in a similar manner), which epitomizes the entire tone and purpose of the Ionian revolt as narrated by Herodotus. Here the Athenians, according to Herodotus, made their sympathy for Miletos clear in many ways (τῇ τε ἄλλῃ πολλαχῇ) but in particular (καὶ δὴ καὶ) in their response to the premiere of Phrynikhos's play *The Capture of Miletos*. This dramatic performance apparently reduced the audience to tears and provoked a fine against the playwright for "recalling their own misfortunes": ὡς ἀναμνήσαντα οἰκήια κακά. The play was banned from further performances by an Athenian decree and does not, in fact, appear in the standard lists of ancient dramas.[21]

The exact historical circumstances of this event are not specified by Herodotus. Its *terminus post quem* is clearly dictated by the destruction of Miletos in 494 B.C. and the most convenient date assigned to the production has been 493/2 B.C., the archonship of Themistokles, who served as *choregos* for another play by Phrynikhos in 476 B.C. (Plutarch, *Themistokles* 5). It has usually been assumed that this play was the *Phoenician Women*, which must have appeared before Aeschylus's *Persians* to account for its influence on the latter (see Chapter 13). However, the archonship of Themistokles is not necessary to the production of the *Capture of Miletos*, merely because he was *choregos* for another play by the same poet. Nor would the disaster have necessarily provoked an instant drama. Herodotus's use of ἀναμνήσαντα (6.21) suggests that more than a few months had elapsed since the disaster, and seven years passed before the battle of Salamis was commemorated in Aeschylus's *Persians*, without diminishing the immediacy of the drama. A far more likely setting for the *Capture of Miletos* and its unhappy reception would be the decade of the 470s, before the ostracism of Themistokles in 472. Although Herodotus offers this story as a demonstration of Athenian sympathy for Miletos, his expression οἰκήια κακά too clearly suggests the experiences of the Athenians themselves.[22] Instead, the play must have had a special poignancy for Athenians after the capture and destruction of their own akropolis by the same enemy, and after the

[21] On Phrynikhos, see G. Freymuth, "Zur ΜΙΛΗΤΟΥ ΑΛΩΣΙΣ des Phrynichus," *Philologus* 99 (1955) 51–69; H. Lloyd-Jones, "Problems of Early Greek Tragedy: Pratinas, Phrynichus, and the Early Gyges Fragment," in *Estudios sobre la tragedia griega*, Cuadernos de la Fundación Pastor 13. (Madrid, 1966), 11–33; J. Roisman, *Eranos* 86 (1988) 15–23.

[22] The meaning of οἰκήια is disputed since antiquity: e.g. Isokrates, 4.76: "They mourned as if for their own" (ἐκήδοντο μέν ὡς οἰκείων), but cf. Ammianus Marcellinus, 28.1.3–4. Modern renderings: "their own misfortunes" (Rawlinson), or "a disaster which touched them so closely" (de Selincourt), or simply "related" (Kierdorf, *Erlebnis und Darstellung*, 118 n. 2). Only J. Roisman, *Eranos* 86 (1988) 17–19, realizes that "their own" means the play must postdate 480/79 B.C.

death and enslavement of their own citizens at Persian hands.[23] The capture of Miletos would have the same effect on an Athenian audience as the fall of Troy, which preoccupied painters and poets in the decades after the Persians burnt Athens (Chapter 12). In this interpretation, οἰκήιος would refer to the events of 480 and 479 B.C., to Athenian misfortunes proper, not to "related" ones suffered by Miletos after Athens had left the Ionian revolt. [24] In other words, the dramatic commemoration of the capture of Miletos drew its effect from events experienced in Athens, just as the narrative of the Ionian revolt draws its meaning from Athenian resistance. The effect of Milesian defeat on Athens is a fitting conclusion, not to mention one literally dramatic, for this narrative, and links the fortunes of the two Greek cities in a pattern intended to demonstrate their differences. Ninety years later, a Milesian poet, Timotheos, returns the compliment to Athens with a lyric poem on the battle of Salamis, performed and reperformed at Greek festivals.[25]

In Herodotus's quest for the moral causes of Greek victory, Ionia, like Lydia, offered opportunities for dramatic demonstrations of failure on a moral plane, disregard for divine retribution (φθόνος), and inability to negotiate democracy. Not until after the repute earned by Athenians and others at Salamis and Plataia reached Asia were the Greeks in Ionia able to defeat the Persians in their own territory (Herodotus, 9.90–105). The Ionian revolt succeeded only at the battle of Mykale, but to the credit of the Athenians, who excelled among Greeks, as Herodotus narrates it (9.105: ἐν δὲ ταύτῃ τῇ μάχῃ Ἑλλήνων ἠρίστευσαν Ἀθηναῖοι). This battle, too, may have figured in a play by Phrynikhos, according to fragments quoted in a papyrus commentary to Homer and assigned to a speech in the Phoenician Women.[26] An account of the battle could have been narrated in a messenger speech toward the end of the play, if the juxtaposition between the disaster at Miletos and its vindication at Mykale formed a dramatic contrast long before Herodotus. The historian synchronizes Mykale and Plataia through their occur-

[23] Thus, e.g., Pollitt, in Greek Art: Archaic into Classical, 103; Nenci Introduzione, 30 n. 21, locates the play in the decade after Marathon, such that οἰκήια κακά recalls the misfortunes of the first Persian invasion. R. J. Lenardon, The Saga of Themistocles (London, 1978), 38, 105, identifies Phrynikhos's Phoenician Women as the (papyrus) title of the play Herodotus knew, and dates the play to 476/5 B.C.

[24] The revival of such a memory as a political tactic could be appropriate to the climate of Themistoklean Athens, after the battle of Salamis and in the early days of the Delian League: cf. W. G. Forrest, "Themistocles and Argos," CQ 54 (1960) 235; E. Badian, "Archons and Strategoi," Antichthon 5 (1971) 15–16 n. 44. However, Themistokles' role in the production

and his political motives remain theoretical: F. Frost, Plutarch's Themistocles: A Historical Commentary (Princeton, 1980), 76; J. Roisman, Eranos 86 (1988) 19–20, argues for a social and cultural suppression of the play, not a political one.

[25] On Timotheos's Persians (Papyrus Berlin, 9865: Page, PMG, frag. 791), see Francis, in Ancient Persia, 53–86, esp. 77–81; Herington, Poetry into Drama, chap. 7.

[26] PapOxy II, 1899, nr. 221, col. III, 2.4ff. (from Ammonios's commentary to Iliad 12); F. Marx, "Der Tragiker Phrynichus," RhM 77 (1928) 352, 355–60; F. Stoessl, "Die Phoinissen des Phrynichos und die Perser des Aischylos," MH 2 (1945) 158–61.

rence on the same day (9.101), a dramatic improbability formulaic since the first such simultaneous Athenian victory (in 506 B.C.: 5.77) and which linked East and West through the defeat of barbarians at Himera and Salamis on the same day (7.166; see Chapter 13 on the symmetry of Greek victories in Sicily and Greece). In addition to linking East and West in space, and Miletos with Mykale through time, Herodotus concludes his work with an overt revelation of nascent Athenian imperialism, and the next war. The oaths of allegiance sworn after Mykale, for example (9.106.4), anticipate those taken in the following year to inaugurate the Delian League (Chapter 12). The last λόγος of the Persian wars engages the first conflict of the Pentekontaetia. The "liberation of allies" abroad through Athenian action, rather than the Spartan victory of Plataia, ends the investigation of Herodotus, and opens the story of an Athenian-led alliance in the Aegean.[27]

This final episode is rendered more dramatic not only by the synchronism of the battles but in divine manifestations (the herald's wand, the protection of Demeter: 9.100, 101) and in the deliberate imagery contrasting land and sea, Athens versus Sparta. Although these narrative devices are often attributed to tragedy, careful analysis has shown how elusive is the influence of tragedy often presumed at work in the histories of Herodotus.[28] In truth, tragedy and history acquired similar patterns at the same time and for the same reasons, which make "comparison" unnecessary. The writing of history, as it first appeared in the work of Herodotus, and the structure of classical tragedy were both determined by their subject matter, the Persian wars. For the former, Robert Drews's analysis of Herodotus pinpointed this fact as the most crucial distinction between his work and that of his predecessors:[29]

> The Persian Wars inspired a number of literary efforts which described, interpreted, and glorified the wars as the climax of a Great Event. The conclusion is inescapable that the authors of the early *Persica* were motivated by the Great Event which they or their fathers had

[27] Immerwahr, *Form and Thought in Herodotus*, 287–303, on the parallelism of Plataia and Mykale and the structure of this last *logos*. Cf. P. Gauthier, "Le parallèle Himère—Salamine au Vème et IVème siècle av. J-C.," *REA* 68 (1966) 5–31. Balcer, *Sparda by the Bitter Sea*, 272–81, on the origins of Athenian imperialism in the last expeditions against the Persians (Mykale, Sestos); Raaflaub, *Entdeckung der Freiheit*, 105–6.

[28] A. Lesky, "Tragödien bei Herodot?" in *Greece and the Eastern Mediterranean: Studies Presented to Fritz Schachermeyr on the Occasion of his Eightieth Birthday*, ed. K. H. Kinzl (Berlin, 1977), 224–30; Chiasson, "Tragic Influence on Herodotus," demonstrates how limited and specific was such influence; cf. his "Tragic Diction in Herodotus: Some Possibilities,"

Phoenix 36 (1982) 156–61; T. Long, *Repetition and Variation in the Short Stories of Herodotus* (Frankfurt, 1987), 176–92, "Tragic Narrative and Herodotean Narrative"; Immerwahr, *Form and Thought in Herodotus*, 12, emphasizes the innovation of Herodotus's narrative, which he claims antedates dramatic and rhetorical patterns, but admits tragic structures in parts (pp. 71, 101, 183).

[29] Drews, *Greek Accounts of Eastern History*, 36; Cf. F. Jacoby, "Griechische Geschichtsschreibung," *Die Antike* 2 (1926) 1–29, esp. 11–15, on how the Persian wars gave the work of Herodotus its unity; L. Pearson, *The Local Historians of Attica* (Westport, Conn., 1972) 148.

witnessed . . . if the earliest Greek accounts of Eastern history were inspired by the Persian Wars, is it not possible that Greek historiography as such was the result of the Persian Wars?

He concludes (pp. 42, 43) that the confrontation with Persia represents "an event so monumental, so historic that it demanded literary commemoration. The early *Persica*, like the *Phoenician Women* of Phrynikhos and the *Persians* of Aeschylus, are inconceivable without the Persian Wars. . . . Greek historiography was, in a real sense, a result of history itself."

But ἱστορίη, "inquiry," was pursued in poetry as it was in prose, and through myth as well as history. The unexpected result of the Persian challenge demanded an explanation, and historians and tragedians alike sought it in human error as much as in heroism. Long before Herodotus applied this tragic pattern to his account of the fall of Lydia, Ionia, and Persia, his subjects had become figures in art and drama. As Herington remarked, the "so-called historical tragedies" (e.g., *Persians* and *Phoenician Women*) hardly represent an extraordinary choice of subject matter, for the unexpected victories were nothing short of miraculous, and entered the realm of myth instantly.[30] The explanatory function that mythology already played in Greek thought made it an adjunct of historiography, such that the Greek experience of history readily took place through myth, and required no extra effort to imagine the one in terms of the other.

The convergence of patterns in tragedy and history is especially vivid in their focus on the figure of a tragic hero, in the form of a king. The Greek image of a tyrant, or great man, and his downfall, was inspired by the fortunes of Kroisos, Dareios, and Xerxes.[31] Lydian, then Persian wealth and power failed in action, and the mystery of that failure not only raised the question of how it happened, but, once a moral conclusion was drawn, how Lydia and Persia had managed to survive so long without failure: "Why was Dareios so long unharmed?" (τίπτε Δαρεῖος μέν οὐ καὶ τότ᾽ ἀβλαβὴς ἐπῆν; Aeschylus, *Persians* 555). The implications of these questions led to Greek portraits of tyrants with Persian attributes. In Aeschylus's *Agamemnon*, the beacon fires that bring the news of Troy's fall to Argos trace a Persian signal route and even bear a Persian name (ἄγγαρος: 282), matching Herodotus's account of the same route and word (ἀγγαρήιον: 8.53–54; 8.98).[32] This dramatic device casts the victorious returning general

---

[30] Herington, *Poetry into Drama*, 129; pp. 65–71 on "The Forests of Myths." Hall, *Inventing the Barbarian*, 62–76.

[31] Immerwahr, *Form and Thought in Herodotus*, 154–88, on the Eastern ruler and his fate; Chiasson, "Tragic Influence on Herodotus," 200–5; W. Burkert, "Demaratos, Astrabakos und Herakles: Königsmythen und Politik zur Zeit der Perserkriege (Herodot 6, 67–69)," *MH* 22 (1965) 166–77. L. Roller, "The Greek View of Anatolia," in *Ancient Greek and Related*

Pottery, 260–63. S. Borzsák, "Persertum und griechisch-römische Antike. Zur Ausgestaltung des klassischen Tyrannenbildes," *Gymnasium* 94 (1987) 289–97. Hartog, *Mirror of Herodotus*, 335–37, on tragedy and history, and 310–70, esp. 322–39, on the portrayal of power. S. Flory, *The Archaic Smile of Herodotus* (Detroit, 1988), 84–87. Hall, *Inventing the Barbarian*, 93–98, 205–10.

[32] S. Tracy, "Darkness from Light: The Beacon Fire in the Agamemnon," *CQ* 36 (1986) 257–60; Hall, *In-*

in the light of Medism, also suggested in the Oriental, purple carpet offered by his wife as part of the "trap" he tries to escape (*Agamemnon* 905–29). If history recasts mythology at the same time as legends became part of history, the tragic view of history also determines historiography. The image of the Persian king is even tarnished in the Near East after his treatment in Greek hands.[33]

Those figures that exemplify a tragic pattern in Herodotus—Kroisos, most prominently—were already the subject of poetry in the early classical period and popular in contemporary art. A famous amphora by Myson depicts the Lydian king on the pyre (Figure 37 left, right), whose juxtaposition with Theseus carrying off an Amazon on the reverse will be examined in Chapter 12; a similar scene with an Oriental king survives on a fragmentary red-figure hydria from Corinth, dated somewhere between 470 and 450 B.C.[34] On both vases, an artist depicted the moment when Kroisos remembers the words of Solon, according to Herodotus (1.86), and is saved by Apollo (or Zeus, according to Bacchylides). Decades before Herodotus told the story of Kroisos, the Lydian king must have inspired an early tragedy, and such a drama survives in a papyrus fragment with an episode from the Mermnad dynasty's rise to power through Gyges, also narrated by Herodotus (1.6–12). Scholarly opinion has divided on the date of this drama since its discovery in 1950; originally assumed to precede Herodotus, it also has been attributed to the Hellenistic period, and no firm evidence has settled the date.[35] The vase paintings, alone, indicate the existence of early classical dramas about the Lydian dynasty, independent of an early date for the Gyges fragment.

The medium of such dramas—whether in painting, poetry, or history—is secondary to their substance, the historical events that inspired artistic commemoration. The historical experience of such figures—wealthy, powerful—who failed against the Persians when the Athenians succeeded first suggested a tragic pattern to the Greek imagination. What is implicit on the Myson amphora (Figure 37 left, right), with its contrast between a Lydian king who lost to the Persians (Kroisos) and the legendary king of a city that won (Theseus), is explicit in the histories of Herodotus, or a comparison made

---

venting the Barbarian, 93; Francis, *Image and Idea in Fifth-Century Athens*, 33–35.

[33] As observed by A. Kuhrt, "The Achaemenid Empire: A Babylonian Perspective," *PCPhS* 214 (1988) 66–68.

[34] Myson amphora: Louvre G 197, from Vulci (*ARV* 238, 1), dated variously between 500 and 480 and associated with historical events such as the capture of Miletos, the burning of Sardis, etc. Hölscher, *Griechische Historienbilder*, 30–31. Hydria from Corinth: J. Beazley, *Hesperia* 24 (1955) 305–19; D. Page, "An Early Tragedy on the Fall of Croesus?" *PCPhS* 8 (1962) 47–49. N. Hammond and W. Moon, "Illustra-

tions of Early Tragedy at Athens," *AJA* 82 (1978) 371–83; Boardman, in *Eye of Greece*, 15–16.

[35] *PapOxy* 2382: E. Lobel, "A Greek Historical Drama," *PBA* 35 (1950) 207–16; D. Page, *A New Chapter in the History of Greek Tragedy* (Cambridge, 1951); H. Lloyd-Jones, "The Gyges Fragment: A New Possibility," *PCPhS* 182 (1952–1953) 36–43; A. Lesky, "Das hellenistische Gyges-Drama," *Hermes* 81 (1953) 1–10. For a summary of the controversy, see Chiasson, "Tragic Influence on Herodotus," 239–48, with fuller bibliography in Holzberg, "Zur Datierung der Gyges-Tragödie, POxy 2382," *ZAnt* 23 (1973) 273–86.

by Bacchylides. In his ode for Hieron of Syrakuse's quadriga victory at Olympia in 476 B.C. (cf. Pindar, *Olympian* 1), the poet praises not only the tyrant's horses but his dedications at Delphi (3.1–23). A formula (ἐπεί ποτε καί) introduces another horse tamer (δαμασίππος), who lost Sardis to the Persians despite his "golden sword" and the patronage of Apollo. On his funeral pyre, the Lydian king calls on Apollo and is saved by the rain of Zeus (55–58, probably a tribute to the chief deity of Olympia, context of Hieron's victory, rather than an "intrusion" or contradiction of Herodotus, 1.87). Apollo rescues Kroisos in recognition of his εὐσέβεια, his generosity in gifts to Delphi. Kroisos's fate as captive advisor to the Persian king is tactfully omitted by Bacchylides, as is the role of Solon in his final appeal to Apollo, unlike the Herodotean version, which includes the Athenian figure of Solon. These discrepancies do not dilute the main point: Kroisos has become a symbol of fallen fortune and the qualities attributed to Greek tyrants in the decade following the defeat of Persia, when historical plays by Phrynikhos and Aeschylus were popular.[36]

On Myson's amphora and in the Athenian imagination, the fate of Kroisos balances the figure of Theseus, just as the defeat of Ionia exaggerates the success of Athens. The wealth of Kroisos and his relationship to Apollo won him the admiration of contemporary Greeks, including aristocratic Athenians who named their sons after him (e.g., the Anavyssos kouros). The failure of that wealth in the face of Persia made the Athenian achievement all the more remarkable, and became a formula beyond the political arena. By the time Aristotle analyzes the nature of the tragic "plot," it is epitomized in the change of fortunes of a single man: virtuous or wicked, ὄλβιος or wretched, he experiences a change from good or bad fortune to the opposite condition (*Poetics* 1453a1). Even the character favored by Aristotle, the μέτριον who falls between the extremes of good and evil, must be a man of great repute and prosperity, a "conspicuous man." The more distinguished the man, the more spectacular his failure; the lesson of Lydia's defeat is delivered by Solon in Herodotus, but adapted to flatter a Greek tyrant by Bacchylides, who still emphasizes the power of wealth, not wisdom.

These patterns explored in painting, poetry, and history are all responses to a new historical experience that demanded new cultural expressions. No examples of historical and dramatic literature prior to the Persian wars survive, but one doubts that they would demonstrate these patterns before the powerful influence of history.[37] In art,

[36] A. H. Smith, "Illustrations to Bacchylides," *JHS* 18 (1898) 276–80; C. P. Segal, "Croesus on the Pyre: Herodotus and Bacchylides," *WS* 5 (1971) 39–51 (although he believes that the Myson amphora is "probably some thirty years prior to *Ode* 3"). B. Snell, "Gyges und Kroisos als Tragödien-Figuren," *ZPE* 12 (1973) 204–5. J.A.S. Evans, "What Happened to Croesus?" *CJ* 74 (1978) 34–40; J. Péron, "Les mythes de Crésus et de Méléagre dans les Odes III et V de Bacchylide," *REG* 9 (1978) 307–39. Hall, *Inventing the Barbarian*, 65.

[37] As maintained by Else, *Origins and Early Form of Greek Tragedy*, 101–2; B. Knox, "Literature," in *Athens Comes of Age: From Solon to Salamis*, ed. W. Childs (Princeton, 1978), 48; Hurwit, *Art and Culture of Early Greece*, 355.

however, both novel forms and older ones survive, with the transition from archaic to classical thought more vividly etched (Chapter 12). In no medium was the impact of the Persian wars instantaneous, but it evolved through newly crafted forms and ideas. Thus the epic tradition provided one source for praise in poetry (the poems and epigrams attributed to Simonides) and in its prose equivalent (the opening λόγοι of Herodotus's histories), but the public commemoration of victory occasioned new vehicles of praise.

In the early λόγοι, the narrative of Herodotus preserves a closer relationship with the age of Aeschylus, in its admiration of Oriental kingship and culture and its patterns of early classical tragedy. It is the later portions of his work, devoted to the achievement of Athens, that display the language of public oration and the propaganda for Athenian hegemony characteristic of the eulogy of Athens. The term οἱ Ἀθηναῖοι, for example, loses its general function and becomes a specific reference to Athenian democracy and the *demos* of Athens.[38] The source of such language emerges in the catalogue of Athenian ἔργα ("deeds") recited just before Plataia, an argument for the privilege of a right-wing position in battle (9.27). Athenian deeds of long ago are praised with citations from epic history (the Herakleidai, Seven against Thebes, the Amazons), including the city's conspicuously modest role in the Trojan War (οὐδαμῶν ἐλειπόμεθα: "We fell short of none"). Finally, all these are dismissed as well known and remote (παλαιῶν μέν νυν ἔργων ἅλις ἔστω): the Athenian performance at Marathon, alone, has earned them the honor (γέρας) they currently seek. In that battle, the Athenians now claim that they alone fought against the Persians (μοῦνοι Ἑλλήνων δὴ μουνομαχήσαντες τῷ Πέρσῃ), a boast contradicted by Herodotus's own account of the battle where the Plataians fought with distinction on the right wing (6.108, 113; 7.10). As noted by many, the language and tone of this "catalogue" recall public rhetoric of post-Persian Athens, in particular the speech inaugurated by the state, the ἐπιτάφιος λόγος or public funeral oration devoted to those fallen in battle, where a catalogue of deeds drawn from mythical history became a traditional element.[39] In between these two poles of praise—the post-Persian era and the Periklean age of public oration—lies the uncharted territory of the Pentakontaetia. Thucydides abbreviates the ellipse between his work and his predecessors' with a brief summary (1.18–19):

The whole period from the Median War to this, with some peaceful intervals was spent by each power in war, either with its rival, or with its own revolted allies, and consequently

---

[38] Immerwahr, *Form and Thought in Herodotus*, 119 n. 126, on the language of the Athenian λόγος; Loraux, *Invention of Athens*, 192–93. Walser, *Hellas und Iran*, 8 n. 22, on Athenian passages in Herodotus (collected by W. Schmid and O. Stählin, *Geschichte der griechischen Literatur* [Munich, 1934], I. 2:585) with a more pronounced bias against barbarians.

[39] W. West, *GRBS* 11 (1970) 274–75; Kierdorf, *Erlebnis und Darstellung*, 97–100, on the speech at Plataia; Loraux, *Invention of Athens*, 60–75; Rosivach, *CQ* 37 (1987) 303–4.

afforded them constant practice in military matters, and that experience which is learnt in the school of war.

It is during this fifty-year period that all three surviving playwrights were active in Athens, when major temples were initiated, built, or embellished in Athens, Olympia, and Aigina, that new art forms like the ἐπιτάφιος λόγος and historical painting became public and familiar. Most visible of these testimonia were monuments commemorating historical events and which functioned as their historical records. For example, Herodotus's description of the battle of Marathon, and the catalogue of deeds recited at Plataia, both derived from autopsy of the paintings in the Stoa Poikile. Commemorative statues in bronze and related inventions in statuary (e.g., herms, portraits) developed directly from military occasions, to make new heroes for Athens. Finally, what inspired the content of many of these new art forms was a new world of ideology, both political and mythological. For if history became manifest in monuments, it also created a new kind of intangible monument, ἔργον as the commemoration of deeds through words.[40] Only the integrated study of these cultural forms is possible: missing links in cycles of myth appear in vase paintings, lost speeches are reflected in poetry or history, while mural paintings where myth mimed history must be pursued in partial reflections and descriptions. It was this fertile period in classical Athens that transformed the figure of Daidalos into an Athenian hero, and his metamorphosis must be traced throughout these forms.

ERGON: HISTORY AND MONUMENT

κλεινὸν ἐλευθερίας τεύχων μέγαν Ἑλλάδι κόσμον . . .

Building a famous monument of freedom, a great honour for Hellas . . .

—Timotheos, *Persians* frag. 788 (Page)

εἶτα διδάξας Πέρσας μετὰ τοῦτ᾽ ἐπιθυμεῖν ἐξεδίδαξα
νικᾶν ἀεὶ τοὺς ἀντιπάλους, κοσμήσας ἔργον ἄριστον.

Then, producing *The Persians* after this, I taught the desire
ever to vanquish one's enemies, embellishing a great deed.

—Aeschylus in Aristophanes, *Frogs* 1026–27

[40] Immerwahr, *AJP* 81 (1960) 261–90; Loraux, *Invention of Athens*, chaps. 3, 6.

The historiography of the Persian wars was more instantly and lavishly articulated in monuments than in words. During the early classical decades, between the Persian and Peloponnesian (Archidamian) wars, commemorative monuments, personal portraiture, and historical painting were virtually invented in a specific historical context and for specific historical purposes, and collaborated in new ways. This section will examine those media in terms of their origins, as a prelude to tracing those aspects of cult and myth that accompanied the new media.

The commemoration of the Persian wars began on the battlefields. One hundred ninety-two Athenians fell at Marathon and were buried on the spot (αὐτοῦ: Thucydides, 2.34.6), a visible reward of their ἀρετή ("excellence") worthy of legendary heroes (Herodotus, 1.30.5) and an instant monument.[41] After Plataia, Greeks were buried according to their city (Herodotus, 9.85), and their tombs became the focus of later ceremonies (Plutarch, *Aristeides*, 19–21; Thucydides, 3.58). In addition to monument and ceremony, celebration in verse commemorated these new heroes, beginning with an epitaph competition after Marathon, won by Simonides (*Life of Aesop* 8). The name of Simonides is connected with at least twenty epigrams, preserved in quotations and on stone, composed for those fallen in the battles of the Persian wars.[42] This surfeit of honors—in monument, cult, and literature—contributed to the "radical re-interpretation of traditional historical terminology and imagery" that inaugurated a new era in Greek culture.[43] The visible afterlife of victory, in the form of public monuments and commemorative ceremonies, kept history alive as a political and intellectual influence.

After the booty was viewed, portions of the spoils, chiefly armor and ships or trophies made from them, were dedicated at Panhellenic sanctuaries, according to ancient accounts and modern discoveries.[44] While a number of these dedications were traditional in Greek warfare, the Persian wars were commemorated in novel forms, whose impact on related arts was rapid and irrevocable. After the battle of Salamis, the most spectacular booty dedicated to the gods included three Phoenician ships, two for Poseidon's sanctuaries at Sounion and at Isthmia, and one to Ajax, local hero of the battle site (Herodotus, 8.121.1). The Akropolis may have displayed one, too, if a set of marble blocks inscribed with an Athenian dedication ἐκ τ[ῶν Μηδῶν] once held such a ship.[45]

[41] N. Robertson, *EchCl* 27 (1983) 78–92. Clairmont, *Patrios Nomos*, 16–23.

[42] C. M. Bowra, *Early Greek Elegists* (Cambridge, 1938) 173–203; A. Raubitschek, "Two Monuments Erected after the Victory of Marathon," *AJA* 44 (1940) 56–59; D. Page, *Epigrammata Graeca* (Oxford, 1975), 10–19; Kierdorf *Erlebnis und Darstellung*, 16–29; W. West, *GRBS* 11 (1970) 271–82; Svenbro, *La parole et le marbre*, 116–35.

[43] Immerwahr, *AJP* 81 (1960), 281. Cf. P. Amandry, "Athènes au lendemain des guerres médiques," *RUB* 14 (1961) 198–223.

[44] Herodotus, 8.121–22; 9.86; Pausanias, 10.19.4; Gauer, *Weihgeschenke*, 21–44; W. West, *CP* 64 (1969) 7–19.

[45] Raubitschek, *Dedications from the Athenian Acropolis*, 198ff. no. 172; Dinsmoor, in Χαριστήριον, 145–55; Gauer, *Weihgeschenke*, 73.

In light of the personal confrontation between Athenians and Phoenicians at the battle and in intellectual history (Chapter 13), these monuments functioned as visual reminders of the chief Eastern opponent at sea. First fruits of the captured booty from the naval victory were sent to Apollo at Delphi, in the form of a statue holding the akroterion of a ship.[46] Representations of gods—particularly Athena, Poseidon, and Nike—holding naval trophies like the ἄφλαστον, become common on early classical vases (Figure 42). Such an image became an emblem of Athenian naval victory, appropriate for later campaigns as at the Eurymedon; the personification of "Salamis" holds an ἄφλαστον facing "Hellas," in one of the paintings by Panainos surrounding the statue of Zeus at Olympia.[47]

After the battle of Plataia, monumental statues were dedicated at Panhellenic sanctuaries, including a bronze Zeus at Olympia and one of Poseidon at Isthmia (Herodotus, 8.81). A tithe was reserved for Delphi and made into the famous golden tripod astride the bronze column of a snake's coils ending in three heads, probably as protomes around the tripod's bowl.[48] The inspiration for this monument was Oriental, in more ways than one. Extravagant metal cauldrons with animal heads adorned Greek sanctuaries since the eighth century, and had already been imitated by Greek artists since the seventh.[49] A specific version of the column made of entwined snakes appears on an Elamite seal of the Late Bronze Age, where it supports a seated snake-god before a worshiper.[50] The motif joins those found in Bronze Age glyptic of the Near East that resurface in Greek Iron Age art (Figures 15, 16), but here it contributes to a symbol of Greek triumph over the Near East, perhaps conceived as a deliberately ironic tribute to the East. The bronze column was one of the monuments taken to Byzantion by the emperor Constantine for his new Hellenic capital, where it experienced another ironic trick of history. For the monument now belongs to Greece's latter-day Oriental conquerors; it has remained in Istanbul, its golden snakes intact until 1700 in Ottoman miniatures (Figure 40).[51]

[46] A. Jacquemin and D. Laroche, "Une base pour l'Apollon de Salamine à Delphes," BCH 112 (1988) 235–46, on base and inscription.

[47] Here on a red-figure lekythos by the Brygos Painter, from Gela: New York 25.189.1; Hausmann, in Charites, 144–51. Völcker-Janssen, Boreas 10 (1987) 16–17, 28, on the Olympia painting and its symbolism.

[48] Herodotus, 8.81. Gauer, Weihgeschenke, 75–92, pls. 1–4. The most convincing reconstruction remains that of B. Ridgway, "The Plataean Tripod and the Serpent Column," AJA 81 (1977) 374–79; cf. Amandry, BCH 111 (1987) 102–15; D. Laroche, "Nouvelles observations sur l'offrande de Platées," BCH 113

(1989) 183–98.

[49] U. Jantzen, Griechische Greifenkessel (Berlin, 1955), pls. 49, 58. A Phoenician gilded cauldron with serpent handles of the type found in the Bernardini tomb at Tarquinia is imitated on a Protoattic amphora: Morris, Black and White Style, 44 n. 32, pl. 6.

[50] R. D. Barnett, "The Serpent-headed Tripod Base," in Michael Avi-Yonah Memorial Volume, ed. D. Barag, G. Foerster, and A. Neger, Eretz-Israel 19 (Jerusalem, 1987), 1; the seal belonged to Ishme-Karab-ilu of Susa and dates around 1600 B.C.

[51] The column signified the topography of Istanbul, as in these two sixteenth-century festival scenes now in the Topkapi Museum, where it appears next

What made the monument Greek were the names of thirty-one city-states inscribed on eleven coils of the serpent-column, a roster of those who chose to defend Greece rather than Medize.[52] Two of the names—those of the Tenians and the Siphnians—were added later, to respect their last-minute embrace of the Greek cause (at Salamis: Herodotus, 8.82). The Tenian ἔργον ("deed") was visible on an actual ἔργον ("work of art"), and the monument served as an official roster of allegiance. States whose names were inscribed claimed themselves among those "who had played an active part in the war," as Tenos eventually did (Plutarch, *Themistokles* 20), and defended themselves on the basis of the monument (e.g., at Plataia: Thucydides 3.57.2). The Plataian tripod also inspired twin monuments nearby, erected on similar occasions. Two Sicilian tyrants, Gelon and Hieron of Syrakuse, dedicated bronze tripods to the right (north) of the temple approach at Delphi to commemorate their Western victory over an Oriental (Punic) enemy, as if in deliberate juxtaposition to a mainland monument for a similar victory.[53] Thus the confrontation between Greek and Eastern enemies, in which Punic and Phoenician forces played a primary role, was visible in complementary monuments.

None of the commemorative statues described in historical sources has survived, but others that have indicate significant changes in design and style in the early classical period. The striding bronze male brandishing a lost weapon, rescued from the sea off Artemision, epitomizes this early classical style of the decades after the Persian wars (Figure 41). Whether identified as Poseidon wielding a missing trident, or Zeus (Soter) hurling a lost thunderbolt, he is readily associated with the events that destroyed the Persian fleet near the cape where he was discovered.[54] The circumstances that assisted the Greek cause at Artemision were commemorated in a cult of Boreas at Athens (Herodotus, 7. 189; see Chapter 12) and associated with other gods like Artemis Proseoa (Plutarch, *Themistokles* 8.4). Thus storm and battle belong to those events that transformed cult and iconography. Even without a specific identity, the bronze god expresses divine action, perhaps against an enemy. His pose is traditional since the Geometric figure and derives, with the usual irony, from an Oriental statuette type, the "smiting god" (see Chapter 5, n. 35). Like the serpent column, this early classical version becomes a symbol of West overcoming East, in this case suggesting the principle

---

to the obelisk also still visible in the Hippodrome. V.-L. Menage, "The Serpent-Column in Ottoman Sources," *AnatStud* 14 (1964) 169–73; N. Atasoy, "The Documentary Values of the Ottoman Miniatures," in *Mélanges Mansel*, ed. E. Akurgal and U. B. Alkim (Ankara, 1974), 2:749–55, pl. 252a.

[52] Tod, *GHI*, 22–24 no. 19; ML, 57–60 no. 27; Jeffery, *LSAG*, 102, no. 15, pl. 13. Gauer, *Weihgeschenke*, 92–96.

[53] Amandry, *BCH* 111 (1987) 79–131, esp. on the Deinomenid tripod; see n. 27, on the synchronization of victories in Greece and Sicily.

[54] Bronze Poseidon: Ridgway, *Severe Style*, 62–64; figs. 98, 99; R. Wünsch, "Der Gott aus dem Meer," *JdI* 94 (1977) 77–111; Artemision storm sent by Boreas: Herodotus, 7.188–91; Zeus Soter: 7.192. Battle: Plutarch, *Themistokles* 8 (celebrated by Pindar, frag. 77, and Simonides, frag. 109: Kierdorf, *Erlebnis und Darstellung*, 39).

of divine φθόνος at work in history (Herodotus, 8.109.3). The radical break with pre-classical postures in statuary may have had more to do with the effect of history on human images of the divine, than with preoccupations in style, as will be examined. Figures like the Artemision god belong to the same era and spirit as the bronze Athena ("Promachos") by Pheidias dedicated on the Akropolis. This was the largest victory dedication in Athens, before the Akropolis building program was launched after 450 B.C.[55] The statue can be dated near the middle of the century from inscribed financial accounts, but its appearance can only be surmised from ancient reports and representations. The tip of the statue's spear still impressed those sailing from Sounion, in the second century A.D. (Pausanias, 1.28.2). Like the Artemision Zeus/Poseidon, this armed Athena was a transformation of a miniature votive type, popular in archaic statuettes and on vase painting, into a monument. Both bronzes represent gods in action with weapons, as they appeared in battle against Persians in the Athenian imagination. Details of Athena's decoration, such as the Centaurs fighting Lapiths on her shield, become formulaic themes in classical art. And like the group of statues to be examined shortly, the Athena Promachos, as the work of Pheidias, links his name and formative development as a sculptor with commemorative monuments of the Persian wars.

Anonymous but inscribed is a second major dedication from the Akropolis which commemorates the Persian wars. A marble figure of a Nike (Victory) on an Ionic column of the same material is inscribed on two flutes with a dedication commemorating Kallimachos, the Athenian polemarch who fell at Marathon (Figure 43).[56] The fragments of the statue indicate a draped figure running right, whose details influence the chronology of red-figure vase painting. Her pose breaks stride, literally, with archaic running winged figures, while her dress suggests that "late archaic" conventions in vase painting outlast the Persian wars. The closest relatives of the Nike's drapery belong to the red-figure painters of the Leagros period, and cannot be contemporary with the earliest Severe Style artists.[57] Along with the Athenian treasury at Delphi, reconciled to its

[55] H.-G. Niemeyer, *Promachos* (Berlin, 1960), esp. 75–86; Gauer, *Weihgeschenke*, 103–5. Meiggs, *Athenian Empire*, 94–95, 416–17, dates it to 460/59. P. Demargne, "Athena," *LIMC* II.1, 118–73; cf. 969–74, 1020.

[56] Raubitschek, *Dedications from the Athenian Acropolis*, 13; Gauer, *Weihgeschenke*, 53, 115–17. The inscription (now *IG* I³ 784) indicates a posthumous dedication by his deme, Aphidna: B. Shefton, "The Dedication of Callimachus, IG I² 609," *BSA* 45 (1950) 140–64, and "The Dedication of Callimachus: A Supplement," *BSA* 47 (1952) 278, in response to E. Fraenkel, "A Marathon Epigram," *Eranos* 49 (1951) 63–64.

E. B. Harrison, "The Victory of Kallimachos," *GRBS* 12 (1972) 5–24, restores μν[ῆμα δ' ἀρετῆς] in the last line, language evocative of history and epigraphy relating to the Persian wars.

[57] M. Brouskari, *The Acropolis Museum* (Athens, 1974), 125–26, figs. 239–40; Gauer, *Weihgeschenke*, 51, 63, 115–17. Hurwit, *Art and Culture of Early Greece*, 324, figs. 140, 141. Chronology: A. B. Follmann, *Der Panmaler* (Bonn, 1968), 22–23; J. Kleine, *Untersuchungen zur Chronologie der attischen Kunst von Peisistratos bis Themistokles*, IstMitt Beiheft 8 (1973) 116–19. R. Tölle-Kastenbein, *AA* (1983) 581 (see n. 91).

proper date after the battle of Marathon, the Nike dedicated in memory of Kallimachos reemerges as a fixed point in the chronology of late archaic and early classical art.

In addition to innovative poses for figures in action, a second, more profound change in statuary inserted representations of historical personalities among the Olympian pantheon. The most dramatic example of this kind of composition was a group of ten figures dedicated from a tithe at Marathon and made by Pheidias (Pausanias, 10.10.1–2). Pausanias indicates only their identities, and their arrangement is unknown, but a single row on a common base is presumed.[58] What is striking about these lost statues is their subject: in the order named by Pausanias, they represented Athena, Apollo, and Miltiades, followed by seven of the ten eponymous heroes of Athens: Erechtheus, Kekrops, Pandion, Leos, Antiochos, Aigeus, and Akamas. A Macedonian appendix to this group was also present by the second century A.D.: Pausanias reports figures of Antigonos, his son Demetrios (Poliorketes), and Ptolemy (III), apparently replacing the missing eponymous heroes, Hippothoon, Aias, and Oineus, to complete the group (cf. 1.5.1–3). In this Hellenistic form the group of statues spanned the poles of Athenian classical history, from Marathon to Macedon, as well as the religious poles represented by Athens and Delphi.

The original composition inaugurated the new spiritual prosopography of the Persian wars by placing gods and men literally on the same pedestal. The portrayal of historical figures was an innovation inspired by history: the first Greek portraits, as such, were invented in commemoration of Greek heroes of the Persian wars.[59] The figure of Miltiades, one of the Athenian generals responsible for the victory at Marathon, is conspicuously mortal among the other nine gods and heroes portrayed by Pheidias; his appearance is usually attributed to his son Kimon's sponsorship of the monument.[60] The presence of the eponymous heroes of Athens includes a recent ingredient of Athenian myth and cult. Although introduced with the reforms of Kleisthenes as symbolic representatives of the ten new "tribes," these ten figures only enter Attic iconography as a group after the Persian wars.[61] These innovations—the portrayal of historical Athe-

---

[58] Thus Schanz, *Greek Sculptural Groups*, 49, following G. Roux, in J. Pouilloux and G. Roux, *Enigmes à Delphes* (Paris, 1963), 51–55. Gauer, *Weihgeschenke*, 65–70. Kron, *Phylenheroen*, 215–27. P. Vidal-Naquet, "Une enigme à Delphes: À propos de la base de Marathon (Pausanias, X, 10, 1–2)," *RH* 238 (1967) 281–302.

[59] Pollitt, in *Greek Art: Archaic into Classical*, 106, on the portraiture of Greek generals; Richter and Smith, *Portraits of the Greeks*, 124–26. See nn. 73–102 on the tyrannicides. W. Gauer, "Die griechischen Bildnisse

der klassischen Zeit als politische u. persönliche Denkmäler," *JdI* 83 (1968) 118–79.

[60] D. Kluwe, "Das Marathonweihgeschenk in Delphi—eine Staatsweihung oder Privatweihung des Kimon," *WZJena* 14 (1965) 21–27; E. Kluwe, "Das Perikleische Kongressdekret, das Todesjahr des Kimon und seine Bedeutung für die Einordnung der Miltiadesgruppe in Delphi," *WZRostock* 17 (1968) 677ff.; Gauer, *Weihgeschenke*, 70 n. 290. Kron, *Phylenheroen*, 215–17.

[61] Kron, *Phylenheroen*, 215–27; cf. review by Gauer,

nians, recent Attic heroes, and divine figures who assisted in battle—were also launched in historical paintings of the same epoch, especially when gods and men appear on the same plane of action in a new, Athenian vision of history.

Pausanias's description of the monument and his attribution of its statues to Pheidias have inspired the usual attempts to correlate Roman copies with lost Greek statues.[62] The association of Pheidias with a monument dedicated as early as forty years before the Parthenon has raised some chronological anxieties. But the date of the Delphi statues is uncertain, for the battle of Marathon provides only a terminus post quem, the reason and the revenues for the monument, whose actual completion could be much closer to the mature period of Pheidias's work. The Parthenon itself was remembered by some as a monument commemorating Marathon (Demosthenes, 23.13), and the statue group at Delphi cannot be fixed more closely within a range of thirty to forty years. The impact of the victory over the Persians was such that several decades were stamped by its visual monuments, as they were by its rhetoric. Like the Athena Promachos and the paintings at Plataia, this monument helped define the early career, even style of Pheidias as one intimately linked to the commemoration of Athenian achievements against the Persians, long before the Parthenon.

The original location of this statue group is unknown and may have reflected its historical occasion. It was moved by the Roman period to the Sacred Way, where Pausanias saw it "below the Wooden Horse" (10.10.1). Many scholars assume its original home was the socle displayed in front of the Athenian treasury, higher up the Sacred Way. This socle bears an inscription, recut after the fourth century, that records that the Athenians dedicated ἀκ[ροθ]ίνια τῆς Μαραθ[ῶ]νι μ[άχης] to Apollo.[63] Pausanias transmits similar information, calling the treasury an Athenian dedication after Marathon (10.11.5). Traditional chronology for archaic and classical sculpture could not reconcile such a date with the sculpted metopes on the building, which appear to be a decade or two before 490 B.C. (Figures 38, 39). But recent adjustments of that chronology to architectural, historical, and ceramic evidence have restored the Athenian treasury to its association with Marathon.[64] Not only the style of the sculpted metopes, but their subject,

GGA 230 (1978) 179ff; D. Kluwe, WZJena 14 (1965) 23; Harrison, in Essays: Margaret Thompson, 71–85, 80–83, on Delphi monument. See Chapter 12, on the eponymous heroes.

[62] Gauer, Weihgeschenke, 68–69. The Riace bronzes have been attributed to this monument: W. Fuchs, "Die Krieger aus Riace?" Boreas 4 (1981) 25–28, and in Praestant Interna, 34–40; Harrison, in Greek Art: Archaic into Classical, 47–48.

[63] Raubitschek,"Zu den zwei attischen Marathondenkmälern in Delphi," in Mélanges Daux, 315–16; Gauer, Weihgeschenke, 45–51, figs. 1–3, and in Fest-

schrift Neutsch, 127–36.

[64] R. Tölle-Kastenbein, AA (1983) 580–81, based on H. Büsing, "Ein Anthemion in Delphi," in Studies in Classical Art and Archaeology, 29–36, which supersedes W. B. Dinsmoor, "The Athenian Treasury as Dated by Its Ornament," AJA 50 (1946) 111–13. Cf. B. Ridgway, "Late Archaic Sculpture," in Greek Art: Archaic into Classical, 4–5; Gauer, in Festschrift Neutsch, 127, and F. Cooper, "Reconstruction of the Athenian Treasury at Delphi in the Fourth Century B.C.," AJA 94 (1990) 317–18, on the architectural unity of treasury and statue base.

a juxtaposition of the deeds of Herakles and Theseus with an occasional appearance by Athena, belongs to Athenian (self-) imagery of the post-Persian decades. Like other monuments of the Persians wars, the treasury is a traditional form of dedication but transmits a new kind of message. For the figures decorating its metopes reflect the divine participants of the battle of Marathon, where Athena, Herakles, and Theseus are said to have appeared in aid of Athens (Pausanias, 1.16.1). The representation together of these two heroes has been identified as a "Marathon motif" in classical art.[65] Even the pediment, with its fragmentary scene of Theseus and Antiope, belongs to a new cycle of myth inspired by the Persian wars (cf. Figures 52, 55).[66] Similar transformations of traditional legend must have been promoted in lost monuments, such as the statue group of Theseus and the Marathonian bull dedicated by the deme of Marathon on the Akropolis (Pausanias, 1.27.9–10; see Chapter 12), which celebrates one of the themes represented in the metopes of the Athenian treasury. Finally, what makes the Athenian treasury distinctive as the last of the archaic treasuries is the early classical statue group in front of it, whether the Pheidian monument or another set of statues appropriate to Marathon stood on those bases. If the ten statues by Pheidias stood there, the figures of Athena, Herakles, and Theseus would have appeared in legendary combat on the treasury, and in a historical moment below. This kind of juxtaposition was writ large in the monumental paintings of early classical Athens, as in the Stoa Poikile, on whose walls the battle of Marathon faced a scene of Greeks fighting Amazons.

The monuments just examined were scattered in sanctuaries and cities of the Greek world, and share few consistent features beyond their sources of funding and their destination. But several of them helped launch certain principles critical to Greek art, especially of the classical era. Gods came alive in sculpture, the way they did in battle; men were elevated to the divine plane, as the gods came down to join them in battle; and a rich store of mythological traditions assumed new meanings in history. These principles developed further in the art of the early classical period, beginning with the rebuilding of Athens, also in the aftermath of the Persian wars. The shift from Panhellenic sanctuaries like Delphi to city centers, especially Athens, has other implications. Delphi, in many ways, lost credibility after the oracle of Apollo failed to prepare Greek city-states adequately for the Persian invasion, and after Athens accomplished what the oracle and those who trusted it failed to do.[67] This transfer of authority is celebrated in

---

[65] By Gauer, *Weihgeschenke*, 64 and in *Festschrift Neutsch*, 131. K. Hoffelner, "Die Metopen des Athener-Schatzhauses. Ein neuer Rekonstruktionsversuch," *AthMitt* 103 (1988) 77–117, arranges the deeds of Herakles on the short sides, those of Theseus on the metopes of the flanks.

[66] Kierdorf, *Erlebnis und Darstellung*, 91 n. 2; Boardman, in *Eye of Greece*, 8–9; also see, Chapter 12.

Gauer, in *Festschrift Neutsch*, 131, and in *Kanon*, 36, calls it "the first 'Persian' Amazonomachy; Hurwit, *Art and Culture of Early Greece*, 302–3, 311–12, 316–19. On the related Eretria pediment with Theseus and Antiope (Figure 52), see Chapter 12.

[67] Shapiro, *Kernos* 3 (1990) 344–45, on the decline of Delphi. The Athenian Stoa at Delphi is now associated with an intra-Greek battle of the Pentekontaetia,

tragedy in unsubtle ways: the dilemma of the house of Atreus in Aeschylus's *Oresteia*, for example, cannot be solved by Apollo at Delphi, and is referred to Athens and a solution from Athena, in the *Eumenides*. Cult images even in Panhellenic sanctuaries are transferred to and by those cities claiming control of lucrative games; hence the statue of Nemean Zeus made its way to Argos (Pausanias, 2.20.3). By the fourth century, the creation of new, artificial cities readily claimed venerated statues from sanctuaries to grace new city centers, the way Arkadian shrines contribute monuments from the sanctuary of Zeus on Mount Lykaion and the statue of Apollo Epikourios at Bassai to the new foundation, Megalopolis (Pausanias, 8.39.3–4).[68] Athens inaugurates what the Macedonians and Romans perfected in centralizing cults for political power; although the city embellished anew its rural sanctuaries in the fifth century, more vital was the transformation of the city's Panathenaic festival into a Panhellenic one where allies were forced to attend and contribute.

The beautification of Athens eventually deplored as tasteless (Plutarch, *Perikles* 12.1–2) began as a reasonable response to disorder. The Persian occupation and destruction of Athens eliminated a body of statues, vessels, and buildings that had accumulated over centuries in sanctuaries and cemeteries. Repair and replacement of parts of the city occasioned new conventions in statuary and architecture, and in some cases deliberate restatements of archaic values. In the reconstruction of the citadel's fortifications, for example, drums from an unfinished temple were eventually incorporated into the north circuit of the Akropolis, as memorials of destruction.[69] According to Herodotus, walls burnt by the Persians were still visible and, in fact, provided a display for trophies earned before the Persian wars, like the fetters of prisoners ransomed from Boiotia and Chalkis in 506/5 B.C. (5.77).[70] That early victory of the Kleisthenic democracy was commemorated with a new dedication in the fifth century that linked it, literally, with a memorial of that same democracy's greatest victory. For Herodotus, Athens' simultaneous victory over two of its greatest enemies was a vindication of ἰσηγορίη, a word he uses only here in his work (see n. 19; also Chapter 13). The synchronization of victories on different fronts anticipated the miraculous events of the Persian wars (c.f. Plataia and Mykale, or Salamis and Himera; see n. 27), with their decisive victory over a nondemocracy. Visible monuments like the wall burnt by the Persians with its display of earlier trophies reinforced this promotion of democracy as much as any written or oral tradition.

---

not the Persian wars: J. Walsh, "The Date of the Athenian Stoa at Delphi," *AJA* 90 (1986) 319–36.

[68] N. Norman, "Moveable Feasts and Sanctuaries: The Case of Nemean Zeus," *AJA* 93 (1989) 269, on these manipulations of cults in Argos and Arkadia.

[69] Travlos, 54–55; H. Thompson, "Athens Faces Adversity," *Hesperia* 50 (1981) 344–46; Hurwit, *Art and Culture of Early Greece*, 336–38, fig. 147.

[70] Dinsmoor, in Χαριστήριον, 147–55; for the epigram of Simonides for the victory, see *IG* I² 394; D. Page, *Epigrammata Graeca* (Oxford, 1975), 9, III.

The buildings of the Akropolis were not fully replaced until the program launched after 450 B.C., but a new gateway and a new temple of Athena were begun in the decades after Marathon and Salamis.[71] From the perspective of the fourth century, the Parthenon was a monument for Marathon (Demosthenes, 23.13), an association scholars have revived more recently through close study of its sculptural decoration.[72] But in the quarter century before the building program was decreed, dramatic changes in monumental art took place, such that the sculpture of the Akropolis program represents the mature version of what was conceived in early classical art.

Some of these changes occurred in the process of replacement and repair of the city's monuments, as the people of Athens restructured their environment and its style, in a literal way. One of the casualties of the Persian occupation was the statue group commemorating Harmodios and Aristogeiton, who attempted to assassinate the tyrants of Athens in 514 B.C. As Thucydides points out, the assassination was only marginally motivated by politics, eliminated the wrong tyrant, and resulted in the execution of the two would-be assassins, with a harsher period of rule by the surviving tyrant, Hippias (1.20; 6.53–59; cf. Herodotus, 5.55; 6.109, 113). Only in retrospect did these two figures become heroes, commemorated in sculpture on two occasions. On the occasion of their replacement, and perhaps even when the first statue group was commissioned, victory over the Persians was a recent event. These statues were the first historical portraits in sculpture, if not the first Greek portraits of a commemorative nature.[73] They add the genre of portraiture to history, rhetoric, drama, and painting, as commemorative media initiated by the Persian wars and thereafter canonical in Western art. The origins of historical portraiture, like the origins of "historical" tragedies, the first portrayal of historical figures in art (e.g., Kroisos: see nn. 34–36), and the origins of history itself, all can be located in these first responses to victory over the Persians. And like some of their companion monuments—the Plataian serpent column—their immediate formal antecedents have Oriental dimensions. Both in sculpture and in coinage, the portrayal of Persian satraps inaugurated a tradition eventually Hellenic.[74] Even famous heroes of

[71] W. B. Dinsmoor, Jr., *The Propylaea to the Athenian Akropolis. Vol. 1: The Predecessors* (Princeton, 1980); J. Bundgaard, *The Excavation of the Athenian Acropolis, 1882–1890* (Copenhagen, 1974), 20–25, suggests that "Hill's Parthenon" was Kimonian; Tölle-Kastenbein, *AA* (1983) 581–83; J. Walsh, "The Athenian Building Program of the 460s B.C.," *AJA* 90 (1986) 179–80.

[72] J. H. Kroll, "The Parthenon as a Votive Relief," *AJA* 83 (1979) 349–52; J. Boardman, "The Parthenon Frieze: Another View," in *Festschrift Brommer*, 39–49. Thomas, *Mythos und Geschichte*, 40. Cf. W. B. Dinsmoor, "The Correlation of Greek Archaeology with History," *Studies in the History of Culture* (February

1942) 216.

[73] Pollitt, in *Greek Art: Archaic into Classical* 106; G.M.A. Richter, *The Portraits of the Greeks*, rev. ed. by R.R.R. Smith (Oxford, 1984), 37–40; Hölscher, *Griechische Historienbilder*, 85; Gauer, *JdI* 83 (1968) 118–79.

[74] H. A. Cahn and D. Gerin, "Themistocles at Magnesia," *NC* 148 (1988) 13–20 (*pace* M. Oeconomides, "Le problème de l'effigie de Thémistoclès sur les monnaies (à propos d'une monnaie de Magnésie)," in *Actes du 9eme Congrès Internationale de Numismatique*, ed. T. Hackens and R. Weiller (Louvain, 1982), 85–87; W. Weiser, "Die Eulen von Kyros dem Jüngeren. Zu den ersten Münzporträts lebender Menschen," *ZPE*

the Persian wars like Themistokles, associated with the first "Greek" portraits, ended life more Persian than Greek (Plutarch, *Themistokles* 23–31).

The tyrannicide statues and their history document the evolution of portraiture as a civic and symbolic, rather than private or dynastic, art form. Commissioned by the city and created by Antenor, the original portraits of these two posthumous heroes of Athenian democracy were removed by the Persians, perhaps even by Hippias himself, descendant and namesake of their victims. The original group by Antenor could have been made as early as the last decade of the sixth century, presumably after the expulsion of Hippias in 510/9 B.C.; since antiquity they have been readily assigned to that precise date (Pliny, *Naturalis Historia* 34.17) to coincide with the expulsion of kings from Rome, a synchronism too neat to be true. At the other end of the spectrum, they could have been made as late as the decade after Marathon, following the ostracism of Hipparchos, another significant date in Athenian history.[75] Ancient plaster casts of the tyrannicides found at Baiae on the bay of Naples are not identical to copies of the later group by Kritios and Nesiotes, dated to 477/6 B.C. by the Marmor Parium, but too similar to them in style and date for any major difference between the original group and its replacement.[76] The originals were probably a pair of statues close in date and style to late archaic kouroi, visibly different or at least more traditional than their replacements. This would explain how the statues stolen by the Persians, recaptured by Alexander, and restored next to their replacements in the Athenian Agora looked ἀρχαίους, "old[er]" to Pausanias (1.8.5).[77] In the absence of the statues by Antenor from Athens for at least 150 years, and because of the special status of the statues that replaced them, the later group played a dramatic role in Athenian art and cult.

As a political gesture, the replacement of tyrannicide statues was a symbolic, even defiant act on the part of Athens, comparable with its display of trophies from earlier victories on the walls burnt by the Persians. The impulse to commemorate historical

---

76 (1989) 267–96; on marble portraits, see the satrap's head published by E. Akurgal, "Bärtiger Kopf mit Tiara aus Herakleia Pontica," in *Archaische und klassische griechische Plastik*, 1:9–14, where Robertson cites his Carian identification for the Sabouroff head (*History of Greek Art*, 111); B. Ridgway, *Fifth-Century Styles in Greek Sculpture* (Princeton, 1981), 179–80. Cf. the origins of the first literary biographies in Persian War narrative: O. Murray, "Herodotus and Oral History," in *Achaemenid History II: The Greek Sources*, Proceedings of the Groningen 1984 Achaemenid History Workshop, ed. H. Sancisi-Weedenberg and A. Kuhrt (Leiden, 1987), 106.

75 Schanz, *Greek Sculptural Groups*, 70–72, follows A. Raubitschek, "Two Monuments Erected after the Victory at Marathon," *AJA* 44 (1940) 58 n. 2, and *Ded-*

ications from the Athenian Acropolis, 481–83, in placing Antenor's group after Marathon.

76 Ch. von Hees-Landwehr, *Griechische Meisterwerke in römischen Abgüssen. Der Fund von Baia* (Frankfurt, 1982), 24–26, no. 24, fig. 24, for a cast of the Aristogeiton head that disagrees in its details with extant copies; W.-H. Schuchhardt and Ch. Landwehr, "Statuenkopien der Tyrannenmörder-gruppe," *JdI* 101 (1986) 85–126. Cf. E. Langlotz, "Aristogeiton des Antenor?" *AthMitt* 71 (1956) 149–52, for a similar argument from a copy in the Capitoline Museum.

77 Thus M. Robertson (Ridgway *Severe Style*, 82 n. 2); J. Boardman, *Greek Sculpture: The Archaic Period* (London, 1978), 25; cf. Hölscher, *Griechische Historienbilder*, 85 n. 395; Taylor, *The Tyrant Slayers*, 30–33.

figures on the level of mythology made heroes out of them, as art elevated Athenians like Miltiades and Kallimachos among gods and heroes in statue groups and paintings.[78] What rehabilitated the tyrannicides from the embarrassing failure of their deed was the victory that surprised Athens and the world: in retrospect, Harmodios and Aristogeiton had struck a blow for freedom from Persia as well as for freedom from tyranny. The defection of Hippias, the tyrant they failed to eliminate, to the Persian cause in order to plan a return to power conflated internal with external history, such that the enemy of Athens in 514 was assimilated to the enemy at Marathon and Salamis. This convergence may have inspired the statues by Antenor to have been commissioned after Marathon, in the first stage of retroactive hero-cult. For this same conflation of the expulsion of the tyrants with the defeat of the Persians was condoned by the most sophisticated historian, Thucydides. In his synopsis of early Athenian history, he expresses this telescoping of significant events as in a public oration, with the usual neglect of non-Athenian combatants (1.18.1): "Not many years after (οὐ πολλοῖς ἔτεσιν ὕστερον) the putting down of the tyrants from Greece, the battle at Marathon of the Medes against the Athenians took place." If battles like Marathon initiated commemoration in painting, the same event could have inspired the heroic portrayal of Athenians in sculpture.[79]

The replacements of these statues in 477/6 presented the heroes in action, weapons raised against their invisible victims (cf. Figures 44, 45).[80] In addition, Harmodios and Aristogeiton were distinguished as heroic images through their nudity, an appearance at odds with the realities of the historical assassination, where they hid daggers under clothing worn in the Panathenaic procession (Thucydides, 6.57–59). An epigram by Simonides inscribed on their base accorded these heroes the same honors bestowed on heroes fallen in battle against the Persians.[81] The reerection of statues of these heroes was accompanied by literary and legislative measures that made an official and private cult of the two heroes.[82] Their families and descendants were honored by the city with such priviliges as σίτησις, ἀτέλεια, and προεδρία (maintenance in the state dining

---

[78] Metzler, *Porträt und Gesellschaft*; Gauer, *JdI* 83 (1968) 118–79. Fuchs, in *Praestant Interna*, 34.

[79] In dating the Antenor statues after Marathon, Schanz, "Greek Sculptural Groups," 72–74, invokes a scheme by Themistokles to undermine the Spartan and Alkmeonid role in the expulsion of the tyrants and the establishment of democracy. Even without his role, this occasion for the statues would agree with the spirit of Thucydides, 1.18.1, and "the meaning of Marathon as a battle of liberation" (E. Harrison, *ArtB* 54 [1972] 362).

[80] B. B. Shefton, "Some Iconographic Remarks on the Tyrannicides," *AJA* 64 (1960) 173–79; Brunnsåker, *Tyrant-Slayers*, 163–64; Schanz, "Greek Sculptural Groups," 74–77. Taylor, *Tyrant Slayers*, 29–46.

[81] Athenian Agora, I 3872, reported by B. Meritt, *Hesperia* 5 (1936) 355–59; Raubitschek, *AJA* 44 (1940) 58 n. 2; Forrest, *CQ* 54 (1960) 237 n. 4; Page, *Epigrammata Graeca*, 8, I. Taylor, *Tyrant Slayers*, 67–70; Tölle-Kastenbein, *AA* (1983) 578; J. Day, "Epigrams and History: The Athenian Tyrannicides, A Case in Point," in *The Greek Historians: Literature and History. Papers Presented to A. E. Raubitschek*, ed. M. Jameson and others (Stanford, 1985), 25–46.

[82] A. Podlecki, "The Political Significance of the 'Tyrannicide'-Cult," *Historia* 15 (1966) 129–41; Ch. Fornara, "The Cult of Harmodios and Aristogeiton," *Philologus* 114 (1970) 155–80. Taylor, *Tyrant Slayers*, 1–28. Clairmont, *Patrios Nomos*, 2, 14, 22–23, 37, 220–21.

room, exemption from fees, and first-row seats at the theater). The names of Harmodios and Aristogeiton generated an anthology of σκόλια or drinking songs popular at Attic symposia and promoting a new heroic image.[83] The way these heroes became models for Athenians surfaces in the speech Herodotus assigns Miltiades to deliver to Kallimachos before the battle of Marathon, which begins (6.109):

Ἐν σοι νῦν, Καλλίμαχε, ἐστί . . . καταδουλῶσαι ἢ μνημόσυνον λίπεσθαι ἐς τὸν ἄπαντα ἀνθρώπων βίον οἷον οὐδὲ Ἁρμόδιός τε καὶ Ἀριστογείτων.

It is now up to you, Kallimachos, . . . whether to be enslaved or to leave a memorial for the entire history of man, such as not even Harmodios and Aristogeiton [did].

The phrase, and most of the speech, is studded with formulaic language characteristic of the aftermath of the Persian wars; like the defense delivered by the Athenians before Plataia (9.27), it was composed years after the event. The challenge to Kallimachos, the general doomed to die in that battle, by Miltiades, who survived it, suggests that a visual image, not just a verbal one, inspired the historian. The statues of the tyrannicides have been compared to this passage, as a possible source in art for the transformation of a visible μνημόσυνον into a metaphorical one.[84] In addition, the painting of the battle of Marathon in the Stoa Poikile may have portrayed the polemarch in the pose of one of the statues by Kritios and Nesiotes.[85] Those poses soon invaded representations of heroes in Athenian painting, most vividly in the iconography of Theseus (Chapter 12), but Kallimachos may have been the first Athenian to be honored through that comparison. In the imagery of Herodotus, whose vision and diction span archaic and classical traditions, the word μνημόσυνον, in the imaginary speech of Miltiades, embraces both the archaic power of a tangible monument and its classical force as a concept.

For sculpture, the tyrant slayers represent the birth of a new style.[86] Because of the visual popularity of the statues, their images proliferated throughout Athenian iconography, in copies of the statues and representations on classical coins, vases (Figure 45), and in relief sculpture, as on the Elgin throne (Figures 44 left, right).[87] Some of these

[83] Athenaeus, 15.695, 10–13; C. M. Bowra, *Greek Lyric Poetry from Alcman to Simonides* (Oxford, 1936), 391ff.; B. Knox, in *Athens Comes of Age*, 49–50; Taylor, *Tyrant Slayers*, chap. 3, "Scolia and Epigram," 47ff.

[84] Immerwahr, *AJP* 81 (1960) 267.

[85] As suggested by E. Harrison, *AJA* 76 (1972) 355, 362, who notes that the statues stood in the Agora not far from the Stoa. A. Stewart, "History, Myth and Allegory in the Program of the Temple of Athena Nike, Athens," in *Pictorial Narrative in Antiquity and the Middle Ages*, ed. H. Kessler and M. S. Simpson, Studies in the History of Art 16 (Washington, D.C.,

1983), 62–63.

[86] E.g., Ridgway, *Severe Style*, 12, calls 477 B.C. "the legal birthday of the Severe style"; Simon, in *Greek Art: Archaic into Classical*, 71–72, calls the statue group "one of the first manifestations of Early Classical sculpture." In addition, as noted in n. 70, they mark the first historical, individualized portraits and the first examples of heroic nudity (Hölscher, *Griechische Historienbilder*, 85–88; Richter and Smith, *Portraits of the Greeks*, 37, 124–26).

[87] Brunnsåker, *Tyrant-Slayers*, chap. 4, pls. 23, 24; Hölscher, *Griechische Historienbilder*, 86–88; Taylor, *Ty-*

reproductions seem politically motivated, like the dissemination of the images of the tyrannicides on the coinage of Kyzikos.[88] Other imitations of the statues appear in historically significant contexts or juxtapositions. A late fifth-century red-figure oinochoe in Boston that represents the two heroes in their familiar "statuary" pose (Figure 45) was buried in the Athenian precinct crowned by the Dexileos stele, the final resting place of latter-day heroes who also died for Athens.[89] The relief on one side panel of the Elgin throne (Figure 44 left) portrays the tyrannicides; the other side (Figure 44 right), whether carved later or at the same time, balances the historical moment that became myth, with a myth that became history: the Amazonomachy of Theseus. This makes the Elgin throne, whatever its date(s), a counterpart in sculpture to the amphora by Myson, which offers a historical event associated with the Persian wars on one side (Figure 37, left) and the story of Theseus and Antiope on the other (Figure 47, right).

A subtler and more fascinating influence exerted by the tyrannicide statues is the way their poses are adapted and borrowed for other heroes, Kallimachos being the first to mime them, in the painting of the battle of Marathon (see n. 85). The postures of Harmodios and Aristogeiton are applied to Herakles and other heroes in early classical red-figure vases by the Pan Painter and Berlin Painter, among others.[90] Representations of these poses, whether in images of the tyrant slayers or of other heroes, are critical to the current debate on the chronology of archaic and early classical art; their appearance in "late archaic" vases, including some work of the Pioneers, may not necessarily "anticipate" the statues but could date these vases after 477/6.[91] Their figures were probably publicized in wall paintings, as well through the display of the statues themselves; eventually they were assimiliated exclusively and thoroughly to representations of Theseus.[92] Their primary impact, however, was on sculptural types of the early classical

rant Slayers, chaps. 4 and 5. Simon, in Greek Art: Archaic into Classical, 71. On the Elgin throne: B. Frischer, The Sculpted Word: Epicureanism and Philosophical Recruitment in Ancient Greece (Berkeley, 1982), 250–60, although new evidence suggests that the prytaneion of Athens lay east of the Akropolis (G. Dontas, "The True Aglaurion," Hesperia 62 [1983] 60–62), and the findspot of the Elgin throne is no longer the home of σιτῆσις, as suggested by Frischer (p. 259).

[88] Brunnsåker, Tyrant-Slayers, 99–100, 107, pl. 24; Meiggs, Athenian Empire, 441–43, on Kyzikene and other staters under the empire; D. Mannsperger, "Das Motif des Waffenläufers auf den Elektronmünzen von Kyzikos," in Der Tübinger Waffenläufer, 75–76, 85, 89.

[89] E. Vermeule, "Five Vases from the Tomb Precinct of Dexileos," JdI 85 (1970) 94–111.

[90] K. Schefold, "Neues zur Gruppe der Tyrannen-

mörder," MH 2 (1945) 263–64, nn. 4–5. Simon argues that this group "has changed the style of [the Copenhagen] painter" (in Greek Art: Archaic into Classical, 71–72).

[91] Harrison, AJA 76 (1972) 355 n. 21, and Taylor, Tyrant Slayers, 39–42, on the "Harmodios" stroke of the Euphronios krater in Arezzo; cf. E. Simon, in Greek Art: Archaic into Classical, 71, who dates the Copenhagen Painter "among the Late Archaic vase painters" despite his allusions to the tyrannicides; Schefold, MH 2 (1945), 263–64, on the tyrannicides and the Pan Painter. Gauer, Weihgeschenke, 53, 57–62, on dated monuments that lower the chronology of the Leagros group, including Euthymides, the Kleophrades Painter, the Brygos Painter (whose work is found in the Akropolis Perserschutt), and Onesimos ("Proto-Painaitios," whose cup was buried at Marathon); Tölle-Kastenbein, AA (1983) 574, 578.

[92] Taylor, Tyrant Slayers, chaps. 4–5; also see Chap-

period. Harmodios and Aristogeiton shared with Greek heroes of the Persian wars, both mortal and divine, the audacity in action that encouraged the Athenians to attack the Persians δρόμῳ, "at a dead run," at Marathon (Herodotus, 6.112.1) and turn the loss of their city into a defeat of the Persian navy, at Salamis. The "rash action" of the would-be tyrant-slayers deplored by Thucydides (ἀλόγιστος τόλμα· 6.59) became a "bold deed" once Hippias had Medized; the same word was used to praise Athenian action against the Persians (1.90.5: τὴν ἐς τὸν Μηδικὸν πόλεμον τόλμα). The aggressive manner in which the Athenians tackled their own fate, and the direct action taken by the gods in human events, transformed the conception of the human figure after the Persian wars. The militant stance of the god from Artemision and the Athena Promachos belong to the same spirit and time as the bold poses bestowed on Harmodios and Aristogeiton by Kritios and Nesiotes. It is no surprise that the same team of sculptors created a statue of a ὁπλιτόδρομος dedicated on the Akropolis by Epicharinos, according to Pausanias (1.23.9) and the remains of an inscribed base.[93] The figure of a running warrior in full armor was popular in the decades after Marathon, in miniature bronzes, on red-figured vases, and on a painted plaque of a running warrior in armor from the Akropolis (Figure 46).[94] The popularity of the motif apparently survived into the fourth century, when Parrhasios painted two pictures of hoplites in *Waffenlauf*, which Pliny praised as *nobilissimae* (*Naturalis Historia* 35.71).

According to Herodotus (6.112.3), the Athenians were the first to use the running attack in battle, as they were the first to face an enemy in Median costume. While ὁπλιτοδρομία had been practiced in Greek athletics and military training since the archaic period, its first triumphant use in battle was associated with Marathon and the Athenian performance on that battlefield. The most famous celebration of that feat took place at Plataia in connection with the festival of Zeus Eleutherios (Pausanias, 9.2.4), a further link between victories in the Persian wars and running in armor.[95] Even without the wearing of armor in motion or a race in full armor, the Greek hoplite was distinguished by fighting on foot in a full suit of body armor, in contrast to the Persians who fought in elaborate dress but without armor, relying on the horse and the bow.[96] In fact, the

---

ter 12, on the political and historical aspects of this transformation.

[93] G. Fischer-Heetfeld, "Die Statue des Epicharinos auf der Acropolis von Athen," in Hausmann, *Der Tübinger Waffenläufer*, 67–74; Raubitschek, *Dedications on the Athenian Acropolis*, 124–25. Brunnsåker, *Tyrant-Slayers*, 136. As Ridgway, *Severe Style*, 80, points out, the statue is dated after 480 B.C. primarily because it was seen by Pausanias.

[94] Neumann and Hausmann, both in Hausmann, *Der Tübinger Waffenläufer*, 40–44, 58–66; M. Brouskari, *The Acropolis Museum* (Athens, 1974), 126–27, no. 6,

fig. 241; M. Robertson, *Greek Painting* (Geneva, 1959), 94–95. A date after Marathon would still allow the name of Megakles to be erased, after his ostracism in 486, and the name of Glaukytes to be substituted in the *kalos* inscription.

[95] Cf. Philostratus, *Gymnasticus* 8. G. Neumann, "Der Waffenlauf im antiken Griechenland: Schriftliche Quellen und bildliche Überlieferung," in Hausmann, *Der Tübinger Waffenläufer*, 34, 37, 38, 44; Raaflaub, *Entdeckung der Freiheit*, 126–35, on the games of Zeus Eleutherios at Plataia.

[96] Herodotus, 7.61. Cf. Plutarch, *Theseus* 35: even

fame of hoplites after they defeated the Persians made an armed warrior as heroic in art as a nude one, in vase paintings depicting Greeks fighting Persians (e.g., Figure 47a).[97] The image of a running warrior in armor became a symbol of Athenian victory over Persia, and the same sculptors who made the sixth-century tyrant-slayers into new classical heroes celebrated the hoplites of Marathon.[98]

These innovations in sculpture have recently recast early classical sculpture—long called "severe" (from German *Streng*) as a prelude to the maturity of the classical style—as the "bold style" in emulation of Pliny's *audacia* (*Naturalis Historia* 34.39), an expression that best captures Greek τόλμα ("daring, boldness") and the spirit of the aftermath of victory.[99] The moment represented by new daring poses in statuary helps make "late archaic" vases such as the name vase of the Foundry Painter more congenial to an "early classical" date.[100] As argued in the opening of Chapter 8, this cup illustrates the early classical migration of the career of Daidalos, thanks to the new prominence of sculpture as an art form. On the inside (Figure 1), the artist familiar from Homer makes armor for a hero; on the exterior (Figure 58), classical sculptors and their apprentices manufacture new heroes: athletes and warriors like Homeric ones, but newly monumental in bronze. The cup also challenges notions of stylistic chronology in the early decades of the fifth century. The statue types on this vase, like the hoplite on the Akropolis plaque (Figure 46), may present no "anachronism" if they were painted in the early classical period—after 490 or even 480 B.C. As suggested in comparing the tyrannicides to the work of the Pioneers (see n. 91), several critical pieces could date after the Persian wars, for historical reasons. Objects found on the Akropolis and assumed to come from the so-called *Perserschutt* can no longer enjoy a terminus ante quem of 480 B.C., thanks to recent investigations.[101] The events of the Persian wars played such a critical role in the conception of human and divine that they are a crucial index to the calibration of stylistic chronology in the sensitive decades between about 510 and 470 B.C.

Theseus appeared in armor at the battle of Marathon, not as the nude hero of art. P. Vidal-Naquet, "The Tradition of the Athenian Hoplite," *The Black Hunter*, trans. A. Szegedy-Maszak (Baltimore, 1986), 85–99; Hartog, *Mirror of Herodotus*, 44–50, on the Persian lack of armor. See How and Wells, 2:397–410, where the postclassical prejudice for heavy-armed foot soldiers over cavalry and archers is expressed in "the superiority of the ordered and disciplined freedom of the city-state to the vast but amorphous empires of the East" (p. 400).

[97] As observed by Hölscher, *Griechische Historienbilder*, 40–44.

[98] Neumann and Mannsperger, both in Haus-

mann, *Der Tübinger Waffenläufer*, 31–44, 90–96 on ὁπλιτοδρομία in athletics, art, and warfare.

[99] E. Harrison, "Early Classical Sculpture: The Bold Style," in *Greek Art: Archaic into Classical*, 40–65; Stewart, in *Pictorial Narrative*, 62–63 on τόλμα, Harmodios, and Kallimachos.

[100] Harrison, in *Greek Art: Archaic into Classical*, 40–41, on the Foundry Painter; see n. 94, on the Akropolis plaque; C. Mattusch, "The Berlin Foundry Cup: The Casting of Greek Bronze Statuary in the Early Fifth Century B.C.," *AJA* 84 (1980) 435–44.

[101] Bundgaard, *Athenian Acropolis*; J. Hurwit, "The Kritios Kouros," *AJA* 93 (1989) 41–80, on the post-Persian date of the Kritios kouros.

The popularity of new action poses for human figures coincides with the dramatic demise in Athens of the traditional archaic male statue type, the kouros.[102] While aesthetic considerations and experiments in the portrayal of movement may have revised theories of motion and anatomy,[103] the archaic kouros was eliminated, in part, through historical events. First, the desecration of sanctuaries and cemeteries destroyed not only many standing examples of the statue type, but also what they represented. The battle cry at Salamis, as imagined by Aeschylus, called for the liberation of θεῶν τε πατρώιων ἤδη | θήκας τε προγόνων (*Persians* 404–5), "the seats of the gods of our fathers and the places of our ancestors": the sanctuaries and cemeteries of their homeland. Later, when the Athenians protest the Macedonians' fear of Medism on their part, they invoke, "first and foremost" (πρῶτα μὲν καὶ μέγιστα), those statues of gods and homes of Greeks burned by the Persians, defining Greek culture ("τὸ Ἑλληνικόν") not only in blood and language but in common sanctuaries, sacrifices, and customs (Herodotus, 8.144.2). The archaic cemetery was as conspicuous as the sanctuary, with its prominent marble stelai and statues proclaiming family and class identities in the landscape.[104] Those monuments that were not toppled and burned by the Persians (or buried beforehand, for fear of such damage) were dismantled hastily and ruthlessly by the Athenians themselves.[105] One occasion for native destruction was the building of a new circuit wall for the city of Athens after the Persian invasion, the so-called "Themistoklean" wall. In defiance of Spartan objections, the entire city population was mobilized en masse (πανδημεί). The task included both men and women and children,

> sparing no structure, private or public, which might be useful at all to the construction, but tearing everything down. . . . In this way the Athenians walled their city in a short time. And it is still clear today that the construction took place in haste; for the foundations are laid of stones of all kinds, and in some places not even fitted together, but placed just as each was brought at the time ; and many tombstones from graves and worked blocks were put in with the rest. (1.90.3; 93)

Like the north wall of the Akropolis, this postwar fortification incorporated debris from the city's occupation into a new form of monument marking the urgency of its

---

[102] Ch. Karusos, *Aristodikos* (Stuttgart, 1961), 26–43, for a study of the "latest" kouros [dated ca. 500 by standard chronology, whose adjustment would place Aristodikos closer to ca. 480]; see review by B. Ridgway, *AJA* 67 (1963) 223: and by F. Eckstein, *GGA* (1964) 164. Ridgway, *Archaic Style*, 49–54; Hurwit, *Art and Culture of Early Greece*, 198–200, 340–53.

[103] As maintained by Hallett, *JHS* 106 (1986) 71–84, and Stewart, *Greek Sculpture*, 133–34; see Chapter 8 on movement and classical sculpture.

[104] On the archaic cemeteries of Attika, see C.W.J. Eliot, "Where did the Alkmeonidai Live?" *Historia* 16 (1967) 279–86; S. Humphreys, "Family Tombs and Tomb Cult in Ancient Athens: Tradition or Traditionalism?" *JHS* 100 (1980) 96–126.

[105] The statues of "Kroisos," the Berlin kore, Phrasiklea and her "brother," may have been buried to avoid damage: Hurwit, *Art and Culture of Early Greece*, 334 n. 10, 334–40, on Attic monuments during the Persian invasion.

construction. Thus defensive architecture belongs to those archaic forms of material culture that were recast by history into historical monuments. The new circuit wall was
also contaminated with the strategies and pretexts of nascent Athenian imperialism, like
the final battles in Herodotus and his retrospective account of pre-Persian history. According to Thucydides, the construction of this wall was one of the clever stratagems in
the career of Themistokles, singled out by the historian to pinpoint the rise of Athenian
power.[106] As the first event after the siege of Sestos narrated by Herodotus, this construction project also bridges the accounts of the two Athenian historians.

This defensive project, still visible in preserved portions of the city wall in Athens,
enlisted all kinds of laborers not accustomed to construction work, nor to burying their
families with lavish marble monuments. Their task required dismantling the archaic
city, including its aristocratic monuments, and may have encouraged deliberate "political vandalism," in some modern views.[107] The corpus of those funerary monuments,
calibrated to traditional dates for vase painting, displayed a significant gap after 500
B.C., correlated by some scholars with sumptuary legislation cited by Cicero *post ali-
quanto Solonem*.[108] This archaeologically overworked passage could refer to later legislation under Demetrios of Phaleron, whom Cicero is citing; among its stipulations is an
ordinance against eulogies "except at public funerals," and the tradition of the
ἐπιτάφιος λόγος this implies did not exist before the Persian wars. Even without new
discoveries such as an early classical statue for a grave from the Kerameikos, a reevaluation of Attic stylistic chronology (as recommended in nn. 64, 91, 101) would allow the
latest sepulchral monuments of Athens a longer life by a margin of ten to twenty years,
such that the apparent "gap" in those monuments would coincide more closely with
the decades after the construction of the Themistoklean wall.[109] Other archaeological

[106] Thucydides, 1.89–95; Diodorus, 11.39–40; Plutarch, *Themistokles* 19; Theopompus, *FGrH* 115 F 85;
Andokides, *On the Peace* 38. Frost, *Plutarch's* Themistocles, 173–214. Travlos, 301, and U. Knigge, *Der Kerameikos von Athen* (Athens, 1988), 32–35, 49–54, for
remains of the Themistoklean wall in the Kerameikos.

[107] H. Thompson, "Athens Faces Adversity," *Hesperia* 50 (1981) 344–45; R. Garland, *The Greek Way of
Death* (Ithaca, N.Y., 1985), 122; and review by Morris,
Phoenix 40 (1986) 470. Knigge, *Kerameikos*, 32–35,
notes "popular" activity in the Kerameikos (post-
Kleisthenic burials intrusive into archaic tumuli)
which suggests a post- or anti-Peisistratid *damnatio* of
aristocratic tombs.

[108] Cicero, *De Legibus* 2.26.24; R. Young, "*Sepulturae
inter Urbem*," *Hesperia* 20 (1951) 72ff.; G.M.A. Richter,
The Archaic Gravestones of Attica (London, 1961), 38–

39, 53; Garland, *Death*, 125, and "The Well-Ordered
Corpse: An Investigation into the Motives behind
Greek Funerary Legislation," *BICS* 36 (1989) 1–15; review by Morris, *Phoenix* 40 (1986) 470. Stewart's use
of the passive voice ("nothing is dated after 500 B.C.,"
in *Corinthiaca*, 68–69) pinpoints the problem: a modern misestimate in chronology, not an ancient gap.
Boardman is one of the few who admits that "the
general dearth of public and private monuments after about 500 B.C. is not easy to explain on the
grounds of politics and only partly explicable in
terms of assumed sumptuary legislation": *Greek
Sculpture: The Archaic Period* (London, 1978), 82.

[109] V. Zinserling, "Das attische Grabluxusgesetz
des frühen 5. Jhdts.," *WZIena* 14 (1965) 29–34, proposed lowering the legislation to 487 B.C. to coincide
with the first ostracism, as does Tölle-Kastenbein
(*AA* [1983] 584); cf. Stupperich, *Staatsbegräbnis und*

configurations would agree with this date: for example, the onset of Attic white-ground
funerary lekythoi would coincide with the aftermath of the Persian invasion and the
decline in sculptural monuments.[110]

Among the monuments that disappeared from the Attic sepulchral repertoire during
these events and as a result of them, the most familar archaic type was the kouros,
including kouroi in relief on stelai and bases.[111] It is perhaps significant that the last of
the Attic kouroi, the "Kritian boy" from the Akropolis, is probably a portrait of Theseus,
the new hero of classical and democratic Athens (Chapter 12, n. 130). Other monumental symbols of aristocratic values disappeared, too, including all forms of marble gravestones, not just those portraying kouroi. The equestrian statue was no longer common
as a votive or a funerary type, and only reappears in historical portraiture under the
Macedonians.[112] Hoplites, not cavalry, were the heroic fighters at Marathon, and the
hippeis were no longer a privileged class after the latest constitutional reforms. These
historical circumstances may have assisted the decline of equestrian images for individuals, although the figure of the mounted horseman still functioned as an ideal type in
relief sculpture, most conspicuously on the Parthenon frieze. Another archaic Greek
favorite that disappears after the Persian invasion is the theme of the lion, especially in
combat with prey or heroes. The animal closely associated with Assyrian, Persian, and
Lydian dynasts, then with Greek aristocratic tastes in archaic temples and tomb monuments, may have become unpopular after those dynasts became enemies of Athens.[113]

Thus historical and social circumstances rather than a state decree discouraged rather
than prohibited certain archaic conventions in the private cemetery. In addition, a new
state burial introduced for those fallen in war, the so-called πάτριος νόμος described
by Thucydides (2.34), replaced private expense with public honors, including a state
funeral and a public oration.[114] This practice was probably inaugurated in the 460s with

Privatdenkmal, 71–86. U. Knigge, "Ein Jünglingskopf
vom Heiligen Tor in Athen," *AthMitt* 98 (1983) 45–56,
publishes a new early classical marble head whose
date implies that sumptuary laws took effect after 480
B.C. under Themistokles, not Kleisthenes.

[110] D. Kurtz, *Athenian White-Ground Lekythoi* (Oxford, 1975), 133, 136.

[111] Hurwit, *Art and Culture of Early Greece*, 198–200,
and A. Stewart, "When Is a Kouros Not an Apollo?
The Tenea 'Apollo' Revisited," in *Corinthiaca*, 54–67,
and *Greek Sculpture*, 134, on the kouros, its social significance, and its demise.

[112] Richter, *Archaic Gravestones*, 53–54, on their disappearance in Attika; Ridgway, *Archaic Style*, 140–43,
on the equestrian statue type, essentially "an Attic
invention"; Stewart, in *Corinthiaca*, 68–69, and *Greek
Sculpture*, 133. R. Stucky, "Überlegungen zum 'Per-
serreiter,' " *AK* 25 (1982) 97–101, on the rider from

the Akropolis; cf. A. Alföldi, "Die Herrschaft der Rei-
terei in Griechenland nach dem Sturz der Könige,"
in *Gestalt und Geschichte. Festschrift für Karl Schefold*,
AK Beih. 4 (Basel, 1967), 13–33; G. Bugh, *The Horsemen of Athens* (Princeton 1986), chap. 1.

[113] Vickers, *RA* (1985) 6–9; G. Markoe, "The 'Lion
Attack' in Archaic Greek Art: Heroic Triumph," *CA* 8
(1989) 86–115, esp. 103–9; cf. U. Magen, *Assyrische
Königsdarstellungen*, "Typus I, Der König als Jäger"
on the image of the Assyrian king as lion-hunter;
C. Ratté, "Five Lydian Felines," *AJA* 93 (1989) 379–
93, on lions in Lydia. Gunter, "Models of the Orient," 137–43, on Near Eastern lion-hunts and other
royal motifs in early Greek art.

[114] Loraux, *Invention of Athens*; N. Robertson, *EchCl*
27 (1983) 78–92. Stupperich, *Staatsbegräbnis und Privatdenkmal*, 31–56. Clairmont, *Patrios Nomos*, 2, 13–14,
254 n. 15.

the return of the bones of Theseus from Skyros, a mythological paradigm for the return of military heroes for burial by the state (Chapter 12). Along with tragedy and history, the funeral oration may have been the most important literary form to evolve from the Persian wars. It inaugurated a new form of historical fame in speech rather than in monuments, collective prose rather than individual sepulchral poem, where a λόγος came to represent an ἔργον or the word replaced marble.[115] In ways like these, history transformed the traditional patterns of material and oral culture in Athens.

The most dramatic impact the Persian wars and their aftermath had on Greek art, and ultimately on Western art, was through a "revolution in painting."[116] As with sculpture, the medium preexisted the Persian wars, often in emulation of Near Eastern traditions, but was transformed through a new format, function, and symbolic meaning. Monumental painting in Greece began with architecture; the earliest temples were decorated with painted panels on plaster applied to limestone or mudbrick walls.[117] Together with painted tiles and antefixes, these panels belong to architectural ornament, and are not true "paintings" of the kind attested in literary sources, especially in the northeast Peloponnese and the Corinthia, the home of early Greek painters as well as temples (Pliny, *Naturalis Historia* 35.15–16, 56). Meanwhile, history inspired "commissioned" paintings in the archaic period, chiefly for private, dynastic purposes in a non-Greek setting. Kandaules of Lydia paid for a depiction of his victory over the Magnesians by the painter Boularches of Samos (Pliny, *Naturalis Historia* 35.55; 7.126), presumably sometime during his reign (690–687 B.C.).[118] At the close of the archaic period, Mandrokles of Samos had painted for himself (ζῷα γραψάμενος) a scene of the bridge of pontoon boats that he designed for Dareios over the Hellespont (Herodotus, 4.87–88). This painting, which showed the bridge in use with Dareios surveying the operation, "sitting in state and his army crossing," (ἐν προεδρίῃ κατήμενον καὶ τὸν στρατὸν αὐτοῦ διαβαίνοντα), was financed by Dareios's reward and offered as a dedication to Hera at Samos, where Herodotus saw it. He quotes the inscription that proclaims the painting a μνημόσυννον of the bridge, a word Herodotus repeats in describing the painting in his own prose (4.89.1). It is an expression he uses metaphorically on only two occasions, in addition to its more common function to denote dedications at Delphi (2.135) or in Egypt (2.110,

[115] Immerwahr, *AJP* 81 (1960) 269, 285; Svenbro, *La parole et le marbre*; Loraux, *Invention of Athens*.

[116] Robertson, *History of Greek Art*, 240–70; A. Snodgrass, *Archaic Greece* (London, 1982), 208, on monumental painting and the Persian wars; Francis, *Image and Idea in Fifth-Century Athens*, 67–90.

[117] Fragments from the temple of Poseidon at Isthmia are disputed in date, disposition, and subject: O. Broneer, *The Temple of Poseidon at Isthmia* (Princeton, 1971), 33–34, pls. A–C; for revised chronology and reconstruction, see R. F. Rhodes, "The Beginnings of Monumental Architecture in the Corinthia"

(Ph.D. diss., University of North Carolina at Chapel Hill, 1984); D. Amyx, "Archaic Vase-Painting Vis-à-Vis 'Free' Painting at Corinth," in *Ancient Greek Art and Iconography*, ed. W. Moon (Madison, 1983), 37–52.

[118] Hölscher, *Griechische Historienbilder*, 34–35; G. Schauss argues that a later defeat of the Magnesians (in 652 B.C.: Strabo, 14.647) would allow a more appropriate date for the painting: "The Beginning of Greek Polychrome Painting," *AJA* 92 (1988) 273, and *JHS* 108 (1988) 107–11.

121, 136, 148, etc.). In the same book, the historian describes the reform of gold coinage by Dareios as a μνημόσυνον (4.166), appropriate for coins that still bear the name of the king ("darics.") The other occasion when μνημόσυνον indicates a memorial both metaphorical and physical is in Miltiades' speech to Kallimachos before Marathon, cited earlier. Appealing to the images of Harmodios and Aristogeiton, Miltiades challenges his fellow general not only to make Athens free and not slave but "to leave a μνημό-συνον for men of all times" (6.109.3). The use of this word helps support the theory that Miltiades' speech was inspired by a painting where the polemarch actually appeared in the posture of one of the statues by Kritios and Nesiotes (see n. 85). The archaic effect of this word still links it with a visible monument in the speech of Miltiades. In Herodotus's fourth book, its use could be ironic: despite gold coinage and invasion by bridge, the Persians lost and their "memorials" survived as a reminder of their failure. The painting of Mandrokles' bridge portrays a grand act that failed, like the Persian invasion itself, and the word μνημόσυνον has become specific to works associated with the Persian wars.

These archaic paintings belong to the Near Eastern tradition of portraying rulers in the context of victorious campaigns and ambitious building projects.[119] Like the art of portraiture, attributed to Greek art but first attested in Persian coins and heads (see n. 74), these monumental panoramas may have resembled "Oriental" compositions like that in the tondo of the Arkesilaos Painter's name vase (Figure 36). Like Kroisos before fate displaced him from throne to pyre (Figure 37, left), King Arkesilaos of Cyrene sits on a δίφρος, supervising the loading and weighing of export products in an Egyptian manner.[120] The focus on the image of the king suggests that lost paintings, such as the depiction of Mandrokles' bridge, were dominated by the figure of the ruler, with Dareios on his throne. Moreover, the painting of Dareios and his troops crossing the Hellespont must have inspired Herodotus's portrayal of Xerxes at the crossing of the same body of water, a decade later (7.44). His description of the Persian king viewing (κα-τορῶν) his army and his ships, then requesting the spectacle of a race among his ships—ironically won by the Phoenicians, their last naval "victory" before defeat at Salamis—stages an early and unnatural sea battle as gratuitous entertainment, characteristic of Oriental caprice and self-indulgence. The Greek image of Eastern monarchy, which contributed to the image of the king or tyrant in Greek tragedy, probably drew as much from art as from ethnography.[121] In Herodotus's description of Dareios at the

---

[119] Hölscher, *Griechische Historienbilder*, 35–37; cf. Magen, *Assyrische Königsdarstellungen*, esp. "Typus II," on the king-as-builder type; Root, *King and Kingship in Achaemenid Art*; Gabelmann, *Antike Audienz- und Tribunalszenen*, 71–72.

[120] Hölscher, *Griechische Historienbilder*, 30. C. M. Stibbe, *Lakonische Vasenmaler des sechsten Jh. v. Chr.*

(Amsterdam, 1972) 115–17, 195–201, no. 194, pls. 61–62; Boardman, *Greeks Overseas*, 149. On the stool as royal seat, see Chapter 10.

[121] Kierdorf, *Erlebnis und Darstellung*, 75–76; Miller, *AK* 31 (1988) 79–89; cf. A. Alfödi, "Gewaltherrscher und Theaterkönig," in *Late Classical and Medieval Studies in Honor of Albert Mathias Friend, Jr.*, ed.

Hellespont, the details seem pictorial, not verbal; as in his reconstruction of the battle of Marathon (see nn. 136–43), the historian's narrative technique and even research were guided by his acquaintance with paintings like the one dedicated by Mandrokles at Samos. The Greek obsession with the throne as an emblem of the Persian king lasts into the fourth century, as on the Darius krater (Figure 62). It was only when Alexander is said to have taken his seat on the throne of another Dareios (Plutarch, *Alexander* 37) that Greece finally displaced Persia as a world power. This makes all the more intriguing the possibility that Athenian tradition might have turned a Persian seat into a chair made by Daidalos, as argued in Chapter 10.

The painting of Mandrokles' bridge already participates in the historical circumstances of the Persian invasion, through its subject. Like other art forms of the early classical period, historical painting was transformed into a new vehicle of public commemoration comparable with statuary. Early classical Athens witnessed the emergence of painting as a Western art form, in murals and panels no longer subsidiary to buildings but independently conceived and displayed. In the absence of preserved paintings, their tremendous impact on surviving art forms—primarily relief sculpture and vase painting, but also in historiography and philosophy—is difficult to appreciate. Ancient and modern scholarship on the paintings of Polygnotos and Mikon has concentrated on their alleged technical innovations in representing perspective, landscape, drapery, features, color, and portraiture. Ancient comments on these details have been explored and compared with potential reflections in classical vase painting as the closest preserved medium.[122] As in other discrepancies noted previously, the subjects of these new paintings correspond with depictions on vases dated a decade or two earlier—the work of the Kleophrades Painter being a conspicuous example.[123] Greater flexibility in chronology would place these vases closer to the major monuments they seem to emulate. Meanwhile, a distinct group of later vases shows the influence of Polygnotan painting in the disposition of figures "behind" rocks and arranged on two levels, but it is the psychological dimensions of character portrayal that experienced a more profound influence.[124] History provided an impetus for the portrayal of character, as explored in the

K. Weitzmann (Princeton, 1955), 15–55. See nn. 31–33 for Oriental monarchs and Greek tyrants in Greek art and literature.

[122] M. Swindler, *Ancient Painting* (New Haven, 1929), 195–223; E. Simon, "Polygnotan Painting and the Niobid Painter," *AJA* 67 (1963) 43–62; cf. her "Early Classical Vase-Painting," in *Greek Art: Archaic into Classical*, 76–77; Robertson, *History of Greek Art*, 240–70; Barron, *JHS* 92 (1972) 23–45, on details of vases and their monumental prototypes. The most recent investigation of Polygnotos's paintings at Delphi finds few reflections on Attic vases: Stansbury-

O'Donnell, *AJA* 94 (1990) 232–34.

[123] Boardman, *AK* 19 (1976) 3–18; B. Cohen, "Paragone: Sculpture vs. Painting, Kaineus and the Kleophrades Painter," in *Ancient Greek Art and Iconography*, 171–92.

[124] J. J. Pollitt, "The Ethos of Polynotos and Aristeides," in *In Memoriam Otto J. Brendel*, 49–54, and in *Greek Art: Archaic into Classical*, 104–6. In his new reconstruction of Polygnotos's paintings at Delphi, Stansbury-O'Donnell explores these qualities: *AJA* 93 (1989) 212–14, and *AJA* 94 (1990) 232.

genres of history, drama, and sculpture, particularly portraiture, which made its debut with tragic heroes and grand gestures in painting after the Persian wars. The importance and novelty of these early classical paintings lies in their symbolic role and their political function, and their impact on other major arts such as sculpture, rhetoric, and drama was more significant than their technical reflections in vase painting.

In the archaic period, few names of mural painters are associated with Athens, compared with the number active in Ionia and the Corinthia: the Persian victories may have attracted major painters to Athens for the first time. A set of buildings and their paintings cluster in the second quarter of the fifth century, in association with several prominent painters and political figures active in Athens. Just as the Persian wars dominated the early career of Pheidias with several conspicuous monuments, the same historical events monopolized the professional output of Polygnotos and Mikon. The careers and talents of sculptors and painters were closely linked in testimonia where the painter Panainos is the brother (Pliny, *Naturalis Historia* 36.77) or nephew (Strabo, 8.3.30, 354) of Pheidias, as well as his collaborator at Olympia (Pausanias, 5.11.5–6). Pheidias himself is said to have begun his career as a painter (Pliny, *Naturalis Historia* 35.54), and worked with Mikon and Polygnotos at Plataia on the decoration of the temple of Athena Area, restored after the battle with its spoils.[125] As frescoes on a temple, these paintings belong to the archaic tradition of architectural decoration, but their subjects betray the kind of allegorical vision of Greek myth appropriate to recent history.[126] Those by Polygnotos represented Odysseus after the slaughter of the suitors, an image suggestive of the battlefield at Plataia, where Greeks had massacred a large number of unwelcome guests, the Persian army. The other paintings whose subject is described are by Onasias, an artist otherwise unknown, who painted the first expedition against Thebes under Adrastos, a legend appropriate for a city that supported the winning side while its enemy, Thebes, sided with the Persians. Pausanias saw these paintings on the walls of the pronaos, where they must have occupied a position similar to the disposition of panels inside the Lesche of the Knidians at Delphi.[127] Their allegorical subject matter and their arrangement both anticipate the design and decoration of subsequent early classical buildings with paintings.

---

[125] Plutarch, *Aristides* 20; Pausanias, 9.4.1–2; Pliny, *Naturalis Historia* 35.123 (the paintings were restored by Pausias in the fourth century).

[126] As observed long ago by Welcker in 1836 (*Allgemeinische Literatur Zeitung*, 205) Reinach, *La peinture ancienne*, 148–49 n. 3; Thompson, *Marsyas* 9 (1960–1961) 49–50; Thomas, *Mythos und Geschichte*, 69–75. Cf. Gauer, *JdI* 105 (1990) 31–65, on the Penelope motif, the revenge on the suitors, and their symbolic value in the Persian Wars.

[127] Stansbury-O'Donnell, *AJA* 93 (1989) 203–15, and *AJA* 94 (1990) 213–35, arranges the two Homeric tab-leaus centered on the west and east ends (cf. Robertson, *History of Greek Art*, 248), spanning three walls apiece (one short wall plus half of each adjacent long wall). Reinach, *La peinture ancienne*, 149 n. 6, assumed a similar arrangement at Plataia; cf. the paintings by Panainos at Olympia: Völcker-Janssen, *Boreas* 10 (1987) 11–31. On the temple at Plataia, see H. S. Washington, "Discovery of a Temple of Archaic Plan," *AJA* 7 (1881) 390–421; P. W. Wallace, "The Sanctuary of Demeter: The Site of the Victory at Plataea," in *La Béotie antique* (Paris, 1985), 97–100; Francis, *Image and Idea in Fifth-Century Athens*, 84.

In Athens, one of the first new building complexes with paintings must have been Themistokles' rebuilding of the shrine of the Lykomidai at Phlya, at his own expense (Plutarch, *Themistokles* 1). Like the temple at Plataia, this shrine had been destroyed by the Persians, and its repair, as at Plataia, occasioned new decoration. The authority of Simonides cited by Plutarch implies that an epigram was inscribed, as on Polygnotos's *Ilioupersis* at Delphi (Pausanias, 9.27.4) and on paintings by Kimon of Kleonai (*Anthologia Palatina* 9.578; 16.84). This reinforces the idea of collaboration between word and image in the commemoration of the Persian wars. It may have been Simonides' collaboration with painters that inspired his famous comparison of the two media (cited by Plutarch, *Moralia* 346): τὴν μὲν ζωγραφίαν ποίησιν σιωπῶσαν [προσαγορεύει], τὴν δὲ ποίησιν ζωγραφίαν λαλοῦσαν: "Painting he calls silent poetry, and poetry—painting with a voice." His pronouncement belongs to a tradition of representing poetry in terms of art (as in Pindar: see Chapter 2) and is hardly "the invention of literary criticism," but more likely a compliment to painters whose works he inscribed.[128] The role of Themistokles in a building with paintings also inaugurates the kind of personal initiative in public projects characteristic of Kimon and even of Perikles, who offered to the Athenians his own sponsorship of the Akropolis program, in lieu of the state expenses they protested (Plutarch, *Perikles* 14). However, the subject of the paintings paid for by Themistokles is not recorded, and their implications for classical art are lost.

Four buildings in Athens were embellished with monumental paintings by Mikon and Polygnotos in the second quarter of the fifth century B.C. Two of them were shrines: the sanctuary of the Dioskouroi or the Anakeion, whose description is obscured by textual corruption (Pausanias, 1.18.1), and the Theseion founded in conjunction with the return of the bones of Theseus (Plutarch, *Kimon* 8, *Theseus* 36). The first contained at least two paintings, one by Polygnotos of the Rape of the Leukippidae by the Dioskouroi, and the other by Mikon depicting Jason's expedition to Kolkhis. Pausanias also mentions a third one, distinguished for its σπουδή, showing Akastos and his horses. Of the paintings surviving in such descriptions, those from the Anakeion are the most elusive in terms of the shrine's location and appearance. However, plausible arguments point to the influence of the Leukippidai painting on other fifth-century art, specifically the metopes of the Temple of Apollo at Bassai.[129] Moreover, the theme of the second painting, from the *Argonautica*, acquired new significance after the Persian wars in Greek iconography, as a confrontation between Greeks and Oriental opponents.[130]

The paintings in the Theseion decorated a shrine whose ancient site and design are

[128] A. Carson, "Simonides Painter," *APA Abstracts, 1987*, 65. Cf. Pollitt, *Ancient View of Greek Art*, 10, on literary analogy in art criticism. See Chapter 2, n. 21, for references in Harriott, Svenbro; also Part III.

[129] According to B. Madigan, "The Sculptured Metopes of the Temple of Apollo at Bassae" (Ph.D. diss., University of Minnesota, 1982), 51–55.

[130] B. Shefton, "Medea at Marathon," *AJA* 60 (1956) 159–63, on the "orientalization" of Medea in the fifth century, which he attributes to the influence of a monumental painting; Meyer, *Kunst und Geschichte*, 18, on scenes of Jason as a confrontation between East and West (see Chapter 12).

still unknown. Pausanias locates the shrine "near the gymnasium" and describes three paintings, with a digression on Theseus that could be construed as the description of a fourth painting (1.17.2).[131] Of the three paintings clearly indicated, Pausanias first names a battle between Athenians and Amazons, a myth not attested earlier than the Persian wars and repeated in the Stoa Poikile paintings. Pausanias himself mentions other versions on the shield of Athena Parthenos and the throne of Zeus at Olympia, appropriate to the promulgation of this myth in early classical art and propaganda. Next is a battle between Centaurs and Lapiths, likewise popular on lost monuments (e.g. the shield of Athena Promachos: Pausanias, 1.18.2) as well as in sculpture and vase painting. The third painting is the only one the periegete clearly ascribed to an artist—Mikon—and was difficult for Pausanias to interpret, as he found it only partially represented. It apparently showed some aspect of Theseus's dive to the bottom of the sea (cf. Figure 56), a myth that Pausanias recounts in more detail than the painting indicates, and which leads him into a digression about the subsequent fate of Theseus that implies a fourth painting, perhaps on the rescue of the Athenian hero by Herakles.

The iconographic implications of these paintings for the mythology of Theseus and Athens have been repeatedly and intensively analyzed, and will be explored in Chapter 12. Presumably the building and its paintings were executed between the return of the hero's remains in 475 B.C. and the ostracism of Kimon in 462/1, within the same range of time to which Polygnotos's paintings at Delphi and in the Stoa are assigned. As a new rather than a restored shrine, the Theseion could have been designed for paintings rather than as a traditional temple like building, but no evidence allows it closer comparison with the innovative design and purpose of the Stoa Poikile.

A third collection of paintings was housed in the Pinakotheke on the Akropolis in the second century A.D., when Pausanias reported a number of epic scenes. He attributes two, depicting Achilles at Skyros and Odysseus with Nausikaa and her maidens, to Polygnotos (1.22.6–7). It is tempting to associate the first subject with Kimon's trip to Skyros to recover the bones of Theseus (see Chapter 12) but the story was also popular in fourth-century monumental painting (Pliny, *Naturalis Historia* 35.134). In the allegorical scenario implied by the painting in the Pinakotheke, Kimon's recovery of the hero's remains for the city of Athens would find its mythological analogy in Odysseus's mission to fetch the hero, Achilles, from the same island, for the Greek expedition to Troy. Two other "pendants" were displayed in the Pinakotheke: two exploits from the Trojan expedition—Odysseus with the bow of Philoktetes, and Diomedes stealing the Palladion—and a pair of scenes contrasting the sacrifice of Polyxena with the murder of Aigisthos.[132] Other paintings are mentioned: Aglaophon's tableau of Alkibiades in the lap

[131] J. Six, "Mikon's Fourth Picture in the Theseion," *JHS* 39 (1919) 130–43; Barron, *JHS* 92 (1972) 20–45, Francis, *Image and Idea in Fifth-Century Athens*, 49–51.

[132] Reinach, *La peinture ancienne*, 144 n. 1; Thompson, *Marsyas* 9 (1960–1961) 50, on these six paintings as pendants. Achilles on Skyros: *LIMC* I.1, 55–69.

of Nemea, for example, and a wrestler portrayed by Timainetos, a painter not mentioned elsewhere. Pausanias describes at least ten paintings still visible (ἔτι δὲ τῶν γραφῶν παρέντι), whose variety in date suggests a range of time over which the paintings were produced, collected, and ultimately displayed. What remains unknown is whether their setting, merely described as an οἴκημα of the Propylaia, was designed to be a picture gallery or acquired that function after the Propylaia was completed.[133] If the latter is true, which would agree with the Roman conversion of Greek sanctuaries into art collections, then the Stoa Poikile retains its claim as the first building in the history of Western art deliberately designed to display paintings.

Recent excavations in the northwest corner of the Athenian Agora have located the foundations of a colonnaded structure, measuring 12.60 by 2.68 meters, with open ends defined by columns rather than walls.[134] Whether or not this structure is the Painted Stoa, it sheds no light on the paintings and their disposition, and simply agrees with Pausanias's location of the building in this general area (1.15.1). The Stoa Poikile, or Painted Stoa, derived its name from four sets of murals, but may have been known more commonly in the century of its construction as the Peisianakteion, in honor of its sponsor, Peisianax, the brother-in-law of Kimon (schol. Aiskhines, Ktesiphon 186; Plutarch, Kimon 4.5; Diogenes Laertius, 7.1.5; Suda s.v. Πεισιανάκτειος στοά). Presumably the building and its paintings were complete before 462/1, the year of Kimon's ostracism, and the building is mentioned in Aristophanes' Wasps (1088–90). Unlike a building decorated with painted plaster, the stoa probably displayed panels of wood on the walls: true "paintings." A late reference describes them as sanides, presumably some kind of (laminated?) panels, which were removed in late antiquity (Synesius, Epistles 54, 135).[135]

Pausanias describes the paintings in the Stoa Poikile in the following order: first, the battle of Athenians against Spartans at Oinoe, in the Argolid; then, "in the middle of the walls" (ἐν τῷ δὲ μέσῳ τῶν τοίχων), a battle with Theseus and the Athenians fighting the Amazons, apparently by Mikon; followed by (ἐπὶ δέ) the capture of Troy by the

[133] The off-center doorway of this room long suggested a dining room, denied by W. B. Dinsmoor, Jr., "The Asymmetry of the Pinakotheke—For the Last Time?" in Studies in Athenian Architecture, Sculpture and Topography in Honor of Homer F. Thompson, Hesperia suppl. 20 (Princeton, 1982), 18–33, but revived by P. Hellström, "The Planned Function of the Mnesiklean Propylaia," OpAth 17 (1988) 107–120, who invokes original paintings (p. 118) for an interior resembling the Lesche of the Knidians; cf. R. A. Tomlinson, "The Sequence of Construction of Mnesikles' Propylaia," BSA 85 (1990) 405–13.

[134] T. L. Shear, Jr., "Excavations in the Athenian Agora, 1980–1982," Hesperia 54 (1984) 5–19; Camp, Athenian Agora, 66–72, figs. 42–44. Late details (triple rebate moldings on the undercut steps) and unusual design (with open wings rather than closed on both ends for paintings, like the Lesche of the Knidians at Delphi) suggest a building other than the Stoa Poikile.

[135] Swindler, Ancient Painting, 217; Robertson, History of Greek Art, 244–45; cf. Polygnotos's tabula in Rome (Pliny, Naturalis Historia 35.59), presumably also a wooden panel. For the testimonia on the Stoa Poikile painting of Marathon, see Harrison, AJA 76 (1972) 370–78.

Greeks, featuring Ajax and Kassandra; and finally (τελευταῖον δέ), the battle of Marathon. With the exception of the battle of Oinoe, which dates from more recent (post-Persian) history, the order in which Pausanias describes these paintings follows closely a formulaic sequence of Athenian ἔργα, deeds from the Athenian past, as they are invoked in a rhetorical context.[136] The catalogue of Athenian achievements recited at Plataia and analyzed previously (Herodotus, 9.27) is the first written version of the *Tatenkatalog*, which becomes a standard feature of the ἐπιτάφιος λόγος or funeral oration.[137] Herodotus may have consulted more than speeches, written or remembered, in imagining the Athenian speech at Plataia and endowing it with innovations actually generated later, as a result of the Persian wars. Other narratives in Herodotus, specifically the battle of Marathon, have been convincingly traced to pictorial sources such as the painting in the Stoa Poikile.[138] Details of action, time, and character at Marathon are likely to have been drawn from the painting, but the actual sequence of paintings in the stoa could have inspired the recital of Athenian deeds at Plataia. This list excludes Oinoe, of course, but that battle postdates Plataia and its painting may have been a later addition to the stoa's collection (see n. 136). The other three battles—against Amazons, Trojans, and Persians at Marathon—constitute the three climactic encounters of Athenian history in art as in rhetoric, and form a "trilogy" in post-Persian narrative, whether in painting or literature.

The connection between public speech and public art is not just inferred from Herodotus but is explicit in references made by orators to the paintings in the stoa. Unlike Herodotus, Demosthenes acknowledges the presence of the Plataians at Marathon (*Neaira* 94) and invokes the evidence of the painting, still visible in his time (καὶ ἔτι καὶ νῦν . . . δεδήλωκεν, although the scholiast thinks otherwise).[139] The language of Demosthenes describes the representation of Athenians in the painting as τῆς ἀνδραγαθίας αὐτῶν ὑπομνήματα, "memorials of their valor." Similar expressions are used by Aiskhines (*Ktesiphon* 186) when he invokes the Stoa as authority: "For you have the monuments of all these noble deeds in the agora" (ἁπάντων γὰρ ὑμῖν τῶν καλῶν ἔργων τὰ ὑπομνήματα ἐν τῇ ἀγορᾷ κεῖται). Aiskhines then describes the figure of Miltiades, who can be recognized even without an inscription, urging on the soldiers in the fore-

[136] L. H. Jeffery, "The Battle of Oinoe in the Stoa Poikile: A Problem in Greek Art and History," *BSA* 68 (1965) 41–57, 51–52, and Hölscher, *Griechische Historienbilder*, 73, on rhetoric. Meiggs, *Athenian Empire*, 469–72. J. Busche *Untersuchungen zur Oinoe-Schlacht des Pausanias* (Frankfurt, 1974). Francis, *Image and Idea in Fifth-Century Athens*, 85–94.

[137] Kierdorf, *Erlebnis und Darstellung*, chap. 3; Loraux, *Invention of Athens*, 60–75, esp. 61, 74.

[138] E. Harrison, "The Victory of Kallimachos," *GRBS* 12 (1971) 7, on the painting's triangular struc-

ture and progressive narrative; *ArtB* 54 (1972) 390–402, esp. 402, and *AJA* 76 (1972) 353–78. *Contra*: Meiggs, *Athenian Empire*, 280 n. 2; M. Vickers and E. D. Francis, "The Oinoe Painting in the Stoa Poikile and Herodotus' Account of Marathon," *BSA* 80 (1985) 99–113, equate the battle of Oinoe painting with Marathon.

[139] Harpocration admits that Δημοσθένης διαμαρτάνει but knows no other written authority: οὐδεὶς εἴρηκεν.

ground. The exchange imagined by Herodotus at Marathon, with Miltiades in the fore-
ground, urging on the army, and Kallimachos in the pose of Harmodios, might be a
caption for the painting by Polygnotos.[140] The gesture may have become a formula in
other monumental art of the classical period. The description of the figure of Miltiades
"extending his arm and indicating the barbarians to the Hellenes, while speaking to
urge them on" (schol. Aristeides, *On the Four* 174: ἐκτείνων τὴν χεῖρα καὶ ὑποδεικνὺς
τοῖς Ἕλλησι τοὺς βαρβάρους λέγων ὁρμᾶν κατ᾽ αὐτῶν) could also describe the figure
of Apollo in the west pediment of the temple of Zeus at Olympia, where he transcends
the Lapiths' struggle with the centaurs by his gesture.[141] The composition of the Marathon painting, and the images of its heroes, continued to inspire public oratory, as if
readily familiar to an Athenian audience. Thus two *declamationes* by Polemon, a teacher
of Aristides, are attributed to an imaginary contest between the fathers of Kynegeiros
and Kallimachos.[142] In coincidences of language and image, it becomes clear how rhetorical gestures and expressions participated and collaborated in the commemoration of
history. Furthermore, the function of rhetoric as a public art, dependent on gesture and
monument as much as formulaic structures in syntax, requires its analysis in terms of
visual and not just verbal traditions.

Harrison's reconstruction of the Marathon painting as a trilogy, "in which successive
dramas are named 'Miltiades,' 'Kallimachos,' and 'Kynegeiros,' or 'attack,' 'victory,' and
'pursuit' " is more than just a convenient analogy to drama.[143] History, tragedy, and
painting all demonstrate the emergence of this structure in the same period of Attic
culture, without requiring arguments for "influence" between the different media. The
architectural layout of the Knidian Lesche at Delphi requires an arrangement in triptych
form, as argued recently (see n. 127), and must have become a standard form of design
for relief sculpture as well as painting. The same tripartite, interior display has been
conjectured for the paintings by Panainos inside the temple of Zeus at Olympia.[144] The
"brother" of Pheidias and painter of the battle of Marathon in the Stoa Poikile at Athens
decorated the throne of Zeus's statue at Olympia with nine pairs of figures, described
in groups of three panels where history and allegory are juxtaposed with legend, as in
the Stoa Poikile (Pausanias, 5.11.5–6). Deeds of Herakles and Theseus are joined by
episodes from the Trojan War depicting Ajax and Kassandra, Achilles and Penthesilea;
the Persian wars are represented by figures of Hellas and Salamis, perhaps holding an

---

[140] Thus E. Harrison, *AJA* 76 (1972) 356.

[141] N. Terzini, "The Gesture of Apollo in the West
Pediment of the Temple of Zeus at Olympia," *AJA* 86
(1982) 287–88; "Unifying Themes in the Sculpture at
Olympia," *CA* 6 (1987) 145–52. This heroic gesture re-
calls the Homeric ὑπερέχειν χεῖρα practiced by
Zeus (*Iliad* 4.249) and Apollo (*Iliad* 5.433).

[142] Analyzed in detail by Harrison, *AJA* 76 (1972)

358–62.

[143] Harrison, *AJA* 76 (1972) 363–64, ill. 1; also argued by V. Massaro, "Herodotus' Account of the Battle of Marathon and the Picture in the Stoa Poikile,"
AntCl 47 (1978) 458–75, esp. 461–62; Stewart, in *Pictorial Narrative*, 61 fig. 18 .

[144] Völcker-Janssen, *Boreas* 10 (1987) 11–31.

ἄφλαστον, the symbol of naval victory (cf. Figure 42).[145] Panainos's collaboration and kinship with Pheidias, however anecdotal in source, expresses in metaphor the close relationship between monumental sculpture and painting in classical Greece. The arrangement of interior sculpted friezes inside classical temples—in two Attic temples and at Bassai—simulates the display of monumental paintings in an interior space, across inside angles. It was in these major aspects of purpose and arrangement that monumental painting influences other classical media, not in minor details of anatomy or angle reflected on vases. Thus the triple register of the Darius krater (Figure 62) could reflect the scheme of a wall painting in "triptych" scheme—the Persian king and his courtiers in the central panel, flanked by a scene of Persians paying tribute facing the panel with Greece, Asia, and "Apate."

The other field where paintings played a role—tragedy—was encouraged by their design and display. The arrangement of paintings in triptych sections juxtaposed not only different episodes of the same subject but figures from two cycles of myth. In the Lesche of the Knidians at Delphi, Ajax and Kassandra form the apex of the *Ilioupersis* triangle, balanced by the symmetry of departure scenes, Greek tents versus Trojan homes, the slavery of Trojan women against the death of Trojan men. Heroes like Agamemnon, Ajax, and Odysseus are portrayed opposite their counterparts in the underworld, on the opposite walls, and the violation of Athena's sanctuary is balanced by her vengeance on the violators, in a pattern familiar in tragedy. Similar arrangements within the Stoa Poikile in Athens would have allowed Persians and Amazons to be juxtaposed as enemies of Athens, the defenders of Athens with the captors of Troy.[146] Thus monumental paintings presented the same comparison of character and destiny that preoccupied Herodotus and vase painters, reflected in literary testimonia on qualities of ἦθος attributed to Polygnotos (see n. 124).

In ways like these, the proliferation of paintings in early classical Athens publicized a new form with its new content. Their historical significance compares with the status of mural painting in the Americas in the twentieth century. Public murals launched a new style of panorama with figures selected and paired for their social and historical symbolism. Thus Miltiades and Theseus shared the same field in classical Athens the way Marx and Montezuma do in the murals of modern Mexico. Like commemorative portrait statues, historical and myth-historical paintings transformed a traditional medium into a newly political one, making legendary material coterminous with current history. The Stoa Poikile is conspicuous as a secular building, not a shrine decorated with paintings; its purpose is not homage to a deity but the glory of Athens, just as Herodotus

---

[145] Reinach, *La peinture ancienne*, 168–71, no. 166 (see my n. 47 on representations of the ἄφλαστον in victory dedications); Swindler, *Ancient Painting*, 220–22; Gauer, in *Festschrift Neutsch*, 133.

[146] Stewart, in *Pictorial Narrative*, 57 table 2, for one such reconstruction. Hölscher, *Griechische Historienbilder*, 78, and Stansbury-O'Donnell, *AJA* 93 (1989) 214; *AJA* 94 (1990) 230–32, on painting and tragedy.

made Athens the "hero of his work."[147] Like history and tragedy, this new medium was inconceivable without certain historical events. Second, the paintings, like the bronze statue groups, juxtaposed Athenians and Olympians—gods, heroes, and citizens— much as history had raised contemporary experience to the realm of legend. It was these transformations that made the Parthenon frieze, with its cast of Olympians, Athenians, and ep/anonymous heroes, a natural legacy of the early classical revolution in painting. The effects of these paintings and their message are traced in Athenian myth and cult, in the next section, but their primary medium was public and visual, not literary. If archaic Greece is remembered as an "oral" or "song culture,"[148] its classical successor used the visible power of monuments to forge new traditions in public art.

[147] Immerwahr, *AJP* 81 (1960) 281.

[148] Herington, *Poetry into Drama*, 3–4; B. Gentili, *Poetry and Its Public in Ancient Greece*, trans. A. T. Cole (Baltimore, 1988), 3–23.

CHAPTER 12

The Invention of Athens: History into Myth

"FOR THE HEROES ARE AT HAND": CULT AND MYTH

For not we have achieved these things ourselves, but the gods and
the heroes, who punished one man for his desire to rule Asia and
Europe, being wicked and reckless; he who treated sacred and private
property alike, who burned and destroyed the images of the gods;
who even whipped the sea and bound it in chains.

—Herodotus 8.109

IKE all speeches delivered in Herodotus's account of the Persian wars, this one may mix irony with authencity or sincerity. When Themistokles abandoned the pursuit of the defeated Persians to the Hellespont, he did so partly to ensure favor (ἀποθήκη) with the enemy as a safeguard for the future, a precaution that later served him well (Plutarch, *Themistokles* 21–33). His public concession to the majority vote against pursuit professed more pious reasons, attributing the Greek victory to good fortune (εὕρημα) in the speech just quoted. Like the speech delivered by Miltiades before Marathon (6.109) cited earlier, the words of Themistokles betray a post-Persian interpretation of the victory and a synthesis of Athenian responses to the Persian wars. In the aftermath of victory, dedications of thanksgiving and repair or renewal of monuments generated new genres in art and literature, as examined in the previous section. More profound innovations were new modes of understanding and explaining the unexpected Greek success; the nature of this intellectual response is the focus of the final chapters.

The first response was traditional, archaic, and pious, like the sentiment attributed to Themistokles in this speech. Only divine action (δαίμων τις: Aeschylus, *Persians* 344, cf. 496, 724) could have sent storms to confound the enemy and allowed a small defensive force to defeat the greatest army and navy then in existence. This response worked itself out in attention to the gods: establishment of new cults and reparation to old ones, with the transformation of legend into a historical precedent for recent events. In art, the gods still occupied a separate sphere in the historical hierarchy generated by the Persian wars. On the Darius Painter's name vase (Figure 62), the figures of Olympian gods and personified nations occupy the upper register, with kings and mortals the next two registers below them, respectively. Even if the vase derives its scheme from a painting of three panels, it divides gods from men (see Chapter 13).

The second response evolved more gradually and insidiously, and was more intimately linked to the continuing ambitions of Athens. The belief arose that the Greeks, and Athenians in particular, were naturally and culturally superior, hence able to overcome an enemy lacking the advantages of democracy and other Athenian institutions. Intellectual developments in Athens, particularly in philosophy and rhetoric, assisted this incremental secularization of history, visible in the critical historiography of Thucydides and his contempt for superstition, in contrast to Herodotus's attention to divine action. Political priorities—the ambitions of the Athenian Empire—may have encouraged the promotion of Athenian achievement, a subset of the secular response, at the expense of the sacred one dependent on divine dispensation. This evolution affected both types of $\xi\rho\gamma o\nu$: the monuments examined in Chapter 11 as well as $\xi\rho\gamma\alpha$ in narrative, the "works" of historiography. The trophies erected after victories over the Persians were restored at critical moments later in the century, when Athens needed to emphasize those victories to defend its right to leadership in the Aegean.[1] These physical restorations complemented the "ideology of Marathon" promoted in public rhetoric, a monumental equivalent to oral communication. This secondary interpretation of Athenian victory was ultimately responsible for the promotion of democracy and other concepts now considered "Western" values.[2] The secular, political evaluation of the victory included the promotion of Athens as the natural home of culture as well as of political leadership, and was probably responsible for the repatriation of Daidalos as an Athenian artist. However, his role in this recasting of Greek cultural history had its origins in the mythological interpretation of victory, the focus of this section.

Through cult and myth, divine personalities were newly integrated into the Attic calendar and landscape to honor their role against Persia. Heroes, old and new, provided a third target for Athenian gratitude toward newly appreciated benefactors. These three domains of Greek religion experience significant transformations in early classical literature and art, with new images of gods and heroes reborn as youthful and benevolent. Ultimately, mythology becomes a historical process in the classical era, transcending other "universal" theories of myth (e.g., structuralism), which might apply to other periods of Greek culture.[3] In particular, the exploration of allegory, as a dialogue be-

[1] W. West, CP 64 (1969) 7–19; see Chapter 11, n. 45.

[2] Euben, Political Theory 14 (1986) 359–90; see Chapter 13.

[3] DuBois, Centaurs and Amazons, 53; N. Horsfall, "Myth and Mythography," EchCl 29 (1985) 394, on "secondary myth." Cf. C. Brillante, "Myth and His-

tween myth and history, was initiated in this period in ways fundamental to ancient and European art.[4] Its sources were not so much an ingenious and original juxtaposition of legend and reality, artificially separated in the modern mind, but the simultaneous experience of them without contradiction, as a convergence of myth and history (Chapter 10). Most vividly, traditional legends such as epic battles against centaurs, Amazons, and Trojans acquired new status in classical art as documents of Athenian history.

Herodotus documents how specific episodes of the Persian wars promoted new cults; the case of the god Pan provides a complete paradigm for their mechanics. On his way to Sparta before the battle of Marathon, the Athenian runner, Pheidippides, met Pan on Mount Parthenion near Tegea in Arkadia (6.105). The god called the athlete by name and bid him convey his complaints to the Athenians, "for they have paid no attention to him, although he is well disposed toward the Athenians and has been useful to them on many occasions, and will be in the future." Accordingly, the Athenians founded a sanctuary to him in a cave below the Akropolis and held an annual festival with torch races in his honor, a cult whose link to the battle of Marathon is confirmed by Pausanias (1.28.4; 32.7). The cave sanctuary appears in classical literature (Euripides, Ion 492–94, 938) and contained a statue of the god dedicated by Miltiades and inscribed with an epigram attributed to Simonides (frag. 136 = Anthologia Planudea 232, 259):

> τὸν τραγόπουν ἐμὲ Πᾶνα, τὸν Ἀρκάδα, τὸν κατὰ Μήδων,
> τὸν μετ᾽ Ἀθηναίων στήσατο Μιλτιάδης.

> Miltiades established me, the goat-footed Pan, the Arkadian,
> the one [who fought] with the Athenians against the Medes.

The torch race held for Pan's new cult represents a contest popular in other rites celebrated in Athens in the fifth century, notably the cult shared by Prometheus and Hephaistos, the rites for Bendis celebrated in the Peiraieus (Plato, Republic 327a, 354a), the Anthesteria, and the cult of Artemis Brauronia.[5] Several traditions involving the declaration of victory or defeat after battle link the torch race to the Persian wars. Pheidippides' trip to Sparta establishes a messenger's journey as a model for an athletic event dedicated to the god he met en route.[6] In a passage immortalized (in stone) by the U.S. Post Office, Herodotus compares the famous mail-route of the Persians to the torch race (λαμπαδηφορίη) familiar to him in the cult of Hephaistos, presumably in Athens (8.98): "Nothing stops these couriers from covering their allotted stage in the quickest possible time: neither snow, rain, heat, nor darkness" (trans. A. de Selincourt). In Aeschylus's Agamemnon, Klytemnestra uses a Persian word (ἄγγαρος) to describe the

tory," in Approaches to Greek Myth, ed. L. Edmunds (Baltimore, 1990), 91–138, and other essays.

[4] Shapiro, Boreas 9 (1986) 4–23.

[5] S. Herbert, "The Torch-Race at Corinth," in Co-rinthiaca, 29–35.

[6] H. W. Parke, Festivals of the Athenians (Ithaca, N.Y., 1977), 172–73; Borgeaud, Cult of Pan, 134.

route of beacons bringing news of the fall of Troy to Argos, and calls the same route λαμπαδηφόρων νόμοι (312), comparing it with a torch race.[7] Finally, the traditional headgear worn in the torch race, the spiked wreath worn by torch runners in vase paintings, recalls an incident from the Persian wars. After the battle of Plataia, Euchidas ran to Delphi, fetched sacred fire from the altar to rekindle that polluted by the barbarians, and returned to the site of the battle, only to collapse and receive a hero's burial in the sanctuary of Artemis Eukleia (Plutarch, *Aristeides* 20). He had returned from Delphi crowned with laurel, as if the image of his arrival at Plataia wearing laurel and carrying the sacred fire became a model and an *aition* for the classical torch race. These historical references suggest that the torch race, like the race in full armor (see Chapter 11), commemorated dramatic episodes from victories against the Persians. The argument that the torch race derives from a "religious ritual in which the sacred fire is transferred from one altar to another"[8] may explain some of its original associations but not its popularity in the fifth century or its link to history.

What kind of assistance Pan promised the Athenians is not specified by Herodotus but was fulfilled at Marathon, according to other sources. Popular (if false) etymology attributed the "panic" experienced by the Persians at Marathon to his influence, and an allusion to this may survive in Herodotus's anecdote about the blinding of Epizelos.[9] A cave sacred to Pan at Marathon (Pausanias, 1.32.7) may have provided sacred protection for the defenders the way the sanctuary of Herakles served as the Athenian camp (6.108), but the cave is not mentioned by Herodotus.[10] The cave at Oinoe (Marathon), like other caves sacred to Pan and the Nymphs in Attika, shows a significant increase in material in the early fifth century, as if a cult of Pan were, indeed, initiated after the battle of Marathon. The island of Salamis was sacred to Pan in Aeschylus's account of the battle (*Persians* 447–49), as if the god's blessing spread to other battle sites of the Persian wars, in the spirit of the epigram by Simonides that praises him as τὸν κατὰ Μήδων, τὸν μετ' Ἀθηναίων. In Greek art, representations of Pan are rare before this period, and cluster in the second quarter of the fifth century.[11] Some of these represen-

---

[7] S. Tracy, "Darkness from Light: The Beacon Fire in the *Agamemnon*," *CQ* 36 (1986) 257–60; Herbert, in *Corinthiaca*, 29, on the torch-race in classical metaphors and similes; Francis, *Image and Idea in Fifth-Century Athens*, 33–35.

[8] Herbert, in *Corinthiaca*, 32; How and Wells, 2:269 cite Frazer, who subscribed to theories on the role of fire in religion that encouraged the ritual origin of the torch race at the expense of history.

[9] Immerwahr, *Form and Thought in Herodotus*, 253–54; Harrison, *AJA* 76 (1972) 368; Borgeaud, *Cult of Pan*, 88–101 and 133–62.

[10] A. Deligiorgi-Alexopoulou, "Attic Caves Dedi-

cated to the God Pan," Ἀρχαιολογία 15 (1985) 45–54; excavation reports: I. Papadimitriou, Ἔργον 1958 (1959) 15–22; Daux, *BCH* 82 (1958) 681; 83 (1959) 587–88. J. Wickens, "The Archaeology and History of Cave-Use in Attica from Prehistoric through Late Roman Times" (Ph.D. diss., Indiana University, 1985) 169–96, on the dramatic rise in cave cults of Pan and the Nymphs in the classical period.

[11] F. Brommer, "Panbilder des fünften Jahrhunderts," *AA* 53 (1938) 376–81; Bovon, *Études de Lettres* 6 (1963) 224–26. C. Edwards, "Greek Votive Reliefs to Pan and the Nymphs" (Ph.D., diss., New York University, 1985).

tations show specific correlations with the new cult: for example, a late black-figured cup by the Haimon Group, dated around 475 B.C., shows Pan running with a torch, an allusion to the race instituted after Marathon.[12] Last but not least, the figure of Pan was included in Polygnotos's painting of the battle of Marathon, along with gods like Athena and Demeter, and heroes like Herakles and Theseus (Pausanias, 1.15.3). This provides as important a historical source on his presence at the battle as the missing account by Herodotus.

The promotion of Pan is matched by the new attention Athens paid to Boreas, god of the north wind, after he destroyed the Persian fleet off Artemision (Herodotus, 7.189). A tradition (λέγεται δε λόγος) held that the Athenians prayed to the god before the battle to assist them, the equivalent of the prebattle encounter between Pan and Pheidippides. As in the complaint of Pan, the god Boreas was remembered as assisting the Greeks before, in this case by having sent a storm off Mount Athos during the expedition under Mardonios (6.44.2). Herodotus himself, with unusual skepticism, reserves judgment on whether Athenian prayers and sacrifice were responsible for the storm at Artemision (οὐκ ἔχω εἰπεῖν. 7.189.3). But he then mentions the foundation of a sanctuary to Boreas on the Ilissos River in southeast Athens, presumably the source of his λόγοι on the storm at Artemision. This site was also remembered as the location of the rape of Oreithyia by Boreas, the incident that made him a γαμβρός (kinsman) of the Athenians. In the *Phaedrus* (229.b–d), Sokrates locates the incident near the sanctuary of Agrai on the same river, and mentions an altar to Boreas, but knows of another version of the myth that attests to the rape of Oreithyia on the Areopagos.[13] The foundation and celebration of the cult must have been accompanied by commemoration in poetry. The equivalent of a hymn to Boreas, a choral (?) poem on the battle of Artemision, was attributed to Simonides, the poet whose name was associated with epigrams and other poems celebrating the Persian wars (*PMG*, frag. 534).[14] The story of Boreas became popular in other Attic poetry and prose of the period, including tragedies by Choirilos, Aeschylus (frag. 281, Radt), and Sophokles (Radt, 768.596), and mythography by Akusilaos and Pherekydes (*FGrH* 3, F 145).

Predictably, the story of the rape of Oreithyia also appears in Attic vase painting for the first time in the early classical period, on about thirty-five extant vases, only to disappear thereafter.[15] What makes this theme more than just a story of the love between gods and mortals, of the kind popular in archaic times, is the connection to Athens. It

---

[12] Martin v. Wagner-Museum, Würzburg (loan): E. Simon, "Ein nordattischer Pan," *AK* 17 (1976) 19–23. Borgeaud, *Cult of Pan*, 134.

[13] G. Ferrari, *Listening to the Cicadas* (Cambridge, 1988), 9–12, on the significance of this myth in the dialogue.

[14] U. Wilamowitz, *Sappho und Simonides* (Berlin,

1913), 206–9; Kierdorf, *Erlebnis und Darstellung*, 23–24.

[15] Bovon, *Études de Lettres* 6 (1963) 223–24; J. Burns, "Boreas and Oreithyia in Greek Vase Painting," *ZAnt* 31 (1981) 215–32; Simon, in *Greek Art: Archaic into Classical*, 75–76; Pollitt, *YUAG Bulletin* (Spring 1987) 13–14. S. Kaempf-Dimitriadou, "Boreas," *LIMC* II.1, 133–40.

was this rape that made not only Boreas a γαμβρός of Athens but Thrace its ἐπίκουρος, or ally. In some representations, including four vases by the Niobid Painter alone, the presence of Athena suggests divine approval of a violation that ends in marriage and a profitable relationship for Athens.[16] Other Athenian figures depicted in attendance, in as many as half of the Attic scenes, include Oreithyia's parents, Erechtheus and Praxithea, her sisters, and the legendary king, eponymous hero, and father of her companions, Kekrops.[17] The presence of figures like Kekrops and Erechtheus legitimates the story as one linked to royal Attic genealogy. Absent from Attic art until the Persian wars, they also indicate a recent innovation perhaps inaugurated in poetry or monumental art. The lost poem of Simonides on Boreas and the Artemision episode may have incorporated these Attic heroes into a standard narrative version adopted by painters. As Simon suggests (see n. 15), the iconography of these vases also suggests that a painting could have decorated the new sanctuary of Boreas on the Ilissos (in the tradition of other post-Persian shrines decorated with paintings: see Chapter 11). The story of the Thracian king is also one of those traditions of the Persian wars that evolve into a myth in support of Athenian ambitions during the Pentakontaetia. Boreas wears Thracian costume in some of his appearances on vases, and his connection to Thrace may have been emphasized during Athenian campaigns in northern Greece.[18] The story of Boreas and Oreithyia was popular as architectural sculpture in at least two akroteria for Attic temples of the late fifth century, including the Athenian temple on Delos, a conspicuous locale for Athenian propaganda.[19] In addition to the specific associations of the god of the north wind with recent storms and battles, the theme of rape or abduction plays a significant role in the historiography of the Persian wars. Herodotus opens his history with a series of abductions explaining legendary and contemporary hostilities, and ultimately the origins of the Persian wars (1.1–5).[20] This mode of explanation coincides with an interest in scenes of abduction in classical art, often involving gods and mortals, as if the miraculous intervention of gods in human history revived interest in their erotic

[16] S. Kaempf-Dimitriadou, "Boreas," LIMC II.1, 137, nos. 53–56; Simon in Greek Art: Archaic into Classical, 76, pl. 71; A. Follmann, Der Pan Maler (Bonn, 1968), 62. Cf. the same pose held by Boreas on a lekythos at Yale (1913.148): Pollitt, YUAG Bulletin (Spring 1987) 13–14, fig. 6. On rape, abduction, and marriage in Attic iconography, see Ch. Sourvinou-Inwood, "A Series of Erotic Pursuits: Images and Meanings," JHS 107 (1987) 131–53 (p. 134 n. 24 on Boreas).

[17] Kron, Phylenheroen, 37–39, 78–82; Kaempf-Dimitriadou, LIMC II.1, 136–37, nos. 19–56.

[18] Boreas in Thracian costume on a pelike in Hamburg by the Painter of the Birth of Athena: Simon, in Greek Art: Archaic into Classical, 76, pl. 72, n. 85. W. Agard, "Boreas at Athens," CJ 61 (1966) 241–46.

[19] F. Courby, EADélos 12: Les temples d'Apollon (Paris, 1931), 237–41, fig. 276; Schanz, "Greek Sculptural Groups," 102–4, pl. 29. U. Wester "Die Akroterfiguren des Tempels der Athener auf Delos" (Ph.D. diss., Heidelberg, 1969), 25–31, no. 66; A. Hermary, EADélos 34: La sculpture archaique et classique I. Catalogue des sculptures classiques de Délos (Paris, 1984), 26–28, no. 15; 36–38 (p. 37 on its political symbolism for Athenian imperialism), pls. 14–16.

[20] P. Walcot, "Herodotus on Rape," Arethusa 11 (1978) 137–47.

interaction.[21] In other words, traditional patterns in myth and art—rape and abduction, as well as the specific identity of a divine figure—were transformed by the historical experience of war and its intellectual interpretation.

The third god who experiences a significant transformation in Athenian cult and myth after the Persian wars is an Olympian one, Poseidon. His new manifestation involves new attributes and epithets, the way traditional gods like Zeus, Athena, or Artemis are newly appreciated in epithets like Eleutherios, Promachos, or Eukleia.[22] Like Boreas, Poseidon was credited with the storm that weakened the Persians at Artemision; he may be represented in the bronze statue found there (Figure 41) and was worshiped thereafter as Poseidon Σωτήρ, or "Savior," an eponym formulaic in the language celebrating Greek victory.[23] Closely linked to this new manifestation of Poseidon as Savior is Zeus Eleutherios, who "liberated" Greece from the Persians and was commemorated with an altar and cult at Plataia and a stoa in the Agora of Athens.[24] The cult is not attested before the Persian wars and is associated only with Zeus; inevitably, it becomes the focus of Athenian propaganda in the Delian League.[25]

Poseidon's debut as a sea god, in particular, coincides with the debut of Athenian naval power at the battle of Salamis. On the Akropolis there are no dedications to Poseidon before the early classical period; even then, his cult may have been introduced there as an adjunct to other Attic heroes like Erechtheus and Theseus.[26] A special story

[21] S. Kaempf-Dimitriadou, *Die Liebe der Götter in der attischen Kunst des 5. Jahrhunderts v. Chr.* (Bern, 1979); F. Zeitlin, "Configurations of Rape in Greek Myth," in *Rape*, ed. S. Tomaselli and R. Porter (Oxford, 1986), 122–51, esp. 129–36. Sourvinou-Inwood, *JHS* 107 (1987) 131–53; "Menace and Pursuit: Differentiation and the Creation of Meaning," in *Images et société en Grèce ancienne*, ed. C. Bérard, C. Brun, and A. Pomari (Lausanne, 1987), 41–58; E. Keuls, "Patriotic Propaganda and Counter-Cultural Protest as Evidenced by Vase Paintings," in *Ancient Greek and Related Pottery*, 256 notes "a sudden outburst of violence on Mount Olympus" around 480 B.C.

[22] Artemis became Eukleia after the Persian Wars at Plataia (Pausanias, 9.17.1–2), Corinth (Xenophon, *Hellenika* 4.4.2), and Athens (Pausanias, 1.14.5); A. Kossatz-Deissmann, "Eukleia," *LIMC* IV.1, 48–51; Gauer, in *Festschrift Neutsch*, 128–29; Shapiro, *Boreas* 9 (1986) 17, 21–22. The temple now known as the "Theseion" or "Hephaisteion" has been attributed to Artemis Eukleia: Harrison, *AJA* 81 (1977) 139 n. 14.

[23] Herodotus, 7.193; Pollitt, *YUAG Bulletin* (Spring 1987) 11. On Σωτήρ, see W. West, *GRBS* 11 (1970) 279–80; Raaflaub, *Entdeckung der Freiheit*, 41–43, 245–46, 319–20 (Zeus Soter/Eleutherios). On the statue

from Artemision (Poseidon or Zeus Soter), see Ridgway, *Severe Style*, 62–63 n. 5.

[24] Plataia: Plutarch, *Aristides* 19; Pausanias, 9.2.5–6; Strabo, 9.2.31. Athens: *Agora III*, 25ff.; inscriptions and stoa: Camp, *Athenian Agora*, 105–7. Raaflaub, *Entdeckung der Freiheit*, 125–39, on cults of Zeus Eleutherios. V. Rosivach, "The Cult of Zeus Eleutherios at Athens," *PdP* 135 (1987) 263–85. A red-figure cup with scenes of warriors and libation excavated under the Stoa of Zeus in Athens (Agora P 42: H. Thompson, "Athens Faces Adversity," *Hesperia* 50 [1981] 345, dates it to the *Perserschutt* but calls it "very new" in 480) has been connected with the founding of the cult: D. Williams, in *Festschrift Schauenburg*, 78. Francis and Vickers, *BSA* 83 (1988) 155–58, on chronology of cup and stoa.

[25] As argued by Raaflaub, *Entdeckung der Freiheit*, 140–47.

[26] J. Binder, "The West Pediment of the Parthenon: Poseidon," in *Studies Presented to Sterling Dow*, 15–22; L. H. Jeffery, "Poseidon on the Acropolis," in *Twelfth International Congress of Classical Archaeology, September 1983*, ed. A. Delivorrias and others (Athens, 1988), 3:124–26. The earliest dedication on the Akropolis

seems to have been invented at this time, about a contest between Athena and Poseidon for the position of supreme deity of Athens. No trace of this legend predates the Persian wars, and it first appears in the west pediment of the Parthenon, one of the most prominent displays in Athens.[27] Herodotus reports μαρτύρια of the contest in the temple of Erechtheus (8.55), and a statue group was still on display on the Akropolis in the second century A.D. (Pausanias, 1.24.3). The myth promotes Athens as a city so attractive that the gods fought to sponsor it, an expansion of mere gratitude for divine assistance in war expressed toward minor deities like Boreas and Pan. Although some sources cast Zeus or other Olympians as judges of the contest, one version that must be Attic has Kekrops, the "first king" of Athens, serve as judge.[28] Revered as a founder of agriculture and cultural institutions and as an eponymous hero of Athens, Kekrops is one of those figures, like Daidalos, newly accredited after the Persian wars, and is promoted as a symbol of "autochthony."[29] Poseidon's new epithets ("Pelagios") and new cults at Phaleron also commemorate Athenian naval action against the Persians.[30] After Salamis, one of the captured Phoenician triremes was dedicated at Sounion, a sanctuary probably more important to Apollo and Athena in the archaic period.[31] If Poseidon was a classical newcomer to Sounion, the new temple begun in the early fifth century and completed in the decades after the Parthenon would have been a logical addition to the sanctuary. Its sculptural decoration, a frieze inside the colonnade before the pronaos, was devoted to three themes expressive of recent myth-historical subjects: the battle of the gods against giants, the centauromachy, and the youthful deeds of Theseus.[32] The appearance of Theseus, in particular, bespeaks one of Poseidon's contributions to Attic fame, for it is through his son, Theseus, that he becomes a more intimate member of the Attic pantheon.

---

was a perirrhanterion for Poseidon Erectheus (Raubitschek, *Dedications from the Athenian Akropolis*, no. 384; *IG* I² 580) appropriate to his striking the sea of Erechtheis from the rock with his trident (Apollodoros, 3.14.1).

[27] F. Brommer, *Die Skulpturen der Parthenon-Giebel* (Mainz, 1963), 158–70; W. Fuchs, "Zur Rekonstruktion des Poseidon im Parthenon-Westgiebel," *Boreas* 6 (1983) 79–80. The central figures of the pediment are lost, but survive in vase painting, e.g., on a red-figure krater from Pella from around 400 B.C: *Greece and the Sea*, ed. A. Delivorrias (Amsterdam, 1987), 202–6, no. 104.

[28] Callimachus, *Iambi* frag. 194, 66–68; Kron, *Phylenheroen* 90 n. 375, 96–99; P. Vidal-Naquet, "Athens and Atlantis: Structure and Meaning of a Platonic Myth," in *Myth, Religion and Society*, ed. R. L. Gordon (Cambridge, 1981), 206, calls this dispute "one of the

mythical foundations of Athenian history."

[29] Kron, *Phylenheroen*, 84–85. On autochthony, see subsequent discussion in the text. Cf. the new Attic agricultural hero "Bouzyges," once Epimenides the Cretan: Shapiro, *Kernos* 3 (1990) 341.

[30] Schachermeyr, *Poseidon* 37 n. 75. Immerwahr, *Form and Thought in Herodotus*, 253 n. 47, on fighting at Phaleron.

[31] Herodotus, 8.121; Pausanias, 1.1.1 (Athena); Apollo: Ridgway, *Archaic Style*, 52–53; Morris, *Black and White Style*, 99–100.

[32] A. Delivorrias, "Poseidon-Tempel auf Kap Sunion: Neue Fragmente der Friesdekoration," *AthMitt* 84 (1969) 127–42, on the frieze; for a new reconstruction, see F. Felten and K. Hoffelner, "Die Relieffriese des Poseidon-Tempels in Sunion," *AthMitt* 102 (1987) 169–84.

Although Poseidon was an Attic cult figure before the Persian wars, he was a local god, Poseidon Hippios, not a maritime deity, and hence primarily represented in art in the company of other gods.[33] In early classical iconography, his role in the naval victory over the Persians is made explicit in scenes where Nike, the goddess of victory, pours a libation into a phiale he holds (Figure 53).[34] Images of gods at libation are concentrated in these decades when new cults and old gods were honored in ceremonies of thanksgiving and sanctuary foundations.[35] Poseidon's new post-Persian image as a naval patron is promoted through his association with other new maritime heroes and heroines, notably his consort, the Nereid, Amphitrite, and his newly recognized son, Theseus (Figure 54). Amphitrite first appears in Attic art in a cluster of vase paintings in the early classical period, including scenes of libation with Poseidon and receiving Theseus (Figure 56), as if to address the new "need for an iconography of sea-power."[36]

The emergence of Theseus as a prominent figure in the iconography and mythology of classical Athens soon eclipses that of all other gods and heroes, such that the reputation of Theseus, a hero, bolsters that of his father Poseidon, a god. The contractual relationship between them is emphasized in scenes where they shake hands, a gesture of oath or contractual obligation rather than of friendship (Figure 54).[37] A number of these scenes seem to represent the moment of recognition, after Theseus's journey to Athens from Troizen to find his father, a story that acquires fresh relevance in Athens after the city's population took refuge at Troizen in 479 B.C.[38] In the absence of Poseidon, it is Theseus, Amphitrite, and Athena who incorporate a trinity of Athenian sea-power, on a red-figure cup by Euphronios difficult to imagine before the naval victories of the Persian wars (Figure 56).[39]

At this point, the proliferation of maritime iconography reflects more than just thanksgiving or self-congratulations for naval victory over Persia. Since 478, the existence of a maritime alliance among the Greek states, and the ambition of Athens to control the Delian League, must have encouraged the popularity of Poseidon and The-

[33] Schachermeyr, *Poseidon*, 35–38, 49; U. Heimberg, *Das Bild des Poseidon in der griechische Vasenmalerei* (Freiburg, 1968), 71–75; P. Siewert, "Poseidon Hippios am Kolonos und die athenischen Hippeis," in *Arktouros: Hellenic Studies Presented to B. Knox*, ed. G. Bowersock, W. Burkert, and M. Putnam (Berlin, 1979), 280–89. Shapiro, *AA* (1982) 291–97.

[34] Here on a calyx krater by the Aegisthus Painter dating to the 470s: Yale University Art Gallery 1985.4.1: S. Matheson, "A Red-Figure Krater by the Aegisthus Painter," and Pollitt, both in *YUAG Bulletin* (Spring 1987) 2–7, 8–13, fig. 1. Cf. Louvre G 348, a column krater by the Mykonos Painter, and New York 06.1021.151, an amphora by the Syracuse Painter, for related scenes of Poseidon and Nike.

[35] E. Simon, *Opfernde Götter* (Berlin, 1953), and *AK*

(1976) 21, on the frequency of gods in early classical art and drama as *Kultstifter*.

[36] E. Harrison, "Athena and Athens in the East Pediment of the Parthenon," *AJA* 71 (1967) 41; cf. *ArtB* 54 (1972) 401–2; "The Portland Vase—Thinking It Over," in *In Memoriam Otto J. Brendel*, 131–42; Heimberg, *Bild des Poseidon*, 35–40, 53–58; Shapiro, *AA* (1982) 296; S. Kaempf-Dimitriadou, "Amphitrite," *LIMC* I.1, 724–35. See *Greece and the Sea*, 188–207, for a selection of objects illustrating "The Persian Wars and Athenian Supremacy at Sea."

[37] Pollitt, *YUAG Bulletin* (Spring 1987) 9–13, figs. 2–5, for a selection of such scenes.

[38] As argued by Shapiro, *AA* (1982) 291–97.

[39] P. Jacobsthal, *Theseus auf dem Meeresgrunde* (Leipzig, 1911). On these historical grounds, W. Klein, *Ge-*

seus.[40] Like the narrative of the Persian wars, their implications become difficult to disentangle from the milieu of subsequent campaigns, both those conducted against Persia and separate strategies for Athenian expansion practiced during the Pentekontaetia. Athenian credit for victory became an Athenian claim to supremacy, culminating in the imperial self-image of Athens mimed in Pericles' funeral oration. This means that the dual interpretation of victory introduced in this section, the attribution to divine blessing and natural supremacy, cannot be separated into two strands or two phases, easily. As Herodotus (9.120–21) and Thucydides (1.89–90) indicate, the aftermath of the Persian wars cannot be distinguished from the growth of Athenian power, a development also manifest in myth and art.

The promotion of Athens emerges in the popularity of certain heroes, sometimes more explicitly in surviving art than in patchy sources. The miraculous appearance of heroes characterized the narrative of numerous battles; Ajax and the Aiakids were summoned to Salamis (Herodotus, 8.64) and Theseus appeared at Marathon, "clad in full armor and charging ahead of them against the barbarians," according to witnesses (Plutarch, *Theseus* 35). Art as well as legend made these anecdotes an ἔργον of history: the Pheidian monument at Delphi portrayed Athena and the eponymous heroes next to Miltiades (Pausanias, 10.10.1–2), while the Stoa Poikile painting of the battle of Marathon included Herakles and Theseus in the company of gods and Athenians. This tableau showed Theseus "rising from the ground" (Pausanias, 1.15.3), an image of reincarnation that may have encouraged other heroes to surface from the earth or their tombs in art and legend (Figures 47–50). On the lid of a red-figured askos in Boston, a bearded warrior appears to rise from his tomb, an egg-shaped mound ornamented with fillets and athletic trophies, and is ready for battle (Figure 48).[41] In the tondo of a cup by the Oxford Brygos Painter two warriors rise from a structure like an altar with drawn swords as if for battle (Figure 47, left).[42] The exterior of the same cup (Figure 47, above) shows Greeks fighting Persians, making explicit the connection between the Persian wars and the "return" of heroes. Some of these heroes already played a role in Athenian cult and mythology before the Persian wars, like the tyrannicides and their statues (Figures 44, 45), but only made their debut in art after epiphany on the battlefield.

The most "political" among these figures should have been the ten eponymous heroes of the city. Their names were selected (with the aid of the Delphic oracle) by lot to personify the ten new tribes designed in the reforms of Kleisthenes, but they attracted

schichte der griechischen Kunst (Leipzig, 1904), 308–13, dated this cup after the Persian wars.

[40] J. Barron, "The Religious Propaganda of the Delian League," *JHS* 84 (1964) 35–48.

[41] MFA 13.169, once attributed to the Tyszkiewicz Painter (*ARV*[1] 188.59). Clairmont, *Patrios Nomos*, 84 n. 54 pl. 5a; Vermeule, *Aspects of Death*, 31–33, fig. 25; cf. Boardman, *AK* 19 (1976) 6, pl. 2, 2.

[42] Oxford 1911.615: A. Barrett and M. Vickers, "The Oxford Brygos Cup Re-Considered," *JHS* 98 (1978) 17–24, connect the scene with the battle of Plataia, while D. Williams, in *Festschrift Schauenburg*, 77–79, identifies the figures in the tondo as the two generals, Kallimachos and Stesilaos, who died at Marathon.

few images in art before the Persian wars. Even then, only three monuments represented them as a group: the statues by Pheidias at Delphi, the east frieze of the Parthenon, and the official monument in the Athenian Agora, near the tyrannicides.[43] As symbols of the Kleisthenic constitution, which met its first great challenge in the Persians, the eponymous heroes were first vindicated by Athenian victory, like the slayers of the tyrants whom the Persian wars made heroes (see Chapter 11). Unlike Harmodios and Aristogeiton, however, no particularized iconography develops for these heroes, as a group or individuals, such that their identification on the Parthenon frieze can still be disputed.[44] Instead, individual heroes attend representations of Attic myths newly critical to the ideology of Athens.

Erechtheus, legendary king and hero since Homer (*Iliad* 2.546–51), boasts a cult on the Akropolis and close associations with Athena and Poseidon.[45] He is often confused in name and personality with Erichthonios, the equally earthborn offspring of Athena and Hephaistos, and is sometimes identified as his father or son. His most popular legend in art is the story of his birth, a frequent theme on early classical vases (Figure 49) and perhaps the subject of larger paintings, according to a reference in Euripides.[46] Eventually the scene was represented on the base bearing the cult images of Athena and Hephaistos by Alkamenes, in the craftsman-god's new temple.[47] The childhood of Erichthonios is also popular in vase painting, in scenes where the goddess Athena appears as nurse and sponsor, if not as mother. The earliest version is on a white-ground cup by the Panaitios Painter, dedicated appropriately enough on the Akropolis. Although associated with *Perserschutt* debris, revision of stratigraphy and chronology may allow this cup to be later and not earlier than 480 B.C. If so, and its subject is part of the argument for its date, there may be even less evidence for interest in this story before the Persian invasion.[48] Like other Attic heroes who become kings, notably Kekrops,

[43] Kron, *Phylenheroen*, 13–31, 202–14 (Parthenon), 215–27 (Delphi), 228–36 (Agora), 215–23 (Delphi); "Die Phylenheroen am Parthenonfries," in *Parthenonkongress Basel*, 235–44. Gauer, *GGA* 230 (1978) 179–80; Harrison, in *Essays . . . Margaret Thompson*, 71–85. The Agora remains date to the fourth century, but a predecessor is known in late fifth-century testimonia.

[44] E.g., by Ian Jenkins, "The Composition of the So-Called Eponymous Heroes on the East Frieze of the Parthenon," *AJA* 89 (1985) 121–27; cf. E. Harrison "Time in the Parthenon Frieze," and Kron, "Die Phylenheroen am Parthenonfries," both in *Parthenon-Kongress Basel*, 230–34, 244, for a table of proposed identifications; cf. Harrison, in *Essays . . . Thompson*, 79–80). Attributes may have identified the lost figures on the Agora monument: Kron, *Phylenheroen*, 232, 246.

[45] Kron, *Phylenheroen*, 32–55; N. Papahatzis, "The

Cult of Athena and Erechtheus on the Akropolis," *Kernos* 2 (1989) 175–85 (see n. 26, for "Poseidon Erechtheus" on the Akropolis).

[46] Here by Hermonax on a celebrated krater in Munich (2413); Kron, *Phylenheroen*, 37–39, 55–67, E 1–22, pls. 1–5. Cf. J. Neils, "A Greek Nativity by the Meidias Painter," *BClevMus* 70 (1983) 278–81; J. Oakley, "A Calyx-Krater in Virginia by the Nikias Painter with the Birth of Erichthonios," *AK* 30 (1987) 123–30. Euripides indicates that the myth was familiar from paintings (ὥσπερ ἐν γραφῇ νομίζεται: *Ion* 271).

[47] The financial documents for the Hephaisteion (*IG* I² 370, 371) indicate that the statues were executed between 421/0 and 416/5 B.C.: Kron *Phylenheroen*, 63–64, E 14; Harrison, *AJA* 81 (1977) 265–87; Brommer, *Hephaistos*, 45–46.

[48] Akropolis 433: Kron, *Phylenheroen*, 72–75, pls. 7–8. On chronology, see Chapter 11, nn. 57, 91, and

Erechtheus can be represented with a lower body in the form of a snake, an indication of connections to the earth, either as a chthonic deity or as an "earthborn" one.

Interest in the native birth of Erechtheus/Erichthonios, their chthonic (serpentine) form, and the parentage of Athena/Athens reflects an Athenian obsession with the concept of authochthony. As recently analyzed, at least three different principles contributed to this. The origin of figures like Erechtheus/Erichthonios, born from the earth with minimal assistance from anthropomorphous parents, was extended to the Athenians when they received the appellation "Erechtheids" in the fifth century. This chthonic origin was synthesized with the historical fiction that the Athenian people were "autochthonous," or had lived in Attika since time immemorial: ᾤκουν οἱ αὐτοὶ αἰεί (Thucydides, 1.2.6 and 2.36.1). Only a population that had in fact been invaded and evacuated and had abandoned its territory during the Persian invasion, as the Athenians did before Salamis, could have claimed this fiction with such ferocity. By the time Thucydides uses this phrase, it had entered the formulaic language of Attic rhetoric, probably through the propaganda of funerary orations.[49] But even in the retrospective speech that Herodotus casts in the mouth of Athenian envoys to Syrakuse, the Athenians are "the oldest race, and the only ones of the Hellenes who have not e/migrated" (ἀρχαιότατον μὲν ἔθνος παρεχόμενοι, μοῦνοι δὲ ἐόντες οὐ μετανάσται Ἑλλήνων: 7:161.3). This claim is allied to a racial one: as exaggerated in parody, the Athenians have never been invaded, hence their blood has never been contaminated by barbarians (in a passage quoted in Chapter 13, from Plato, *Menexenus* 245d).[50] This resistance to outside invasion argues from nature what happened in history: because the Athenians defended their territory, and "saved" Greece from the Persians, it become logical to imagine an infinite past when this was true. The object of these claims was the present and the future, not the past: the state that had defended itself in the past deserved to lead a defensive alliance among other states, once vindicated by a historical myth.[51] The claim to autochthony also assisted two other ambitions of classical Athens. Possession of ter-

---

compare the chronology of the cups found under the Stoa of Zeus: this chapter, n. 24. Other Persian contexts for this artist include his early career at Marathon (Proto-Panaitian cup from the Athenian tumulus) and a cup with Persians now reattributed to the Antiphon Painter (Agora P 43: J. Mertens, *Attic White Ground. Its Development on Shapes Other Than Lekythoi* [New York, 1977], 182, no. 70, pl. XXXIV, 1); also see n. 24; Williams, in *Festschrift Schauenburg*, 78; Francis and Vickers, *BSA* (1988) 143–63, on the chronology of Attic deposits.

[49] As parodied in Plato's *Menexenus* 237c. N. Loraux, "L'autochthonie: Une topique athénienne, le mythe dans l'espace civique," *AESC* 34 (1979) 3–26; *Invention of Athens*, 148–50: "In short, autochthony is not so much a weapon as the Athenian myth par ex-

cellence" (p. 150). A. Saxonhouse, "Myths and the Origins of Cities: Reflections on the Autochthony Theme in Euripides' Ion," in *Greek Tragedy and Political Theory*, 252–73; Rosivach, *CQ* 27 (1987) 284–94; Tyrrell, *Amazons*, 114–28.

[50] Saxonhouse, in *Greek Tragedy and Political Theory*, 256, 265, on the connection between autochthony and aristocracy; Loraux, *Invention of Athens*, 146, 149 for the coincidence of εὐγενία and autochthony in, e.g., Aristotle and Demosthenes.

[51] As argued by Loraux, *Invention of Athens*, 148–50; Rosivach, *CQ* 27 (1987) 305, on the rise of this concept as an ideological tool between 475 and 450 B.C; Tyrrell, *Amazons*, 114–15, on the Athenian link between autochthony and imperialism justified by nature.

ritory, a vital concern during the battles of the Pentekontaetia and the Peloponnesian War, was defended by arguments of "natural" rights and ownership without conquest or concession. The rights of citizenship, the subject of frequent reform and debate in Athens, including on the stage (in Euripides' *Ion*), were also involved in the claim to perpetual "native" residence.[52]

The emphasis on this concept in rhetoric was accompanied by a proliferation of scenes that suggested the "earthborn" nature of Athenians, the mythological counterpart of their permanent residence in Attika. Not only the infant Erichthonios was born from the earth, without "parents" except for the unconsummated union between Athena and Hephaistos and his foster-gestation by Earth, Ge (Figure 49). The creation of Pandora, a figure created by "all the gods" in Hesiod's version of her origins (*Theogony* 570–74; *Works and Days* 60–82, especially 80–82), is recast as a native Athenian event in the fifth century. The most prominent display of this myth was on the statue base of the Athena Parthenos (Pausanias, 1.24.7; Pliny, *Naturalis Historia* 36.19), as if to recapitulate the creation of the cult image itself.[53] Fragments of a sculptured frieze found in the Athenian Agora have been restored as another representation of the birth of Pandora, perhaps from a lost monument from the Akropolis.[54] Representations of Pandora in Attic vase painting (Figure 50) focus on her birth, and may reflect the popularity of Sophokles' satyr play *Pandora* or the *Sphyrokopoi*.[55]

What is distinctive about these representations is their divergence from the account by Hesiod. Pandora is shown rising from the earth like Erichthonios or Ge, as if she, too, were a native Athenian, or a hero like Theseus who "rises from the earth" to help Athens (Pausanias, 1.13.5). She is even labeled in some scenes by an epithet shared with Demeter, "Anesidora," or "She who sends up gifts," to emphasize her connection to the earth.[56] Even the birth of Athena comes to play the same role in Attic ideology, as a cerebral achievement, a triumph of the brain unassisted by natural gestation or reproduction, without benefit of a mother, as Athena herself remembers (Aeschylus, *Eumenides* 736–40). This final play of the trilogy has been called "an apparatus for escaping birth from women," in which the artificial naturalization of the Erinyes as "native

[52] Saxonhouse, in *Greek Tragedy and Political Theory*, 255–56 (territory) and 268 (citizenship); G. Walsh, "The Rhetoric of Birthright and Race in Euripides' Ion," *Hermes* 106 (1978) 301–15. R. Parker, "Myths of Early Athens," in *Interpretations of Greek Mythology*, 194–95, on the myth of autochthony as an expression of "collective snobbery."

[53] As suggested in Chapter 1; cf. Fehr, *Hephaistos* 2 (1980) 113–25, and *Hephaistos* 3 (1981) 67–72.

[54] E. Harrison, "The Classical High-relief Frieze from the Athenian Agora," in *Archaische und klassische griechische Plastik*, 2:109–17; A. Delivorrias, "Τὸ Βάθρο

τῆς Ἀθῆνας Παρθένου καὶ ὁ γλυπτικὸς τοῦ διακόσμος," in *Twelfth International Congress of Classical Archaeology, September 1983*, ed. A. Delivorrias and others (Athens, 1988), 3:53–64.

[55] Radt, frags. 482–85; Sutton, *Satyr-Play*, 55. E. Simon, "Pandora," *EAA* 5 (1963) 930–33, and in *Eye of Greece*, 145–47.

[56] E. Simon, "Anesidora," *LIMC* I.1, 790–91; Cl. Bérard, *Anodoi* (Rome, 1974), 161–64; N. Loraux, *Les enfants d'Athèna*, 30–31, 122–25, etc. See the Oxford Brygos cup (Figure 47b) for related images of heroes who rise from the earth.

Athenians" and Athena's denial of motherhood are allied claims in the city's displacement of nature.[57] In a comparable exclusion of women, the same city reduces the role of female mourners and rites in favor of public funerals at state expense and substitutes new citizenship laws for "naturalization," displacing nature with the city as regulator of natural relationships.[58]

The role of Hephaistos as "parent" to earthborn offspring like Erichthonios and Pandora introduces the leadership of Athens in the world of art, a theme promoted in the Attic cult of Athena and Hephaistos as craftsmen and in the city's claim to Daidalos as a native son. On the level of myth and image, Athens portrayed itself as patron of the arts just as orators claimed that the city was the παίδευσις or μουσεῖον of Greece (Thucydides, 2.41; Figures 58–61, and Chapter 13). The political dimensions of these artificial creations and earthborn epiphanies ultimately emphasize the unusual origins of Athenian leadership in politics and culture. The city's claim to priority (ἀρχή) in origins of cultural institutions served its claim to political ἀρχή: hegemony of the Delian League and the Aegean.

In addition to representing Athenian cultural claims to autochthony, the eponymous heroes also contributed to the mythology of Attic kingship in the fifth century. Beginning with Kodros, a line of Attic kings in classical sources arranges Kekrops, Erechtheus, Pandion, Aigeus, and other eponymous heroes—some, like Pandion of Megara, shared with other cities.[59] Judging from Herodotus's version of this descent (8.44), the revised list was not established until the late fifth century under political motives.[60] The use of a foreign word, τύραννος, for an absolute monarch supports the idea that kingship was not native either, as the model of foreign rulers admired by the Greeks in the archaic period contributed to the image of kingship.[61] Like other responses to the Persian wars that become ironic, the adoption of kingship derived from an admired Oriental tradition was intended to embellish a native victory over those very institutions. The fabrication of a genealogy of hereditary kings in the fifth century agrees with the

[57] Tyrrell, *Amazons*, 116–24, "Autochthony and Birth in the Oresteia." Cf. birthright and autochthony in Euripides' *Ion*: Walsh, *Hermes* 106 (1978) 301–15; F. Zeitlin, "Athenian Mythmaking in the *Ion* of Euripides," *APA Abstracts, 1987*, 15; B. Goff, "Euripides' *Ion* 1132–65: The Tent," *PCPhS* 214 (1988) 42–54, on authochthony and birthrights in Athenian rites such as the Arrephoria and the Ephebia.

[58] Saxonhouse, in *Greek Tragedy and Political Theory*, 259, 269–73; Loraux, *Les enfants d'Athèna*, and *Invention of Athens*, esp. 45–49; Keuls, "Patriotic Propaganda."

[59] F. Jacoby, "Die attischen Königliste," *Klio* 2 (1902) 406–39; Drews, *Basileus*, 86–94. See chart in Brommer, *Theseus*, 142. Pandion: Kron *Phylenheroen*

104–9.

[60] As argued by F. Brommer, "Attische Könige," in *Charites*, 153–64; Kron, *Phylenheroen*, 100. Cf. Drews, *Basileus* on the absence of hereditary monarchy in early Greece before a late and restricted βασιλεύς; Schachermeyr, *Rückerinnerung*, 283, on the manipulation of genealogy to make Minos and Theseus contemporaries.

[61] E.g., in tragedy, history, and art, as argued in Chapter 11: see the Oriental image of Arkesilaos on the Lakonian cup (Figure 36) and the influence of Persian images of kingship on Attic iconography: Root, *AJA* 89 (1985) 103–20; Miller, *AK* 31 (1988) 79–89, and "Priam, King of Troy," forthcoming; and see Chapter 10.

need to invent a more continuous and glamorous history than Attic tradition offered, to provide historical precedents for present and future power. It also accommodated new cultural heroes, most conspicuously Theseus, but allowed him to claim Daidalos as cousin (Plutarch, *Theseus* 19) just as Sokrates did (Chapters 8 and 9), and helped legendary figures in the history of Greek art became royal and Athenian. Thus the creation of new "autochthonous" heroes helped Daidalos, like Pandion, became a native Athenian.

In art, figures like Kodros first appear in the fifth century, in the company of new personifications of sovereignty like the Attic deity "Basile."[62] Like Hephaistos, Daidalos, and Erechtheus, or newly honored gods like Pan and Boreas, Basile was installed in the hearts and minds of Athenians with a home in the city, a place in Athenian topography that was essential to a legitimate and effective cult.[63] The attendance of figures like Basile at scenes of the birth of Erichthonios "reaffirms the Athenians' belief in an autochthonous line of kings in their heroic past."[64] Mythical battles of the Athenian past give the eponymous heroes a role in legendary glory, as in the early war against Eumolpos of Eleusis where Erechtheus distinguished himself. This war was celebrated in at least two lost tragedies, Aeschylus's *Eleusinians* and Euripides' *Erechtheus* represented in a statue group on the Akropolis; and eventually cited among legendary deeds of the Athenian past, in fourth-century orations.[65] Chronological and other details of this early war against Athens' neighbors are vague and the event is deliberately projected back into the mythical past, where it functioned as "the great event of the period of the kings."[66] Other king/heroes, like Akamas, son of Theseus, are remembered as founder-heroes (in the Troad and Thrace) and represented in combat against Amazons and Trojans.[67]

Among the ten eponymous heroes, three are related to Theseus as grandfather, fa-

[62] H. A. Shapiro, "The Attic Deity Basile," *ZPE* 63 (1986) 134–36.

[63] *IG* I³ 84 for the sanctuary of Kodros, Neleus, and Basile in a decree dating to 418/7 B.C., also attested in Plato, *Charmides* 153a; R. Wycherley, "Neleion," *BSA* 66 (1960) 60–66.

[64] Shapiro, *ZPE* 63 (1986) 136; cf. F. Brommer, "Attische Könige," in *Charites* 161, on the late and artificial invention of Kodros; D. Kluwe, *WZJena* 14 (1965) 23, on the role of Neleid (e.g., Ionian) connections in the propaganda of the Delian League. See n. 46 for scenes of the birth of Erichthonios.

[65] E.g., Plato, *Menexenus* 239b. As late as Sulla's sack of Athens, three legends—Theseus, Eumolpus, and the Persian wars—saved the lives of Athenians: Plutarch, *Sulla* 13–14. Kron, *Phylenheroen*, 50, 76–77,

for testimonia; Pausanias, 1.27.4 (cf. 9.30.1) for monument. A. Hauvette, "Les *Eleusiniens* d'Eschyle et l'institution du discours funèbres à Athènes," in *Mélanges Henri Weil* (Paris, 1898), 159–78; Loraux, *Invention of Athens*, 65. C. Austin, "De nouveaux fragments de *l'Erechthée* d'Euripide," *Recherches de Papyrologie* 4 (1967) 11–67; C. Carrara, *Euripide Eretteo: Papyri Florentini* 3 (Milan, 1977); E.A.M.E. O'Connor-Visser, *Aspects of Human Sacrifice in the Tragedies of Euripides* (Amsterdam, 1987), 148–76; Hall, *Inventing the Barbarian*, 105–6.

[66] Jacoby, *Atthis*, 124–25; R. Padgug, "Eleusis and the Union of Attika," *GRBS* 14 (1972) 138–40.

[67] Kron, *Phylenheroen*, 141–70. Harrison, in *Essays . . . Margaret Thompson*, 75–76, on Akamas.

ther, and son, respectively, in the figures of Pandion, Aigeus, and Akamas. Some of them appear first in his company, as in a symposium scene on a ram's head rhyton with figures inscribed with the names of Kekrops, Theseus, Pandion, and Aigeus.[68] Others attend the deeds of Theseus in classical art to the exclusion of other appearances.[69] Like Poseidon himself, heroes of the city of Athens, including the tyrannicides and the eponymous heroes of the ten tribes, received vicarious promotion from the figure of Theseus, whose image eclipsed them all. Thus Theseus could provide two sons for eponyms, and Plato can have Kritias reduce the tribal heroes to "Kekrops, Erechtheus, Erichthonius, and those other heroes before Theseus" (*Critias* 110a). The new image of kingship revolves around the figure of Theseus: the only royal image in archaic Athens, he is singled out for elaborate iconography and mythology in the classical period.[70] In the imagination of the fifth century, Theseus assumed not only the glory of the remote past but the achievements of more recent times, particularly the democratic reforms of Athens and the defeat of the Persians. Of all the gods and heroes newly appreciated after the Persian wars, he played the most active role in the development of the image of Athens, such that his career in classical mythology requires separate treatment (see the next section).

Beyond individual gods and heroes with names and cults, the world of Greek mythology was reborn after the Persian wars, in a series of legends that pitted anonymous Greeks against centaurs, Amazons, and Trojans. Of the major monuments erected in the early classical period (see Chapter 11), most included one or more of these subjects, whether in sculpture or painting. The Athenian treasury may have set a standard with its assembly scenes of Herakles and Theseus fighting Amazons and other figures; the murals of the Theseion and the Stoa Poikile arranged paintings of Greeks fighting Amazons next to Greeks fighting Persians in a display that emphasized their similarity. The later pediments of the temple of Aphaia on Aigina depict the Aiakid heroes, who distinguished themselves in both Greek expeditions to Troy (remembered by Pindar in *Isthmian* 5), in both confrontations with Trojans. The role of the Aiakids at Salamis (Herodotus, 8.64) and new perspectives on the chronology of these sculptures make these pediments one of the most significant and explicit monuments to commemorate the Persian wars.[71] The metopes of the Parthenon displayed Greeks in combat with all three

[68] R. Guy, "A Ram's Head Rhyton signed by Chairinos," *Arts in Virginia* 22 (1981) 2–15; K. Schefold, "Pandion's Sorge," *Boreas* 5 (1982) 67–69.

[69] E.g., Pandion at the struggle with the Marathonian bull, an implicitly post-Persian deed: Kron, *Phylenheroen*, 114–16, 119; Aigeus: Kron, *Phylenheroen*, 127–39, and "Aigeus," *LIMC* I.1, 359–67. For Theseus and the Marathonian bull, see subsequent discussion.

[70] Davie, "Theseus the King in Fifth-Century Athens," *GR* 29 (1982) 25–34. See next section for discussion of Theseus.

[71] D. Williams, *AA* (1987) 629–80, and D. Gill, "The Temple of Aphaia on Aegina: The Date of the Reconstruction," *BSA* 83 (1988) 169–77; Stewart, *Greek Sculpture*, 137–38. The later pediments are now dated after Marathon, although the heroism of Aigina at Salamis makes a date after 480 B.C. attractive.

"Persian war" enemies (centaurs, Amazons, and Trojans); these themes were repeated on the friezes of the Hephaisteion, the Nike temple, and the temple of Apollo at Bassai.

It has become as common in modern scholarship as it may have been in classical Athens to identify mythical barbarians with recent historical ones; the literature on this transformation is copious, thorough, and convincing.[72] But the complexity of the Greek attitude toward the Orient should not be underestimated, for in tragedy, history, and painting the Greeks' admiration for non-Greek peers was as generous as their consternation at their own upset victory. This attitude is found in the Greek reaction to the fall of Miletos, discussed in Chapter 11: οὐδὲν ὁμοίως καὶ Ἀθηναῖοι: "not so the Athenians," an expression that encompasses the surprises of Greek culture. The first celebration of the Greek victory preserved in poetry was a Greek lament over the downfall of the enemy, in Aeschylus's *Persians*. The most poignant view of the Persian invasion of Athens appears in new representations of the Greek capture of Troy, whether in tragedy or painting. The Vivenzio hydria by the Kleophrades Painter expresses this early classical sympathy, in a lament for the destruction of the Athenian Akropolis that is a simultaneous expression of sorrow for the defeat of the enemy.[73] More than analogy made the misfortune of Troy popular in art and poetry: the sack of Troy linked the fortunes of Persia and Greece in a chain of events that brought them eventually into conflict with each other, according to a popular account (Herodotus, 1.5.1); and the sacking of cities, like the stories of stealing of women, joined the fates of Troy, Sardis, Miletos, and Athens. Individual details of the historical narrative were conceived in terms of epic precedents, such as in the comparison of the Persian army to the Homeric "catalogue of ships" (Herodotus, 7.20.2). Episodes from Homer are suddenly popular themes in vase painting, those from the sack of Troy most conspicuously: seventy-five percent of Greek vases with this scene belong to this first quarter of the fifth century. But even eccentric episodes like the mission of spying and betrayal, the Doloneia, may only have become compelling to a city betrayed by Ephialtes (cf. δόλον in Aeschylus's *Persians* 361).[74] The motif of deception or trickery—ἀπάτη—has been described as "the

---

[72] For recent works, see duBois, *Centaurs and Amazons*; Tyrrell, *Amazons*; and Thomas, *Mythos und Geschichte*; also Hall, *Inventing the Barbarian*, 53, 67–69; important articles include Boardman, in *Eye of Greece*, and Gauer, in *Kanon*, 28–41.

[73] Boardman, *AK* 19 (1976) 3–18, on this vase and other early classical scenes of the *Ilioupersis*; Simon, in *Greek Art: Archaic into Classical*, 67: "The sack of Troy seems to have been painted after the sack of Athens by the Persians." The Kleophrades Painter's hydria may not be an "anticipation of Early Classical

wall-painting" (Boardman *AK* 19 [1976] 15) if it belongs to the 470s, but Robertson, *History of Greek Art*, 233–35, emphasizes the difference between vase and mural; cf. B. Cohen, in *Ancient Greek Art and Iconography*, ed. W. Moon (Madison, Wis., 1983), 177–79.

[74] F. Lissarrague, "Iconographie de Dolon le Loup," *RA* (1980) 3–30. The earliest Attic red-figured version of the Doloneia is by Onesimos, also the first to paint an *Ilioupersis* (Sparkes, in *Greek Art: Archaic into Classical*, 37 n. 51) and other scenes (Theseus, Gigantomachy, etc.) relevant after the Persian wars.

single most common motif in Herodotean military accounts," and played a critical role in many a stratagem of the Persian wars.[75] One hundred and fifty years after the defeat of Dareios, the figure of Ἀπάτη still stood between Hellas and Asia as a symbol of the Persian wars on Apulian vases (Figure 62). Like Diabole ("Slander"), the personification of Apate may have appeared in a classical wall-painting, especially if the figure of Dolus described by Pliny in a painting of Odysseus at Troy by Polygnotos's brother, Aglaophon, represents her Latin sister, conceived in the same historical milieu that reappreciated Trojan episodes in the light of the Persian wars.[76]

Legendary battles outside of the Trojan cycle also recall the Greek confrontation with the Persians. In the Gigantomachy popular in the archaic period, the Greek pantheon defeats creatures of a larger and older race; its popularity, after Greeks inferior in number and experience defeated the formidable Persians, may derive from analogy.[77] The tradition that Mikon was fined thirty minae for representing the Persians as larger than the Greeks in his painting of the battle of Marathon may reflect an iconographic scheme that imagined the Persians as giants, in the tradition of archaic iconographic conventions.[78]

More significant than the new interpretation of traditional legends are the implications of this change for the history of art. This innovation encouraged the interpretation of any legend in the light of history and its juxtaposition with contemporary events. The effect of history could produce radical inversions, under radical circumstances. For example, legendary figures like Theseus could appear in the guise of historical heroes like the tyrannicides, in a period when contemporary events seemed more astonishing than mythical ones. In the history of art, the use of allegory to express an image of nations is taken for granted in the modern world, but was first developed in this period.[79] The world of early classical Athens, and the circumstances of its unlikely victory over a formidable enemy, first caused myth and history to converge, appropriate to a culture that barely distinguished them to begin with. This attitude marks classical art as distinct from archaic: not stylistic traits or new media alone, but the capacity to see

---

[75] Immerwahr, *Form and Thought in Herodotus*, 243–44.

[76] Pliny, *Naturalis Historia* 35.138; Shapiro, *Boreas* 9 (1986) 4–7, on Diabole, Dolos, and Apate; cf. M. Schmidt, "Asia und Apate," in ΑΠΑΡΧΑΙ. *Nuovi ricerche e studi in onore di Paolo Enrico Arias*, ed. L. Beschi and others (Pisa, 1982), 2:505–20.

[77] F. Vian, *La guerre des géants* (Paris, 1951); Thomas *Mythos und Geschichte*, 19–28, on the Gigantomachy; B. Sparkes, "Aspects of Onesimos," in *Greek Art: Archaic into Classical*, 26–27, 28–29, pl. 32, on the Doloneia.

[78] Lykourgos, in Harpokration s.v. Μίκων; debated by Sopater, Διαίρεσις Ζητημάτων 1.8.120 = 340.26 in C. Waltz, ed., *Rhetores Graeci*, vol. 8 (repr. Osnabrück, 1968), 126–45, and Reinach, *La peinture ancienne*, nos. 141–42. See Chapter 13, on Persians in Greek art.

[79] Hölscher, *Griechische Historienbilder*, esp. chap. 3; Thomas, *Mythos und Geschichte*; Meyer, *Kunst und Geschichte*, 9–122; Shapiro, *Boreas* 9 (1986) 4–23. Gauer, in *Kanon*, 41, claims the Athenian Amazonomachy not only as the earliest *Staatsmythos* but as the first allegory in the history of art.

familiar faces in the forests of myth, and the fate of a nation newly reflected in legends long awesome.

"THIS OTHER HERAKLES": THE INVENTION OF THESEUS

πολλὰ γὰρ δράσας καλά
ἦθος τόδ᾽ εἰς Ἕλληνας ἐξελεξάμην
ἀεὶ κολαστὴς τῶν κακῶν καθεστάναι

For having performed many noble deeds
I have become a tradition among the Greeks for this:
to be always a punisher of evils.

—Euripides, *Suppliants* 339–41

No figure exemplifies the ingenuity of Athenian mythmaking in the fifth century as vividly as Theseus, most celebrated of kings and most democratic of heroes. His transformation in classical art and literature from an archaic hero into a symbol of democratic Athens has been recognized for nearly a century, but rewards a fresh, if selective, survey. Ultimately, he is responsible for the naturalization of Daidalos as an Athenian; together their evolution epitomizes the invention of Athenian culture.

Theseus occupies, with unusual privilege and some contradiction, the symbolic position of king as well as founder of Athenian democracy. In legend, he proposed "a constitution without a king" (Plutarch, *Theseus* 24) and became a symbol of democracy's origins. At the same time, his image as king was the most fully developed of all Athenian figures, before the fifth century. Theseus already played a significant role in archaic Athens, if literature and art are any indication (Figure 10a).[80] Tradition connects him to Peisistratos, albeit in sources that are late and suspect. The tyrant is said to have mustered his troops at the Theseion in his first rise to power (*Athenaion Politeia* 16.5). Given that the Theseion was only founded by Kimon in the early classical period (Plutarch, *Theseus* 8.7), while Polyainos locates the muster of Peisistratos in the Anakeion (1.21.2), another classical building known for its murals, the *Athenaion Politeia* reference may be dubious. But the passage demonstrates that by the fourth century the image of Theseus as king was powerful enough for deliberate retrojection to the reign of the tyrant, perhaps to improve the status of Peisistratos by association with a positive example of Athenian kingship. In another celebrated and disputed set of testimonia, Homeric scholars in antiquity accused Peisistratos of "interpolating" references to Theseus in the *Iliad* and

[80] Shapiro, *Art and Cult under the Tyrants*, 142–49, esp. 146–47, on Kleitias and Exekias, and the hero's   early association with Athena.

Odyssey.[81] The tyrant was also held responsible for suppressing references unfavorable to Theseus, such as the hero's treatment of Ariadne, in Hesiod (frag. 147, 298 M-W). Although these accusations have been disputed since antiquity and in Homeric philology, the association of Peisistratos with Theseus was strong enough to inspire and sustain them.

It is important to emphasize the role of Theseus in preclassical Athens in relation to Herakles', and the rise of political mythology in the archaic period. Recent scholarship has exaggerated the symbolic value of Herakles in ideology of the age of Peisistratos.[82] While Herakles enjoys enormous popularity in archaic Athenian art, in sculpture as well as vase painting, that does not guarantee that the tyrant Peisistratos deliberately cultivated a popular image of himself in the style of the hero. There is no explicit association between the tyrant and the hero in literature, where Theseus (*Athenaion Politeia* 16.5; Plutarch, *Theseus* 20) and Odysseus (Plutarch, *Solon* 30) are mentioned instead.[83] Rather, a dramatic new focus on Theseus in cult, myth, and art begins in the late archaic period and increases after the Persian wars. Because Theseus became "another Herakles" (ἄλλος οὗτος Ἡρακλῆς: Plutarch, *Theseus* 29) in popular expressions does not necessarily mean that the archaic Herakles was likewise the object of deliberate political propaganda, that he was "a prior Theseus." The promotion of Theseus may have concentrated on a hero with specifically Attic associations, rather than a figure too Panhellenic in popularity like Herakles. As one historian put it, "Theseus was destined for greatness at Athens for no other reason than the absence of a rival there."[84] And just because Theseus became a hero of Athenian democracy does not mean that his predecessor was a Peisistratid figure or a representative of tyranny. Instead, Herakles was a model for the figure of a new hero, both in the creation of his biography and in the Greek imagination. Thus Plutarch has the young Theseus dream of Herakles at night and emulate his ἀρετή (prowess, heroism, valor) by day, an anecdotal complement to the deliberate creation of a new hero by Athens (*Theseus* 6). When Plutarch compares this obsession with the one Themistokles had about Miltiades, whom he envied for his victory (*The-*

---

[81] Plutarch, *Theseus* 20; J. A. Davison, "Peisistratos and Homer," *TAPA* 86 (1955) 1–21; W. R. Connor, "Theseus in Classical Athens," in *Quest for Theseus*, 144. For a revival of the sixth-century canonization of Homer, see M. Jensen, *The Homeric Question and the Oral-formulaic Theory* (Copenhagen, 1980).

[82] First argued by Boardman in a number of articles: "Herakles, Peisistratos, and Sons," *RA* (1972) 57–72; "Herakles, Peisistratos, and Eleusis," *JHS* 95 (1975) 1–12; "Exekias," *AJA* 82 (1978) 11–25; "Image and Politics in Sixth Century Athens," in *Ancient Greek and Related Pottery*; "Herakles, Theseus and Amazons," in *Eye of Greece*, 1–28. Cf. R. Cook, "Pots and Pisistratan Propaganda," *JHS* 107 (1987) 167–71,

with Boardman's response, "Herakles, Peisistratos and the Unconvinced," *JHS* 109 (1989) 158–59; Shapiro, *Art and Cult under the Tyrants*, 157–63.

[83] W. Agard, "Theseus—A National Hero," *CJ* 24 (1928) 85; H. Herter, *RhM* 85 (1939) 284–85, even argues for a Peisistratid *Theseis* on the basis of, e.g., the François vase; Brommer, "Attische Könige," in *Charites*, 153–64; Connor, in *Quest for Theseus*, 144–50; Taylor, *Tyrant Slayers*, 77–79; Shapiro, *Art and Cult under the Tyrants*.

[84] Tyrrell, *Amazons*, 3. Cf. Thomas, *Mythos und Geschichte*, 80, who argues that Theseus was promoted precisely because Herakles was too Panhellenic.

mistokles 3), the biographer juxtaposes a legend with the very historical moment that promoted it. The figure of Theseus in art eventually assumes the posture of Miltiades (e.g., in the Olympia pediment) and of the tyrannicides (in classical relief sculpture and vase painting). This transformation suggests that the image of Theseus was fresh enough in the Athenian imagination for comparison with more familiar heroes: Miltiades, Themistokles, and the tyrannicides, whose historical fame belongs to the same era that promoted Theseus. By the end of the century, Theseus had eclipsed his model to the degree that Herakles could describe him as a hard act to follow: Θησεῖ πανώλεις ἐψόμεσθ᾽ ἐφολκίδες (Euripides, *Herakles* 1424).

The next phase of the Attic promotion of Theseus is associated with Kleisthenes. The exclusion of the name of Theseus from the roster of the ten eponymous heroes is more than balanced by the inclusion of his father (Aigeus), grandfather (Pandion), and son (Akamas). Furthermore, it suggests that he was already too important a figure to monopolize the identity of a single tribe.[85] Instead, during this phase of Athenian constitutional reform, it is likely that Theseus was first cast as the practitioner of *synoikismos*, that unification of Attika in the legendary past that was invented as a precedent for the Kleisthenic distribution of representative units. As the legendary agent of a new constitution, he acquired the reputation of "the king who abdicated for his people."[86] According to Thucydides (2.15) and Plutarch (*Theseus* 24), he transformed the separate communities of Attika into "one city," abolished local bouleuteria, prytaneia, and magistracies, replacing them with ἓν βουλευτήριον and ἓν πρυτανεῖον in Athens. This tradition is suggested as early as Herodotus, who does not discuss the *synoikismos* of Attika but alludes to it in his description of how the Ionians resisted the advice of Thales to found "one bouleuterion" with the other states to remain independent δῆμοι (1.170; see Chapter 11). The phrase ἓν βουλευτήριον became a classical formula for Athenian democracy as a superior system of government, as in the speech of Perikles to the Athenian assembly in 432 B.C. (1.141.6).[87]

Philologists and archaeologists have applied the testimonia on *synoikismos* to various dates in early Attic history as plausible occasions for the "unity" of Attika, on the basis of material culture and history.[88] Like the historicity of the "Minoan thalassocracy," there may not be a configuration of evidence proving or disproving a historical occasion for the unification of Attika. This myth must have developed no earlier than the Kleis-

---

[85] Thus Connor, in *Quest for Theseus*, 150.

[86] Tyrrell, *Amazons*, 3–4. Cf. Connor, in *Quest for Theseus*, 152–53, and the image of Theseus in Euripides' *Suppliants* as a "constitutional monarch."

[87] P. Culham, "The Delian League: Bicameral or Unicameral?" *AJAH* 3 (1978) 29.

[88] E.g., R. Padgug, "Eleusis and the Union of Attica," *GRBS* 14 (1972) 135–50, esp. 140–43 (Late

Bronze Age); S. Diamant, "Theseus and the Unification of Attica," in *Studies in Attic Epigraphy History and Topography Presented to Eugene Vanderpool. Hesperia* suppl. XIX (Princeton, 1982), 38–47 (Geometric); C. G. Thomas, "Theseus and Synoicism," *SMEA* 22 (1982) 337–49, argues for post-Mycenaean consolidation of regional Attica.

thenic reforms and for the express purpose of attributing a recent and radical reorganization of Attika to a mythical precedent. This pattern—the invention of a legendary event to complement recent political or historical events—originates with and for the sake of Athenian constitutional democracy. It becomes an organic component of Athenian mythmaking, and inaugurates a specific species of myth rooted in history.[89]

Contemporary interest in the new deme-units of Attika has been claimed in late archaic representations of Theseus fighting the Marathonian bull, a symbol of the special Tetrapolis or four demes of Marathon. This was the first of the deeds of Theseus performed after his journey to Attika from Troizen and the most frequently portrayed in all Greek art next to his contest with the Minotaur. It is attested copiously in literature, although no earlier than in Sophokles' *Aigeus*.[90] Eventually, the people of Marathon dedicated a statue of the bull on the Akropolis, seen by Pausanias in the second century (1.27.9–10). His autopsy suggests the dedication was not set up before 480/79 B.C., since it was unlikely to have survived the Persian destruction of the Akropolis monuments. However, a number of scholars prefer to identify it as a post-Persian replacement of the original dedication, in the spirit of the Athenian replacement of the tyrannicides, to celebrate the new significance of Marathon.[91] Fragments of a marble torso and muzzle have been identified as the remains of such a replacement, while the original dedication is restored as a bronze bull. An appropriate display for this replacement would be the same wall where the fetters of the miraculous victory of 506 B.C. were on view, on the wall burned by the Persians (Herodotus, 5.77).[92] However, it seems unnecessary to assume the marble fragments belong to a replacement of an original bronze bull. Related evidence of monuments celebrating the Persian wars suggests the myth did not seize the imagination until after the battle of Marathon, and only became an Attic *topos* in classical literature (as in Sophokles' *Aigeus*). The myth first appeared in art in late archaic vase painting as one of the deeds celebrated on the "cycle" cups, joining other more familiar deeds of Theseus—the Minotaur—as a new and Athenian event.[93] The occasion for such a marble monument on the Akropolis is more likely to have been the victory at Marathon, not the Kleisthenic creation of the Tetrapolis. New interest in the myth is also suggested by a new version of the story, where Theseus captures the bull and leads

[89] Boardman, in *Eye of Greece*, 1, and duBois, *Centaurs and Amazons*, 53, on myth in literate cultures and its transcendence of elaborate "universal" theories of mythology; N. Horsfall, "Myth and Mythography," *EchCl* 29 (1985) 394, calls this "secondary myth"; Gauer, in *Kanon*, 37 (*Staatsmythos*; Keuls, in *Ancient Greek and Related Pottery*) on the early classical rise of "nationalistic" myth.

[90] Brommer, *Theseus*, 27–34; Neils, *Youthful Deeds of Theseus*, 37–53, 73–74; H. A. Shapiro, "The Marathonian Bull on the Athenian Akropolis," *AJA* 92

(1988) 377–78. Boardman, in *Eye of Greece*, 2–3.

[91] As argued by U. Hausmann, *Hellenistische Reliefbecher aus attischen und böotischen Werkstätten* (Stuttgart, 1959), 75; Shapiro, *AJA* 92 (1988) 377–82.

[92] In a recent proposal by Shapiro, *AJA* 92 (1988) 374–75, 382; see Chapter 11.

[93] The earliest "indisputable representation" is on a red-figure cup from Orvieto by Kachrylion, the "progenitor of the cycle vases" (Florence 91456); a related cup by Oltos (Madrid 11267) is "disputed": Neils, *Youthful Deeds of Theseus*, 37.

it to the Akropolis for sacrifice, rather than killing it in battle. The latter, more violent version is popular in the archaic period but disappears in early classical art.[94] The more civilized version of the story agrees with the new emphasis on ceremony and rituals commemorating the Persian wars, with a sacrifice to Athena (Pausanias, 1.27.9–10) or Apollo (Plutarch, *Theseus* 24). The monument on the Akropolis may have represented this ceremony, since Pausanias narrates that version of the myth. On the so-called cycle cups, the bull of Marathon often occupies the tondo, as if it played a special role in the early classical imagination reflecting the significance of the battle of Marathon. The presence of Athena in some scenes lends the figure of legitimate historical authority to the adventure, and the occasional appearance of Medea also bespeaks a special post-Persian view of Marathon.[95] Apparently the story even became the subject of a satyr play: silens are present on three cups that illustrate Theseus and the bull.[96] Moreover, the struggle with the bull gradually replaces, as it were, the equivalent scene where Herakles struggles with the Cretan bull, in the process whereby Theseus becomes "another Herakles" (Plutarch, *Theseus* 29).[97] In other words, a concentration of evidence points to a context after the battle of Marathon for a dedication by the demesmen of the Tetrapolis. A complementary occasion can be imagined for the bronze dedication on the Akropolis representing Theseus lifting the rock at Troizen to discover the tokens of his identity and the weapons of his manhood (Pausanias, 1.27.8; 2.32.7, 34.6). Although represented rarely and late in Attic art, such a monument belongs to the spirit of Salamis, when the Athenians were evacuated to Troizen and the arrival and departure of Theseus from Troizen become popular in Attic art.[98] Likewise, the first marble monument representing Theseus in Athens survives in the fragments of two statues from the Akropolis, showing the hero in combat with a creature like a giant, most plausibly Prokroustes (Figure 51). Because this statue was found in "Persian debris," a late archaic date (before 480) has been assumed, which would place the monument in the vicinity of the cycle cups where the adventures that included the struggle with Prokroustes first appear.[99]

Discussing the date of these Theseus monuments on the Akropolis raises a delicate problem of chronology. According to traditional dating, there is a proliferation of scenes with multiple deeds of Theseus, especially those performed in his youth, in late archaic (late sixth and early fifth century) red-figure vase painting (Figures 55–57). The so-called

[94] Brommer, *Theseus*, 28–29; Shapiro, *AJA* 92 (1988) 373, 378.

[95] F. Brommer, "Theseus—Deutungen, I" *AA* (1979) 504–5, and *Theseus*, 30–31; B. Shefton, "Medea at Marathon," *AJA* 60 (1956) 159–63.

[96] Brommer, *Theseus*, 30 n. 17; cf. Simon, in *Eye of Greece*, 130.

[97] Boardman, in *Eye of Greece*, 2–3; Brommer, *Theseus*, 30; Neils, *Youthful Deeds of Theseus*, 144–45, on the conflation/contamination between the two he-

roes' versions of the adventure.

[98] Plutarch, *Theseus*, 6; Brommer, *Theseus*, 1–2; C. Sourvinou-Inwood, "Theseus Lifting the Rock and a Cup near the Pithos Painter," *JHS* 91 (1971) 94–109; Shapiro, *AA* (1982) 293–94, cf. A. Raubitschek, "Theseus at the Isthmus," in *Corinthiaca*, 1–2.

[99] Akropolis Museum 145 and 171: Neils, *Youthful Deeds of Theseus*, 45–46, figs. 16–17, and p. 48, for metope with the same subject on the Athenian treasury.

cycle cups begin around 510 B.C. and present several myths for the first time, as well as the first representations of more than one deed performed by Theseus. The exceptions are his combat with the Minotaur and with the Marathonian bull, already known in earlier act. New scenes make their debut on these red-figure cups in compositions that repeat the figure of Theseus some 125 times on twenty-three cups.[100] Elsewhere in art, a "cycle" of the deeds of Theseus first appears on the metopes of the Athenian treasury at Delphi. If this monument is dated by its ancient terminus post quem of 490 B.C. (see Chapter 11), it suggests a similar date for related vases and sculptures after 490, too, rather than before 500 B.C. This might solve more problems than it would create. A chronological chart of the deeds of Theseus plotted in art and literature shows a consistent gap, where scenes in art "anticipate" the earliest references in literature by a regular interval of about fifteen to twenty years.[101] An adjustment in chronology in the vicinity of about a decade, as recommended in recent scholarship (see Chapter 11, nn. 57, 91; Chapter 12, nn. 24, 71) would reduce this "gap" and prevent the invention of lost monuments and poems to justify dates that are artificially early. Independent of the correlation between art and sources, a margin of uncertainty of about ten years is assumed in the calibration of vase-painting chronology. This makes it extremely difficult, if not dangerous, to pin the cycle cups to particular events in Athenian history, whether it be the reforms of Kleisthenes, the Persian wars, or any event in between them. The decades between the assassination of the tyrants (514 B.C.) and the first ostracism (487 B.C.) are poorly documented in Athenian political history. It is especially difficult to ascertain how and when the reforms of Kleisthenes were actually implemented, much less advertised or reflected in art.[102]

If political events cannot be ascertained as a source for late archaic art, a second and widespread assumption maintains the existence of a major poem, a *Theseid*, dated to the last decade of the sixth century. Although poems about Theseus were apparently abundant (Plutarch, *Theseus* 28–29; Aristotle, *Poetics* 1451a), their composition in the late sixth century is entirely a modern theory, largely derived from the (estimated) chronology of the vases.[103] Once the uncertain chronology of those vases is admitted, there may no

---

[100] E.g. Figure 55: J. Neils, "The Loves of Theseus: An Early Cup by Oltos," *AJA* 84 (1981) 177–79; *Youthful Deeds of Theseus*, 31–40, 143–48ff.; Brommer, *Theseus*, 67–68, 73–74; Shapiro, *AA* (1982) 292–97, and *AJA* 92 (1988) 378.

[101] Brommer, *Theseus*, fig. 10; pp. 8, 25, 28, 34, 74–75, on the consistent interval between art and literature, attributed to circumstances of preservation (p. 28: "Zufall der Erhaltung").

[102] E. Badian, "Archons and Strategoi," *Antichthon* 5 (1971) 1–34. Cf. D. Knight, "Athenian Politics, 510–480 B.C.: Some Problems," *Historia* 13 (1970) 28–30;

D. J. McCargar, "The Relative Date of Kleisthenes' Legislation," *Historia* 25 (1976) 385–95; D. H. Kelly, "The Athenian Archonship 508/7–487/6," *Antichthon* 12 (1978) 1–17; G. R. Stanton, "The Tribal Reform of Kleisthenes the Alkmeonid," *Chiron* 14 (1984) 1–41; E. David, "A Preliminary Stage of Cleisthenes' Reforms," *CA* 5 (1986) 1–13.

[103] Other testimonia include: scholia to Pindar, *Olympian* 3.50 and 10.83; Diogenes Laertius, 2.59; *FGrH* 3b 309–11, 3b II 343, n. 23; 3b II 344, n. 20: G. Huxley, *Greek Epic Poetry* (London, 1969), 116–18. Kleisthenic date argued by Herter, *RhM* 88 (1939)

longer be compelling reasons for assuming the existence of such a poem in a Kleisthenic context. The political circumstances of that context, which first attributed *synoikismos* to Theseus, could have been responsible for new interest in other deeds, if not a cycle.[104]

More significant attention to the myth of Theseus can be charted in later decades. For example, the hero's departure from Troizen and arrival in Athens appear suddenly on Greek vases in the decade after the Athenian evacuation to Troizen.[105] The same city may have dedicated the bronze monument with Theseus lifting the rock at Troizen (Pausanias, 1.27.8) in this period, as argued previously. The decades of the Delian League, Kimon's recovery of the hero's bones, and founding of the Theseion, might be a more logical period to imagine the proliferation of poems about Theseus.[106] Simonides, Bacchylides, and Aeschylus are the first to celebrate the hero in verse, and the stories that Plutarch transmits as the subject of poems about Theseus include post-Persian inventions like the Amazon invasion of Attika (*Theseus* 27–28). Like the tyrannicides in their earlier incarnation (by Antenor), the fame of Theseus may not have been simultaneous with the reforms of Kleisthenes. Not until the vindication of the new democracy in battle, especially against the Persians, did democracy need and find a special hero.

New images and stories develop around the figure of Theseus after Marathon. The Athenian treasury at Delphi represents several of them, in deliberate association with complementary exploits of Herakles, a *Nebeneinander* that has been identified as a "Marathonian motif."[107] The earliest monumental versions of Theseus's struggles with Skiron, Prokroustes, Kerkyon, the bull of Marathon, the Minotaur, and Amazons are depicted on the north and south metopes (Figure 39); both heroes fight Amazons on the east metopes; a pedimental sculptural group probably depicts another encounter with Amazons.[108] Not only the depiction of both heroes together was inaugurated by history. The appearance of Herakles and Theseus in an individual narrative of deeds represents

282–86, and "Griechische Geschichte im Spiegel der Theseus-Sage," *Die Antike* 17 (1941) 222. Cf. K. Schefold, "Kleisthenes," *MH* 3 (1946) 65–67; Jacoby, *Atthis*, 219, 394–95. Brommer, *Theseus* 65–76, 93.

[104] Gauer, in *Festschrift Neutsch*, 130, doubts a Kleisthenic *Theseid* and attributes the new scenes on vases to "einem Wandel des politischen Selbstverständnis der Athener"; cf. Taylor, *Tyrant Slayers*, 79–83, and Neils, *Youthful Deeds of Theseus*, 11–12, 144.

[105] As argued by Shapiro, *AA* (1982) 290–97; Neils, *Youthful Deeds of Theseus*, 31. Cf. Bacchylides, *Ode* 17.

[106] Herter, *RhM* 88 (1939) 285 n. 197; J. Barron, "Alkamenes at Olympia," *BICS* 31 (1984) 209 n. 37; Neils, *Youthful Deeds of Theseus*, 12, notes the absence of such a tradition in Pherekydes (*FGrH* 3 frags. 145–

55).

[107] By Gauer, in *Festschrift Neutsch*, 130–31; cf. Davie, "Theseus the King in Fifth-Century Athens," *GR* 29 (1982) 27; Boardman, in *Eye of Greece*, 3–5. See Chapter 11, n. 64.

[108] Ridgway, *Archaic Style*, 236–38 (she now accepts a date after Marathon: above, Chapter 11, n. 64). Brommer, *AA* (1979) 498–500; Boardman, in *Eye of Greece*, 3–15; Brommer, *Theseus*, pls. 1a–4a. Hurwit, *Art and Culture of Early Greece*, 311–19; Neils, *Youthful Deeds of Theseus*, 47–51. Hoffelner, "Die Metopen des Atheners Schatzhauses: Ein neuer Rekonstruktionsversuch," *AthMitt* 108 (1988) 79–117, for new arrangement of metopes.

the earliest known portrayal of a "cycle" of exploits by a single hero in ancient art or mythology. Herakles himself does not manifest such a cycle in classical art or literature, except for the twelve metopes of the temple of Zeus at Olympia, whose number dictated what became a canon much later.[109] If the "cycle cups" are allowed to agree with this monument in date as they do in style (as recommended in Chapter 11), the earliest representations of these deeds and of the phenomenon of the cycle belong to the same decade, after the battle of Marathon. This allows the possibility that the concept of a cycle, of a heroic biography of a hero, developed under the influence of the series of campaigns with which the Greeks eventually defeated the Persians. Certain deeds of Theseus allude to specific episodes in the Persian wars: his combat with the bull of Marathon commemorates the battle there, his defense against the Amazon invasion involves a myth that did not exist before the Persian invasion of Athens, his journey from Troizen is involved with the Athenian evacuation to that city, and his maritime adventures (recovery of the ring, defeat of Minos) are appropriate to the triumphs of the Athenian navy. It is possible that the narrative structure of mythical deeds participated in other narrative patterns with which Greece recounted its victory and its self-image.[110] A new genre of postepic biography, formed by history, adds itself to those literary and artistic traditions inspired by the Persian wars.

One metope of the treasury at Delphi (now with headless figures) shows Theseus with the goddess of Athena, helper of heroes since Homer and commonly seen with Herakles in vase painting. Nowhere else in contemporary art does she appear with Theseus alone, although she assists him in many other adventures. In literature, she sends a favorable wind for his ship, bound for Crete in the story of his confrontation with Minos (Bacchylides, *Ode* 17.5–7); in art, she appears on vases with him in at least seven of his adventures (e.g., Figure 56).[111] On the Athenian treasury she represents the blessing of the city of Athens, duplicated below the building where she appears in the lineup of gods and heroes dedicated after Marathon. The complementary pediment at Eretria where Theseus carries off Antiope (Figure 52) is dominated by the figure of Athena on a temple presumably sacred to Apollo but near the place where Theseus brought the captured Amazon queen.[112] The "archaistic" traits of hair and drapery are no more anachronistic than the folds on Kallimachos's Nike (Figure 43), once it is recognized that

[109] Brommer, *Theseus*, 65, 115.

[110] Thus Loraux contrasts the biographies of hero and city: "Theseus' 'historical' career is one with the history of Athens and is gradually enriched by the experiences of the city" (*Invention of Athens*, 119).

[111] F. Brommer, "Theseus—Deutungen, II," *AA* (1982) 83, and *Theseus*, 130 n. 11. Boardman, in *Eye of Greece*, 4–5.

[112] Boardman, in *Eye of Greece*, 8–9; Brommer, *AA*

(1979) 503–4, and *Theseus*, 113, pl. 19; E. Touloupa, "Τὰ ἐναέτια γλυπτὰ τοῦ ναοῦ τοῦ Ἀπόλλωνος Δαφνηφόρου στὴν Ἐρέτρια" (Ph.D. diss., Ioannina, 1981), maintains a date before 490. A. Delivorrias, *Attische Giebelskulpturen und Akrotere* (Tübingen, 1974), 180, does not assign Athena to the same pediment as Theseus and Antiope; Neils, *Youthful Deeds of Theseus*, 45.

the parallels for this in vase painting, including the "cycle" cup in London where Theseus is first seen carrying off Antiope (Figure 55), may be later than 490 B.C.[113] The figure
of Theseus on the Eretria pediment is close enough to those heads from the Athenian
treasury at Delphi, especially in the details of their snail-shell curls, to belong to the
same decade, if not the same Attic style.[114] A recent proposal to lower the date of the
Eretria pediment would allow the figures of Athena, Theseus, and Antiope to join those
from Delphi as an expression of Athenian victory over the East, in this case by Athens'
ally against the first Persian expedition.[115] Newly lowered dates for the Aphaia temple
pediments on Aigina (see n. 71), also dominated by the figure of Athena, would accom-
modate a post-Persian date for the Eretria pediment. However, the instability in absolute chronology of these monuments limits discussions of iconography and its significance. If the Eretria pediment predates the invasion of Dareios, the city was a significant
and solitary ally of Athens in the expedition against Persia in Ionia, in 499 B.C., and its
sculpture apparently participates in the Attic imagery of Theseus and Antiope also seen
on the amphora by Myson (Figure 37, right) and the Athenian treasury (Figure 39).

What emerges from these sculptures and red-figure vases of the first decades of the
fifth century is a lively interest in struggles against Amazons. What had been a love
story between Theseus and the Amazon queen, in the tradition that paired Achilles and
Penthesilea, or Herakles and Hippolyta, is discarded as unsuitable for the king of a city
that defeated the Persians; instead, Theseus and Antiope become antagonists.[116] The
Athenian treasury, for example, repeats this theme four times: in the akroteria, on one
north metope with Theseus (Figure 39), in another with Herakles (metope 22, possibly
from the east frieze), and probably in the pediment. On this monument, both heroes,
Theseus and Herakles, collaborate in battle, as if this were an adventure central to their
image as saviors of Greece. Certainly combat with Amazons was a skill required of numerous Greek heroes, including Achilles, Peleus (Pindar, frag. 172), and Bellerophon
(Pindar, *Olympian* 13.83–92). The paintings in the Stoa Poikile make this classical version
historical: the Athenians defeat the Persians at Marathon, with the help of Herakles,
Theseus, and Athena, next to the painting with Theseus and the Athenians in combat
against the Amazons (Pausanias, 1.15.15; cf. Arrian, *Anabasis* 7.13.5). The same Athe-

[113] Ridgway, *Archaic Style*, 107, 316 n. 5. See Chapter 11, on the Nike of Kallimachos and on the "man-
nerism" of the Pan Painter; n. 100 for cup in London.

[114] Ridgway, *Severe Style*, 17 compares the curls,
which appear "old-fashioned" or "conservative" unless the Pausanian date for the Athenian treasury is
accepted. W. Deyhle, "Meisterfragen der archaischen
Plastik Attikas," *AthMitt* 84 (1979) 44–45, argues for
an Attic sculptor (Antenor) at Eretria.

[115] E. D. Francis and M. Vickers, "Signa priscae artis," *JHS* 103 (1983) 49–87, propose a date in the 470s

for the Eretria pediment; the 480s would be more reasonable. J. Boardman, "Signa tabulae priscae artis,"
JHS 104 (1984) 161–62, disagrees but admits elsewhere (in *Eye of Greece*, 9 n. 29) that the Eretria pediment could be later than 490. Francis, *Image and Idea
in Fifth-Century Athens*, 8–16, 24–26.

[116] Boardman, in *Eye of Greece*, 8, 12–13, invoking a
late archaic *Theseis* and the Athenian expedition to Ionia in 499 B.C. as inspirations; Shapiro, *Art and Cult
under the Tyrants*, 148–49.

nian battle against the Amazons was represented in the new sanctuary for Theseus, along with a Centauromachy and a painting of his dive into the sea (Pausanias, 1.17.2). In his identification of the Theseion painting, Pausanias mentions its two most prominent representations in classical art: the shield of the Athena Parthenos and the paintings on the throne of Zeus at Olympia, both associated with the hand of Pheidias. Eventually this became a favorite theme in the art of classical Athens, where it appears on the Akropolis in the metopes and friezes of the Parthenon. The Athenian treasury is the first monument to illustrate the theme as a celebration of Attic victory over the Persians.

The locale of the Amazonomachies represented on the Athenian treasury is unclear. In archaic art, Herakles appears in hundreds of Amazonomachies alone, never with Theseus, but this solo expedition is no longer represented in the classical period, when another Amazonomachy becomes popular. Herakles and Theseus participated in a joint expedition to Themiskyra on the Thermodon, to recover the belt of Hippolyte (Euripides, *Herakleidai* 215–17), and some scholars identify this story on the treasury.[117] The east metopes of the Athenian treasury could be the earliest representation of both heroes together on this expedition, marking "the transformation of the Amazonomachy from Herakles to Theseus," an important step in the creation of the new hero.[118]

However, yet another new legend of Greek combat with Amazons developed in Athens, after and because of the Persian invasion of Athens. It is first attested in classical literature in Aeschylus's *Eumenides*, performed in 458 B.C. The goddess Athena, an appropriate witness to a glorious, if newly invented, episode from the Athenian past, describes the Areiopagos (685–90):

> πάγον δ' Ἄρειον τόνδ', Ἀμαζόνων ἕδραν
> σκηνάς θ', ὅτ' ἦλθον Θησέως κατὰ φθόνον
> στρατηλατοῦσαι, καὶ πόλιν νεόπτολιν
> τὴνδ' ὑψίπυργον ἀντεπύργωσαν τότε
> Ἄρει δ' ἔθυον, ἔνθεν ἔστ' ἐπώνυμος
> πέτρα πάγος τ' Ἄρετος.

> This is the hill of Ares, and the camp of the Amazons
> and their tents, that time when they came for revenge on Theseus
> in campaign for a siege, and against the newly founded city,
> this high-towered one, they built towers at that time
> and sacrificed to Ares, from whence comes the name
> of this rock: the hill of Ares.

---

[117] D. von Bothmer, *Amazons in Greek Art* (Oxford, 1947); Boardman, in *Eye of Greece*, 8–10; Tyrrell, *Amazons*, 2–3; duBois, *Centaurs and Amazons*, 57–60.

[118] DuBois, *Centaurs and Amazons*, 58–59, on how this theme becomes the cultural property of Athens.

The locale remembered as the camp of the Amazons is the Areiopagos, the same spot
chosen by the Persians for their assault on the Akropolis in 479 B.C. (Herodotus, 8.52).
One version of this adventure known to Plutarch (*Theseus* 27, citing Kleidemos) even
mentions the shrine of the Eumenides as a landmark in battle, another link between the
post-Persian cult first attested in Aeschylus and the new story of Amazons invading
Attika. Shrines and tombs of Amazons were maintained in Athens (Pausanias, 1.2.1,
1.41.7, reports monuments to Antiope and Hippolyta; cf. Plutarch, *Theseus* 27), suggesting the interest in topography common to Greek cults. The motive assigned to the Amazons—φθόνος toward Theseus for his prior expedition to Themiskyra—mirrors the
motive of vengeance against the Athenians for their role in the burning of Sardis, which
Herodotus assigns to the Persians (5.105; 6.94). The revenge the Amazons seek is, instead, exacted by Athens, and the amphora by Myson juxtaposing Theseus capturing
Antiope, with Kroisos on his pyre (Figure 37), expresses this connection.[119] The successful capture of Antiope is an Athenian achievement, in contrast to the failure of Kroisos
to defend his empire against the Persians, the historical equivalent of the Amazons. For
historical reasons, such a juxtaposition is unlikely to have occurred to an Athenian artist
before the Persian wars, just as the counterpoint of Ionia and Athens and the fall of
great men and cities entered historiography as a result of history (Chapter 11). As mythical equivalent to Persians and other Eastern barbarians, the Amazons came to represent
the opposite of Hellenism in the creation of "the other" which succeeded Greek victory
over the East.[120] Against an adversary like Theseus, they also had to fight democracy
and other Greek cultural institutions, in a formulaic confrontation between East and
West whose dimensions will be explored in (Chapter 13).

Even this early classical version is improved to exclude the rape of Antiope, one of
the deeds of Theseus (along with his mistreatment of Ariadne, Helen, etc.), which was
suppressed for the sake of nobler behavior. Like other interpretations favorable to Theseus, this one is first attested in the Atthidographers and is promoted by Attic orators
in the late fifth and fourth centuries. Without the theme of rape as a motif for revenge,
the Amazons become imperialists, their invasion of Attika more outrageous, and Theseus's defense of Athens all the more inspiring.[121]

---

[119] As recognized recently by Gauer, in *Festschrift
Neutsch*, 132, and Boardman, in *Eye of Greece*, 12–16,
although they connect amphora and treasury with
the Athenian expedition to Ionia in the 490s. Shapiro,
AJA 92 (1988) 379–81, fig. 8, associates the bull-device
on Peirithoos's shield (Figure 37b) with an earlier
dedication of the Marathonian bull; the adjustment
in chronology advocated in this chapter would coor-
dinate representations like these with a post-Mara-
thon monument. See Gauer, *JdI* 105 (1990) 31–65, on
another vengeance motif in early classical art.

[120] duBois, *Centaurs and Amazons*, chaps. 1–3; Tyrrell, *Amazons*, chaps. 1 and 6. F. Hartog, "Les ama-
zones d' Hérodote: Inversions et tiers exclus," in *Pour
Leon Poliakov: Le racisme. Mythes et sciences* (Paris,
1981) 177–86, and *Mirror of Herodotus*, 216–24, includes the Scythians in a triangular construction of
cultural identities.

[121] Connor, in *Quest for Theseus*, 156–57; Tyrrell,
Amazons, 9–22, "Theseus's Defense of Athens";
Neils, *Youthful Deed of Theseus*, 146–47, on the rape of
Antiope and how it disappears after 490 B.C.

This development accompanies the creation of a new image of Athens as defender of autonomous states and agent of just wars, an image deliberately designed to suppress the imperial behavior of Athens that contradicted it. If encounters with the bull of Marathon and Amazons in Athens allude to two experiences of the Persian invasion, a more calculated image of Theseus grew out of the victory at Salamis and the rise of the Delian League. Thus Theseus bridges the gap between the older, Marathon-oriented ideology of hoplite victory with a conservative state, and the more radical maritime democracy.[122] This division, already alluded to also separates a victory due to the gods from those where men (specifically, Athenians) claim credit for victory, and also distinguishes the more old-fashioned perspective of Herodotus and Aeschylus from the critical attitude of Thucydides. Unlike the battle of Marathon, where gods, heroes, and Athenians performed nobly, only Theseus and his father, Poseidon, emerge as the heroes of Salamis. The aftermath of naval victory, with the pursuit to Mykale and Sestos and the establishment of a defensive naval alliance in 478 B.C., usher in a new era of Athenian naval power and the need for a new ideology. Before Themistokles' exploitation of the silver from Laureion, Athens had had no serious navy and in fact expected to beat a longtime foe, Aigina, with her new triremes (Plutarch, *Themistokles* 4). In the development of a new ideology for this navy, Theseus played many a convenient role by providing different adventures appropriate to Athenian history.

His adventures en route to Troizen have already been cited as a reflection of the Athenian evacuation to that city. His reception by Aigeus established his claim to the throne of Athens, and scenes of Theseus and his Athenian father are most common in the decades after the Persian wars.[123] More evocative are those scenes where Theseus is greeted by his other father, Poseidon, often with the exchange of a handshake, which marks a contractual, legal relationship in Greek iconography (Figure 54).[124] In this case, the gesture may establish paternity, a claim challenged by Minos, son of Zeus, in the story narrated by Bacchylides in *Ode* 17 (52–66). Even if all scenes with Theseus and Poseidon do not allude to that test of paternity, they emphasize the relationship between father and son also attested in cult. They shared a festival day in Athens, and the games at Isthmia were established by Theseus in honor of his father (Plutarch, *Theseus* 25; 36). The emphasis on a divine father may be another episode in the hero's biography modeled on the iconography of Herakles, whose reception or "introduction" in Olympos by Zeus makes him more than an ordinary hero.[125]

---

[122] For an analysis of these two themes, see N. Loraux, "Marathon—ou l'histoire idéologique," *REA* 75 (1973) 13–42, and Euben, *Political Theory* 14 (1986) 359–90.

[123] U. Kron, "Aigeus," *LIMC* I.1, 359–63; Shapiro, *AA* (1982) 291–97, on arrival in Athens.

[124] Pollitt, *YUAG Bulletin* (Spring 1987) 10–12; cf.

U. Heimberg *Das Bild des Poseidon in der griechischen Vasenmalerei* (Freibourg, 1968), 53–58; Brommer, *Theseus*, 78, 140–41; Neils, *Youthful Deeds of Theseus*, 110, 113. Compare scenes of Theseus meeting with his father at the bottom of the sea: Figure 56, and nn. 139–45.

[125] As argued by P. Jacobsthal, *Theseus auf dem*

As well as bringing Theseus from Athens to Troizen, the Athenian imagination of the early classical period made a more literal home for him in Athens. In 476/5 B.C., the Delphic oracle instructed the Athenians to "bring home the bones of Theseus, give them honorable burial in Athens, and guard them as sacred relics" (Plutarch, *Theseus* 36). The general, Kimon, captured the island of Skyros and there "found" the bones of the hero, which he brought home in triumph on his ship "with great pomp and ceremony" (Plutarch, *Kimon* 8). According to Plutarch's account, this was the most popular achievement in the lifetime of Kimon (ἐφ᾽ ᾧ καὶ μάλιστα πρὸς αὐτὸν ὁ δῆμος ἔσχεν). This ceremony culminated in the establishment of a cult and sanctuary in Athens (Pausanias, 1.17.2; Philokhoros: *FGrH* 328 F 18a), the ultimate means of legitimacy for myth and ideology in Athens. The return of the bones of Theseus completes the hero's new ideology by making a place for him inside the city in imitation of archaic "founder-heroes" whose tombs and cults, often in the Agora, played an active role in archaic politics and history (e.g., in Sikyon: Herodotus, 5.67). In a city as proud of its "autochthony" as Athens was, it would be indelicate to suggest that the city had to be "founded," a contradiction of the belief that the the city and its citizens had "always been there" (Thucydides, 1.2.6; see previous section on autochthony). But the new shrine of Theseus provided Athens with a substitute for such a founder-hero.

The date of this repatriation of the hero's remains is not necessarily that of the oracle, dated by Plutarch to the archonship of Phaedo; the return of the relics could have been celebrated later in the 470s or even in the early 460s. The occasion is complicated by a link presumed by many between the return of Theseus's bones and the institution of the πάτριος νόμος, the Athenian state funeral for those fallen in battle, which Thucydides describes (2.35).[126] Pausanias identifies the tomb of those fallen at Drabeskos in Thrace (465 B.C.) as the first such state burial (1.29.4–5), and this coincides approximately with some of the first inscribed casualty lists (e.g., *IG* I³ 1147, from the tribe of Erechtheis). However, some documents indicate an earlier date for the inception of this practice, and the date may remain more elusive—somewhere during the generalship of Kimon, in the late 470s or early 460s—than the connection with Theseus.

It seems clear that the custom of bringing home the remains of those fallen in battle, for state burial in Athens rather than the traditional honor of burial on the battlefield, was a deliberate and political invention of imperial Athens. This state appropriation of a private responsibility turned family mourning into a public occasion for rhetorical de-

---

Meeresgrunde (Leipzig, 1911) 6–7; Barron, *JHS* 92 (1972) 40; Tyrrell, *Amazons*, 11; Neils, *Youthful Deeds of Theseus*, 145–46.

[126] F. Jacoby, "Patrios Nomos: State Burial in Athens and the Public Cemetery in the Kerameikos," *JHS* 64 (1944) 36–66; J. D. Smart, "Kimon's Capture of Eion," *JHS* 87 (1967) 136–37; Connor, in *Quest for Theseus*, 158–60; A. Podlecki, "Cimon, Skyros and Theseus' Bones," *JHS* 91 (1971) 141–43; Loraux, *Invention of Athens*, 28–30; Tyrrell, *Amazons*, 10–11; Clairmont, *Patrios Nomos*, chap. 1, 7–15; N. Robertson, *EchCl* 27 (1983) 78–92.

fense of the state and of the policies that sacrificed citizens to imperial strategies.[127] With the return of the bones of Theseus himself for state burial and funeral, this new custom received the blessing of myth and was legitimized through a heroic precedent.[128] Theseus himself performed the πάτριος νόμος in myth, by burying the bodies of Athenians after the war with Eleusis (Aeschylus, *Eleusinians*; cf. Plutarch, *Theseus* 29).[129] In the tradition of epic heroes like Achilles who return the bodies of the slain to the enemy, Theseus also arranged for the burial of the Argive dead after the epic battle of the Theban tradition and their graves were noted at Eleutherai (Plutarch, *Theseus* 29).[130] According to Plutarch, most of the sources on this tradition have Theseus arrange for burial by means of a truce. Philokhoros, whom he cites, claims this was the first such truce arranged for the burial and recovery of bodies, although Plutarch knows of a prior claim to this invention by Herakles, and Homeric warfare suggests a precedent (*Iliad* 7.331–35, 394–97, 408–11). Other Atthidographers present the same image of Theseus as a civilized hero with diplomatic skills as well as courage in battle. According to Kleidemos (Plutarch, *Theseus* 27), the battle against the invading Amazons also was concluded with a truce and, presumably, with the burial of Amazons whose tombs became Athenian landmarks. The proliferation of truces in the campaigns of the Pentekontaetia and the Peloponnesian War, and the emphasis on the role of the state in burying those fallen in battle, must have encouraged stories of heroes negotiating truces and burial. Thus Theseus continued to demonstrate his versatility in the creation of Athenian ideology throughout the fifth century.

In the aftermath of the Persian wars, the rise of Athenian imperialism transformed Theseus into a symbol of continuing expansion, rather than a mere symbol of victory. The institution of the πάτριος νόμος and its funeral oration were an opportunity for the state to advertise its policies and encourage public support for the war effort, and Theseus served to legitimize this institution. The ultimate celebration of Theseus as hero of Athenian democracy took place in iconography, where his figure was assimilated to the poses of the tyrannicides, Harmodios and Aristogeiton. These poses may have been adopted earlier, by heroes of the Persian wars like Miltiades and by legendary figures like Herakles and Telamon, on vases painted by the Pioneers. By the middle of the fifth century, first in vase painting and thereafter in relief sculpture, Theseus strides in the posture of both heroes. On a cup by the Codrus Painter, the deeds of Theseus are de-

[127] K. Walters, "Rhetoric as Ritual: The Semiotics of the Attic Funeral Oration," *Florilegium* 2 (1980) 1–27; Loraux, *Invention of Athens*; Tyrrell, *Amazons*, 13–19.

[128] Hauvette, in *Mélanges Henri Weil*, 169–73; Clairmont, *Patrios Nomos*, 2, 13–15, 254 n. 15 (he dates the return of the bones to the year of the oracle, 475 B.C.).

[129] Hauvette, in *Melanges Henri Weil* 168–78, dates the play between 475 and 470 and calls it "un hymne à la gloire de Thésée et d'Athènes" (p. 169); Bovon, *Études de Lettres* 6 (1963) 222; A. Podlecki, *The Political Background of Aeschylean Tragedy* (Ann Arbor, 1966), chap. 4; Loraux, *Invention of Athens*, 63–64, 195, 204–6.

[130] Euripides, *Suppliants*; Loraux, *Invention of Athens*, 107–8, 206, 216, 306.

picted in the tondo (Figure 57, above), around it, and on the exterior, in two of which adventures his attitude and weapons imitate the statues by Kritios and Nesiotes (Figure 57 center, below).[131] Thereafter, friezes of classical Athenian temples like the Hephaisteion and the temple of Poseidon at Sounion present the hero in these poses in traditional battles against Centaurs and Amazons, not just in individual deeds particular to his own cycle. At the same time, and perhaps through the influence of these portraits of mature men, Theseus appears as a young warrior with a beard, no longer as an ephebe. The source that disseminated the new images of Theseus may have been one of the monumental paintings of the early classical period that portrayed the hero in historical and legendary events.[132] At least one marble portrait from early classical Athens has been linked to the image of Theseus. The Kritios kouros from the Akropolis, newly restored and attributed to a context after the *Perserschutt*, wears the same haircut as Theseus in the west pediment at Olympia, one suggestive of the *Theseis* haircut attested by Plutarch (*Theseus* 5.2.1).[133] The new historical context for this statue and its new interpretation emerge as more important features in the history of Greek sculpture than its pose or stylistic date. The Kritian "boy" concludes the history and demise of the kouros in Athens with its rebirth as a new historical hero, in the hands of an artist related to those who produced the first historical portraits in Greek sculpture, the tyrannicides. The new identity of the Kritios "kouros" is all the more attractive, given the ultimate convergence of the image of Theseus with the statues of the tyrannicides.

These two poses link Theseus to the constitutional identity of Athens as a democratic city and promote his image as the hero of Athenian democracy, both Kleisthenic and radical. This image was one of the longer lived in his repertoire: in the fourth century, Euphranor painted Theseus in the company of Demos and Democracy, in a painting displayed in the Stoa of Zeus Eleutherios along with murals of the twelve gods and the battle of Mantinea.[134] Pausanias reports that, in some manner that can only be imagined, "the painting shows it was he who instituted Athenian political equality" (τὸν

---

[131] London E 84: Brommer, *Theseus*, pl. 13. Chr. Kardara, "Theseus and the Tyrannicides," *AJA* 55 (1951) 293–300; Taylor, *Tyrant Slayers*, 74–143, esp. 88–129. Taylor suggests (pp. 39–42) that Kritios and Nesiotes adopted the pose of Euphronios's Herakles on the Arezzo krater for Harmodios (or vice versa? See Chapter 11, n. 91). Neils, *Youthful Deeds of Theseus*, 129–32, no. 111.

[132] Taylor, *Tyrant Slayers*, 144–57, including earlier scholarship by Barron, Woodford, etc.

[133] The identification of the Kritios kouros as Theseus was made by E. Harrison, "Greek Sculptured Coiffures and Ritual Haircuts," in *Early Greek Cult Practices*, 250; by J. Neils, "Heroes and Hairdoes: The

Quest for Theseus in Classical Sculpture," *AJA* 84 (1984) 254; *Youthful Deeds of Theseus*, 108; and by J. Hurwit, "The Kritios Boy: Discovery, Reconstruction, and Date," *AJA* 93 (1989) 76–77.

[134] Pliny, *Naturalis Historia* 35.129; Pausanias, 1.3.3; Thompson, *Marsyas* 9 (1960–1961) 48–49. O. Palagia, *Euphranor* (Leiden, 1980), 60–61; Shapiro, *Boreas* 9 (1986) 23. For a fourth-century representation of Demokratia crowning Demos, on a decree against tyranny, see an inscription from the Athenian Agora, inventory no. 6524 = *SEG* 12.87 (337/6 B.C.); Oliver, *Demokratia*, 164, pl. II; C. Lawton, "Attic Document Reliefs of the Classical and Hellenistic Periods" (Ph.D. diss., Princeton 1984), 196–200.

καταστήσαντα Ἀθηναίους ἐξ ἴσου πολιτευέσθαι). This suggests a pose like those of Harmodios and Aristogeiton, if Pausanias reflects the grammar of Attic iconography familiar in the fifth century. But the painting, and its description in terms that associate the image of the hero with Athenian democracy, maintains the political symbolism of art inaugurated in the fifth century and inspires the relationship between rhetoric and art manifest in the painting of the battle of Marathon and its reflection in oratory (Chapter 11). Like the reputation of Athenian democracy itself, its symbol, Theseus, far outlived its original political circumstances.

Meanwhile, the maritime side of Theseus's adventures supported the image of Athens abroad as "natural" leader of the Delian League. In conjunction with the return of the bones of Theseus, the Theseion founded in Athens was decorated with paintings of the hero's exploits, against Amazons and Centaurs, and his dive into the sea.[135] It is tempting to associate the first major poems devoted to Theseus with the publicity generated by this new sanctuary and its ceremonies, including lost works like Aeschylus's *Eleusinians* (see nn. 65, 128). Theseus is the subject of two poems by Bacchylides, one (*Ode* 18.1–60) devoted to his arrival in Athens from Troizen.[136] Performed as a dramatic dialogue in lyric meters between the king, Aigeus, and a chorus or its leader, the poem inaugurates not so much the arrival of the hero from Troizen but the emergence of a new figure renowned for ἄφατα ἔργα, "untold deeds" (line 18). The king recounts five of the deeds performed on the road from Troizen to Athens (18–30), and describes him as a young man (παῖδα πρώθηβον: 56–57). The poem has been dated to the 470s and associated with a festival like the Thargelia, but can be generally assumed to belong to the era of Kimon's promotion of the hero. The description of the hero as youthful and wearing sword, cloak, and so on, as well as the catalogue of his youthful deeds, suits the iconography of the early classical cycle cups.[137] His arrival in Athens, in particular, appears on vases as a reception scene with his father and other Athenian relatives present.[138]

The other poem by Bacchylides that celebrates Theseus (*Ode* 17) concentrates on his dive to the bottom of the sea, a choral hymn (dithyramb) that ends in praise of Apollo

[135] Pausanias, 1.17.2; Barron, *JHS* 92 (1972) 20–45; duBois, *Centaurs and Amazons*, 61–62; Davie, *GR* 29 (1982) 27–28. J. Koumanides, "Θήσεως Σηκός," *AE* (1976) 194–216, makes the shrine with paintings separate from the site where the bones were buried.

[136] D. Campbell, *Greek Lyric Poetry* (London, 1967), 440 (citing Jebb on the Thargelia); Barron, *BICS* 27 (1980) 1–8; R. Merkelbach, "Der Theseus des Bakchylides (Gedicht für ein attisches Ephebenfest)," *ZPE* 12 (1973) 56–62; Herington, *Poetry into Drama*, 251 n. 73; Burnett, *Art of Bacchylides*, 117–23.

[137] Neils, *Youthful Deeds of Theseus*, 32–40. Barron, *BICS* 27 (1980) 1–8, connects several of these attributes to Kimon.

[138] Neils, *Youthful Deeds of Theseus*, 96, 103, 146. Cf. Brommer, *Theseus*, 125–28; Kron, "Aigeus," *LIMC* I.1, 359–67, esp. nos. 27–32, "Aigeus bei der Begrüssung des Theseus"; C. Sourvinou-Inwood, *Theseus as Son and Step-Son. BICS* suppl 40 (London, 1979), on some peculiarities of these reception scenes (e.g. the cup by Makron showing Theseus attacking [?] Aithra).

as Delian and Kean, suggesting the context of some (Cycladic?) festival.[139] The story of
the dive forms an episode within the longer subject of Theseus's voyage to Crete, slaying of the Minotaur and rescue of Athenian youths and maidens, and triumphant return
to Athens via Naxos, where he abandons Ariadne. The poem takes place on board the
ship that carries Theseus, the seven Athenian youths, and seven maidens to Crete, with
Minos. The first event narrated in the poem is Minos's attempt to violate Eriboia, one
of the Athenian maidens, who is defended by Theseus in a verbal attack on Minos (6–
46). This preliminary incident attributes to Minos the weaknesses of unbridled lust, βία
(violence), and ὕβρις (outrage), formulaic weaknesses in classical literature, while Theseus appears as an advocate and model of civilized restraint. This is one of the few
surviving classical testimonia to the unfavorable portrait of Minos attributed to Attic
poets of the classical period (Plutarch, *Theseus* 16). This passage characterizes that portrait in terms of the typical wickedness of a tyrant in the Herodotean image. Theseus
challenges Minos's descent from Zeus by appealing to his own father, Poseidon, to
which Minos's response is a prayer to Zeus, answered by a thunderbolt. With his
prayer, Minos throws his golden ring into the sea (60–62) and challenges Theseus to
recover it and win κλέος from his father, Poseidon. Without hesitation, the hero plunges
into the waves, where dolphins carry him to the home of Poseidon and Amphitrite. The
ring is never mentioned again, but Theseus receives a crown and a robe from Amphitrite, with which he emerges dry from the sea.

Pausanias tells a slightly different version of this story, in describing Mikon's painting
of the dive in the Theseion (1.17.3). The Athenian maiden seized is known as Periboia
to him, not Eriboia; Pausanias also confirms that the story (if not the painting) has Theseus return to the surface with ring, as well as crown. His explanation implies that the
painting, which only told part of the story (οὐ τὸν πάντα . . . λόγον), may have presented only Theseus and Minos, or Theseus, Poseidon, and Amphitrite. A number of
vases present such a tableau with the hero flanked by Poseidon, Amphitrite, and other
figures like Nereus and his daughters (Figure 54).[140] The only other source on this story
is Hyginus (*Astronomica* 2.5), who narrates the story of the dive on the Cretan coast, not
on board ship. Of the other vases that may illustrate the story, none show the ring, and
may be based on another painting.[141] The most magnificent of these vases is the cycle

[139] Jacobsthal, *Theseus auf dem Meeresgrunde*; A. Sev-
eryns, *Bacchylide* (Liege, 1933), 56–59; Campbell,
GLP, 433–39; Barron, *BICS* 27 (1980) 1–8; Burnett, *Bacchylides*, 15–37; R. Scodel, "The Irony of Fate in Bacchylides 17," *Hermes* 112 (1984) 136–43; Neils, *Youthful Deeds of Theseus*, 10–11; D. A. Schmidt,
"Bacchylides 17: Paean or Dithyramb?" *Hermes* 188
(1990) 18–31.

[140] The first juxtaposition of Theseus and Poseidon

is on a late work of the Berlin Painter (Metropolitan
41.167.17) dated 470–465: Neils, *Youthful Deeds of Theseus*, 73, 82, 89–90, 103, 146; cf. versions by the Har-
row Painter in the Fogg Art Museum and by the Syr-
iskos Painter in Paris. Figure 54 is the name vase of
the Painter of the Yale Oinochoe: Pollitt, *YUAG Bulletin* (Spring 1987) 12–13, figs. 4, 5. S. Kaempf-Dimitriadou, "Amphitrite," *LIMC* I.1, 724–35.

[141] Thus Barron, *JHS* 92 (1972) 40; Brommer, *The-*

cup of Euphronios painted by Onesimos, depicting deeds of Theseus on the exterior and the young hero in the tondo, supported by a triton (?) and receiving a crown or wreath from Amphitrite (Figure 56).[142] The central figure of the scene, as in the pediments at Eretria and Aigina, is the goddess Athena, not involved in the story according to the literary sources and not commonly seen underwater in Greek art. The political implications of her presence are difficult to dissociate from the imagery of Athenian sea power, not celebrated in poetry before the Delian League. The cup is usually cited as an "anticipation" of the painting by Mikon and the poem by Bacchylides, although its historical associations have persuaded some of a lower date.[143] Like other scenes favored by Onesimos that acquire new significance after 480 B.C.—the *Ilioupersis*, most conspicuously—his depiction of the dive by Theseus recommends a reevaluation of the late work of the Pioneers in connection with the imagery of the Persian wars.

The conspicuous absence of the ring in the finale of Bacchylides' poem, after the theatrical gesture when Minos casts it into the sea and taunts Theseus, whispers of classical history. Xerxes performs a barbarian rite at sunrise before he crosses the Hellespont (Herodotus, 7.54). Pouring a libation from a golden phiale, the Persian king prays to the sun, then submerges the phiale, a golden krater presumably used to mix the libation, and a Persian dagger, an ἀκινάκης, in the sea. Xerxes' prayer was for συντυχίη (good fortune) to permit him to destroy Europe, a wish not granted, so that his offerings were made in vain. The image of Minos formed an anti-Athenian figure with Oriental trappings in Athenian mythology, as a foil to Theseus, and the Persian king who offers gold to the sea, in vain, parallels the Cretan king who also throws precious metal into the sea, trusting in his god in vain. The episode in the Bacchylides poem suggests another tantalizing link with history, specifically with the Delian League. A ring cast into the sea that does not reappear suggests the imagery of oaths, when iron is cast into the sea to symbolize the swearing of an agreement that will only be dissolved when the metal floats. Such oaths were anticipated in the first episode of Athenian alliance and imperialism, after Mykale in 479 B.C. (Herodotus, 9.106.4), and eventually sworn at the establishment of the Delian League in 478/7 B.C. (Plutarch, *Aristeides* 25; *Athenaion Politeia* 23.5). Recent research traces them to Near Eastern formulas, another irony of the victory over an Oriental enemy.[144] In a process of suppression and substitution familiar in Greek poetry and mythology, the ring of Minos may not resurface in the poem pre-

seus, 77–83, on sources and illustrations.

[142] Louvre G 104, from Caere: Neils, *Youthful Deeds of Theseus*, 59–62, no. 15, calls this "the finest graphic expression of Theseus's youthful adventures" (p. 61).

[143] W. Klein, *Geschichte der griechischen Kunst* (Leipzig, 1904), 308–13.

[144] H. Jacobson, "The Oath of the Delian League," *Philologus* 119 (1975) 256–58, on its Near Eastern origins; R. Winton, "The Oaths of the Delian League," *MH* 40 (1983) 125. For archaic legends of submerged rings that reappear (e.g. the ring of Amasis: Herodotus 3.41–42), see Chapter 6.

cisely because a recent public ceremony has emphasized the submergence of metal. Instead, another symbol from the cycle of Theseus—the gift of a wreath or garland, perhaps the one with which he eventually crowns Ariadne—replaces it in this poem as it appears in art.[145]

Theseus's adventures in Crete involve further triumphs over Minos, his navy, and his power. The Minotaur is slain, the Athenians saved from human sacrifice, and Ariadne carried off to Naxos, where she is abandoned, only to be seduced by Dionysos. Many of these episodes were familiar in archaic art and literature, and some have Near Eastern roots. As argued previously, the Minotaur misrepresents Levantine rituals of men wearing bulls' masks and, ultimately, Near Eastern iconography, which imagines gods as bulls (Figures 20–22: Chapter 6). The dispatch of youths and maidens to Knossos for sacrifice coincides with a locale settled by Phoenicians where infant sacrifice may indeed have been practiced, and is expressed in terms of the same interval, nine years, formulaic to the image of Minos (Plutarch, *Theseus* 15; Chapter 6). In the classical period, these separate myths were synthesized into the heroic biography of Theseus.

The Minotaur is attested in Greek literature as early as the *Kypria* (Proclus, *Chrestomathia* 1), and was the earliest and most popular of the deeds of Theseus in art. It was more frequently represented than other deeds of Theseus combined (over four hundred vases) and belongs, in fact, to the most popular legends in the history of Greek art.[146] The Boiotian skyphos (Figure 10) examined earlier shows the slaying of the monster in connection with Ariadne and her thread, the seven youths and seven maidens, and a mysterious flying creature who may be Daidalos or Ikaros. This suggests there was already a developed narrative of the Cretan deeds of Theseus, in archaic Athenian art, and that this tradition included Daidalos. In the late archaic–early classical era, the period of the cycle cups and the Athenian treasury at Delphi, the slaying of the Minotaur and the events that accompany it (Ariadne, Naxos, and Delos) are incorporated into the cycle of other deeds of Theseus, many of which seem to be reconstituted from the adventures of Herakles. The hero now appears younger than he did in archaic art (i.e., unbearded) and often in traveler's garb such as boots and *pilos* or *petasos* hat. These details make the slayer of the Minotaur as youthful in the classical period as Bacchylides and the vase painters of his other deeds make him, appropriate to the young image of Athenian naval power.

Minos and Daidalos do not appear in art in connection with Theseus in Crete, but must have received a new image on the Attic stage, according to the titles and fragments of lost plays (Chapter 8). Plutarch (*Theseus* 16) blames the reputation of Minos on

---

[145] Brommer, *AA* (1982) 69–88, on wreath; Blech, *Studien zum Kranz*, 259–67.

[146] Brommer, *Theseus*, 35–64; E. R. Young, "The Slaying of the Minotaur" (Ph.D. diss., Bryn Mawr College, 1972), reviews Near Eastern and Greek representations; Neils, *Youthful Deeds of Theseus*, 22–30, 143–45; B. Schmaltz, "Theseus, der Sieger über den Minotaur," *AA* (1989) 71–79 (Roman painting).

the tragedians, as did Sokrates, who knew Minos as "harsh, cruel, and unjust" (ἄγριόν τινα καὶ χαλεπὸν καὶ ἄδικον: *Minos* 318d; cf. *Laws* 4.706a-b). At least seven known plays represented Athenians as victims of Cretans, of which only one is preserved (Euripides, *Hippolytos*).[147] The absence of favorable portraits of Cretans in early tragedy accompanies the gradual evolution of the image of Athens as superior to other cultures, including barbarians.[148] As Plato and Plutarch observe, the classical portrait of Minos as cruel and violent contradicts his image of lawmaker and judge in Homer and Hesiod. In his rare appearances in Greek art, Minos is bearded and wields scepter or spear, in the image of kingship.[149] The sources for the contradiction lie in the same mythography that made Theseus a new and positive hero. As his opponent, Minos had to represent adverse qualities, and those Levantine institutions still associated with Crete—infant sacrifice expressed as "tribute" and the worship of gods as bulls—contributed to an unfavorable portrait of the Cretan king. After the Persian wars, their resemblance to (or known derivation from) Levantine customs could only help make the image of Minos more negative, to a culture that had confronted Persian armies and Phoenician ships.

This last item, in particular, probably played a crucial role in the most important new attribute of Minos to emerge in the classical period: his thalassocracy. For classical historians, his navy represented the earliest known in the Greek tradition (Herodotus, 3.122; Thucydides, 1.4). Because of the modern identification of Minos with the culture of the Middle Bronze Age, much research has been devoted to tracing the historical reality of this myth in Aegean archaeology.[150] Few discussions of this myth and its possible archaeological correlations have appreciated the late and artificial nature of this myth, which probably developed to emphasize how Minos was defeated by Theseus. The thalassocracy of Minos was probably invented by Athens, as a historical precedent for a powerful navy defeated by Athens, the way the Athenians of the fifth century defeated a superior navy, that of the Persians. Whether the Levantine associations of Crete and the "Phoenician" parentage of Minos (Chapter 10) contributed to the pejorative attitude toward Minos, as an appropriate paradigm for a navy primarily Phoenician, may only be a coincidence that appears convenient to this theory.[151] In the most

---

[147] Haft, *The Myth That Crete Became*, 166 n. 102. The other six include plays named *Theseus* by Sophokles, Euripides, and an anonymous playwright; Sophokles' *Phaidra* and *Kamikoi*, and Euripides' *Cretans*. K. Reckford, "Phaedra and Pasiphae: The Pull Backward," *TAPA* 104 (1974) 307–28; Chr. Eucken, "Das anonyme Theseus-Drama und der *Oedipus Coloneus*," *MH* 36 (1979) 136–41.

[148] Bacon, *Barbarians in Greek Tragedy*, 167–72, on the rise of the "symbolic foreigner" in the works of Euripides, modified by Hall, *Inventing the Barbarian*, 160–61, 169–70.

[149] Brommer, *AA* (1982) 86–87.

[150] See the essays in *Minoan Thalassocracy*; J. Warzeski, "Minoan Cultural Hegemony and the Myth of the Minoan Thalassocracy" (M.A. thesis, Yale University 1985), 1–4. Also see my Chapter 6.

[151] C. Starr, "The Myth of the Minoan Thalassocracy," *Historia* 3 (1954–1955) 282–91; "Thucydides on Sea Power," *Mnemosyne* 31 (1978) 343–50; *The Influence of Sea Power on Ancient History* (Oxford, 1989), esp. 12–13, on the projection of Athenian naval imperialism into the past, by Thucydides. M. Miller, *The Thalassocracies* (Albany, 1971), on the historiography

flattering version of this myth, it is Theseus who launches an expedition against the sons of Minos to make the seas safe and clear them of piracy, a service Minos himself claimed in older traditions (Thucydides, 1.4). This epilogue to the early classical myth of the thalassocracy of Minos is, not surprisingly, the invention of Atthidography (Kleidemos, *FGrH* 3b, 74–75). It belongs to the era when Kimon drove the Dolopians out of Skyros and "freed the Aegean of pirates" (Plutarch, *Kimon* 8), as well as defeating Phoenicians and Cilicians by sea (18). Ultimately, this myth belongs to the same ideology of Athenian maritime power that promotes Theseus as son of Poseidon and deep-sea diver, and Athens as a natural naval power.

The return of Theseus to Athens involved several episodes in cult and myth that address the new image of the Athenian hero. A sanctuary was founded in Athens for Theseus under the sponsorship of his first hosts, the Phytalidae; commemorative sacrifices were offered to the hero by the families whose children had been rescued in Crete (Plutarch, *Theseus* 23). In early Greek art, Ariadne leaves Crete with Theseus, after helping him escape, but dies on Dia (Naxos?), according to Homer (*Odyssey* 11.321), through the arrows of Artemis. However, by the time Plutarch compiled his biography of Theseus, "there are many different accounts of these events, and of the story of Ariadne, none of which agree in their details."[152] For the classical period under consideration, the significant changes are the reform of the character of Theseus and his role in the unkind desertion of Ariadne. Pherekydes (frag. 106 = schol. *Odyssey* 11.320) is the first to present an "Athenian" version of the abandonment, where the goddess Athena bids Theseus to return to Athens. This intervention of divine authority anticipates the kind of *pietas* bestowed on Aeneas, who leaves Dido not out of cruelty but out of a sense of duty.[153] As argued by Webster, "at a time when Theseus was becoming more and more important as their national hero the Athenians were offended by his desertion of Ariadne."[154] One of the virtues newly appreciated in the classical period was the rescue of maidens, not their abandonment, as Theseus himself exemplifies by defending Eriboia against Minos (Bacchylides, 17.16–46). However, the whitewashing of Theseus was attributed to Peisistratos: according to Plutarch, the tyrant excised from the poetry of Hesiod the lines that blamed Theseus's callous behavior on infidelity, the love of another woman (*Theseus* 20, citing Hereas of Megara). This passage belongs to a general pattern

---

of thalassocracies; Barron, *BICS* 27 (1980) 4, suggests a correspondence between Minos, son of Phoinix, and the primarily Phoenician fleet of Xerxes (on which see Chapter 13).

[152] Plutarch, *Theseus*, 20; Brommer, *Theseus*, 86–92. T.B.L. Webster, "The Myth of Ariadne from Homer to Catullus," *GR* 13 (1966) 22–31, pl. 1; E. Richardson, "The Story of Ariadne in Italy," in *Studies in Classical*

Art and Archaeology, 189–95. M.-L. Bernhard and W. Daszewski, "Ariadne," *LIMC* III.I, 1050–70. Sh. McNally, "Ariadne and Others: Images of Sleep in Greek and Early Roman Art," *CA* 4 (1985) 152–92.

[153] Richardson, in *Studies in Classical Art and Archaeology*, 191; Servius on *Aeneid* 3.125.

[154] Webster, *GR* 13 (1966) 26.

of implicating Peisistratos in the manipulation of poetic tradition, although it does help support the evidence that Theseus, not Herakles, was the tyrant's hero.

Artists of the early classical period were the first to depict the abandonment of Ariadne and with it the "honorable" departure of Theseus, supporting Webster's argument that it was the Kimonian era, not the sixth century, that revised the motives of Theseus. A lekythos in Taranto near the Pan Painter is the earliest representation of the episode, and shows an unusual scene. Ariadne is asleep, with Hypnos perched on her head, next to Theseus, who is awake and being addressed by Athena.[155] The image is saturated with the quality of $\mathring{\eta}\theta os$ or "character" attributed to Polygnotos and missing in lost paintings. At least one monumental painting in Athens depicted this scene, a tableau in the temple of Dionysos that showed the sleeping Ariadne and the departing hero, along with the arrival of Dionysos (Pausanias, 1.20.21; Philostratos, *Imagines* 1.15). A number of vase paintings include Dionysos, in substance or symbol, or a bridge between the departure of Theseus and arrival of Dionysos, and some cast Hermes in the role of messenger.[156] The abandoned Ariadne continued to preoccupy romantic artists in antiquity and post-Renaissance times, unperturbed by the classical reform of Theseus.[157] In terms of the new image of the hero, classical painters and mythographers apparently made him respectful of the gods in this adventure, as he was in others.

A second passenger on Theseus's return to Athens was the artist, Daidalos. According to Kleidemos, Daidalos joined the Cretan adventure of Theseus as accomplice who actually left Athens for Crete, having already escaped Minos himself (Plutarch, *Theseus* 19). The same source names Daidalos as a blood relative of Theseus and grandson of Erechtheus, one example of the Athenian genealogy of Daidalos newly fabricated in classical Athens (Chapter 8). Pherekydes has Daidalos, not Ariadne, provide the escape stratagem of a thread for Theseus.[158] Finally, Hyginus has Daidalos return to Athens with Theseus, an explicit link between craftsman and city (*Fabellae* 40). This displacement is matched in other sources where the death of Ikaros, for example, takes place between Athens and Crete, not during the escape from Minos (Menekrates, quoted by Servius on *Aeneid* 6.14). This gesture of repatriation links the hero associated with Athe-

---

[155] Taranto 4545 (ARV² 560, 5): L. Curtius, "Lekythos aus Tarent," *ÖJh* 38 (1950) 1–16; E. Simon, "Zur Lekythos des Panmalers in Tarent," *ÖJh* 38 (1954) 77–90; Richardson, in *Studies in Classical Art and Archaeology*, 190, gives the hero more credit than he deserves: "To do him justice, Theseus seems to be expostulating with the goddess." Brommer, *Theseus*, 88–91, 130. Other versions with Athena include Berlin 2179 (Syleus Painter) and the work of the Lewis Painter (Vienna 1773).

[156] E.g., Tarquinia cup (RC 5291: *ARV²* 405, 1; per-

haps by the Foundry Painter in his Brygan phase); Brommer, *Theseus*, 89 (Hermes: Servius on *Georgics* 1.222).

[157] Webster, *GR* 13 (1966) 22–31, and Richardson, in *Studies in Classical Art and Archaeology*; M. Meiss, "Sleep in Venice: Ancient Myths and Renaissance Proclivities," *PAPhS* 110 (1966) 348–82; S. Tidworth, "From the Renaissance to Romanticism," in *Quest for Theseus*, 195–230.

[158] Pherekydes, *FGrH* 1A 3F, 148; Brommer, *AA* (1982) 69ff., and *Theseus*, 36.

nian cultural institutions (e.g., democracy, festivals) with the benefaction of Athenian art.[159] With the incorporation of Daidalos into Athenian genealogy, and as eponym for a Kleisthenic deme, the Cretan artist joins the cultural agenda of Athens as παίδευσις of Greece.

The atmosphere that promoted legendary artists as Athenian also rediscovered the craftsman Hephaistos as a native. Like Daidalos, Hephaistos, has origins in the Bronze Age and in the Near East. The evidence of the Linear B tablets and some legends and epithets suggest his tentative connection with Crete in the Bronze Age (Chapter 4), but no closer than that of Daidalos. In the Greek world, his strongest associations are with the island of Lemnos, and cults of Hephaistos are rare outside of Athens.[160] Miltiades' conquest of Lemnos in the last decade of the sixth century may have been the first occasion when the god of Lemnos became interesting property for Athens.[161] In archaic art, scenes of the return of Hephaistos to Olympos are highly popular, and the god appears as a bearded and lame figure in the company of silens.[162] In his second most popular archaic adventure, the birth of Athena, Hephaistos appears brandishing an ax with which he dispells the headache of Zeus and helps bring Athena into the world.[163] As suggested previously, both scenes may derive from Near Eastern traditions. Craftsmen-gods like Kothar are summoned to the palace of the king of the gods, and often travel by donkey. The birth of Athena, in its earliest Greek illustrations (Figures 13, 14), translates a Levantine image (cf. Figure 15) into a Greek story, and incorporates a multiple company of craftsmen into its story. It is only in the fifth century that scenes of Hephaistos as a craftsman, independent of mythological occasions for his services, become popular for a brief period, when the god acquires a new image. Homeric episodes like the manufacture of the arms of Achilles, from *Iliad* 18, are first illustrated in the decades following the Persian wars (Figures 1, 3).[164] Hephaistos appears as a youth for the first time, the way Herakles and Theseus first lose their beards in these decades. He is also more consistently represented as a craftsman, with workman's cap and tunic (*exomis*), as Alkamenes probably portrayed him as a cult image inside his new temple.[165]

[159] Robertson, in *Festschrift Brommer*, 80–87, and in *Parthenon-Kongress Basel*, 207–8. Compare the repatriation of Epimenides, another Cretan who becomes an Attic cultural hero, "Bouzyges:" Servius on *Georgics* 1.19; Shapiro, *Kernos* 3 (1990) 341.

[160] Delcourt, *Hephaistos*, chaps. 8–9; Brommer, *Hephaistos*, 1–3, 195–96, etc. Burkert, *Greek Religion*, 167: "Only in Athens does Hephaistos have a special importance in mythology and cult" (primarily through his association with Erichthonios and Athena).

[161] As suggested by N. Robertson, "The Riddle of the Arrephoria at Athens," *HSCP* 87 (1983) 288.

[162] Brommer, *Hephaistos*, 10–17; G. Hedreen, "Si-

lens in Attic Black-figure Vase-painting: Myth and Performance" (Ph.D. diss., Bryn Mawr College, 1988), chap. 1, "The Return of Hephaistos."

[163] Brommer, *Hephaistos*, 18, 36–38; *LIMC* II.1, 985–90 (Birth of Athena).

[164] Brommer, *Hephaistos*, 20–21, for vases by early classical artists like the Tyszkiewicz Painter, the Foundry Painter, the Dutuit Painter (dated between 490 and 480 B.C.; the adjustment of Attic chronology advocated in this chapter would relocate them to the 470s and 460s).

[165] Harrison, *AJA* 81 (1977) 146–50, 413–14.

This iconography was borrowed for one of the few representations of Daidalos in vase painting, on a phlyax vase from South Italy where only the inscription confirms that the craftsman in battle with Enyalios is not Hephaistos himself (Figure 11).[166] This overlap suggests that images of both gods were conceived under similar circumstances and without an exclusive or established icononographic tradition, just as their biographies were newly refurbished to emphasize their connection with Athens.

Another significant innovation in these early classical scenes of Hephaistos at work is the appearance of Athena, even on occasions such as the manufacture of arms for Achilles where no tradition requires her presence.[167] The goddess also accompanies the craftsman in other scenes critical to the image of the city as a center of art and culture: at the birth of their "son," Erichthonios and in scenes of the manufacture of Pandora (Figures 49, 50). Athena and Hephaistos eventually appear together on the east frieze of the Parthenon in the assembly of gods, where they suggest a husband-and-wife couple appropriate to their parentage of Erichthonios. Hephaistos's other wives—Charis in the *Iliad* (18.382–83) and Aphrodite in the *Odyssey* (8.267)—are discreetly absent in classical mythology, although the craftsman's traditional role as "midwife" to Athena, somewhat compromising of his status as her husband, is still portrayed and appears on the same monument (in the east pediment of the Parthenon). It is their conjugal relationship that becomes paramount in the later fifth century and is celebrated in the pair of cult statues sharing a single base in the Hephaistion. That base probably portrayed the event that made them a couple, the birth of Erichthonios, according to modern reconstructions.[168] It was the association of Hephaistos with Athena in early poetry (e.g., *Odyssey* 6.223; Solon, frag. 1, 49–50) that helped usher Hephaistos into Attic topography, mythology, and genealogy. Like Poseidon, first honored on the Akropolis in connection with a new native deity, Erechtheus (see Chapter 12, n. 26), Hephaistos became Athenian through his connection to a newly autochthonous creature, Erichthonios. In becoming parents of Erichthonios, Athena and Hephaistos also became "parents" of Athenians, who are celebrated as κελευθοποιοὶ παῖδες Ἡφαίστου by 458 B.C. (Aeschylus, *Eumenides* 13). The process by which Athenian citizens became "children" of Athena and of Hephaistos belonged to the city's appropriation of natural properties examined previously, in the concept of autochthony.[169]

[166] London F 269, from Bari: A. D. Trendall, *Phlyax Vases*, 2d ed., BICS suppl. 19 (London, 1967), 52 no. 81; Delcourt, *Héphaistos*, 93–94 n. 5; Brommer, *Hephaistos*, 118, 203 D 1. In a review of Brommer, M. Robertson, *AJA* 84 (1980) 104–5, suggests another scene where Daidalos, not Hephaistos, was intended: Brommer, *Hephaistos*, 74, 236, pl. 39, 2.

[167] Brommer, *Hephaistos*, 20, for two vases (Oxford 1911.620 and Villa Giulia 50441), both by the Tyszkiewicz Painter.

[168] S. Karouzou, *AthMitt* 69–70 (1954–1955) 67–94; Harrison, *AJA* 81 (1977) 265–87; N. Robertson, "The Riddle of the Arrephoria at Athens," *HSCP* 87 (1983) 288, emphasizes how the *birth* of Erichthonios as a child of Athena and Hephaistos is a classical innovation.

[169] Loraux, *Les enfants d'Athèna*, 28–30 (Hephaistos); also on Pandora, Athena and Erichthonios.

The craftsman-god was introduced to Athens in two festivals, the Chalkeia and the Hephaisteia; shared a new temple with Athena (Pausanias, 1.14.5); and acquired an altar in the Erechtheion (Pausanias, 1.26.5) and also a place in Attic genealogy that made him an ancestor of Daidalos.[170] The only Homeric Hymn composed for Hephaistos (21) concentrates on his relationship to Athena and his contribution to the lively arts, in this case architecture (2–7):

> ὅς μετ᾽ Ἀθηναίης γλαυκώπιδος ἀγλαὰ ἔργα
> ἀνθρώπους ἐδίδαξεν ἐπὶ χθονός, οἳ τὸ πάρος περ
> ἄντροις ναιετάασκον ἐν οὔρεσιν, ἠΰτε θῆρες.
> νῦν δὲ δι᾽ Ἥφαιστον κλυτοτέχνην ἔργα δαέντες
> ῥηιδίως αἰῶνα τελεσφόρον εἰς ἐνιαυτὸν
> εὔκηλοι διάγουσιν ἐνὶ σφετέροισι δόμοισιν.

> He who taught, along with gray-eyed Athena,
> shining gifts for mortal men, they who used to live
> in caves in the mountains, like beasts,
> But now, having learned arts through Hephaistos, famous in crafts,
> easily they dwell all the year round in their own homes.

The hymn suggests an Attic festival in a century where the city distinguished itself with building programs, perhaps in celebration of a new temple for Hephaistos. Like Daidalos in Sicily, Hephaistos is newly praised for building as well as metalwork in fifth-century Athens.[171] A third new hero of Athenian invention was the Titan, Prometheus. Dormant since Hesiod's tales of fire and sacrifice, he reappears in fifth-century Athens, home to his only Greek cult with festival and torch race linked to Hephaistos, and enjoys newly native credit for cultural inventions like fire.[172]

The emphasis on gods as craftsmen and manufacturers in early classical art and myth is but a specialized aspect of a new interest in artists at work. Representations of workshops with potters, painters, and smiths at work abound in early classical vase painting, the most famous of them being the Foundry Painter's name-vase (Figure 58).[173] Satyrs assist Hephaistos in workshop scenes, including the manufacture of Pandora and the arms of Achilles (*Anthologia Graeca* 16.15, 15a); some illustrations must derive from

[170] [Plato], *Alkibiades* 121.1.4. H. Jeanmaire, "La naissance d'Athéna et la royauté magique de Zeus," *RA* 47–48 (1956) 28–35, on the genealogy of Attic kings and craftsmen; Delcourt, *Héphaistos*, chap. 8; Harrison, *AJA* 81 (1977) 414–16. See Chapter 10.

[171] T.B.L. Webster, "Homeric Hymns and Society," in *Le monde grec. Hommages à Claire Préaux* (Brussels, 1975), 93, dates the Hephaistos hymn to the fifth century, comparing it to the *Prometheus Bound*.

[172] Aeschylus's *Prometheus Pyrkaios* (472 B.C.) is the first of Attic dramas on Prometheus; Plato, *Protagoras* 320c–323a; H. W. Parke, *Festivals of the Athenians* (Ithaca, N.Y., 1977), 171–72, on the Prometheia.

[173] Berlin 2294, from Vulci: *ARV*, 400, 1; Mattusch, *AJA* 84 (1980) 435–44. Philipp, *Tektonon Daidala*, 109–11, lists over fifty classical representations of artists and workshops.

themes popular in satyr plays.[174] Athena appears in another workshop scene by the Foundry Painter, where she accompanies the presentation of a marble (?) horse by craftsman to customer (Figure 61).[175] The goddess herself takes a hand at finishing a statue of a horse, probably clay as a model for bronze, on a red-figured oinochoe near the Foundry Painter in date (Figure 59).[176] Some of these scenes appear on special vases like white-ground cups, one of which, by the Tarquinia Painter, is the first to show Hephaistos as a young man.[177] Simon attributes this "rejuvenation of gods and heroes at the beginning of the high classical period" to satyr plays, according to their illustrations on vases.[178] Others have suggested that craftsmen themselves were responsible not only for the proliferation of scenes of manufacture but for the mythological traditions that inserted legendary craftsmen into Attic genealogy.[179] The appearance of Athena in workshop scenes dedicated on, and probably made for, the Athenian Akropolis (as in Figure 60, by the Euergides Painter), home of the goddess in her capacity as Ἐργάνη or patroness of craftsmen, makes this suggestion attractive. Just as sculptors apparently contribute to popular traditions about craftsmen known to Sokrates (*Hippias Major* 282a.1; see Chapter 9), other artists promoted the image of divine craftsmen or sponsors in their own work.

In images like these, in stories of Athenian inventions in architecture or achievements in road building, and in the tremendous impact of a monumental building program extraordinary in its cost and speed, Athens became the city of art in more ways than those monuments alone express. The appropriation of Daidalos as a newly native son, perhaps as early as the Kleisthenic constitution, which used his name for a deme (see Chapter 8), is not an isolated event but belongs to the process whereby Athens also adopted Hephaistos and made him, together with Athena, a figurehead of the city's artistic production. In fact, the promotion of Hephaistos, as a figure already linked to the city's patron goddess, Athena, since the earliest poetic tradition, may have prevented Daidalos from gaining greater prominence in Athens through a major cult. His relationship with Theseus, however, guaranteed him a special place in Attic genealogy and mythology. How this repatriation reflects a wider evolution in the Athenian attitude toward the Orient will emerge in the next and final chapter of this book.

[174] R. D. Gempeler, "Die Schmiede des Hephäst—eine Satyrspielszene des Harrowmalers," *AK* 12 (1969) 16–21, pls. 13–14. Th. Hadzisteliou Price, "Bird-Dancers and Satyr-Craftsmen on an Attic vase," *GRBS* (1972) 239–45, for the earliest satyrs as craftsmen. Simon, in *Eye of Greece*, 134–36, 145–46.

[175] Munich 2650, from Vulci: Mattusch, *AJA* 84 (1980) 441 n. 40.

[176] Berlin F 2415; Mattusch, *AJA* 84 (1980) 438–39, pl. 55, fig. 3.

[177] J. Mertens, *Attic White Ground: Its Development on Shapes Other than Lekythoi* (New York, 1977), 174, no. 61, pl. XXXII.3; Simon, in *Eye of Greece*, 146, pl. 39a.

[178] Simon, in *Eye of Greece*, 134–36, 145–47; also see my n. 173.

[179] Jeanmaire, *RA* 47–48 (1956) 27–39.

CHAPTER 13

"Greeks" and "Barbarians": The Origins of Orientalism

Such was the natural nobility of this city, so sound and healthy
was the spirit of freedom among us, and the instinctive dislike
of the barbarian (φύσει μισοβάρβαρον), because we are pure
Hellenes, having no admixture of barbarism in us.
For we are not like many others, descendants of Pelops or
Cadmus or Aegyptus or Danaus, who are by nature barbarians,
and by custom Hellenes, but we are pure Hellenes,
uncontaminated by any foreign element, and therefore the
hatred of the foreign has passed unadulterated into the
lifeblood of the city.

—Plato, *Menexenus* 245d (trans. Jowett)

ὅ τί περ ἂν Ἕλληνες βαρβάρων παραλάβωσι, κάλλιον τοῦτο
εἰς τέλος ἀπεργάζονται.

Whatever Greeks receive from barbarians, they transform this
into a better result.

—Plato, *Epinomis* 987d

I N THE PAINTINGS by Panainos surrounding the statue of Zeus at Olympia, it is no
surprise to find the representation of Salamis paired with the figure of Hellas (Pausanias, 5.11.6: see Chapter 11). The image and self-image of Greece as a nation only
developed after an external enemy forced a definition of what it meant to be a Hellene.
In a poet's perspective on the same battle, Queen Atossa dreams of two sisters in Doric
and Persian robes who represent, respectively, ἡ μὲν Ἑλλάδα, ἡ δὲ βάρβαρον (Aeschylus, *Persians* 186–87). Consciousness of distinctions and commonalities emerged in response to victory, and with them developed the concept of what it meant to be non-
Greek, as well as what it meant to be Greek. The personification of these new concepts

in visual images and legends emerged in the early decades after the Persian wars, as examined in the last two chapters.[1] The intellectual defense of Hellenism developed later, under circumstances of internal debate and external ambitions. In a premature definition of Hellenism imagined by Herodotus before the battle of Plataia, the Athenians remind the Spartans of what keeps them loyal to the Greek cause (Herodotus, 8.144.2–3, trans. Rawlinson):

> The first and chief of these is the burning and destruction of our temples and the images of our gods, which forces us to make no terms with their destroyer, but rather to pursue him with our resentment to the uttermost. Again, there is our common brotherhood with the Greeks (τὸ Ἑλληνικόν): our common blood and common language, the altars and the sacrifices of which we all partake, the common character (ἤθεα) which we bear.

The term complementing τὸ Ἑλληνικόν appears later in classical literature, where τὸ βαρβαρικόν only becomes pejorative in the works of Euripides.[2] In a gradual and complex sequence of reactions to victory and ambitions for expansion, the Athenians transformed their moment of triumph into an intellectual and political resource. Beyond impressive monuments and innovative legends, their third medium and its message was subtler but more profound, its origins secular rather than theological, its purpose strategic and political rather than celebratory or thankful. Despite Themistokles' false modesty (Herodotus, 8.109), the gods were not exclusively responsible for success in battle. The spirit of ἱστορίη discovered qualities innate to Greek (especially Athenian) character and culture that made victory not only possible but inevitable. Aspects of this attitude emerge in the praise of Athenian τόλμα in battle and in art (Chapter 11) and in the emphasis on Athenian leadership in art and culture promoted in literature and vase painting. The articulation of these sentiments, implicit in tragedy and art, was made explicit in explanatory prose, both rhetorical and exegetical, and actually inspired new forms of discourse to express the implications of Greek victory.

The most famous portrayal of the Athenian self-image is the funeral oration attributed to Perikles in 432/1 B.C. by Thucydides (2.36–46), a passage that also reveals the context of that image. More of a military *adlocutio* (or διδασκαλία: 2.42.1) than a lament for the dead, the speech addresses current campaigns, as the speaker and general admits (2.42.1): "Indeed, if I have dwelt at some length upon the character of our country [τὰ περὶ τῆς πόλεως], it has been to show that our stake in the struggle is not the same as theirs who have no such [blessings to lose]." As spelled out in the preceding sentence (2.41.5), those who fell in battle are meant to inspire survivors to similar sacrifice. In the

---

[1] Also summarized by Picard, in *Les Grecs devant la menace perse*, 115–27, on monuments (116–19) and epigrams (119–21) defining Greek unity.

[2] At *Hekabe* 1129, Agamemnon reproaches Polymestor, the king of Thrace blinded by Hekabe, for his "barbarian" impulse to tear her limb from limb:

Bacon, *Barbarians in Greek Tragedy*, 12–13, 152–53, on Euripides; Hall, *Inventing the Barbarian*, who admits (p. ix) that her title "might . . . almost as well have been *Inventing the Hellene*," applies Herodotus's definition of Hellenism to tragedy.

context of this war effort, Perikles' catalogue of praises lists virtues like autochthony (2.36.1: οἳ αὐτοὶ αἰεὶ οἰκοῦντες) next to self-sufficiency, or the ability to wage war and withstand siege (καὶ ἐς πόλεμον καὶ ἐς εἰρήνην αὐταρκεστάτην: 2.36.3), and the power to acquire additional territory (2.36.2). He dismisses as too familiar the military ἔργα of the past (2.36.4: presumably Marathon), choosing instead to praise the Athenian πολιτεία (2.37), the city's opportunities for leisure (2.38), and, most of all, its military policy (2.39). All these virtues are demonstrated in action: Athens does not need the verses of Homer for praise and posterity, for its τόλμα has been implemented abroad with "perpetual memorials of good and evil deeds" (μνημεῖα κακῶν τε κἀγαθῶν ἀΐδια): not monuments but historical action. In the era of the Peloponnesian War and after, these metaphors mark the replacement of the concept of ἔργον in a monument by its afterlife in δόξα (2.43.2), as examined previously in the analysis of historiography.[3]

This eulogy also reveals how concepts and words like ἐλευθερία, τόλμα, εὔνοια, εὔκλεια, and other classical virtues derived from performance against the Persians came to serve military strategy among Greeks. What these intellectual concerns inherited from the confrontation with the Orient was an exclusively Greek (if not Athenian) claim to their invention or perpetuation. The poles of freedom and slavery were planted in the struggle against a foreign slave-master, Persia, by an internally free populace, one governed by a democracy. The battle of Salamis formalized the struggle between "freedom" and "slavery" in the rhetoric of Aeschylus's Persians, later in history and philosophy.[4] Eventually, Athens itself exercised a form of despotism over other Greek cities more palpable than that attributed to the Persians.[5] The concept of Panhellenism likewise was sponsored by inter-Greek conflict, not the reality of an external, non-Greek enemy. It became "a tool of propaganda for the hegemonial or imperial rule of a polis; it served to justify the hegemony and the mastery of one polis over other states by proposing a common aim, war against the barbarians."[6] Other specific terms appear for the first time in the context of Athenian victory. Ἰσηγορίη (as noted in Chapter 11) is used once by Herodotus to explain why Athens beat long-time enemies in 506 B.C. (5.78). The word does not denote an equal voice in Athenian democracy as much as it connotes the absence of tyranny and (therefore, according to the logic of historical events) the ability to defeat one's enemies. When Herodotus staged a constitutional debate among the Persians over the relative virtues of monarchy, oligarchy, and de-

---

[3] See Chapter 11; Immerwahr, AJP 81 (1960) 261–90. Loraux, Invention of Athens, on the funeral oration as an Attic genre of self-praise.

[4] Raaflaub, Entdeckung der Freiheit, esp. chap. III.1; Euben, Political Theory 14 (1986) 363–72, on "freedom."

[5] Raaflaub, Entdeckung der Freiheit, 162; Hall, Invent-ing the Barbarian, 59–60, 193–94.

[6] S. Perlman, "Panhellenism, the Polis and Imperialism," Historia 25 (1976) 5; cf. Thébert, Diogenes 112 (1980) 101–10, on Pan-Hellenism and Athenian imperialism; Hall, Inventing the Barbarian, 59–60, 162–65; P. Cartledge, "Herodotus and 'the Other': A Meditation on Empire," EchCl 9 (1990) 27–40.

mocracy, history had predetermined this debate as a lesson in the superiority of democracy (3.80–82). In these and other intellectual arguments defending the superiority of Greek and Athenian nature, culture, and politics, it was inevitable that the corresponding Eastern institutions acquired a negative image. The first Oriental target of Greek derision was directly related to the historical circumstances that inspired it: that is, the political differences between Greece and Persia, or between democracy and monarchy.[7] As in modern uses of the term in official rhetoric and colloquial debate, the term "democracy" became an accomplice to claims for alliance, control, or enmity with other nations.

Eventually, the attention focused by history on aspects of Greek constitutions developed into an embryonic form of political theory as we know it. Historical events as much as intellectual ones encouraged the exploration of politics and culture for the sake of laudatory, then explanatory purposes. The first reaction and explanation involved the gods; the secondary explanation, where Salamis played the role of promoting human factors as Marathon did the divine, involved mortal responsibility. As Euben put it recently and succinctly: "The victory at Salamis made political theory possible and necessary."[8] The convergence of Greek political theory with historical events—first, the Persian wars, then the decades of the Peloponnesian War and its influence on thinkers like Thucydides—adds the genre of political philosophy to the intellectual developments engendered by victory over the Persians.[9] That genre was perpetuated in public rhetoric and private discourse devoted to the maintenance of Athenian superiority, of which the funeral oration was the most conspicuous example of a public forum that functioned as a political platform.[10]

Political science was but one modern intellectual discipline that developed from a quest for natural and cultural explanations of human fortune and misfortune, in reaction to the Persian wars. If theology and democracy determined destiny, so did geography and biology. In initial and final passages of his narrative, Herodotus explores the relationship between natural habitat and human character, or νόμος and φύσις, as a means for explaining which ethnic groups succeeded and which failed to defeat the Persians.[11] For example, in opening the story of the Ionian revolt and its failure, he praises the air and climate of Ionia as the best of all known areas (1.142.1), but then

---

[7] Meier, *Entstehung des Politischen*, esp. 144–244, on the *Oresteia* and early classical political consciousness; 142, 344, 378–83, 422–23, on the role of the Persian wars; cf. his "Historical Answers to Historical Questions: The Origins of History in Ancient Greece," *Arethusa* 20 (1987) 41–57.

[8] Euben, *Political Theory* 14 (1986) 380. Cf. Jouanna, *Ktema* 6 (1981) 3–15, particularly on the two levels of answers, divine and secular, to the puzzle of Persian

defeat.

[9] On the intellectual background to political theory, see Farrar, *Origins of Democratic Thinking*; Hall, *Inventing the Barbarian*, 160–200.

[10] Loraux, *Invention of Athens*, esp. chaps. 4 and 5.

[11] F. Heinimann, *Nomos und Physis* (Basel, 1945); Immerwahr, *Form and Thought in Herodotus*, esp. 306–23, "History and the Order of Nature."

describes its natives as the weakest of all known nations (ἀσθενεστάτον· 1.143.2) and elsewhere calls them ἀνανδρότατοι ("most unmanly") and φιλοδέσποτα, a word coined first here to describe subservience in captivity (4.142). The Athenians are cited as an exception to the weakness of the Ionians, thanks to their home far from Ionia, in a land noted for its harsh terrain (cf. Aeschylus, *Persians* 792, 794). Their performance at Marathon confirms this lesson, and in fact must have inspired it, according to the logic subscribed to by Herodotus. His account of the Persian wars ends with an extraordinary lesson from history that Kyros transmits to the Persians, in advising them to move to more rugged country, which will make them "men good in war" ἄνδρας ἀγαθοὺς τὰ πολέμια (9.122). Herodotus concludes with the opinion that soft places breed soft men (φιλέειν γὰρ ἐκ τῶν μαλακῶν χώρων μαλακοὺς ἄνδρας γίνεσθαι), the final statement of his book. It suggests that the paramount conclusion to be drawn from his investigation was the relationship between climate and character, if not the superiority of Greece's rough territory for producing fighting men. The role of nature was eventually more fully defended in the Hippokratic essay *On Airs, Waters and Places*, in passages often compared with Herodotus', where Europe and Asia are compared in terms of moral as well as natural differences.[12] These reflections become commonplace in the fourth century, when the Greeks are said to occupy a τόπος nature made best for excellence (ἄριστος for ἀρετή: Plato, *Epinomis* 987d). Thus, like other forms of intellectual enterprise that first emerge in the fifth century, certain principles of Greek scientific and medical theory were inspired by historical events and the need to explain them.

Political distinctions also divide Europe and Asia in Hippocratic writings long before they appear in history and rhetoric. A prominent example is αὐτονομία, a term that develops closely with ἐλευθερία and expresses a specific form of independence allowing cities the right to govern themselves.[13] The word is rare in Greek references before Thucydides and is first attested epigraphically in 427/6 B.C. (*IG* I² 60), but receives its first political treatment in *Airs, Waters and Places* sometime before 430 B.C. In sections 16 and 23, the Hippokratic author praises Europeans as μαχιμώτεροι ("more warlike") and εὐψυχότεροι ("stronger in spirit") than Asians, on the basis of their αὐτονομία or freedom from despotism. Like other phrases promoted, if not inspired, by the Persian wars, "autonomy" is abused in the policies and rhetoric of the Athenian Empire. What began as "a peculiarly political understanding of freedom, and one embodied in the capacity for self-determination exercised by the Athenians with the advent of de-

---

[12] W. Backhaus, "Der Hellenen-Barbaren-Gegensatz und die hippokratische Schrift Περὶ ἀέρων ὑδάτων τόπων," *Historia* 25 (1976) 170–85; Thébert, *Diogène* 112 (1980) 97, on nature, regime and character in Hippokrates; Jouanna, *Ktema* 6 (1981) 11–15, on the centrality of Greek courage in the Hippokratic es-

say and the ethnography of Herodotus; Hall, *Inventing the Barbarian*, 133–43, 191.

[13] M. Ostwald, *Autonomia, Its Genesis and Early History* (New York, 1982); Raaflaub, *Entdeckung der Freiheit*, 189–93; Farrar, *Origins of Democratic Thinking*, 103–5.

mocracy" became a claim to independence from Athens and the right to revolt, reproached in Antigone's behavior (Sophokles, *Antigone* 821, 877).[14] In an intellectual pattern sadly frequent in the fifth century, a concept born in the Greek struggle against Persia became a term of conflict amid Athenian designs on other Greek states.

If political institutions were singled out to distinguish Greeks and Persians, cultural dimensions of the contrast between East and West were next in the roster of differences discovered between Greek and non-Greek. The word "barbarian" and the characterization of foreignness first appear in Aeschylus's *Persians*.[15] In a pattern Bacon described as "the reverse of orientalizing," foreign features became specific, detailed, and consistent qualities in literature as well as essential to the narrative.[16] Trappings of *Perserie*, eventually equated with ὕβρις, political Medism, and tendencies toward tyranny, as in the experience of the Spartan general Pausanias, were applied in literature to portraits of foreigners and tyrants.[17] In Aeschylus's *Agamemnon*, for example, the king is implicated in Medism by being offered the royal robe and προσκυνῆσις, in his method of conveyance (a "throne on wheels": ἀμαξήρης θρόνος, line 1054: cf. Xerxes' ἁρμαμάξα: Herodotus, 7.41) and in his dispatch of signal fires along a Persian route.[18] In the works of Sophokles, Trojans (and Phrygians) carry Persian weapons, maintain eunuchs, and observe other Persian customs, and even speak Persian language.[19] Sophokles' fascination with themes from Trojan legend inspired some thirty lost plays on Trojan subjects (in addition to the three that survive, *Philoktetes*, *Ajax*, and *Elektra*). This agrees with the lively interest in episodes from the *Ilioupersis* and other Trojan topics on murals and vases of the early classical period (Chapter 12). Persian terms already carry pejorative qualities in Sophokles, as when Oidipous calls Teiresias a μάγος to express his fear of a plot against him.[20] Persian exotica also provided humorous episodes in Old Comedy, as in the mockery of Persian envoys in Aristophanes' *Acharnians* (91–122), which be-

---

[14] Farrar, *Origins of Democratic Thinking*, 103, 105.

[15] Bacon, *Barbarians in Greek Tragedy*, 5–15, 62–63; cf. essays in *Grecs et Barbares*, Fondation Hardt, Entretiens 8 (Geneva, 1961), esp. H. Diller, "Die Hellenen-Barbaren Antithese im Zeitalter der Perserkriege"; H. Dörrie, "Die Wertung der Barbaren im Urteil der Griechen: Knechtsnaturen? Oder Bewahrer und Künder heilbringender Weisheit?" in *Antike und Universalgeschichte. Festschrift H. E. Stier*, ed. R. Stiehl and G. A. Lehmann (Münster, 1972), 146–75; Thébert, *Diogène* 112 (1980) 91–110; Walser, *Hellas und Iran*, 5–8; duBois, *Centaurs and Amazons*, 78–94; Hall, *Inventing the Barbarian*.

[16] Bacon, *Barbarians in Greek Tragedy*, 62, on Oriental motifs in Aeschylus; Hall, *Inventing the Barbarian*, chap. 2.

[17] Pausanias: Herodotus, 8.3; Thucydides, 1.128–34; Walser, *Hellas und Iran*, 73–76. W. Burkert, "Demaratos, Astrabakos und Herakles: Königsmythen und Politik zur Zeit der Perserkriege (Herodot 6, 67–69)," *MH* 22 (1965) 166–77.

[18] On the robe of Agamemnon, see Chapter 11. Francis, in *Ancient Persia*, 56 n. 11, suggests that "Agamemnon, in conquering the Trojans, had become one of them"; Hall, *Inventing the Barbarian*, 93–98. Francis, *Image and Idea in Fifth-Century Athens*, 33–35.

[19] Bacon, *Barbarians in Greek Tragedy*, 101–4; Hall, *Inventing the Barbarian*, 76–98.

[20] Sophokles, *Oidipous Tyrannos* 387; Bacon, *Barbarians in Greek Tragedy*, 67–68; K. Rigsby, "Teiresias as Magus in Oedipus Rex," *GRBS* 17 (1976) 109–114; Francis, in *Ancient Persia*, 58.

speaks some familiarity with diplomatic relations as well as foreign culture.[21] The same terms used to convey an atmosphere of Oriental despotism in tragedy—for example, Agamemnon's Persian-sounding vehicle (*Agamemnon* 1054)—amused comic audiences (Aristophanes, *Acharnians* 70). While comedy has been accused of appearing too late in the fifth century to reflect conflict with Persia, and of limiting its portrayal of barbarians to humorous stereotypes, tragedy as well enjoys an exaggerated status for its perspective on classical Athenian consciousness.[22] Performances were limited to specific festival occasions, and those dramas that survive represent three playwrights and a fraction of their oeuvre, a pitiful proportion of what was written and produced. Daily impressions from speeches in the assembly, in law courts, in conversation, and in private art, especially indestructible vases, offer a more extensive source of Athenian ideology, however patchy and in need of connection to literature.

The same detail that invades literature with foreign words and customs after the Persian wars contributes to a new image of the Persians and other barbarians in early classical art.[23] The anecdote that Mikon was fined for representing Persians as larger than Greeks in his painting of the battle of Marathon (Harpokration s.v. Μίκων, citing Lykourgos; see Chapter 12, n. 78) implies that other iconographic techniques were more acceptable in creating an image of Persians. However, Herodotus records the story of the giant figure with a long beard seen by Epizelos, who imagined this creature as the opponent who blinded him, and claimed he saw this φάσμα slay the Greek next to him (6.117; cf. 9.25, 83, 96). As has been suggested, the iconography of creatures larger than life, such as giants, may have influenced the representation of Persians, an enemy more numerous and more formidable than any previous antagonists except those in Greek legend. But the primary means of representing Persians applied exotic elements—costume and weapons, primarily—to images of familiar (Greek) figures. The proliferation of details in Persian equipment, dress, and even language in classical art and literature derived from Greek acquaintance with objects admired, captured, or even purchased from the Orient. It is characteristic of the archaic Greek fascination with material culture that Herodotus describes the different ἔθνεα of the Persian army and navy in terms of their armor and equipment (7.61–98). It also implies that he was familiar with visual evidence, such as a painting of the battle or captured examples of equipment. The Greek image was adjusted to accompany the new picture of an enemy: heroic warriors were

[21] Ch. Chiasson, "Pseudartabas and His Eunuchs: *Acharnians* 91–122," *CP* 79 (1984) 131–36; T. Long, *Barbarians in Greek Comedy* (Carbondale, Ill., 1986), esp. chap. 6, on the ideology of the barbarian image.

[22] Hall, *Inventing the Barbarian*, x, finds comedy too late a source for the Persian wars and inadequate to the complexity of Greek attitudes toward barbarians; her own excellent book expands Bacon's treatment of

[23] Bovon, *BCH* 87 (1963) 579–602; Hölscher, *Griech-barbarians in tragedy to include history.*
ische Historienbilder, 38–49, and "Ein Kelchkrater mit Perserkampf," *AK* 17 (1974) 78–85. K. Schauenburg, "ΕΥΡΥΜΕΔΟΝ ΕΙΜΙ," *AthMitt* 90 (1975) 104–18, and "Siegreiche Barbaren," *AthMitt* 92 (1977) 91ff.; W. Raeck, *Zum Barbarenbild in der Kunst Athens im 6. u. 5. Jh. v. Chr.* (Bonn, 1981).

more likely to be represented in full armor in the decades after the Persian wars, as a compliment to hoplites recently victorious.[24]

The attitude toward Persian culture was ambiguous, for Oriental luxury continued to fascinate Greeks and was as popular in private taste as it was disdained in public rhetoric.[25] The Persian invasion introduced many Greeks to Oriental splendors in autopsy, some never imagined before their first glimpse of the Persian army and their equipment. The invaders themselves made their material culture popular through gifts of ξεινίη like the suit of clothing presented to the Akanthians by Xerxes (Herodotus, 7.116). They successfully bribed the Thebans with gifts of gold and silver plate (Herodotus, 9.41), contributing to the association between political Medism and a taste for Oriental luxuries. After the defeat of the Persians, the display and distribution of booty introduced armor, jewelry, and furniture from the East into Greek households. Persian treasures also washed up on Thessalian shores after the storm off Artemision for scavengers (e.g., Ameinokles of Magnesia: Herodotus, 7. 190) but were more systematically circulated after major land battles. The richest booty was collected at Plataia, where it formed the first demonstration, for many Greeks, of the magnitude of the enemy they had defeated. The splendor of this treasure was exaggerated in a spectacle arranged by the general Pausanias (and by the historian Herodotus: 8. 80), displaying the furniture, vessels, jewelry, and clothing that accompanied the Persian army on an expedition of conquest. The distribution of such booty among those who had fought at Plataia (8.81.1.10: ἔλαβον ἕκαστοι τῶν ἄξιοι ἦσαν) and of captured clothing and jewelry from Sestos and Byzantion (Plutarch, *Kimon* 9) contributed to the popularity of Persian luxuries in private Athenian circles.[26] Conspicuous examples of the influence of Persian luxuries on Greek taste were the imitation of metal vessels in clay and the adoption of Persian dress as a status symbol in life and art.[27] More monumental responses to Persian forms included the design of the Odeion of Perikles, which resembled and may have imitated deliberately the shape of a Persian tent.[28] Like the captive Greeks who con-

[24] As pointed out by Hölscher, *Griechische Historienbilder*, 40–44.

[25] Picard, *Les Grecs devant la ménace perse*, chap. 12; Miller, "Perserie," chaps. 4 and 5; D. Graf, "Medism: The Origins and Significance of the Term," *JHS* 104 (1984) 15–30. Gunter, "Models of the Orient," on Persian and pre-Persian imagery adopted by Greek status-seekers.

[26] Miller, "Perserie," chap. 2. J. Balcer, "The Greeks and the Persians: The Processes of Acculturation," *Historia* 32 (1983) 257–67; M. Vickers, "Attic Symposia after the Persian Wars," in *Sympotica*, ed. O. Murray (Oxford, 1990), 105–21.

[27] H. Hoffmann, "The Persian Origin of Attic Rhyta," *AK* 41 (1961) 21–26; on garments, see F. von Lorentz, "ΒΑΡΒΑΡΩΝ ΥΦΑΣΜΑΤΑ," *RömMitt* 52 (1937) 165–222; Miller, "Perserie," chap. 4, and "The *Ependytes* in Classical Athens," *Hesperia* 58 (1989) 313–29.

[28] O. Broneer, *The Tent of Xerxes and the Greek Theater*, University of California Publications in Classical Archaeology 1.12 (Berkeley, 1944); A. Alfödi, "Gewaltherrscher und Theaterkönig," in *Late Classical and Medieval Studies in Honor of Albert Mathias Friend, Jr.*, ed. K. Weitzmann (Princeton, 1955), 32ff.; H. von Gall, "Das persische Königszelt und die Hallenarchitektur in Iran und Griechenland," in *Festschrift Brommer*, 119–32; Francis, in *Ancient Persia* 82–83.

quered their Roman victors in taste (Horace, *Epistles* 2.1.156–57), the defeated Persians may have sponsored a new level of prosperity and ostentation in private material wealth in Athens, different from the way material culture functioned as propaganda in the archaic period.[29] The taste for Persian imports and imitations perpetuates the Orientalizing phenomenon in Greek culture that flourished in the fifth and fourth centuries B.C. much as it did in the seventh, or even a thousand years earlier. Atossa's vision of Greece and Asia as "sisters" (in Aeschylus's *Persians* 185) reflects the kinship of their cultures since the previous millennium (see Chapter 4). By dressing these personifications in native costume, the Persian queen also conjures up images familiar through material culture in circulation in classical Greece, in contributing to the personification of nations that became a legacy of the Persian wars. The figures of Hellas and Asia on the Darius Painter's name vase (Figure 62) maintain this tradition in the fourth century (see n. 43).

The incorporation of Persian images into Greek tradition included ironic transformations of Orientalizing images to conform to new myths of Hellenic superiority, as in the design of the Plataian tripod (Chapter 11). An eloquent example of this dialogue between art and ideology, the figure of the caryatid, was adopted from Near Eastern forerunners to serve as an anthropoid support in archaic Greek sculpture and architecture. At some point after the Persian wars, this sculptural type acquired an *aition* attributing its name to Karyai, a city in Arkadia that Medized and was punished with a permanent image of its women serving as slaves, bearing an architectural burden (Vitruvius, 1.2. 4–5).[30] A second story blaming the Persian wars for images of enslavement incorporated into buildings is also transmitted by Vitruvius (1.1.6), in a scenario of oppression where barbarians, women, and slaves share common burdens. A Spartan victory monument called the "Persian Stoa" commemorated the victory over the Persians by portraying barbarian prisoners in postures of perpetual punishment, a description more appropriate to Roman columnar facades of barbarian captives than to extant early classical monuments. In a western Greek variant on this *aition*, the Atlas figures (Telamones) supporting the entablature of the colossal Olympieion at Akragas could represent the Carthaginian prisoners who were forced to work on the Sicilian temple (Diodorus, 11.25).[31] By the time caryatids were installed in the porch of the Erechtheion, whose epigraphic accounts simply call them κόραι in 409/8 B.C., several such traditions could have been in circulation, giving these figures a special historical burden not shared by

---

[29] Argued by M. Vickers, in *Sympotica*, 105–21, and in "Dates, Methods, Icons," in *Images et société en Grèce ancienne*, ed. C. Bérard, C. Bron, and A. Pomari (Lausanne, 1987), 20, along with some unacceptable chronological revisions.

[30] Despite the efforts of M. Vickers (*RA* [1985] 3–28) and E. D. Francis (Francis and Vickers, "Signa pris-

cae artis," *JHS* 103 [1983] 49–67), this *aition* does not justify an early classical date for the Siphnian treasury and other caryatid figures. On archaic caryatids and Levantine forerunners, see Carter, *The Beginning of Greek Sculpture*.

[31] G. Hersey, *The Lost Meaning of Classical Architecture* (Cambridge, 1988), 173 n. 2.

their archaic forerunners.[32] These architectural anecdotes resemble the one that made Daidalos the manufacturer of a throne possibly Oriental in origin, stored inside the same temple supported by caryatids (in the second century A.D.: Pausanias 1.27.1; see Chapter 10). These monuments form archaeological props with which new Athenian myths in circulation in prose and poetry were made concrete, particularly in the Erechtheion whose syncretistic display of cults old and new made it more of an encyclopedia of Atthidography than a traditional temple.

The Persian expedition introduced a double standard of Medism among the people of Athens, who condemned Persians, or heard them condemned, in public rhetoric, while admiring Persian institutions (including kingship) and enjoying Oriental luxuries in dress and household property. Throughout a conflict that lasted until the conquests of Alexander, admiration for *Persika* was not extinguished in private taste and romantic history of the fifth and fourth centuries, only replaced in official language by the rejection of Oriental τρυφή and the character it bred. It makes the evaluation of the classical attitude toward the Orient a delicate process, where material culture must be balanced against the rhetoric of the state. Classical art alone does not reveal how Athenians and artists conceived of ethnic identities beyond costume and accessories. It is through mythological conceptions that new attitudes worked themselves out, while details of material culture continued to be popular in private life, and new attitudes must be explored in a comparison of history and mythology.

A special dimension of Greek enmity with the East involved the Phoenicians, who formed the majority of the Persian fleet. The confrontation between Greek ships, specifically Athenian ones, and vessels primarily Levantine under Mesopotamian command helped dissolve a long-term intimacy that this book has traced in the kinship of Kothar and Daidalos. The role of Phoenician ships in the Persian fleet allows an opportunity to examine a selected target of Athenian hostility toward the Orient. The importance of Phoenician vessels for Persia is illustrated in several martial episodes predating the invasion of Greece. Under Kambyses, the Persians were not able to pursue a campaign against Carthage, because the Phoenicians refused to make war on their own kin and their withdrawal left the Persian fleet too weak for such an expedition (Herodotus, 3.19). Herodotus links Persian sea power with the eventual subjection of the Phoenicians in his explanation of why the Ionians had nothing to fear from Persia in 498 (1.143).[33] During the expedition to Cyprus prior to the Ionian revolt, Greek ships faced

---

[32] Vickers invokes Lakonian imagery (as in Vitruvius, 1.1.6) and specific Spartan invasions of Attika to make the Erechtheion caryatids "collaborators and quislings, ready to place Greece beneath a Persian yoke" (*RA* [1985], 28).

[33] This does not mean that the Phoenicians first acquired their reputation as sailors after 498 B.C.

(T. Kelly, "Herodotus and the Chronology of the Kings of Sidon," *BASOR* 268 [1987] 50), which contradicts the long history of Phoenician maritime and mercenary enterprise (see Chapter 5), independent of their subjection by Persia (after 546 B.C.): H. T. Wallinga, "The Ancient Persian Navy and Its Predecessors," in *Achaemenid History I*, Proceedings of the

Phoenicians and Cilicians (Herodotus 5.108–9), as they did later at Lade (6.6–17; see Chapter 11). In the Persian fleet assembled at Lade, the Phoenicians were described as most keen in battle (προθυμότατοι) compared with the contingents from Cyprus, Cilicia, and Egypt (Herodotus, 6.6), a compliment that makes them the equal of the Athenians, who earned the same superlative before Plataia (in the words of Pausanias: 9.60.3). During the engagement off Miletos, the Persian fleet is simply called οἱ Φοίνικες (6.14.1); afterward, the Phokaian general, Dionysios, made a special target of merchant ships in Phoenicia itself, then sailed west where he raided ships belonging to their cousins, the Carthaginians, as well as the Etruscans (6.17). Meanwhile, in the following year, the Persian fleet—in the form of Phoenician ships—attacked the coastal cities of Thrace across the Hellespont, then in the Proconnese and Chersonese (6.33). It was during this naval campaign that the future hero of Marathon, the Athenian Miltiades, first met Phoenician ships, losing one of his five triremes and nearly losing his life to them (6.41, 104).

Thereafter, Phoenician ships played a leading role in the expeditions of Dareios and Xerxes into Greece. The first Persians ever to enter Greece from Asia came as spies (κατάσκοποι) for Dareios, on an expedition launched from Sidon on two Phoenician triremes and one merchant ship (γαῦλος, a word and vessel Phoenician in origin: 3.136; cf. 138.4). Dareios may have been the first Persian monarch to expand the Persian Empire across the sea as well as over land by invading Scythia (Herodotus, 4.80–86), and his expedition to Greece was only possible with the help of subjects and allies with naval experience, especially the Phoenicians.[34] Moreover, his motives for invading Thrace, its resources in silver mines and timber suitable for shipbuilding (Herodotus 5.23), may have developed precisely because his informants and reconnaissance experts were Phoenicians, who had long pursued the same resources in northern Greece (Chapter 5).

At Salamis in Cyprus in 498, the Ionians faced a choice of fighting the Persians on land or the Phoenicians at sea (Herodotus 5.108–9; see Chapter 4.1), a balance of tactical forces repeated throughout the Persian campaigns in Greece. At the later battle of Salamis, the Phoenicians accounted for one-quarter of the Persian fleet, or some 300 ships out of 1207 (7.89), along with other Levantine allies of Persia like "the Syrians of Palestine." Their dismissal from the fleet before Mykale (9.96), along with desertion by Greek allies, may have contributed to the Persian defeat in that battle, just as their absence prevented Kambyses from fighting the Carthaginians (3.19). For in reputation as well as number, the Phoenicians were conspicuous: their ships were the best (ἄριστα πλειού-

Groningen 1983 Achaemenid History Workshop, ed. H. Sancisi-Weerdenburg (Leiden, 1987), 47–77.

[34] H. Hauben, "The King of the Sidonians and the Persian Imperial Fleet," *Ancient Society* 1 (1970) 1–8;

"The Chief Commanders of the Persian Fleet in 480 B.C.," *Ancient Society* 4 (1973) 23–37; Kelly, *BASOR* 268 (1987) 43–52, on Phoenicians in the Persian fleet. Balcer, *Sparda by the Bitter Sea*, 174, 243.

σας) in the fleet of Xerxes, particularly those of the Sidonians, who won the rowing-match watched by the king from his throne at Abdyos (7.44, 96.1). The Persian king took his seat on such a Sidonian ship, enthroned under a golden tent, for his review of the fleet in Thrace (7.100), and after his defeat at Salamis he escaped to Asia from Eion on a Phoenician ship (8.118.1). Thus the image of the Persian king must have been identified with a Phoenician vessel the way the Persian fleet, in general, meant Phoenician ships. The display of Phoenician triremes as trophies in Greek sanctuaries after the Greek victories (Herodotus, 8.121; see Chapter 11) kept alive the image of Phoenicians as naval enemies of Greece, a visual prop for the political and mythological propaganda that promoted Athenian deeds.

In other skills, Phoenicians were essential to the invasion of Xerxes, notably as naval engineers. In the excavation of the canal across the Mount Athos peninsula, their σοφίη was praised by Herodotus as a conspicuous example of their renowned skill (7.23.3: οἱ Φοίνικες σοφίην ἔν τε τοῖσι ἄλλοισι ἔργοισι ἀποδείκνυνται καὶ δὴ καὶ ἐν ἐκείνῳ). This skill recalls Thales' engineering feats performed for Kroisos at the Halys (1.75); his Phoenician ancestry (1.170) may be more than a coincidence, or perhaps talents like his inspired the tradition of such ancestry. The same quality (σοφίη) also attracts praise in the handiwork of Daidalos (Euripides, *Eurystheus* frag. 188; Xenophon, *Memorabilia* 4.2.32), a coincidence appropriate to the Near Eastern background of the craftsman and his kind of handiwork. In Herodotus's account, Phoenicians also built one of the two bridges across the Hellespont at Abydos of flaxen cables, the destruction of which by a storm provoked Xerxes to order the lashing of the Hellespont (7.25, 34). Phoenician merchant ships were as tactically essential as their warships throughout Persia's pursuit of Greece; they were dispatched with the reconnaissance mission sent by Dareio (3.136) and lashed together as a bridge to Salamis after the battle (8.97).

It was Phoenician ships that the Athenians, in particular, faced at Salamis (Herodotus 8.85), and Simonides' epitaph for those who died at Salamis represents the Median enemy, on land and sea collectively, as Φοινίσσας νῆας καὶ Πέρσας: "Phoenician ships and Persians" (Plutarch, frag. 90c). The first enemy ship to be rammed by a Greek one was a Phoenician vessel, in Aeschylus's account of the battle (*Persians* 409–11), and Mikon's painting of the battle of Marathon closes with the Athenian attack on the prows of the Phoenician ships (Pausanias, 1.15.2): ἔσχαται δὲ τῆς γραφῆς νῆές τε αἱ Φοίνισσαι καὶ τῶν βαρβάρων τοὺς ἐσπίπτοντας ἐς ταύτας φονεύοντες οἱ Ἕλληνες. Thus the confrontation between Greeks and Persians was remembered in some instances as a conflict between Athenians and Phoenicians, in art as well as poetry and prose accounts of the war.

This concentrated exposure in battle at sea to Phoenicians during the Persian wars continued in the campaigns of the 470s and 460s, both east and west. In Sicily, Phoenicians and Greeks had competed for territory since the early Iron Age, in history and legend (Chapter 7; cf. Herodotus, 5.46, on Spartans and Phoenicians in conflict in Sicily). The western descendants of the Phoenicians, the Carthaginians, were defeated at Himera in 474 along with another non-Greek naval opponent, the Etruscans. Pindar's ode for Hieron's chariot victory at Delphi, a few years later, also celebrates the tyrant's military triumph in Sicily over the two non-Greek naval forces. Pindar's words reflects the kinship perceived among Greeks between eastern and western Phoenicians in calling the Carthaginians ὁ Φοῖνιξ, in a conflation of Punic and Phoenician common in Greek tragedy (e.g., Euripides, *Trojan Women* 221). Pindar expresses sentiments familiar in Herodotus and Aeschylus by invoking Zeus's justice on the enemies' "nautical hybris" (ναυσίστον ὕβριν) and praising the Greek victor for "leading Greece out of heavy slavery" (Ἑλλάδ᾽ ἐξέλκων βαρείας δουλίας: *Pythian* 1.72–74, 76; cf. Simonides' epigram on the same victors: *Anthologia Palatina* 7.650). The threat of Phoenician ships both east and west helped encourage the parallelism maintained in Greek tradition, the synchronicity of the two miraculous victories.[35]

In the eastern Mediterranean, the Athenians pursued the enemy in a series of encounters inevitably compared in contemporary accounts with the battles of the Persian wars; Phoenicians continued to represent Persians at sea. In Plato's parody of an Athenian funeral oration, the Persian wars are linked with the ambitious campaigns of Kimon (*Menexenus* 242a): "The war against Xerxes was brought to its ultimate completion by Athens after 479 B.C. in campaigns at the Eurymedon, Cyprus, Egypt and elsewhere." In the first of these campaigns, around 467 B.C., Kimon met the Persians, including 80 Phoenician ships, on Cyprus and defeated them in two victories on a single day, an achievement that surpassed the miracles of Salamis and Plataia (Plutarch, *Kimon* 12–13; cf. Diodorus, 11.60.3–62). The 80 ships he pursued and destroyed were exaggerated to 350 or even 600 in the popular imagination and in pro-Athenian sources (according to Ephoros and Phanodemos, cited by Plutarch, *Kimon* 12). The miracle of simultaneous victories—by land and sea on a single day—was praised in prose (Aristeides, 2.209) and in poetry (Diodorus, 11.62.3; Simonides, frag. 171):

οἱ δὲ γάρ ἐν γαίῃ Μήδων πολλοὺς ὀλέσαντες
Φοινίκων ἑκατὸν ναῦς ἕλον ἐν πελάγει.

For destroying many Medes on land
they captured one hundred Phoenician ships at sea.

The battle of the Eurymedon formed almost as dramatic a landmark in classical history as those fought at Marathon and Salamis, thanks to its commemoration in Athe-

---

[35] P. Gauthier, "Le parallèle Himère-Salamine au   Chapter 11.
Vᵉ et IVᵉ siècle av. J. C.," *REA* 68 (1966) 5–31; also see

nian art and monuments.[36] As in Aspasia's imaginary *epitaphios* (Plato, *Menexenus* 242a), this battle was the finale in the heroic Athenian victories against the Persians, although it also inspired the first allied refusals to contribute ships, men, or money and the first revolts against Athens (Thucydides, 1.99.1; Plutarch, *Kimon* 11.1). The first casualty lists of Athenians fallen in battle, the monumental equivalent of the funeral oration, were set up in the 460s and specify Egypt, Cyprus, and Phoenicia as the locale of heroic death.[37] Other Greek cities shared the Athenian vision of an enemy at sea as Phoenician, as early as 498 B.C. according to Herodotus (1.143). The monument for the Samian dead in the 460s describes the conflict between "the Medes and the Hellenes," but singles out the capture of (fifteen) Phoenician ships.[38]

In other words, throughout the campaigns of Dareios and Xerxes but even into the sea battles of the Pentekontaetia, the naval enemy of Greece was primarily Phoenician, in Persian employ. It was the threat of that Phoenician fleet in the Aegean that justified the Athenian transfer of the Delian treasury to Athens in 454 B.C. The final Greek victory over this Eastern threat was the achievement of Alexander, who captured impregnable Tyre with the help, predictably, of Phoenician ships, except for those of Tyre (Diodorus, 17.41.1, 42.3; Arrian, 2.20.2). To capture Babylon, he had Phoenician ships transported overland from the Levantine coast to Mesopotamia (Arrian, *Anabasis* 7.19.3). The burning of Persepolis, with its symbolic seizure of the Persian throne and recapture of the tyrannicide statues, formed the final act of vengeance in the series of raids narrated, at an earlier stage, by Herodotus, and the capture of Phoenician cities like Tyre repaid what Greeks had suffered from Phoenicians at sea. In western Greece, the Phoenician presence, in Punic guise, threatened Greeks in Sicily and invaded the island's Greek cities under Hannibal in 409–6 B.C. Athenian ambitions in the West probably influenced attitudes that claimed Greeks preceded Phoenicians at Sicilian settlements (Chapter 7). Those ambitions culminated in the disastrous Sicilian expedition, which crippled the Athenian naval empire, reviving the specter of Sicily as a challenge, Greek or Punic, to Hellenic sea power. For several centuries thereafter, the Punic city of Carthage, especially its fleet, remained the greatest challenge facing the growing power

[36] Hausmann, in *Charites*, 144–51; M. Sordi, "La Vittoria dell' Eurimedonte e le due spedizioni di Cimone a Cipro," *RivStudAnt* 1 (1971) 33–48; Schauenburg, *AthMitt* 90 (1975) 97–122; S. Th. Parker, "The Objectives and Strategies of Cimon's Expedition to Cyprus," *AJP* 97 (1976) 30–38; G. Pinney, "For the Heroes are at Hand," *JHS* 104 (1984) 181–83; Balcer, *Sparda by the Bitter Sea*, 370.

[37] E.g., in the Erechtheid casualty list (*IG* I³ 1149) ca. 459 B.C. Meiggs, *The Athenian Empire*, chap. 6, "War on Two Fronts," 92–108, whose title expresses

the miraculous and the disastrous in Athenian foreign policy during the Pentekontaetia; pp. 28, 28–29, 126–28, 105, 107 267, 481, on Phoenician ships; on Kimon's campaigns in Cyprus and Egypt, pp. 92–128.

[38] Jeffery, *LSAG*, no. 21; Tod, *GHI*, no. 34; Meiggs, *The Athenian Empire*, 107, takes this to mean that Samos contributed as many as one hundred ships to the Athenian expedition to Egypt, but this is not certain: C. Fornara, *Archaic Times to the End of the Peloponnesian War* (Cambridge, 1983), p. 78, no. 77.

of Rome. Thus the establishment of Athens, Macedon, and Rome as naval powers in
the Mediterranean, as for Egypt, Assyria, and Persia in earlier times, depended on the
challenge (or service) of Phoenician/Punic ships, specific target of naval strategies
against an Oriental enemy.

An irony central to Greek and Roman history is the contribution made by this Oriental enemy to Western navies and their empires, in the field of naval engineering. The
invention of the quadrireme was attributed to the Carthaginians by Aristotle (Pliny,
Naturalis Historia 7.207) and certain naval maneuvers were famous as Phoenician specialties, notably the διέκπλους (according to Sosylos of Sparta, cited in a papyrus commentary on the campaigns of Hannibal: *FGrH* 176 F1). Even the Athenian trireme, chief
instrument of its classical empire, may have been a lesson learned from Phoenician nautical specialists, just as Rome designed its first warships from the example of a captured
Carthaginian vessel (Polybius, 1.20.150). Disagreement reigns over the origins of the
Greek trireme and its relationship to Phoenician warships, probably because European
classicists prefer this warship as a Greek invention, along with democracy and other
historic contributions to Western civilization.[39] Much of the controversy thrives on the
lack of information about preclassical and non-Greek triremes, such as those employed
in the Saite navy of Egypt where both Greeks and Phoenicians served and may have
exchanged skills in shipbuilding.[40] Spokesmen for both sides of the argument, however,
agree on one crucial issue: "It was probably the conflict with Persia which brought the
crucial breakthrough."[41] Two occasions inspired rapid Athenian engineering of the trireme, both aimed at the Persians. The first occurred in the decade between Marathon
and Salamis, when Themistokles persuaded the Athenians to apply their new silver
resources toward a fleet, ostensibly against Aigina (Herodotus, 7.144). The second was
Kimon's improvement of the trireme in time for his victory at the Eurymedon (Plutarch,
Kimon 12.2). This source of Athenian triumph over the Persians may have derived from
an Oriental tradition in naval warfare, in which other Greeks (e.g., Polykrates of Samos:
Herodotus, 3.39.3) had excelled in the archaic period, with the conspicuous exception
of the Athenians.

This historical scenario may explain much of the elaborate imagery about Athens and
the sea that developed during the decades of the Delian League. As suggested in the

[39] L. Casson, *Ships and Seamanship in the Ancient
World* (Princeton, 1971), chap. 5 (pp. 94–96 on the
Phoenician trireme). M. Lucien Basch, "Trières
grecques, phéniciennes et égyptiennes," *JHS* 97
(1977) 1–10; A. B. Lloyd, "The Trireme Controversy,"
JHS 100 (1980) 195–98; Basch, "M. le Professeur Lloyd
et les trières: Quelques remarques," *JHS* 100 (1980)
198–99. J. S. Morrison and R. T. Williams, *Greek Oared
Ships 900–332 B.C.* (Cambridge, 1968); Morrison and

J. T. Coates, *The Athenian Trireme* (Cambridge, 1986),
38–39. Interest in this topic, as in the thalassocracy of
Minos (Chapter 6, n. 164), is intensified by the conflicts of modern naval powers.

[40] A. B. Lloyd, "Triremes and the Saite Navy," *JEA*
58 (1972) 268–79; Basch, *JHS* 107 (1977) 1–10; Lloyd,
Herodotus Book II. An Introduction (Leiden, 1975) 32ff.

[41] Lloyd, *JHS* 100 (1980) 196, with which Basch
agrees (p. 199).

analysis of the legends of Theseus (Chapter 12), Minos and his Cretans formed convenient antagonists to the young hero representing the new Athenian naval empire. Several factors assisted the decline of Minos's reputation. The first was his legendary connection to Phoenicia, emphatic in classical Athenian literature (e.g., Euripides, *Cretans* frag. 472, 1–4). The Phoenician reputation as pirates and kidnappers on the high seas was established since Homer (*Odyssey* 13.272, 14.288–300, 15.415–30, etc.) and maintained by Herodotus, who links their activity as pirates and kidnappers with the origins of the Persian wars (1.1–5). This tradition contributed to the classical image of Phoenicians as an enemy of Athens at sea. Then, the failure of the Cretans to join the Greek cause at Salamis (Herodotus, 7.169) added to their sins, as enemies of Athens and suspects for Medism. The Cretan excuse for missing the battle introduced the legend of Daidalos, in the version known to Herodotus (7.169–71) and presumably the substance of the many dramatic versions of the myth in classical Athens (see Chapters 7 and 8). Thus the amplification, if not the origin, of Athenian legends about Daidalos and Minos belonged to the new vision of the past inspired by recent history.

Unlike Persians, Phoenicians make rare appearances in Greek literature and are difficult to identify in art, making it a special challenge to explore the Greek image of Phoenicia in the classical period. Phrynikhos wrote a play about the battle of Salamis with a chorus of Phoenician women, which Aeschylus reworked (παραπεποιῆσθαι) in his play about the same event, the *Persians*.[42] The title of Phrynikhos's play may also have been the *Persians*, according to the list of seven titles in the Suda, which omits the *Phoenician Women* but calls one play Δίκαιοι ἢ Πέρσαι ἢ Συνθῶκοι. The date of the play is unknown: presumably its production predated 472, when Aeschylus's *Persians* was produced, if Glaukos could claim the latter was influenced by Phrynikhos; it could be the play for which Themistokles served as *choregos*, produced in 476 B.C. (Plutarch, *Themistokles* 5), whose title is not known. According to Glaukos's observations reported in the hypothesis, the play opened with a eunuch of the Persian court arranging seats for Persian councillors (hence the alternate titles reported in the Suda), presumably in a costume as exotic to the audience as the royal θρόνους he prepared for the king's councillors. Such theatrical details must have been deliberately designed to look Persian, in the spirit of the early classical fascination with *Persika*. Vase paintings indicate some of these trappings, as in the personification of new images like Greece and Asia, which survive in the fourth century on the name vase of the Darius Painter (Figure 62).[43] The

[42] According to Glaukos of Rhegion, quoted in the hypothesis to *Persians*: F. Stoessl, "Die *Phoinissen* des Phrynichus und die *Perser* des Aischylos," *MH* 2 (1945) 148–65. F. Marx, "Der Tragiker Phrynichus," *RhM* 77 (1928) 348–60, rejects the testimony of Glaukos and claims Aeschylus's play was the earlier one. For ancient testimonia on Phoenicians, see F. Mazza,

S. Ribichini, and P. Xella, *Fonti Classiche per la Civiltà Fenicia e Punica*, vol. 1 (Rome, 1988).

[43] Naples 3253; C. Anti, "Il vaso di Dario e i *Persiani* di Frinico," *ArchClass* 4 (1952) 23–24; Oliver, *Demokratia*, chap. 4, "The Darius Vase of the Naples Museum," 118–20; Hölscher, *Griechische Historienbilder*, 177–79; Francis, in *Ancient Persia*, 84–85; M. Schmidt,

chorus of Phoenician women, presumably the relatives of those lost in the fleet, must have sung odes of lament at the news of Xerxes' defeat reported by the eunuch; the only two fragments of these odes (frags. 9 and 10) speak of their home in Sidon. Biblical lamentation for cities that fell to Assyria include not only Tyre (Ezekiel 27–28) but Sidon itself (Isaiah 23.1–4), and their defeat had dramatic consequences in the Aegean (Chapter 6). These laments may have inspired a Greek response, but in a play where a Greek victory precipitates a choral lament by the wives of those on defeated ships. The choice of Phoenician, rather than Persian, wives and mothers reflects the preponderance of Phoenicians in the fleet, who must have been the chief victims in the battle of Salamis, hence Xerxes' special sorrow for them in Aeschylus's *Persians* (962–65). What remains extraordinary about the Greek mind is how different it became from the Orient in ways like this, perhaps precisely because of their historic conflict. No other ancient nation was curious as well as compassionate enough to experience victory from the vanquished side, whether in composing laments for the enemy or in reacting to drama in sympathy so extreme that its source was censored (as the Athenians did to Phrynikhos's *Capture of Miletos*).

Phrynikhos's *Phoenician Women* belongs to this early classical spirit of sympathy and respect for the enemy, matched in Aeschylus's *Persians* of 472 B.C. and reflected in the popularity of episodes from the *Ilioupersis* in art and literature. The attitude for which Herodotus was condemned as φιλοβάρβαρος (Plutarch, *De Malignitate Herodoti* 12.1) included acknowledging the Phoenician ancestry of figures admired in the classical period. Athens' greatest historical heroes, Harmodios and Aristogeiton, belonged to the Gephyraeans who arrived with Kadmos in Boiotia (Herodotus, 5.57). Thales of Miletos, one of Ionia's wisest figures and numbered among the "Seven Sages" of Greece, was Phoenician by birth, according to a passage in Herodotus (1.170), attacked by Plutarch for "making Thales barbarian" (*De Malignitate Herodoti* 15). Other sources—Diogenes mentions Douris and Demokritos in addition to Herodotus—support Thales' descent from the Theleids, whom he admits as Phoenician (οἱ εἰσι Φοίνικες, εὐγενέστατοι τῶν ἀπὸ Κάδμου καὶ Ἀγήνορος), although Diogenes also indicates that most call him "Milesian born" (ἰθαγενὴς Μιλήσιος: 1.22). His father's name, however, sounds Carian (Examyes), making Thales "barbarian" through other relatives, or as one scholar put it wittily, "half Carian, half Phoenician, and all Greek."[44] As with other sages of early Greece (e.g., Solon), Thales' reputation was enhanced by a visit to Egypt in his youth, and his contributions to geometry and geography attributed in antiquity to the lessons

---

"Asia and Apate," ΑΠΑΡΧΑΙ. Nuovi ricerche e studi in onore di Paolo Enrico Arias (Pisa, 1982), 2:505–20.

[44] E. Vermeule, "The Hittites and the Aegean World: Response to Hans Güterbock," *AJA* 87 (1983)

142. On the ancestry of Thales, see G. S. Kirk, J. E. Raven, and M. Schofield, *The Presocratic Philosophers* (Cambridge, 1983), 76–77, who call Thales "as Greek as most Milesians."

of this visit.[45] And as in shipbuilding and geometric urban planning, the source of such practical learning may have been acquired by Greek mercenaries in Egypt who settled there with Phoenicians.[46] The association of wisdom with the East was a belief that survived Greek political enmity with the Orient, was a reality in the Phoenician background of philosophers like Zeno of Kition, and even became a European tradition.[47] Pherekydes "Syrios," for example, not only demonstrates Near Eastern elements in his own writings but was alleged to have taught himself from τὰ Φοινίκων ἀπόκρυφα βιβλία (Suda, s.v. Φερεκύδης); was he from the Greek island of Syros, or from As/syria, and literate in cuneiform? His Oriental debt is supported by Jewish apologists like Philo of Byblos (Eusebius, *Praeparatio Evangelica* 1.10.50), while Pythagoras was accused by Josephus of imitating and claiming as his own the δόξαι of the Jews (*Contra Apionem* 1.162–65). Thus the tribute to Phoenician wisdom associated with ancient portraits of philosophers is just as misleading as the denial of Phoenician sources maintained by Greek and modern prejudice: both claims illustrate attitudes toward the Orient. A telling example of this complexity of ancient thought on East and West is the thanks Thales is said to have expressed to Tyche (Fortune) for making him "a human rather than an animal, a man rather than a woman, and a Greek instead of a barbarian" (Diogenes Laertius, 1.33). Usually dismissed as a posthumous sophistic apophthegma, the sentiment not only postdates the tradition that maintains the "barbarian" ancestry of Thales, but duplicates a traditional Hebrew prayer (where "Jew" and "Gentile" replace "Greek" and "barbarian," respectively), making his ancient portrait and intellectual persona all the more "barbarian," if not specifically Semitic. The ambiguous image of Thales epitomizes the Greek attitude toward the Orient, where admiration for vastly more ancient and learned cultures was mixed with prejudice inspired by political conditions. The enrichment of early Greek philosophy by the Orient is demonstrated in explicit and implicit debts, especially during the period when Persia ruled Ionia (ca. 550–480) and when intellectuals like the Magi may have been influential residents. The Persian wars coincide with an abrupt decline in this influence, suggesting how much the early Greek *polis* lost in intellectual resources as it gained in military victories.[48] But images of figures

[45] Aetius, 1.3.1; Proclus, *In Euclidem* 65 (geometry); Plutarch, *De Isis et Osiris* 34, 364d, attributes Thales' theory of water as the first principle to Egyptian learning.

[46] On the derivation of archaic Greek geometry from Egyptian and Babylonian principles, see T. D. Boyd and M. H. Jameson, "Urban and Rural Land Division in Ancient Greece," *Hesperia* 50 (1981) 334–35. Lloyd, *Herodotus Book II*, 14–17.

[47] A. Momigliano, *Alien Wisdom: The Limits of Hellenization* (Cambridge, 1975); Bernal, *Black Athena*, 98–

188, emphasizes ancient and modern admiration of Egypt. Kirk, Raven, and Schofield, *Presocratic Philosophers*, 79–80, on Thales and Egypt. H. Tarrant, "The Distribution of Early Greek Thinkers and the Question of 'Alien Influences'," in *Greek Colonists and Native Populations*, 621–28.

[48] West, *Early Greek Philosophy and the Orient*, esp. 226–41, for Iranian influence on Ionian thinkers between 550 and 480 B.C. M. Papatheophanes, "Heraclitus of Ephesus, the Magi and the Achaemenids," *IrAnt* 20 (1985) 101–61, esp. 104–6. Cf. Van Effenterre,

like Thales, Pherekydes, and Zeno survived as descendants of Homeric δημιοεργοί, prehistoric "wise men from the East" like Kothar and Agaptari, circulating wisdom often falsely but always significantly associated with the Orient.

The same historian who still retains Phoenicians in the traditional ancestry of heroes and sages ranks them below Persians and Ionians in the treatment they experience at the hands of Xerxes (Herodotus, 8.90, 119). The pretext used by Histiaios to persuade the Ionians to revolt against Persia was the threat of a transfer of populations between Phoenicia and Ionia allegedly planned by Dareios (Herodotus, 6.3). The alarm it caused the Ionians suggests that they felt more than commercial rivalry toward Phoenicians at the time and responded in order to ensure their homes. Most conspicuous of all in Herodotus's treatment of Phoenicians is the role they play in his mythological scenario of the origins of the Great War. Claiming Persian sources, Herodotus reports that those who began the conflict were the Phoenicians, in an account that blames their traditional activity as pirates and kidnappers for the capture of Io, the first of the ἀδικήματα ("injustices") that resulted in the Persian invasion of Greece (1.1–2). Herodotus sounds skeptical of this explanation, repeating his reference to Persian and Phoenician sources and offering his own account as the result of his investigation (the Lydian λόγος: 1.5.3). Even his elaborate disclaimer of Phoenicians as a cause suggests that they were more widely blamed for the war, in popular opinion, than in his informed judgment.

The origins of Greek ambiguity toward the Orient may have been predominantly Athenian, in sentiments etched more vividly in poetry and mythology than in the prose history of Herodotus. In the sixty years between the defeat of the Persians as narrated by Aeschylus and the performance of plays like Euripides' *Phoenician Women* (412 B.C.), the campaigns of the Pentekontaetia and the Peloponnesian War had contributed to an increasing sense of Greek (and Athenian) superiority. The plays of Euripides contain fewer specific and exotic details of barbarian language and practice than the early classical fascination transmitted in the plays of Aeschylus, but exhibit to some a more monolithic and morally superior attitude to foreign culture, visible in the first use of the word βάρβαρος in a pejorative sense.[49] Euripides hardly represents mainstream opinion, and in fact is often eccentric to it; hence his sympathetic portraits of foreigners (e.g., in *Andromakhe, Trojan Women*) could reflect a divergence from general attitudes in Athens. If his plays express sentiments about the natural Greek rule of barbarians (*Andromakhe* 665–67; *Iphigeneia in Aulis* 952–54, 1264–65, 1400–4001) and the superiority of

---

La cité grecque, chap. 14, 268–84 "La Défaite de Marathon," on what Athens (and Greece) stood to lose from the "defeat" of the Greek *polis* at Marathon.

[49] Bacon, *Barbarians in Greek Tragedy*, 151–55, 167–72, on the lack of concrete foreign details and the rise of the "symbolic foreigner," inferior to Greeks in law and culture, in the plays of Euripides. E. Said, *Ori-*

entalism (New York, 1979) 56–57, on the two poles of Aeschylus and Euripides as "essential motifs of European imaginative geography" (p. 57); S. Saïd, "Grecs et Barbares dans les tragédies d' Euripide. La fin des différences?" *Ktema* 9 (1984) 27–53; Hall, *Inventing the Barbarian*, 211–23, defends a more "noble barbarian" in the plays of Euripides than Bacon did.

Greek law (*Helen* 273–76; *Medea* 536–38), which became commonplace in classical wisdom, it has also been claimed that few specific portraits emerge from his references, where "the genus non-Greek" is more important than individual barbarians.[50]

An exception worth exploring in the context of this chapter is his *Phoenician Women*, the next preserved classical drama after Phrynikhos' play of the same name to present Phoenicians on stage. The play derives its name from the chorus of Phoenician slave women on their way to Delphi, although the play presents an episode from the epic siege of Thebes linked to the violence of the city's foundation myths. After its Medism, the city of Thebes formed a convenient polarity with the city of Athens in tragedy, whose details imply what is barbarian in Thebes, some with a link to Oriental culture. In this play of Euripides, the chorus of Phoenician women are the equivalent of those slaves belonging to Persians, in earlier plays of Phrynikhos and Aeschylus.[51] The need to sacrifice the king's son to save the city, an episode unique in literature on the Theban cycle and presumably invented by Euripides in analogy to his *Erechtheus*, singles out Menoikeus, who averts a taboo by offering himself in suicide. The episode betrays links to the Phoenician and Punic practice of infant sacrifice: for example, Menoikeus offers himself to Ares, the god who received Phoenician-inspired offerings of human sacrifice at Sparta (Porphyry, *De Abstinentia* 2.55.4, citing Apollodoros; see Chapter 5), and the chorus of Phoenician women describes itself as ἀκροθίνια (214–15, 203), votive offerings like those set up by Athenians after their victory over Phoenician ships at Salamis (see Chapter 11). Such details could have been colored by Athenian enmity with Phoenicians and their equivalent in the West, Carthage, a city familiar to other playwrights who also know its god, Kronos, as the recipient of human sacrifice (e.g., Sophokles, *Andromeda* frag. 126; *Triptolemos* frag. 602).[52] Oriental rituals were readily appropriate to Thebes, a city remembered for its association with Medism (in this case, Persian luxuries argued the Persian cause: Herodotus, 9.41) and its claim to Phoenician ancestry, through the legends of Kadmos. The first distinction helped reinforce the second: the Medism of Thebes made its kinship in foundation legends with Phoenicians, a constant enemy to Athens if not Greece, more conspicuous in the Athenian imagination. It has even been argued that the Phoenician parentage of Kadmos was primarily a product of classical mythology, in reproach of the city's Medism.[53] However, evidence for Phoeni-

---

[50] Bacon, *Barbarians in Greek Tragedy*, 152.

[51] Cf. M. B. Arthur, "The Curse of Civilization: The Choral Odes of the *Phoenissae*," *HSCP* 81 (1977) 163–85; F. Zeitlin, "Thebes: Theater of Self and Society in Athenian Drama," in *Greek Tragedy and Political Theory*, 114–16; Hall, *Inventing the Barbarian*, 116, 119, on the chorus of the *Phoenician Women*.

[52] R. Rebuffat, "Le sacrifice du fils de Créon dans les *Phéniciennes* d'Euripide," *REA* 74 (1972) 14–31,

makes Euripides' chorus of "Phoenicians" into women of Carthage. Cf. H. Foley, *Ritual Irony: Poetry and Sacrifice in Euripides* (Ithaca, N.Y., 1985), 106–46, on the *Phoenician Women*; E.A.M.E. O'Connor-Visser, *Aspects of Sacrifice in the Tragedies of Euripides* (Amsterdam, 1987), 73–98, "The Sacrifice of Menoiceus," and appendix, 211–30, on "The Evidence for Human Sacrifice"; Hall, *Inventing the Barbarian*, 147–48.

[53] Vermeule, "Kadmos and the Dragon," 183;

cian exploration of Boiotia and Euboia is well attested in the Late Bronze and early Iron Ages (Chapter 5) and provides some historical support for the ancestry of Kadmos. New emphasis on his heritage makes classical sense, especially in the light of continued hostility between Thebes and Athens. In Attic drama, the Theban cycle was the source of numerous plays, but in many of them the city of Thebes functions as the "anti-Athens," an image assisted by the Boiotian city's barbarian founders.[54] Close examination of the treatment of places like Thebes in classical Athenian literature reveals how Athens could undermine richer mythology in rival cities for the sake of promoting itself, and how reference to the Orient assisted this process.

In this way the Phoenicians acquired new dimensions not in art but through new insights into traditional stories about new enemies. Crete, like Thebes, was punished for its Medism with a Phoenician cudgel. Discredited in Greek eyes by their absence at Salamis, Cretans had their Phoenician ancestry newly emphasized in classical legends about Minos, in lost tragedies and in mythography, all the work of Athenians. The chorus preserved from Euripides' *Cretans*, for example, emphasizes the Phoenician parentage of Minos and describes unusual rites such as *omophagia*, cast as "romantically exotic rather than realistically foreign."[55] The passages closest to these appear in the same playwright's *Bacchae*, describing the rites of Dionysos in terms similar to those that invoke Cretan ritual (and emphasize "Asian" origins), set in the city of Thebes whose un-Greek traits were noted in the *Phoenicians*. Thus the contrast between Greek and barbarian, axiomatic since the Persian wars, shares with other Persian war legacies (the repute of democracy and other virtues) their use and abuse against Greek enemies of Athens, who accumulate Oriental vices in order to appear less favorable. Conversely, when barbarians behave in ways superior to Greeks in works by the same playwright— notably his *Andromakhe* and *Trojan Women*—a similar concern with immediate history may be at work. The production of the *Trojan Women* in 415 b.c. has long been noted for its coincidence with the Athenian massacre of the population of Melos (Thucydides, 5.84–116), and Euripides' sympathy for the citizens of a defeated city, Troy, may be directed in criticism against Athenian cruelty toward Melos. In other words, the close link in classical Athens between mythology and history, claimed in the preceding chapter, is essential to specific fluctuations of sentiment toward barbarians, which re-

---

N. Demand, *Thebes in the Fifth Century* (London, 1983), 53; A. Collinge, "Aristaios, or his Father-in-Law?" *AK* 31 (1988) 13–14, in an article that identifies the scene on the Sotades Painter's white-ground cup (London D7) as Kadmos and the dragon. F. Vian, *Les origines de Thèbes. Cadmus et les Spartes* (Paris, 1963), on Theban myths; see Chapter 5, n. 181, on Thebes and the legends of Kadmos.

[54] As argued by Zeitlin, in *Greek Tragedy and Politi-*

cal Theory, 115–41. Athens receives Oidipous when Thebes rejects him, in Sophocles' *Oidipous at Kolonos*, and produces Teiresias as a solution sent from Athens (Euripides, *Phoenician Women* 852–57).

[55] Bacon, *Barbarians in Greek Tragedy*, 141; Hall, *Inventing the Barbarian*, 169. On the archaeological basis for Cretan human sacrifice and cannibalism, see Chapter 6.

flect more than an enigmatic or deliberately ambiguous streak on the part of Euripides. The image of non-Greeks was a useful foil for Greek political opinion, and could be positive to express dissatisfaction with Greek behavior as easily as it could be hostile to promote Greek interests. Moreover, the monolithic model of "Greek" and "barbarian" was so explicitly promoted by Athens, and often directed against specific targets like Phoenicians, that it deserves careful definition and analysis in its modern usage, and should not be applied as the broad cliché it became in the words of Athenian orators.

The latters' claim of Athenian superiority over other cities is fully articulated in statements like the exaggerated chauvinism of the funeral oration parodied in Plato's *Menexenus*. In the passage (245d) quoted at the head of this section, it is the very lack of a foreign ancestor that makes the Athenians "pure Hellenes," in the spirit of artificial autochthony promoted in art and literature (see Chapter 12). In reality, Athens had made a virtue out of an inadequacy: despite its rich prehistory, the city had no native epic cycle or colorful myths claiming founders from abroad, which became an opportunity for creative inventions in mythology. Argos and Thebes were conspicuously rich in the kind of legends absent in Athens: in the archaic period, Athens not only lacks a native cycle of myth, but contributes no major figures to Panhellenic experiences like the Trojan expedition, and is sensitive enough about this last omission, in particular, to defend its Trojan performance in the catalogue of heroic deeds imagined by Herodotus at Plataia (9.27.4: οὐδὲν ἐλειπόμεθα). As West summarizes Attic mythology:

> There is virtually no saga here, only an unstable combination of cult, myth (Kekrops and his daughters, Erechtheus), political myth (Kreiousa, Sikyon, Orneus), clan and parish antiquarianism (Keryx, Metion, Melite) and folk tale. The stemma has neither breadth, depth, nor strength. We feel we are in a region that possesses plenty of uncoordinated story material but no tradition of putting it together in connected account.[56]

Even those legends cited by West are only common after the classical period, and Attic genealogies in general "have a makeshift appearance, as if they were cobbled together to fill gaps in the corpus," and as a result "Athenian propaganda seems to be particularly prominent."[57] The lack of a major poet or poetic tradition in Athens before the late archaic period explains some of this spotty record, and the classical impulse toward mythography as compensatory history explains its sudden, political refurbishing. This phase and genre of mythography corresponds to what has recently been recognized as "secondary myth," well defined as "the products of antiquarian industry, literary activity, a desire for impressive antecedents, a good nose for suggestive analo-

[56] West, *Catalogue of Women*, 164, in evaluating the Attic contribution to the Panhellenic catalogue of women. Cf. Jacoby, *Atthis*, 221 on the Athenian ab- sence from legends outside Athens.

[57] West, *Catalogue of Women*, 169.

gies, and for what might pass as a credibly antique story, a talent for creating a seductive but illusory patina of hoarily ancient authenticity, and, lastly, wide reading."[58] The Athenian myth of the Amazons follows such a recipe, with historical causes paramount: "The development of the Amazon myth resumes in an atmosphere of intense antipathy towards Persians and other foreigners. . . . at this time [the Athenians] became aware of the paucity of their past and the need to expand upon it in order to substantiate their pretensions abroad."[59]

The activity that produced new myths, or new versions of old ones, favoring Athens at the expense of other Greek traditions, is reflected by poets and orators but originated in prose writers. Mythographers like Pherekydes, Kleidemos, and Philokhoros inaugurated an important branch of Attic historiography, and constituted the first generation who practiced Atthidography, best defined as a "distinctive literary genre specifically concerned with the country's antiquity, including its mythology."[60] The bulk of these writings date from the fourth century, and one of the most prolific and pro-Athenian practitioners, Philokhoros, was active in the third century. But the genre of Atthidography belongs to those intellectual endeavors stimulated by the Persian wars to discover and justify Athenian victory from the Athenian past. A conspicuous example of Athenian mythmaking is the legend of Theseus, whose promotion in art and literature as legendary king, founder-hero, and father of democracy was examined in Chapter 12. This hero was the research topic of five Atthidographers, fragments of whose writings reveal the classical reform of the hero into a civilized and civilizing negotiator, peacemaker, and civic ideal.[61] The first prose equivalent of the *Theseis* poem appears in the writings of Pherekydes, and many of the pro-Athenian revisions of the hero's career are the work of these industrious, imaginative, and creatively dishonest classical Athenian researchers.

In one conspicuous example of propaganda promoting Athens, Phoenicians became victims of the nationalization of cultural institutions. The origins of the alphabet are usually attributed to Kadmos and the Phoenicians, even in classical writers (Herodotus, 5.59; Diodorus, 3.67). But as Diodorus claims, Greeks kept reinventing the science of writing, having known letters long ago, then lost them in the flood and forgotten how to write (ἔδοξαν ἀεί τι προσευρίσκειν περὶ τῶν γραμμάτων, κοινῆς τινος ἀγνοίας κατεχούσης τοὺς Ἕλληνας: 5.57.5). Explanations like these were presumably aimed

---

[58] N. Horsfall, "Myth and Mythography," *EchCl* 29 (1984) 394, analyzing a similar phenomenon in Roman mythology. Cf. R. Parker, "Myths of Early Athens," in *Interpreting Greek Mythology*, and P. Veyne, *Did the Greeks Believe in their Myths? An Essay on the Constitutive Imagination* (Chicago, 1988).

[59] Tyrrell, *Amazons*, 9.

[60] Parker, "Myths of Early Athens," in *Interpreting*

Greek Mythology, 187. Jacoby, *Atthis*, esp. 71–79 and 215–25; cf. J. H. Schreiner, "Historical Methods, Hellanikos and the Era of Kimon," *OpAth* 15 (1984) 163–71.

[61] Pearson, *Local Historians of Attica*, 149–56; Jacoby, *Atthis*, 135–41, on the *aitia* predating Atthidography proper, which he begins with Hellanicus.

at playing down the obvious primacy of Egypt and other Near Eastern countries in the use of writing, and reconciling traditions about Phoenicians with a Greek desire to claim the invention. Eventually, a source no doubt Athenian reassigns this invention to an Athenian king, Aktaion, who named the letters in memory of his daughter, "Phoinike."[62] This king belongs to the Athenian royal line as father of Kekrops (Pausanias, 1.2.6) and hence to the tradition of local, Attic inventors of civilized institutions. Testimonia for such figures are late (e.g., Philokhoros) and those on heroes who are dated "before Kekrops" particularly so, but classical sources tend to include the alphabet within the sphere of Athenian accomplishments. "Phoinike" is not the only Athenian claim to the invention of the alphabet: γραμμάτων τε συνθέσεις, | μνήμην ἁπάντων, μουσομήτωρ᾽ ἐργάνην are attributed to Prometheus (*Prometheus Bound* 460–61) in a play where his kinship with Hephaistos is stressed (lines 14, 39) in agreement with the Attic cult they share (Chapter 12, n. 172). In a tradition that can be traced to Stesikhoros (*PMG* F 213), if not to the *Kypria*, Palamedes makes a similar claim. In a long eulogy of the civilizing benefits of letters from a lost play of the trilogy by Euripides that included the *Trojan Women*, Palamedes praises his invention (frag. 581 = Stobaeus, 81.7) as Τὰ τῆς γε λήθης φάρμακ᾽ . . . ἄφωνα καὶ φωνοῦντα, δέλτος διαιρεῖ, κοὐκ ἐᾷ ψευδῆ λέγειν· "The remedy of forgetfulness, voiceless and voiced . . . the writing tablet decides, and does not allow to speak untruths." While associating the alphabet with the Argolid, home of Palamedes, rather than Athens, passages such as these illustrate how readily Greek tradition could claim foreign inventions as native, and how an institution as admired as the alphabet attracted new stories. Other legends and locales that claim to have "invented" or discovered the Phoenician alphabet include Egypt (according to Hekataios) and Miletos, home to a Kadmos homonymous with the Phoenician founder of Thebes.[63]

The Athenian claim, however, belongs to a wider campaign to establish the roots of civilization in Attica, to make the city-state the first home of Greek culture as well as its classical leader, and justify present hierarchy through priority in the past. Much of this new mythology was perpetuated by Atthidographers like Philokhoros, who "propounded a local Attic theory for the origins of civilization," apparently "in opposition to that of Hekataios of Abdera."[64] New figures like Kekrops and Kodros are associated with the origins of agriculture and constitutional government, while local heroes like Triptolemos develop classical contributions to similar institutions.[65] Kekrops is credited

[62] Skamon, at Photios, s.v. Φοινίκη, cf. Hesychius, Suidas, etc. Joanna Schmidt, "Phoinike," *RE* 20.I, 349; Astour, *Hellenosemitica*, 168; Jeffery, in *Europa*, 152–66, for ancient testimonia on the origins of the alphabet.

[63] Jeffery, in *Europa*, 152–56.

[64] M. J. Miller, "The Athenian Autochthonous He-

roes from the Classical through the Hellenistic Period," *HSCP* (1984) 59–62. Cf. Jacoby, *Atthis*, 133–34, on the promotion of Athens as the "first civilized city" by Philochoros and other Atthidographers.

[65] L. Lacroix, "Formes de la vie primitive et de la vie civilisée dans les traditions légendaires de la Grèce," in *Le rayonnement grec. Hommage à Charles Del-*

with the invention of laws, the first census, the foundation of certain cults (of Hermes and Zeus Hypatos), and the development of cities, including a version of *synoikismos* that united the settlements of Attica into a dodekapolis.[66] Non-Attika heroes are recruited as founders of institutions in Athens, sometimes from the same locales derided for their foreign or "Phoenician" connections. Crete, for example, not only offered Daidalos and perhaps Hephaistos for Athenian mythology; a learned Cretan, Epimenides, is born again as "Bouzyges," native Athenian who first yoked ox to plow.[67] Pandion and Tereus, once native to Attika's neighbor and rival, Megara, become Athenian heroes, the first as a legendary king and eponymous hero, the second as a "Thracian" ancestor of Athens.[68] The creation of Athens through mythology not only involved amplifying a scanty local tradition, but appropriating or undermining other mythologies.

This classical milieu of monuments and literature promoting Athens was what encouraged the legend of Daidalos into a local tradition anchored in cult, topography, iconography, and myth (Part III). The Athenian desire to incorporate inventors of art and culture into its legendary past embraced the Cretan figure of Daidalos in its own genealogy, in ignorance or defiance of origins possibly as Levantine as those of Minos or Kadmos. The ancestry of Daidalos points beyond Crete to the Near East, according to the evidence of comparative philology and mythology (Chapter 4), adding another layer of irony to one fiction with which Greece, and Athens, constructed its talents as native. One possible consequence of this appropriation of the Orient, by the same spirit that professed to despise it, made an item of furniture in the Erechtheion the work of Daidalos (Pausanias, 1.27.1; see Chapter 10). The quantity of Persian booty stored on the Akropolis makes it plausible that Pausanias saw an Oriental throne, perhaps even one captured as spoils, whose craftmanship was associated with an artist believed to be Athenian, originally Cretan, and perhaps from the Levantine world that produced such a throne for a Persian king. Whether or not such an episode made a Persian artifact "Greek," it brings the itinerary of this book back to its departure in the East. It forces Athens, home to many literary and political traditions inherited as "Western," into a new light. Many of its classical achievements deserve to be reexamined as more than reflections of "the Greek genius" but as deliberate Athenian strategies to distinguish itself from other Greek states and from a more formidable East. Daidalos is neither the first nor the last import from the East to be incorporated into a Western heritage, but his case illustrates how *Kunstgeschichte* is insufficient as *Motifgeschichte*, or even *Künstlergeschichte*, but requires the history of their incorporation into the fictions that make us human.

---

voye (Brussels, 1982), 59–67, on Athens and agriculture.

[66] Kron, *Phylenheroen*, 84–85, for a discussion of these contributions and their literary sources.

[67] Shapiro, *Kernos* 3 (1990) 341.

[68] K. Hanell, *Megarische Studien* (Lund, 1934), 35–40; Kron, *Phylenheroen*, 104–9 on Pandion; Hall, *Inventing the Barbarian*, 103–5, on how Tereus becomes a Thracian.

BIBLIOGRAPHY

Adams, L. *Orientalizing Sculpture in Soft Limestone from Crete and Mainland Greece*. *BARep* Series 42. Oxford, 1978.

The Aegean and the Near East: Studies Presented to Hetty Goldman. Ed. S. Weinberg. Locust Valley, N.Y, 1956.

Amandry, P. "Trépieds de Delphes et du Péloponnèse." *BCH* 111 (1987) 79–131.

Ancient Greek and Related Pottery. Ed. H.A.G. Brijder. Allard Pierson Series 5. Amsterdam, 1984.

Ancient Israelite Religions: Essays in Honor of Frank Moore Cross. Ed. P. Miller, P. Hanson, and S. D. McBride. Philadelphia, 1987.

Ancient Persia: The Art of an Empire. Ed. D. Schmandt-Besserat. Malibu, Calif., 1980.

Antichità Cretesi: Studi in onore di Doro Levi. *CronArch*, vols. 12–13. Catania, 1973–1974.

Archaische und klassische griechische Plastik. 2 vols. Ed. H. Kyrieleis. Mainz, 1986.

Arend, W. *Die typischen Szenen bei Homer*. Berlin, 1933.

Astour, M. *Hellenosemitica: An Ethnic and Cultural Study in West Semitic Impact on Mycenaean Greece*. Leiden, 1967.

Attridge, H., and R. Oden. *Philo of Byblos, The Phoenician History: Introduction, Critical Text, Translation, Notes*. *CBQ* Monograph 9. Washington, D.C., 1981.

Aux origines de l'Hellénisme. La Crète et la Gréce. Hommage à Henri Van Effenterre. Paris, 1984.

Bacon, H. *Barbarians in Greek Tragedy*. New Haven, 1961.

Bakhuizen, S. C. *Chalcis-in-Euboea, Iron and Chalcidians Abroad*. Chalcidian Studies 3. Leiden, 1976.

Balcer, J. *Sparda by the Bitter Sea: Imperial Interaction in Western Anatolia*. Brown Judaic Studies 52. Chico, Calif. 1984.

Barletta, B. *Ionic Influence in Archaic Sicily: The Monumental Art*. *SIMA* pocketbook 23. Göteborg, 1983.

Barron, J. "New Light on Old Walls: The Murals of the Theseion." *JHS* 92 (1972) 20–45.

———. "Bakchylides, Theseus, and a Wooly Cloak." *BICS* 27 (1980) 1–8.

Bass, G. "A Bronze Age Shipwreck at Ulu Burun (Kaş): 1984 Campaign." *AJA* 90 (1986) 269–96.

———. "Oldest Known Shipwreck Reveals Splendors of the Bronze Age." *National Geographic* 172, no. 6 (1987) 693–733.

Bass, G., C. Pulak, D. Collon, and J. Weinstein. "The Bronze Age Shipwreck at Ulu Burun: 1986 Campaign." *AJA* 93 (1989) 1–29.

Baumgarten, A. *The Phoenician History of Philo of Byblos: A Commentary*. *EPRO* 89. Leiden, 1981.

Beazley, J. D. "Icarus." *JHS* 47 (1927) 222–33.

Becatti, G. "La leggenda di Dedalo." *RömMitt* 60–61 (1953–1954) 22–36.

———. *Oreficerie antiche dalle minoiche alle barbariche*. Rome, 1955.

Benveniste, E. *Problèmes de linguistique générale*. Paris, 1966.

Bérard, J. *La colonisation grecque de l'Italie méridionale et de la Sicile dans l'antiquité. L'histoire et la légende.* Paris, 1957.

Bérard, V. *Les Phéniciens et l'Odyssée.* 2 vols. Paris, 1902.

Bernal, M. *Black Athena: The Afroasiatic Roots of Classical Civilization*, vol. 1: *The Fabrication of Ancient Greece 1785–1985.* New Brunswick, N.J., 1987.

——. *Cadmean Letters: The Transmission of the Alphabet to the Aegean and Further West before 1400 B.C.* Winona Lake, Ind., 1990.

Betancourt, P. *The Aeolic Style in Greek Architecture.* Princeton, 1977.

Beyer, I. *Die Tempel von Dreros und Prinias und die Chronologie der kretischen Kunst des 8. u. 7. Jhs. v. Chr.* Freiburg, 1976.

Bikai, P. *The Pottery of Tyre.* London, 1978.

——. *The Phoenician Pottery of Cyprus.* Nicosia, 1987.

Billigmeier, J. C. "Kadmos and the Possibility of a West Semitic Presence in Helladic Greece." Ph.D. diss., University of California at Santa Barbara, 1978.

Blankenhagen, P. von. "Daedalus and Icarus on Pompeian Walls." *RömMitt* 75 (1968) 106–43.

Blech, M. *Studien zu dem Kranz bei den Griechen.* Religionsgeschichtliche Versuche und Vorarbeiten 28. Berlin, 1982.

Blome, P. *Die figürliche Bildwelt Kretas in der geometrischen und früharchaischen Periode.* Mainz, 1982.

Boardman, J. *The Cretan Collection in Oxford: The Dictaean Cave and Iron Age Crete.* Oxford, 1961.

——. "The Kleophrades Painter at Troy." *AK* 19 (1976) 3–18.

——. "Daedalus and Monumental Sculpture." In *Fourth Cretological Congress*, 43–47.

——. *The Greeks Overseas.* 3d ed. London, 1985.

Bonnet, C. *Melqart. Cultes et mythes de l'Héracles tyrien en Méditerrannée.* Leuven/Namur, 1988.

Borgeaud, P. *The Cult of Pan in Ancient Greece.* Trans. K. Atlas and J. Redfield. Chicago, 1988.

Bourriot, F. "L'influence des guerres médiques sur la civilization artistique grecque." *L'Information Historique* 42 (1980) 193–202.

Bovon, J. "Les guerres médiques dans la tradition et les cultes populaires d' Athénes." *Études de Lettres* 6 (1963) 224–26.

——. "La représentation des guerriers perses et la notion de barbare dans la 1ère moitié du Ve siècle." *BCH* 87 (1963) 579–602.

Brommer, F. *Hephaistos: Der Schmiedegott in der antiken Kunst.* Mainz, 1978.

——. *Theseus: Die Taten des griechischen Helden in der antiken Kunst und Literatur.* Darmstadt, 1982.

Bronzeworking Centres of Western Asia. Ed. J. Curtis. London, 1988.

Brown, J. P. "Kothar, Kinyras, and Kytherea." *JSS* 10 (1965) 197–219.

Brunn, H. *Geschichte der griechischen Künstler.* 2 vols. Stuttgart, 1889.

Brunnsåker, S. *The Tyrant-Slayers of Kritios and Nesiotes.* Lund, 1955.

Bunnens, G. *L'expansion phénicienne en Méditerranée: Essai d'interpretation fondé sur les traditions littéraires.* Brussels and Rome, 1979.

Burkert, W. "Resep-Figuren, Apollon von Amyklai, und die 'Erfindung' des Opfers auf Zypern." *Grazer Beiträge* 4 (1975) 51–79.

——. *Structure and History in Greek Mythology and Ritual.* Berkeley, 1979.

——. *Die orientalisierende Epoche in der griechischen Religion und Literatur.* Heidelberg, 1984.

———. *Greek Religion of the Archaic and Classical Periods*. Cambridge, Mass., 1986.

Burnett, A. *The Art of Bacchylides*. Cambridge, Mass., 1980.

Camp, J. *The Athenian Agora*. London, 1986.

Canciani, F. *Bronze orientali e orientalizzanti a Creta nell' VIII e VII sec. a. C*. Rome, 1970.

———. *ArchHom II: N. Bildkunst, 2*. Göttingen, 1984.

Carlier, P. *La royauté en Grèce avant Alexandre*. Strasbourg, 1984.

Carter, J. B. *Greek Ivory-Carving in the Orientalizing and Archaic Periods*. New York, 1985.

———. "The Masks of Ortheia." *AJA* 91 (1987) 355–83.

———. "Masks and Poetry in Early Sparta." In *Early Greek Cult Practice*, 89–98.

———. "The Chests of Periander." *AJA* 93 (1989) 355–78.

———. *The Beginning of Greek Sculpture*. New Haven, forthcoming.

Catling, H. *Cypriote Bronze Work in the Mycenaean World*. Oxford, 1974.

———. *Cyprus and the West 1600–1050 B.C.* Ian Sanders Memorial Lecture. Sheffield, 1980.

———. "Workshop and Heirloom. Prehistoric Bronze Stands in the East Mediterranean." *RDAC* (1984) 69–91.

The Challenge of Black Athena. Ed. J. Peradotto and Molly Myerowitz Levine. *Arethusa*, Special Issue, Fall 1989.

Chantraine, F. *Dictionnaire étymologique de la langue grecque*. 4 vols. Paris, 1968–1980.

Charites. Festschrift Ernst Langlotz. Ed. K. Schauenburg. Bonn, 1957.

Chiasson, C. "The Question of Tragic Influence on Herodotus." Ph.D. diss., Yale University, 1979.

Clairmont, C. *Patrios Nomos: Public Burial in Athens during the Fifth and Fourth Centuries B.C.* 2 vols. *BARep* International Series 161. Oxford, 1983.

Coldstream, J. N. *Deities in Aegean Art*. Inaugural Lecture, Bedford College. London, 1978.

———. "Cypriaca and Cretocypriaca." *RDAC* (1984) 122–39.

———. *The Formation of the Greek Polis: Aristotle and Archaeology*. Opladen, 1984.

Colloquium Mycenaeum. Ed. E. Risch and H. Mühlestein. Geneva, 1979.

The Coming of the Age of Iron. Ed. T. A. Wertime and J. Muhly. New Haven, 1980.

Coogan, M. *Stories from Ancient Canaan*. Philadelphia, 1985.

Cook, R. M. "Origins of Greek Sculpture." *JHS* 87 (1967) 24–31.

Corchia, R. "Genealogia dedalica e scultura arcaica: Un 'canone' in forma di Mito?" *MEFRA* 93 (1981) 533–45.

Corinthiaca: Studies in Honor of D. A. Amyx. Ed. M. del Chiaro and W. Biers. Columbia, Mo., 1986.

Creta antica. Centi anni di archeologia italiana (1884–1984). Scuola Archeologica Italiana di Atene. Rome, 1984.

Curtin P. *Cross-Cultural Trade in World History*. Cambridge, 1984.

Cyprus and the Eastern Mediterranean in the Iron Age. Ed. V. Tatton-Brown. London, 1989.

Cyprus at the Close of the Bronze Age. Ed. V. Karageorghis and J. Muhly. Nicosia, 1984.

Cyprus between the Orient and the Occident. Ed. V. Karageorghis. Nicosia, 1986.

Dädalische Kunst auf Kreta im 7. Jh. v. Chr. Ed. P. Démargne. Hamburg, 1970.

Davaras, K. *Die Statue aus Astritsi. Ein Beiträg zur dädalischen Kunst auf Kreta und zu den Anfängen der griechischen Plastik*. *AK* Beiheft 8. Bern, 1972.

Delcourt, M. *Héphaistos ou la légende du magicien*. Paris, 1957.

Demargne, P. *La Crète dédalique. Études sur les origines d'une renaissance*. Paris, 1947.

Desborough, V. "The Background to Euboean Participation in Early Greek Maritime Enterprise." In *Tribute to an Antiquary: Essays Presented to Marc Fitch*, ed. F. Emmison and R. Stephens, 27–40. London, 1976.

Dinsmoor, W. "Two Monuments on the Athenian Acropolis." In Χαριστήριον εἰς Α. Κ. Ὀρλάνδος, 4:145–55. Athens, 1967–1968.

Dombrowski, B. *Der Name Europa auf seinem griechischen and altsyrischen Hintergrund*. Amsterdam, 1984.

Donohue, A. *Xoana and the Origins of Greek Sculpture*. American Classical Studies 15. Atlanta, 1988.

Drews, R. *The Greek Accounts of Eastern History*. Washington, D.C., 1973.

———. "Phoenicians, Carthage and the Spartan *Eunomia*." *AJP* 100 (1979) 45–58.

———. *Basileus: The Evidence for Kingship in Geometric Greece*. New Haven, 1983.

duBois, P. *Centaurs and Amazons: Women in the Prehistory of the Great Chain of Being*. Ann Arbor, Mich., 1982.

———. *History, Rhetorical Description and the Epic*. Cambridge, 1982.

Dunbabin, T. W. *The Western Greeks*. Oxford, 1948.

———. *The Greeks and Their Eastern Neighbors*. London, 1952.

Early Greek Cult Practice. Ed. R. Hägg, N. Marinatos, and G. Nordquist. Stockholm, 1988.

Early Metallurgy in Cyprus, 4000–500 B.C. (Larnaca 1981). Ed. J. Muhly, R. Maddin, and V. Karageorghis. Nicosia, 1982.

Ebla to Damascus: Art and Archaeology of Ancient Syria. Ed. H. Weiss. Washington, D.C., 1985.

Eckstein, F. *ArchHom II: L. Handwerk, 1. Die Aussagen des frühgriechischen Epos*. Göttingen, 1974.

Edwards, G. P. *The Language of Hesiod in Its Traditional Context*. Oxford, 1971.

Edwards, R. *Kadmos the Phoenician. A Study in Greek Legends and the Mycenaean Age*. Amsterdam, 1979.

ΕΙΛΑΠΙΝΗ. Τόμος Τιμητικὸς γιὰ τὸν Καθηγητὴ Νικόλαο Πλάτωνα. Heraklion, 1987.

Elayi, J. *Pénétration grecque en Phénicie sous l'empire perse*. Nancy, 1988.

Else, G. *The Origins and Early Form of Greek Tragedy*. Cambridge, Mass., 1965.

Erbse, H. *Scholia Graeca in Homeri Iliadem*. 7 vols. Berlin, 1969–1988.

L'espansione fenicia nel Mediteraneo. Ed. F. Barrecca and others. Rome, 1971.

Euben, J. Peter. "The Battle of Salamis and the Origins of Political Theory." *Political Theory* 14 (1986) 359–90.

Europa. Studien zur Geschichte und Epigraphik der frühen Ägäis. Festschrift für Ernst Grumach. Ed. W. Brice. Berlin, 1967.

The Eye of Greece: Studies in the Art of Athens. Ed. D. Kurtz and B. Sparkes. Cambridge, 1982.

Faraone, C. A. "Hephaestus the Magician and Near Eastern Parallels for Alcinous' Watch-Dogs." *GRBS* 28 (1987) 257–80.

Farrar, C. *The Origins of Democratic Thinking: The Invention of Politics in Classical Athens*. Cambridge, 1988.

Faure, P. *Ulysse le Crétois (XIIIe s. av. J-C.)*. Paris, 1980.

Fenik, B. *Typical Battle Scenes in the Iliad: Studies in the Narrative Technique of Homeric Battle Description*. *Hermes* Einzelschriften 21. Wiesbaden, 1968.

Fehr, B. "Zur religionspolitischen Funktion der Athena Parthenos im Rahmen des Delisch-Attischen Seebundes: II." *Hephaistos* 2 (1980) 113–25.

———. "Zur religionspolitischen Funktion der Athena Parthenos im Rahmen des Delisch-Attischen Seebundes: III." *Hephaistos* 3 (1981) 67–70.

———. "Die 'gute' und die 'schlechte' Ehefrau: Alkestis und Phaidra auf den Südmetopen des Parthenon." *Hephaistos* 4 (1982) 37–66.

Festschrift für Frank Brommer. Ed. U. Höckmann und A. Krug. Mainz, 1977.

Festschrift für Konrad Schauenburg zum 65. Geburtstag am 16.4.1986. Studien zu Mythologie und Vasenmalerei. Ed. E. Böhr and W. Martini. Mainz, 1986.

Fittschen, K. *ArchHom II: N. Bildkunst, 1. Der Schild des Achilleus.* Göttingen, 1973.

Ford, A. L. "A Study of Early Greek Terms for Poetry: 'Aoide,' 'Epos,' and 'Poiesis.' " Ph.D. diss., Yale University, 1981.

Forrest, W. G. "Themistocles and Argos." *CQ* 54 (1960) 221–41.

Francis, E. D. "Greeks and Persians: The Art of Hazard and Triumph." In *Ancient Persia*, 53–86.

———. *Image and Idea in Fifth-Century Athens: Art and Literature after the Persian Wars.* London, 1990.

Francis, E. D., and M. Vickers. "The Agora Revisited: Athenian Chronology c. 500–450 B.C." *BSA* 83 (1988) 143–63.

Frankenstein, S. "The Phoenicians in the Far West: A Function of Neo-Assyrian Imperialism." In *Power and Propaganda*, 263–94.

Freedberg, D. *The Power of Images. Studies in the History and Theory of Response.* Chicago, 1989.

Frisch, B., W.-R. Mansfeld u. Thiele. *Kamīd el-Lōz 6. Die Werkstätten der spätbronzezeitlichen Paläste.* Bonn, 1985.

Frontisi-Ducroux, F. *Dédale. Mythologie de l'artisan en Grèce ancienne.* Paris, 1975.

Fuchs, W. "Die Krieger aus Riace?" *Boreas* 4 (1981) 21–28.

———. "Zu den Grossbronzen aus Riace." In *Praestant Interna. Festschrift Ulrich Hausmann*, ed. B. von Freytag, D. Mannsperger, and F. Prayon, 34–40. Tübingen, 1982.

Gabelmann, H. *Antike Audienz- und Tribunalszenen.* Darmstadt, 1984.

Gaster, Th. *Thespis: Ritual, Myth and Drama in the Ancient Near East.* Garden City, N.Y., 1961.

Gauer, W. "Die griechischen Bildnisse der klassischen Zeit als politische und persönliche Denkmäler." *JdI* 83 (1968) 118–79.

———. *Weihgeschenke aus den Perserkriegen.* IstMitt Beiheft 2. Tübingen, 1968.

———. "Das Athenerschatzhaus und die marathonische Akrothinia in Delphi." In *Forschungen und Funde. Festschrift Bernard Neutsch*, ed. F. Krinzinger, B. Otto, E. Walde-Psenner, 127–36. Innsbruck, 1980.

———. "Parthenonische Amazonomachie und Perserkrieg." In *Kanon*, 28–41.

———. "Penelope, Hellas, und der Perserkönig." *JdI* 105 (1990) 31–65.

Gawantka, W. *Die sogenannte Polis. Entstehung, Geschichte und Kritik der modernen althistorischen Grundbegriffe der griechische Staat, die griechische Staatsidee, die Polis.* Stuttgart, 1985.

Gérard-Rousseau, M. *Les mentions religieuses dans les tablettes mycéniennes.* Incunabula Graeca 29. Rome, 1968.

Gibson, J.C.L. *Canaanite Myths and Legends.* 2d ed. Edinburgh, 1978.

Gifts to the Gods. Proceedings of the Uppsala Symposium, 1985. Ed. T. Linders and G. Nordquist. *Boreas* 15. Uppsala, 1987.

Gill, D. "Silver Anchors and Cargoes of Oil: Some Observations on Phoenician Trade in the Western Mediterranean." *BSR* 56 (1988) 1–12.

Gillis, D. *Collaboration with the Persians. Historia* Einzelschriften 34. Wiesbaden, 1979.

Gordon, C. H. "Homer and Bible: The Origin and Character of East Mediterranean Literature." *Hebrew Union College Manual* 26 (1955) 43–108.

Greek Art: Archaic into Classical. Papers presented at a symposium held at the University of Cincinnati, April 2–3, 1985. Ed. C. Boulter. Cincinnati Classical Studies 5. Leiden, 1985.

Greek Colonists and Native Populations. Proceedings of the First Australian Congress of Classical Archaeology held in honour of A. D. Trendall. Ed. J.-P. Descoeudres. Oxford, 1990.

The Greek Renaissance of the Eighth Century B.C.: Tradition and Innovation. Ed. R. Hägg. Stockholm, 1983.

Greek Tragedy and Political Theory. Ed. P. Euben. Berkeley, 1986.

Griechenland, die Ägäis und die Levante während der "Dark Ages." Papers presented at the Symposium Zwettl, 1980. Ed. S. Deger-Jalkotzsky. Vienna, 1983.

Gunter, A. "Models of the Orient in the Art History of the Orientalizing Period." In *Achaemenid History V. The Roots of the European Tradition*, Proceedings of the 1987 Groningen Achaemenid History Workshop, ed. H. Sancisi-Weerdenburg and J. Drijvers, 131–47. Leiden, 1990.

Haft, A. "The Myth That Crete Became: The Thematic Significance of Crete and Cretan Topoi in Homer's Odyssey and Vergil's Aeneid." Ph.D. diss., Princeton University, 1981.

Hall, E. *Inventing the Barbarian: Greek Self-Definition through Tragedy*. Oxford, 1989.

Hallett, C. H. "The Origins of the Classical Style in Sculpture." *JHS* 106 (1986) 71–84.

Harriott, R. *Poetry and Criticism before Homer*. London, 1969.

Harrison, E. B. "The Composition of the Amazons on the Shield of the Athena Parthenos." *Hesperia* 35 (1966) 107–33.

———. "The Nike Temple Frieze and the Marathon Painting in the Painted Stoa." *AJA* 76 (1972) 353–78.

———. "Preparations for Marathon, the Niobid Painter and Herodotus." *ArtB* 54 (1972) 390–402.

———. "Alkamenes' Sculptures for the Hephaisteion: Part I, The Cult Statues." *AJA* 81 (1977) 137–78; "Part II, The Base," 265–87; "Part III, Iconography and Style," 411–26.

———. "The Iconography of the Eponymous Heroes on the Parthenon and in the Athenian Agora." In *Greek Numismatics and Archaeology: Essays in Honor of Margaret Thompson*, ed. O. Mørkholm and N. Waggoner, 71–85. Wetteren, 1979.

Hartog, F. *The Mirror of Herodotus: The Representation of the Other in the Writing of History*. Trans. J. Lloyd. The New Historicism. Studies in Cultural Poetics 5. Berkeley, 1988.

Hausmann, U. "Akropolisscherbe und Eurymedonkämpfe." In *Charites*, 144–51.

Hausmann, U., ed. *Der Tübinger Waffenläufer*. Tübingen, 1972.

Helck, W. *Beziehungen Ägyptens zu Vorderasien im 4. und 3. Jt. v. Chr.* Wiesbaden, 1971.

Helm, P. R. " 'Greeks' in the Neo-Assyrian Levant and 'Assyria' in Early Greek Writers." Ph.D. diss., University of Pennsylvania, 1980.

Herbert, S. "The Torch-Race at Corinth." In *Corinthiaca*, 29–35.

Herington, J. *Poetry into Drama: Early Tragedy and the Greek Poetic Tradition*. Berkeley, 1985.

Herter, H. "Theseus der Athener." *RhM* 88 (1939) 244–326.

Hodges, R. *Dark Age Economics: The Origins of Towns and Trade A.D. 600–1000.* London, 1987.

Hoekstra, A. *Epic Verse before Homer: Three Studies.* Amsterdam, 1981.

Hoffmann, H., with A. Raubitschek. *Early Cretan Armorers.* Fogg Art Museum Monographs in Art and Archaeology 1. Mainz, 1972.

Holloway, R. *Italy and the Aegean 3000–700 B.C.* Archaeologica Transatlantica I. Louvain-la-Neuve, 1981.

Hölscher, T. *Griechische Historienbilder des 5. u. 4. Jahrhunderts v. Chr.* Beiträge zur Archäologie 6. Würzburg, 1973.

Householder, F., and G. Nagy. *Greek: A Survey of Recent Work.* The Hague, 1972.

Hurwit, J. *The Art and Culture of Early Greece, 1100–480 B.C.* Ithaca, N.Y., 1985.

Immerwahr, H. "*Ergon*: History as a Monument in Herodotus and Thucydides." *AJP* 81 (1960) 261–90.

———. *Form and Thought in Herodotus.* American Philological Association Monographs 23. Cleveland, 1966.

In Memoriam Otto J. Brendel: Essays in Archaeology and the Humanities. Ed. L. Bonfante and H. von Heintze. Mainz, 1976.

Interpretations of Greek Mythology. Ed. J. Bremmer. London, 1987.

Jacoby, F. *Atthis: The Local Chronicles of Ancient Athens.* Oxford, 1947.

Jenkins, R.J.H. *Dedalica: A Study of Dorian Plastic Art in the Seventh Century.* Cambridge, 1936.

Jouanna, J. "Les causes de la défaite des barbares chez Eschyle, Hérodote et Hippocrate." *Ktema* 6 (1981) 3–15.

Kanon. Festschrift Ernst Berger zum 60. Geburtstag am 26. Februar 1988. Ed. M. Schmidt. *AK* Beiheft 15. Basel, 1988.

Kanta, A. *The Late Minoan III Period of Crete.* SIMA 58. Göteborg, 1980.

Kantor, H. *The Aegean and the Orient in the Second Millennium B.C.* Bloomington, Ind., 1947.

Kassel, R. "Dialoge mit Statuen." *ZPE* 51 (1983) 1–12.

Kaulen, G. *Daidalika. Werkstätten griechischer Kleinplastik des 7. Jh. v. Chr.* Munich 1967.

Kierdorf, W. *Erlebnis und Darstellung der Perserkriege. Studien zu Simonides, Pindar, Aischylos und den attischen Redern.* Hypomnemata 16. Göttingen, 1966.

Knapp, A. B. "Alashiya, Caphtor/Keftiu and Eastern Mediterranean Trade." *JFA* 12 (1985) 231–50.

———. *Copper Production and Divine Protection. Archaeology, Ideology, and Social Complexity on Bronze Age Cyprus.* Göteborg, 1986.

Kokalakis, M. "The Iconography of Icarus." In *Concilium Eirene* 16, ed. P. Oliva and A. Frolíková, 2:25–30. Prague, 1983.

———. "Οἱ Κρῆτες τοῦ Εὐριπίδου καὶ ἡ ἰκωνογραφία τοῦ Ἰκάρου." In *XII. International Congress of Classical Archaeology*, ed. A. Delivorrias and others, 116–20. Athens, 1988.

Konstan, D. "Persians, Greeks and Empire." *Arethusa* 20 (1987) 59–73.

Kris, E., and O. Kurz. *Legend, Myth and Magic in the Image of the Artist.* New Haven, 1979.

Kron, U. *Die zehn attischen Phylenheroen. Geschichte, Mythos, Kult, und Darstellungen.* AthMitt Beiheft 5. Berlin, 1976.

Lacroix, L. "Ikmalios." In *Hommages à W. Déonna*, 309–21. Collection Latomus 28. Brussels, 1957.

Lang, M. "Herodotus and the Ionian Revolt." *Historia* 17 (1968) 24–36.

Lefkandi I: The Iron Age. Ed. M. R. Popham, L. H. Sackett, and P. G. Themelis. BSA suppl. 11. London, 1979.

Lembesi, A. Οἱ Στῆλες τοῦ Πρινιᾶ. Athens, 1976.

―――. Τό Ἱερό τοῦ Ἑρμη καί τῆς Ἀφροδίτης στή Σύμη Βιάννου. I: Χαλκινά κρητικά τορευματα (I). Athens, 1985.

Leumann, M. *Homerische Wörter*. Basel, 1950.

Lloyd, A. B. *Herodotus Book Two. An Introduction*. EPRO 43. Leiden, 1975.

Loraux, N. *Les enfants d'Athèna. Idées athéniennes sur la citoyenneté et la division des sexes*. Paris, 1981.

―――. *The Invention of Athens: The Funeral Oration in the Classical City*. Trans. A. Sheridan. Cambridge, Mass., 1986.

Lorimer, H. L. *Homer and the Monuments*. London, 1950.

Magen, U. *Assyrische Königsdarstellungen—Aspekte der Herrschaft. Eine Typologie*. Mainz, 1986.

Magia. Studi di storia delle religioni in memoria di Raffaela Gariosi. Ed. P. Xella. Rome, 1976.

Manni, E. "Sémites et Grecs en Sicilie jusqu'au Vème siècle." *Bulletin de l'Association Guillaume Budé* (1974) 63–84.

Markoe, G. *Phoenician Bronze and Silver Bowls from Cyprus and the Mediterranean*. University of California Classical Studies 26. Berkeley, 1985.

Mattusch, C. "The Berlin Foundry Cup: The Casting of Greek Bronze Sculpture in the Early Fifth Century B.C." *AJA* 84 (1980) 435–44.

Meier, C. *Die Entstehung des Politischen bei den Griechen*. Frankfurt, 1980.

Meiggs, R. *The Athenian Empire*. Oxford, 1972.

Mélanges Syriens Offerts à René Dussaud. Paris, 1939.

Merkelbach, R. "Gefesselte Götter." *Antaios* 12 (1971) 549–65.

Mesopotamien und seine Nachbarn. Politische und kulturelle Wechselbeziehungen im alten Vorderasien vom 4. bis 1. Jt. v. Chr. Ed. H.-J. Nissen and J. Renger. Berliner Beiträge zum Vorderen Orient 1. Berlin, 1980.

Metallogenetic Map of Greece. K. Zachos and M. Maratos. Athens: I.G.M.E., 1965; Explanatory Volume (Athens: I.G.M.E., 1973). In Greek.

Metzler, D. *Porträt und Gesellschaft: Über die Entstehung des griechischen Porträts in der klassischen Kunst*. Münster, 1971.

Meyer, H. *Kunst und Geschichte. Zur antiken Historienkunst*. Münchener Archäologische Studien 4. Munich, 1983.

Miller, M. C. "Perserie: The Arts of the East in Fifth-Century Athens." Ph.D. diss., Harvard University, 1985. Abstract: *HSCP* 90 (1986) 254–55.

―――. "Midas as the Great King in Attic Fifth-Century Vase-Painting." *AK* 31 (1988) 79–89.

The Minoan Thalassocracy: Myth or Reality? Ed. R. Hägg and N. Marinatos. Stockholm, 1984.

Morris, S. *The Black and White Style: Athens and Aigina in the Orientalizing Period*. Yale Classical Monographs 6. New Haven, 1984.

―――. "Daidalos and Kadmos: Classicism and 'Orientalism.' " In *The Challenge of* Black Athena, 39–54.

―――. "Greece and the Levant." *JMA* 3, no. 1 (1990) 57–66.

Muhly, J. "Homer and the Phoenicians: The Relations between Greece and the Near East in the Late Bronze and Early Iron Ages." *Berytus* 19 (1970) 19–64.

Murnaghan, S. *Disguise and Recognition in the Odyssey*. Princeton, 1987.

The Mycenaeans in the Eastern Mediterranean. Acts of the International Symposium. Ed. V. Karageorghis. Nicosia, 1973.

Nagler, M. *Spontaneity and Tradition: A Study in the Oral Art of Homer*. Berkeley, 1974.

Nagy, G. *The Best of the Achaeans: Concepts of the Hero in Archaic Greek Art and Poetry*. Baltimore, 1979.

Naveh, J. *The Early History of the Alphabet: An Introduction to West Semitic Epigraphy and Palaeography*. Jerusalem, 1982.

Negbi, O. "The Continuity of the Canaanite Bronzework of the Late Bronze Age into the Early Iron Age." *Tel Aviv* 1 (1974) 159–72.

————. *Canaanite Gods in Metal: An Archaeological Study of Ancient Syro-Palestinian Figurines*. Tel Aviv, 1979.

————. "Evidence for Early Phoenician Communities in the East Mediterranean Islands." *Levant* 14 (1982) 179–82.

————. "Levantine Elements in the Sacred Architecture of the Aegean." *BSA* 83 (1988) 339–57.

Neils, J. *The Youthful Deeds of Theseus*. Rome, 1987.

Niemeyer, H.-G. "Die Phönizier im Mittelmeer im Zeitalter Homers." *JRGZM* 31 (1984) 1–94.

Nilsson, M. *The Mycenaean Origin of Greek Mythology*. Rev. ed. Berkeley, 1972.

Nouvelle contribution à l'étude de la société et de la colonisation eubéenne. Cahiers du Centre Jean Bérard 6. Naples, 1981.

Oliver. J. *Demokratia, the Gods and the Free World*. Baltimore, 1960.

Orient and Occident: Essays Presented to Cyrus H. Gordon on the Occasion of His Seventy-fifth Birthday. Ed. H. Hoffner, Jr. Neukirchen, 1973.

Overbeck, J. A. *Die antiken Schriftquellen zur Geschichte der bildenden Künste bei den Griechen*. Leipzig, 1868.

Parry, M. *The Making of Homeric Verse: The Collected Papers of Milman Parry*. Ed. A. Parry. Oxford, 1987.

Parthenon-Kongress Basel: Referate und Berichte. 2 vols. Ed. E. Berger. Mainz, 1984.

Pearson, L. *The Greek Historians of the West: Timaeus and His Predecessors*. Atlanta, 1987.

Pernicka, E. "Erzlägerstätten in der Ägäis und ihre Ausbeutung im Altertum—Geochemische Untersuchungen zur Herkunftsbestimmung archäologischer Metallobjekte." *JRGZM* 34, no. 2 (1987) 607–714.

ΦΙΛΙΑ ΕΠΗ εἰς Γ. Ε. Μυλῶνα διὰ τὰ 60 Ἔτη τοῦ Ἀνασκαφικοῦ τοῦ Ἔργου. Athens, 1987.

Philipp, H. *Tektonon Daidala. Die Geschichte des Künstlers in vor-platonischer Zeit*. Berlin, 1968.

The Phoenicians. Ed. S. Moscati. Milan, 1988.

Phönizier im Westen. Ed. H.-G. Niemeyer. *MadrMitt* Beiheift 8. Madrid, 1982.

Photos, E. "Early Extractive Iron Metallurgy in Northern Greece: A Unified Approach to Regional Archaeometallurgy." Ph.D. diss., University of London, 1987.

Picard, O. *Les Grecs devant la ménace perse*. Paris, 1980.

Pollitt, J.J. *The Art of Greece: Sources and Documents*. Englewood Cliffs, N.J., 1965.

Pollitt, J.J. *Art and Experience in Classical Greece*. Cambridge, 1972.

―――. *The Ancient View of Greek Art: Criticism, History and Terminology*. Yale Publications in the History of Art 26. New Haven, 1974.

―――. "Pots, Politics and Personifications in Early Classical Athens." *YUAG Bulletin* (Spring 1987) 8–17.

Poulsen, F. *Der Orient und die frühgriechische Kunst*. Leipzig, 1912.

Power and Propaganda: A Symposium on Ancient Empires. Ed. M. T. Larsen. Mesopotamia 7. Copenhagen, 1979.

Prehistoric Production and Exchange: The Aegean and the Eastern Mediterranean. Ed. A. B. Knapp and T. Stech. UCLA Institute of Archaeology Monograph 25. Los Angeles, 1982.

Preisshofen, F. "Phidias-Daedalus auf dem Schild der Athena Parthenos? Ampelius 8, 10." *JdI* 89 (1974) 50–69.

Primo Congresso Internazionale del Micenologia (Atti e Memorie). Ed. C. Gavalotti. Incunabula Graeca 25. Rome, 1967.

Prinz, F. *Gründungsmythen und Sagenchronologie*. Zetemata 72. Munich, 1979.

Problems in Greek Prehistory: Papers Presented at the Centenary Conference of the British School of Archaeology at Athens, Manchester, April 1986. Ed. E. French and K. Wardle. Bristol, 1988.

Pucci, P. *Hesiod and the Language of Poetry*. Baltimore, 1977.

Puech, E. "Présence phénicienne dans les îles à la fin du IIᵉ. millénaire." *RB* 90 (1983) 365–95.

The Quest for Theseus. Ed. A. Ward. New York, 1970.

Raaflaub, K. *Die Entdeckung der Freiheit. Zur historischen Semantik und Gesellschaftsgeschichte eines politischen Grundbegriffes der Griechen*. Vestigia 37. Munich, 1985.

Raubitschek, A. *Dedications from the Athenian Acropolis*. Cambridge, Mass., 1949.

Redfield, J. *Nature and Culture in the Iliad: The Tragedy of Hector*. Chicago, 1975.

Reinach, A. *Recueil Milliet. Textes grecs et latins relatifs à l'histoire de la peinture ancienne*. Paris, 1921.

The Relations between Cyprus and Crete, 2000–500 B.C. Acts of the International Archaeological Symposium. Ed. V. Karageorghis. Nicosia. 1979.

Renfrew, C., and others. *The Archaeology of Cult: The Sanctuary at Phylakopi*. BSA suppl. 18. London, 1985.

Richter, G. M.A. *Korai: Archaic Greek Maidens. A Study of the Development of the Kore Type in Greek Sculpture*. New York, 1968.

―――. *Kouroi: A Study of the Greek Kouros Type from the Late Seventh to the Early Fifth Century B.C.* 3d ed. New York, 1970.

Ridgway, B. *The Severe Style in Greek Sculpture*. Princeton, 1970.

―――. *The Archaic Style in Greek Sculpture*. Princeton, 1977.

Rizza, G., and V. Santa Maria Scrinari. *Il santuario sull'acropoli di Gortina*. Vol. 1. Rome, 1968.

Robert, C. *Archäologische Märchen aus alter und neuer Zeit*. Berlin, 1886.

Robertson, M. *A History of Greek Art*. 2 vols. Cambridge, 1977.

―――. "Two Question-Marks on the Parthenon." In *Studies in Classical Art and Archaeology*, 78–87.

―――. "The South Metopes: Theseus and Daidalos." In *Parthenon-Kongress Basel*, 206–8.

Robertson, N. "The Collective Burial of Fallen Soldiers at Athens, Sparta and Elsewhere: 'Ancestral Custom' and Modern Misunderstanding." *EchCl* 27 (1983) 78–92.

Roisman, J. "On Phrynichos' *Sack of Miletus* and *Phoinissai*." *Eranos* 86 (1988) 15–23.

Romano, I. "Early Greek Cult Images." Ph. D. diss., University of Pennsylvania, 1980.

Root, M. C. *The King and Kingship in Achaemenid Art: Essays on the Creation of an Iconography of Empire*. Acta Iranica 9. Leiden, 1979.

———. "The Parthenon Frieze and the Apadana Reliefs at Persepolis: Reassessing a Programmatic Relationship." *AJA* 89 (1985) 103–20.

Rosivach, V. "Autochthony and the Athenians." *CQ* 27 (1987) 294–306.

Ruigh, C. J. *Études sur la grammaire et le vocabulaire du Grec mycénien*. Amsterdam, 1967.

Rumpf, A. "Daidalos." *BonnJbb* 135 (1930) 74–83.

Said, E. *Orientalism*. New York, 1979.

Sakellarakis, I. *L' Antro Ideo. Cento anni di attività archeologica (1884–1984)*. Rome, 1985.

Salamine de Chypre. Ed. M. Yon. Paris, 1980.

Sanctuaries and Cults of the Aegean Bronze Age. Ed. R. Hägg and N. Marinatos. Stockholm, 1984.

Sandars, N. *The Sea Peoples: Warriors of the Ancient Mediterranean 1250–1150 B.C.* London, 1978.

Saxonhouse, A. "Myths and the Origins of Cities: Reflections on the Autochthony Theme in Euripides' *Ion*." In *Greek Tragedy and Political Theory*, 252–73.

Schachermeyr, F. *Poseidon und die Entstehung des griechischen Götterglaubens*. Munich, 1950.

———. *Die griechische Rückerinnerung im Lichte neuer Forschungen*. Vienna, 1983.

Schachter, A. *The Cults of Boiotia*. BICS suppl. 38. London, 1981–1986.

Schanz, H. "Greek Sculptural Groups: Archaic and Classical." Ph.D. diss., Harvard University, 1969.

Shapiro, H. A. "Theseus, Athens and Troizen." *AA* (1982) 291–97.

———. "The Origins of Allegory in Greek Art." *Boreas* 9 (1986) 4–23.

———. *Art and Cult under the Tyrants of Athens*. Mainz, 1989.

———. "Oracle-Mongers in Peisistratid Athens." *Kernos* 3 (1990) 335–45.

Simon, E. "Polygnotan Painting and the Niobid Painter." *AJA* 67 (1963) 43–62.

———. "Versuch einer Deutung der Südmetopen des Parthenon." *JdI* 90 (1975) 101–20.

———. "Early Classical Vase Painting." In *Greek Art: Archaic into Classical*, 66–82.

———. "Satyr Plays on Vases in the Time of Aeschylus." In *Eye of Greece*, 122–48.

Sjöqvist, E. *Sicily and the Greeks: Studies in the Interrelationships between the Indigeneous Populations and the Greek Colonists*. Ann Arbor, Mich. 1973.

Smith, M. S. "Kothar-wa-Hasis. The Ugaritic Craftsman God." Ph.D. diss., Yale University, 1985.

Smith, W. Stevenson. *Interconnections in the Ancient Near East*. New Haven, 1965.

Society and Economy in the Eastern Mediterranean c. 1500–1000 B.C. Ed. M. Heltzer and E. Lipiński. OLA 23. Leuven, 1988.

Stambolides, N. "Eleutherna on Crete: An Interim Report on the Geometric-Archaic Cemetery." *BSA* 85 (1990) 375–403.

Stansbury-O'Donnell, M. "Polygnotos' *Iliupersis*: A New Reconstruction." *AJA* 93 (1989) 203–15.

———. "Polygnotos' *Nekyia*: A Reconstruction and Analysis." *AJA* 94 (1990) 213–35.

State and Temple Economy in the Ancient Near East. Ed. E. Lipiński. Leuven, 1979.

ΣΤΗΛΗ. Τόμος εἰς μνήμην Νικολάον Κοντολέοντος. Ed. N. Zapheiropoulos and others. Athens, 1980.

Stella, L. *Tradizione Micenea e Poesia dell' Iliade*. Rome, 1978.

Stewart, A. *Greek Sculpture: An Exploration*. New Haven, 1990.

Strange, J. F. *Caphtor/Keftiu: A New Investigation*. Leiden, 1980.

Strasser, F. *Zu den Iterata der frühgriechischen Epik*. Beiträge zur klassischen Philologie 156. Königstein/Ts, 1984.

Studia Phoenicia, vol. 3: *Phoenicia and Its Neighbours*. Ed. E. Gubel and E. Lipiński. Leuven 1985.

Studia Phoenicia, vol. 4: *Religio Phoenicia*. Ed. C. Bonnet, E. Lipiński, and P. Marchetti. Namur, 1986.

Studia Phoenicia, vol. 5: *Phoenicia and the Eastern Mediterranean in the First Millennium B.C.* Ed. E. Lipiński. Leuven, 1987.

Studia Phoenicia, vol. 6: *Carthago*. Ed. E. Lipiński. Leuven, 1988.

Studies in Classical Art and Archaeology: A Tribute to Peter H. von Blanckenhagen. Ed. G. Kopke and M. Moore. Locust Valley, N.Y., 1979.

Studies in Greek, Semitic and Indo-European Languages in Honor of Leonard Palmer on the Occasion of His Seventieth Birthday. Ed. A. M. Davies and W. Meid. Innsbruck, 1976.

Studies in Sardinian Archaeology, vol. 1. Ed. M. S. Balmuth and R. J. Rowlands, Jr. Ann Arbor, Mich., 1984.

Studies in Sardinian Archaeology, vol. 2: *Sardinia in the Mediterranean*. Ed. M. S. Balmuth. Ann Arbor, Mich., 1986.

Studies in Sardinian Archaeology, vol. 3: *Nuraghic Sardinia and the Mycenaean World*. Ed. M. S. Balmuth. *BARep* International Series 387. Oxford, 1987.

Studies Presented to Sterling Dow on His Eightieth Birthday. Ed. A. L. Boegehold and others. *GRBS* Monograph 40 (1984).

Stupperich, R. "Staatsbegräbnis und Privatdenkmal im klassischen Athen." Ph. D. diss., Münster, 1977.

Sutton, D. *The Greek Satyr Play*. Meissenheim am Glan, 1980.

Svenbro, J. *La parole et le marbre: Aux origines de la poétique grecque*. Lund, 1976.

Symposia Celebrating the Seventy-Fifth Anniversary of the Founding of ASOR (1900–1975). Ed. F. M. Cross. Cambridge, Mass., 1979.

La Syrie au Bronze Récent. Recueil publié à l'occasion du cinquantenaire de la découverte d'Ougarit–Ras Shamra. Ed. M. Yon. Extraits de la 27e. Rencontre Assyriologique Internationale. Paris, 1982.

Taylor, M. *The Tyrant Slayers: The Heroic Image in Fifth-century Athenian Art and Politics*. New York, 1981.

Teixidor, J. *The Pagan God*. Princeton, 1977.

Temples and High Places in Biblical Times. Ed. A. Biran. Jerusalem, 1981.

Temples et Sanctuaries. Ed. M. Yon. Lyon, 1984.

Thalmann, W. *Conventions of Form and Thought in Early Greek Poetry*. Baltimore, 1984.

Thébert, Y. "Refléxions sur l'utilisation du concept d'étranger: Evolution et fonction de l'image du Barbare à Athènes à l'époque classique." *Diogène* 112 (1980) 96–115.

Thomas, E. *Mythos und Geschichte. Untersuchugen zum historischen Gehalt griechischer Mythosdarstellungen*. Cologne, 1976.

Thompson, D. B. "The Persian Spoils in Athens." In *Aegean and the Near East*, 281–91.

Thompson, M. L. "The Monumental and Literary Evidence for Programmatic Painting in Antiquity." *Marsyas* 9 (1960–1961) 36–77.

Tölle-Kastenbein, R. "Bemerkungen zur absoluten Chronologie spätarchaischer und frühklassischer Denkmäler Athens." *AA* (1983) 573–84.

Tyrrell, Wm. Blake. *Amazons: A Study in Athenian Mythmaking*. Baltimore, 1984.

Van Effenterre, H. *La cîté grecque des origines à la défaite de Marathon*. Paris, 1985.

Verbruggen. H. *Le Zeus Crétois*. Paris, 1981.

Vermeule, E. "Kadmos and the Dragon." In *Studies Presented to G.M.A. Hanfmann*. Ed. D. G. Mitten, J. G. Pedley, and J. A. Scott, 177–88. Fogg Museum Monographs in Art and Archaeology 2. Mainz, 1971.

———. *Greece in the Bronze Age*. Rev. ed. Chicago, 1972.

———. *Aspects of Death in Early Greek Art and Poetry*. Berkeley, 1979.

———. "Priam's Castle Blazing." In *Troy and the Trojan War*, ed. M. Mellink. A Symposium Held at Bryn Mawr College, October 1984. Bryn Mawr, 1986.

Vernant, J. *Myth and Society in Ancient Greece*. Trans. J. Lloyd. London, 1972.

Vickers, M. "Persepolis, Vitruvius, and the Erechtheum Caryatids: The Iconography of Medism and Servitude." *RA* (1985) 3–28.

Völcker-Janssen, W. "Klassische Paradeigmata. Die Gemälde des Panainos im Zeustempel von Olympia." *Boreas* 10 (1987) 11–31.

Wachsmann, S. *Aegeans in the Theban Tombs*. Louvain, 1987.

Waldbaum, J. *From Bronze to Iron in the Eastern Mediterranean: The Transition from the Bronze Age to the Iron Age in the Eastern Mediterranean*. SIMA 54. Göteborg, 1978.

Walser, G. *Hellas und Iran. Studien zu den griechisch-persischen Beziehungen vor Alexander*. Erträge der Forschung 109. Darmstadt, 1984.

Wandlungen. Studien zur älteren und neueren Kunst Ernst Homann-Wedeking gewidmet. Ed. I. Scheibler and H. Wrede. Wald-Sassen Bayern, 1975.

Warner, M. *Monuments and Maidens: The Allegory of the Female Form*. New York, 1985.

Warren, P. "Circular Platforms at Minoan Knossos." *BSA* 79 (1984) 307–23.

Weinfeld, M. " 'Justice' and 'Righteousness' in Ancient Israel against the Background of Social Reforms in Israel and the Ancient Near East." In *Mesopotamien und seine Nachbarn*, 2: 491–519.

Wells, P. *Culture Contact and Culture Change: Early Iron Age Europe and the Mediterranean World*. Cambridge, 1980.

———. *Farms, Villages and Cities: Commerce and Urban Origins in Late Prehistoric Europe*. Ithaca, N.Y., 1984.

Wertime, T. "The Furnace and the Goat." *JFA* 10 (1983) 445–52.

West, M. L. *Hesiod* Theogony. Oxford, 1966.

———. *Early Greek Philosophy and the Orient*. Oxford, 1971.

———. *The Hesiodic Catalogue of Women: Its Nature, Structure and Origins*. Oxford, 1985.

———. "The Rise of the Greek Epic." *JHS* 108 (1988) 151–72.

West, W. C., III. "The Monuments of the Persian Wars." *CP* 64 (1969) 7–19.

———. "Saviors of Greece." *GRBS* 11 (1970) 271–82.

Western Cyprus: Connections. An Archaeological Symposium. Ed. D. Rupp. SIMA 57. Göteborg, 1987.

Wiesner, J. "Der Künstlergott Hephaistos und seine aussergriechischen Beziehungen in kretisch-mykenischer Zeit." *AA* (1968) 167–73.

Williams, D. "The Antiphon Painter and the Battle of Marathon." In *Festschrift Schauenburg*, 75–81.

———. "Aegina, Aphaia-Temple XI: The Pottery from the Second Limestone Temple and the Later History of the Sanctuary." *AA* (1987) 629–80.

Woodhead, A. G. *The Greeks in the West*. London, 1962.

INDEX OF ANCIENT SOURCES

GENERAL INDEX

Illustrations

1. Hephaistos, Thetis, and the arms of Achilles, 480–470 B.C. Interior of red-figure cup by the Foundry Painter, from Vulci. D. .305 m. Berlin F 2294. (For exterior, see figures 58a, b.)

2. Young helmet-maker, ca. 480 B.C. Red-figure cup by the Antiphon Painter, from Orvieto. D. .243 m. Oxford G.267 (ex-Bourguignon).

4. Manufacture of the chest for Danae and Perseus, ca. 490 B.C. Red-figure hydria by the Gallatin Painter, from Gela. H. .417 m. Boston MFA 13.200.

3. Hephaistos, Thetis, and the arms of Achilles, ca. 470 B.C. Red-figure Nolan amphora by the Dutuit Painter. H. .342 m. Boston MFA 13.188.

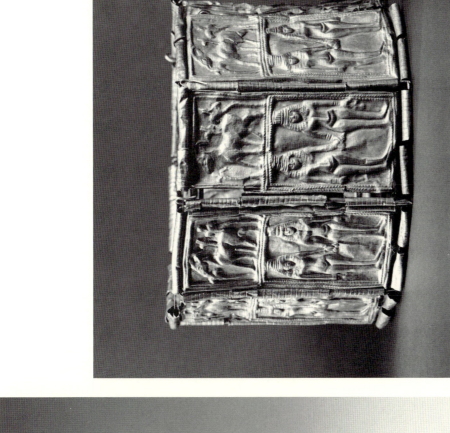

6. Gold crown, Syrian or Phoenician, late second millennium B.C. H. .116 m. Baltimore 57.968.

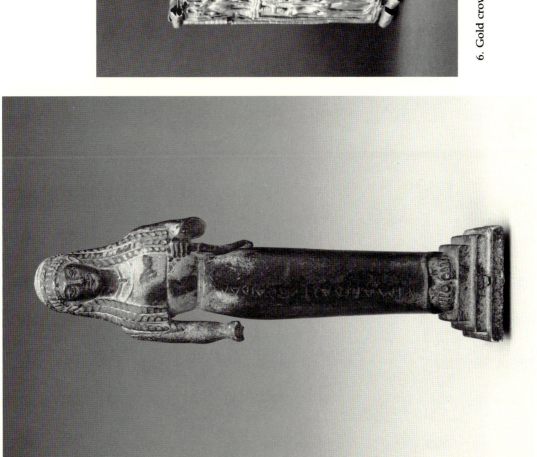

5. Lakonian bronze statuette, ca. 525 B.C. From Mazi (Elis). H. .191 m. Boston MFA 98.658.

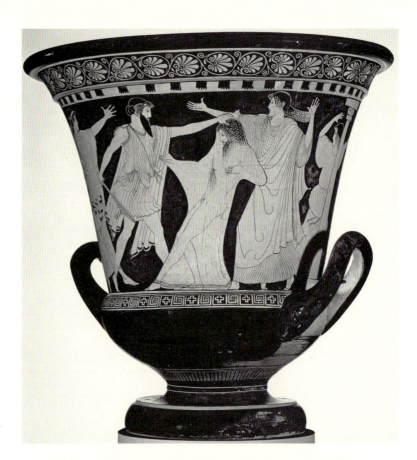

7a, b. Death of Agamemnon (a), and death of Aigisthos (b), ca. 470 B.C. Red-figure calyx-krater by the Dokimasia Painter. H. .51 m. Boston MFA 63.1246.

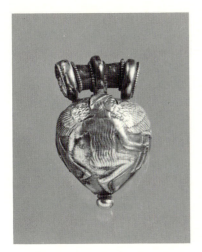

8a, b. Daidalos (ΤΑΙΤΛΕ) and Ikaros (VIKAPE) in flight, 475–450 B.C.
Etruscan gold bulla. H. .04 m, D. .024 m. Baltimore 57.371.

9. Birth of Athena, with Hephaistos; Ikaros, ca. 560 B.C. Fragments of black-figure vase
by the Painter of Akropolis 601, from Athens. Akropolis 601.

10a

10b

10. Theseus, Ariadne, and the Minotaur (a); Athenian youths and maidens (b); rider: Minos or Daidalos? (c); in flight: Daidolos or Ikaros? (d), ca. 540 B.C. Black-figure skyphos ("Rayet skyphos") from Tanagra, Boiotia. H. .115 m., D. (rim) .164, (foot) .087 m. Louvre MN 675.

10c

10d

11. Daidalos fights Ares before enthroned Hera, late fourth century B.C.
Phlyax vase from Bari. H. .378 m. London F 269.

12. Daidalos fastening wings on Ikaros, 420–400
B.C. Apulian skyphos fragment. Oxford 1922.208.

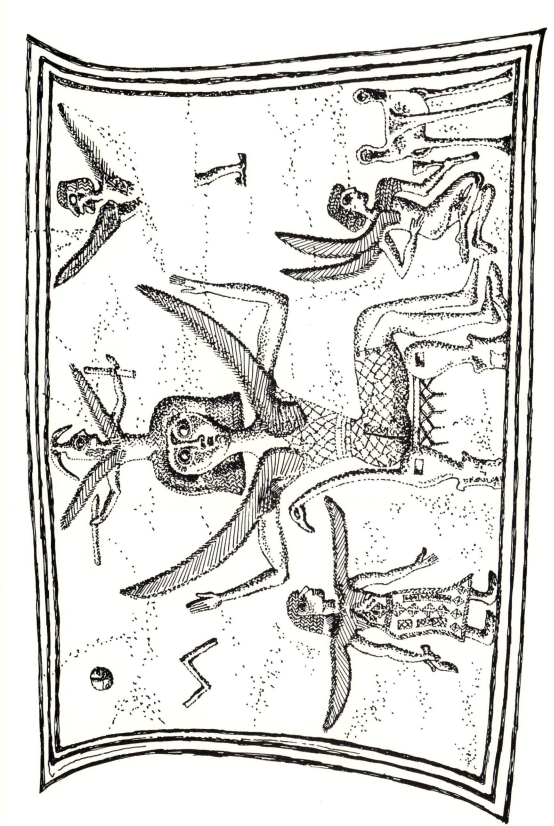

13. **Birth of Athena from the head of Zeus, with winged artist-attendants, seventh century B.C. Neck scene on relief pithos from Tenos. Drawing by Deborah Nourse Lattimore.**

14a. View of neck of relief pithos from Tenos with birth of Athena (figure 13).

14c. Female attendant to left of throne, with sickle or knife: Eileithyia?

14b. Central figure on throne (Zeus?), giving birth to Athena.

14d. Winged figure to upper right of birth scene: Daidalos or Ikaros?

14e. Winged assistant seated at cauldron, to right of birth scene: Hephaistos or Daidalos?

16. Egyptianizing cylinder seal, fourteenth century B.C. From Beth Shean, Israel. Drawing by Deborah Nourse Lattimore.

15. Egyptianizing cylinder seal, second millennium B.C. From Byblos. H. .05 m. Drawing by Deborah Nourse Lattimore.

17. Phoenician gilded silver bowl, eighth
century B.C. From Idalion, Cyprus. D. .185 m.
Louvre, AO 20134.

18. Achilles and Penthesilea (restored drawing),
seventh century B.C. Terracotta shield from
votive deposit on akropolis of Tiryns.
D. ca. .38 m.

19a, b. Animal sacrifice, worship before altars with horns of consecration (above), and libations of liquid, lyre music, and offerings to dead (statue, tomb) (below), thirteenth century B.C. (Late Minoan III). Hagia Triada sarcophagus, Crete. H. .895 m., L. 1.375–85 m., W. 45 m.

20. Limestone statue of man wearing bull's head, sixth century B.C. From Golgoi, Cyprus. H. .435 m. (mask .205 m.). Louvre AM 2758.

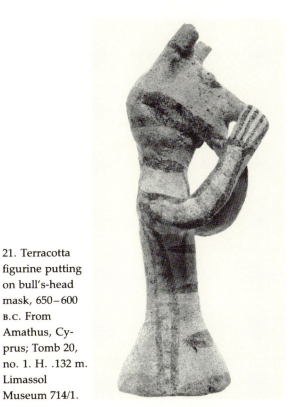

21. Terracotta figurine putting on bull's-head mask, 650–600 B.C. From Amathus, Cyprus; Tomb 20, no. 1. H. .132 m. Limassol Museum 714/1.

22. Terracotta figurine of ram-headed god (Baal-Hammon? 600–550 B.C. From archaic sanctuary at Meniko (Litharkes), Cyprus. H. .185 m. Nicosia M.L. 1952/S83.

23a. Wheel-made terracotta statuette of "hermaphrodite," sixth century B.C. From Ayia Irini, Cyprus. H. .362 m. Stockholm A.I. 2316.

23b. Wheel-made terracotta statuette of warrior, sixth century B.C. From Ayia Irini, Cyprus. H. .353 m. Stockholm A.I. 1276.

24a, b. Terracotta votive statues in situ around altar at Ayia Irini, Cyprus, sixth century B.C.

25. Syrian bronze mold-made plaque (nose or chest piece) from horse harness made for King Haza'el of Damascus, ninth century B.C. From sanctuary of Hera on Samos in a late sixth-century context. L. .273 m., W. .175 m.

26. Ivory lion's head, eighth to seventh century B.C. From Thasos. H. .05 m.

27. Marble leaf drum in Aeolic style, sixth century B.C. From Thasos. D. .313–.22 m. Thasos 1385.

28. Unfinished marble statue of ram bearer, early sixth century B.C. From quarries on Thasos. H. 3.5 m.

29. Limestone capital, seventh century B.C. From Arkades, Crete. Lower D. .247 m.

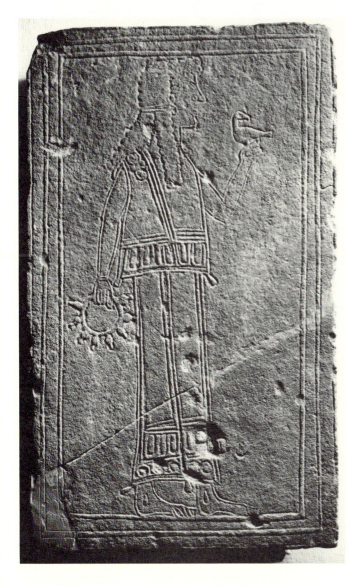

30. Limestone frieze of horsemen, seventh century B.C. From temple at Prinias, Crete. H. .84 m. Heraklion 232.

31. Limestone stele with maiden holding wreath, bird, seventh century B.C. From Prinias, Crete. H. .485 m. Heraklion 396.

32. Two winged demons confronting each other, below sun disk in crescent, ninth or eighth century B.C. Basalt stele found at Aleppo, Syria. H. .95 m, W. .131 m. Aleppo 9955.

33. Bronze helmet with pair of winged young men, snakes, late seventh century B.C. From Crete, said to be from Arkades. H. of helmet .21 m. New York L. 1979.49.2.

34. Black-glazed sherd with graffito scene of "goblins" in workshop, last quarter of fifth century B.C. From workshop of Pheidias, Olympia. Pres. W. .115 m.

35a, b. Archaic bronze kouros, "Daedalic" style, ca. 600 B.C. From Delphi. H. .197 m.

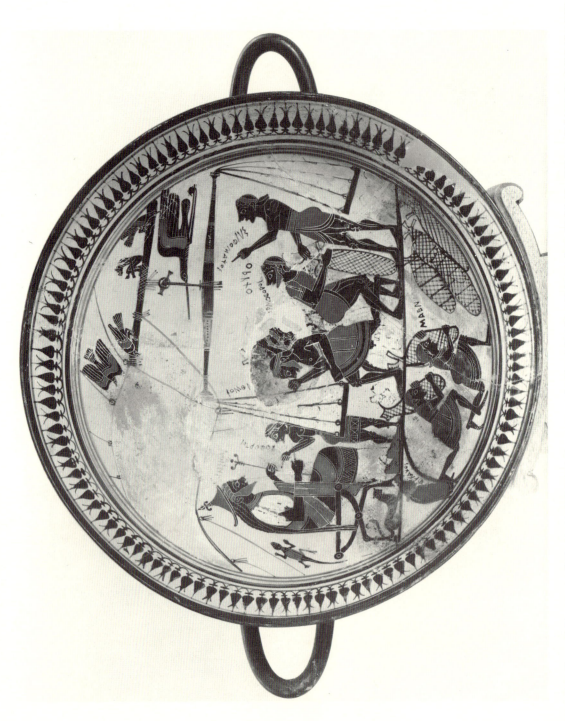

36. King Arkesilaos of Cyrene on diphros, ca. 560 B.C. Lakonian cup by the Arkesilaos Painter, from Vulci. D. .293 m. Cabinet des Médailles 189.

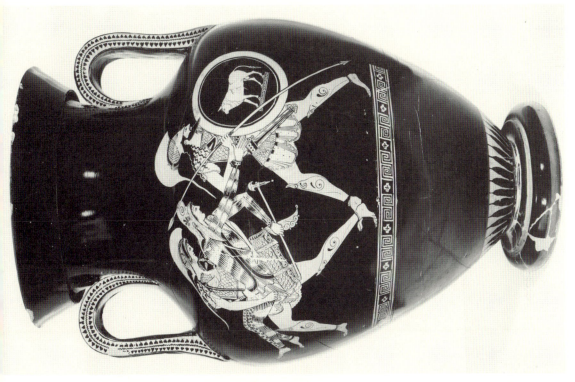

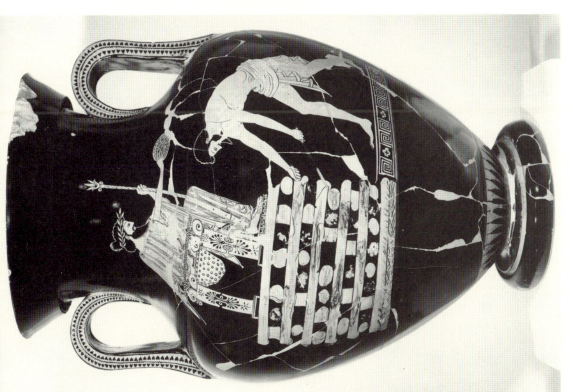

37. Kroisos on the pyre (left), and Theseus and Antiope, Peirithoos (right), after 490 B.C. Red-figured belly amphora by Myson. H. .585 m. Louvre G 197.

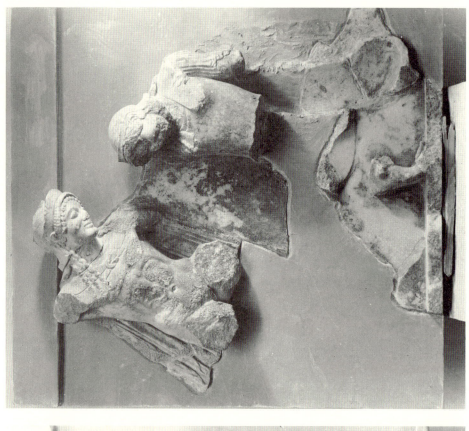

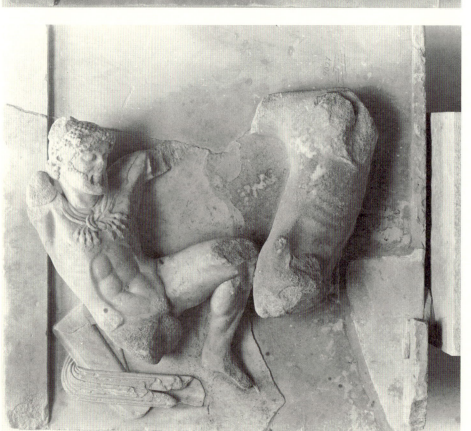

38. Herakles and the Kerkynian deer, after 490 B.C. Metope 19, east frieze (Hoffelner), from the Athenian treasury. .67 × .63 m. Delphi Museum.

39. Theseus and Antiope, after 490 B.C. Metope 8, north frieze (Hoffelner), from the Athenian treasury. .67 × .63 m. Delphi Museum.

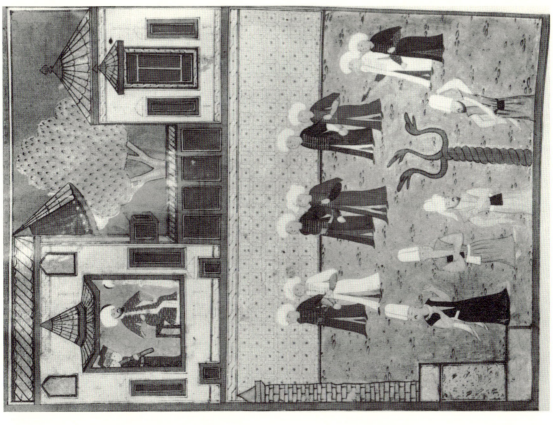

40. The serpent column of the Plataian tripod from Delphi, in Constantinople. Ottoman miniatures (Şur-name), sixteenth century A.D. Topkapi Museum, Istanbul.

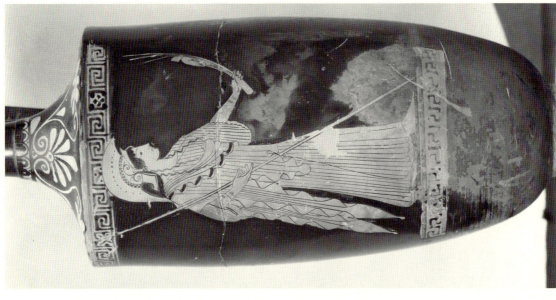

42. Athena with ἄφλαστον, 480–460 B.C. Red-figure lekythos by the Brygos Painter, from Gela. H. .34 m.

41. Bronze statue of god (Zeus or Poseidon), 470–460 B.C. Found off Artemision, Euboia. H. 2.09 m. Athens, National Museum (inv. 15161).

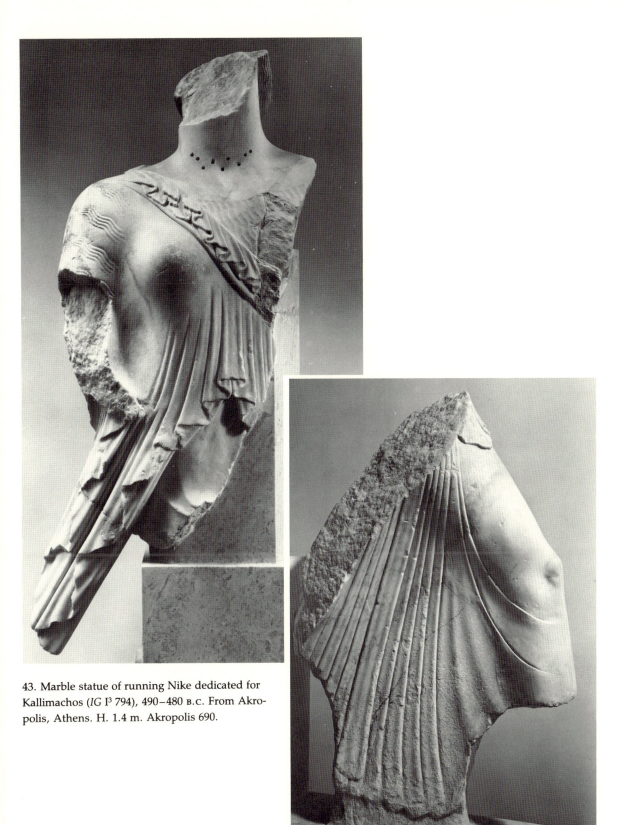

43. Marble statue of running Nike dedicated for Kallimachos (*IG* I³ 794), 490–480 B.C. From Akropolis, Athens. H. 1.4 m. Akropolis 690.

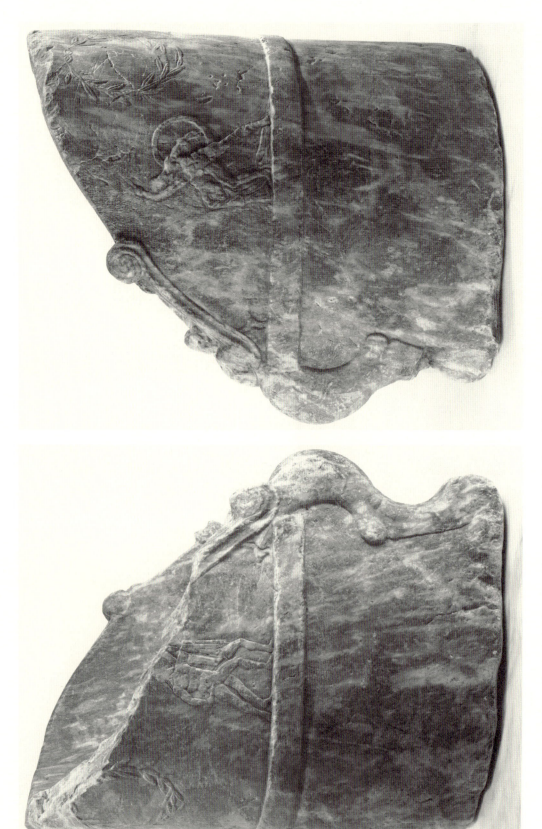

44a, b. Harmodios and Aristogeiton (the tyrannicides), (left), and Greek and Amazon (right), late fourth century B.C. The Elgin Throne. H. .815 m., Malibu 74 AA 12.

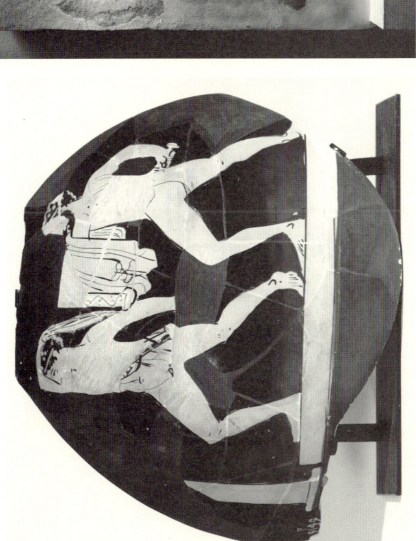

45. Harmodios and Aristogeiton, ca. 400 B.C. Red-figure oinochoe, from the Dexileos grave precinct, Kerameikos, Athens. Pres. H. .14 m. Boston MFA 98.936.

46. Clay plaque from Akropolis, Athens, with running hoplite, after 490 B.C. "(ΜΕΓΑΚΛΕΣ) ΓΛΑΥΚΟΣ ΚΑΛΟΣ." By Euthymides. W. .52. m. Akropolis 1037.

47. Greek fighting Persian (above, exterior), and two Greek warriors climbing out of tomb or altar (left, interior), ca. 460 B.C. Red-figure cup, name vase of the Painter of the Oxford Brygos Cup. D. .33 m. Oxford 1911.615.

48. Hero rising from tomb, ca. 470 B.C. Top of red-figure askos, near the Tyszkiewicz Painter (*ARV*[1] 188.59). Boston MFA 13.169.

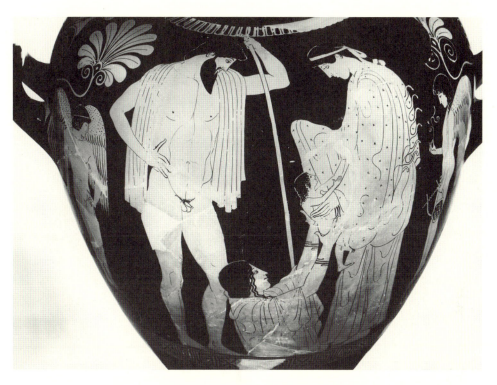

49. Hephaistos and Athena at the birth of Erichthonios from Ge, ca. 460 B.C. Red-figure stamnos by the Painter of Munich 2413. H. .39 m. Munich 2413.

50. Hermes, Hephaistos, Athena, and Ge at the Birth of Pandora, ca. 450 B.C. Red-figure volute krater, related to group of Polygnotos. H. .482 m. Oxford 525 (G 275).

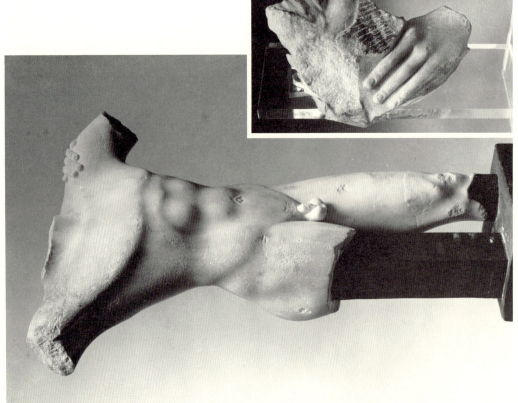

51. Theseus and giant (Prokroustes?), marble statue group from Akropolis, Athens, before 480 B.C.? Akropolis 145 (Theseus: Pres. H. .63 m) and 370 (fragment: hand, beard).

52. Theseus and Antiope, after 490 B.C.? Pediment of the temple of Apollo, Eretria. H. 1.12 m.

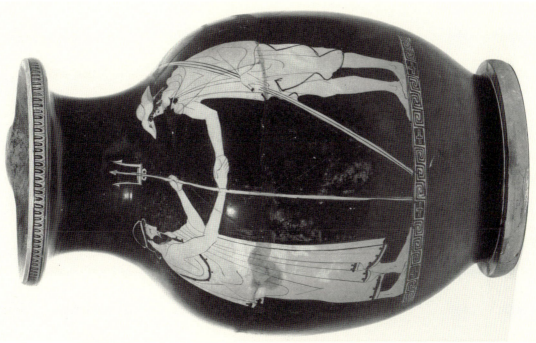

54. Poseidon and Theseus, ca. 470–460 B.C. Red-figured oinochoe, name-vase of the Painter of the Yale Oinochoe. H. .403 m. Yale 1913.143.

53. Poseidon receiving libation from Nike, ca. 470–460 B.C. Calyx-krater by the Aegisthus Painter. H. .405 m. Yale 1985.4.1.

55. Theseus and Antiope, ca. 490 B.C. Exterior of red-figure cup by Euphronios. D. .324 m. London E 41.

56. Theseus, Athena, and Amphitrite, ca. 500–490 B.C. Interior of red-figure cup by Onesimos (painter) and Euphronios (potter). D. .40 m. Louvre G 104.

57. Theseus and the
Minotaur (above, tondo)
and deeds of Theseus
(center and below, exte-
rior), ca. 460 B.C. Red-
figure cup by the Cod-
rus Painter. D.
.325 m. London E 84.

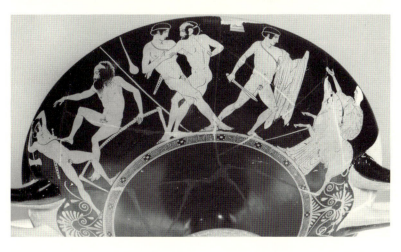

58. Bronze sculptor's workshop: manufacture of hoplite statue (above), and manufacture of athlete statue (below), 480–470 B.C. Exterior of red-figure cup by the Foundry Painter from Vulci. D. .305 m. Berlin F 2294. (For interior, see Figure 1.)

60. Athena in workshop of potter, metalworker, 490–480 B.C. Red-figure cup by the Euergides Painter, from the Akropolis, Athens. Pres. H. .13 m., D. .24 m. Athens, National Museum. Akropolis 166.

59. Athena modeling a horse in bronze or clay, 470–460 B.C. Red-figure olpe from Capua, name-vase of the Group of Berlin F 2415. H. .215 m. Berlin F 2415.

61. Athena in bronze-sculptor's workshop, 480–470 B.C. Red-figure cup by the Foundry Painter, from Vulci. Munich 2650.

62. King Dareios on his throne with Persian nobles, hearing Greek "warner"? Upper register: personifications of Hellas, Asia, Athena, and Apate. Late fourth century B.C. Apulian krater by the Darius Painter from Canosa. H. 1.30 m. D. 1.93 m. Naples 3253.